A HISTORY
OF HISTORICAL
WRITING

BY

HARRY ELMER BARNES

Second Revised Edition

DOVER PUBLICATIONS, INC.

NEW YORK

Manufactured in the United States of America

Dover Publications, Inc.
180 Varick Street
New York 14, N.Y.

To

FERDINAND SCHEVILL

*A master craftsman in the field of history,
and a generous friend*

PREFACE TO DOVER EDITION

THIS new edition of *A History of Historical Writing* is the result of many inquiries and requests from university and college teachers of history who have contended that it remains the only adequate survey of the whole course of historical writing in a single volume. They have represented to me that there has been and remains a great need for this work to serve as a guide and textbook for courses in historiography and historical method—that it is literally indispensable for these purposes. These requests have been made in increasing numbers over the past decade during which the book has been out of print. The intellectual enterprise and generosity of Mr. Hayward Cirker of Dover Publications, Inc., have now made it possible for me to comply.

It is desirable in the interest of candor and guidance to indicate just what is the nature of this revised edition. Since it is an offset product, it is obvious that it remains essentially the same book that was originally published in 1937 and reprinted with some corrections in 1938. But this is no disadvantage for the purposes in mind. It is this book that has been demanded by those who have been interested in its reproduction, and it is this book which meets the purposes which they have had in mind and those of all other historians who may wish a textbook for the courses for which it is intended and suitable.

The author may further say that even if this edition had permitted a resetting of the type and complete freedom in revision, it would not have been in any essential way different from the book here reprinted. I did my best on the 1937 edition and have seen no reason for modifying it in any important manner over the years. This might not have been the case if a much larger book were envisaged, but even so the increased size would only have augmented accordingly the difficulty of using it as a manageable textbook.

In preparing the present revision, the author has taken full account of all criticisms of the 1937 edition together with all other comments and suggestions that have come to him since that time. He has read carefully the more notable books on the history of historical writing which have appeared since 1938, notably the monumental work of James Westfall Thompson, the able writings on American historiography by Michael Kraus, and the several books which have appeared dealing mainly with the developments associated with the writings of

Carl Becker and Charles Austin Beard, and with the problems of "historical relativism."

A primary change in the new edition has been the insertion of historical works of first-rate importance which have been published since 1938 on all periods of history from the preliterary age to the Cold War of today. Bibliographies and footnotes have been brought up to date, including important books that have appeared in 1961. Due consideration has been given to those changes in historical methodology and to new technological developments since 1938 which have modified historical perspectives, research, documentation, and writing.

While the author has given far more careful and extended attention to the historiography of the second World War and its aftermath than any other living historian, he has resolutely resisted the temptation to treat this problem at any length in the present edition. Those who desire to discover and present the author's views on this matter are fully aware of where they can be found.

HARRY ELMER BARNES

Malibu, California
June, 1962

PREFACE TO FIRST EDITION

THIS book is an introduction to the history of historical writing. It presents a survey of the development of the art and science of historical writing from the earliest days to our own era, viewed throughout in relationship to the cultural background and intellectual forces which have conditioned its evolution. Due attention is given to the leading individual writers who have produced the historical works of the past, and an effort has been made to indicate both the special personal contributions of such writers and the intellectual influences which have helped to shape their historical conceptions. Historical writing, like other forms of culture, is truly a historical product and must be considered against the background of the civilization out of which it grew. So, a history of historical writing must necessarily be, to a large degree, a phase of the intellectual history of mankind. Intelligent historical writing must give proper consideration to both the great man theory and to the notion of cultural determinism. The history of historical writing illustrates to an unusual degree the potency of both of these factors in cultural evolution.

There are three main ways in which the subject of the history of historical writing may be approached. The author might select a score or so of the major historians from Herodotus to Eduard Meyer and then devote to each a literary essay. This mode of procedure is more entertaining than any other and lends itself better to literary artistry. Such a work is Moritz Ritter's *Die Entwicklung der Geschichtswissenschaft in den führenden Werken betrachtet*. But whatever such a work gains in reader interest and literary merit it loses from the standpoint of thoroughness and comprehensive information.

Another way of getting at the matter is to present an encyclopedic bibliography of historical writing, such as has been done in the *Guide to Historical Literature* by William Henry Allison and others, and by Charles V. Langlois in his *Manuel de bibliographie historique*. This achieves the thoroughness which is lacking in the first mode of treatment mentioned, but it produces something which must of necessity be purely a work of reference. It is not suited for consecutive reading.

A third possible method of procedure is to characterize the intellectual background of each major period of human advance in western civilization, show how the historical literature of each period has been related to its parent culture, point out the dominant traits of the historical writing in each era, indicate the advances, if any, in historical science, and then make clear the individual contributions of the major historical writers of the age.

This mode of treatment makes it possible to set forth both the significant advances in each epoch and to indicate the nature of the major personalities involved. It makes possible a combination of both readability and comprehensive information. It is this method which has been followed by Eduard Fueter in his notable *Histoire de l'historiographie moderne* and it is the method chosen for the present volume. I am convinced that it is the desirable way of going at the subject in any introductory survey. It is for others to judge how well the method selected has been carried out.

The conventional chronological stages of the development of historical writing have been retained in blocking out the earlier portions of the volume, and the treatment is roughly chronological throughout. But in the later parts of the book some concession has been made to the topical arrangement. This is unavoidable, since different trends in historical writing have developed parallel to each other in time. For example, the seventeenth and eighteenth centuries witnessed the origins of modern historical scholarship, the rise of the philosophy of history, rationalistic strains in historical writing, and the origins of the nationalistic tone in historical literature. Likewise, the last hundred years have seen the perfection of erudite historical writing, the rise of *Kulturgeschichte,* and the very significant impact of the social sciences upon historical writing. To lump these developments all together in a single chronological treatment would only result in confusion. A slight modification of strictly chronological treatment which will permit an illuminating topical arrangement is greatly to be preferred.

Obviously, selection has been necessary in deciding upon the historians to be listed or characterized individually. Otherwise, the book would have degenerated into a mere catalogue, especially in the later portions. I have endeavored to make the selection as fair and intelligent as possible, but it is inevitable that others would have chosen differently in many cases. At least, I can say that no names have been included because of my own favoritism as to any particular attitude towards history or as to personalities. Nor has anybody been excluded because of my prejudices or because of personal malice. Any omissions of undoubted importance will gladly be taken care of in subsequent editions if anyone will be kind enough to call them to my attention.

I have been as candid and straightforward in treating contemporary historical writing and living historians as I have been in estimating the historical literature and historians of antiquity and the Middle Ages. This is a departure from usual and approved procedure, but I believe that it is indispensable in any history of historical writing which assumes to bring the story down to date. The most important historical writing of all time has been done in the last fifty years and many of the ablest historians are now living. To exempt living historians and their work from comment and criticism would leave a serious gap in the critical estimates and evaluations which such a book as this may be expected to contain. Works on history and the social sciences, which refuse to deal with contemporaries, seriously, if not fatally, weaken their utility for those of us who are living in this day. An essay like that of Charles Austin Beard on "That Noble Dream" is of greater practical import than a whole volume criticizing the medieval chroniclers. To deal frankly, though fairly, with contemporaries is also more "sporting." A living man can protest but a dead man cannot defend himself against criticism.

Much attention is here given to the broadening of the interests of historians and to the extension of the studies upon which they rely in our day. A more expansive conception of the scope of historical interests, the notion that a study of the past should tell us how things have developed as well as how they have been in bygone days, the conviction that the history of the human past will help us better to understand the human present and better to plan for the human future, and the recognition of the importance of the several social sciences in equipping the historian to ply his trade, have been the chief innovations in historical writing in the twentieth century. They also definitely forecast the developments in historical writing in the immediate generations to come if civilization survives. Even the erudite school has finally admitted this fact, as exemplified by the elaborate report of a committee of the American Historical Association on the social studies. Yet, a recognition of the significance of the so-called "New History" for our generation has not led me to scrimp with respect to the space allotted to the triumph of conventional historical scholarship. It is accorded full respect and given its due credit.

This volume is intended to be something more than a compendium of esoteric learning. It may possibly bring together loose ends in the reading of scholars and it may introduce the beginner in historical studies to the main developments in, and the giants of, his future craft. But it is hoped that the general reader will be interested as well. The great historians have always possessed a glamour and romance for cultivated readers of the world's literature. Here Thucydides, Tacitus, Hume, Gibbon, Motley, Parkman, Macaulay and the rest are placed against the cultural and professional background from which their writing proceeded and are evaluated properly with their contemporaries. The whole history of history should be both more entertaining and instructive than any account of a single historian and his work. Further, a survey of the history of history is inevitably a relevant and important excursion into the always diverting and edifying history of the growth of human ideas and mundane intelligence. Finally, a study of past historical writing, as well as of past historical facts, should prepare us the better to deal with the problems of today and the current interpreters thereof.

I have executed the task to the best of my ability within the conceptions of the enterprise that have guided me and within the space at my disposal. If anybody thinks he can do better at the project, he will assuredly find plenty of elbow-room. This is the only book of its kind in any language. So I wish any potential competitor godspeed and no one will be more highly pleased to discover a superior work emerging from the presses.

HARRY ELMER BARNES

Auburn, N.Y.
May 1, 1937.

NOTE OF ACKNOWLEDGMENT

DEAN Carl Wittke of Oberlin College and Professor Ralph H. Records of the University of Oklahoma each read the entire manuscript and made many constructive criticisms which have aided me in revising the material. Others have given special attention to sections of the manuscript falling within their particular fields of interest. Professor Nathaniel Schmidt of Cornell University read Chapter I. Professor Wallace E. Caldwell of the University of North Carolina read Chapters I-II. Professor Edward Maslin Hulme of Leland Stanford University and Professor Josiah C. Russell of the University of North Carolina read Chapters III-VI. Professor Albert H. Lybyer read the sections of Chapter IV dealing with Byzantine and Muslim historians. Professors James E. Gillespie of Pennsylvania State College and Leo Gershoy of Long Island University read Chapter VII. Dr. H. C. Engelbrecht of New York City read Chapters VIII-IX. Professor David S. Muzzey of Columbia University read Chapter X and a preliminary draft of Chapter XI. Professor Louis M. Hacker read portions of Chapter X. Professor Benjamin B. Kendrick of the North Carolina College for Women read Chapters XII-XIII and XV. Professor Merle Curti of Teachers College, Columbia University, and Dr. Fulmer Mood of the Huntington Library, Pasadena, California, read Chapter XIV. These men detected a number of slips and made many constructive suggestions as to the improvement of the material which have been embodied in the revision.

I am indebted to Mr. Savoie Lottinville of Norman, Oklahoma, for checking the names and dates in the proofs and for making the Index. It is a pleasure to acknowledge the courteous and competent supervision of editorial and publishing details by Mr. Joseph A. Brandt of the University of Oklahoma Press. Mr. Anthony Netboy aided me by reading the galley proofs.

The author has not imposed on anybody for assistance in preparing this edition. But he has profited by the criticisms and comments which have been sent to him since 1938. He would especially wish to express his gratitude to Mr. Robert Hutchinson and his editorial associates at Dover Publications, Inc., for their competent professional assistance and for their patience and consideration in working with me on the project.

TABLE OF CONTENTS

A HISTORY

OF HISTORICAL WRITING

I

THE ORIGINS OF HISTORICAL WRITING

THE NATURE OF HISTORY

THE term "history," in popular usage, has carried with it two very different meanings. It is often used to designate the sum total of human activities in the past. It is when employed in this sense that one often hears the remark, at a particularly active or critical period in human events, that "now history is being made." A more common usage is that which looks upon history as the record of the events rather than the events themselves. In this latter and more generally accepted meaning, two definitions may be offered. In an objective sense history is, to use the words of Professor James Harvey Robinson, "all we know about everything man has ever done, or thought, or hoped or felt." Subjectively or psychologically expressed, history may be regarded as a record of all that has occurred within the realm of human consciousness.

When viewed as the record of the past activities of the human race, history has been regarded by some, particularly in earlier eras, as primarily an art—a branch of literature. By a continually increasing number of authorities it is coming to be considered as, in the main, a genetic social science, which is concerned with reconstructing as far as may be possible, the past thoughts and activities of humanity.

Prior to those important discoveries made by students of prehistoric archeology, which have done so much to extend our knowledge of human activities in the distant past, it was the conventional practice to limit the term history to a record of the events which are described or preserved in literary remains. Now, however, archeology tells one much more of certain phases of the life of early man than was once known about more recent periods through literary evidence. It is no longer accurate or logical to use the term "prehistoric," unless it is employed to designate that vague and hypothetical period at the very beginning of human development, of which there exists no positive and tangible record, or unless one is limiting his conception to the notion of history as a branch of literature. In the place of the now generally discarded term, the "prehistoric" period, there has been substituted the concept of "preliterary history." This is descriptive of that period of human development where information is revealed by archeological rather than literary evidence.

In short, it has been agreed that a fundamental fallacy and contradiction are involved in the use of the term prehistoric for any period of which there is any considerable record preserved, whether in writing or in the stone, bone and metal artifacts of daily life. With recent writers the word prehistoric has followed the term "pre-Adamite" into that repository of discarded concepts which is being continually expanded as an inevitable result of the growth of our knowledge of human activities in both time and space.

It is deemed inadvisable at this point to discuss in detail the various interpretations of what history means or should be mainly concerned with narrating. It is in great part the task of this entire book to reveal the diverse interpretations of history, and this much-debated problem of what history means or has been thought to mean will be shown in its historical mutations and transformations.[1]

THE DEVELOPMENT OF PRELITERARY HISTORY

Having seen that history, in our contemporary usage, goes back to the beginning of any record whatever of human existence and activities, one must look for the ultimate origins of history in those early artifacts which were sufficiently distinctive in form and durable in material composition to have been preserved through the ages as evidence of what mankind was accomplishing in the vast expanse of time before the art of writing was mastered. History, thus, probably may be said to have had its real origin in the vague, distant and conjectural Eolithic period. The first historical document may be accurately held to have been the first indisputable "eolith," or, if the Eolithic period be denied, the first definite paleolith of the river-drift period.

The space at our disposal allows only the briefest résumé of that most interesting story of the early development of mankind as revealed by the artifacts which have been preserved. The thrilling evidences of man's interests and activities in that almost immeasurable period of more than a quarter of a million years which are revealed by the *coup de poings* of the river-drift period, the remarkable flaked flints of the cave period, the engraving on animal bones and the early paintings from such cave sites as Altamira and Font-de-Gaume, and the wonderful products of the bronze and iron ages, are of the most compelling interest, for the complete treatment of which the reader must be referred to such books as C. R. Knight's *Before the Dawn of History*,[2] George Grant MacCurdy's *The Coming of Man*,[3] and Stanley Casson's *Progress of Archeology*.[4] We can only pause for a rapid summary of the outstanding facts.

Two profound and revolutionary discoveries bearing on the origins of the human race were made during the nineteenth century. The first destroyed the notion that the living things upon this earth, with the accent

---

[1] See also below, pp. 344 ff.
[2] McGraw-Hill Book Co., 1935.
[3] University Society, 1932.
[4] McGraw-Hill, 1935.

on man, were created by divine impulse all within a certain week, said in the Jewish and Christian literatures to have been a trifle more than four thousand years before the advent of Christ. It showed, instead, that erect living beings, with something of the intelligence of man as we know him today, many of his fundamental habits, and, in all outstanding aspects, his physical characteristics, put their footprints upon the sands of time around five million years ago.

Paradoxically enough, the second discovery served to make of man again a mere infant in years, when compared to the newly revealed age of the earth itself. The conventional story of Genesis has been compelled to give way before the new perspective forced upon us by a realization of the vast period of time that has elapsed since our planet was first separated as a gaseous mass from the parent sun, or whirled about as fragments in a great planetesimal disc. However widely the estimates of the age of the earth may vary, we know that a staggering stretch of time, quite transcending the finite understanding of man, has gone by since the gas began to solidify or the particles to collect which were to give rise to our planet. Yet, as astronomers measure time, the birth of our planet is but a recent incident in the history of our universe. "Long, long before," says Professor Shapley, "for trillions of years, in the absence of the 'Lords of all Creation,' the stars had poured out their radiant energy, the celestial bodies had rolled on, law had governed the universe."

To geology we are heavily indebted for our revised views as to the age of the earth. It was geology that made the first breach in the orthodox stronghold. The theory accepted until the early part of the nineteenth century assumed a series of "complete catastrophes in the history of the globe," the handiwork of God, to explain the physical formation of the earth's surface. The English geologist, Sir Charles Lyell, was the first to prove that the earth's surface is not the result of cataclysmic catastrophes, but of natural causes—now well known—most of which can still be seen in operation. In his famous *Principles of Geology,* published in 1830-33, Lyell made clear the natural processes which, after countless eons, had resulted in the formation of the various geological strata and of mountains, valleys, and the like. Since his day, the elaborate works of later geologists have confirmed his views. Another work of Lyell, published thirty years later, was no less significant at the time. In 1863 his *Antiquity of Man* appeared. This summarized the impressive body of evidence then in existence in favor of the theory that man was much older than was generally believed at the time. From the biological point of view, Charles Darwin soon showed in his *Descent of Man* that man could have evolved from earlier forms of simian life.

Geologically, the evolution of organic life on our planet falls into four major subdivisions: (1) the Primary or Paleozoic, (2) the Secondary or

Mesozoic, (3) the Tertiary or the Age of Mammals, and (4) the Quaternary or the Age of Man. Sometimes the term "Cenozoic" is employed to include both the Tertiary and the Quaternary ages. An enormous period of time elapsed during the first two ages, the Paleozoic and the Mesozoic —perhaps some three hundred million years. Estimates of geological time vary greatly with different authorities, and we have to be satisfied with approximations. The Tertiary age is believed to have lasted between five and thirty million years, and at present it is generally held that the length of the Quaternary age has been something over a million years. These last two ages are both subdivided: the Tertiary into the Eocene, Oligocene, Miocene, and Pliocene periods; the Quaternary into the Pleistocene and Recent periods. The chronology of the Quaternary age is of prime importance in computing the age of man. It is based upon the four glacial and three interglacial periods which succeeded one another down to the close of the Pleistocene period. We may be living today in the fourth interglacial period.

Not so very long ago the origins of human culture, like those of the human race, were shrouded in total darkness. As long as Adam was accepted as the first human being, there could be no notion of any history of man before his day. The science of "prehistoric" archeology had no reason for existence, since the origins of human writing go back to a period almost coeval with the "first" man of biblical history. The discovery of human skeletal remains in ancient geological deposits, proving the presence of early types of man at this remote period, and the disclosure of the artificial products of human handiwork in similar deposits soon made it clear, however, that the history of man and his culture must have extended back over a very long space of time. Now we have sufficient knowledge, though it is far from complete, to follow in broad outlines the history of human culture from its remote origins through its various stages of development to our day.

The science that has made this possible, "prehistoric" archeology, is little more than a hundred years old. Since there was no calendar in the days of preliterary man, the archeologist is forced to classify and date evidence with which he deals—that is, the stone and bone and metal remains that he has uncovered—in a time sequence which is directly related to the progressive development of material culture. To his aid come the geologist and the paleontologist, who make it possible to give such objects approximate datings. They estimate as closely as possible the age of the geological formations in which human bones and artifacts are deposited and the age of the animal bones found in them. The Carbon 14 technique enables us to date deposits made as far back as fifty thousand years. The Potassium-Argon method can carry this dating back two million years or more.

The existence of stone implements, which we of today know to have been the work of primitive man, led some writers during pagan antiquity to sense their true significance. The great Roman poet-philosopher, Lucretius, writing in the first century B.C., seems to have recognized intuitively the sequence of the Stone, Bronze and Iron ages. Usually, however, the stone implements were then believed to have been "thunderstones" hurled by the gods, and they were so regarded for many centuries. They were even treasured as possessing potent magic power. When, in the sixteenth century, the Tuscan, Michael Mercate, advanced the theory that the "thunderstones" might be implements manufactured by early man, he was years ahead of his time. In the following century, one Tollius could write for a believing world that "thunderstones" were "generated in the sky by a fulgurous exhalation conglobed in a cloud by the circumposed humor."

Not until the nineteenth century was the human origin of these ancient stone implements fully established. In part, it was demonstrated by C. J. Thomsen, a Danish museum curator, but much more thoroughly by the industrious and courageous Jacques Boucher de Perthes, a French archeologist. Thomsen revived and reduced to a scientific basis the more or less vague intuition of Lucretius. He classified his museum exhibits according to the sequence of Stone, Bronze and Iron ages by an early use of the stratigraphic method of geology. What Thomsen did, however, added little to our knowledge of the significance or the antiquity of the exhibits thus classified. It was the task of Boucher de Perthes to show that the early stone implements, already known for years, were actually used by members of the human family many thousands of years ago. About 1830 he began to explore systematically the cultural remains of the Somme Valley, where he recovered vast quantities of stone implements and weapons from the ancient river gravels. In 1846 he published his *De l'industrie primitive*. In this significant work Boucher de Perthes contended that the stone implements he had found were unquestionably of human manufacture. At first he met with sharp ridicule. But he persisted in the face of strenuous opposition, and before long his hypothesis was not only accepted, but even earnestly defended by the leading students of man's early history on the earth, such as Sir John Evans.

Once the human origin of these stone implements was thoroughly established, Thomsen's earlier classification became meaningful. Now the tools of primitive man could be arranged in the order of their historical and technical evolution. From the middle of the nineteenth century onward, rapid progress was made in archeology. More accurate and specialized classification paralleled the discoveries of much new material in stone, bone and metal.

In the 1860's Sir John Lubbock divided the Stone age into two distinct periods, Paleolithic and Neolithic. The period when stone implements were made roughly, he called the Paleolithic or Old Stone age. The following period, when polished stone implements were produced, he called the Neolithic or New Stone age. Sir John's clear and forceful writings also did much for the young science of archeology. Especially noteworthy was his *Prehistoric Times,* published in 1865. A Frenchman, Édouard Lartet, had already (in 1861) made the discoveries that enabled him to divide the Paleolithic age into an Upper and Lower Paleolithic. The work of subdividing each of these broad ages into sub-periods descriptive of cultural advance went on apace.

Gabriel de Mortillet in his *Essai de classification* (1869) laid the basis for prehistoric chronology and for our present detailed subdivision of the Paleolithic, in order of age, into Mesvinian, Chellean, Acheulian, Mousterian, Aurignacian, Solutrean, Magdalenian, Azilian and Tardenoisian periods. These are really subdivisions within the larger divisions of Lower, Middle, and Upper Paleolithic. Sometimes the Azilian and Tardenoisian sub-periods are not included under the Paleolithic but are regarded as transitional between the latter and the Neolithic. The term "Mesolithic" has recently been applied to them. The work on the Paleolithic age was continued by scholars like Henri Breuil, and that on the Neolithic by such students as R. R. Schmidt, August Schenk and Oskar Montelius. Within our century, the Belgian archeologist, Aimé Rutot, and J. Reid Moir of England have apparently definitely established the existence of a long Eolithic age preceding the Paleolithic. At the other end, the metal ages have been related to the stone ages, and a chronology for the former has also been worked out.

When the discovery and classification of primitive artifacts, or crude implements, had made possible a general chronology for the preliterary period, the next step was to develop the archeological synthesis for the various European areas. Rutot has admirably described the unity of the preliterary cultures of Belgium and the Somme Valley. Joseph Déchelette, Henri Breuil, Pierre Marcellin Boule, and Emil Cartailhac prepared the archeological synthesis for France. Cartailhac and Hugo Obermaier did the same for Spain, and T. E. Peet for the Italian peninsula. R. R. Schmidt and Obermaier have synthesized German archeology. Montelius worked over Scandinavian material in a scholarly fashion. Other students have concerned themselves with the remaining countries, and the first complete and up-to-date synthesis of the entire preliterary period has been the work of an American scholar, George Grant MacCurdy.[5]

To the beginner in the study of prehistoric archeology, names like Solutrean, Mousterian, Tardenoisian, and so on, may well seem cumbersome and disconcerting. When properly explained, they become simple and intelligible. These terms represent the sequence of cultural evolu-

---

[5] *Human Origins* (D. Appleton and Co., 1924, 2 vols.).

tion. At the same time, they attest the growth of technical perfection in the manufacture of the early stone implements and weapons, as indicated by the changes and improvements in the number, design, shape and cutting edge of the stone artifacts (weapons and implements). This, as we have said, is the only means of establishing a chronology for the preliterary period. Contrary to what may appear at first sight, the strange names given to the various cultural periods were not arbitrarily chosen to puzzle the student or to offer him practice in spelling and pronunciation. They have an understandable and natural derivation. Each of these periods is named from what is called the "type site" for the form of culture thus designated. By the type site is meant the locality in which the most typical or complete remains of a particular form of stone culture were first discovered. The Mousterian type site is the cave of Le Moustier; the type site of the Aurignacian culture is the cave of Aurignac. The cave of Lascaux in France best reveals the art and picture writing of the preliterary age.

Though there was no writing in this long age of man, lasting for around five million years, and hence no historical literature, the archeological discoveries mark the real beginnings of the historical record of man's "rough road" from savagery to civilization. Indeed, they tell us more about the life of mankind than does much of our later historical literature which ignored many of the more vital and important aspects of human living.[6] And they are of immense historical importance, since more than ninety per cent of human existence on our planet had passed before the art of writing was mastered. It is for this reason that we have come to discard the term prehistoric and to substitute for it the conception of preliterary history.

Along with the reconstruction of the material culture of preliterary man by the archeologists has come the social anthropologists' study of the institutional life of primitive society. We have, of course, slight remains of the institutions and the group life of man in preliterary days, save for the implications of such things as evidences of religious observances and certain work, mainly in stone, which must have required much coöperative endeavor. We have to reconstruct the group life of man, by implication and comparison, through a study of the institutional life of existing savages whose material culture is roughly like that of preliterary peoples. This reconstruction was aided by the adoption of the theory of evolution and its application to the explanation of social development. Lewis Henry Morgan's *Ancient Society* was the most representative example of this type of "evolutionary" anthropology. While it made many important contributions, it over-simplified matters. Morgan's important approach to the

6 See below, pp. 291 ff.

study of primitive society was brought into better accord with the facts by his disciple, Leslie A. White, in his *Evolution of Culture*. This, and Robert H. Lowie's *Primitive Society*, are roughly comparable to Mac-Curdy's synthesis of archeological materials in his *Human Origins*.

THE MASTERY OF THE ART OF WRITING

Though the non-literary archeological remains of early man are of the utmost aid and importance in reconstructing his modes of life and activity, no extensive record of past events was possible until some progress had been made in giving permanent expression to human thought and action —in other words, until the art of writing had been mastered.

The obscure origins of the art of writing must be regarded as dating back to the picture-writing which first appears on the implements and the cave walls of the middle and later Paleolithic periods. Before these pictograms could be regarded as real writing, however, it was necessary that they should pass through three well-defined stages of development. In the first place, the pictures had to become conventionalized, so that they always had the same appearance and designated the same object. Next, it was necessary that they should not only refer to a concrete object but also become the symbols of abstract conceptions. Finally, it was essential that these conventionalized symbols should pass into that stage where they combined a representation of an abstract conception and the sound of the human voice. This last stage itself went through a number of developments. First, we probably had a primitive type of agglutinative speech. Then, in the simplest and most elementary form of "sound writing," each symbol represented an entire word. Some languages, such as the Chinese, have never passed beyond this primitive monosyllabic stage. Normally, however, the symbols usually came to represent not a whole word but a syllable. Sooner or later, various sounds of the human voice were analyzed and came to be represented by separate symbols or letters, and the alphabet came into existence therewith.

By some time around 3000 B.C., the Egyptians had taken an important step in this direction by using some twenty-four hieroglyphic signs to indicate as many consonantal sounds. They did not, however, consider these alone to be sufficient for their needs, but continued to employ a large number of other symbols for words and syllables, and consequently missed what was essential to a true phonetic alphabet. The first real phonetic alphabet has recently been discovered in inscriptions turned up on the Sinaitic peninsula and in southern Palestine. The author of this alphabet had forced himself free from the limitations of the imperfect Egyptian alphabet. He may have been a Phoenician from Byblos, or perhaps was of some other Semitic nationality, and probably lived during the nineteenth century B.C. Important inscriptions have lately been discovered at Rasesh Shamra near Latakiyeh in ancient Ugarit. Some of these are written in an alphabetic cuneiform script and in a northwestern Semitic dialect. Whether the inventor attempted to substitute cuneiform signs for a Semitic alphabet already known, or independently devised this system is as yet uncertain. But it is evident that we must modify the common view that the Phoenicians invented the first phonetic alphabet. Our earliest inscription in the fully developed Phoenician alphabet is that of Ahiram, a contemporary of Ramses II in the thirteenth century B.C. This alphabet contained twenty-two letters, all consonants. It remained for the Greeks to complete the alphabet by employing some of its consonants as designations of vowel sounds. With some modifications, this Greek alphabet spread through the Romans to the western world, and through the Byzantines to various peoples in eastern Europe. The Romans gave us the particular style of letters which have become conventional in most countries in the modern western world. By the Roman period the now common differentiation between capitals and small letters [lower case letters] came into being. But respectable literature was written in capitals during the Greek and Roman period. Only in commercial and highly personal communications were lower case letters employed. In the reign of Charlemagne the monkish copyists at his court began to use the lower case letters, along with capitals, for reputable literature, and this procedure has since been followed.

Along with the mastery of the art of writing went the provision of materials on which to set down the desired letters and words. Stone columns and walls, or even the clay tablets of the Babylonians, whatever their virtues from the standpoint of permanence, were clumsy, awkward and restricted writing materials. The Egyptians solved the difficulty by utilizing the membrane of the papyrus reed to make a form of paper. Later, parchment was fashioned from the skin of animals for the use of those peoples where papyrus was not available. Paper, made originally from silk and the pulp of the mulberry tree, first appeared among the Chinese about the beginning of the Christian era. The Arabs devised a paper made from cotton fiber, about A.D. 750. This was brought into Spain, where flax was substituted for cotton and the modern linen paper came into use about 1250. Rag paper became common by the fourteenth century in western Europe. The earliest ink was made by mixing water, which had been thickened with vegetable gum, with soot obtained from blackened pots. Later, ink was produced from mixtures of animal and vegetable dyes, and in our day it is made with various chemical colors. The first pens were made from reeds sharpened and pointed by hand. Next, the quill, made from goose and other feathers, was introduced and remained in use until the steel pen was invented in the nineteenth century.

With the provision of an alphabet and writing materials, historical writing could start on the long course of development which was to bring it from Herodotus and Thucydides to von Ranke, Aulard, Gardiner, Osgood and Haskins. Professor James H. Breasted has well stated the importance of this step in the evolution of civilization in general and of historical writing in particular: "The invention of writing and of a convenient system of records on paper has had a greater influence in uplifting the human race than any other intellectual achievement in the career of man. It was more important than all the battles ever fought and all the constitutions ever devised."[7] Before a true historical perspective could develop, however, it was indispensable that some method of measuring time should be discovered and a scientific system of chronology established.

THE DISCOVERY OF TIME AND THE RISE OF CHRONOLOGY

Indispensable as some method of measuring time was for chronicling the thoughts and actions of man, it was not for this purpose that the calendar was originally developed. As Professor James T. Shotwell has remarked, and Professor Hutton Webster has shown in greater detail, it was the deeds of the gods and not of men that the early calendars were originally designed to fix and record. The methods of measuring time grew up about the need for determining the dates of tabooed or holy days and for fixing and recording the occurrence of unusual natural phenomena which were believed to have religious significance. In other words, the concept of time was produced by the consciousness of nature's repetitions and the necessity of differentiating between days on the basis of their particular sacred virtues or qualities. The improvement in the methods of measuring time has been a gradual transition "from luck to mathematics." It was not until long after crude calendars had been provided for these religious uses that they were utilized to fashion a chronology for recording secular historic events.

The simplest and most primitive type of calendar was the lunar calendar related to the phases of the moon. The basis was the lunar month of twenty-nine and one-half days. From this it was possible to provide roughly for convenient units of measurement, both longer and shorter than the month. The lunar fortnight was widely accepted as a unit of time, and weeks were derived from the quarters of the moon or from a division of the months into three periods of ten days each, the latter being the closest feasible mathematical solution. Twelve lunar months produced a lunar year of 354 days, and to keep the months synchronized with the

---

[7] J. H. Breasted, *Ancient Times* (Ginn and Co., 1916), p. 45.

seasonal divisions a thirteenth month was interpolated at appropriate intervals. A longer interval was the lunar cycle of some nineteen years, which came into use among the Greeks about 750 B.C.

Though the lunar calendar provided no exact divisions of time, either long or short, and was constantly getting out of adjustment, it was tolerated and retained by all the peoples of antiquity except the Egyptians, who share with the aboriginal inhabitants of Mexico the honor of having first devised what was essentially a solar year and the beginnings of the modern calendar. The agricultural life of the dwellers in the Nile Valley and the importance of the sun god in Egypt tended to increase the importance of the sun at the expense of the moon. Accordingly, as early as 4236 B.C.,[8] the earliest fixed date in history, the Egyptians seem to have worked out a solar year of 365 days, with twelve months of thirty days each and five feast days at the end of each year.[9] The seven-day week of the modern calendar, cutting through both month and year, was the product of the religious arrangements of the Sumerians and the Hebrews. As early as 238 B.C. Alexandrian scientists had devised the quadrennial leap year, and during the Hellenistic period the Hebrew week was adapted to form the planetary week of our modern calendar. In 46 B.C. Julius Caesar introduced this solar year into the Roman world, but the planetary week did not come into general use in Rome before the second century A.D. The final step in perfecting the calendar was taken by the authority of Pope Gregory XIII in 1582. Eleven days were dropped from the calendar and centennial years were regarded as leap years only when divisible by 400.

The provision of some sort of crude calendar was an essential prerequisite of systematic history, but the process had to be carried a step further before the mechanism for measuring and recording time was sufficiently advanced to be of any considerable service to the historian. It was not enough to be able to measure time by the year and its fractions; it was also necessary to have some method of identifying successive years, in other words, to provide a chronology.

While the Egyptians had an admirable instrument for fashioning a scientific chronology in the astronomical "Sothic cycle" of 1461 years, they made no use of it in historical reckoning and never worked out a scientific chronology. The earliest Egyptian approximation to a chronology was the annalistic expedient of naming the years by some great event which happened therein. The famous "Palermo Stele" constitutes the

---

[8] Some scholars believe that the date was 2776 B.C. rather than 4236 B.C.

[9] While essentially a solar year and only a quarter of a day shorter than the exact solar year, the Egyptian calendar year was computed on a basis of the stars as well as the sun. The Egyptian year began on the day the dog-star, Sirius, first appeared on the eastern horizon at sunrise in the latitude of the lower Delta.

earliest remaining record of these year-lists and is supposed, in its original and complete form, to have identified the seven hundred years
from 3400 B.C. to 2700 B.C. An advance in methodology was made when
the years were named from the regnal years of a particular king. The only
comprehensive list of Egyptian regnal years which has been preserved,
even in a fragmentary condition, is the precious "Turin Papyrus," which
has to be supplemented by the lists inscribed on the temple walls of the
later dynasties. About 275 B.C., Ptolemy Philadelphus commissioned a
learned Egyptian priest, Manetho, to collect and translate into Greek all
the Egyptian annals and regnal lists. The fragmentary remains of the
labors of Manetho have constituted the skeleton upon which modern
Egyptologists have reconstructed the chronology of ancient Egyptian
history.

The Babylonians never passed beyond the annalistic stage of chronology—namely, the identification of years by some conspicuous occurrence.
But they were rather profuse and competent in compiling lists of kings.
A contemporary of Manetho, Berossos, a Babylonian priest at the court
of Antiochus I, tried to systematize Babylonian chronology as Manetho
had the Egyptian. But, to judge from what remains of his work in the
fragments of copyists, he seems to have been less successful in chronological thoroughness and precision. In the Assyrian period, royal annals begin to appear in the fourteenth century B.C., and by the time of Tiglath-
pileser I (*ca.* 1100 B.C.) they became reasonably complete and reliable for
dating purposes. Moreover, far greater exactness was given to Assyrian
chronology by the fact that the years of a given king were identified by
the annual appointment of an official known as a *limmu*. As the name of
the contemporary *limmu* was given in the notices of events contained in
the clay records, the lists of *limmi* enable the historian to reconstruct Assyrian chronology with a high degree of accuracy. In the later period of
Assyrian and Babylonian history there developed some conception of an
"era," which dated from the reign of Nabonassar, 747 B.C.

The Hebrew chronology never developed greater precision than the
crude genealogical system of reckoning by generations, the conventional
length of which was forty years. Some vague conception of eras seems also
to have arisen, as, for example, the period from Abraham to David, or from
David to the "captivity." The classic examples of the Hebrew chronological system are to be found in the opening of the first book of Chronicles
and in the first chapter of Matthew.

The early Greek historians, in spite of an admirable starting point for
the Greek era in the semi-mythical siege of Troy and an unusually ingenious mechanism for measuring time in the nineteen-year—lunar-solar
"cycle of Meton," did no better than their predecessors in creating a chronology. Down to the middle of the fifth century B.C. the only chronolog-

ical records possessed by the Greeks were the local genealogies and the names of archons, priests and priestesses. The early attempt of Hellanicus of Lesbos, in the latter half of the fifth century B.C., to fashion a chronology from genealogies was "an ingenious edifice erected on foundations that had no solidity," but even the effort had some significance. Neither Herodotus nor Thucydides made any serious attempt at solving the problems of chronology, and the later Greek historians finished their work with no more satisfactory system of chronology than the clumsy method of reckoning by Olympiadic years, introduced by Timaeus about 300 B.C. The Olympic "era" was dated from the supposed founding of the Olympic games in 776 B.C. The laudable effort of Eratosthenes, about eighty years after Timaeus, to put Greek chronology on the firm basis of astronomical reckoning was little utilized or encouraged by the historians, though the astronomical researches of the Alexandrian scientists were of the utmost importance for the future of chronology.

The practical-minded Romans were the first people of antiquity to devise a rational and reliable system of chronology. In due time they dated their years from the mythical foundation of Rome in 753 B.C. The fantastic Christian chronology, introduced by Julius Africanus, Eusebius and Jerome, as well as the real foundations of modern scientific chronology in early modern times with Joseph Scaliger's *De emendatione temporum* and Dom Clément's *L'Art de vérifier les dates* will be dealt with later.[10] It is sufficient here to bear in mind the fact that only the Roman chronology enabled a historical writer of antiquity to deal with assurance, in respect to dates, with anything save contemporary history. This serves in part to explain why the great historical works of Greece had to be mainly records of recent and contemporary events.

Closely related to the development of historical chronology was the notion of the possible periodization of history, familiar to us in the conventional divisions of ancient, medieval and modern history. This usage did not, however, come into being until the close of the seventeenth century.

The earlier notions of periods or stages of history were pensive and retrospective. The Jews and Christians looked back to a primordial paradise, and the chief periods of history were held to be those before and after the "Fall of Man," and the expulsion from Paradise. The Jews also used the exiles in their chronological reckonings. The Greeks developed a comparable idea in the conception of a decline from an original "Golden Age." This found its best-known expression in the doctrine of the five ages of man expressed by Hesiod, i.e., gold, silver, bronze, heroes and iron. With the Patristic Christians the notions of primordial paradise and a golden

[10] See below, pp. 172 ff.

age were fused, and the pagan idea of decline was identified with the Christian dogma of the "Fall." Even more general among the Greeks and Romans was the notion of cycles of human development. Culture was held to pass through definite stages of ascent and decline, with the process repeating itself indefinitely.

The medieval historians, for the most part, were wont to stress the continuity of history rather than periodization. They tended to regard the medieval period as a continuation of the Roman Empire. One of the first to break away from this view was the learned Humanist historian, Flavius Blondus (1388-1463).[11] He came to conceive of the Middle Ages as the period in which the peoples of western Europe had broken away from Rome and had created a history and culture of their own. Blondus thus clearly had in mind the notion of at least two periods of history—antiquity and the Middle Ages. But it was a Dutch Humanist, Christoph Keller [Cellarius], who gave us our conventional historical periods in a work written near the end of the seventeenth century. He divided history into three periods: (1) *Historia antiqua* [ancient history] to Constantine the Great; (2) *Historia medii aevi* [medieval history] to the fall of Constantinople in 1453; and (3) *Historia nova* [modern history] from 1453 onward. These divisions of history have been followed, at least in a general way, from Cellarius to our own day. We shall later indicate their misleading character and their utter inadequacy in the light of our present perspective of human development—indeed, the inadequacy of any type of periodization designed to apply to the cultural history of the human race as a whole.[12]

Now that the development of the indispensable prerequisites of historical writing has been briefly touched upon, attention may be turned to the origins of historical writing in antiquity.

ORIENTAL BEGINNINGS OF HISTORICAL WRITINGS

With the exception of the Hebrew historians, ancient oriental historical literature was relatively slight and informal until very late times, when the Hellenistic Greek culture had deeply affected the ancient Near Orient. Historical material was limited mainly to inscriptions and lists of kings. These inscriptions were devoted chiefly to the glorification of the kings, and set forth their building operations, military victories and hunting exploits. Most of them, while presumably written by priest-scribes, were attributed to the monarchs or to the gods. There was no critical sense whatever, and nothing was included which would be in any way disparaging to the monarchs or to the gods who were supposed to guide them.

---

[11] See below, pp. 105 ff.   [12] See below, pp. 330 ff.

While climatic conditions have made Egypt a veritable archeological museum, or, as Professor Breasted has termed it, "a vast historical volume," and have made possible the preservation of valuable and extensive sources of historical information in the architecture, the engineering facts, rich remains in royal tombs, the plastic arts, and even the inscriptions cut on the stone surfaces of tombs, palaces, temples and monuments, few Egyptian historical writings have been preserved. An exception is the work of a scribe of Thutmose III, which describes with ability the notable conquests of that capable and energetic monarch. Except for this work and a few fragmentary annals, such as the Palermo stele and the Turin papyrus, there is no historical treatise of importance by an Egyptian which is known to us that dates from earlier than the Hellenistic period. In this latter age, when the culture of Egypt was more Hellenic than Egyptian, a thoroughly Hellenized Egyptian scribe, the aforementioned Manetho, compiled an Egyptian chronology and a narrative history of Egypt which seem to have been of a high order for the time. Manetho appears to have had intelligence and objectivity in assembling and interpreting his materials. Unluckily, little is preserved of his important work save garbled and incomplete excerpts in such books as those of the Jewish historian, Josephus, and the early Christian historical writers, Julius Africanus and Eusebius.

The Babylonians and Assyrians seem to have done a little better than the Egyptians in compiling historical documents, though there was no Mesopotamian historian comparable to Manetho until a Hellenized Babylonian priest, Berossos, brought together his history of Babylonia in the same century that Manetho wrote. The earliest Asiatic historical writings were the records set down by the Sumerian scribes, but we have no systematic narratives which can be assigned to them. Early sources, dating from the third millenium B.C., were the Babylonian votive inscriptions, giving the names of kings, reciting their genealogies, and describing the buildings they erected. The Babylonians also compiled many lists of kings. For the Sumerian period the great cylinder inscriptions of Gudea of Lagash (2070 B.C.) are also a valuable historical source, especially in relation to the manners and customs of the age. About three centuries later came the Code of Hammurabi, not only an invaluable source for Babylonian social history, but the most important single document in early legal history. Nothing else of importance as historical writing can safely be attributed to the early Sumerian and Babylonian eras.

The facts and chronology of Assyrian history must be gleaned chiefly from three types of sources: (1) "Display Inscriptions," written mainly on slabs of stone, intended for architectural adornment, and having little relation to precise accuracy in historical narration; (2) the Royal Annals type of inscriptions, giving a brief chronological summary of the events of each year and constituting the most important source-material for Assyrian history; and (3) the *Eponym canon* which gave a list of the *limmi* and the years of their appointment. The importance of this latter source for Assyrian chronology has already been made clear. The two historical works of the Assyrians which made some pretense to being serious compilations were the so-called *Synchronous History* and the *Assyrian Chronicle*. The former was an ostensible history of the relations between Babylonia and Assyria from about 1600 to about 800 B.C., giving a list of the kings involved. It devoted special attention to boundary disputes. It was once regarded as a serious historical work, but later research seems to have established the fact that it was only an elaborate "display inscription," designed to glorify Assyria and its gods and to portray the evil deeds of the wicked Babylonians. Yet the paucity of other material at times makes it a precious source of information. The *Assyrian Chronicle* was a dry but invaluable compilation of officials, their term of office and the seemingly most important event of each year. The closest approximation to literary art in Assyrian historiography is to be detected in the picturesque language of the royal annals. The reign of Ashurbanipal (668-626 B.C.) was of special importance for the development of Assyrian historical writing. This king ordered composed and assembled a great library which not only preserved earlier historical materials, but contained the inscriptions of the reign of Ashurbanipal which came closer to historical narrative in style than any earlier royal annals.

From the later Babylonian and Chaldean periods come two meritorious narratives. One is the *Babylonian Chronicle* which covers the time from 745 to 668 B.C. Its viewpoint is different from that of the Assyrian records which it supplements and corrects, and it relates with notable impartiality the wars of Assyria with Elam. The other is the so-called *Gadd Chronicle* which, in the parts preserved, deals with the years from 616 to 610 B.C., describes the fall of Assur in 614, of Nineveh in 612, and Harran in 610. It gives full credit to the Medes for their military prowess. The *History* of Berossos, written in Greek at the beginning of the third century B.C., was obviously compiled from native records in Babylon, the characteristic style of which it preserved. To the Greco-Roman world it became an important source, and it continues to have a distinct value, owing to the paucity of other material, though we have only late and unreliable excerpts from it.

The royal annals of the Babylonians and Assyrians were continued in general style and manner by the Median and Persian kings. One of the most important, that of Darius upon the great rocky crag at Behistun, has proved of special significance for the reconstruction of our modern knowledge of ancient oriental history and languages. This elaborate inscription was set down in Persian, Susian, and Babylonian script. By copying and deciphering this inscription, Sir Henry Rawlinson was able to unravel the mysteries of the cuneiform languages nearly a century ago.

It has more recently been ascertained that the Hittites produced a respectable historical literature. We have a vast mass of historical material, mostly in cuneiform tablets, read and interpreted, and also in later hieroglyphic texts which have now been deciphered. In addition to historical annals, there are treaties referring to earlier political relations. Especially noteworthy is the *History* of Telepinus (*ca.* 1100 B.C.) which covers more than three centuries. It has a definite didactic purpose, namely, to show the evils of blood feud as a means of settling crimes and disputes. The author shows how it helped to extinguish the dynasty and led to the adoption of the institution of *wergild* in the Hittite Code of Hattusil III. Attention might also be called to one of the first examples of historical autobiography, namely, that of Hattusil III (*ca.* 1281-1260 B.C.).

The honor of having first produced a truly historical narrative of considerable scope and high relative accuracy must be accorded to the Hebrews of ancient Palestine. These Hebrew historical writings were contained mainly in the Bible, and we may profitably look briefly into the rise of the scholarly views relative to the nature of the Hebrew Bible.

Doubts were voiced in regard to certain traditional notions of the authorship of the Bible by some of the more critical Church Fathers in the later Roman Empire, but the first scholar to raise serious questions about the conventional views was an able medieval Jewish scholar, Aben Ezra, who, about A.D. 1150, seriously challenged the notion of the Mosaic authorship of the Pentateuch. In the seventeenth century the distinguished critical philosopher, Thomas Hobbes, questioned the Mosaic authorship on the basis of considerations of logic and common sense rather than textual and historical scholarship. He pointed out how unusual it was for an author (Moses), while still writing his autobiography, to be able to call attention to his death and to boast that he was so well buried that no one, for many years, had been able to locate his grave. Yet the Pentateuch tells of this successful secrecy in the burial of Moses and describes in detail the grief of the Jews following his death. The Jewish scholar, Baruch Spinoza, a younger contemporary of Hobbes, began the truly critical study of the origin of Genesis, showed that Genesis could not have been written by a single author at any one time, and offered evidence to discredit the theory of the Mosaic authorship of the Pentateuch.

In the middle of the eighteenth century a brilliant French physician, Jean Astruc, outlined crudely what has come to be accepted as the accurate version of the nature and composition of the Pentateuch. The next decisive step was taken by Karl David Ilgen at the very close of the eighteenth century. He pointed out that there were at least seventeen different documents in Genesis, with three major sources which we have since accepted as correct. In the century following Ilgen there was remarkable progress in the difficult problem of unraveling the authorship of the Old Testament. Among the leading names associated with this great conquest of scholarship are W. M. L. DeWette, Hermann Hupfeld, Bishop John William Colenso, Bernhard Stade, Abraham Kuenen, Bernhard Duhm, and Julius Wellhausen. Wellhausen greatly advanced Old Testament criticism and has been looked upon as the master scholar in this field. Since his day splendid work has been done by T. K. Cheyne, S. R. Driver, B. W. Bacon and others.

The critical process has been carried beyond a mere study of the text of the Old Testament. The brilliant Cambridge professor, William Robertson Smith, in his famous *Religion of the Semites,* demonstrated that there was nothing unique about the Jewish religion and indicated many points of similarity between the religion of the ancient Hebrews and the religious beliefs and practices of the other branches of the Semitic peoples. Pursuing this line of investigation more thoroughly and precisely, scholars like Delitzsch, Winckler and Rogers have made more clear the profound influence of Babylonian mythology and religious tradition upon the religion of the Hebrews, particularly in the way of the adoption of the Babylonian cosmology, creation tales and early historical myths, such as the stories of the Tower of Babel and the Deluge. R. H. Charles and others have done equally significant work in indicating the Persian foundations of the late Jewish version of what became the typical Christian doctrine of the devil, hell, and a literal immortality of the soul.

As we have already pointed out, it is the opinion of the pious Jew and Christian that the Pentateuch was dictated by God to Moses, a great Hebrew statesman and faithful amanuensis, sometime during the thirteenth century before Christ. Biblical scholars have shown that, in the first place, the very term Pentateuch is a misconception and a misnomer. Instead of being made up of five books it really constitutes a block of eleven, namely, the first twelve books of the Bible, leaving out the Book of Ruth, which is a late product of the Persian and Greek periods. Far from being the creation of a single author who brought out his work within a period of a few years, the Pentateuch was actually compiled by at least four groups of authors, writing over a broad sweep of time which extended from the close of the tenth century B.C. to the middle of the fifth century B.C. There are at least four basic strains making up this section of the Bible. The earliest, or so-called "J" source, is a product of the late tenth or early ninth century. It is called "J" because the writers give to the Hebrew God the term "Jahveh." The second source in chronological order is known as the "E" source, because the authors here use the term "Elohim" to describe the Deity. It comes from the eighth century. The third foundation document is the Book of Deuteronomy, written some time between 650 and 620 B.C.

Scholars refer to this as "D". The fourth and final document is the so-called "priestly" or "P" source and it dates from somewhere between 586 and 450 B.C. Each of these four sources was the product of a group of writers rather than a single author.

None of these four foundation documents exists in the Bible in exactly the same form in which it was written down. All were altered in differing degrees by subsequent editors. Nor is the Pentateuch made up of "J", "E", "D", and "P" strung along in serial and chronological order. These sources were combined by later editors and intermingled in an almost inextricable fashion. It is this fact of subsequent editing and combination which made the unraveling of the authorship and composition of the Pentateuch so complex a problem as to require a century of scholarly endeavor. "J" and "E" were edited and combined some time around the close of the eighth century B.C. Then "J", "E" and "D" were combined and edited between 620 and 450 B.C. Finally, in the middle of the fifth century B.C., "J", "E" and "D", already much modified and edited and re-edited, were joined with "P" to constitute the historic Pentateuch as we have it in the Old Testament. These facts about the Pentateuch, altogether too briefly and incompletely recounted to give any true conception of the complexity of the situation, will show how far from the truth is the simple pietistic notion of the Pentateuch which we described above. Perhaps we can make the nature of the Bible somewhat more clear by quoting Professor James T. Shotwell's striking comparison of the Bible with a hypothetical Greek work of similar character and composition:

> Let us imagine, for instance, that instead of the Jewish scriptures we are talking of those of the Greeks. Suppose that the heritage of Hellas has been preserved to us in the form of a Bible. What would be the character of the book? We should begin, perhaps, with a few passages from Hesiod on the birth of the gods, and the dawn of civilization mingled with fragments of the *Iliad* and both set into long excerpts from Herodotus. The dialogues of Plato might be given by Homeric heroes and the text of the great dramatists (instead of the prophets) be preserved, interspersed one with another and clogged with the uninspiring comments of Alexandrian savants. Then imagine that the sense of their authority was so much obscured as centuries passed, that philosophers—for philosophers were to Greece what the theologians were to Israel—came to believe that the large part of this composite work of history and philosophy had been written down by Solon as the deliverance of the oracle of Apollo at Delphi. Then, finally, imagine that the text became stereotyped and sacred, even the words taboo, and became the heritage of alien peoples who knew nothing more of Greek history than what this compilation contained. Such, with some little exaggeration, would be a Hellenic Bible, after the fashion of the Bible of the Jews. If the comparison be a little overdrawn there is no danger but that we shall make sufficient mental reservations to prevent us

from carrying it too far. Upon the whole, so far as form and structure go, the analogy holds remarkably well.[13]

The beginnings of the historical narrative among the Hebrews were stimulated by the great expansion of Hebrew prosperity and prestige under the kings of the united kingdom, Saul, David and Solomon. As Professor George Foote Moore has said: "The making of great history has often given a first impulse to the writing of history, and we may well believe that it was so in Israel, and that the beginning of Hebrew historical literature, in the proper sense of the word, was made with Saul and David."[14]

The first Hebrew historical writing, which marks the earliest appearance of the true historical narrative of which any record has anywhere been preserved, is to be found in the work of the uncertain authors of the "Jahvist" sources of the Pentateuch, Joshua, the Books of Samuel and the opening of the first Book of Kings. On this Professor Breasted makes the following comment: "They are the earliest example of historical writings in prose which we possess among any people, and their nameless author is the earliest historian whom we have found in the early world."[15] Eduard Meyer remarked of the best passages in this historical writing: "It is astonishing that historical literature of this character should have been possible in Israel at this time. It stands far above anything we know elsewhere of ancient Oriental historical writing." Far and away the outstanding example of this Hebrew historical narrative is the so-called *History of David,* written possibly by the high priest, Abiathar. Of this Professor A. T. Olmstead has written:

> Whether written by Abiathar or not, the modern professional historian must do justice to his predecessor of three thousand years ago. He has presented us with a genuine history and so far as we know he had no forerunners. Here are no inspired annals of a monarch's wars, no brief dry chronicle or folk tale of past heroes, such as we find among the Egyptians, Babylonians and Assyrians, but a contemporary history which would suffer little in essentials if compared with present day records of reigns. Our historian has been behind the scenes, he writes simply yet vividly, not propaganda for his monarch, but an account of the facts for coming generations.
>
> His complete objectivity is uncanny. David is, to be sure, his hero and we realize why he stole the hearts of all with his winning ways, but he paints David's weaknesses as unsparingly, the banditry of his early life, his repeated lies, his flight to the enemy of his people, his forgetfulness that Michal had saved his life, his intrigue with Bathsheba and its

---

13 J. T. Shotwell, *An Introduction to the History of History* (Columbia University Press, 1922), pp. 82-83.
14 G. F. Moore, *Literature of the Old Testament* (Henry Holt, 1911), p. 96.
15 Breasted, *op. cit.,* p. 208.

terrible consequences in his family, his degeneration through success and luxury. The other members of the court, even the Zadok who supplanted Abiathar as chief priest, are treated with equal objectivity. Whether Abiathar or not, he is our first great historian.[16]

The remaining historical books in the Old Testament canon were the Books of Kings, which were written about 560 B.C.,[17] and Chronicles-Ezra-Nehemiah, written about 300 B.C. The Books of Kings were the first practical illustration of the notion of history as "philosophy teaching by example." The author sought primarily to convince his people of the value of religious fidelity by citing historical illustrations of the disasters that had come to the Hebrews because they deserted their national religion. The author of Kings, in the synchronous history of Israel and Judah and the story of the later Judean kings, drew upon valuable early records whose factual accuracy has, in the main, often been corroborated by contemporary inscriptions. The chronicles are distinctly inferior in accuracy. Chronicles-Ezra-Nehemiah constitute mainly the work of a single author, a priest of Jerusalem, who by genealogies and narrative surveyed the whole of Hebrew history with the aim of glorifying, through tremendous exaggerations, the splendor of the Hebrew kingdom under David and Solomon, and of re-emphasizing the warning of the author of the Books of Kings respecting the penalties imposed for deserting the true religion. The most important materials contained in Chronicles-Ezra-Nehemiah are the rich and interesting personal memoirs of Nehemiah, which have been embodied in the general narrative. These are far superior in character to the work of the priest-author. The latter is believed to have forged the memoirs of Ezra. In addition to the Old Testament narratives there are other valuable historical materials in this religious anthology. Among them is the Hebrew legislation (religious and secular laws) which the Higher Critics have finally arranged in historical order. Others of importance are the poems and hymns, and the folk tales like the legends of the patriarchs, the Samson stories and the stories about David and Solomon.

One of the ablest products of Hebrew historiography was the First Book of Maccabees. Not being in the Hebrew canon of the Bible used by the translators, it was not included in the Protestant Bible. This narrative, written about 125 B.C. by a devout and vigorous Sadduccee and an ardent admirer of the Asmonean house—a sort of Judean Treitschke—tells the stirring story of Hebrew history from the conquest of Palestine by Alexander the Great to the accession of John Hyrcanus. The work centers about the deliverance of Palestine from Syrian domination as a result

---

[16] A. T. Olmstead *et al.*, *Persecution and Liberty: Essays in Honor of George Lincoln Burr* (Century, 1931), p. 33. See footnote on this page for references to specific biblical passages in the Books of Samuel which go to make up this *History of David*.

[17] The last event referred to is the reign of Amit Marduk (562-560 B.C.).

of the military exploits of Judas Maccabaeus and his successors. While fired by the thrills of patriotic pride, the author produced a work unique for his time in its secular attitude. He attributed the victories of the Hebrews to the personal ability and courage of the Asmoneans and not to the direct intervention of the Deity in behalf of the Jews. Unfortunately, however, the Christian historians of medieval Europe did not take as their Hebrew model the brilliant secular narrative of First Maccabees, but sought rather to strengthen their followers' zeal and to terrorize their opponents by imitation of the more conventional Hebrew historical tales of the miraculous interposition of the Deity in rewarding the faithful and punishing the sinners.

The last of the distinguished Hebrew historians was Flavius Josephus (*ca.* A.D. 37-105). He was the national historian of the Jews and, writing mainly after the destruction of the power and unity of his people in A.D. 70, he tried to compensate for the contemporary distress of the Jewish people by emphasizing the glories of their past. Consequently, he almost outdid the author of Chronicles-Ezra-Nehemiah in his exaggeration of the wealth, population and international prestige of ancient Palestine. His two chief works were the *War of the Jews,* and the *Antiquities of the Jews.* The first mentioned gave an account of the history of the Jews in the centuries immediately prior to the Great Jewish War, which ended in the destruction of Jerusalem, and then narrated in detail the events of the final struggle. The *Antiquities,* an even more elaborate work, was devoted to the glories of the Jewish past. A shorter work, *Against Apion,* was a defiant challenge to Gentile historians for their alleged failure to do justice to the importance of Jewish history and culture.

In his treatment of the Old Testament period his narrative was highly unreliable, but the discussion of the post-Maccabean era was far more free from exaggeration and credulity. He wrote in Greek with a considerable degree of literary skill and he has been referred to as the "Livy of the Jews." While the comparison is not without some basis in fact, Josephus did not quite equal the national historian of Rome in literary merit though he perhaps matched him in accuracy of statement.

Though the Hebrews brought into being the true historical narrative, Hebrew historiography did not affect the general current of historical writing until after the Christians had taken over the sacred books of the Jews. The Christians used these not only as the basis of much of their theology, but also as the foundation of their chronology and their synthesis of the history of the past. It is to the Greeks that attention must be turned in describing the chief source of the origins and development of the type of historical writing which dominated classical antiquity and prevailed until the time of Julius Africanus, Orosius and Eusebius. Indeed, all the major systematic historical narratives of the ancient Orient, with the exception of the early Hebrew historical writing, were profoundly affected by Greek culture. Manetho, Berossos and Josephus were all pretty thoroughly Hellenized, and all of them wrote in Greek.

SELECTED REFERENCES

H. E. Barnes, *The New History and the Social Studies*. The Century Co., 1925.

A. C. Haddon, *History of Anthropology*. G. P. Putnam's Sons, 1910.

B. J. Stern, *Lewis Henry Morgan, Social Evolutionist*. University of Chicago Press, 1931.

Stanley Casson, *Progress of Archeology*. McGraw-Hill Book Co., 1935.

B. L. Ullman, *Ancient Writing*. Longmans, Green and Co., 1932.

W. A. Mason, *History of the Art of Writing*. Macmillan, 1920.

Hutton Webster, *Rest Days*. Macmillan, 1916.

J. C. McDonald, *Chronologies and Calendars*. London, 1927.

J. T. Shotwell, *Introduction to the History of History,* chaps. i-xi. Columbia University Press, 1922.

Adolf Erman, *Literature of the Ancient Egyptians*. E. P. Dutton and Co., 1927.

A. T. Olmstead, *Assyrian Historiography*. University of Missouri Press, 1916.

D. D. Luckenbill, *Ancient Records of Assyria and Babylonia*. University of Chicago Press, 1927, 2 vols.

G. A. Barton, *The Royal Inscriptions of Sumer and Akkad*. Yale University Press, 1929.

R. W. Rogers, *Cuneiform Parallels to the Old Testament*. Abingdon Press, 1912.

G. F. Moore, *Literature of the Old Testament*. Henry Holt, 1911.

A. T. Olmstead, "Hebrew History and Historical Method," in Olmstead *et al., Persecution and Liberty*: *Essays in Honor of George Lincoln Burr,* pp. 21 ff. Century, 1931.

Hans Schmidt, *Die Geschichtschreibung im Alten Testament*. Tübingen, 1911.

J. W. Thompson, *A History of Historical Writing*, Vol. I, chap. i. 2 vols., Macmillan, 1942.

H. E. Barnes and Howard Becker, *Social Thought from Lore to Science,* Vol. I, chap. iii. 3 Vols., Dover, 1961.

Herbert Wendt, *In Search of Adam*. Houghton Mifflin, 1956.

J. H. Robinson, *The New History*. The Macmillan Co., 1912.

L. A. White, *The Evolution of Culture*. McGraw-Hill, 1959.

Julius Lippert, *The Evolution of Culture*. Macmillan, 1931.

Will Durant, *Our Oriental Heritage*. Simon and Schuster, 1938.

Jack Finegan, *Light from the Ancient Past*. Princeton University Press, 1959.

Werner Keller, *The Bible as History*. Hodder Stoughton, 1956.

F. J. Teggart, *The Theory of History*. Yale University Press, 1925.

J. O. Hertzler, *Social Thought of the Ancient Civilizations*. McGraw-Hill, 1936.

J. H. Breasted, *Ancient Records of Egypt*. Univ. of Chicago Press, 1906-7.

J. A. Bewer, *Literature of the Old Testament*. Columbia Univ. Press, 1951.

Alexander Heidel, *The Babylonian Genesis*. Univ. of Chicago Press, 1951.

II

HISTORICAL WRITING AMONG THE GREEKS AND ROMANS

HISTORICAL WRITING AMONG THE GREEKS

IT has been said, with some solid basis, that the first notable historical writing in Greece is to be found in the poems attributed to Homer. At least, as a source of information concerning culture and society, the Homeric poems contain materials superior in scope and content to most of the traditional Greek historical writing. The works of T. D. Seymour, Andrew Lang and A. G. Keller on Homeric society well illustrate how clear and adequate a picture of the civilization of the age can be gleaned from a study of the Homeric writings.

The birth of formal historical writing in Greece, however, required several essential conditions in the cultural background which did not exist before the sixth century B.C., namely, the easy and conventional writing of prose, the critical rejection of the current mythology concerning Greek beginnings, and the stimulation of interest in social origins and institutions. By the middle of the sixth century these indispensable prerequisites of historical narrative had come into being in the city of Miletus in Ionia. Cadmus of Miletus, at the beginning of the sixth century, had introduced the practice of writing prose instead of poetry and he ranks as one of the earliest of Greek prose writers or *logographoi*. In the same period there came into existence that speculative Ionic philosophy which brought the world the origins of free thought and critical philosophy. As Professor Bury has said: "Our deepest gratitude is due to the Greeks as the originators of liberty and thought and discussion . . . . Ionia in Asia Minor was the cradle of free speculation. The history of European science and European philosophy begins in Ionia. Here, in the sixth and fifth centuries B.C., the earliest philosophers by using their reason sought to penetrate into the origin and structure of the world . . . . They began the work of destroying orthodox views and religious faiths."[1]

The colonizing movement, trade, and travel in the East were also powerful aids in civilizing the Ionic and Aegean Greeks and in developing that culture and critical spirit which lay at the basis of the origins of Greek philosophy, literature and historical writing. This contact of cultures stimulated curiosity and intellectual growth. It is not without significance

[1] J. B. Bury, *The History of the Freedom of Thought* (Holt, 1913), pp. 22-23.

that Hecataeus, the first of the Greek historians, had traveled extensively in Egypt.

Finally, the Persian absorption of Ionia tended to bring a broader cultural perspective to the Ionic Greeks through the further operation of this all-important process of the contact of cultures. It also aroused the interest of the Ionic Greeks in the civilization of the diverse peoples who dwelt in the great empire of which they had recently become a part.

The origin of Greek historical literature, then, was a part of that great intellectual movement conventionally known as the rise of the *logographoi* and of the critical Greek philosophy in Ionia. Along with these more general or cultural explanations of the appearance of the first Greek historical literature, there should be noted the personal impulse arising from the dominating desire of the more prominent citizens of the time to provide their families with a distinguished genealogy. Hesiod had favored the Greek gods by providing them with a respectable ancestry, and a similar service was rendered to the nobles by the *logographoi*. Interest in geography and ethnography supplemented the genealogical element in helping on the origins of Greek historical writing. This serves to explain the prevalence of geographical description, descriptive sociology and ethnography in Greek historical literature.

In view of the foregoing sketch of the intellectual environment of early Greek critical prose, it seems to have been in the natural course of events that the first Greek historian should have been Hecataeus (born 550 B.C.), a traveler and a native of Miletus, the birthplace of both Greek prose and Greek critical philosophy. His main significance lies in the fact that he foreshadowed two important developments of scientific historical method by setting up truth as the test of his statements and assuming a frankly critical attitude toward the conventional Greek creation myths. The opening paragraph of his *Genealogies* is, perhaps, the first close approach on the part of any writer to a consciousness of the nature of historical criticism: "What I write here," he said, "is the account which I considered to be true: for the stories of the Greeks are numerous, and in my opinion ridiculous."

The intellectual trends which had produced Hecataeus grew apace, and the essential achievements between his *Genealogies* and the *History* of Herodotus were rapidly consummated. Charon of Lampsacus and Dionysius of Miletus compiled histories of Persia during the middle of the fifth century, and Scylax of Caryanda produced the first historical biography. In the latter part of the fifth century Antiochus of Syracuse composed the first history devoted to the peoples of Greece, and Hellanicus of Lesbos prepared the way for Herodotus by the breadth of his interests. He not only dealt with the history of Persia and Greece from a broad social point of view, but was also the earliest of the Greek historians to recognize the necessity of a comprehensive system of chronology. The latter, with relative success, he attempted to supply.

The first comprehensive and systematic historical work composed by a Greek author was the account of Greco-Asiatic relations from the reign of Croesus of Lydia (560-546 B.C.) to the defeat of the Persian invaders of Greece in 478 B.C. by Herodotus. The Persian wars had awakened the interest of the Greeks in the character of the civilizations of the Near Orient. Hence, any writer who linked up a description of oriental cultures with the absorbing patriotic theme of the Greeks' rebuff of the Persians was bound to have many and enthusiastic readers. The opportunity was seized by Herodotus of Halicarnassus (*ca.* 484-425 B.C.). He was interested not only in civilized peoples but in the uncivilized as well. Hence, he is correctly regarded as not only the father of history but also as the father of anthropology. Of the general character and import of his work Maurice Croiset has written:

> An Asiatic Greek, Herodotus of Halicarnassus, undertook this task [of revealing more of the Orient to his countrymen] and succeeded very well with it. An indefatigable traveler, whose desire to see and to know led him successively to Egypt, to Asia, to almost all parts of Greece, to Sicily, and to Italy, where he finally settled down and probably died, he succeeded in carrying out a most profitable inquiry—questioning men, visiting monuments, informing himself about everything, about customs, laws, forms of government, and religions, without preconceived ideas or prejudices, but with a singular mixture of acuteness and credulity, of insatiable curiosity and religious discretion. And from everything which he had seen, read and heard, he produced by the power of his genius, by his keen sense for beautiful things, by his talent as a story-teller, and by the charm of his style, a truly admirable work. In an immense frame, as in a sort of moving panorama, he gives his readers a picture of the life of twenty different peoples. How much instruction was offered in this encyclopedic collection, wherein the variety of human types, the multiplicity of religions, and the history of diverse institutions, were so interestingly set forth! Scarcely did the contemporary tragedy itself present so rich a collection of human documents.[2]

The central theme of the *History* of Herodotus was the Persian wars, especially the destruction of the forces of Xerxes by the Greeks. But the background which he sought for his work provided even more important and interesting material than his specific history of the Persian wars. Indeed, Herodotus was at his worst as a reporter of military history, where he showed much carelessness and little capacity for checking up on details. In one sense, however, his work here was both unusual and commendable. He did not allow patriotic bias to overcome his judgment and

---

[2] Maurice Croiset, *Hellenic Civilization* (Alfred A. Knopf, 1935), pp. 143-44.

sense of fairness. He was so just to the Persians and so willing to concede their valor that he was bitterly criticized on this point by his patriotic Greek readers.

To Herodotus the Persian wars represented the clash of two important and distinct types of civilization—the Hellenic and the oriental. Hence, he "backed off" to analyze these conflicting cultures. This exercise in historical perspective led to the very entertaining and illuminating descriptions which he gave of the peoples of the western Mediterranean and Asiatic world in the sixth and fifth centuries B.C. This material was a sort of mixture of cultural history and descriptive sociology. He ranged from the climates of various areas to the regimen of everyday life among the peoples he dealt with. And he described the diverse peoples with unusual freedom from race prejudice. For a long time regarded as the victim of a boundless credulity, contemporary archeological research has confirmed not a few of his vivid tales and descriptive flights. He differentiated with remarkable success for his age between the popular tales and what he himself saw and believed. By his broad interests, Herodotus really qualified as a cultural historian, and it is worth noting that the first comprehensive historical work ever composed was at the same time a history of civilization.

In his specific treatment of the Persian wars Herodotus was somewhat less happy and successful, though perhaps no less interesting. Professor Shotwell has described him as "the Homer of the Persian wars," and the comparison is not without much merit and cogency. This part of his work was a prose epic. Herodotus was an admirer of Athenian "democracy." Though praising Persian bravery, he eulogized Athens and its triumph over the autocratic Persian imperialism with all the fervor of a Bancroft describing the winning of American independence from the British Empire. But he had none of that solicitude for accuracy and precision in his reporting of military facts which characterized his distinguished successor, Thucydides. Nor did he free himself fully from deference to the doctrine of the intervention of the gods in human affairs. The theory of supernatural causation appeared not infrequently in his work.

But the fame of Herodotus will endure as the first constructive artist in the field of historical writing, as the author of the earliest comprehensive historical work, as the first writer to imply that the task of the historian is to reconstruct the whole past life of man, and as one of the most absorbing story-tellers in the entire course of historical writing. His prestige and importance have been enhanced in our generation as a result of the growing popularity of the history of culture and the gradual eclipse of the long-popular episodical military and political type of history which prevailed from Thucydides until the twentieth century of our era.

The second major Greek historian, Thucydides (*ca.* 456-396 B.C.), ap-

proached historical problems in a far different spirit from that of Herodotus. He abandoned entertaining story-telling in favor of sober and earnest narration of historical truth as he conceived it. He rigorously excluded
the myths and legends in which Herodotus reveled. Thucydides divorced
history from both epic poetry and supernaturalism in his attitude towards
historical causation. He attributed historical events to rational causes or
secular pretexts. There were none of the long and diverting digressions
which we find so profusely scattered through the writing of Herodotus.
Instead, Thucydides selected a definite theme for his historical enterprise
and he hewed closely to the line thus chosen. His materials were not only
always relevant to the general topic, but were invariably closely cogent to
the specific matter under discussion.

The major subject of Thucydides' historical writing, the Peloponnesian
War (431-404 b.c.), was much more narrow and restricted a field than that
covered by Herodotus. Compared to the work of the latter, it was much
like a history of the American Civil War would be when set off against
an account of the evolution of Anglo-American civilization since the sixteenth century. Since Thucydides' history was in part prepared during the
course of the conflict, it was as much the work of a scholarly and philosophic war correspondent—an antique Frank Simonds—as that of a dispassionate historian reconstructing the events of the distant past from a
study of the documents. His sketch of the rise of Greece from early city-
states to the Athenian Empire, with which he prefaced his account of the
Peloponnesian War, showed, however, that Thucydides had rare capacity
to portray the past if he had seen fit. But his great work was preëminently
contemporary history which he beheld as a prominent eyewitness, being
himself an Athenian general and politician.

The main contribution of Thucydides to historiography lay, as we have
implied, in the realm of criticism and methodology. He set forth with
vigor the thesis that the permanent worth and enduring fame of a historical work should depend more upon the accuracy of its statements than
upon the entertainment furnished by the narrative. Leopold von Ranke,
at the opening of the nineteenth century, did not expound more earnestly
than Thucydides had at the close of the fifth century b.c. the basic tenet of
scientific history, namely, that accuracy of data must be the foundation of
true historical writing. The second main historical canon of Thucydides
was that of relevance and cogency of material—a vast step in advance, as
we have seen, over Herodotus. To these should be added his ability in
the mastery of details and their subordination to the forward movement
of the whole narrative. In these respects Thucydides may rightly be held
to have been the founder of scientific and critical history. Further, Thucydides was probably the first historian clearly and definitely to state the
alleged "pragmatic" value of the writing and study of history. In the

opinion of Thucydides, "the accurate knowledge of what has happened will be useful, because, according to human probability, similar things will happen again."

Thucydides insisted not only upon sifting his sources and basing his narrative upon accurate documentation. He was also highly competent in organizing and interpreting his materials. If he was mainly interested in political data, he was at the same time the first historian to treat politics with the grasp of a philosopher. He carefully considered what he understood to be the problems of historical and political causation, recognizing and treating remote as well as immediate causes. And he possessed real astuteness in psychological analysis, as applied to both individuals and groups. This is well illustrated by his masterful series of character studies and by his analysis of public opinion in such instances as the Athenian revolution of 411 b.c. Thucydides was also an impressive literary artist. While he made wide use of documents and oral sources, he adroitly concealed them and subordinated the external mechanics of scholarship so that he might produce a smooth and flowing narrative.

In spite of his sterling contributions to historical science, the writings of Thucydides were not free from some major defects. He was unable fully to grasp the concept of time or to view his facts in their true historical perspective. Nor did he possess Herodotus' keen appreciation of the importance of geographical factors in historical situations. He not only narrowed the field of history to a consideration of contemporary political phenomena, but even restricted the latter to the external military and diplomatic phases of political activity. He missed the vital significance of the deeper cultural, social and economic forces in history, a weakness perhaps overemphasized by Mr. F. M. Cornford. In his *Thucydides Mythistoricus* Cornford contends that Thucydides did not understand the real nature and background of the Peloponnesian War. Cornford holds that the war was brought about by the policies of the commercial and industrial groups of the Piraeus—in other words, the mercantile middle class. This fundamental fact is not even mentioned by Thucydides. Being a characteristically snobbish Athenian gentleman he seemed averse to noticing the activities and aspirations of this mercantile class. He took Pericles' public utterances on the issues of the war at their face value. G. F. Abbott and others have undertaken to defend Thucydides on these points, though not with entire success.

Above all, Thucydides neglected the magnificent opportunity to portray the glories of Athenian civilization. This was due to his restricted conception of the mission of the historian, not to any lack of ability as a cultural historian. His famous reconstruction of the funeral speech of Pericles gives one an inkling of what he might have done in the field of cultural history if he had chosen to treat this theme. It can scarcely be

doubted, moreover, that he carried the test of "relevance" too far. If Herodotus had introduced many long digressions into remote fields of
description, Thucydides plainly omitted much relevant material essential
to a full comprehension of his narrative. This was especially true of non-
political and non-military elements in historical situations. Again, he illustrated Carlyle's weakness in his dramatic interpretation of events in
terms of great personalities, though he did not possess Carlyle's ability to
portray a personality in its entirety. Accepting the notion of purely personal causes in history, he was somewhat superficial even here, too often
putting down mere pretexts for real causes. Lastly, there appeared little
or none of Mabillon's profound discussion of the critical use of documents. His sources, as we have indicated, were carefully concealed in
order that the style of the narrative might not suffer.

One may agree entirely with Bury that "the work of Thucydides
marks the longest and most decisive step that has ever been taken by a
single man towards making history what it is today," without regarding
that statement as an unmixed compliment. Thucydides certainly was influential in bringing historiography under the domination of the "political
fetish" and the spell of episodes, from which it suffered from classical
times to the end of the nineteenth century. It must not be forgotten that,
as Lamprecht has insisted, true historical accuracy requires a consideration
of the genesis and cultural setting of a situation as certainly as it does the
mere formal truth of such facts as are narrated.[3] From the standpoint of
this broader and more fundamental view of historical accuracy, Thucydides will scarcely rank as the equal of Herodotus. The ardent admirers of
the former have too often forgotten that scope and content are quite as
important in history as refinement of the methodology of research or the
cogency and tightness of the narrative.

The last of the major Greek historians was Polybius (*ca.* 198-117 B.C.).
From the standpoint of both productivity and profundity he was superior
to Thucydides and he was fully equal to the latter with respect to the accuracy of historical statements. Due, however, to the fact that his style is
labored and diffuse Polybius has been less popular with the learned reading public than his two great predecessors. His *History* was an ambitious
work in forty books dealing with the expansion and constitutional development of the Roman Empire to 146 B.C. Polybius was, if anything, more
emphatic than Thucydides in maintaining that the qualified historian
must be an eminent man of affairs, preferably a general and a statesman.

As Herodotus had mirrored the interest of early Greek historians in the
East, and Thucydides had written of Athens and its foreign relations at
the height of Athenian civilization, so Polybius reflected the decline

---

[3] See below, pp. 316 ff.

of Hellas and the shifting of interest to the new Roman power in the West. A native Greek who spent most of his adult life in Rome, Polybius came closer to the ideal of impartiality in treating Greek and Roman history than any other historical writer of antiquity. He sought in a well-organized work to explain the rise of Rome to power. His sixth book is the best extant ancient analysis of Roman political ideals and military methods. He found the unique political genius of the Romans to reside in their adoption of a mixed form of government—monarchical, aristocratic, and democratic. It was by thus adopting all three major forms of government that the Romans had escaped from the otherwise almost inevitable trend towards a cyclical movement from monarchy to tyranny, aristocracy, oligarchy, democracy and mob rule, and then around the cycle again. Polybius possessed shrewd judgment in assessing policies and was a keen student of events and personalities. His character sketches—as, for example, that of Hannibal—were often masterpieces.

Even more than in the case of Thucydides, the contributions of Polybius to the advancement of historical science consisted in his furtherance of the ideals of sound historical methodology. In the twelfth book of his work is found, as a critique of the antiquarian, Timaeus, the first great treatise on the methodology of scientific history. Conceived independently of Thucydides, this discussion has scarcely been surpassed to our own day, and his impartiality could well be a model for all historians. Especially noteworthy was his Ritter-like insistence upon the value of a knowledge of geography and topography to the historian. Like Thucydides, he intended his history to be intensely pragmatic—to be "philosophy teaching by example." He believed that the major practical value of history resides in the provision of accurate historical facts which might help to guide the administration of public affairs in the present. But he rarely allowed the philosopher in him to overcome the historian. Greatly interested in the problem of causation, he went deeper in his analysis of impersonal causes than Thucydides, though even his interpretation was ethical rather than economic or social. As Croiset observes: "It was in his work that there was defined the idea of continuity of human life, of an intimate logic of things, and of an interdependence among nations, which until then had been able to appear isolated. . . . . Thereafter history could no longer consider either geography, or the constitution of states, their laws and customs and their economic and military organization, as episodical subjects calculated to satisfy the curiosity of readers in a more or less transitory way."[4] The following brief quotation from his twelfth book admirably epitomizes his views as to the scope, methods and purpose of history:

> The science of history is threefold: first, the dealing with written documents and the arrangement of the material thus obtained; second, topog-

4 Croiset, *op. cit.*, p. 218.

raphy, the appearance of cities and localities, the description of rivers and harbors, and, speaking generally, the peculiar features of the seas and countries and their relative distances; thirdly, political affairs. . . . . The special province of history is, first to ascertain what the actual words used were; and secondly, to learn why it was that a particular policy or arrangement failed or succeeded. For a bare statement of an occurrence is interesting indeed, but not instructive; but when this is supplemented by a statement of cause, the study of history becomes fruitful. For it is by applying analogies to our own circumstances that we get the means and basis for calculating the future; and for learning from the past when to act with caution, and when with greater boldness, in the present.

Analyzing and criticizing the Greek antiquarian, Timaeus, Polybius carefully considered the matter of the reliability of the sources which a historian must use. He denounced partisanship and was a relentless foe of rhetoric, which was already beginning to debauch Greek and Roman historical writing.

All in all, one may almost agree with Professor George Willis Botsford that "a careful reading of this author is the best possible introduction to the spirit and method of history as we of today regard it." Or, as Professor Shotwell puts it, "Polybius' discussion of the guiding principles of historical writing are the first and noblest statement of scientific ideals for the historian until the days of Ranke."

A historian far inferior to Herodotus, Thucydides and Polybius was Xenophon (*ca.* 430-354 B.C.) who, chronologically, preceded Polybius by over two centuries. His literary ability was of a high order, but his capacity for profound historical analysis was most limited. He was a good memoir writer and his *Anabasis* was one of the most absorbing of Greek memoirs. In his *Hellenica* he attempted to continue the narrative of Thucydides from 411 to 362 B.C. While this book is most valuable as a historical source for the period, it is superficial and owes much of the historical merit it possesses primarily to its imitation of the method and arrangement of Thucydides' work. Xenophon also composed the best historical biography in Greek literature, his life of Agesilaus. And his *Ways and Means* afforded the only example among Greek historians of a thorough consideration of economic factors in politics. On the whole, however, it is safe to agree with Bury that Xenophon owes his reputation as a historian to the fact that an uncritical generation later preserved his writings while allowing more meritorious works to perish and that "if he had lived in modern days, he would have been a high-class journalist and pamphleteer and would have made his fortune as a war-correspondent."[5] It would not be fair, however, to deny the remarkable versatility of Xenophon's literary

[5] J. B. Bury, *The Ancient Greek Historians* (Dover, 1958), p. 151; see also L. V. Jacks, *Xenophon: Soldier of Fortune* (Scribner's, 1930).

talents, which were exhibited in memoirs, biography, systematic history, constitutional analysis and economic theory.

Polybius was unique in his age as a historian. Long before he composed his great work Hellenic historiography had begun to decline from the standards set by Thucydides, and it came under the influence of rhetoric in the fourth century. With their tendency to insipid moralizing, the interpolation of florid and fictitious speeches, and their "passion for panegyrics," the historical works of the rhetorical school, like those of Froissart and Lamartine in later days, "exhibited artistic but not historical genius." This capitulation to the popular demand for rhetoric Hermann Peter believes to have been the main reason for the decline and stagnation of Greek historical writing and its Roman imitations.[6]

Of the rhetoricians of the fourth century the leader was Isocrates and the chief historians of the school were Ephorus and Theopompus. The work of Ephorus was probably the nearest approach in Greek historiography to a "national history" of Hellas. Of quite a different character was the work of Timaeus of Tauromenius, who devoted a lifetime of labor to the patient compilation of a vast repository of reliable facts concerning the history of Sicily and Italy. He was the first and the ablest of the antiquarians that flourished in the third century B.C., and he may be regarded as the prototype of Blondus and Leland. Two later ambitious compilations—the *World History* of Diodorus of Sicily (*ca.* 90-21 B.C.), and the *Roman History* of his younger contemporary, Dionysius of Halicarnassus, published in A.D. 7, were of inferior accuracy, though far ahead of the work of the rhetoricians. The latter is supposed to be the first to have stated specifically that history is "philosophy teaching by example."

Historical biography among the Greeks was promoted by Isocrates, a leader of the rhetoricians, and one of the earliest products was the biography of Agesilaus by Xenophon. Subsequent historians devoted considerable space to biography. Plutarch's (*ca.* A.D. 50-125) polished *Parallel Lives* have remained at the head of the world's biographical product in perennial popularity on account of their compelling interest, if not for their high historical accuracy. It must be remembered that Plutarch was a moralist and that he wrote his *Lives,* not as strictly historical biographies, but in order to furnish a concrete vindication of his ethical principles for the moral edification of his readers.

In the period of the Hellenic revival in Rome a number of Greek historians made contributions to historical writing of widely different merit. Among the less notable productions were the *Anabasis of Alexander* by Arrian (*ca.* A.D. 95-175), and the *History of Rome* by Appian, in the same period. Far superior to these were the incisive *History of Rome* by Dio

[6] Hermann Peter, *Wahrheit und Kunst* (Leipzig, 1911).

Cassius (*ca.* A.D. 155-240), and the broadly conceived history of the Roman Empire from A.D. 96 to 378, in its social as well as its political conditions, by Ammianus Marcellinus (*ca.* A.D. 330-401), the last of the long and honorable list of Greek historians. Seeking a Roman reading public, he wrote his work in Latin. Ammianus lacked grace in his adopted tongue, but his narrative was straightforward and generally reliable.

An important incidental contribution of the Greeks to historical science was their creation of passable notions of historical chronology. The antiquarian, Timaeus (*ca.* 350 B.C.), introduced the method of reckoning by means of the cycle of Olympiads, the four-year period of the Olympic games. Scientific chronology was carried further by the learned librarian at Alexandria, Eratosthenes (*ca.* 276-194 B.C.), who first fixed the dates of the major periods of Greek history, making use of astronomical calculations as well as of conventional historical references. His work was popularized by Apollodorus of Athens (*ca.* 120 B.C.) in the leading handbook of Greek chronology. It was continued to 61 B.C. by Castor of Rhodes. This Greek chronological work was later exploited by Julius Africanus, Eusebius and Jerome in their fashioning of the early Christian calculations of world history.[7]

ROMAN HISTORICAL WRITING

Rome added few original contributions to historiography. As in all other phases of its culture, Rome here followed the models set up by the Greeks. While there were distinguished Roman historians, none equaled Thucydides or Polybius for careful adherence to critical methods, and only Livy and Tacitus matched the best of the stylists among Greek historians.

The immediate dependence of the Roman historiography on the Greek is evident from the fact that down to the second century B.C. most Roman historical literature was actually written in Greek. These early historical works in Greek were chiefly *Annals,* of which the first and most famous were those of Fabius Pictor (b. 254 B.C.). The work which first suggested the myth of the Trojan origin of Rome was the *Annals* of the poet and adapter of Greek literature, Ennius (d. 169 B.C.). The earliest important Roman historical literature in Latin was the *Origins* of Cato the Censor (*ca.* 234-149 B.C), in which he narrated the history of Rome, interpreted according to his ever-evident patriotic, bucolic and aristocratic prejudices. The best-known Roman antiquarian was that versatile and indefatigable writer, Varro, whose chief work here was his *Roman Antiquities* (47 B.C.).

The first major historian among the Romans in point of time was that leader of all Romans in point of ability, Julius Caesar (100-44 B.C.). Gen-

[7] See below, pp. 44 ff.

erally accurate and always clear, forceful and direct in his style, Caesar's apologies for his public career—the *Commentaries on the Gallic Wars* and the *Civil War*—were the best historical memoirs produced in the ancient world and rank well with those of any period. Caesar's historical writing represents about the cleverest *ex parte* exposition in all historical literature. By maintaining a subtle self-restraint and an apparent personal modesty, he adroitly argued his case and portrayed his genius with the utmost effect. His *Commentaries* are almost as important for our knowledge of pre-Roman Gaul as is Tacitus' *Germania* for information about pre-Roman Germany.

A more systematic Roman historian was Sallust [Gaius Sallustius Crispus] (*ca.* 86-34 B.C.) the Roman disciple of Thucydides. His chief work, a *History of Rome,* from 78 to 67 B.C., has never been recovered, but from his monographs on the *Conspiracy of Catiline* and the *Jugurthine War* one can appreciate his vigorous yet dignified style and his power in the analysis of personalities and political forces. Commentators on his work have especially praised Sallust's evident effort to maintain impartiality in the face of political conditions about which he felt deeply, and his high ability in the portrayal and analysis of historical personalities. He was not able, however, wholly to conceal his pessimism with regard to the future of the Roman state in the stirring and confusing period that marked the decline of the republic. Sallust never fully appreciated the underlying historical trends in Roman politics in his day, he was very careless in his chronology and geography, and he hired secretaries to do most of his historical research.

The great national history of Rome was that of Livy [Titus Livius] (59 B.C.-A.D. 17), one of the greatest story-tellers of all time. His work was a massive prose epic of the growth of the Roman world-state. While he had a decent general appreciation of the value of accuracy in historical statements, he subordinated precision in statement to perfection of style. The Greek rhetoricians, rather than Thucydides, were his stylistic models. The high literary merit of Livy's history, its caressing of the national vanity of the Romans and their cult of modern admirers, and its wide popularity with the later Humanists, have all combined to give it a position in historical writing higher than its purely historical value would warrant.

Livy wrote frankly to glorify Rome, to flatter national vanity, and to inspire in Roman youth patriotic ardor and affection. And his piety was only less than his patriotism. The supernatural returned to history with a vengeance. Few medieval historians outdid him in assigning historical events to the interference of the gods. He was careless in his use of sources, possessing little capacity or inclination for rejecting the fabulous and traditional elements. All earlier historical material was grist for his mill. Especially unreliable was his treatment of the origins of Rome, where he gathered together a veritable synthesis of myths, marvels, and portents. And it is, unfortunately, the earlier part of his history which has been preserved for posterity. The contrast between the patriotic story-teller and the scientific historian was never better illustrated than by the two widely variant histories of Rome by Livy and Polybius.

It is desirable, however, to remember that Livy himself was probably not very credulous personally. He knew what he was about. He recognized the near-worthlessness of his sources for early Roman history, but he used them regardless of this fact. He knew that if the material he wrote was not good history in a scientific sense it was excellent literary and patriotic propaganda, and that was what he was interested in writing.

A less successful example of Roman historical writing of the rhetorical school was the history of Rome under the early empire by Velleius Paterculus in the period of Tiberius.

The last of the major Roman historians was Publius Cornelius Tacitus (*ca.* A.D. 55-120). Like Thucydides and Polybius, he was a man of action. Being an ardent admirer of the aristocratic Roman Republic, his view of early imperial Roman politics and society was even more pessimistic than Sallust's story of the fall of the republic. Tacitus wrote with great vigor, had rare power in portraying personalities and was generally accurate. Yet, the subjective moralizing element in his writings, while adding to their literary reputation, greatly reduced their historical value. Tacitus and Juvenal were primarily responsible for that venerable but very misleading myth of the "moral causes" of the decline of the Roman Empire, which was later received and elaborated with such deplorable results by Charles Kingsley and others.

The two chief historical works of Tacitus were his *Annals,* which dealt with the period from the death of Augustus to the year A.D. 69, and the *Histories* that began with the political crisis of A.D. 69 and covered the period of the Flavian emperors. As a scientific historian he stood about midway between Livy and Polybius. He was less careless and credulous than Livy, but he did not have Polybius' sober impartiality. His bias against the Empire and his penchant for dramatic writing made him less reliable than Polybius. He wrote from the standpoint of the senatorial class and with a definite affection for the old republican institutions, even though he recognized that the republic had been brought to an end by its own weaknesses.

In the dissection of political intrigues and the delineation of prominent personalities, however, Tacitus stood at the head of antique historians. His portrait of Tiberius is unrivaled in ancient historical writing. If Polybius believed that history should be the handmaiden of statecraft, Tacitus felt that it should buttress private and public morality. He held that "history's highest function is to let no worthy action be uncommemorated, and

to hold the reprobation of posterity as a terror to evil words and deeds."
Tacitus introduced the popular classical cyclical theory of history into the
field of morals. In his *Annals* (III, 55), he wrote: "Perhaps there is in
all things a kind of cycle, and there may be moral revolutions just as there
are changes of seasons. Nor was everything better in the past. Our age,
too, has produced many specimens of excellence and culture for posterity
to imitate." The works of Tacitus suffered from lack of a broad plan such
as that which guided Polybius, coupled with a mass of somewhat confusing detail. Hence, the forest of Roman imperial evolution is obscured by
the trees of personal episodes and the complicated maze of current intrigues and partisan actions.

In addition to his purely historical works, Tacitus' *Germania* was one
of the earliest excursions into the field of descriptive sociology. Being the
only extensive source of our information regarding the institutions of the
Germans of his day, the *Germania* acquired a vast importance in later
years. It has been the most controverted historical document in existence,
excepting only the Pentateuch and the Synoptic Gospels. Recovered in
the period of the Humanists and brought before the learned public by
Poggio, Enoc of Ascoli, and Conrad Celtis, it has been the center of historical conflict between the modern Teutonist and Gallican historians, in
the same way that Alsace-Lorraine has been the pivotal point in the political and military rivalry of their respective national states.[8] More than
this, the tendency of Tacitus to idealize the early Germans at the expense
of the Romans gave rise to that amusing but disastrous perversion of the
history of the Germanic "invasions" which culminated in the vagaries of
Charles Kingsley's *The Roman and the Teuton*.[9]

The last Roman historian of any repute, unless it be the vague figure
that Kornemann has endeavored to reconstruct,[10] was Suetonius Tran-
quillus (A.D. 75-160), the erudite secretary of Hadrian's praetorian prefect.
His anecdotal and diffuse *Lives of the Caesars,* while reliable in its description of public affairs, was one of the earliest examples of historical muck-
raking and scandal mongering. Rich in episodes and personal description,
the biographies by Suetonius cover the period from Augustus to the
Flavians. In spite of his love for spicy detail, Suetonius eschewed the
current rhetorical methods and let his facts tell their own story. Suetonius' chief significance in historiography lies in the fact that he became
the model of style and arrangement for historical biography during the
period of Humanism.

One should not close this brief account of Roman historical writing
without mentioning a writer who, while not a professional historian, was
probably the most historically-minded of all the ancients, the great poet of

---

[8] See below, pp. 178 ff.   [9] See below, pp. 218 ff.

[10] Cf. Ernst Kornemann, *Kaiser Hadrian und der letzte grosse Historiker von
Rom*, Leipzig, 1905.

evolution, Lucretius (95-55 B.C.). His *De Rerum Natura* was the ablest statement of universal evolution until the publication of Herbert Spencer's *First Principles* in 1860. It included the evolution of material culture, institutions, manners and customs. Professor Shotwell says that it is "perhaps the most marvelous performance in all antique literature."

Though the Roman historians were not original and were always more or less under the spell of the Greek rhetoricians, Roman historiography was incomparably higher in respect to reliability than the type of historical writing which was about to succeed it and to bring history back under the spell of mythology and religious prejudices from which it was beginning to escape with Hecataeus of Miletus eight centuries earlier.

SELECTED REFERENCES

J. T. Shotwell, *An Introduction to the History of History,* chaps. xii-xxiii.

Thompson, *History of Historical Writing*, Vol. I, chaps. ii-vii.

Moritz Ritter, *Die Entwicklung der Geschichtswissenschaft.* Munich, 1919.

C. Wachsmuth, *Einleitung in das Studium der alten Geschichte.* Leipzig, 1895.

————, *Über Ziele und Methoden der griechischen Geschichtshchreibung.* Leipzig, 1897.

J. B. Bury, *The Ancient Greek Historians.* Dover, 1957.

Hermann Peter, *Die Geschichtliche Litteratur über die römische Kaiserzeit bis Theodosius I.* Leipzig, 1897.

————, *Wahrheit und Kunst.* Leipzig, 1911.

T. R. Glover, *Herodotus.* University of California Press, 1924.

Lionel Pearson, *Early Ionic Historians.* Oxford University Press, 1939.

J. E. Powell, *The History of Herodotus.* Cambridge University Press, 1939.

F. M. Cornford, *Thucydides Mythistoricus.* London, 1907.

G. B. Grundy, *Thucydides and the History of His Age.* London, 1911.

G. F. Abbott, *Thucydides: A Study in Historical Reality.* London, 1925.

C. N. Cochrane, *Thucydides and the Science of History.* London, 1929.

Otto Cuntz, *Polybius und Sein Werk.* Leipzig, 1902.

R. A. Laquer, *Polybius.* Leipzig, 1913.

T. S. Brown, *Timaeus of Tauromenium.* University of California Press, 1958.

A. J. Toynbee, *Greek Historical Thought.* Macmillan, 1924.

Wilhelm Soltau, *Livius Geschichtswerk.* Leipzig, 1897.

————, *Römische Geschichtschreibung.* Leipzig, 1909.

Gaston Boissier, *Tacitus.* London, 1906.

Wolf Steidle, *Sallusts Historische Monographien.* Wiesbaden, 1958.

M. L. W. Laistner, *The Greater Roman Historians.* University of California Press, 1947.

Willy Strehl and Wilhelm Soltau, *Grundriss der alten Geschichte und Quellenkunde.* Breslau, 1913. 2 vols.

Arthur Rosenberg, *Einleitung und Quellenkunde zur römischen Geschichte.* Berlin, 1921.

W. S. Teuffel and L. Schwabe, *History of Roman Literature.* 2 vols., London, 1900.

III

EARLY CHRISTIAN HISTORICAL WRITING

THE INTELLECTUAL BACKGROUND OF CHRISTIAN HISTORICAL WRITING

THE triumph of Christianity over paganism brought with it sweeping changes in the conceptions of historical writing and in the ideas which guided it. Pagan culture was at least formally rejected as a product of the Devil. The historical writings of the pagans were held in far less esteem than the holy writings of the Jews which were embodied in the Old Testament, even though the major part of the Old Testament was far inferior as history to the works of the better pagan histories. Likewise, the Christians debased reason, which had held so important a place in the mental life of the Greeks, and elevated faith to a predominant position. Credulity, especially with respect to the supernatural, became a major intellectual, as well as a spiritual, virtue. Professor Shotwell has admirably summarized the essential facts in this great intellectual revolution, in so far as it affected historical writing:

> There is no more momentous revolution in the history of thought than this, in which the achievements of thinkers and workers, of artists, philosophers, poets, and statesmen, were given up for the revelation of prophets and a gospel of worldly renunciation. . . . . The sacred scriptures of the Jews had replaced the literature of antiquity. A revolution was taking place in the history of History. Homer and Thucydides, Polybius and Livy, the glory of the old régime, shared a common fate. The scientific outlook of the most luminous minds the world had known was classed with the legends that had grown up by the campfires of primitive barbarians. All was pagan; which meant that all was delusive and unreliable except where it could be tested in the light of the new religion or where it forced itself by the needs of life into the world of common experience. . . . . It was, therefore, a calamity for historiography, that the new standards won the day. The authority of a revealed religion sanctioned but one scheme of history through the vast and intricate evolution of the antique world. A well-nigh insurmountable obstacle was erected to scientific inquiry, one which has at least taken almost nineteen centuries to surmount.[1]

Nevertheless, despite the formal and conscious bias of the Christian Fathers against pagan culture, they could not escape wholly from the indirect and unconscious influences of paganism which existed in the intel-

---

[1] Shotwell, *Introduction to the History of History*, pp. 284-86.

lectual environment that surrounded them. Thus, by an interesting irony of fate, it came about that the pagan culture they assumed to abhor actually influenced their cosmic and historical philosophy almost as much as the cultural traditions of Judaism. The Christian Fathers used the classical languages and were always under the spell of classical rhetoric; many of them, before their conversion, were educated as pagans; their syncretic theology was deeply colored with pagan elements; and their political ideals and practices were so thoroughly modeled after those of the Roman Empire that Professor George Lincoln Burr has very aptly described the origins of the Christian ecclesiastical polity as "the rise of the new Rome."

Next to the influence of classical style, rhetoric, and grammar, perhaps the most influential pagan contribution to Christian historical attitudes came from neo-Platonism, which served to give a dignified philosophical justification to the somewhat simple and naïve Christian eulogy of faith. With its thesis of the superiority of the emotions and intuition over reason and intellect and its advocacy of "unbounded credulity" in matters religious, it fitted in admirably with the patristic mental reactions and became an integral part of the mental attitude of the patristic and medieval historians. Augustine flirted with it in his youth and it loomed large in his later philosophy. Its great medieval impulse came later on, partly as a result of the popularity of the *Celestial Hierarchy,* a Christianized version of neo-Platonism, written in the fifth century by a Syrian monk, the so-called pseudo-Dionysius, and partly from the philosophical and literary activities of John Scotus Erigena. Along with the allegorizing tendency, it served to make quite impossible the development of any resolutely sceptical and critical attitude towards the sources of historical knowledge.

THE CHRISTIAN PHILOSOPHY OF HISTORY

Comparable to the break with classical historiography with respect to the formal status of pagan culture was the far greater emphasis placed on pragmatism and teleology in the patristic historical literature. To the early Christian historians the "process of history" had a real significance and meaning. It was a part of a greater cosmic process in which God and man were the chief participants. "The Christians were perhaps the first to suspect a real grandeur in history," says Professor James Harvey Robinson, "for to them it became a divine epic, stretching far back to the creation of man and forward to the final separation of good and evil in a last magnificent and decisive crisis." This Christian philosophy of history, which has been so felicitously termed by George Santayana the "Christian Epic," was gradually evolved by the Fathers and received its final and decisive expression in Augustine's *City of God.* This philosophy, actually drawn as much from Persian and Hellenic doctrines as from Hebrew sources, considered the historic process to be the practical manifestation of the cosmic struggle between the forces of Good and Evil. In its earthly and historical significance, this conflict was a struggle between the "City of God" —the community of the elect believers in the Hebrew and Christian God —and the "City of Satan"—the collective name for the previous and contemporary adherents to paganism and for the lost souls among the Christians. Its final outcome was to be a glorious triumph for the former and the utter discomfiture and destruction of the latter. With such a philosophical background, it is not difficult to understand that Christian historiography was pragmatic to a degree not dreamed of by either Polybius or Dionysius; it was "philosophy teaching by example" with a real vengeance. With such issues at stake the most insignificant event could not fail to have its vital import. This "Epic," which received its philosophical exposition in the works of Augustine and was illustrated from history by Orosius, was given a vivid and pleasing literary statement in the *Chronica* of Sulpicius Severus (A.D. 363-423).[2]

EARLY CHRISTIAN NOTIONS OF HISTORICAL METHOD

The Christian historians also departed widely from the canons of historical method laid down by Thucydides and Polybius. In addition to their tremendous bias against paganism, which made objectivity out of the question, it was necessary to devise a special method for handling "inspired" documents. To assume towards the Hebrew creation tales, for example, the same critical attitude that Hecataeus maintained toward Greek mythology would have been impious and sinful. Therefore, if the obvious content of the "inspired" statement was preposterous or seemingly incredible, some hidden or inner meaning must be found.

In response to this necessity, allegory and symbolism replaced candor and critical analysis as the foundations of historical method. "Not even Holy Writ," says Professor Burr, "was prized for the poor literal facts of history, but for those deeper meanings, allegorical, moral, anagogical, mystical, to be discerned beneath them." The allegorical method of interpreting the Old Testament had been promoted by the Alexandrian Jew, Philo Judaeus, and appeared in early Christian writings in the *Book of Revelation,* in *The Epistle of Barnabas,* and in *The Shepherd of Hermas.* Its main early impulse among the Fathers came from the Alexandrian Father, Origen (186-255). According to Origen, writes Frederick Cornwallis Conybeare:

> Whenever we meet with such useless, nay impossible, incidents and precepts as these, we must discard a literal interpretation and consider of what moral interpretation they are capable, with what higher and mysterious meaning they are fraught, what deeper truths they were intended

2 See below, pp. 52 f.

symbolically and in allegory to shadow forth. The divine wisdom has of set purpose contrived these little traps and stumbling-blocks in order to cry halt to our slavish historical understanding of the text, by inserting in its midst sundry things that are impossible and unsuitable. The Holy Spirit so waylays us in order that we may be driven by passages which, taken in the prima facie sense cannot be true or useful, to search for the ulterior truth, and seek in the Scriptures which we believe to be inspired by God a meaning worthy of him.[3]

This allegorizing tendency, which vaulted over criticism, was almost universally accepted by the Fathers and received its classical expression in the *Moralia,* or *Commentary on the Book of Job,* of Gregory the Great (540-604), and the *Allegoriae quaedam sacrae scripturae* of Isidore of Seville (d. 636), which gave in chronological order the allegorical significance of all the persons mentioned in the Old and New Testaments. These became standard medieval manuals on allegory.

Not only were there two widely variant standards created for the use and interpretation of historical documents, but there were also delimited two sharply defined fields of history, the *sacred* and *profane,* the first relating to religious and the latter to secular activities.[4] It is needless to remark that an incomparably greater importance was attached to sacred history and that the working of a miracle was considered much more significant than the establishment of a dynasty. The Fathers were willing to devote the most extended labor to the allegorical explanation of dubious and contradictory statements in Scripture, but it is impossible to imagine one of them gathering and analyzing, as Aristotle had done, the contents of 158 constitutions.

It is only fair to point out, however, that the evident decline of historical scholarship in the patristic period cannot be attributed wholly to the Christian attitude towards historical data and problems. Though there were the reasons enumerated above why Christian historiography was likely to be less sound than its pagan counterpart, it cannot be denied that the period of the later Roman Empire was one of general intellectual decline, or that the lapse from the ideals and achievements of the height of classical culture affected pagan as well as Christian writers.[5]

THE HISTORICAL PERSPECTIVE OF THE CHRISTIANS: CHRISTIAN CHRONOLOGY

One of the most effective aids in allaying suspicion and attracting converts to a movement is the ability to point to a glorious past. The Chris-

[3] F. C. Conybeare, *A History of New Testament Criticism* (G. P. Putnam's Sons, 1910), pp. 14-15.

[4] J. H. Robinson, "Sacred and Profane History," in *Annual Report of the American Historical Association,* 1899, I, 527-35.

[5] Cf. H. O. Taylor, *The Classical Heritage of the Middle Ages* (Macmillan Co., 1911).

tians felt this keenly, and, having adopted the sacred books of the Jews as the official record of their antecedents, they were faced with the immediate and pressing necessity of giving to ancient Hebrew history a prestige and an antiquity which had been withheld from it in the works of pagan historians. The latter had assigned to the history of the Jewish people only that slender allotment of space and attention to which their inconspicuous political history had entitled them. Therefore, the two world histories which had already been produced by Diodorus Siculus and Pompeius Trogus, and were certainly much superior to any universal history compiled by patristic historians, were utterly unsuited to the requirements of Christian propaganda. Neither was the general Jewish history of Josephus acceptable, for, while it exaggerated tremendously the rôle of the Jews, it paid very little attention to the Christians. Therefore, the Christian literati set about to produce a synthesis of the past which would give due weight to the alleged glories of Hebrew antiquity and would, at the same time, show why the Jews were no longer worthy of their antique heritage. This the Jews had forfeited, and their former glory had now passed over to the Christians.

The first task of the Christian historians was to provide an imposing historical background for the Christian faith and to establish the importance and antiquity of sacred history—that is, Jewish and Christian history. The historical development of the Jews and Christians became the central thread in the whole history of the past. The historical events in the record of the pagan nations were set off incidentally against the background and basic chronology of Jewish and Christian history and were regarded as distinctly inferior to the latter in importance. As Professor George Lincoln Burr has written with characteristic lucidity and charm:

> That long history which was now their preamble was the sacred story of the chosen people, with its Jacob's ladder linking earth and heaven. The central actor was Jehovah, now the God of all the earth. About that story and its culmination all history must now fall into place; and from the sacred record—for the record too is sacred—may be learned the plans of the Omnipotent. It was Jerome who now found them in the interpretations and the visions of Daniel—in the image of the head of gold and belly of brass, in the four great beasts that came up out of the sea—and from his day on almost to ours the changing empires of earth have been forced to find a place within that scheme. Whatever in non-sacred annals was found in conflict with Holy Writ must be discarded. What was left must be adjusted to its words. Man's career on earth became a fall. Nor might human wit exalt itself: Pythagoras and Plato had learned from Moses; Seneca from Paul.[6]

[6] G. L. Burr, "The Freedom of History," in *American Historical Review*, January, 1917, pp. 259-60.

The earliest Christian writer who attempted to provide a suitable chronology of the human past designed to harmonize with the needs and perspective of the new religion was Sextus Julius Africanus (*ca.* A.D. 180-*ca.* 250). His *Chronographia* was a work in five books which epitomized the Jewish and pagan past from the Creation to A.D. 221. Africanus made use of previous writers on chronology, both Jewish and pagan. Among those upon whom he relied were Manetho, Berossos, Apollodorus of Athens, Josephus and Justus of Tiberius. The latter had worked out a rough chronology of the Jewish kings. According to the chronological scheme of Africanus, Creation took place 5,499 years before Christ. The world was to endure for five hundred years after the birth of Christ, whereupon the millennium was to intervene. Africanus summarized the events and chronologies of the Jewish and pagan nations in brief fashion, assigning primary importance to the Jewish record. Symbolism and fantasy, no less than mathematics, dominated his chronological scheme.

Far more complete, systematic and influential was the famous *Chronicle* of Eusebius Pamphilus (*ca.* A.D. 260-*ca.* 340), Bishop of Caesaria and the foremost of the early historians of the Christian Church. Eusebius was moved to prepare his *Chronicle* in order to provide the appropriate historical and chronological background for his projected *Church History* and also to enable him to establish the priority of Moses to the sages of Greece and Rome.

Eusebius wrote his work just prior to A.D. 303 and he made much use of the earlier efforts of Africanus. The *Chronicle* was divided into two major parts. First came the *Chronographia,* which was a summary of the chronological systems of the Jews and pagans and an epitome of universal history based upon excerpts from the conventional historians of each country. For the Chaldeans he relied upon Alexander Polyhistor, Abydenos and Josephus; for the Jews, upon the Old Testament, Josephus and Clement of Alexandria; for the Egyptians, upon Diodorus, Manetho and Porphyry; for the Greeks, upon Castor, Porphyry and Diodorus; for the Romans, upon Dionysius of Halicarnassus, Diodorus and Castor. Many of the ablest and most reliable of the pagan historians were, thus, overlooked or ignored by Eusebius.

More important was the second portion of the *Chronicle,* the *Chronological Canons,* which represented the real chronological contribution of Eusebius. The dates, in which the Jewish events were given primary consideration, ran down through the center of each page. The events of pagan and Jewish-Christian history were then synchronized in parallel columns, with those assigned to the latter taking the commanding position. Indeed, the events of history were now divided into two major categories—*sacred* [Jewish-Christian] and *profane* [pagan]. The events in sacred history were placed on the left of the column of dates, while the materials from the pagan past were arranged on the right.

A brief biblical chronology led the reader back to Creation, but the detailed comparative chronology did not begin until the alleged date of the birth of Abraham (2016 B.C.). From here on, the chronological history was divided into five stages or epochs: (1) from Abraham to the capture of Troy; (2) from the capture of Troy to the first Olympiad; (3) from the first Olympiad to the second year of the reign of Darius; (4) from the second year of the reign of Darius to the death of Christ; and (5) from the death of Christ to the twentieth year of the reign of the Emperor Constantine.

As we have hinted, the materials were arranged in parallel columns, the number of which differed according to the epoch under consideration. They started with columns devoted to the Assyrian kings, the Hebrew prophets, the Sicyonian kings, and the Egyptian pharoahs. The columns were most numerous in the second to the fourth epochs and wound up in the last period with three rows of tables, devoted to the Jews, Greeks and Romans, respectively. Marginal comments by Eusebius were included. In assembling and selecting his materials Eusebius revealed not only great industry and learning but also a large amount of credulity. The late President Andrew D. White pointed this out when he wrote that, "in these tables Moses, Joshua and Bacchus; Deborah, Orpheus and the Amazons; Abimelech, the Sphinx and Oedipus appeared together as personages equally real, and their positions in chronology equally ascertained."[7]

Eusebius wrote in Greek, which at that time could only be read by a very few scholars in the Western Empire. So there was a real need to transmit it in Latin to the western Christians. This service was rendered by the learned western Father, Jerome. In the year 379 he hurriedly dictated a Latin translation of Eusebius' *Chronicle,* with certain revisions and additions. He translated the *Chronographia* without important changes. In order to make the work more useful in the West Jerome added to his translation of the *Chronological Canons* more facts of general history, and especially more material dealing with Roman history and Roman literature. He also continued the chronological summary down to the year A.D. 378.

In Jerome's translation Eusebius' *Chronicle* provided the authoritative chronology for the Christian West until it was revised by Joseph Justus Scaliger in 1583 and by Bishop James Usher in 1650. It entered systematic church history in the *Chronica* of Sulpicius Severus (*ca.* 360-*ca.* 410), and the *Historia Tripartita,* compiled by the associates of Cassiodorus. It had

---

[7] A. D. White, *A History of the Warfare of Science with Theology* (Dover, 1960), I, 250.

a tremendous vogue in all medieval historical writing, since the chroniclers of that time were wont to prefix it to their accounts of national and regional historical developments, which were thus linked up with Creation. Jerome's *Chronicle* was continued to 455 by Prosper of Aquitaine, and to 468 by Idatius, a Spanish bishop. Victor Tonnennensis, an African monk, drew up a general chronicle from Creation to A.D. 566. Better known was the early seventh century *Chronicle* of the Spanish savant, Isidore of Seville. This was based on Eusebius and Jerome, but was also influenced by Augustine, from whom Isidore derived his division of the history of the world into six epochs, corresponding to the six days of Creation. It summarized the history of mankind chronologically from the beginning to 615, but it added nothing substantial to the earlier chronologies. The Venerable Bede also wrote an influential work on chronology in the eighth century, his *De Temporum Ratione*. This divided history since creation into six ages and was widely copied by medieval historians. Bede was the first to give currency in chronologies to our practice of using the birth of Christ as the dividing point in historical dating—i.e., the use of B.C. and A.D. This procedure had been introduced by Dionysius Exiguus (d. *ca.* 550).

In this Christian synthesis of world history, aside from the artificiality of its chronology and synchronisms, two characteristics are noteworthy, namely, the absurd relative importance attached to Hebrew history and the serious bias against pagan civilization which made an objective historical perspective out of the question. Of the former tendency Professor James Harvey Robinson has said, "this theological unity and meaning of history was won at a tremendous sacrifice of all secular perspective and accuracy. The Amorites were invested with an importance denied the Carthaginians. Enoch and Lot loomed large in a past which scarcely knew of a Pericles."[8] It is an ironical but incontestable fact that the Jewish nation owes its prominence in world history in no inconsiderable part to these distortions in the historical perspective of the early Christian historians.

OROSIUS AND CHRISTIAN WORLD HISTORY

It was hardly to be expected that the Christian Fathers would remain satisfied with bare chronologies of the pagan past. It was desirable to prepare a systematic and official Christian history of mankind which would vindicate Christianity. This achievement actually came about as a by-product of a charge leveled against the Christians by the pagans, to the effect that Christianity had been responsible for the calamities that had

[8] J. H. Robinson, *The New History* (Macmillan, 1912), p. 30.

overtaken the later Roman Empire, especially the sack of Rome by Alaric early in the fifth century. The task of refuting this charge by an appeal to world history was assigned by Augustine to his devoted and industrious lieutenant, Paulus Orosius (*ca.* 380-*ca.* 420). Orosius had been born in Spain and later went to Africa. He became attached to Augustine and studied under him for about five years. Before he composed his main historical work he had already written some doctrinal and anti-heretical treatises at Augustine's suggestion. His historical refutation of pagan charges against the Christians, the famous *Seven Books of History Against the Pagans,* was compiled between A.D. 415 and 418.

The historical treatise of Orosius was based upon Augustine's providential theory of history, namely, the assumption that God's plan had controlled the destinies of the pagan empires as well as the Jewish and Christian history. Babylonia and Rome were selected as the two pagan states most directly influencing the historical evolution of the Jews and Christians. Egypt was not seriously brought into the picture. Macedonia and Carthage were introduced as supplementary empires which helped to transmit Babylonian culture to Rome—and also to bear out the symbolism of the "four great beasts which came up out of the sea," derived from Daniel's vision and established in the Christian historical perspective by Jerome. The chronology of Orosius' manual was based on Jerome's version of Eusebius' *Chronicle.* For the materials used in constructing his history Orosius did not trouble himself to consult the classic historians of the Orient, Greece and Rome. He used secondhand Latin abstracts of Herodotus, Polybius, Livy, Tacitus and the like.

The *Seven Books of History Against the Pagans* opened with a geographical sketch of the world as Orosius knew it, especially of those areas treated in his work. Then the history of man from the Creation began with an adaptation of Jerome's *Chronicle.* Babylonian history was sketched and Orosius next dealt with early Roman history down to the sack of Rome by the Gauls, which he delighted in portraying as far more awful and devastating than the spoliation by Alaric. Then came the history of Greece and Macedonia from Pericles to the defeat of Pyrrhus of Epirus. Orosius next passed on to Carthage, which he treated from the days of settlement to its destruction. In conclusion, Orosius reverted to the later history of Rome, which he portrayed with special emphasis upon its paternal relation to the rising Christian church, but not neglecting the horrors wrought by the pagans in their sins and persecutions. The narrative came down to A.D. 417.

It will be evident that there were great gaps in the history of the past by Orosius, as a result both of the exclusion of certain countries from consideration and the incomplete and arbitrary treatment of those included. The main weakness of the book as history did not arise, however, from its sketchiness, but rather from its purpose, namely, to prove that any calamities which had come to Rome since the origins of Christianity were far surpassed in number and devastation by the disasters which had come to pass in pagan societies. Ignoring the more pleasing aspects of pagan culture, Orosius gathered a veritable *historia calamitatum* by combing pagan history to present an almost unrelieved picture "of all the most signal horrors of war, pestilence and famine, of the fearful devastation of earthquakes and inundations, the destruction wrought by fiery eruptions, by lightning and hail, and the awful misery due to crime." "All the achievements of Egypt, Greece and Rome," wrote Professor Robinson, "tended to sink out of sight in the mind of Augustine's disciple, Orosius; only the woes of a devil-worshipping heathendom lingered."[9]

Nevertheless, one should not overlook some forward-looking and constructive incidental phases of Orosius' vivid book. In his history of pagan wars and their wholesale massacres he lets us see clearly the implication that, however thrilling war may be for the nobility, its impact upon the humble folk is horrible to the last degree. He hinted that there is an important story to be told about the history of the common people to whom war is a veritable calamity. Further, his treatment of the later Roman Empire gives us the impression that he knew he was living in a transitional age, and that what we have come to know as the Middle Ages was then beginning. In this attitude he took a step in advance of his master Augustine, or of any other Christian writer of his age.

Despite the fact that it was intended as a polemical work in defense of the Christian faith, Orosius' book became the standard manual on profane history—that is, ancient pagan world history—during the Middle Ages. This was a highly unfortunate occurrence for students of history during the medieval period, for several very evident reasons. In the first place, the work was decisively biased against the pagan nations and culture. Second, it ignored the more peaceful and constructive elements in pagan life. Third, its treatment of ancient history was sketchy and inadequate as to countries and subject matter alike. Finally, even the sketchy materials were unreliable, having been compiled from secondhand abstracts and then fitted into a pre-determined scheme of historical interpretation.

SYSTEMATIC CHURCH HISTORY

The most creditable performances in the realm of patristic historiography were achieved in the field of systematic history of the Christian church. Though the world outlook of the writers marred their perspective and warped their interpretation, the resulting damage to historical schol-

[9] Robinson, *op. cit.*, p. 30.

arship was least in this department. While the anti-pagan bias, the lust for the miraculous, the pious credulity of the writers and the Christian philosophy of history were all in evidence, the very nature of the subject-matter made their operation less disastrous here than in the synthesis of the history of antiquity. Attention was centered almost entirely upon ecclesiastical matters and the writers dealt in a large degree with their co-religionists of the immediate past, who scarcely received the reverence accorded to personages that had figured in scriptural events.

The earliest semi-narrative sources for the history of Christianity are the recently recovered *Dead Sea Scrolls*, the Pauline Epistles of the first century and the Synoptic Gospels, written probably in the last third of that century. Of the Gospels, the most reliable is the straightforward narrative of Mark, written about A.D. 70, though the Gospel of Luke is a more polished and finished historical work. The Acts of the Apostles, the remaining canonical historical work of the first century, was written by the author of Luke about A.D. 100. The Christian apologists of the second and third centuries are also valuable sources of information, though their writings are highly controversial.

The one outstanding product of systematic ecclesiastical historical writing in the age of the Fathers was the *Ecclesiastical History* of Bishop Eusebius of Caesaria, the founder also, as we have noted, of authoritative Christian chronology. Eusebius was an important ecclesiastical statesman, a friend and confidant of the Emperor Constantine, and a learned Christian antiquarian. He prepared himself for his work by wide reading and much research in the library of his benefactor, Pamphilus of Caesaria, who was martyred in the persecutions of Maximinus. In his religious outlook, Eusebius had been influenced by the most scholarly of the Eastern Fathers, Origen of Alexandria. His *Ecclesiastical History* was an account of the origins and triumph of the Christian religion and a narrative of the growth and organization of the Christian church in apostolic and patristic times. Eusebius was more of a scholar, antiquarian and philologian—a sort of Christian Timaeus—than a historical philosopher or a creative literary artist. As Professor Defarrari summarizes his talents and contributions: "Eusebius was the first to grasp clearly the concept of a Christian literature, and to employ with it the ancient methods, fixing the dates of writers and cataloguing their works. He translated the tradition of Alexandrian philology to Christian soil."[10]

Eusebius had treated the rise of the Church briefly in his *Chronicle,* and his *Ecclesiastical History* was really a massive expansion of that outline. The main divisions of his work were the following: (1) the succession of bishops in the more important sees; (2) outstanding Christian

[10] In Peter Guilday, ed., *Church Historians* (Kenedy, 1926), p. 24.

teachers and writers; (3) the major heresies and heretics; (4) the various punishments which came to the Jews as a result of their execution of Jesus; (5) the Roman persecutions of the Christians; and (6) the martyrs and miracles of Eusebius' own day.

The outlook which pervaded the whole work was, as might be expected, thoroughly apologetic for Christianity. All history attests the divinity and mission of Christ. Yet the tone of Eusebius' history was remarkably fair and calm for an early Christian scribe, especially one whose teacher and close friend had been martyred by the pagan government. The work gave evidence of wide reading and careful study. Indeed, the history was, in a sense, an anthology of the important documents in early Christian history, woven into a guiding and organizing text. A Church history, to Eusebius, was primarily "a collection of materials handed down." While this resemblance to a source book makes Eusebius rather slow reading, the inclusion of many documents proved invaluable for later historical work on the early Church. Most of these documents were subsequently lost and we have record of them only in Eusebius' history. The rich documentation, however, prevented the history from being a work of literary artistry, and the rambling and diffuse style did not aid in enlivening the narrative. It was preëminently a work of patristic scholarship. Eusebius revised his work four times, bringing it down to A.D. 323 in the final edition.

The *Ecclesiastical History* of Eusebius was continued in the fifth century by the Church historians Socrates, Sozomen and Theodoret. There was much duplication in their work. Socrates dealt with the period from 306 to 439; Sozomen with the years from 323 to 439; and Theodoret with those from 325 to 427. The whole was combined, condensed and translated into Latin by Epithanius and others at the direction of Cassiodorus in the sixth century, and the narrative was carried down to A.D. 518. Cassiodorus himself wrote the introduction to this Latin paraphrase and is thought to have personally supervised the abridgment, having decided upon the selection and arrangement of materials. This product of Cassiodorus and his disciples, known as the *Historia Tripartita* [*The Tripartite History*], was the manual of church [sacred] history generally used throughout the Middle Ages. Though confused, incoherent, inaccurate, and annalistic, it was certainly superior in scholarship to the companion textbook on secular [profane] history which had been provided by Orosius.

The one history of the Christian church written during patristic times which possessed real literary merit was the *Sacred History* of Sulpicius Severus. It was a brief and interesting epitome of church history, including a résumé of Christian chronological conceptions of world history, based on Eusebius' *Chronicle*. Sulpicius brought the story down to A.D.

400. He wrote avowedly to interest the learned public in the history of the Church and he executed his project in capable fashion. Despite this, his little book was all but forgotten in the Middle Ages, being dropped in favor of the longer, crude and disjointed *Historia Tripartita*. But it became popular with the early modern Humanists who could appreciate the stylistic excellences.

The greatest defect in these early church histories was their failure to analyze the deeper forces and the more significant events in the great religious movement which they were describing. This was due, in part, to the belief that Christianity was advanced solely through divine favor and, in part, to the fact that the writers all succumbed to the temptation to treat primarily of wonders, miracles, martyrs and saints.

CHRISTIAN BIOGRAPHIES

The growth of the Christian church depended in no small part upon the work of its illustrious converts and holy men. It is not surprising, therefore, that historical biography should assume an important rôle in patristic historiography. The first step in this direction was taken in the earlier portions of Eusebius' *Ecclesiastical History,* where he mentions the life and work of eminent churchmen. But the first formal collection of biographies of illustrious Christians was *De Viris Illustribus* [*Illustrious Men*], written by Jerome in Bethlehem in 392. Suetonius, the Roman biographer, had published in A.D. 113 a work of the same title, listing and describing the chief figures in Latin literature down to this time. The pagans tended to ridicule the literary pretensions of the Christians and to revile them as illiterates and ignoramuses. So Jerome decided to compile a list of those whom he considered had graced the Church by their literary performances in order that he might rebuke the pagan detractors. He laid down his challenge to comparison in the following words:

> Let them learn then—men like Celsus, Porphyry and Julian, those mad dogs raving against Christ—let their partisans learn, men who imagine that the Church has neither philosophers, orators or doctors, the breadth and the talent of the men who founded, developed and embellished her; let them cease accusing our faith of having nothing else to show than rustic simplicity, and let them rather recognize their own ignorance.[11]

Jerome listed and described, in rather uneven and arbitrary fashion, those whom he believed to be eminent Christian literati, from Simon Peter to his own self. More than half of his figures were taken directly from Eusebius. In order to make his exhibit as impressive as possible,

[11] Cited in Pierre de Labriolle, *History and Literature of Christianity* (Knopf, 1925), p. 362.

Jerome included not a few heretics and some non-Christian writers, such as Josephus, Philo and Justus of Tiberius. The space allotted and the tone of the treatment depended chiefly on Jerome's personal appraisal of each particular writer.

Jerome's example was continued about 470 by Gennadius of Marseilles, whose biographical collection was given the same title as Jerome's anthology. In the early seventh century the Spanish bishop and encyclopedist, Isidore of Seville (570-636), brought the collection down to date, still employing the same title. His work was supplemented by that of a fellow-countryman, Ildephonsus of Toledo (d. 667). In the twelfth century, Honorius of Autun carried the work down to that period. The process of addition continued through the medieval period to culminate in the collection of 963 biographies in the *Liber scriptorum ecclesiasticorum* of Johannes Trithemius (1462-1516), abbot of Sponheim. The astonishing credulity of even the most learned of these early biographers, and their zeal for "miracle-mongering" can best be appreciated by a perusal of such a work as Jerome's *Life of Paul the First Hermit,* or Athanasius' *Life of Saint Anthony.* The great autobiography of this period—and one of the most influential ever written—was, of course, the *Confessions* of Augustine.

SELECTED REFERENCES

Shotwell, *Introduction to the History of History,* chaps. xxiv-xxvi.

Thompson, *History of Historical Writing,* Vol. I, chap. viii.

E. J. Goodspeed, *A History of Early Christian Literature.* University of Chicago Press, 1942.

Millar Burrows, *The Dead Sea Scrolls.* Viking, 1958.

T. H. Gaster, *The Dead Sea Scriptures.* Doubleday, 1956.

M. A. Larson, *The Religion of the Occident.* Philosophical Library, 1959.

E. F. Scott, *The Literature of the New Testament.* Columbia University Press, 1932.

C. J. H. Hayes, *An Introduction to the Sources Relating to the Germanic Invasions,* chaps. x-xi. Columbia University Press, 1909.

Peter Guilday, ed., *Church Historians,* pp. 3-70. Kenedy, 1926.

Ritter, *Die Entwicklung der Geschichtswissenschaft,* Book II, chap. i.

Gustav Krüger, *History of Early Christian Literature,* London, 1897.

Pierre de Labriolle, *History and Literature of Christianity.* Knopf, 1925.

A. C. McGiffert, ed., *The Church History of Eusebius,* "Nicene and Post-Nicene Fathers."

I. W. Raymond, ed., *Seven Books of History Against the Pagans: The Apology of Paulus Orosius.* Columbia University Press, 1936.

J. C. Ayer, *Source Book for Ancient Church History.* Scribner, 1913.

IV

HISTORICAL WRITING DURING THE MIDDLE AGES

THE MEDIEVAL HISTORICAL PERSPECTIVE

IT will have been evident from the foregoing discussion that Orosius and Cassiodorus were the standard historical authorities for Christendom during the Middle Ages and that there was no decisive break with the patristic philosophy of history or historical methods. "The Middle Ages," says Professor Burr, "did not dissever history and theology. Nay, to forbid it there grew to completeness that consummate preserver of the unity of thought, the procedure against heresy. And to the end of that long age of faith history did not escape the paternal eye."

The chief representatives of historiography in the Middle Ages, as of other phases of medieval culture, were churchmen of one type or another —mainly the monks. The same zeal for the miraculous and diabolical and the same relative disregard for such essential facts for the historian of today as the foundation and disruption of states and epoch-making political, economic, social and intellectual movements still persisted. The "Christian Epic" kept its prestige unshattered and almost unchallenged for twelve centuries, disturbed only slightly by the later medieval pagan "revival," the growth of Humanism, and the controversies of the Reformation period. It never received a staggering blow until, in the seventeenth and eighteenth centuries, the English Deists and the French Philosophes revealed its weaknesses and inconsistencies by their penetrating and disconcerting criticism.

If anything, during at least the first centuries after the close of the patristic period, there was a decline in scholarship and historical understanding. The medieval writers not only retained the patristic defects but themselves lacked the wide classical or theological erudition of many of the Fathers. They also frequently revealed the presence of those cultural crudities incident to a recent emergence from barbarism. The eminent German historian, Heinrich von Sybel, once summarized the outstanding characteristics of medieval historiography in a manner which brings out clearly its close relation to patristic historical literature:

> This period possessed no idea of historical judgment, no sense of historical reality, no trace of critical reflection. The principle of authority, ruling without limitation in the religious domain, defended all tradition, as well as traditional dogma. Men were everywhere more inclined to be-

lieve than to examine, everywhere imagination had the upper hand of reason. No distinction was made between ideal and real, between poetical and historical truth. Heroic poems were considered a true and lofty form of history and history was everywhere displaced by epics, legends or poetical fiction of some kind. A course of slow historical development was traced back to a single great deed, a single personal cause. Almost no one felt any scruples in giving to existing conditions the sanction of venerable age by means of fabricated history or forged documents. The question whether the ascribed derivation was true interested no one; it was enough if the result harmonized with existing rights, dominating interests and prevalent beliefs.[1]

Another important characteristic of medieval historical writing, its child-mindedness, has been emphasized by Professor George Gordon Coulton:

> The medieval historian as compared with the ancient and modern has the child's keen interest in men and things, the child's directness of observation and picturesqueness of expression and often just that little point of naïve malice which lends such charm to a child's report of what he has seen and heard. But his calculations of numbers, for instance, can scarcely ever be trusted, and nearly always exceptionally great allowance must be made for his professional or religious bias. . . . . The typical medieval history, at least up to the thirteenth century, may be fairly compared with Red Indian natural history—curiously true and observant where daily hunting contact is concerned but beyond that lacking all sense of probability or evidence or sequence of cause and effect.[2]

While it is necessary to recognize these various limitations upon, and defects in, medieval historical writing, it is only fair to point out at the same time the great difficulties under which the historical writing of the early Middle Ages was carried out. The decline of Roman civilization had brought in its wake confusion and violence. Learning became sterile, lost its originality and vigor, or faded out altogether. Many of the more important books of classical antiquity were lost in whole or in part or deliberately destroyed. Christian fanaticism accounted for much of this malicious pillage of the literary treasures of antiquity—especially the destruction of the library of Alexandria. Travel being hard, expensive and dangerous, culture tended to be local and provincial in nature, and the possibility of a large view of European or world society was extremely remote. The monks were the only large learned class in medieval Europe and they were naturally its historians. While we owe much to their industry and devotion, their religious superstitions and prejudices, as well as

[1] Cited in Ernst Bernheim, *Lehrbuch der historischen Methode und Geschichts-philosophie* (Leipzig, 1903), pp. 190-91.

[2] Article, "Historiography," *Encyclopedia of Social Sciences.*

their preponderantly religious interests, warped, distorted and limited their historical work. The fact that the monasteries produced most of the chronicles in the West was not due solely to the leisure or libraries which monks possessed. The cathedral chapters usually had learned men and good libraries, but they failed to produce many chronicles. The monasteries possessed a sense of historical continuity and a vast pride in the achievements of their order, abbey and monks.

Several other important considerations affecting medieval historical writing should be taken into consideration. The medieval historians, like other medieval writers, had many purposes in mind in their work besides the glory of God. They were influenced by personal ambition, patronage, and group loyalty. Their methods were affected by their education, contacts and the libraries available to them. There was no such uniformity of literary resources as is the case today. Personal ambition played an important rôle. Many medieval historians were monks and held monastic office. They were not usually loath to accept advancement, and the production of a laudatory chronicle was a possible means of increasing prestige and stimulating promotion, just as the writing of a book in our day might achieve similar results. This personal ambition might also take the form of seeking patronage by playing up the deeds of a man or his family or of his predecessors in office. This influence seems to have been especially powerful in the Byzantine and Muslim worlds where there were many secular lords who appreciated good literature. The medieval chronicles were thus deeply influenced by the factor of patronage. Today, historians usually write for a general reading public, while in the Middle Ages they wrote mainly for a patron or a small and selected group of readers. Another important point is related to the fact that most medieval chroniclers were connected in one way or another with the monastic records. They were officials of the monastery and thus leaders of great corporations. Their religious interests did not differ much from those of laymen; all were Catholic. However, their economic interests were constantly in opposition not only to laymen but to bishops and other monasteries. The same zeal which led them to write history—that is, group loyalty—also led them into the defense of their group's position. Occasionally, the medieval historians wrote mainly to satisfy their creative impulses. They produced beautiful manuscripts of their works and were obviously proud of their literary ability. In every age there are men who can best express their creative genius in this way.

HISTORICAL WRITING DURING THE TRANSITION FROM CLASSICAL TIMES TO MEDIEVAL CULTURE

It is a fundamental truism of European cultural history that there was no sharp break between classical civilization and medieval culture. Classical civilization gradually dried up because of a growing fondness for rhetoric, the lack of originality of thought, the proclivity to paraphrase previous writers, and the marked shift in intellectual interests brought about by the rise of Christianity.[3] Medieval culture set in with a definite, if fading, background of classical learning, which was gradually subordinated to medieval Christian intellectual concerns. The historical writing of the transitional period from the classical era to the medieval age reflected these same tendencies. From the age of Theodoric to the epoch of Charlemagne there were historians who reflected a vanishing classicism as well as an interest in the religious and political trends of early medieval society. Before turning to a consideration of typical medieval "annals" and "chronicles" we should, perhaps, note the works of some relatively important historians of the transitional period, recognizing, of course, that this period is by no means clear-cut and that the historians considered are not a well-defined group, sharply set apart from their predecessors, contemporaries or successors.

The first of these historians whom we may fittingly present was one of the most important figures in the transmission of classical and early Christian thought to the Middle Ages, Marcus Aurelius Cassiodorus (*ca.* 480-*ca.* 570). He had been an important official in the civil service of Theodoric—a sort of chief of chancery for that king of the Ostrogoths. His most valuable historical work was not his pretentious *History of the Goths,* but rather his *Variae,* or voluminous letters and state papers written by him mainly while in the service of Theodoric. They were official documents of indispensable value. While turgid and rhetorical in style, pedantic and sententious in tone, and always adulatory of Theodoric and the Ostrogoths, they were invaluable as a source of information in regard to the Ostrogothic kingdom in Italy. They covered every phase of the life of the times, economic and cultural as well as political and diplomatic.

The more ostensible and formal historical work of Cassiodorus was his *History of the Goths* in twelve books, written between 526 and 533. No complete text remains and our knowledge of its character has to be derived mainly from the epitome made by the relatively incompetent monk, Jordanes. From this and other references, the *History of the Goths* seems to have been colored by the same bias in favor of Theodoric and the Ostrogoths that was manifested in the *Variae.* Cassiodorus relied for his information mainly upon a Gothic author named Ablavius. He tried to accommodate his sympathy for Theodoric to his admiration for the Latin culture of Rome by resorting to the fanciful theory of the Roman origin of the Goths, and he then traced the Romans back to Troy. We have

3 Cf. Taylor, *The Classical Heritage of the Middle Ages*; and *The Medieval Mind* (Macmillan, 1925), vol. I.

already mentioned the *Historia Tripartita* prepared under Cassiodorus' direction—that crude and spotted manual which served as the popular history of the Christian church during the Middle Ages.

We have stated that we owe most of what we know of the Gothic history by Cassiodorus to the résumé made by the ill-educated Gothic monk, Jordanes, who paraphrased Cassiodorus' work in his *Origins and Deeds of the Goths,* written about 550. He tells us that he was able to have access to Cassiodorus' history for only a few days, though many modern commentators doubt the truth of this assertion. The book by Jordanes is rather fantastic in its treatment of Gothic origins, though it appears to be somewhat more plausible in descriptions of events in his own lifetime. But Jordanes was not so much prejudiced against the Romans as one might have expected a Goth to be. By culture and sympathies he was a Roman and a Catholic. He was especially impressed with the idea of the universality of the Roman Empire, which he linked up with the Old Testament in its antecedents and for which he predicted an indefinite future. Jordanes' writing lacked distinction of style no less than scholarship and intellectual shrewdness.

A historian far superior in all ways to Cassiodorus and Jordanes was the Byzantine recorder of the wars of Justinian, Procopius (*ca.* 500-565), who wrote in Greek.[4] His main historical work was known as *The History of His Own Time,* treating chiefly of the wars against Persia, the wars in Africa, and those against the Goths. Though he rather too obviously aped the classical Greek historians, such as Herodotus and Thucydides, Procopius was a smooth and polished writer. Moreover, being a man of education, wealth and affairs, he was able to assume a breadth of vision not usual in his time. Having accompanied the great Byzantine general, Belisarius, on his campaigns, Procopius wrote in part as an eyewitness of the events he described in his history. But he was not without some major weaknesses as a historian. He was very careless and undiscriminating in his use of sources. He was biased in favor of the Byzantine Empire and especially admired Belisarius. He was thoroughly imbued with the idea of the civilizing mission of Rome, as continued by the Byzantine Empire. Finally, he was a formal apologist for the aristocracy of wealth and official position. Procopius wrote another shorter work, the so-called *Secret History* [*Historia Arcana*], which may have embodied Procopius' private views, and which regaled the reader with tales of the palace intrigues and moral debauchery in the Byzantine capital. As Bury and others have pointed out, it is regarded today as exaggerated and partisan. Some scholars have even doubted that Procopius was its author. At

---

[4] There is an excellent account of Procopius by J. B. Bury in the Appendix to the latter's edition of Gibbon's *Decline and Fall of the Roman Empire.*

any rate, such books as *The Secret History* were a natural product of the times. In an absolutism such as that of Justinian's day, literature of this type tends to flourish, since it is one of the few outlets for suppressed exasperation. The court of Louis XIV fostered the same type of historical writing.

Perhaps the most interesting of this whole group of transitional historians was the famous Gregory, Bishop of Tours (538-594). He provided the most important history of the Franks during the critical period of their invasion of Gaul and their creation of Merovingian civilization out of the fusion of Gallo-Roman and Teutonic elements. Gregory's book was entitled *History of the Franks*. It began with a dull and careless history of the world from antiquity to the fifth century A.D., and then proceeded with a treatment of Frankish history from about the year 417, which was carried along to the year 591. Gregory was contemporary with the events described in the last fifty years of his narrative. Much of his history was written from first-hand information, to gather which he was in a very favorable position. He was a prominent churchman and a friend and associate of secular lords. He was a wide traveler throughout Gaul. After he became Bishop of Tours he was able to mingle with the many pilgrims who came to visit the tomb of the revered Martin.

One of the most quoted passages in all medieval literature is Gregory's complaint with respect to the decline of letters in Gaul after the invasions and his own asserted determination to write in a rustic Latin that the average learned man of his day could read and understand. Yet, despite Gregory's modesty as to his Latin diction, his history is more notable as a piece of vivid, personal literature than as an exacting and critical historical composition. He had a keen sense of the dramatic and the work as a whole was interesting, graphic and colorful. Whatever its faults in syntax, the vernacular Latin employed by him is immensely to be preferred to the florid and pedantic imitations of classical Latin by writers such as Cassiodorus.

The *History of the Franks* is significant for two major reasons: In the first place, it gives us our only unified and relatively complete picture of the genesis of Merovingian culture out of the fusion of Gallo-Roman and Frankish contributions. In the second place, it reflected very fully the ascendent position that the Church was coming to occupy in medieval civilization, and illustrated profusely the credulity that flourished in the Age of Faith. His work reveled in miracles, wonder-working, and holy marvels. Indeed, the element which served to give unity to Gregory's work as a whole was the emphasis placed on the Church as the central and dominating institution in Frankish Gaul.

Gregory's history was far removed from a straightforward and sober historical narrative. It was full of digressions, anecdotes, allegories, sermons and the like, and Gregory made effective use of dialogues to heighten the interest of his tale. Yet there is everywhere evidence of sincerity and intellectual integrity. The fair-minded reader, even though fresh from an account of a batch of breath-taking miracles, will be likely to concede that Gregory wanted and intended to tell the truth. He was at pains to keep the reader informed as to his main sources of information. Perhaps his strongest point as a historian was his ability to delineate personalities, where he showed a psychological talent, if not a literary artistry, rivaling that of Tacitus. In short, Gregory provided the modern reader with the best history of the transition from Roman to medieval culture, and one reason for his success lay in the fact that he was himself so perfect a personal reflection of this transitional age. Gregory's work was epitomized and carried down to 768 in the *Chronicle* of the pseudo-Fredegarius. This work was the product of three authors, a Burgundian, an Austrasian and a Frank. The best sections are those covering the years 631-642 and 742-768. Although a hodgepodge, it is about the only source for Frankish history during these years. From it comes the legend of the Trojan origin of the Franks.

While he was a far more learned man than Gregory, Isidore of Seville's *History of the Kings of the Visigoths, Vandals and Suevi* in no way compared with the *History of the Franks*. It was brief and mainly a second-hand compilation made up of scraps from earlier chroniclers and commentators. There was however, a valuable digression on the place of Spain in early medieval civilization. Isidore's ingenious imagination played a large rôle in his history, as in his other literary efforts.

It is rather generally agreed that the ablest historical work produced during the transitional age was the *Ecclesiastical History of the English People* by the Venerable Bede (672-735). This work provides us with our only thorough and reliable history of the triumph of Christianity in England and of the establishment of Anglo-Saxon culture in that island. After an unoriginal and trivial general historical introduction, Bede's history swung into serious action with the coming in 597 of Augustine, the missionary monk, to convert England. The narrative was carried down to 731, the very year in which Bede completed the book. Bede's history rested on careful research. He read most of the important written sources and also consulted many leading churchmen. And he was honest and sincere in his discussion of the nature and reliability of the sources he used. While introducing many miracles, he showed much more restraint in accepting them as well-substantiated historical truth than did Gregory of Tours. Though Bede wrote primarily to tell his readers the story of the triumph and organization of English Christianity, he treated most of the political events which had any bearing on the progress of religion and ecclesiastical organization in England. The result was that his history not only gives us a record of the early days of English Christianity but also provides a fairly adequate account of the fusion of Anglo-Saxon culture with the native elements in England and of the rise of the Anglo-Saxon polity. The history was also important in a biographical sense, because Bede embodied the biographies of many early English churchmen and saints. It closed with a long chronological summary of English history from Julius Caesar to A.D. 731.

Bede was no clumsy and plodding annalist or compiler. He took much preliminary pains in drafting a general outline of his history and he created a well-organized structure for his whole narrative. The book possessed organic unity and balance, and was written in an easy and vivid Latin style. Bede was one of the best classical scholars of his time in western Europe. If he was not Gregory of Tours's equal in portraying the dramatic and colorful, he had far better intellectual balance and his historical writing was far more reliable. The difference is not unlike that between Herodotus and Thucydides. Bede's *De Temporum Ratione,* with its six ages of the world, from Creation to A.D. 729, had a wide influence on the chronology of many later medieval chronicles.

The appearance of the Lombards on the European historical scene was depicted by a Lombard monk, Paulus Warnefridus (*ca.* 730-800), more usually known as Paul the Deacon. Paul was a fairly well educated churchman who had traveled rather widely in northern Italy and Gaul, having associated with men of state as well as of the faith. His *History of the Lombards* was written late in his life, while he was a resident at the famous monastery of Monte Cassino. He did not live to complete the history, which, in six books, tells the story of the Lombards from their legendary origins to the year 744. Paul used a variety of sources—Pliny, the *Origo Langobardum,* the historical writings of Secundus of Trent, Gregory of Tours, Isidore of Seville and Bede, biographies of churchmen, the theological writings of Gregory the Great, information he had picked up on his travels, oral traditions and legends. He had little critical power in sifting and assessing this mass of source material, and he was especially uncritical in his treatment of early Lombard legends. But he was apparently intellectually honest and sincere, and his handling of more recent Lombard history seems to have been relatively reliable. Even his myths of early times may have accurately reflected the spirit and culture of those times. As Dr. Balzani has written: "Whenever the *History of the Lombards* deals with real events, it is worthy of the utmost consideration, and its testimony is important; when, on the other hand, it introduces legendary matter, we feel at least that it depicts the manner of the Lombards, just as the magic pen of Walter Scott has reproduced, better than any historian, the early history of Scotland."[5] A major weakness in Paul's history

[5] Ugo Balzani, *Early Chroniclers of Europe: Italy* (London, 1883), p. 90.

was its careless and sloppy chronology, which led to much confusion in the narrative. The book was written in clear, fluent and unpretentious style, and certain passages possess high dramatic interest. It was very popular in the Middle Ages and not the least of its value resides in the fact that it preserved many sources which have subsequently been lost.

The first layman to compose an important historical work in the Middle Ages was Nithard (*ca.* 795-843), who received a remarkably good education for one outside the clerical profession. He is regarded as the ablest historian during the later Carolingian age. He was himself an illegitimate grandson of Charlemagne, being the son of a lay-abbot and one of the daughters of Charlemagne. His *Four Books of History* dealt mainly with the civil wars among the grandsons of Charlemagne and covered the time from Louis the Pious to 843, being especially detailed for the years 839 to 843. He was an eyewitness of much he described, and he made unusually discriminating use of the written sources which he consulted. He wrote in a straightforward, lucid and non-rhetorical style. Even the picturesque matter in his history was always relevant. He permitted no discursiveness or digressions to gain dramatic effects. The work was of importance in linguistic history also, since it is our sole source for the famous Strassburg oaths. Though Nithard was a partisan of Charles the Bald and a bitter critic of Lothar II, his historical writings have stood up well under the critical examination of specialists in our own day. Even his harsh judgments of Lothar are now rather generally accepted.

A surpassingly brilliant and competent biographer for his period was Einhard (or Eigenhard, *ca.* 770-840), whose *Life of Charlemagne* is one of the most distinguished historical biographies of the whole medieval period. Einhard was a man of affairs, being both a friend and an official of Charlemagne and a lay-abbott. Long associated with the court of Charlemagne and his successor he had ample opportunity to gather at first hand the information which he required for his biography. Joined to these unusual opportunities for personal observation was an excellent education for that day. Einhard was a splendid classical scholar, having received the best training available in his day, that at Fulda and in the school of Alcuin. He exceeded any other early medieval historian in his ability to follow classical models of expression in his writings. He took Suetonius particularly for his master, making special use of the latter's *Life of Augustus*. But he showed that he had read in all of the major Roman historians at the Fulda library, which was especially rich in historical manuscripts. Einhard's biography of Charlemagne was thus a finished product of Latin diction, far removed from the rustic Latin of Gregory's *History of the Franks* or the florid diction of Cassiodorus.

Einhard's book was in every way an invaluable historical document, but it was not without some notable defects. He followed Suetonius rather too slavishly and specifically, and the picture of Charlemagne suffers at times from being forced too precisely into the Augustan mould. Again he has been accused, and with some reason, of glossing over or omitting entirely some of the less creditable acts of Charlemagne particularly in the early life of the king. Finally, although it does possess dignity, the work is Carolingian propaganda. In order to emphasize the glories of that Carolingian age, Einhard threw into too dark a contrast the Merovingian period and its rulers. There seems little doubt today that the Merovingians, especially the later rulers, have been too harshly judged as a result of Einhard's strictures being taken at their face value. As a whole, however, the permanent verdict of historians is that Einhard's biography was a unique masterpiece of literary expression and historical exposition for the early medieval age.

We may now turn to the more strictly medieval historical literature, the annals and chronicles, which grew from crude and simple beginnings into the systematic historical writings of the Middle Ages.

MEDIEVAL ANNALS AND CHRONICLES

An excellent illustration of the rudimentary nature of early medieval culture is the fact that during the first centuries following the decline of classical culture, the main form of historical writing was the "annals" which had been common in early Egypt and Babylonia. The medieval example of this type of historical writing originated in the early Carolingian period as an incident of the religious need of determining the exact date of the shifting Easter festival. The general absence of any precise knowledge of astronomy and chronology among most of the clergy made it necessary for the more erudite churchmen to prepare and to distribute to monks and priests Easter tables giving dates upon which Easter would occur for some years in advance. There was a fear that the less educated clergy might make a mistake in selecting the date of Easter and thus upset their whole series of movable feasts. This led to the quest for authentic Easter tables. It is thought that this practice of sending out Easter tables originated in Northumbria in England, spread from there over England, and was carried by Alcuin and his monks to the Continent.

An almost universal practice arose of indicating on the margin opposite each year, the events which, in the mind of the recorder, seemed to make that year most significant in the history of the locality. Charlemagne ordered the monasteries in his realms to keep regular and systematic annals. Not only were these early annals very scanty in the information they contained, since they mentioned only a few conspicuous events which occurred during the year. They were rendered still less valuable because the medieval annalist frequently considered most important for his record some insignificant miracle or the transfer of the bones of a saint, information of little value to the modern historical investigator, except in so far as it revealed the state of mind of the medieval annalist and illustrated his limited historical perspective. Professor Haskins well illustrates this by his citation of the early entries in the *Annals* of St. Gall:

709. Hard winter. Duke Gottfried died.
710. Hard year and deficient in crops.
712. Great flood.
714. Pippin, Mayor of Palace, died.
718. Charles Martel devastated Saxony with great destruction.
720. Charles fought against the Saxons.
721. Theudo drove the Saxons out of Aquitaine.
722. Great crops.
725. The Saracens came for the first time.
731. The blessed Bede, the presbiter, died.
732. Charles fought against the Saracens at Poitiers on Saturday.[6]

As Professor Haskins observes, there is no further mention in the entry for the year 732 of the battle of Tours, ranked as one of the decisive battles of the world. In time, however, entries became more frequent and the interests of the annalist grew wider. Eventually, the annals became, with such a work as Roger of Hoveden's *Annals of English History*, in the early thirteenth century, a valuable record of the development of a nation. The more comprehensive later annals were composed from collections based on the earlier and briefer annals.

The origin and development of the "chronicle" was directly related to the growth of the annals. The annals were primarily a yearly record set down by a contemporary. The chronicle was more comprehensive. It normally consisted in the summarizing of the history of a considerable period on the basis of one or more sets of annals, preserving, however, the chronological and strictly annalistic arrangement of the basic annals. Some of the events written about might have occurred before the chronicler's own period and he might need to combine the records contained in several annals in order to obtain a more complete and comprehensive story. To this collection of annals to form a chronicle, there was usually added, as an introduction, Jerome's version of Eusebius' *Chronicle,* which linked the local chronicle with the Christian synthesis of world history from the Creation. The authorship and nature of medieval chronicles differed greatly. Some were personal narratives of an experience or of local history. Others preserved the record of a monastery or an abbey, the life

---

[6] C. H. Haskins, *The Renaissance of the Twelfth Century* (Harvard University Press, 1927), p. 231.

therein and the contacts with the outside world. Again, a chronicle might record the doings in a particular medieval town, like the famous annals of London, Florence, Genoa and Cologne. Some chronicles dealt with a great episode such as the Crusades. But the most notable chronicles usually rose at least to the level of a regional or national record, and some even ventured to narrate the international events of Europe.

Professor T. E. Tout has made a number of illuminating comments on the nature of medieval chronicles.[7] The chief object of the authors of chronicles was not usually literary distinction: "Their object in general was not a piece of literary composition but to fulfil a practical need, to supply information, or to prove some case." The medieval chroniclers had little perspective in dealing with the ancient past. They interpreted it in terms of medieval society and interests, thus lacking fundamental "historical sense." Nor were they able to do very accurate work in treating of medieval periods earlier than their own age. They had little capacity for discriminating between the value of the sources they used. They were at their best on their own age, where they were in part eyewitnesses of the events described. Even here, however, there were certain rather uniform biases and tendencies. Since most of the chroniclers were monks, the monkish point of view and characteristic monkish distortions were common. The main advantage possessed by monkish authors was the stability, peace and security of their lives, conditions conducive to authorship. At first, there was little interest in titles. The works were indiscriminately called Annals or Chronicles, but later, styles in titles became common. In one period "Flowers of History" might be popular, and in another "Polychronicons."

With the expansion of the underlying annals in scope and relevance, the chronicles came to be more of an approximation to a history until, in such products as the *Anglo-Saxon Chronicle,* the *Chronicle* of Hermann of Reichenau (d. 1054), the *Universal Chronicle* of Ekkehard of Aurach in the early twelfth century, the *Chronicle* of Otto of Freising (d. 1158), and the *Greater Chronicle* of Matthew of Paris (d. 1259), this characteristic vehicle of medieval historiography became one of the most thorough and reliable sources of historical information available in that age.

Inasmuch as nearly all the eminent historians of the Middle Ages were either annalists or chroniclers, we shall also be treating the products of this type of historical composition when we survey the works of the major medieval historians. But we might mention, in passing, some of the more important annals and chronicles which are not so closely identified with the personal narrative of some leading medieval historian. Since the annalistic structure was more simple than that of the chronicle, it was only

[7] T. F. Tout, *The Study of Medieval Chronicles* (Longmans, Green, & Co., 1922).

natural that the early medieval products would take the form of annals. Most of them, indeed, cover Carolingian times and the period immediately following. The age of Charlemagne was dealt with in the *Greater Annals of Lorsch* and their continuation to 829 in the *Royal Annals*. From Charlemagne to the tenth century the leading annals were the famous *Annals of Fulda,* the *Annals of St. Bertin,* covering the period from 830-882 and written by such men as Prudentius and Hincmar of Rheims, their sequel in the *Annals of St. Vaast* which carried the story from Creation to 889, and the *Annals of Metz* dealing with the generation from 883 to 903. Among the latest of the major annals were the *Greater Annals of Cologne,* coming down to 1237, and the famous *Annals of Genoa* dealing with the period from 1100 to 1293.

Some representative medieval chronicles were the following: For England there was the all-important *Anglo-Saxon Chronicle,* one of the few written in the vernacular, coming down to about 1154, but losing its vitality after the Norman conquest; the *Chronicle* of Florence of Worcester and continuators, which was important for the period from the conquest to the reign of Edward I; the *Acts of Stephen,* covering the reign of King Stephen and written by a friendly churchman; and the extremely valuable *Chronicle of St. Albans,* dealing with events from 1250 to 1422. In France there were such important chronicles as the *Chronicle of Nantes,* covering matters down to 1049; and the famous *Chronicle of Saint Denis,* written in the great abbey of that name near Paris, dealing with the period from 1250 to 1380. Most of the German and Italian chronicles were the product of medieval historians with whom we shall deal shortly. City as well as regional and national chronicles became common in the later Middle Ages. Representative of these were the famous French *Chronicle of London,* extending from the forty-fourth year of Henry III to the seventeenth year of Edward III; the English *Chronicle of London,* modeled after the French predecessor, compiled in the reign of Henry VI and continued to that of Edward IV; and the notable *Chronicle of Florence* by Dino Campagni (1260-1323). The other major medieval chronicles we shall mention in connection with the review of the more important medieval historians.

Some authorities on medieval historiography, such as the eminent scholar, Reginald Lane Poole, differentiate between medieval chronicles and medieval histories on the basis of the excellence of composition. If a medieval historical work is dry and plodding it is a chronicle, if interesting and vigorous in style and independent in judgment it is a history. Following the medieval writer, Gervaise of Canterbury, Poole makes the following distinction:

> The historian and the chronicler have the same intention and use the same materials, but their manner of treatment is different and their form

unlike. For the historian proceeds in ample and elegant style, whereas the chronicler writes simply and with brevity. The historian aims at relating facts as they really happened, but he does this in a literary form; he pleases his readers by the gracefulness with which he describes men and manners. The chronicler, on the other hand, sets down the years of Grace, calculates the months and days, notes shortly the doings of kings and princes, and records events, portents or miracles.[8]

This is interesting, but can hardly be accepted in full, especially for the height of the medieval period. It might be suitable as a contrast between early medieval and later medieval chronicles, or between a mere compiler and a writer with a conscious philosophy of history. We can hardly say that when we have dry narrative it is a chronicle and when we find an excellent piece of medieval historical composition it is a true history and not a chronicle. Rather, we first come upon real histories in the medieval period when the author broke away from the annalistic method and organized his materials by topics or reigns. The topical treatment occurred rarely in any conscious or systematic fashion until the close of the Middle Ages when the tendency appeared in such writings as those of Machiavelli and Guicciardini. The histories in the medieval period which were based on reigns were often of little historical significance, since they were chiefly given over to genealogies.

The majority of medieval historians were, therefore, mainly men who wrote chronicles according to the annalistic method of chronology and arrangement. Only a few like Roger of Hoveden, Matthew Paris, Villehardouin, Lambert of Hersfeld, and Otto of Freising were able to break away from this method to some degree. But even these writers were primarily chroniclers with only a broader viewpoint and more generalized interest than most of their contemporaries. Most of their writing was constructed on a year-by-year basis.

SOME LEADING MEDIEVAL ENGLISH HISTORIANS

English medieval historical writing began with the gloomy *Book of Complaint Touching the Destruction of Britain* by the outspoken monk, Gildas (*ca.* 516-70). The book was written in vigorous language, in spite of the "decayed Ciceronionism" of its rhetorical Latin. It dealt with the disruption of English culture brought about by the Anglo-Saxon invasion, and is almost our only continuous source of information for this period. The outlook of Gildas is well indicated by his description of the coming

---

[8] R. L. Poole, *Chronicles and Annals: A Brief Outline of their Origin and Growth* (Oxford University Press, 1926), pp. 7-8.

of the Saxons: "Then a litter of whelps bursting forth from the lair of the barbaric lioness in three *keels*, as they call them in their language, or long ships as we would say in ours, with their sails wafted by the wind, and with omens and prophecies favorable, by which it was foretold that they should occupy the country to which they were sailing three hundred years, and half of that time, a hundred and fifty years, should plunder and despoil the same."[9] While Gildas is held to be unreliable in the details of his narrative, most historical scholars today accept his general picture of the havoc and confusion wrought by the Teutonic invasions though they reject the completeness of the destruction of the pre-Anglo-Saxon culture which Gildas implies.

The main source for the period following that dealt with by Gildas was Bede's history, which we have already discussed. The remainder of the Anglo-Saxon period was covered in the *Anglo-Saxon Chronicle*.

The history of the English church from Edgar to Henry I, including the relations between church and state, was the theme of *The History of His Own Time* by Eadmer (*ca.* 1060-*ca.* 1124), a Canterbury monk. His history in six books was an indispensable source for the subject and time covered. The work was lucidly written and dignified in tone, but distinctively biased against William II in treating of his relations with the Church. Another very important and original contribution to English ecclesiastical history was *The History of the Church of Durham* by Symeon of Durham (d. 1119). It was a thorough and independent work. His *History of Kings* traced the history of Northumbria from 731, the date at which Bede's *History* stopped. While a compilation from earlier historians, it contains much valuable material.

Probably the ablest and most reliable of English medieval historians down to his day was another monk, William of Malmesbury (*ca.* 1096-*ca.* 1143), whose major historical work was his *Acts of the English Kings,* which dealt with events from the Saxon invasion to 1128, and was continued in his *Modern History* to 1142. Being by birth half English and half Norman, he was able to preserve relative impartiality in dealing with matters before and after the Norman Conquest, a matter upon which he prided himself . Few historians during the whole medieval period were as conscientious in consulting the available sources. William seems to have looked up every extant source before writing his book. But he was no mere dry and plodding compiler. His history was well organized, he had a fine sense for the dramatic, and he could depict personalities with much skill. Moreover, his historical judgments were uncommonly shrewd, and he showed ability in tracing the development of institutions. He also made important contributions to English ecclesiastical history in his *Gesta pon-*

9 James Gairdner, *Early Chronicles of Europe: England* (London, 1883), p. 6.

tificium anglorum, which reviewed English episcopal and monastic history down to 1125, following roughly the pattern of Bede's history.

A contemporary of William also gave evidence of capacity for independent judgments and critical powers. This was Henry of Huntingdon (*ca.* 1084-1157), whose *History of the English* was brought down to the accession of Henry II in 1154. Henry both loved his profession as a historian and believed that it had some practical utility. He wrote: "There is nothing in this world more excellent than accurately to investigate the course of worldly affairs. . . . . History brings us to view the past as if it were present, and enables us to judge of the future by picturing to ourselves the past."[10] Henry had unusual poise and scepticism for his time in rejecting both legends and the marvels of the supernatural. In addition to being an accurate and well-balanced chronicler, he wrote in a very pleasing manner. The age of Henry II produced the first venacular history, the *Roman de Brut,* by Master Wace of Jersey, composed in verse, as were the first vernacular writings in general. Far more important was the later vernacular history of England by Robert of Gloucester to the year 1270, an important source for the years 1256 to 1270 and valuable for English philology.

The *Chronicle* and *Royal Deeds* of Gervase of Canterbury (*ca.* 1200) provided much information on the struggles between church and state and were one of the main sources for the later Norman kings and the rise of the Plantagenets. The narrative was carried down to King John. Though lacking stylistic brilliance, the writings of Gervase are laborious and conscientious compilations which contain a large fund of reliable information.

The outstanding medieval historian of Normandy was the monk, Ordericus Vitalis (1075-*ca.* 1143), who was born in England but spent most of his life in Normandy. Hence, he is claimed as both an English and a French chronicler. His *Ecclesiastical History* was offered as a general world history from the time of Christ to his own day, but it became detailed only for the period after the Norman Conquest. He dealt with Norman affairs, not only in Normandy and England, but in Italy and Sicily as well. Even more than Bede's work, his *Ecclesiastical History* embraced political and diplomatic history.

In certain ways Ordericus revealed many defects as a writer. He failed to draw up any well-conceived plan for his work as a whole, as Bede had done. Hence, it was ill balanced and discursive. He did not work systematically, with the result that there are many repetitions and some inconsistencies in his book. And he was all too careless in his chronology, which led him into errors and confuses his readers. His style was rather labored and pedantic. Yet, despite all these defects, he was a very

[10] Gairdner, *op. cit.,* p. 99.

important historian because of his comprehensive scope and his breadth of interests. As Professor Charles W. David writes: "No other historian of his time had his breadth of human interest or his zeal for full and detailed knowledge. All things modern and human interested him, whether the local affairs of his abbey or distant events in England, Italy or the Orient, whether military, ecclesiastical, religious, or literary and artistic. Especially was he interested in people. . . . . He saw and comprehended the life of all classes. . . . . No other writer of his time is so rich in local color."[11]

On the reign of Richard the Lion-Hearted and the Third Crusade the main English historian was Richard of Devizes (fl. *ca.* 1190), noted particularly for his cynical wit. His work was reasonably accurate and penetrating and it succeeded admirably in portraying the spirit of the age. It was especially important for its dramatic account of the preparation for the Third Crusade and for the state of England after King Richard left for the East. Richard's style was somewhat affected and his story was clogged with frequent classical quotations. His account of the politics, diplomacy and wars of the age was well supplemented by the chronicle of Joceline of Brakeland (fl. *ca.* 1200), who wrote a record of the monastery of St. Edmundsbury. This was a veritably unique memoir on English social and monastic life in the twelfth century. It was invaluable as a description of medieval monastic administration. Joceline was highly autobiographical in his writing, and he thus gives us much insight into the thoughts and actions of a lively, entertaining and able monk.

The unmatched historical fakir of medieval England was Geoffrey of Monmouth (*ca.* 1100-1154). He even faked the origin and nature of his *History of the Kings of Britain*. He pretended that it was his translation into Latin of an old and hitherto unknown Anglo-Saxon history of early Britain. Especially notorious and influential was his fantastic legend of the Trojan origin of the British people. However worthless his book may have been as history, it was very important in its influence on the literature of chivalry and romance in England. The stories of King Lear and of the prophet-magician, Merlin, were derived from his writings, as also were the majority of the Arthurian romances.

Giraldus Cambrensis (1146-1220) attacked Geoffrey as an imposter, but he turned out almost as many marvels and wonders in his own history of the conquest of Ireland, the *Vaticinal History of the Conquest of the Island*. In spite of his ardent patriotism, his vivid imagination and his gullibility, Giraldus' book was the best medieval work on the subject and he was one of the most gifted literary artists among all the English chroniclers. He wrote in a simple, vigorous and eloquent style and he was one

---

[11] In Guilday, *Church Historians*, pp. 121-22.

of the most talented delineators of character and personality among all the English medieval historians. Giraldus included much illuminating material on manners, customs, traditions and scenery. He was also interested in historical geography, as exemplified by his *Topography of Ireland* and his *Itinerary of Wales*.

More effective as a critic of Geoffrey of Monmouth was William of Newburgh (b. *ca*. 1135), whose *History of England* covered the period from the reign of Stephen to the end of the reign of Henry II. He took Bede as a model for the historian and he produced an accurate, clear and interesting book marked by unusually discerning judgments. An even greater advance is to be noted in the *Annals of English History* by Roger of Hoveden (d. *ca*. 1201), who continued Bede's history down to his own day. He broke away from the crude annalistic methods more successfully than any other historian of his day and produced a well-organized and broadly conceived history of the reigns of Henry II and Richard I and of the beginning of the reign of John. He was especially notable for his knowledge of, and attention to, foreign affairs.

Among the ablest of English medieval historians were a group of monks from the monastery of St. Albans. Roger of Wendover (d. 1236) was the author of a compendium of world history which he entitled *Flowers of History*. It went back to Creation and came down to 1235. It dealt mainly with English affairs after it reached the Norman Conquest and it was the best original source for the reign of John. His work was written in straightforward style, was restrained in expression, and was relatively impartial in its judgments.

It is quite generally agreed that the ablest historian of medieval England was Matthew Paris (*ca*. 1200-1259), who continued Roger of Wendover's chronicle. Better than any other historian of the age, he freed himself from religious and mythical interests and devoted himself to the story of political development. He was the incomparable authority on English constitutional developments between Magna Carta and the rise of Parliament. He included many important public documents in his book. His work was especially notable for its presentation of foreign affairs and of their implications for the internal political history of England. He was a plain and direct writer and showed plenty of capacity for independence of judgment, even on the acts and policies of the kings of England. Professor Tout calls him the most independent and individual of all medieval chroniclers. His work was continued to the death of Henry V by another monk of St. Albans. Among the important continuators of the work of the St. Albans monks was Robert of Reading (d. 1318), himself a Westminster monk, who showed marked partiality for the Earl of Lancaster.

The last of the major St. Albans historians was Thomas Walsingham (fl. *ca.* 1400), who revised the work of earlier chroniclers and carried the story down to the death of Henry V (1422) in his *English History.* Though hostile to the radical movements, he is our best source on Wycliffe and Wat Tyler's rebellion. His work was also valuable for its account of contemporary constitutional developments.

An important source for Edward I was the work of a Dominican monk, Nicholas Trevet (*ca.* 1258-1328). He was a passable classical scholar, and his account of English history in this period was relatively accurate, though a little dry and mechanical. It possessed more of the characteristics of a textbook than most works of the time. The treatment of foreign history was chiefly a digest of the work of the German historian, Martin of Troppau.

Walter Heminburgh (d. *ca.* 1315), in his *History of England,* covered the period from the Norman Conquest to the reign of Edward III. He is our most valuable source for the reigns of the Edwards. His account was reliable, and his style vigorous and distinguished, despite the fact that he embodied many documents such as charters, letters and state papers. His judgments, moreover, were very sound and his opinions moderate and impartial.

On the reign of Edward III, to 1356, an important historical work was that of Robert of Avesbury (*ca.* 1350), one of the few lay historians of medieval Europe. He was keeper of the registry of Canterbury. Robert devoted his book chiefly to military history, especially the wars with France from 1339 to 1356. He gave little attention to matters of internal political or constitutional history or to the religious history of England. As a historian of military affairs he was accurate and painstaking and relatively impartial. His work is particularly important because of the many original documents and letters which he incorporated in his narrative.

A novel historical enterprise was undertaken by Ralph Higden (*ca.* 1299-1364), a monk who lived in the time of Edward III. His *Polychronicon* was an ambitious and compendious world history, divided into seven books, after the seven days of Creation. It also included an elaborate account of historical geography as it was then known. As Gairdner puts it: "No such voluminous, exhaustive and interesting history had ever yet been written. No work was ever so wonderfully popular."[12] Yet it is of little value as a source for any period of history. Its significance lay chiefly in the originality of the whole conception for the author's period and in Higden's emphasis on the geographical basis of history.

A general synthesis of English medieval historical writing was undertaken by Robert Fabyan (d. 1512) in his *Concordance of Histories,* which

---

[12] Gairdner, *op. cit.,* p. 279.

was based not only on the major English chronicles, but also upon the more important French medieval historians.

OUTSTANDING FRENCH MEDIEVAL HISTORIANS

The first important strictly medieval historian in France was Richer, who lived in the first half of the tenth century. He wrote a *History of His Times,* covering the period from 887 to 998. The work was divided into four books. While somewhat prolix, rhetorical and prejudiced, it was well informed and honest for that age. It is invaluable as a source of information on the period which marked the decline of the weak Carolingians and the rise of the Capetian dynasty. Less reliable was the *Chronicle* of Raoul Glaber (Ralph the Bald, d. *ca.* 1050), which extended from 900 to 1046. It was often inaccurate, and was notorious for legend-mongering. It was from Ralph the Bald that we derived the famous legend of the panic which was supposed to have come over Christendom as the year 1000 approached. It passed into historical tradition through the works of Baronius, Robertson and Michelet. But Ralph's book was important because of the paucity of other material bearing on this age. Far more reliable were two other eleventh-century works, the general *Chronicon* of Adhemar of Chabannes, and the *Deeds of William the Conqueror* by William of Poitou, an invaluable source for Norman history.

Sigebert of Gembloux (*ca.* 1030-1112) was the author of a general world chronicle, the *Chronographia,* which was widely used by later writers. He was a monk in the monastery of Gembloux in Belgium. His chronicle, which he completed about 1106, began with Creation and became more voluminous when it reached the year 381. It ended with the year 1101, and was based in large part on the earlier work of Marianus Scotus. The earlier portions are worthless as history, but the later sections are rather valuable, even though here Sigebert was careless in his use of sources.[18] It was frequently continued by later writers and much used, especially as a chronological guide. It was easily the most popular medieval summary of universal history. Robert of Torigni (d. 1186), abbot of Mont-Saint-Michel, wrote an *Appendix to Sigebert,* covering the period from 1154 to 1186, which was good in its chronology and valuable for ecclesiastical history. It was one of the most important sources for the reign of Henry II of England. Another able chronicler was Robert of Auxerre (*ca.* 1156-1212), who wrote a *Chronicon* or universal history. The material down to 1181 was taken chiefly from Sigebert and others, but from 1181 to 1211 it is valuable as an original and contemporary source. It

---

[18] Some authorities give Sigebert a higher rating. Molinier, in his *Les Sources de l'histoire de France* (II, 310), calls him the best of the universal chroniclers of the Middle Ages.

is important as a source of information on Philip Augustus and the Crusades. Robert was a diligent reader and a man of good judgment. He is ranked as one of the best of medieval French chroniclers.

The French took a leading part in the Crusades and there were a number of medieval French historians, in addition to Robert of Auxerre, who contributed to our knowledge of this period. The *History of the Crusades* by Foulcher of Chartres (1058-1127) was egotistical and partisan, but it provided much detail on the early Christian settlements in the Near East. Better known was *The Deeds of God Through the French* by Guibert of Nogent (1053-1124). It was based chiefly on an earlier Norman narrative and the author floundered badly when he lost his guide. The style was full of stilted affectations, but the work was a valuable authority on the First Crusade. The story of the Second Crusade was told in the *History of the Crusade of Louis VII* by Odo de Deuil (d. *ca.* 1162), concise in statement and eloquent in describing the heroism of the Crusaders. It was particularly interesting for its vivid, if unfriendly, description of Constantinople and its inhabitants. The best general French history of the Crusades was that by William of Tyre (1130-*ca.* 1193). He was Archbishop of Tyre and his book described the course of events in the Holy Land from 1095 to 1184. He gathered his information carefully and widely, was cautious in his statements, and was reasonably impartial. His work was continued by several later chroniclers.

The *Conquest of Constantinople* by Geoffrey de Villehardouin (*ca.* 1167-1213) was one of the more notable historical works of the Middle Ages. It was the first medieval historical book of importance written in the vernacular. While modest in speaking of his own deeds, the book was somewhat of an apology for Villehardouin's own policy in the Fourth Crusade. It is still the best source from which to learn of the spirit of the Crusaders on this holy sacking expedition. It was written in a vigorous and concise style, full of personal touches and throbbing with virile human interest. Gustave Masson observes that: "the slightest study of Villehardouin's prose will convince the reader that no medieval French author can be named more noteworthy for clearness of style, neatness of composition, and admirable delineation of character."[14] In his political philosophy, Villehardouin was an apologist for chivalry and feudalism.

Far and away the longest historical work written in France during the Middle Ages was the historical section of the vast *Speculum majus* of the Dominican friar, Vincent of Beauvais (1190-1264). This was called *Speculum historiale,* divided into thirty-one books and 3,793 chapters. It would run to about twenty volumes of the size of an ordinary present-day book. It covered all of human history from the Creation to St. Louis. It

---

[14] Gustave Masson, *Early Chroniclers of Europe: France* (London, 1883), p. 129.

was culled from many medieval chroniclers. While not original, it was a skillfully compiled mosaic, and the most impressive monument to industry in all medieval writing.

Guillaume de Nangis (d. *ca.* 1330) wrote a *Chronicle* from Creation to the reign of Philip the Fair. The general historical introduction, which comes down to 1300, was based on Eusebius, Jerome and Sigebert of Gembloux and was of no special importance. The later and original portion is our best account of the early part of the reign of Philip. The author eulogized the monarchy and the centralizing policies of Philip. Guillaume's narrative was continued by Jean de Venette (b. *ca.* 1308), a writer of much greater independence of judgment and critical spirit. He was no mere annalist but a historian who rose above his material. He freely criticized the monarchy and the feudal lords, especially the latter. While no democrat, he believed that if the people paid heavy taxes they were at least entitled to justice and security. One of the most prolific of French medieval historians was the Dominican, Bernard Guy (*ca.* 1261-1331), a special authority on the medieval Inquisition. His most elaborate work was a universal chronicle, *Flowers of Chronicles,* which was valuable for his own age. He also wrote, in addition to manuals on the Inquisition, brief chronicles of the popes, the emperors, the kings of France and the counts of Toulouse.

The most vivid stylist among medieval French historians was Jean Froissart (1337-1410). He was a poet as well as a chronicler, and his *Chronicles of France, Flanders, England, Scotland and Spain,* were written primarily to delight his readers. In this he succeeded very well indeed. His chronicle was episodical history in its most extreme form. He had remarkable talent in portraying stirring scenes and in painting characters. Masson says that "in point of style and brilliant coloring, Shakespeare alone can be placed on the same line with Froissart."[15] He rewrote his work three times and each draft was different in character. The first was more fresh and vivid and pro-English. The last was more philosophic and anti-English. It went more into matters of cause and effect, and gives us much on manners, customs and institutions. Froissart was not a nationalistic historian, but was rather the chronicler and eulogist of the deeds of chivalry in the declining period of feudalism. He was not too careful of his facts and his chronological errors also were many and confusing. But his work was the foremost contemporary account of the Hundred Years' War, and it faithfully reflects the chivalric age and ideals.

Much different in style and tone was the *Chronicle* of Enguerrand de Monstrelet (1390-1453), covering the period from 1400 to 1444. He wrote

15 Masson, *op. cit.,* p. 176.

in a sober style and he manifested much sympathy for the populace ravaged by the wars of the nobles. He copied many documents and was accurate in most details, save for chronology. He went far beyond most contemporaries in rejecting miracles, magic, prodigies and the like. His major defect was his provincialism; a native of Flanders, he magnified beyond reason the importance of events taking place therein. Monstrelet was continued to 1461 by Mathieu de Coucy (b. *ca.* 1420). He was a vivid stylist, at times rivaling Froissart, but he was more conscientious and accurate in handling historical materials. He was sober and honest and admitted the paucity of sources when such was the fact. His work was particularly valuable for the latter part of the reign of Charles VII.

A very bitter work was *The History of the Reigns of Charles VII and Louis XI* by Thomas Basin (1412-91). It was decidedly anti-English and anti-monarchical, being very severe on the tyranny of Louis. The author was careful with his facts, but his judgments were highly colored.

The so-called *Scandalous Chronicle* of Jean de Troyes covered the period from 1460 to 1483. But its contents were more gossipy than scandalous. Much of the material was superficial, secondhand description, but it was valuable for the light which it threw on Parisian life during the period.

The last and the ablest of French medieval historians was Philippe de Commines (1445-1509), whose *Memoirs* reflect the transition to early modern forms in historical writing. They were a vigorous narrative exhibiting most of the traits of the true historian—an intelligent grasp of the trend of events, penetrating analysis of motives, a consideration of cause and effect in historical matters, a description of the cultural environment, and sound generalizations. Commines delighted in unraveling complicated political intrigues and diplomatic plots. Especially did he emphasize the pragmatic and political value of history. He advised statesmen, politicians and diplomats to "study it well, for it holds the master key to all types of frauds, deceits and perjuries." His *Memoirs* covered the period of 1464-83 and of 1488-94. It is our best source for the reigns of Louis XI and Charles VIII. Commines was generally favorable to Louis, and his glorification of the rôle of the prince in politics reminds one of Machiavelli. The classic English historian, Hallam, said of Commines: "He is the first modern writer . . . . who in any degree has displayed sagacity in reasoning on the characters of men, and the consequences of their actions, and who has been able to generalize his observation by comparison or reflection."[16]

[16] Masson, *op. cit.*, p. 260.

SOME IMPORTANT MEDIEVAL ITALIAN HISTORIANS

The most important early medieval historian of Italy was Paul the Deacon, whom we have mentioned as one of the writers intermediate between classical historiography and the medieval chroniclers. Italy was the country which contained the capital city of western Christendom, except for the brief Babylonian captivity at Avignon during the later Middle Ages. Hence, material on the popes constituted an important item in medieval Italian historical writing. Most interesting here was the *Liber Pontificalis* [*Book of the Popes*]. It began in the fourth century with brief statements of fact relative to the official life of each pope. It gradually developed until it included fairly complete biographies of the popes. Another work of importance for church history was the history of the Bishops of Ravenna from Apostolic times to the middle of the eighth century by Angellus of Ravenna (b. 805). As might be expected, he included plenty of miracles and legends along with the authentic historical materials.

The first outstanding and strictly medieval historian in Italy was the active and interesting Bishop Liutprand of Cremona (*ca.* 922-72). He was far the ablest Italian historian of his age and probably the most competent historical writer in all medieval Europe in the tenth century. He was the author of three important historical works. Best known and most valuable was his *Antapodosis* or *Book of Retribution* which dealt with the period from 888 to 950. While mainly Italian history, it also contained much material on German, Byzantine and Muslin history. He was bitter against King Berengarius, who had exiled him. This accounts for the title of the book. It presented a great mass of material of the most varied detail. For a writer of his day, Liutprand admitted singularly little of the miraculous and legendary. His *History of Otto* was a full picture of the events from 960 to 964, of which Liutprand was an eyewitness. His *Account of the Mission to Constantinople* was an interesting but satirical picture of the Byzantine court at this time. Liutprand also was a good classical scholar, something relatively rare for his time and almost unknown in the other historians of his age. He took Boethius as his model in style and he freely cited passages from the classics, even quoting Greek authors in Greek. His main weakness was his proclivity to deep emotional attitudes —biases and hatreds such as his animus against Berengarius. He also had a tendency to overcolor his materials, and his judgments were at times rash. But he stood head and shoulders above the other chroniclers of his day.

An interesting and important contribution to historical science in the Middle Ages was the compilation of the *Farfa Register* by Gregory of Catino in the eleventh century. He arranged the archives of the monastery of Farfa and copied them in order in one work. He labored on this enterprise for some fifteen years and the experience helped him to develop a considerable sense of the historical criticism of documents. Gregory then wrote a chronicle in the form of a historical narrative based on the *Register*. Also from the eleventh century was the important historical poem on the Conquest of Southern Italy by the Normans, written by William of Apulia.

A valuable contribution to the religious and cultural history of Italy in the Middle Ages was the official history of the great monastery of Monte Cassino by Leo Ostiensis (d. *ca.* 1116). He wrote a complete history of Monte Cassino and its activities from the foundation to 1075. It was one of the best examples of Italian historical writing during the whole medieval period, well-organized, impartial, instructive and pleasingly written. The author was relatively cautious in admitting wonders and legends. Leo's narrative was continued to 1138 by Petrus Diaconus (d. *ca.* 1140), whose work was far inferior to that of Leo. Petrus was vain and emotional, and he was uncritical in utilizing legendary material.

In his *Liber ad Amicum,* Bonizo, Bishop of Sutri (b. *ca.* 1060), provided a history of the papacy in his day. He possessed a good knowledge of ecclesiastical subjects and his book was mainly a pro-papal history of the famous investiture struggle, including the bitter conflict between Gregory VII and Henry IV. Of the investiture struggles Bonizo wrote as an eye-witness, but he was prone to rely upon scriptural and canonical quotations to prove his points.

The history of Sicily, especially Norman Sicily, claimed the attention of Hugo Falcandus, who was regarded as "the Tacitus of Sicilian history." He was born in France but lived for a considerable time in Italy and Sicily. His work was completed in 1169. While a definite partisan of the Norman feudal nobility in Sicily, Hugo was capable of keen and independent judgments. His history included invaluable material on the institutions, manners and customs of medieval Sicily, and it was written in a vigorous and polished style.

One of the most interesting books in all medieval Italian historical writing was the chronicle of Fra Salimbene (1221-*ca.* 1290) a Franciscan friar. Salimbene traveled widely and mixed with all types of people from popes and kings to the common people and paupers. His chronicle was a discursive, episodical and disorganized description of all he had seen and heard, down to 1288. Despite the diffuse character of his chronicle, Salimbene was a discerning spectator of his times and a born story-teller. Hence, his work was extremely interesting and valuable for its description of the manners, customs, dress and culture of his day. He dwelt much on the dramatic political events of his period, especially the struggles between Frederick II and the Italian towns. His chronicle was written in a vigorous but crude medieval Latin.

Almost the opposite in his historical methods from Salimbene was Ferretus of Vincenza (b. *ca.* 1295), whose *History of Italian Affairs* covered Italian history and foreign relations from 1250 to 1318. His history was carefully planned and admirably organized, and the author showed great skill in selecting his facts. The book was written in elegant Latin style. Its main defect consisted in the author's flair for the dramatic, which led him at times to stretch the truth to attain colorful description.

One of the main political issues in medieval Italy was the struggle between the Guelphs and Ghibellines. Among the best histories of this conflict was the *Historia Augusta* of Albertinus Mussatus (1261-*ca.* 1330). Albertinus was a soldier, statesman and diplomat who had traveled extensively in European countries. He wrote with striking impartiality and was a fine Latin stylist.

The interesting story of medieval Venice attracted many historical writers. Martin de Canale, of whose life we know little, wrote a history of Venice to the year 1275. His book was half romance and half history, but it was valuable for its description of the manners, customs and art of Venice. Far more reliable was the *Chronicle of Venice* by Andrea Dandola (*ca.* 1309-54). Andrea was a statesman, jurist and historian. He carefully studied the earlier histories of Venice and copied in his work many documents which would otherwise have perished. He was an impartial writer and was reliable in all save the earlier portions of his history and in his chronology. His chronicle was indispensable as a source of information for the life and institutions of medieval Venice, especially the evolution of the Venetian constitution.

Genoa also provided her annalists, such as Caffaro, Obertus and Ogerius Panis. Caffaro was one of the most reliable and straightforward of medieval historians of the Crusades. His *Annals,* in addition to his special works on the Crusades, give a good picture of his age. But it was in late medieval Florence that Italian historical writing of the Middle Ages reached its highest development. The two best representatives were Dino Compagni (*ca.* 1260-1323) and Giovanni Villani (d. 1348). Dino's *Chronicle of Florence* gave a brief review of the origins of the city and then supplied a rather full account of Florentine history from 1280 to 1312, with which period Dino was personally acquainted. He was not purely an annalistic narrator. He often gave an intelligent and independent interpretation of his facts. The book was dominated by civic pride and was written in a vivid and picturesque style. Balzani says of its spirit: "In this history he lives, breathes and moves, and in such a way that we know of no modern historian who equals him in his gift of lighting the same flame in his readers' breasts as burned in his own."[17]

It is fairly generally admitted that Giovanni Villani was the foremost Italian historical writer of the Middle Ages. With him historical writing entered the modern stage in Italy. He was a soldier, traveler and important Florentine official. His *Florentine Chronicle* dealt with the whole sweep from biblical times to 1346, but it became important only with the medieval period. On Florentine origins Villani was prone to accept legendary accounts. His work was far more inclusive than Dino's chronicle, both as to time and space. It supplied a complete picture of the history of Florence in the Middle Ages and also much material on the general history of medieval Europe as a whole. The book was based on wide reading and some critical study of earlier authorities. It was written in a sincere and honest fashion, nothwithstanding the Guelph sympathies of the author, which made him a partisan of the merchant group. The organization was carefully thought out and Villani possessed plenty of capacity for critical and independent judgments. As Professor Ferdinand Schevill observes, Villani had a "feeling for factual reality which no medieval writer before his time possessed in the same degree."[18] His style was serene and lucid. The book provided not only a narrative of Florentine development, but also a good survey of its society and culture. As Professor Schevill puts it: "His immense achievement, for which we of a later period can never be too grateful, is the accurate description of the town under his eyes, his story of its trade, its industry, its social classes, its religious customs, its relation to its neighbors, its ceaseless and passionate domestic conflicts."[19] The book was also one of the few historical works of the Middle Ages to include statistical information of a relatively accurate character. The chronicle was continued by Matteo and Filippo Villani to the year 1364.

LEADING GERMANIC HISTORIANS OF THE MIDDLE AGES

Among Germanic historians of the Middle Ages we would certainly have to list writers like Jordanes, Einhard, Nithard and others whom we have treated as transitional figures between classical historiography and medieval historical writing. Perhaps the first strictly medieval German historical writer of importance was one Flodoard, a priest of Rheims, who died in 966. He compiled some well-informed *Annals* covering the period from 919 to 966. They were apparently composed as the events took place and Flodoard wrote as an eyewitness of the episodes which he de-

---

[17] Balzani, *Early Chroniclers of Europe: Italy*. pp. 321-32.
[18] Ferdinand Schevill, *A History of Florence* (Harcourt Brace, 1936), p. xiv.
[19] *Ibid.*, p. xv.

scribed. Historians regard him as accurate in his facts for a writer of this period and his works are of high value on the end of the Carolingians and the rise of the Capetians in France and for the origins of the Saxon dynasty in Germany. An interesting source for the latter part of the tenth century was the writings of the poet-nun, Hroswitha (b. *ca*. 935). She wrote a number of versified chronicles dealing with her age. Most famous was her epic poem of the Ottoes, the *Carmen de gestis Oddonis* [*Song of the Deeds of Otto*], which brought the story down to 968. She also produced a number of comedies.

In the next generation came Widukind (d. 1004), a Benedictine monk of Corvey. His main historical work, which is known as *The Deeds of the Saxons,* was divided into three books. It covered the period from the origins of the Saxons to the death of Otto the Great in 973. His treatment of the early history of the Saxons was largely legendary, but his work was of high value for Henry the Fowler and Otto the Great. He began to write about 968, at the height of the reign of Otto. He was very proud of the Saxon emperors and extolled their virtues and accomplishments. In his style he imitated the classical historians, especially Sallust. His Latin grammar was, however, not flawless. Following Widukind was Thietmar, Bishop of Merseburg, who completed in 1018 a chronicle which covered the reigns of the three Ottos and Henry II. On the reign of Henry III the most important work was the *Chronicle* of Hermann of Reichenau (1013-54). Hermann was a learned and versatile scholar as well as an able historian. He distinguished himself by works in mathematics, astronomy and music. His historical work consisted of a general European chronicle from the beginning of the Christian era to 1054, which was continued to 1080 by his disciple, Berthold. He was one of the ablest historians of his time and his work was particularly valuable as a survey of his own period. On the previous century also, his book was important, for it relied upon a highly valuable source which has since been lost.

Inspired by Livy and Sallust, Lambert of Hersfeld (d. *ca*. 1080), a Benedictine monk, composed the most polished and elegantly written historical work of the time in any European country. His *Annals* were one of the more important contributions to the history of the relations of Germany and the papacy. They began with a chronology extending from Creation to 1040. This portion was only repetition of the customary general world chronicle, together with materials from the old *Annals of Hersfeld*. From 1040 onward the work was more important and original and the best section was that treating events from 1069 to the end in 1077. In the last portion Lambert sometimes dropped the annalistic method and rose to the level of an original historian. He succeeded far better than his contemporaries in attaining a respectable notion of time perspective in history, and he not only chronicled events but discussed intelligently the problem of cause and effect in the flow of historical developments. Also, he possessed high talent in describing historical scenes. Hence, it is not surprising that, for three centuries after his *Annals* were first printed in 1525, Lambert was vastly admired. But beginning with Leopold von Ranke's criticisms in 1854, his reputation has suffered rather severely in our day. A generation after von Ranke, Hans Delbrück examined Lambert's writings even more thoroughly. He showed that Lambert often was in error with respect to simple historical facts, that he was definitely biased in favor of the papacy and allowed this to distort his account of the investiture struggle and the deeds of the emperors, and that he ignored or minimized the position of secular law and procedure in the struggle. It was Lambert who invented the tale concerning the alleged humiliation of Henry IV before Gregory VIII at Canossa. Yet, his work possessed distinct historical value and it far surpassed that of any contemporary as polished historical literature.

From Constance came two chronicles of some value for the reign of Henry IV and his struggles with the Church. Berthold of Constance (d. 1088) wrote a considerable work on the investiture struggle, taking the side of the pope against Henry. More valuable and impartial, though still anti-monarchical, was the *Chronicle* of Hermann of Constance (1046-1132). Bruno's *History of the Rebellion of Saxony* was important for the Germanic events of Henry's reign. Valuable information on northern Germany was embodied in the *Ecclesiastical History of Hamburg and Bremen* by Adam of Bremen, written in the last part of the eleventh century. It dealt with the period from 788 to 1072. Adam was learned in the classics and his history contained much cultural material and information on the history of the Church, as well as an account of the conquest of the Slavs of the Elbe district. Some information of importance was included on the reign of Henry IV. Adam also wrote a very important work on the antiquities of early Scandinavian history and the early Norse trade.

A pretentious general history was the *Universal Chronicle* of Marianus Scotus (1028-84), a scholar in Mainz, but a native of Ireland. His chronicle was in three books, the first devoted to ancient history, the second to the life and times of Jesus, and the last to the Middle Ages. The first portion of the last book was based on Cassiodorus and early medieval annals. The work was of real value only for the period of the author's own life. It contained much information on Irish history and still more on the history of Mainz. Marianus was a mathematician as well as a historian, and his books included interesting discussions of chronological problems in history. His work was continued by Florence of Worcester in England and then widely exploited by Sigebert of Gembloux in fashioning his universal history.

The most comprehensive of all the general medieval chronicles was the

Chronicle of the World by Ekkehard of Aurach, who began his writing in the last decade of the eleventh century. Ekkehard's work was not only very inclusive, but it also showed a high order of historical conscientiousness in its composition. He used good sources, especially for the latter part of his chronicle, and he used them carefully. He was patient in historical research and revised his work several times, bringing it down in the latest version to 1106, from which point it was continued to 1125 by his successors. In Ekkehard's version it ended with an account of the First Crusade which Ekkehard rewrote after a pilgrimage to the Holy Land. He was far more impartial than Lambert in his narrative of events, and he showed good judgment in selecting his materials. His *Chronicle* was divided into five books, the first three of which brought the story down to Charlemagne. The last two dealt with events from Charlemagne into the reign of Henry V. The final book, which treated of Henry's reign, was by far the most important and reliable portion, and it was much the best source for Henry's activities. His work was one of the most valuable sources of information for the history of Northern Germany in the Middle Ages. While not as polished a writer as Lambert, Ekkehard wrote in a clear and simple style and his work as a whole is very lucid. At the request of Henry V, Ekkehard wrote a history of the Holy Roman Empire from Charlemagne onward, but this was of less value than his great chronicle.

A valuable source for Germany and the early Crusades was the *Chronicle* of Albert of Aachen, about whose life we know little, except that he wrote before 1158. His chronicle was in twelve books and came down to 1121. It was important chiefly for its discussion of the First Crusade and of the Latin kingdom of Jerusalem. Albert's work was much used by William of Tyre.

The most noted and influential German historian of the Middle Ages was Bishop Otto of Freising (*ca.* 1114-58), uncle of the Emperor Frederick I [Barbarossa]. He was not only an able chronicler of events but also the first medieval philosopher of history of any proportions. His two most important books were his *Chronicle* or *Book of Two Cities*, and his *Deeds of the Emperor Frederick I*. The *Book of Two Cities*, which came down to 1146, was the first important medieval philosophy of history. The historical method was that of Orosius and the historical philosophy that of Augustine. The book rested upon the Augustinian antithesis of the City of God and the City of the Devil. Otto illustrated their struggles, after the manner of Orosius, from Creation to his own time. The work was carried on to 1209 by another monk, Otto of St. Blaisen. The treatise was in eight books, the final one of which was devoted to the Last Judgment and the world to come. It was the first attempt of a medieval historian, says Balzani, to force "the whole story of humanity into a foreordained system of causes and effects." Otto's philosophical approach lessened the historical value of his work in two ways. In the first place, it biased him against secular and pagan affairs. In the second place, his primary interest in the philosophy of history led him to be careless at times in his handling of details. This carelessness with respect to facts was also intensified by his striving for rhetorical effects and for dramatic contrasts—the form was as important as the content to him. His account of the important Concordat of Worms in 1122 was, for example, both wrong-headed and shaky in details. Despite all this, Otto's material was very valuable as he approached his own time. He used reliable sources, depending especially on Ekkehard. And no other historian of his day gave as much attention to cause and effect or so earnestly endeavored to explain the present by light from the past.

The *Deeds of the Emperor Frederick* was a less impressive book but more important for contemporary history. It was an invaluable source for the relations of Frederick and the Church. Otto was an eyewitness and fully informed for his task. His premature death prevented him from carrying the work beyond 1158. He was sympathetic with German imperialism at the expense of the Italians, but his churchly background often led him into partisanship in behalf of the pope. This work was completed and continued by Otto's assistant, Rahewin. Otto also is supposed to have written a work on the history of Austria, which has been lost. As a stylist Otto was polished and dramatic, but somewhat rhetorical and affected. A sympathetic Catholic critic, Franz X. von Wegele, pays the following tribute to Otto:

> A writer possessing such extraordinary literary talent as Otto of Freising did not appear again in German historical writing for many a century. However much Lambert of Hersfeld may have excelled him as a polished narrator, Otto more than made up for this by the deep seriousness of his world-philosophy and by the loftiness of the viewpoint which he invariably maintained. Whatever one may think of his philosophy, he was the only medieval German historian who was able to grasp in a philosophical manner the march of world history and who sought to give its progress a judicious exposition. And he occupies no less conspicuous a position as a narrator of the history of his times.[20]

Godfrey of Viterbo (1120-96) is claimed by both Germans and Italians. He seems to have been born and educated in Germany, but he died in Viterbo, which was his home during the later years of his life. He was a chaplain and secretary in the employ of Frederick I, and he also was sent on important diplomatic missions. His main historical work was *The Deeds of Frederick I,* covering the period from 1155 to 1180 and written mainly in verse. It dealt chiefly with events in Italy and was highly

[20] F. X. von Wegele, *Geschichte der deutschen Historiographie seit dem Auftreten des Humanismus* (Leipzig, 1885), p. 20.

episodical and distinctly inferior to most of the German medieval works mentioned above.

A curious but very popular work was *The Chronicle of the Popes and Emperors* by Martin of Troppau (d. 1278), a Dominican friar and later a bishop. Martin was papal chaplain for a time and wrote his chronicle at the bidding of the pope. The work was curiously arranged. The popes and emperors appeared on opposite pages; each page contained fifty lines; and each line dealt with a year. This plan worked passably well down to 1276, when there were three popes. So Martin abandoned this scheme and launched out into a discussion of the major events of the time. The work was not too reliable but it was highly popular and much used by later chroniclers, such as Nicholas Trevet in England.

HISTORICAL BIOGRAPHY IN WESTERN EUROPE DURING THE MIDDLE AGES

Some of the best historical writing of the Middle Ages consisted of biographies of leading political and ecclesiastical figures. The prowess of the great political and military personages in the Middle Ages made attractive subjects for historical biography. Often the monarch subsidized or otherwise favored a biographer to insure a properly flattering record of his deeds. Needless to say, strict impartiality was never observed, and sycophancy was often added to the other defects of medieval historiography. In addition, the theological coloring of all medieval thought often led the biographer to represent the great secular figures of the period as the chosen agents of Divine Providence in their age.

One of the two or three best medieval historical biographies was Einhard's *Life of Charlemagne,* which we have already described. Also very close to historical biography was such a work as Otto of Freising's *Deeds of the Emperor Frederick.* Perhaps the first important and typically medieval historical biography was Asser's *Life of Alfred.* It was the work of a Welsh priest of the late ninth or early tenth century. The work began with 849, the traditional year of Alfred's birth. It went beyond a mere biography, in that it dealt also with the major events of Alfred's reign. The author used as a basis for his biography and narrative the *Saxon Chronicle.* The book was full of interesting episodes and the tone was usually adulatory of Alfred. It was written in simple and interesting fashion. There have been innumerable interpolations by later writers. These furnished many of the classic tales about Arthur, such as the legend of his carelessly letting the cakes of a cowherd burn. Asser's *Life* was copied almost *in toto* by Florence of Worcester (d. 1118).

Better known was the biography of Louis VI [the Fat], one of the more important of the early Capetians, by Suger, Abbot of Saint Denis and an adviser to Louis VII. The work was not a full annalistic narrative; it was a biography of Louis, and one must look elsewhere for a complete chronicle of the events of his reign. The story was, of course, very partisan in Louis' favor, but not so partial as to lead to the falsification of facts. Suger was also very fair to the English in his work. The style of the book was rather dull, but it brightened up considerably in the narration of dramatic events. The Latin grammar in the book was bad indeed. The biography of Emperor Conrad II (1024-39) by his chaplain, Wipo, was an intelligent and competent work, even if very flattering to Conrad.

One of the most colorful ecclesiastical figures in the Middle Ages was Pope Gregory VII. He found his biographer in an Italian priest, Paul of Bernried, who completed his *History of Gregory VII* in 1128. Paul prepared himself carefully for his work by much study and the questioning of many eyewitnesses. The result was a very able book—the best Italian historical work on the investiture conflict. Paul used good sources and studied many official documents. He was, to be sure, not exceedingly critical in his handling of sources, but he made few major blunders save in his proclivity to admit the miraculous and the legendary. Even here the reader is able to distinguish between what Paul took from legends and what he derived from substantial historical sources. The work was strongly biased in favor of Gregory, whose great moral strength was emphasized in the book.

The able and colorful French king, Philip Augustus, found his biographers in Rigord (d. *ca.* 1207) and Guillaume le Breton (d. *ca.* 1227). Rigord was, like Suger, a monk of Saint Denis. He began his *Life of Philip Augustus* about 1190 and devoted many years to it. It covered the period from 1179 to 1207. The narrative was broken into by myths of the origins of the French nation and by chronologies of the French kings. Rigord was neither a great mind nor a great historian, but his partiality for Philip pleased the latter and led to his warm approbation of Rigord's book. Guillaume le Breton, the chaplain of Philip, was a far abler historian than Rigord. He was entrusted with several political and diplomatic missions and he accompanied Philip on many of his campaigns. He continued Rigord's *Life* to 1219, and his work was invaluable for the period from 1209 to 1219. Guillaume's poem, the *Philippid,* shed much light on geographical matters and on the manners and customs of the time.

Perhaps the only medieval biography which equaled or surpassed Einhard's *Life of Charlemagne* was the biography of Louis IX by Joinville (1224-1319). Joinville was the friend, adviser and confidant of the king. His *History of St. Louis* was written or dictated after he had attained an advanced age. The Seventh Crusade formed the framework of the book, and the emphasis was on the events from 1248 to 1254. But the historical material, while relatively reliable, was subordinated to the fundamental aim of stressing the saintly qualities of the monarch. Joinville was far less sceptical than Villehardouin had been in rejecting the miraculous. In political philosophy, he was a protagonist of the growing royal centralization, as Villehardouin had been of feudal independence and chivalry. The work is written in a beautiful and lucid style, whether the subject-matter be description, eulogy or satire.

The *Life of Matilda,* countess of Tuscany, in Latin verse by her chaplain, Donnizone, from the eleventh century, was the first important Italian contribution to historical biography. From Italy in the fourteenth century came the anonymous *Life of Cola di Rienzi,* the most notable historical work produced in Rome during the whole century. The author exhibited high skill in the difficult problem of reconstructing the composite character of Cola and of portraying the evolution of his power and personality. The work was also valuable for its account of the political intrigues in church and state. The narrative was vivid and the work as a whole absorbing.

Next to the work of Joinville the most important French historical biography in the medieval period was *The History of Charles VI* by Jean Juvenal des Ursins (1388-1473). The author was both an eminent French lawyer and Archbishop of Rheims. Hence, he was at home in both secular and ecclesiastical law and politics. His work covered the period from 1380 to 1422, the whole reign of Charles, and it was of high value for both state and church affairs. The style was simple and interesting, and the book as a whole highly readable. The author possessed a lofty, masterful and impartial view of the affairs of his day.

Among medieval autobiographies, the one outstanding product was the *Historia calamitatum* of Abelard, the mental autobiography of one of the most original minds of the Middle Ages. More intimate and popular but more morbid were the famous *Confessions of Augustine* from the age of the Church Fathers, to which we have already referred.

There was much rich historical material in medieval times in poems or chansons, romances, fables, myths, and public charters, but we do not have space to deal with these accessory but valuable sources of historical information.[21]

BYZANTINE HISTORIANS OF THE MIDDLE AGES

Until recently there has been an unfortunate tendency to regard medieval history as overwhelmingly the history of Latin Europe during the Middle Ages. Hence, accounts of the leading medieval historians have been limited to the major historical writers of western Europe, thus ignor-

21 See J. W. Thompson, *The Middle Ages.* Vol. II, chap. xxviii (Knopf, 1931), 2 vols.

ing the many and relatively excellent historians of the Eastern, Roman, Greek or Byzantine Empire (whichever name one may prefer) and of the far-flung Muslim realms. To such writers of history during the medieval period we may now briefly turn our attention.

Among early Byzantine historians would be certain writers whom we have already mentioned, such as the ecclesiastical historians Eusebius, Socrates, Sozomen, and Theodoret, and the military and political historian, Procopius. Perhaps the first of the secular historians of the East was Eutropius, the soldier-secretary of Constantine, who died some time after 378. He wrote in Latin at a period before Greek had become the official language of the East. His chief historical work was a compendious survey of Roman history down to the time of Valens, *Brevarium ab Urbe Condita,* which was used and enlarged by Paul the Deacon. One of the more important early Byzantine historians was Zosimus, who was flourishing about the middle of the fifth century. His work was entitled *The New History,* and it covered the period from Augustus to A.D. 410. Zosimus was a pagan in religion and was keenly conscious of the decline of the power and prestige of the Roman Empire. The responsibility for this he placed mainly upon the rise of Christianity and its adoption by the Roman state. He was, accordingly, rather severe on Constantine and sympathetic towards Julian the Apostate. His view of history was the opposite of that of Orosius and was much needed as a corrective in perspective.

The important *History* of Procopius, dealing with the wars of Justinian and eulogizing the military genius of Belisarius, was supplemented by the history of the Roman Empire to Julian the Apostate, written by a contemporary of Procopius, Peter the Patrician, a Byzantine lawyer and diplomat. During the reign of Justinian, Hesychius of Melitus compiled the first Byzantine *Universal History.* It covered the period from Assyrian history to A.D. 518. Hesychius continued it in a historical survey of the reign of Justin I and the early part of the reign of Justinian, most of which has been lost. Contemporary with this *Universal History* was the *Chronicle* of John Malalas (*ca.* 491-578) who dealt with events from early Egyptian history to the age of Justinian, introducing much legendary and fabulous material into his account. His work was no more than relatively accurate even for the age of Justinian. Antioch was the center of his narrative. He was a warm supporter of the church and monarchy. His book was very popular, even if unreliable, since it was the first historical treatise written in Byzantine realms in idiomatic language for general consumption.

On the reign of Justinian, and especially important for the years 552-58, was the *History of the Reign of Justinian* by the able lawyer, Agathias the Scholastic, of Myrina in Asia Minor, who lived in the latter part of the sixth century. This work was continued in inferior style to the beginning of the reign of Maurice in 582 by Menander the Protector, who wrote his history during the reign of Maurice (582-602). It was particularly valuable because of the ethnographic and geographical material included. Also covering the period from Justinian to Maurice was the history of Theophanes of Byzantium, written at the end of the sixth century. It contained, incidentally, one of the first important references to the Turks. In the same generation, Evagrius the Scholastic (b. *ca*. 536), of Syria, continued the church histories of Socrates, Sozomen and Theodoret from 431 to 593 in his *Ecclesiastical History*. On the reign of Maurice the most valuable work was *The History of the Emperor Maurice* in eight books by Theophylact of Simocratta (d. *ca*. 630), an Egyptian scholar. It was affected and rhetorical in style and much given to the allegorical method, but it was the only important contemporary treatment of the period of Maurice. During the reign of Maurice, John of Ephesus (d. *ca*. 586) compiled in Syriac his *Ecclesiastical History* which surveyed religious developments from Julius Caesar to 585. It was of special significance for its account of the last struggles and extinction of paganism and for the political and cultural history of the Eastern Empire in the sixth century.

For the reign of Heraclius (610-14) there were the versified histories of the wars of Heraclius against the Persians and Avars by George of Pisidia, who lived during this same period. In this reign also John of Antioch composed his *Universal Chronicle* from Adam to 610. It was a more competent work than that of John Malalas, the author being much colder towards legends and fables, having a broader historical point of view, and making far more intelligent use of better sources. The Iconoclastic age witnessed the production of three important historical works. George Syncellus, who died in the early ninth century, surveyed the period from Creation to Diocletian. His *Chronicle* (or *Chronography*) was continued in the very valuable *Chronicle* of Theophanes the Confessor (758-818), who brought the story down to 813. Theophanes' compilation was highly informing in its treatment of the Iconoclastic controversy. It was anti-Iconoclast in tone. Theophanes used and preserved many important earlier sources and his work was much exploited by later Byzantine historians. Nicephorus Patriarcha (*ca*. 758-829), patriarch of Constantinople, produced a valuable compendium of Byzantine history for the years 602-770. It is one of the most important sources describing the emergence of the Bulgars on the historical scene in the Balkans. Nicephorous also brought out a less valuable chronological summary of events from Adam to his own day.

At the very end of the period of the Iconoclastic controversy (*ca*. 850) the extensive *Chronicle* of George Hamartolus was written. It surveyed the whole period from Adam to 842. In the later portions of his chronicle the author wrote as an eyewitness. His book was full of valuable information on the cultural, religious and artistic history of the period, and was particularly useful for the light it threw upon life in the monasteries of the East. Hamartolus' chronicle was very popular with later Byzantine historians and had an even greater influence upon the Russian chroniclers of the Middle Ages. In the period of Constantine VII (912-58), Joseph Genesius wrote his valuable *History of Constantinople* on the era from Leo V to Leo VI (813-86). In four books, it was a reliable narrative written in clear and simple style. In the early tenth century the influential statesman, Simeon Metaphrastis, compiled his famous *Lives of the Saints,* a notable collection which dealt with the saints of the Eastern church. The emperor Constantine Porphyrogenitus (905-59) is credited with a life of the Emperor Basilius I. It was probably composed by some scholar under the auspices of the emperor. In any event, it contains much information on the legal and military history of that period.

Leo Diaconus' *History* was the chief authority for the period 959 to 975, giving particular attention to the wars against the Muslims and Bulgars. Perhaps the greatest scholar of the whole Byzantine culture was Michael Constantine Psellus (*ca.* 1018-1110). He wrote a valuable and scholarly history of the period from 976 to 1077, continuing the work of Leo Diaconus. His style was a good example of the best rhetorical Greek of the Byzantine age. Also important for the eleventh century was the history by Michael Attaliata (*ca.* 1075), who dealt with the period from 1034 to 1079. An able jurist, his history was particularly strong on legal and administrative developments. John Scylitza wrote a substantial *Chronicle* on the years 811 to 1057, and this was embodied in the more notable *Universal Chronicle* of George Cedrenus (*ca.* 1100).

In this same general period came two world histories. George Cedrenus (*ca.* 1100) produced the chronicle just mentioned, covering the period from Creation to 1059. John Zonaras (d. *ca.* 1130), perhaps the ablest Byzantine chronicler of the Middle Ages, did a much better piece of work in writing a real world history in eighteen books on the period from Creation to 1118. His *Chronicle* departed from the style of the conventional chronicle and was reasonably reliable as to facts, especially for the later period. He made wide use of the Greek and Roman classics. Zonaras also wrote less important works on the history of the Eastern church. One of the most popular historical works of the Middle Ages written in the Byzantine Empire was the *World History* of Michael Glycos, composed in the twelfth century.

An interesting work was the history of the reign of Alexius I by his daughter, Anna Comnena (b. 1083). She plotted to secure succession to the throne but failed and was sent to a convent. Here she compiled the history of the Alexiad from 1081 to 1118. She wrote in a rhetorical style, consciously modeled after that of the classical Greek historians. Her adu-

lation of her father led to gross favoritism and to exaggeration of petty
episodes connected with him, and thus to neglect of important public
events. The chronology was most defective. But the work had special
value as a pro-Byzantine account of the early Crusades.

The age of the Comneni produced one of the most eminent of Byzantine historians, the imperial secretary, John Cinnamus (fl. *ca.* 1175.) He
consciously imitated the methods of Xenophon and Procopius. His *History* in six books dealt with the reigns of John II and Manuel I, covering
the period from 1118 to 1176. His narrative was highly eulogistic of Manuel and he vigorously defended the Eastern Empire against the pretensions of the pope and Latin Christianity. The work was written in excellent and forceful style.

The Crusades, especially the Fourth Crusade, provoked much interest
on the part of Byzantine historians. The most notable product was the
history by Nicetas Acominatus (d. *ca.* 1216). He was, roughly, a sort of
Byzantine Villehardouin. His *History* was a large work in twenty-one
books covering the period from 1180 to 1206, thus including the capture
of Constantinople by the Crusaders in 1204. It was in form a series of
studies of the emperors of the period. It was the best work for the facts
about the reign of Manuel I and the capture of Constantinople. The author argued in spirited fashion for the superiority of Byzantine civilization
to what he not unreasonably regarded as the barbarism of the West. He
had a better understanding of the background of the relations of East and
West than any other contemporary historian in either region. His *History*
was written in picturesque but unaffected style.

The autobiography of Nicephorus Blemmydes, who flourished in the
first half of the thirteenth century, gave a good account not only of the
ecclesiastical developments of the time but also of political and social conditions. His pupil, the diplomat, George Acropolita (1217-82), was the
author of one of the major Byzantine historical works, *A History of the
Byzantine Empire, 1203-61*. It was the best history of the critical period
from the capture of Constantinople to the restoration of the Greek Empire. Of many of the developments and events of which he wrote George
was an eyewitness. The style of his history was as excellent as its contents.
For the following period we have the historical writings of George Pachy-
meres (1242-1310). They covered the imperial history of the East from
1261 to 1308. Though his works were pedantic, in imitation of antique
historians, they were valuable as a source of information on the bitter
religious and dogmatic disputes of this age. They were relatively impartial
for his day.

In the fourteenth century came the important *Byzantine History, 1204-
1359* of Nicephorus Gregoras (*ca.* 1295-*ca.* 1360). Nicephorus' work, in
thirty-eight books, was an erudite study of religion, philosophy and sci-

ence, and his history was especially valuable for its light on the civilization and religious disputes following the restoration. The period of the final eclipse of the Greek Empire and its capture by the Turks was treated by three able historians, all eyewitnesses of the capture of Constantinople. The courtier and diplomat, Ducas (fl. *ca.* 1460), dealt with the period from 1341 to 1462; George Phrantzes (*ca.* 1401-78) with the years from 1258 to 1476; and Laonikas Chalkondyles (fl. *ca.* 1460) with the era from 1298 to 1463. Of these three histories of the end of the Greek Empire, the *Chronicle* of Phrantzes was probably the ablest and most satisfactory. Phrantzes wrote as an eyewitness and in reliable and interesting fashion. Chalkondyles was one of the first to appreciate the significance of the Turks in history and to assess fairly their strength in the fifteenth century. Also worthy of mention was the history by the Greek author, Critobulus of Imbros, on the times of Sultan Mohammed II, to 1467.

As a general characterization one may say that the Byzantine historians were usually far more learned than the comparable historians of Latin Europe. The erudition of classical times held over much more completely in the Byzantine Empire than it did in the West. But this greater erudition was offset to a certain degree by the less fresh and original character of all varieties of Byzantine literature. Both style and content were more stereotyped and there was less opportunity for originality and growth than in the West. In western Europe during the Middle Ages culture was developing from near-barbarism to a fairly high civilization. In the East it was declining from classical levels and becoming more decadent and reminiscent. One was a growing, the other a dying culture. In both areas, however, the Christian world philosophy permeated the historical writings, the Byzantines being even more absorbed in dogmatic disputes than the western Christians.

The Russian medieval chronicles were deeply influenced by the Byzantine models. There was little historical writing in Russia in the early Middle Ages, for the country was illiterate save in the south. Anonymous chronicles appeared from the middle of the eleventh century onward. Most important of them were the *Nestor Chronicle* and the *Galician Chronicle* of the thirteenth century. After 1400 the Byzantine influence, especially of Hamartolus, became more noticeable. The chronicles then became official compilations. Many works were compiled in late medieval Russia on the lives of the saints, a literature which was full of fables and marvels.

SOME LEADING MUSLIM HISTORIANS OF THE MIDDLE AGES

In many ways the most advanced civilization of the Middle Ages was not a Christian culture at all, but rather the civilization of peoples of the faith of Islam. Likewise, some of the ablest medieval historians were Muslims. And the greatest of them, Ibn Khaldun, completely outdistanced any Christian historian of the Middle Ages in his fundamental grasp of the principles of human and cultural development. Not until the time of Voltaire in the eighteenth century was there a historian in Christendom who equaled him in this respect.[22] As a group, the Muslim historians, compared with the Christian historians of the period, were characterized by independent judgment, relative impartiality, and a better grasp of chronological methods. They dated their materials and events far more precisely than most Christian writers.

The main incentives to Muslim historical writing in the first centuries after Mohammed lay in the desire to hand down the authoritative traditions of Islam, in the zeal for establishing genealogical relationship to the Prophet, and in the wish to celebrate the Muslim conquests and to laud the Muslim conquerors. For a considerable time, historical documentation consisted chiefly of the unbroken transmission of supposedly authoritative traditions concerning the origin and dissemination of the Islamic faith. Historical scholarship and criticism were mainly a matter of choosing among traditions and between the transmitters .of these traditions. Muslim historical writing was primarily religious and political history. Only the ablest and most original of the Muslim historians gave much attention to social and economic history. And the Muslim historians adopted much the same providential theory of historical development that the Christian historians embraced, Allah being substituted for Yahweh. The style of writing was much influenced by Persian models, especially the *Book of Kings,* by Al-Firdausi (935-1020), which was quickly translated into Arabic.

The earliest important Muslim historical works were, naturally enough, biographies of Mohammed and accounts of the Mohammedan conquests. The first notable biography of Mohammed was *The Biography of the Prophet* by Ibn Ishaq (d. 768). It was a sincere and devout attempt to gather together the traditions and facts relative to Mohammed and the origins of Islam. It was most reliable for the period after Mohammed's visions. This book was widely used by later Muslim historians and almost completely and literally embodied in Ibn Hisham's (d. 834) *Biography of Mohammed.* The earliest important chronicler of the wars of Islam was Al-Waqidi (747-823), the favorite historian at the court of the Abbasids. His chief work was a *History of the Wars of the Prophet.* A definite advance was taken by Al-Baladhuri (d. 892), who wrote the standard version of early Muslim conquests and triumphs. He brought together the earlier accounts of the main Muslim conquests into one general narrative,

---

22 See below, pp. 149 ff.

his *Conquests of the Countries.*[23] In the same generation Al-Dinawari (d. 895) composed his standard *History of Arabia and Persia.* The best work on the Caliphate of Bagdhad was *The History of Bagdhad and Its Caliphs* by Ibn Abi Tahir (d. 902).

The leading political and narrative historian of the Muslims was Al-Tabari (838-923), a traveler and a writer learned in the Muslim law and lore. His chief work was *The Annals of the Apostles and Kings,* bringing his account to 915. He perfected the use of the annalistic method among Muslims and his work was a model for extensive imitation by later writers. He has been called "the Livy of the Muslims," but the comparison is not fitting. He was more accurate than Livy but far inferior as a stylist. In fact, his great work was a vast assemblage of materials with little order and organization—a sort of source book which could be delved into by later historians. Al-Masudi (d. 956) was not only a great Muslim encyclopedist, but also one of the leading Muslim historians. He rejected the simple annalistic method of Al-Tabari and organized his materials according to kings, dynasties and topics. His *Meadows of Gold* and other works were unusual in containing much enthnographic material and cultural and social history, as well as a record of political events. He has been fairly appropriately designated "the Herodotus of the Arabs," for he possessed the same avid curiosity and zeal for information as did "the father of history." But he was more gullible than Herodotus in accepting legends and wonders.

One of the ablest of Muslim historians was Miskawaihi [Ibn Miskawaih] (fl. *ca.* 970). He was a great admirer of Al-Tabari. His intelligence was of a high order and he possessed a great deal of first-hand information on administrative and military matters. His *Experiences of the Nations* was also distinguished for its impartiality and its outspoken judgments even on eminent Muslim rulers. In his review of Muslim historians, Professor Margoliouth says of Miskawaihi: "In the work of Miskawaihi Arabic historical composition seems to reach its highest point." But he was no match for Ibn Khaldun as a philosopher of history.

Between 982 and 994, Ali al-Tanukhi (939-94) brought out his *Collection of Histories,* a vast assemblage of Muslim historical anecdotes and episodes. On Damascus and the eminent Muslims who dwelt there we have *The History of Damascus* by Ali al-Hasan (1121-93). The most prolific of the Muslim historians dealing with Muslim Egypt was Makrizi (1360-1442). He was not an original scholar, but he was a learned and sagacious compiler. His chief work was a topographical description and history of Muslim Egypt, especially notable for its unrivaled account of medieval Cairo. He also wrote histories of the Fatimite and Mameluke

[23] Translated by P. K. Hitti and F. C. Murgotten as *The Origins of the Islamic State* (Columbia University Press, 1916, 1924), 2 vols.

sultans and a vast encyclopedia of Egyptian biography. Important Muslim world histories were written by Abu-l-Faraj al Isfahani (897-967), Ibn-al-Athir Izz al-din (d. 1234), and Abu-l-Fida (1273-1331). Ibn-al Athir was one of the first Muslim historians to have a philosophical grasp on cause and effect in historical development.

Far and away the ablest and most significant figure in Arab historiography was Ibn Khaldun (1332-1406). His importance lies in the unique feat, for the time, of having been able to rationalize the subject of history and to reflect upon its methods and purposes. He was the Roger Bacon of medieval historiography. He believed that history should be a science and that it should treat of social development, which he held to be an outgrowth of the interaction between the physical environment and the group life of man. At the outset, in his *Prolegomena to Universal History,* which was the systematic presentation of his theoretical views, he drew a sharp distinction between the conventional annalistic and episodical historical writing of his time and history as he conceived it, namely, the science of the origin and development of society and civilization. Anticipating Vico and Turgot, he comprehended the unity and continuity of historical development. Ibn Khaldun had a remarkable grasp upon the conception of time and the modification of institutions wrought by time. In marked contrast with the static or eschatological conceptions of contemporary Christian historiography was his dynamic thesis that the process of historic growth is subject to constant change, comparable to the life of the individual organism. He made clear the coöperation of psychic and environmental factors in the evolution of civilization. There was a pre-Marxian flash in his observation that the usages and institutions of peoples depend upon the way in which they provide for their subsistence. Ibn Khaldun's elaborate *Universal History* in seven volumes applied these theories to history, especially to Arabic social and cultural development. Robert Flint makes the following estimate of the significance of his work:

> The first writer to treat history as the proper object of a special science was Mohammed Ibn Khaldun. Whether on this account he is to be regarded or not as the founder of the science of history is a question as to which there may well be difference of opinion; but no candid reader of his *Prolegomena* can fail to admit that his claim to the honor is more valid than that of any other author previous to Vico.[24]

Historical biography attracted the attention of many Muslim historians. We have already called attention to the more important early biographies of Mohammed. Important also was the able biography of Saladin by Baha al-Din (1185 to 1234). Ibn Sa'd (d. 845) produced the first valuable classified biographical collection of leading Muslims. Yaqut (1179-1229), an

---

[24] Robert Flint, *The Philosophy of History in France* (Scribner, 1894), pp. 158 ff.

eminent Muslim geographer, also compiled a useful dictionary of learned men. But the main Muslim biographical collection was the massive *Biographical Dictionary* of Ibn Khallikān (1211-82), which brought together material on no less than 865 leading personages in the history of Islam. It was comparable to the Christian work of Trithemius. Muslim antiquities were explored in such works as *The Book of Songs* of Abu-l-Faraj, and the *History of Egypt* to the Ottoman conquest of Ibn Iyas. The eminent Muslim encyclopedist, mathematician and astronomer, Al-Biruni (973-1048), did the best work on Muslim historical chronology, trying to clear it up and to systematize it through placing it on an astronomical basis. Not until the time of Scaliger was there as able a chronologist in Christendom.

CONCLUDING OBSERVATIONS ON MEDIEVAL
HISTORICAL WRITING

While one is not likely to exaggerate the inferiority of medieval historical writings as compared with modern historiography, it is possible to be unfair to the historians of the Middle Ages—especially those of western Europe. The more readily available models of historical writing, such as Orosius and Cassiodorus, were of an inferior type. There was no systematic collection of sources and there was no formal technique of scholarship. The canons of historical scholarship were demoralizing rather than helpful. There was little communication of information between communities which would make possible a masterly grasp of situations as a whole. The primitive and superstitious outlook of medieval historians upon life was something for which they could not be held responsible. There was no natural science to furnish a basis for the rejection of miracles and no social science to furnish a valid criticism of social institutions. The wonder is that these historians were able to do as well as they did.

Several facts stand out from even the foregoing brief survey of medieval historiography. In the first place, like most of the classical historiography, the substantial historical works of the Middle Ages were chiefly concerned with strictly contemporary history. The treatment of a remote period was almost invariably in the nature of a rude and scanty chronicle of events. In the second place, it is almost impossible to differentiate sharply between chronicles, systematic histories and biographies on account of a common methodology. Thirdly, it is apparent that the vast majority of the historians were churchmen, mostly monks. Therefore, while the ecclesiastics cannot be too severely criticized for their vitiation of historical methods, it is also well to remember that without them medieval historical literature would have been practically a blank. Fourthly, it will readily be apparent that medieval history was almost exclusively episodical, there being virtually no attempt to analyze the deeper social, economic and intellectual forces in historical development. Finally, one can easily discern the fact that, with the stimulation of intellectual interests during and following the Crusades, there came an increase in the volume of historical output and an improvement in its quality that were prophetic of the future recovery of the lost historical standards of classical antiquity.

SELECTED REFERENCES

Hayes, *An Introduction to the Sources Relating to the Germanic Invasions,* chaps. viii-xv.

Guilday, *Church Historians,* pp. 71-127.

Ritter, *Die Entwicklung der Geschichtswissenschaft,* Book II, chaps. ii-iii.

Thompson, *History of Historical Writing,* Vol. I, Books II-IV.

Charles Gross, *Sources and Literature of English History.* Macmillan, 1915.

M. L. W. Laistner, *Thought and Letters in Western Europe A.D. 500-900.* Dial Press, 1931.

R. L. Poole, *Chronicles and Annals.* Oxford University Press, 1926.

C. H. Jenkins, *The Monastic Chronicler.* London, 1922.

Marie Schulz, *Die Lehre von der historischen Methode bei den Geschichtschreibern des Mittelalters.* Berlin, 1909.

James Gairdner, *Early Chroniclers of Europe: England.* London, 1883.

Gustave Masson, *Early Chroniclers of Europe: France.* London, 1883.

Ugo Balzani, *Early Chroniclers of Europe: Italy.* London, 1883.

Wilhelm Wattenbach, *Deutschlands Geschichtsquellen im Mittelalter, bis zur Mitte der dreizehnten Jahrhunderts.* Berlin, 1893-94. 2 vols.

Ottokar Lorenz, *Deutschlands Geschichtsquellen im Mittelalter seit der Mitte des dreizehnten Jahrhunderts.* Berlin, 1886-87. 2 vols.

A. A. Vasiliev, *History of the Byzantine Empire,* "University of Wisconsin Studies." Madison, Wis., 1928-29. 2 vols.

Karl Krumbacher, *Geschichte der byzantinischen Litteratur.* Munich, 1897.

D. S. Margoliouth, *Lectures on Arabic Historians.* Calcutta, 1930.

R. A. Nicholson, *Literary History of the Arabs.* Macmillan, 1929.

Nathaniel Schmidt, *Ibn Khaldun.* Columbia University Press, 1930.

J. H. Robinson, ed., *Readings in European History,* Vol. I. Ginn, 1904. 2 vols.

J. A. Giles, ed., *Six Old English Chronicles.* London, 1888.

L. R. Loomis, ed., *The Book of the Popes.* Columbia University Press, 1916.

Ernest Brehaut, ed., *The History of the Franks by Gregory, Bishop of Tours.* Columbia University Press, 1916.

C. C. Mierow, ed., *Two Cities by Otto, Bishop of Freising.* Columbia University Press, 1929.

P. K. Hitti and F. C. Murgotten, eds., *The Origins of the Islamic State* (Translation of Al Baladhuri). Columbia University Press, 1916, 1924. 2 vols.

J. M. Hussey, *Church and Learning in the Byzantine Empire.* Oxford University Press, 1937.

V

HUMANISM AND HISTORICAL WRITING

THE NATURE OF HUMANISM AND ITS GENERAL INFLUENCE ON HISTORICAL WRITING

RECENT research and a more critical examination of the intellectual currents in European history have profoundly modified the exaggerated opinions of Jacob Burckhardt and John Addington Symonds with regard to the relation of the so-called "Renaissance" to the development of European thought and culture. It has been shown that, at the best, this period did not mark a direct and conscious advance toward modern concepts. The Renaissance grew naturally out of medieval antecedents. It was distinctly a revival of interest in an antique culture, which was in many fundamental ways opposed to the present-day outlook. This revival indirectly contributed to the development of the modern outlook chiefly through its aid in breaking through the ecclesiastical "fixation" of medieval thought and in bringing to the front again an interest in secular matters.

In its broadest sense, the literary phase of this movement is now conventionally designated as "Humanism." This meant not only a revival of interest in classical literature, but also a renewed appreciation of the broadly human interests and secular outlook of pagan culture. It was primarily an emotional and poetic reaction against the narrow and ascetic attitude of the theologians, without constituting any real or conscious revolution in theology or social philosophy. The Humanist was a person intermediate in interests and ideals between the medieval Scholastic thinker and the modern sceptic and social philosopher.

There were great differences in the nature and quality of the product of the historians of this period, as, for instance, between the works of a Poggio and a Guicciardini. Yet certain fundamental characteristics of the historiography of Humanism were sufficiently general and universal to justify enumeration.

The reaction of Humanism upon historical writing was strictly in accordance with the fundamental aspects of the movement as a whole. Humanism, as applied to history, meant, in the first place, a search for classical texts and the comparison, criticism and perfection of those recovered. The criticism of literary texts produced at least an elementary sense of the value of a critical handling of historical documents.

Humanism also markedly reduced the element of the miraculous in historical interpretation and lessened the "emotional thrill" of the "Christian Epic." One should not, however, imagine that the majority of the Humanists were anti-theological or sceptical of Christianity. For the most part, they ignored rather than denied the theological claims and controversies. This was due in part to the urbanity of Renaissance Catholicism.

Pagan history was, to an extent, restored to the prominent position from which it had been cast down by the Christian writers in general, and by Augustine and Orosius in particular. This was due, in some degree, to the admiration of the Humanists for classical culture, and also to the fact that for the first time since the passing of Rome, a majority of the leading historians were laymen and practical men of affairs rather than churchmen and theologians. Naturally, also, the classical models of historiography were often effective in promoting an improvement in style and, what was more important, a greater attention to political events and forces. This meant, in short, the re-secularization of history. Another powerful impulse to this trend came from civic pride in the Italian city-states, and from the beginnings of modern nationalism elsewhere.

Humanist historical writing, beginning in Italy, was first primarily local, a record of civic achievements and the doings of city princes. Later it was affected by the rise of modern nationalism and broadened its political perspective. Finally, with the Humanists history became more historical. With their main center of interest in the culture of a period long past, their historical writing could no longer be limited mainly to contemporary history or to a mere elaboration with variations, of the threadbare *Chronicle* of Jerome. Creditable world histories appeared in the books by Sabellicus, Giovanni Doglioni, François de Belleforest, Johannes Clüver and Sir Walter Raleigh.

Obviously, however, Humanism brought to historical writing more literary and cultural improvement than progress in scientific method. It constituted a great impulse to history as literature but not as a critical or social science. The rhetorical canons of Isocrates, Livy, Tacitus, Plutarch and Suetonius, rather than the historical ideals of Thucydides and Polybius, were the main guide of Humanist historians. If the Humanists threw out most of the miracle-mongering of the medieval historians, they showed considerable regard for the traditional fables of antiquity, though not always swallowing them in too credulous a fashion. Historical facts and situations were too frequently distorted in order to accommodate them to the requirements of rhetorical forms and oratorical declamations. And European facts of, say, 1500, were often interpreted in terms of classical civilization, and vice versa, with a great sacrifice of historical sense and perspective in either case.

Nor did Humanism bring to historical writing as full freedom from subserviency to vested interests and authority as is commonly supposed. Humanism emancipated history to some degree from the theological bias, but it substituted a secular restraint which was often equally damaging to historical objectivity and accuracy. And hero worship continued. If the medieval historians had revered and eulogized churchmen, martyrs, virgins and the like, the humanist celebrated the deeds and praised the personalities of the princes of the city-states and then of the kings of the national states. Professor Burr has well stated the case:

> When the Middle Ages waned, the revived study of the ancients and the rise of a lay republic of letters did not at first, one must confess, greatly advance the freedom of history. The courtier Humanist charged with a biography of his princely patron or a history of his dynasty, the Humanist chancellor commissioned by the city fathers to write the history of the town, was perhaps less free to find or tell the truth than had been the churchly chronicler unhampered by hereditary lords or local vanity. The audience, too, was Humanist, and the tyranny of rhetoric, never wholly dispelled throughout the Middle Ages, now reasserted itself with double power. It was the Humanist historian's very function to make the glories of his prince or of his city a vehicle for the display of the Latin style to which he owed his post. And if history, thus again an art, a branch of literature, dared in a field so secular to shun the mention of ecclesiastical miracle and even to forget the great plan of salvation, it was too often to borrow from the ancients a strange varnish of omen and of prodigy.[1]

While it bore little direct or casual relation to Humanism, it should be remembered that it was during this period that the printing press was introduced into general use. It gave a great stimulus to the "making of books" in the field of history, as in other branches of literary effort. In its larger significance for the future of historical science, the invention of printing can be compared only to the original mastery of the art of writing. It is not too much to say that neither Thucydides, Polybius, Blondus, Mabillon nor von Ranke was as influential or indispensable in making possible the present status of historiography as was the inventor of the art of printing by movable type, be he Coster, Gutenberg or someone yet to be discovered.

HUMANIST HISTORICAL WRITING IN ITALY

Before dealing with particular Humanist historical writers we should say a word about an important phase of their contribution to historical science, namely, the enthusiastic search for copies of the manuscripts of classical writers in monasteries and other out-of-the-way hiding places. In this men like Poggio and Enoc of Ascoli took the lead. Lost manuscripts

[1] Burr, *loc. cit.*, p. 261.

of Cicero, Quintilian, Nepos, Plautus, Martial, Ovid, Pliny, Varro and Tacitus were brought to light. Especially important was the discovery of the *Germania* of Tacitus by Enoc of Ascoli. This, as we have seen, became one of the most bitterly controverted historical documents of all time. Not only were important historical sources thus uncovered, but the task of editing these manuscripts gave birth to scientific practices in editing and to acute criticism of documents.

Petrarch (1304-74) was the father of Italian Humanism. He was likewise the first important Humanist historian. He wrote a *History of Rome* as an intellectual satisfaction of his deep, but unrealized, yearning for a united Italy in the form of a revived Roman Empire. His history was constructed and interpreted in terms of this yearning. While he rejected most of the myths about Rome which had been concocted during the Middle Ages, he accepted without much criticism the writings of those Roman historians whose views suited his purposes. Their myths did not worry him. Another offense against the historical perspective was his tendency to interpret Roman institutions, procedure and terminology in terms of his own day, not taking into account the vast modifications in meanings and application wrought by more than a thousand years of historical development.

The next important product of Humanist historiography was *The Twelve Books of Florentine History* by Leonardo Bruni (1369-1444), a lawyer, papal secretary and prominent Florentine official. In this and his later *Commentaries* are to be found many of the characteristics of the historiography of the Humanist school—a decided adherence to the canons of style of the Greek and Roman rhetoricians; the opinion that classical rather than contemporary culture was the most promising source of historical inspiration; the elimination of many pagan and Christian miracles and legends; and a primary concern with the practical analysis of political events and activities. Bruni generally rejected miracles and legends, even many of those surrounding the origins of Florence. But what he gained here, he offset by introducing the oratorical fictions of the rhetoricians and accommodating his facts to such requirements. He used Roman terms to describe Renaissance facts. He did consider the criticism of his sources to be an important historical principle, and he would have done far better if he had not capitulated to the canons of antique rhetoric. Florence was the center of the world in his narrative, though he was impartial enough to admit that not all Florentines or all Florentine policy had been infallible. And he set the pace for the typical Humanist proclivity to attribute political events to personal causes and to paint dramatically the deeds and personalities of political leaders.

The standards and methods of Bruni deeply affected the first important Venetian historian of the Humanist school, Marcantonio Coccio

(1436-1506), better known by his classicized name of Sabellicus. He was a professor of oratory and was employed by the Venetian government to compile an official history of Venice. This he did, bringing together in a well-rounded story the various traditions and chronicles of Venetian history, and relying especially on Dandola. Sabellicus supplied his own share of imaginary rhetorical embellishments. His history was greatly weakened because he all but ignored both ecclesiastical and economic history, matters of special importance in the development of Venice. Also, Sabellicus wrote a eulogistic discourse on Livy. But more important was his attempt at a universal history, the so-called *Enneades*—the first important Humanist excursion into world history.

Sabellicus was not professionally prepared for such a work and the fact that he succeeded as well as he did is an indication of how much Humanism was aiding historical-mindedness and perspective. There were far greater scholars among the medieval world chroniclers, but their biased and limited view of the pagan past largely nullified the value of their writings on the premedieval period. Though Sabellicus took his chronology of events mainly from Eusebius and Jerome, he restored to the history of antiquity some degree of perspective and proportion in his allotment of space to the several ancient nations. He rejected the absurd absorption with Hebrew history that had been the fashion for a millenium. This was not the only contrast between *Enneades* and the medieval world histories. Sabellicus was sceptical of biblical miracles and placed them on the same level as the classical fables, Samson being a sort of Hebrew Hercules. There was no mention of the famous "four monarchies," in spite of his familiarity with Jerome's *Chronicle*. Sabellicus consulted relatively few classical historians for his history of antiquity, but he tried to create a false impression of erudition by implying that he had also consulted all the sources used by his guides. He also fell into a typical Humanist fallacy of looking at a good deal of ancient history through Roman eyes. For the Middle Ages his work was greatly improved as a result of his wide use of good historians, such as Paul the Deacon and Flavius Blondus; but his book was especially weak in its treatment of social, economic and cultural history. In tone and content, however, it marked a vast advance over Orosius and the medieval writers on antiquity and the Middle Ages. A more mature Italian Humanist achievement in world history was the work of the Venetian writer, Giovanni Doglioni, *Compendio historico universale* (1601).

If Bruni was the Herodotus of Humanist historiography and Sabellicus its Diodorus, Poggio Bracciolini (1380-1459) was its Ephorus. Poggio was, like Bruni, a papal secretary and a prominent Florentine official, and he apparently wished to surpass his predecessor as a historian. He especially desired to show himself a greater master of classical Latin. His *Eight*

Books of Florentine History illustrated in extreme form the influence of classical rhetoric on Humanist historical literature and one may agree with Fueter that "what he gained as a literary artist he lost as an historian." Still Poggio was a good observer and his work was more broadly conceived and more impersonal than that of Bruni. He would have done far better had he not been cramped by the rhetorical obsessions that grew out of his efforts to ape classical masters. Also, his official position prevented him from being more frank and penetrating in analyzing the internal politics of Florence. Poggio's activity and success as an enthusiastic searcher for ancient texts must, however, be remembered and honored.

Of a widely different character from the work of Poggio was that of the most distinguished Italian historical critic of the period, Lorenzo Valla (1407-57), the first Humanist historian to write in Naples. Valla's only systematic historical work, *The History of Ferdinand I of Aragon,* was not conspicuously successful. It proved the author to be more a scandal-monger than a historian in the field of narrative. He was little interested in political and military matters. It is probable, however, that the weaknesses of Valla's *History of Ferdinand* were due in no small degree to the fact that it was an "official" history, a task for which Valla's critical mind was poorly fitted.

The achievement for which Valla received great acclaim in the field of criticism was the final proof of the forgery of the Donation of Constantine, the authenticity of which had already been doubted by Cusanus and disproved by Bishop Reginald Peacock in England. As Fueter has clearly shown, Valla acquired his fame as much because of the venerable nature of the document he attacked as through the skill or erudition he displayed in its analysis. It was a testimonial to his courage rather than to his critical powers, which could be matched by several other Humanists. As Emerton has well said: "The most interesting thing about the exposure is the amazing ease of it. It does not prove the great learning or cleverness of the author, for neither of these was needed. The moment that the bare facts were held up to the world of scholars the whole tissue of absurdities fell to pieces of its own weight."[2]

More skill and originality were shown in Valla's *Duo Tarquinii,* an attack on Livy's treatment of certain phases of early Roman history. This work showed that the most highly esteemed of secular classical authorities was no more immune from critical examination by Valla than were venerable ecclesiastical documents. It took more courage for a Humanist to doubt classical legends than to question medieval miracles and forgeries. Most Humanists were sceptical of medieval miracles and legends, but few dared to question great classical authorities like Livy. Humanism produced no other critic equal in ability to Valla until the days of Erasmus.

[2] Ephraim Emerton, *The Beginnings of Modern Europe* (Ginn, 1917), p. 504.

Valla's methods were applied by his Venetian contemporary, Bernardo Giustiniani (1408-89), to dissipate the legends connected with the founding of Venice, in his *Origins and Growth of the City of Venice to 809*. Giustiniani was a statesman rather than a literary Humanist. Hence, he escaped the more serious rhetorical blemishes of Humanist historical writing. And he was no official historian. He thought and wrote with real independence of mind.

Far the greatest historical scholar that Italian Humanism produced was Flavius Blondus (1388-1463)—or, to give him his Italian name, Flavio Biondo—"the Timaeus of Humanism," who devoted his life to a study of the antiquities of ancient Rome and the rise of the medieval states. Blondus' work on Roman history was chiefly antiquarian and archeological. His *Illustrated Italy, Rome Established,* and *Rome Triumphant,* were the first serious Humanist contributions to the topography and archeology of ancient Rome. His *Histories of the Decadence of the Roman Empire* were also primarily archeological. He estimated the excellencies of the reigns and epochs of Roman imperial history chiefly in the light of the degree of peace and scholarly effort which prevailed.

Important as was the work of Blondus in Roman antiquities, his major contribution lay in his original view and relatively accurate portrayal of the history of the Middle Ages. His chief work here was *Decades of History Since the Decline of the Power of the Romans* (from 472 to 1440), in thirty-one books. The most notable thing about this work, aside from the careful scholarship, was the original attitude that the author displayed in his interpretation of the significance of the medieval period. "The novel element in the attitude of Blondus," writes Professor Burr, "is that instead of thinking of the Middle Ages as the continuous history of a Roman Empire, as medievals had been wont to do, he left Rome to the past and told the story of the rising peoples who supplanted her."[3] He contributed more, says Fueter, to our knowledge of the Middle Ages and of Roman antiquity than all the other Humanists combined.[4]

It is the best possible illustration of the canons of Humanism that Blondus, its greatest historical scholar and savant in Italy, was never given formal recognition or adequate reward for his notable contribution to scholarship, because he did not possess an elegant literary style. In a more fundamental sense, perhaps, his work was given the greatest testimonial possible. Of all products of the historical scholarship of the period, it was the most exploited and plagiarized for information by later writers. In this way it also contributed indirectly to the improvement of Humanist historical scholarship. The unpopularity of scholarship for its own sake,

[3] Personal letter to the author.
[4] Eduard Fueter, *Histoire de l'historiographie moderne* (Paris, 1914), p. 131.

as shown by the experience of Blondus, explains why he had but one true Italian disciple, Tristan Calchi (1462-*ca.* 1516), the intelligent and independent historian of Milan. Blondus was the true precursor of Leibnitz, Mabillon and Tillemont.

The Humanist pope, Aeneas Sylvius Piccolomini (1405-64), deserves mention in a sketch of Humanist historiography more from the nature of his personal career and the influence he exerted on later German writers than from the intrinsic value of his own contributions to systematic historical writing or to the improvement of historical method. His numerous historical works, among them *Commentaries on the Council of Basel, The History of Europe, Universal History,* and *Commentaries,* or his autobiography, were superficial, without deep philosophical grasp, fragmentary and frequently unfinished. He did not actually equal Bruni as a historical critic, to say nothing of Valla or Blondus. Nevertheless, he was a man of action in politics to a degree scarcely equaled by Thucydides, Polybius or Tacitus. No contemporary knew more of European politics and culture than he, and the most valuable aspect of his historical works was the fact that they were full of personal reminiscences. As a member of the imperial chancery of Frederick III and through his later ecclesiastical relations with the Empire, his interest in German history and culture was greater than that of any of his Italian contemporaries. His significance in the development of historiography rested primarily upon his use of earlier German historians. In his *History of Frederick III* he made large use of Otto of Freising and brought him to the attention of contemporaries. He also recovered and popularized Jordanes. His *History of Bohemia* was probably the first attempt of a Humanist historian to introduce ethnographic materials into historical literature. Finally, his *History of Europe* and his *Universal History* sought to bring out the inter-relation between history and geography. It was in these respects, chiefly, that he influenced later German historians. Fueter says on this point that Aeneas Sylvius was mainly responsible for the tendency of many later German Humanist historians to introduce into historical works excursions into the origin and growth of law and into the relations of geography to historical development, to assume at least a semi-critical attitude toward the legends of racial origins, and to display a boisterous chauvinism in matters touching the question of nationality.[5]

The transition from strictly Humanist historiography to the beginnings of modern political and national historical writing in Italy was well illustrated by the works of the two famous Florentine historians, Machiavelli and Guicciardini. The cultural supremacy of Florence at the time, and the intensity of its political life, combined to make it a particularly fav-

[5] Fueter, *op. cit.,* p. 143.

orable environment to stimulate the production of historical works of high value. In common with Blondus, these authors valued truth more than rhetoric, but they escaped the former's obscurity and unpopularity by avoiding a labored and pedantic style. With them history became mainly an account of secular matters, and was limited primarily to a straight-forward narrative and the analysis of political events. Some attempt also was made to substitute a psychological and material theory of causation for the abandoned supernaturalism.

Professor Schevill thus explains the "intense preoccupation" of Machiavelli and Guicciardini "with government in general and with Florentine government in particular":

> They were prompted to this view, to a certain extent, by their classical examplars, but in the main they came to it from the actual, perplexing developments of their own country. For several generations, indeed since the collapse of feudalism in the thirteenth century, governments devised by individuals or groups had been hopefully set up at one point or another throughout Italy only to be replaced by a fresh and more promising invention before as much as a year or even a month had gone round.[6]

Niccolo Machiavelli (1469-1527) was primarily a political philosopher without any particular emotion for history unless it was utilized in the interests of political theory. It was this tendency which gave his major historical work, the hastily written *History of Florence,* in eight books, its distinctive characteristics. From the standpoint of style or accuracy it was not equal to some other histories written at the time, but it is doubt-ful if any previous historian since Polybius, with whom Machiavelli was familiar, had exhibited such power in grasping the nature of historical causation in its political aspects or in presenting a clear picture of the pro-cess of political development. It was as a political thinker and an organizer of causal factors in civic evolution that Machiavelli excelled, even more than as an objective narrator of political events. This concern with politi-cal reflection was prompted, as Professor Schevill points out, by the "extra-ordinary spectacle of an Italy culturally predominant but politically too feeble to defend itself against the attack and invasion" of neighboring powers. This led him to make of his work "a political laboratory in which all the doctrines of the ancients and his own as well were put to the test of practice."[7]

Machiavelli had a better insight into the historical background of po-litical developments than any other Humanist historian down to his day. He fully understood the inter-relation between foreign and domestic pol-itics and between military activities and political developments. He also

---

[6] Schevill, *op. cit.,* p. xix.
[7] *Ibid.,* p. xviii.

recognized the place of Florence in the history of Italy as a whole, and he was devoted to the ideal of a united Italian state. He tended to eulogize those men and groups that had tried to found such a state and was antagonistic to the papacy, which he conceived to be an obstacle to Italian unity. This helps to explain his romantic biography of Castracani, a famous condottiere. Yet, on the whole, he minimized the personal element as a causative factor in history, and Fueter says that no writer since Polybius went as far as Machiavelli in making history "a natural history of politics."[8] A frank materialistic theory of causation was substituted for the old supernaturalism and hero worship. This historical philosophy reflected the doctrines of *The Prince*. Machiavelli also abandoned to a large degree the conventional annalistic arrangement of his materials and organized his work by topics. He also eschewed the stereotyped rhetorical devices and wrote in a slashingly realistic fashion. He used few sources but good ones, mainly Blondus, Giovanni Villani and Simonetta. The best part of his work was that on the evolution of the internal politics of Florence. Here he not only described events in detail, but added much personal comment—"copious reflections on government and parties and on the actions of leaders diversely moved by jealousy, zeal, ambition, and all the other passions to which man is heir." The narrative is of less value than "this savory by-product of comment."[9] As a narrative historian, his work was, judged by modern standards, characterized by "innumerable errors of fact and feeble documentation."

Not nearly so philosophical, but more truly historical than Machiavelli, was Francesco Guicciardini (1483-1540). His *History of Florence,* written when he was a young man, was one of the truly original works in historiography. The author broke almost completely with both patristic and earlier Humanist historiography and even went beyond the classical historical conventions in that he eliminated the use of direct discourse in his narrative. In his lucid style, relatively free from digressions and irrelevant details, there was no trace of florid rhetoric, and his primary concern with contemporary political history allowed him, in the latter part of the work, to dispense, to a considerable extent, with the annalistic and strictly chronological arrangement followed in the conventional historical writing of his time. He made a slighter attempt than Machiavelli at philosophical analysis, and devoted himself mainly to a vigorous and incisive narrative of events and a candid criticism of men and policies. He had rare ability in selecting the essential facts. If he had any theory of history it was a rationalistic assumption that political circumstances rest at bottom on calculation and intrigue. He was personally disillusioned and this helps to

---

8 Fueter, *op. cit.,* pp. 79-82.
9 Schevill, *op. cit.,* pp. xx-xxi.

account for his relative impartiality. This somewhat cynical note in his writing is illustrated by such observations as the one to the effect that no reproach attached to Ferdinand of Aragon "save his lack of generosity and faithlessness to his word." His personal affiliations were with the old families and governing clique of Florence. "With the *Florentine History*," says Fueter, "modern analytical historiography and political ratiocination in history began."[10] Most critics contend that with Guicciardini's *History of Florence* historical writing in western Europe attained once again the level reached by Thucydides and Polybius. It had, however, little influence on historiography in the Renaissance, since it was not published until 1859.

From the standpoint of style and arrangement Guicciardini's other major work, the *History of Italy*, written in his mature years, was less original, because here he compromised with those rhetorical conventions of Humanism which he had so rigorously excluded from his first work, such as for example, concern with battles on the grand scale, the use of direct discourse and the introduction of speeches. But with respect to breadth, scope and original mode of approach, the second work was even more epoch-making. For the first time since classical days a historian was able to break with tradition and to free himself from primary concern with any particular state or dynasty and to devote his attention to a much broader field—"the history of a geographical unity." This—the first general history of Italy ever written—gave him an unprecedented opportunity to study the growth and decline of states, the interaction between states, the character of international relations, and the processes of political evolution. In other words, the subject matter offered rare possibilities for the study of universal history reproduced on a small scale. Though Guicciardini lacked the unique philosophical insight into social and political processes that Machiavelli possessed, and was thereby prevented from making a classic analysis of social and political evolution, the very scope and novelty of his historical enterprise constituted a great advance in historical method and perspective.

Few will deny that Guicciardini's books reached the highest level which post-classical historiography attained until the time of Camden, Thuanus, and Clarendon. But the great progress that was necessary before modern scientific political history could be written is best appreciated by a perusal of the perhaps over-severe criticism of Guicciardini by Leopold von Ranke, the first distinguished representative of the modern scientific school. Even the best of these Renaissance historians, like Machiavelli and Guicciardini, were primarily interested in "political reflections, deductions and apothegms" and had only a secondary interest in the accuracy of the facts,

10 Fueter, *op. cit.*, p. 88.

"taking them generally with the greatest unconcern and often without changing a single word from earlier authors who had gone over the same ground. Even Machiavelli and Guicciardini followed a practice which by our present standards would lay them open to a clear charge of plagiarism." They did not distinguish sharply between the earlier secondary narrators they followed and such original documents as they used. This basic discrimination of scientific history appeared in their works only in rudimentary form.[11]

The modern standards might have been reached more quickly had not the Reformation set back the progress of historical writing by the resurrection of those theological interests and religious controversies which Humanism was gradually and peacefully smothering. Not until the theological monopoly had been crushed by the Rationalism of the eighteenth century and secular interests had been reinforced by expansion of Europe, the commercial revolution, and the rise of modern nations, could many fundamental advances be achieved.[12]

Humanistic historical biography started with the *Life of Dante* by Giovanni Boccaccio (1313-75). It was valuable for the understanding of Dante as a literary artist, but it was weak on the political side of Dante's interests, for Boccaccio had little concern with politics. The next important step was taken by Filippo Villani (*ca.* 1325-1405). He took Boccaccio for his model and originally started simply to edit the *Life of Dante* by Boccaccio. But this led him into preparing a series of biographies on the most illustrious men of Florence. His precedent set the pace and model for later Humanist biography, which consisted mostly of similar series of biographical studies. There was in them, all too often, a rather slavish copying of the mannerisms and style of Suetonius, to whom Humanist biographers tended to look back as their classical model.

This subservience to ancient rhetorical style was repudiated to a considerable degree by the most famous of all Humanist biographers, Giorgio Vasari (1511-74), author of the immortal *Lives of the Most Eminent Painters, Sculptors and Architects*. Vasari was a painter and architect who was much interested in the lives and works of the great Italian artists of the Renaissance. He was encouraged to prepare a series of lives by Cardinal Farnese, Paolo Giovi, and others. He had already traveled widely, talked to many artists and taken many notes. He continued this procedure, also studying the great pictures, statues and public buildings. Everything was grist for his mill, and the indiscriminate information he gathered accounts in part for both the charm and the weaknesses of his work. The first edition came out in 1550. He traveled and interviewed still more and brought out an improved version in 1568.

The work as a whole was the first important and comprehensive his-

[11] Schevill, *op. cit.*, pp. xxi-xxii.   [12] See below, chap. VII.

tory of art of which we have any record in the whole history of historical literature. Its merits and defects were equally apparent. Vasari understood the technique of art and handled his subject competently from a professional viewpoint. He wrote with unrivaled charm and fascination and had rare power in making his characters living personalities. And he was reasonably fair and impartial in a field where bias and favoritism would have been easy. The amount of information he assembled was vast and indispensable for the history of Renaissance art. On the other hand, he was not careful in sifting his sources of information. He accepted a great deal of gossip and hearsay. He was careless in his chronology and there are many contradictions in his work. And at times he included too much information on trivial artists while he denied adequate attention to major figures. With all his weaknesses, however, his work stands out as the most interesting product of all Humanist biography in Italy or elsewhere and is one of the permanent landmarks in the history of art.[13] The outstanding Humanist autobiography was the famous work of Benvenuto Cellini (1500-71), a masterly portrait of a man and his age.

HUMANIST HISTORICAL WRITING OUTSIDE OF ITALY

Outside of Italy, Humanism found many distinguished converts, not the least of them in the field of history. In general, the conventional canons of Humanist historiography were faithfully followed, though some variations were introduced as a result of different cultural surroundings. As the movement was somewhat belated beyond the Alps, it became complicated by the religious conflicts of the Reformation period and often took on a concern with ecclesiastical controversy which was foreign to the Italian historical writing of the fifteenth century. Again, the classical literary tastes underwent a change. In the zeal for florid rhetoric and sharp invective, Tacitus, rather than Livy, became the model of many of the northern Humanists in the sixteenth century. Further, the nationalistic impulses arising from the Reformation, the expansion of Europe and the rise of capitalism gave a nationalistic and patriotic coloring to much of the north European Humanistic historical writing. Party conflicts also arose in the new political systems, and Humanistic historical writing gradually merged with the beginnings of modern political historiography.

The most scholarly product of historical writing among the Swiss Humanists were the histories of Saint-Gall and the Swiss forest cantons by Joachim von Watt, better known as Vadianus (1484-1551). Vadianus is often considered superior even to Blondus as a historian. He not only rivaled Blondus in textual criticism, but also advanced a step further to-

---

[13] The biography of Ignatius Loyola by Ribadeneira, which we shall treat later, may be regarded as an outstanding Humanist biography, even though it was a product of the period of religious controversy. See below, p. 132.

ward von Ranke by making some rudimentary progress with internal criticism, namely, an examination of the "tendencies" of the authors of documents. He was especially adroit in tracing out and exploding ecclesiastical legends. Vadianus was able, further, to combine erudition with a clear and vigorous style and a good grasp upon the leading factors in historical development. He was capable of a high order of independence in his judgments and was eminently sensible in his ideas. But it was his marked ability to trace the evolution of religious and political organization and to sense the notion of social development which, more than anything else, placed him in the front rank of Humanist historians. And he adopted a broad-minded doctrine of historical causation, rejecting the conventional tendency to attribute historical developments solely to personalities or trivial episodes. Fueter regards his achievement as the most broadly conceived product of the whole historiography of Humanism, on account of the intelligent and detached attitude of the author and the wide scope of the subjects and interests his works embraced. Vadianus' history was, however, doomed to an even longer period of obscurity than awaited Guicciardini's *History of Florence,* since it was not published until the third quarter of the nineteenth century.

In Germany, the list of distinguished Humanist historians begins with the name of Albert Krantz (1450-1517), who, following Aeneas Sylvius, was one of the first to apply the literary and historical methods of Humanism to a study of primitive peoples in his histories of the early Saxons and Wends. More famous was Johannes Turmair, known as Aventinus (1477-1534). In his *Annals of the Dukes of Bavaria* and his history of early Germany, Turmair tried to combine the literary canons of Bruni with the scholarship of Blondus, but he fell short of both. His strong Protestant bias prevented any objective treatment of the Catholic church, the popes or contemporary affairs. To this he added ardent German nationalism and special enthusiasm for Bavaria and Bavarians. While he was unusually industrious in collecting his sources, he was not especially critical in using them. His work was marred also by lack of proportion. He gave as much space to the Roman emperors as though he were writing a universal history. The major merits of his work consisted in his prefacing the historical narrative by a description of the lands and peoples he proposed to treat and in his rare ability in describing the manners and customs of the populations he studied. His style and expression were also very clear and vigorous.

Ulrich von Hutten (1488-1523) was more distinguished for brilliant satire in his campaign against bigotry than for his contributions to historical literature. But his recovery and publication, with extended comments, of a manifesto of Henry IV against Gregory VII was both a shaft of Protestantism against Rome and a valuable addition to historical knowledge.

The only distinguished representative of the erudite and critical tendencies of Blondus among the German Humanist historians was Beatus Rhenanus (1486-1547), the friend and disciple of Erasmus and author of *A History of German Affairs* [*Rerum Germanicarum*]. He examined the sources of early German history with the same objective, philological scholarship that Erasmus had applied to the ecclesiastical records and doctrines. His labors in research represented the highest level of scholarship to which the historiography of German Humanism attained. Beatus always went back to the original sources, examined them carefully and cited them with exactness. He rejected classical fables as relentlessly as he did ecclesiastical legends. He had a real love for historical research and good judgment in sizing up his discoveries. Though nationalistic in sympathies, his patriotism did not notably warp his judgments. His main defect was inability to weld his materials into a coherent and complete narrative. His history of the Germans was fragmentary. It came down only to the Saxon Emperors, and it was reasonably complete only for the period of Roman domination and the invasions.

Among the many publicists and jurists who have a place in the literature of German Humanism, Samuel Pufendorf (1632-94) was the leader as a historian. His works included a *History of Sweden,* a *History of Charles Gustavus* [*X*], a *History of Frederick William the Great Elector,* and *An Introduction to the History of the Leading Powers and States of Europe.* Pufendorf maintained a lofty tone and possessed a distinguished and lucid classical style. Unfortunately, this was the best thing about his historical writing. Since he often arranged materials according to the date and the nature of the documents he used, he failed to present a clear and consistent narrative of events. He was given to an extreme form of the personal and biographical interpretation of history. The emperors, kings, and electors were his heroes, and, to Pufendorf, their acts accounted for the trend of historical events. He did not interpret historical events in relation to the general historical movements of the times or indicate clearly the inter-relation between internal political policies and foreign affairs. As a semi-official historian, he concealed much relevant material. He wrote primarily to instruct the world outside Germany. Therefore, he depicted Germany as a unified and coherent empire and said little about the very diversified and complicated internal politics of the many German states. There is much truth in Fueter's observation that he wrote for the empire rather than about it.

As Guicciardini had written of the politics and foreign relations of Florence and as Pufendorf was soon to write of Brandenburg and the German Empire, so Bogislaw Philippe de Chemnitz (1605-78) dealt with the kingdom of Sweden and its foreign involvements, especially the Thirty

Years' War in Germany. His book was much used by Pufendorf when the latter touched on Swedish affairs.

The most distinguished personage among Dutch Humanist historians was Hugo Grotius (1583-1645), famed as the father of international law. He wrote historical works on the Goths, Vandals and Lombards, and on the history of Belgium and Holland. His style, imitating Tacitus, was pompous, prolix and involved. But he surpassed even Tacitus in his ability to apply psychology to the analysis of historical situations. This was especially evident in his tracing of the underlying causes of the wars between Spain and the Netherlands. He rejected the personal and episodical interpretation of historical movements which Pufendorf later found so congenial. Grotius adopted a broad and detached attitude towards religious problems and, like Thuanus, deplored religious wars as a menace to the public order and general welfare. In treating internal politics, he wrote as an aristocrat rather than an ardent republican. An abler historian was Pieter Cornelissen Hooft (1581-1647), who exceeded even Grotius in admiration for Tacitus. He translated Tacitus into Dutch and followed his master in method and style. But he was much more of a scholar than his Roman model. He carefully examined and sifted his historical sources and wrote with independent judgment. His writings were mainly on French and Dutch history, and included a history of Henry IV, the House of Medici, and Dutch history in the last half of the sixteenth century. Johannes Clüver's *Historium totius mundi epitome* (1637) was a creditable world history.

Humanist historiography in England was closely related to the origins of the literary movement in Italy. Indeed, the first example of this type of historical literature in England was the scholarly and well-written *History of England,* through the reign of Henry VII, by Polydore Vergil (1470-1535), an Italian ecclesiastic and friend of Erasmus who had made his home in England. His scholarship was not matched in the British Isles until the time of Camden, nearly a century later. He showed critical powers in all parts of his history. He not only devastatingly attacked the myths in Geoffrey of Monmouth's history of British origins, but also produced the best narrative history of the reign of Henry VII.

England's earliest native Humanist historian of note was Sir Thomas More (1478-1535), whose polished style found expression in his brief *History of Richard III.* More wrote this work in both Latin and English and in each version it is a narrative of the highest literary art. The English edition was especially important, since it was the first rendition of the pure classic Humanist diction in the vernacular language. More's highly colored portrait of the character of Richard III was not, however, wholly accurate or free from the superstitions and legends of that age. But it was adopted by Shakespeare and has furnished the popular impression of that monarch from More's day to our own. Scholarly antiquarianism was founded in England by John Stow (1525-1605), and by John Leland (1506-52), who traveled extensively to secure materials on the history and archeology of England and Wales. The writings which grew out of his travels were not published until the beginning of the eighteenth century.

The dashing courtier and intrepid colonizer, Sir Walter Raleigh (1552-1618), wrote a *History of the World* while imprisoned in the Tower of London. His history combined the Humanist love for the classics with the Puritan relish for the Bible and liberty. Familiar with all the leading classical historians, he was especially influenced by Plutarch. Interesting and well written, his history added nothing, however, to our knowledge or to the synthesis of the history of the past. Its later sections were chiefly devoted to English history.

The English representative of the erudite and critical school of Blondus was the court historian, William Camden (1551-1623), an avowed admirer of Polybius. Camden's *Britannia* was an admirable handbook of the antiquities, chronology, and geography of the British Isles. He recounted but mildly ridiculed the myths surrounding the theory of British origins. In his *Annals of English and Irish History in the Reign of Elizabeth* he showed, like his French contemporary Thuanus, that the political history of the sixteenth century could not be safely divorced from ecclesiastical questions. He was less impartial than Blondus in his historical writings, being frankly a conservative royalist and a partisan of the Established Church of England.

Machiavelli and Guicciardini found their English disciple in the philosopher and publicist, Francis Bacon (1561-1626). His point of view and style resembled his Florentine predecessors. His main historical work was a *History of the Reign of King Henry VII*. It was excellent in design and expression and in its philosophical tone. But its severe judgments have been sharply criticized by later writers. He showed surprising respect for the Church, in the light of his scientific predilections, but he was an English gentleman even more than a philosopher, and this demanded respect for the Church of England. Perhaps more important than any of his historical writings was Bacon's thorough grasp of historical perspective in his assertion that "we are the ancients." "These be the ancient times, when the world is growing old. Our own age is more truly antiquity than is the time which is computed backward, beginning with our own age."[14] Equally original and significant was his eloquent appeal for an intellectual history of Europe,[15] which, ironically, was first executed by Bacon's bitterest critic, the American scientist, John William Draper.

[14] A view stated even more thoroughly by Pascal. See Preserved Smith, *A History of Modern Culture* (Holt, 1930), I, 255.

[15] See below, p. 296.

Humanist historical writing merged with modern political and party history in the works of Selden, Clarendon and Burnet. John Selden (1584-1645) wrote mainly monographs on English law and government, including the government of England before the Norman Conquest, the history of English titles, and the history of tithes in England. He was an ardent anti-royalist and libertarian, which led to his imprisonment for a time by James I.

The Civil War which broke out in Selden's last year of life stimulated political and party history. The general arrangement of the Earl of Clarendon's (Edward Hyde, 1609-74) *History of the Rebellion and Civil Wars in England* resembled the French "memoirs." Though he was most superficial in his analysis of the fundamental religious, economic, social and political causes of the first Civil War, it is doubtful if any previous historian, classical or Humanist, surpassed his power of vivid delineation of personalities. While royalist in sympathies, he gave the "devil's due" to Hampden, Cromwell and other rebel leaders. He interpreted the Civil War as an issue of constitutional law, and his theory of causation was a personal and moralistic one—most inadequate for the subject but helpful to his art of character painting.

Bishop Gilbert Burnet (1643-1715), in his *History of the Reformation of the Church of England,* and *The History of My Own Time,* was the first historian of party intrigues and parliamentary debates, a subject not so fully available to any previous writer. He belongs as much with the forerunners of modern political history as in a list of disciples of Humanism. Burnet's *History of the Reformation,* while partisan to the Protestant position and often inaccurate in detail, was broadly conceived, looked into the matter of cause and effect, and was far superior to Clarendon's work in understanding of the intellectual and social background of religious developments. His *History of My Own Time* was an able account of the rapidly changing political scene, of party intrigues and of court gossip. It was an ardent defense of Whig policy.· It contained much cultural history but embraced a providential interpretation of historical events. Though he accepted an Anglican bishopric, Burnet was always fair to Non-Conformists. He wrote in a clear and vivid style.

The outstanding ornament of Scottish Humanism was the erudite George Buchanan (1506-82), distinguished as a poet, political philosopher, historian, religious reformer and political partisan. Few of the best Italians equaled him in the purity of his Latin diction and the vigor and clarity of his narrative. Buchanan's chief historical work was a *History of Scotland* from the earliest times to 1580. It was brilliant in style but partisan in tone and unreliable in content. In the early period it took a vigorously anti-English and pro-Scottish attitude. While Buchanan could analyze miracles and legends he was loath to discard them. The book was most valuable for the contemporary period, but even here it was partisan in behalf of Scottish Presbyterianism. It failed also to give a well-rounded picture of Knox and the Scottish Reformation. Buchanan was anti-rationalist as well as anti-royalist. He was one of the most ardent opponents of the Copernican system.

The most notable product of the historical scholarship of the French Humanists was the work of that polished classical scholar and immensely learned man, Joseph Justus Scaliger (1540-1609), in the field of historical chronology. His *De Emendatione Temporum* [*The Restoration of Chronology*] was a bold attempt to put chronology on a scientific basis by revising the "sacred" chronology in the light of the evidence from the history of the gentile and pagan nations of antiquity. It included a survey of all the known chronologies and methods of reckoning time. His *Thesaurus temporum* [*Repertory of Dates*] was a most notable performance of scholarship, including as it did a valuable and skillful reconstruction of the lost *Chronicle* of Eusebius from Jerome and a Greek chronicle. This work was the most important and reliable reconstruction of the chronology of ancient history prior to the researches of Dom Clément, and especially of our contemporary historical specialists.

Scaliger's publicist contemporary, Jean Bodin (1530-96), in his *Method for Easily Understanding History* (1566) produced the first extensive treatise on historical method, with the emphasis on interpretation rather than upon criticism of sources. Especially significant was the stress which Bodin placed upon the influence of geographical factors in historical development, thus opening the way for Montesquieu and Ritter. His book was, therefore, more a forerunner of the first chapter of Buckle's *History of Civilization in England* than of Bernheim's *Lehrbuch*. Humanist world history appeared in François de Belleforest's *L'histoire universelle du monde* (1577).

While Bodin's notion of geographical influences was based on crude astrological premises, its general implications were important and forward looking. He also clearly recognized the nature of the philosophy of history and divided man's historical development into three stages—that of the Oriental peoples, the Mediterranean nations, and the ascendency of northern Europeans. He first introduced a rudimentary theory of progress into the historical writing of a Christian author by doubting the then common doctrine of decline from Paradise or a Golden Age. He thought mankind had steadily advanced since Creation.

French Humanist scholarship was turned to a study of French politics and the religious wars of the last half of the sixteenth century in the *Universal History* of Theodore Agrippa d'Aubigné (1552-1630). He was a Protestant and copies of his valuable work were burned by the Parlement of Paris. The account of this period was continued in the work of Jacques

Auguste de Thou (1555-1617), conventionally known as Thuanus. He was probably the most notable French contributor to systematic historical writing during the epoch of Humanism. His *History of His Own Time,* designed as a continuation of a work of the same title by the Italian Humanist, Paulus Jovus [Paolo Giovi] (1483-1552), described the civil and religious wars in France in the latter part of the sixteenth century according to the spirit of an enlightened and tolerant French Catholic. It covered the period of 1546-1607. Thuanus introduced into historiography the laudable tendencies displayed in statesmanship by his royal master and friend, Henry IV. As might be expected in the work of one of the jurists who aided in drafting the Edict of Nantes, he was scarcely fair to the Guises and the extreme Catholic party, but his theme was a lofty and noble plea for mutual religious toleration in the larger interest of France. He exhorted the French monarchy to maintain toleration and peace. His work exhibited much ability for extended intellectual labor and it uniformly maintained a real dignity of tone. Thuanus might have equaled Machiavelli and Guicciardini if he had not defended the providential theory of history and if he had possessed the constructive historical imagination to enable him to organize his work into a coherent narrative. He may be said, however, to have improved upon them in one regard, namely, in that he showed how essential a proper consideration of ecclesiastical affairs may be to a thorough understanding of political and constitutional developments. Thuanus' style was clear but overaddicted to classical affectation.

The contributions of Thuanus' contemporary, Isaac Casaubon, will be discussed in another connection.[16] Thuanus' successors in French historical writing were inferior to him in ability and accuracy. Enrico Caterino Davila (1576-1631), a soldier in the French religious wars, retired to Italy and wrote in Italian a popular history of the French civil wars. His understanding of the Huguenot movement was superficial. A *bourgeois* history of France from the beginnings to 1610 was compiled by François Eudes, better known as de Mezeray (1610-83). It was not reliable in matters of detail and throughout it reflected the *bourgeois* sympathy for a strong French monarchy. Hence, it glorified the French kings, especially the strong ones. The book was written in polished French.

The finest literary product of historical writing among the French Humanists was the brilliant but gossipy memoirs of the Duke of Saint-Simon (1675-1755) dealing with France under the Bourbons. Saint-Simon was far from a profound and accurate scholar or a philosophical historian. He was unreliable in regard to details, unable to discriminate between the value of his materials, and highly partisan to his own class, the nobility. He was little interested in foreign politics and had a keen nose for gossip. But he was unrivaled in recreating historical scenes of court circles and in

16 See below, p. 128.

painting personalities. His work was one of the most entertaining historical compositions ever set down. George Peabody Gooch calls it "hyp-
notic" in its influence and writes of "the position of the author at court,
his intimate acquaintance with its leading figures, the unparalleled full-
ness of detail, the extraordinary power of observation, the wonderful gal-
lery of portraits, and the unflagging vivacity of style." Saint-Simon's in-
accuracies were exposed after the rise of critical scholarship by Chéruel
and Boislisle.

Spain contributed three important figures to Humanist historical literature in Diego Hurtado de Mendoza (1503-75), Geronimo de Zurita
(1512-80) and Juan de Mariana (1535-1625). Mendoza was a writer with
plenty of military and administrative experience. He had once been in
favor with Philip II at the court, but had been banished. This provided
him with the psychological basis for the critical attitude which he frequently displayed in his *History of the War of Granada,* an independent
and intelligent narrative. The author knew his materials and he was often
as candid and searching in his judgments as Guicciardini or Bacon. But
his Humanistic yearning to ape the ancients, and that very awkwardly,
served greatly to reduce the clarity and value of his work. He aimed to
follow Sallust and Tacitus, but he did not do so cleverly or gracefully.
He mixed his own acute observations with hackneyed and threadbare
formulas and phrases from Tacitus. He would even try to reconstruct
contemporary historical situations in terms of descriptions by Tacitus. All
of this sadly confused and marred what might otherwise have been a
creditable and straightforward narrative.

A more exacting scholar was Geronimo de Zurita, the official historian
of the kingdom of Aragon and the most prominent and faithful disciple
of Blondus among the Spanish historians of this period. His work, the
Annals of the Kingdom of Aragon, covered the area from the origins to
1516. It was especially significant, in that Zurita was one of the first historians to make an extensive and fairly critical use of archives and diplomatic correspondence in reconstructing the record of political events in
the distant past. His history was of high value for the reign of Ferdinand.

Mariana, a famous political philosopher and an opponent of royal tyranny, was the best known of the Spanish Humanist historians. Stimulated by patriotic emotions, he decided to give Spain a creditable national
historical work and also to reveal to foreigners in this manner the greatness of Spain. So he composed his *History of Spain* from the time of its
alleged settlement by a grandson of Noah to the discovery of America in
1492. Later he continued it in brief fashion to 1621. He used convenient
and well-known sources and was not anywhere near as critical as Zurita
in sifting them. He was prone to accept both classical and Christian miracles and legends. Mariana was discreet in his handling of Spanish poli-

tics, particularly in the period closest to his own day. His narrative contained a good bit of moralizing on politics and the course of events. Since he aimed to be popular he wrote in a clear, flowing and picturesque style. This had led to his being called "the Spanish Buchanan." There is some justification for this, but Mariana did not possess as pure and dignified a classical style as the great Scottish Humanist. He was, however, far superior as a historical scholar. Here also should be mentioned the work of Nicholas Antonio (d. 1684), who wrote the first national literary history of Spain.

We have already alluded to the religious controversies which arose in the sixteenth century with the Protestant Reformation. With the reaction of these on historical writing we must next concern ourselves.

SELECTED REFERENCES

Articles, "Humanism," and "Renaissance," in *Encyclopaedia of the Social Sciences.*

E. M. Hulme, *The Renaissance, The Protestant Revolution and the Catholic Reformation in Continental Europe,* chaps. v, xix, xxix. Century, 1915.

E. P. Cheyney, *The Dawn of a New Era, 1250-1453.* Harpers, 1936.

Thompson, *History of Historical Writing,* Vol. I, chaps. xxviii-xxix.

M. P. Gilmore, *The World of Humanism.* Harper, 1952.

Will Durant, *The Renaissance.* Simon and Schuster, 1953.

James Gairdner, *Early Chroniclers of Europe: England,* chap. vii.

Ugo Balzani, *Early Chroniclers of Europe: Italy,* chap. vii.

Ritter, *Die Entwicklung der Geschichtswissenschaft,* Book III.

Preserved Smith, *A History of Modern Culture,* I, 252-57, 270-78. Holt, 1930.

Robert Flint, *Historical Philosophy in France,* pp. 183-207. Scribners, 1894.

John Morley, *Critical Miscellanies,* IV, 1-108. Macmillan, 1908.

Ferdinand Schevill, *A History of Florence,* Introduction. Harcourt, Brace, 1936.

W. K. Ferguson, *The Renaissance in Historical Thought.* Houghton Mifflin, 1948.

Eduard Fueter, *Histoire de l'historiographie moderne,* Books I-II. Paris, 1914.

F. X. von Wegele, *Geschichte der deutschen Historiographie seit dem Auftreten des Humanismus,* Book I. Leipzig, 1885.

Paul Joachimsen, *Geschichtsauffassung und Geschichtschreibung in Deutschland unter dem Einfluss des Humanismus.* Berlin, 1910.

A. A. Tilley, *The Literature of the French Renaissance.* Macmillan, 1904. 2 vols.

A. W. Ward and A. R. Waller, eds., *Cambridge History of English Literature,* Vols. III-VI. Macmillan, 1907-17. 15 vols.

J. E. Spingarn, *History of Literary Criticism in the Renaissance.* Columbia University Press, 1908.

Sir J. E. Sandys, *History of Classical Scholarship.* Putnam, 1906-8. 3 vols.

Merrick Whitcomb, *Literary Source Book of the Renaissance.* University of Pennsylvania Press, 1904.

VI

ECCLESIASTICAL HISTORICAL WRITING DURING THE REFORMATION AND COUNTER-REFORMATION

THE GENERAL IMPORT OF THE REFORMATION AND COUNTER-REFORMATION FOR HISTORICAL WRITING

IN the same year that Machiavelli received his commission to write his *History of Florence,* Luther burned the papal bull at Wittenberg and the Protestant Revolution was soon in full swing. A rude shock was thus given to the strong Humanistic impulse toward a healthy secularization of historical literature. Historical interests were again forced back into the rut of theological controversies from which they had been trying to free themselves since the days of Petrarch and Boccaccio. Again to quote relevantly from Professor Burr:

> To the freedom of history there came, indeed, a sudden check with the great religious reaction we call the Reformation. Once more human affairs sank into insignificance. Less by far than that of the older Church did the theology of Luther or Calvin accord reality or worth to human effort. Luther valued history, it is true, but only as a divine lesson; and Melanchthon set himself to trace in it the hand of God, adjusting all its teachings to the needs of Protestant dogma. Had either Papist or Lutheran brought unity to Christendom, history again must have become the handmaid of theology.[1]

Not only were ecclesiastical matters, involving both dogma and organization, deemed the all-important sphere of historical investigation, but universal history was also once more portrayed as a great struggle between God and the Devil. Two new "Cities of Satan," however, replaced the pagan "City" of Augustine and Orosius—"the Devil's Nest at Rome," and the followers of "the crazy Monk of Wittenberg," respectively. The struggle was now limited to Christendom, which had become a house divided against itself. The methods of Orosius were employed in a "family quarrel."

It is scarcely necessary to point out that this revival of the religious

[1] Burr, *loc. cit.,* p. 262.

orientation of historical interests was as fatal to the fine objectivity of Guicciardini's type of historical product as it was to the maintenance of the secular point of view of the Florentine school. There was no longer any thought of prosecuting historical studies for the mere love of acquiring information or of enriching the store of knowledge with respect to the past, as Blondus had labored for these purposes. History again became as violently pragmatic as with Augustine and his disciples. The past was viewed mainly as a vast and varied "arsenal" from which the controversialists could bring unlimited supplies of ammunition for the conflict and put their enemies to an inglorious rout. The embryonic canons of criticism which had been in part restored by the best of the Humanist historians were lightly ignored. Each party consciously strove to produce what was literally the most partisan account of past events in order to exhibit their opponents in the most unfavorable light. Sources of information were valued not so much for their authenticity as for their potential aid in polemic exercises; and invective replaced calm historical narrative. Finally, for a long time after the period of the Reformation there was little opportunity for a completely free and impartial study of the medieval period. An epoch whose interpretation was so vital to the two great religious groups of Christendom could scarcely remain a field for calm and dispassionate analysis.

It would be inaccurate, however, to hold that the Reformation gave no impulse to historical investigation. Never in the palmiest days of classical or Humanist historical writing was more feverish energy exhibited in scanning the records of the past. The main evil did not consist in a decline in activity or interest, but in the character of the impulse that led to this vigorous quest for information and the manner of use to which the knowledge was put after it had been acquired. Protestant historians were "aided by the God of Saint Paul" in the search for evidence that would prove, beyond a shadow of doubt, that the elaborate ritual and dogmas of the Roman Catholic church had been wholly an extra-scriptural and semi-pagan growth, and that the pope was the real antichrist. Catholic investigators were "specially guided by the Blessed Virgin" in their counter-demonstration that the Church and all its appurtenances were but the rich and perfect fulfilment of Scripture, and that the Protestants were inviting a most dreadful and certain punishment by their presumptuous and sinful defection from the organization founded by Saint Peter in direct obedience to the words of Christ.

The controversy's most important contribution to historical scholarship was the recovery and publication of important early documents on Church history and the production of telling criticisms by both factions which could be exploited a century later by the Rationalists, to the mutual discomfiture of both camps.

SOME LEADING HISTORICAL WORKS OF THE PERIOD

The first important contribution of the Protestant camp was *The Lives of the Popes of Rome* by Robert Barnes (1495-1540), an English Lutheran who had fled to Germany for protection. Composed under Luther's direct supervision, it endeavored to prove the popes and the Catholic church responsible for the disasters of the Middle Ages and praised the virtues of their secular opponents. At last the procedure of Orosius had been turned against the Church itself.

Another favorite historical expedient of the Protestants was to turn the light, exaggerated if need be, upon the persecutions of the Reformers by the Catholic parties in the various states of Europe. The martyrs made by the Catholics were thus turned to the service of Protestant propaganda, as the Christian martyrs slain by the Romans in the old days had been exploited to the glory of the early Catholic church. The first of such works was *The Book of Martyrs* by the French Protestant, Jean Crespin, published in 1554. It was a colorful and frank polemic, not over-conscientious in its statements, but it showed the possibilities in this type of historical literature. It was perfectly designed to stir passions and to enlist the support of the enemies of Rome.

More complete and effective was the next book of its kind, this time the work of an English author. This was *The Acts and Monuments of the Christian Martyrs* (1563) by John Foxe (1516-87). It was definitely based on Crespin's book as a model of procedure. Beginning with Wycliffe, it traced the record of Protestant martyrs in such a manner as especially to represent the current theological struggle as one between the purity and the perversion of Christianity—between Christ and antichrist. As an afterthought, Foxe decided to widen his work into a general and critical history of the Christian church and he plagiarized in extensive fashion the *Magdeburg Centuries,* which we shall shortly describe. Foxe, having all the arts of the literary demagogue, won a large and enthusiastic group of partisan readers. His character and reliability were bitterly assailed by Catholic critics, but later students, like Professor Preserved Smith, have carefully checked his work with the sources he used and have contended that he was less culpable than his enemies asserted. But his work needs to be taken *cum grano salis*.

Protestantism found its Scottish champion in the Calvinist, John Knox (1505-72), who wrote his *History of the Reformation of Religion Within the Realm of Scotland* to prove the particular solicitude of the Devil for the welfare of the Catholic cause. Despite its obvious Protestant bias, and the ever-evident egotism of the author, Knox's work was greatly superior to that of the Magdeburg Centurians and Foxe. From the standpoint of literary quality, his history was a work of genius, "displaying a marvelous precision and sureness in the selection and presentation of the significant and striking details." For a polemic-writer of the time he showed an unusual mastery of and reliance upon humor, sarcasm and irony. Nor did Knox fail to condemn in the most vigorous terms those who adopted Calvinism as the means of gaining selfish material ends or resorted to violence in the name of religion in order to revenge political or personal grievances. While Knox saw his facts through decidedly partisan eyes he did not consciously falsify or suppress facts.

The most ambitious and famous of the Protestant polemics were the voluminous *Magdeburg Centuries,* a composite work planned and edited by Matthias Vlacich Illyricus (1520-75), better known by his Latinized name of Flacius. He was aided by a number of prominent Protestant scholars, such as Aleman, Copus, Wigand and Judex. Their method was that of Orosius on the grand scale and turned against the Catholic church. All the facts of church history which could be used against the Catholics and popes were eagerly seized upon. The history of the Church and of Christian doctrine was reviewed by centuries down to 1300 in the effort to prove the assured historicity of the Lutheran position and to show that the Catholic doctrines and organization had been an exotic and unholy trend away from the purity of Apostolic Christianity. The first edition appeared between 1539 and 1546. While proposing to examine the whole history of the Christian church, the authors limited themselves mainly to the dreary history of Christian doctrines and dogmas, thus both slighting and misinterpreting the political and legal history of the Church. Though the authors displayed considerable ability in dissecting the papal doctrine and dogmas, they exhibited equal gullibility or malice in accepting preposterous sources and tales to bolster up their side of the controversy. They found two types of miracles. Those which seemed to help their case were regarded as genuine; those that were favorable to the Catholics were held to be spurious inventions and pious frauds. Their powers of criticism were evident only when advantageous, but in such cases they showed ability, as in the first important exposure of the forged pseudo-Isidorian Decretals. The main significance of the *Centuries* lay in the fact that they founded church history in its modern phase.

Less ambitious than the *Magdeburg Centuries* but more creditable to the Protestant side of the controversy were the histories of the Reformation by Sleidanus and Bullinger.

The ablest history of the Reformation written by either a Catholic or a Protestant before Bishop Gilbert Burnet was the *Commentaries on Political and Religious Conditions in the Reign of the Emperor Charles V, 1517-1555* by John Sleidan (1506-56), more generally known by his Latinized name of Sleidanus. Sleidanus' intellectual background was that of a Humanist scholar and a student of late medieval historical writings. He was early a disciple of Erasmus and before he wrote on the Reformation he had translated Froissart and Commines. This helped to give him a more tolerant and broad-minded viewpoint than the usual controversial historian and supplied him with the ideals of urbane historical writing—no man could translate Commines without being helped to view history in a detached and interpretative fashion. He gained first-hand knowledge of the Reformation through his work as a diplomat and jurist. Further, Sleidanus spent some ten years collecting materials for his history of the Reformation. His political and legalistic attitude was stimulated by his studies of Calvinism.

The great importance of Sleidanus' work is that it was the first primarily political analysis of the Reformation movement and the Protestant revolt. He was the official constitutional apologist of Lutheran states in northern Germany, and his task was to justify at the bar of public opinion the entire legality of the secession of the Protestant princes from the Church. He therefore approached the history of the movement from a political and constitutional as well as a theological point of view. He limited himself mainly to authentic documents and his work was the product of a restrained advocate. Though not a polemic, it was a sort of dispassionate lawyer's brief carefully marshaling the historical evidence to be presented. As might be expected in such circumstances, his *Commentaries* exhibited great power in the cogent organization and presentation of material, an admirable lucidity of expression, and a dignified tone, designed to make an appeal to the learned public of Europe.

While it contained none of von Ranke's mystical religious fervor and in no way anticipated the social studies of Janssen, or the economic analysis of Weber and Sombart, Sleidanus' work was of the highest significance as a direct foreshadowing of the now widely accepted thesis of Professor James Harvey Robinson and others that the Protestant revolt was far more a political than a religious movement—that it looked more distinctly toward the political adjustments of the Peace of Augsburg and the Treaty of Westphalia than towards the triumph of "justification by faith alone." Sleidanus anticipated this interpretation, not only through the general mode of his approach to the problem, but also by his specific comments upon the outstanding political phases of the revolt. As Sleidanus himself put it: "In describing religious affairs I was not able to omit politics, for, as I said before, they almost always interact, and in our age, least of all, can they be separated."[2]

Sleidanus' work was, in short, in no sense a profound and complete history of the causes, nature or doctrines of the Protestant Reformation.

[2] Preserved Smith, *The Age of the Reformation* (Holt, 1920), p. 705.

It was only relatively superior, by contrast with the low order of most other works at the time. It had enduring value chiefly because it hit upon and emphasized the fundamental truth concerning the political aspects of the Protestant movement. Also Sleidanus gave impetus to the tendency of political historians, like Camden and Thuanus, to consider religious developments. As might have been expected, his wise and tolerant work was bitterly attacked by both Protestant and Catholic fanatics. Melanchthon, the great Lutheran scholar, said that it was not fit to be put into the hands of Protestant youth, and Catholics thought less well of it.

Heinrich Bullinger (1504-75), a Swiss reformer and a disciple of Zwingli, was one of the ablest Protestant writers of the Reformation period. His work was influenced by the precedent set by Sleidanus. He wrote, from full knowledge, a *History of the Reformation, 1519-32,* dealing with the early years of the movement. It was far different in tone from the works of Knox and the Centurians. While a partisan Protestant history, it was an apologetic treatise and not a polemic, like the vivid history by Knox. Bullinger resembled Knox in the care he used in selecting his facts and his words; he was moderate and restrained in his attitude and, on the whole, aimed to be fair and honest. But even he could not resist at times the temptation to suppress embarrassing facts which had occurred in the course of the Protestant movement. Bullinger was an industrious collector of facts and he followed the method of Blondus in copying entire documents, but he wove these skillfully into his narrative. A patriotic Swiss, Bullinger endeavored to portray the Swiss Reformation as independent of the German movement and he limited his treatment primarily to religious matters. He touched on politics only when they were directly involved in the program of Zwingli.

The history of the Reformation in France was told by the eminent Calvinist and Humanist scholar, Theodore Beza (1519-1605), in his *Ecclesiastical History of Church Reforms in the Kingdom of France* (1580), an account of the rise of Calvinism in France. Beza was the successor of Calvin. His work was a sort of supplement and continuation of Crespin's *Book of Martyrs* and did not possess the scholarly quality which one might have expected from a man of Beza's learning. It appeared without Beza's name, but the weight of evidence seems to show that he was the author.[3]

The formal Catholic reply to the *Magdeburg Centuries* was the even more voluminous *Ecclesiastical Annals* of Cardinal Caesar Baronius (1538-1607). His methods were, on the whole, no great improvement over those of the Centurians. If, having the Vatican library at his disposal, he used more documents, he also was less frank in arraying his sources and in fac-

---

[3] Beza's authorship is, however, still challenged by important modern authorities.

ing difficult issues in straightforward fashion. As our chief authority on the Reformation writes:

> However poor was the work of the authors of the *Magdeburg Centuries,* they were at least honest in arraying their sources. This is more than can be said of Caesar Baronius, whose *Annales Ecclesiastici* was the official Catholic counterblast to the Protestant work. Whereas his criticism is no whit better than theirs, he adopted the cunning policy, unfortunately widely obtaining since his day, of simply ignoring or suppressing unpleasant facts, rather than of refuting the inferences drawn from them. His talent for switching the attention to a side-issue, and for tangling instead of clearing problems, made the Protestants justly regard him as "a great deceiver."[4]

Baronius had enjoyed a long training in Christian humility and church history under the popular Philip Neri. He early decided to consecrate his life to the writing of church history and he lectured on the subject before he began to write his *Annals*. Since his first lectures were given about 1559, he may be said to have devoted nearly a half-century to the study of the history of the Christian church. He was chief librarian of the Vatican after 1597. The *Annals* covered church history from the beginning down to 1198 and appeared in many volumes from 1588 to 1607. The book proceeded by years, which was valuable in establishing historical synchronisms but confusing to the clarity of the narrative. Baronius was an indefatigable searcher after materials and he examined almost everything which had ever been written on the history of the Christian church, even plowing through a good deal of profane history. He included a large amount of hitherto unpublished documentary material. And his work had more personal warmth and charm than the volumes of the Centurians.

Baronius was very reverent towards all Christian sources dealing with the early centuries of Christianity, but he showed more critical ability in handling the later medieval materials. He accepted Valla's demonstration of the fictitious character of, the Donation of Constantine, but he did not heed the demolition of the pseudo-Isidorian Decretals by the Centurians. The *Annals* were obviously apologetic and partisan, and Baronius selected his materials as definitely for partisan uses as did the Centurians. But he uncovered a far wider range of historical sources for this purpose, and this was the great merit of his vast work. His main defects were a tendency to ignore or suppress damaging evidence and his introduction of the practice of shuffling, quibbling and evasion which later particularly characterized the Jesuit controversialists. He all too often endeavored to avoid meeting dangerous or embarrassing issues by trying to obscure the vital points and to turn the discussion into secondary and

---

[4] Preserved Smith, *The Age of the Reformation,* p. 585.

rather irrelevant channels. Baronius' *Annals* were continued in more scholarly fashion by Odoricus Raynaldus, who even surpassed Baronius in the publication of new and important documentary materials.

Far less dignified than Baronius was Nicholas Sanders, an English Catholic, who wrote a book on *The Origin and Progress of the English Schism* which came out in 1585. This was the most ambitious collection of scandal-mongering which appeared in the whole literature of religious controversy in this period. Sanders even accused Henry VIII of incest by alleging that Anne Boleyn was really Henry's daughter. Sanders' methods led him to be known popularly among Protestants as "Dr. Slanders."

Even intelligent and honest Protestants did not hesitate to criticize the *Magdeburg Centuries*. As an example, we may cite Gottfried Arnold, whose *Impartial Church and Heresy History* appeared in 1699. He was a Pietist who hated the violence and political aspects of Lutheranism. His critique was more doctrinal and moral than historical. In the latter respect, he did not differ much from the *Centurians*.

Many of the fallacies and errors in the work of Baronius were revealed in the searching criticism of the great French Humanist scholar, Isaac Casaubon (1559-1614), to whom Baronius' weaknesses, due to his inability to handle Greek, were readily apparent. He devoted the last years of his life to a refutation of Baronius in his *Exercitationes in Baronium,* undertaken at the request of King James I of England. Casaubon was a moderate Huguenot who accepted the truth of the Christian Epic and this limited his criticism to historical mistakes, formal textual errors, philological defects and the like. He was also as credulous of the legends and wonders recounted by classical authors as Baronius was of Christian miracles. Had he united his learning with the perspective of a Bayle or a Voltaire he might have destroyed the whole fabric of Baronius' vast work.

One of the ablest historians of the age of religious controversy, and certainly the most interesting, was the Venetian friar and diplomat, Paolo Sarpi (1552-1623). Though bitterly hated by the papal entourage, and wounded in an assassination plot fostered by some of its members, Sarpi was actually a Catholic. He desired, however, to reform his church and hence incurred the enmity of the Curia. He deplored the superstitions, abuses and political entanglements of Catholicism and wished to advance the cause of enlightenment, tolerance and purity within the Catholic church. He was a sort of seventeenth-century Döllinger. He launched a bitter battle against the Pope, and in 1607 he was attacked by religious gangsters and left for dead on one of the numerous little bridges in Venice. Recovering, he continued the struggle with even greater zeal. It was his theory that the Reformation was caused by the abuses in the Catholic church and by the jealousies between the Augustinian and Dominican friars.

Sarpi wrote a number of tracts, but his chief work was a *History of the Council of Trent* (1619). After an introductory treatment of the Reformation, based on Sleidanus, he sailed into the Council of Trent and denounced it as an example of papal bulldozing and Jesuit intrigue and manipulation. The major weakness of Sarpi was that, in his intense interest in the details and spirit of the Council, he failed to see it in the proper historical perspective. He neither fully appreciated its causes nor appraised its reaction upon the nature and course of the Catholic church. Sarpi wrote in a vivid style, exhibited keen psychological insight, and ever defended liberty and enlightenment. His work has been attacked by Catholics as fiercely as some of them had attacked his body. But Preserved Smith, in the latest appraisal, comes to Sarpi's defense in the following manner: "My final judgment is that, whereas the Venetian historian's narrative was occasionally warped from the strict truth by bias, it generally conformed to the better standards of criticism and of accuracy prevailing when it was written."[5] Opinions regarding Sarpi have differed greatly. Macaulay, a great liberal, called him the best of early modern historians, while Lord Acton, an eminent Catholic historian, said he was no better than a jailbird.

In his own age Sarpi was answered by a Jesuit historian, Cardinal Sforza Pallavicino (1607-67), whose *History of the Council of Trent* appeared in 1657. It was an attempt at a detailed refutation, but it was less able and less reliable than Sarpi's own account. It was the work of an advocate attacking point by point the brief of his opponent. Pallavicino went more deeply into the sources, having at his hand an abundance of material not available to Sarpi. It was little wonder that he overwhelmed Sarpi with details on many minor issues. But on most major matters he equivocated or evaded altogether. He was a master at suppressing embarrassing facts, outdoing in this respect even Baronius.

More openly bitter and antagonistic to the Catholic church than Sarpi was Pietro Giannone (1676-1748), like Valla a Neapolitan historian. His *Civil History of the Kingdom of Naples* passionately assailed the usurpations of political power by the Church in general and denounced with particular sarcasm and sharpness the privileged position of the Church in Naples. But the very great importance of the work of Giannone for historiography did not lie in his bitter attacks against the Church. It consisted in the fact that he was the first historian to make the history of law and institutions a legitimate field of general historical research and exposition. In order to prove his case with respect to the political usurpations of the Church and to show them illegal, Giannone was compelled to go into the history of law, administration and constitutions. Incidental-

---

[5] *History of Modern Culture*, I, 267.

ly, this helped to make clear the primarily political character of the Catholic church, whether legitimate or not. Giannone very ably assembled the researches of specialists in the history of law and administration and put them effectively into a general historical treatise. He wrote clearly and spiritedly with the aim of reaching a large body of readers.

An extremely popular attack on Lutheranism was embodied in the work of a French Jesuit, Louis Maimbourg (1610-86). His *History of Lutheranism* appeared in 1680. He brought together most aspects of the conventional Catholic polemic against Lutheranism, but not in the usually dull and deadly serious fashion. His book was written cleverly in a piquant style designed to satisfy the literary taste of the age and to secure a wide popular following. As a lively and ingratiating popularization of the literature of historical controversy Maimbourg's book was a great success. As a work of independent scholarship it was of trivial importance. Maimbourg also wrote a less substantial critical *History of Calvinism*. While anti-Protestant, Maimbourg was no slavish devotee of the papacy. He vigorously defended the liberty of the Gallican church and, as a result, he was ousted from the Jesuit order by the pope in 1682, whereupon he was pensioned by Louis XIV.

Maimbourg's book was snowed under by the voluminous answer of Ludwig von Seckendorf (1626-92) of Saxe-Gotha in his large and well-informed *Historical and Apologetic Commentary on Lutheranism and the Reformation* (1688-92). Seckendorf was of the school of Sleidanus and produced little that was original. But his work was a dignified and sound historical summary of the Protestant position. Seckendorf desired to combat not only Maimbourg but also a more dangerous enemy, namely, scepticism and indifference to the basic issues of the Reformation. The Saxon princes opened their archives to Seckendorf and he was thus able to use many sources not hitherto touched by Protestant historians. His major work was a paragraph-by-paragraph refutation of Maimbourg by recourse to the sources, with the addition of much in the way of elaboration and comment. Seckendorf also wrote a useful survey of church history for university textbook purposes, his *Compendium of Ecclesiastical History*.

If Baronius appealed to church history to vindicate Catholicism, the chief historical apologist of Catholicism appealed to all history. This writer was the French bishop, Jacques Bénigne Bossuet (1627-1704). In his *History of the Differences Among Protestant Churches* he endeavored to convince the Protestants of the error of their ways by showing them that there could be no logical end to sectarian divisions, once the crucial initial break had been made with unified ecclesiastical authority. The ultimate result would inevitably be atheism, anarchy and immorality, and Bossuet tried to find ample justification for this prediction in the historical course of the Protestant movement to his own day. His importance here lies in the fact that he alone of the controversialists, Protestant or Catholic, was able to get beneath personalities and events and to view the conflict in its deepest philosophical aspects as a struggle between liberty and authority, in which the victory of liberty meant to him indifference, atheism and religious anarchy. Bossuet made an honest effort to be fair in this work, for he was appealing directly to Protestant readers whom he sought to convert and restore to the Catholic fold. He admitted that there had been bad popes, that the Church needed reform in Luther's day, and that Luther had some decent qualities. But he was only too eager to exploit any charges against the Protestants which served to support his thesis.

Bossuet's appeal to the whole history of mankind was embodied in his *Discourse on Universal History*. His ideas were those of Augustine and his methods those of Orosius. Indeed Bossuet has been called the "Orosius of the Counter-Reformation." Though incomparably abler and more philosophic than the *Seven Books of History against the Pagans*, his book was less truly historical than the *Enneades* of Sabellicus. His *Discourse*, says Fueter, was not a historical work. It was merely a sermon in which the biblical text was supplanted by historical subject matter carefully edited and prepared in the interest of the Church.[6] It was an elaborate effort to demonstrate the potency of the divine hand in history. Bossuet believed that God figured directly in profane as well as sacred history, though the latter more directly and invariably reflected His handiwork. He divided his work into three major parts. In the first, he dealt with a review of history from Creation to Constantine. In the second, he traced the history of religion, showing it to have been always under divine control. In the last section, Bossuet described the rise and fall of empires through the bestowal of God's favor or the impact of his wrath.

The Discourse on Universal History was one of the last serious attempts at a providential interpretation of universal history in terms of the old theology. After Voltaire had published his *Essay on the Manners and Spirit of the Nations* in the middle of the next century, few historians of repute dared to risk their reputations by a revival of the doctrines of Orosius and Bossuet.[7]

THE JESUITS

Next to Protestantism, the most important religious and institutional product of the Reformation was the Society of Jesus, now generally known as the Jesuits. The Jesuit contribution to ecclesiastical history was

[6] Fueter, *op. cit.*, p. 360.
[7] For more sophisticated vestiges, see below, pp. 192 ff.

voluminous, and we must note some of the major works. The ablest auto-biography of the whole age was that of the founder of the Jesuits, Ignatius Loyola. This was dictated in the years 1553-56 and was a masterpiece of rationalized self-analysis. Loyola had prepared himself for this work by years of pious introspection. A modern psychiatrist would explain Loyola's personal experiences in quite a different manner than he did, but it was a unique achievement for his day.

The best biography of Loyola in this period was *The Life of Ignatius Loyola* by the Humanist Jesuit, Pierre Ribadeneira (1527-1611). Fueter regards it, indeed, as the finest biography produced by a Humanist historian. Ribadeneira consciously broke with the credulity of the medieval biographies of saints and rejected the more crude miracles. He copied most of the autobiography of Loyola in this work and made a serious effort to place Loyola intelligently in church history and in the course of the Catholic developments. He was a frank partisan of the Catholic cause and a great admirer of Loyola, but he did not leave the subject of his biography hanging loosely in the historical air. He linked him with the developments of the epoch. He was a master of a fine and clear Latin style. Far less capable was the *Life and Habits of St. Ignatius Loyola* by Giampietro Maffei (1553-1603). This was superficial and worshipful and introduced a mass of alleged miracles of Loyola. It was written in florid rhetoric, in imitation of the style of Cicero.

The first good history of the Society of Jesus was written by a Florentine Jesuit, Niccolo Orlandini (d. 1606). He was an able historian and his work was a capable performance. He inclined towards the mild scepticism of later Italian Humanism and suppressed the majority of the miraculous inventions which surrounded Loyola and the growth of the Jesuit order. Orlandini was also honest enough to reveal fully the political operations of the Jesuits and he gave much attention to their cultural activities, especially in the field of education. Like Ribadeneira, he wrote in a pure and lucid Latin style.

The foremost contribution of the Jesuits to historical scholarship in this period was the systematic assembling of a vast collection of lives of the saints. This work was initiated by Father Heribert Rosweyde (1569-1629), but the major figure was Jean Bolland (1596-1665), a Jesuit of the Spanish Netherlands.[8] This great collection, which is still in process of completion, is known as the *Acta Sanctorum*. It arranged the saints according to their feast days, that is, the date of their deaths, or their "birthdays" into the future life. All the saints who died, according to fact or tradition, on January 1, come at the beginning, and last of all, when the work is complete, will come those who died on December 31. This ar-

[8] I.e., present-day Belgium.

rangement is historically confusing and less desirable than a strictly chronological arrangement. In Bolland's day the volumes dealing with the saints who died in January and February were completed. The first volume appeared in 1643. The work was continued by his pupils, Henschen and Papebroch. The *Acta* constitute a vast collection and are especially valuable in bringing together a great body of biographical material. The collection also made some slight contribution to the development of the principles of historical criticism. Cardinal Robert Bellarmine, whom we remember gratefully for his friendship with Galileo, had warned that many of the facts in the original lives of the saints were more conducive to humor than to edification. Therefore, Bolland and his associates rejected many of the traditional miracles and retained mainly those which were passably edifying.

The age of controversy wound up in the beginnings of scientific church history in the works of Johann Lorenz von Mosheim (1694-1755), an eminent German university professor of theology and church history. He wrote a number of books in this field, but the most complete was his *Institutes of Church History: Ancient and Modern* (1755). Mosheim brought together Protestant scholarship and the Protestant version of church history in the form of a voluminous textbook for university instruction in his field. It was moderate in tone and tended at least slightly towards Rationalism, though not sharing at all the Rationalistic critique of the fundamental doctrines of Christianity. Mosheim rejected the crass supernaturalism of both the Protestant and Catholic partisans and tried to effect a compromise between the various Protestant interpretations of church history. He was weak in his treatment of the Middle Ages not only because he viewed the period through Protestant eyes but also because he ignored the all-important elements of church law and administration. And his narrative of the causes and launching of the Reformation was strictly a Protestant interpretation. His account of the Protestant Revolt was a moderate Protestant presentation of the case, more complete than any by earlier Protestant historians. As Fueter well says, Mosheim's work was that of "an able professor and a trained writer but not that of a great historian or an original thinker."[9]

The controversial and supernatural type of history of the Reformation did not die with Mosheim. The most popular supernatural and Protestant history of the Reformation ever written was that produced by the Swiss author, Jean Henri Merle d'Aubigné (1794-1872). His *History of the Reformation of the Sixteenth Century* (1835-53), a very partisan work, gained an immense reading public. It was the last massive echo of the spirit of the Magdeburg Centurians.

[9] Fueter, *op. cit.*, p. 336.

We have treated Bishop Burnet in another connection, but one should not forget that his *History of the Reformation in England* was probably the ablest historical work on any phase of the Reformation down to the time of Mosheim. It was especially notable in that it took into account the economic, social and cultural causes and results of the Reformation.

CHRISTIAN CHRONOLOGY

In this chapter on religious history and controversy in the period of the Reformation and Counter-Reformation a word should be said about the controversies concerning historical chronology which had occupied the attention of historians since the beginning and had been settled tentatively for Christians by Eusebius, Jerome and Bede.

All computations in Christendom were still based upon the biblical statements of Creation, and human history was supposed to begin with Adam. An accepted Jewish computation reckoned Creation as having taken place in the year 3761 B.C. The Christian chronologers varied this to conform with their symmetrical scheme of history. This was based upon the idea that there would be seven symbolic ages of man—a cosmic week—each enduring a thousand years. Creation was placed at 4000 B.C., and it was believed that the Christian era would last for two thousand years more, after which the final millenium would come. Luther sanctified this scheme, placing Noah at 2000 B.C. The great scholar and student of chronology, Scaliger, estimated that Creation took place in 3947 and that Christ was born in 4 B.C. He held that Adam was created on April 23. Johannes Kepler, relying on astronomy as well as the Bible, put Creation in 3992 B.C. and the birth of Christ in 5 B.C. Most influential of all these chronological reconstructions was that of Bishop James Usher, who reached great exactness in his *Annals of the Old and New Testament* (1650-53). He held that the week of Creation began on Sunday, October 23, 4004 B.C., and that Adam was created on Friday, October 28, 4004 B.C., while Christ was born in 4 B.C. This was made more precise a little later by Lightfoot, who dated Creation to the hour by contending that Adam was created on Friday, October 28, 4004 B.C., at 9 A.M. But contemporaneously with this most precise of all the pious chronologers, the early geologists were bringing forth ideas and information which made the whole scheme appear infantile and preposterous.[10]

The works of controversy mentioned are only the more notable ones selected from the great volume of lesser contributions to the historical literature of the Reformation and Counter-Reformation, but they sufficiently illustrate the general tendencies in historical method and interpretation.

[10] See p. 173.

The debate had not entirely ceased in contemporary times as one can readily perceive by a comparison of the works of von Ranke and Schaff with those of Döllinger and Janssen.

While Humanists and religious controversialists were writing, a new Europe was being shaped by the effects of geographical expansion and the Commercial Revolution, out of which was to come modern civilization, and with it the birth of scientific and rationalistic historiography.

SELECTED REFERENCES

Preserved Smith, *The Age of the Reformation,* pp. 579-88, 699-750.

———, *A History of Modern Culture,* I, 258-69; II, 24 ff.

Guilday, *Church Historians,* pp. 153-211.

Thompson, *History of Historical Writing,* Vol. I, chaps. xxx-xxxvi.

Will Durant, *The Reformation.* Simon and Schuster, 1958.

H. O. Taylor, *Thought and Expression in the Sixteenth Century.* 2 vols., Macmillan, 1920.

T. M. Lindsay, *History of the Reformation.* 2 vols., Scribner, 1928.

A. C. McGiffert, *Protestant Thought before Kant.* Scribner, 1915.

R. H. Tawney, *Religion and the Rise of Capitalism.* Harcourt, Brace, 1926.

Pierre Janelle, *The Catholic Reformation.* Bruce, 1949.

J. H. Robinson, "The Study of the Lutheran Revolt," *American Historical Review,* January, 1903, pp. 205-16.

Fueter, *Histoire de l'historiographie moderne,* pp. 305-60.

Wegele, *Geschichte der deutschen Historiographie,* Books I-II.

Hippolyte Delehaye, *The Work of the Bollandists through Three Centuries, 1615-1915.* Princeton University Press, 1922.

Gustav Wolf, *Quellenkunde der deutschen Reformationsgeschichte.* Gotha, 1915-22. 2 vols.

VII

THE RISE OF SOCIAL AND CULTURAL HISTORY: THE ERA OF DISCOVERY AND THE GROWTH OF RATIONALISM

THE GENERAL INFLUENCE OF THE EXPANSION OF EUROPE ON HISTORICAL WRITING

INASMUCH as history, down to very recent times, has been regarded as primarily the domain and province of the literary artist or theologian, it was only natural that the Renaissance and the Reformation were long accepted as marking the origins of the modern phase of the development of historical writing. Now, however, when it has come to be rather generally conceded that, in its broadest interpretation, history is a branch of social science and is related generically to the whole body of science, it has become necessary to search elsewhere for the causes which brought modern historical writing into being. Its origins are to be found in the intellectual results of that great period of transformation which marks the beginnings of the present social and intellectual order, namely, the "expansion of Europe." By this term is meant the extended movement of exploration and discovery which occurred in the three centuries from 1450 to 1750, and its almost incalculable intellectual and institutional consequences.[1] The isolation, repetition, stability and provincialism of the old order could not endure in the face of the widespread contact of contrasting cultures—that most potent of all forces in arousing intellectual curiosity and promoting striking changes of every sort.

The reaction of the expansion of Europe upon the writing of history was in no way more notable and far-reaching than in its revolutionary influence upon the scope of the historian's interests. The narrowness and superficiality of the field of historical investigation since the ideals of Thucydides or of Orosius had come to prevail could no longer endure unimpaired. The new era meant a return to the vision that Herodotus had to some extent created for the historian. Writers, to some degree at least, ceased to be absorbed by those superficial phases of political and ecclesiastical history which had hitherto claimed their attention. They be-

---

[1] H. E. Barnes, *A History of Western Civilization*, Vol. II, Part I. (Harcourt Brace, 1935) 2 vols.

came for the first time interested in the totality of civilization. There arose a more definite impulse to that broadening and secularizing process which had been revived by Humanism. Not only were there vast stores of new knowledge to be obtained from the contact with the older civilizations of the East; in the culture of the natives, historians and philosophers also at last seemed to find the "natural man," who had hitherto been thought to exist only in the mythical period before the Deluge. No greater contrast could be imagined than the vast difference in the type of subjects which interested such a historian as Pufendorf and those with which Gómara concerned himself.

Again, the new range of historical interests offered more opportunity for originality of thought. There were fewer erroneous preconceptions to handicap the writer at the outset. Neither Thucydides, Polybius and Livy, nor Augustine and Aquinas had provided the final authoritative verdict on the marriage customs of Borneo or the kinship system of the Iroquois. The only exception in this respect was the prevalent doctrine of a "state of nature," which had come down from the Stoics and Roman lawyers and now seemed to have practical confirmation in the life of natives.

The influence of the expansion of Europe upon historical writing was effective indirectly through the intellectual and social changes which it produced, and the reaction of these changes upon historical interests and methods.[2] But there were also many important immediate results apparent in the historical writings of those who dealt directly with the record of the discoveries. In the first place, there were radical changes in style and exposition. The old arrangement, in the form of chronological annals, was no longer suitable. What was needed now was a vehicle for comprehensive description rather than mere chronological narration. The majority of the early historians of the movement of exploration and discovery were practical men of affairs and wrote in a direct and unpretentious style. Though there was later, with such writers as Herrera, a tendency to lapse into the affected literary style of Humanism, an important break had already been made with both the form and the style of the conventional historical literature. The content of historical works was also greatly altered by these writers. The recital of political and ecclesiastical intrigues was replaced in part by comprehensive accounts of the manners and customs of peoples. This tendency reacted strongly even on those writers who dealt exclusively with European affairs. The Spanish Humanist, Juan Paez de Castro, in the middle of the sixteenth century, even suggested the educational value of comparing the manners and customs of oversea peoples with those of the inhabitants of Europe. The *Chronicle* of Jerome or the genealogy of reigning monarchs, as the introduction to

[2] See below, pp. 147 ff.

historical works, was now generally displaced by a description of the land and its inhabitants. Excepting only the feeble anticipations by Giraldus Cambrensis and Ralph Higden in England and by Aeneas Sylvius and his numerous German disciples, now for the first time since the days of the Ionic historians of the fifth and sixth centuries b.c., ethnography and geography began to have a conspicuous place in historiography. Finally, though the earlier members of this new school of writers were primarily collectors of descriptive information, they later became speculative and encyclopedic. In the works of Voltaire and Herder there appeared attempts at world history, conceived according to the new orientation, possessing a degree of comprehensiveness and showing some grasp of causal forces.

The effect of European explorations and discoveries upon historical knowledge and writing was first apparent in the travel literature of the medieval explorers and adventurers of the thirteenth and fourteenth centuries, such as John of Plano-Carpini, William of Rubruck, Marco Polo, John of Monte Corvino and Ibn Battuta. The impact of these on historical literature was most evident in the famous and authentic *Travels* of Marco Polo (1254-1324) and the fictitious but illuminating *Travels of Sir John de Mandeville,* which appeared shortly after the middle of the fourteenth century. Marco Polo spent twenty years in the Far Orient holding important posts which enabled him to study oriental customs and habits to great advantage. In the years following 1298, while in prison in Genoa after his return from the East, Polo dictated his reminiscences to a fellow captive, Rusticiano of Pisa, who fortunately possessed remarkable literary ability. The resulting *Travels* were among the most important of all the journals ever written. Eileen Power says of them:

> It is almost impossible to speak too highly either of the extent of his observation or of its accuracy. It is true that he repeats some of the usual travelers' tales, and that where he reports from hearsay he not infrequently makes mistakes; but where he had observed with his own eyes he was almost always accurate; he had a great opportunity and he was great enough to make the most of it.[3]

The *Travels of Sir John de Mandeville* were of quite a different character. This was a fanciful work, drawn indiscriminately from ancient encyclopedists like Pliny, medieval compilers such as Vincent of Beauvais, and the reports of contemporary travelers in the Far East. Though a weird mixture of fact and fiction, the book caught the popular imagination and did much to arouse general curiosity about the riches, wonders and culture of the East. We are here, however, concerned mainly with the historians of the discoveries, explorations and colonization after 1492.

Christopher Columbus never completed his ambitious plans for a de-

[3] In A. E. Newton, *Travel and Travellers in the Middle Ages* (Knopf, 1926), p. 135.

scription of the new world, but he did write rather voluminously of his own discoveries. His pride and desire for self-glory led him into many fanciful elaborations, inventions and exaggerations. But what he did actually see he described with reasonable exactness, moderation and impartiality. His reputation as a "myth-monger" has grown chiefly out of his account of "things not seen." Very valuable as an account of nature and culture in the new world were the reports sent back to Spain by Hernando Cortez, the conqueror of Mexico. They were masterpieces of clear and condensed description, colored somewhat by Cortez' desire for self-justification. Fueter compares them, not without some basis, with the *Commentaries* of Julius Caesar. We may now turn to the series of historians who gave us the first historical account of the discoveries and conquests.

Since historiography was completely dominated by the canons of Humanism at the beginning of the period of discovery, it was only natural that the earliest of the historians of the expansion of Europe should be Humanists who turned their attention to the new movement. Their style and arrangement of material, however, had to be altered to some extent, and the center of their interests was profoundly changed. We shall consider first the writings of Spanish, Italian, and Portuguese chroniclers.

The first important historian of the New World was Pietro Martire d'Anghiera (1455-1526), more frequently known as Peter Martyr. He was an Italian Humanist and a disciple of Aeneas Sylvius and Poggio. He went to Spain to live, and in 1520 was made official chronicler for the Council of the Indies. His *Decades of the New World,* which appeared between 1516 and 1530, were written in the unique form of "news letters." The work showed ability in literary composition and descriptive powers, and abandoned Humanist conventions when desirable. While exhibiting little profundity or critical capacity, Peter provided a fairly complete summary of the extant reports of the peoples of the New World down to 1525. For historiography, the main significance of his book lies in the fact that it was the first work in modern times which described the culture of peoples, divorced from the cramped framework of political and religious annals.

Of less literary merit, but of far greater historical value, was the *General and Natural History of the Indies* by Gonzalo Fernández de Oviedo y Valdés (1478-1557), a Spanish naturalist turned historian. Having spent more than twenty years in America, he wrote from first-hand information. He possessed the objectivity of the naturalist, and what he put down from his own observations was highly reliable.

Most of the writers on the discoveries and conquests were eulogistic of the conquerors, but the native Indians found their champion in the Dominican bishop, Bartolomé de Las Casas (1474-1566), author of *A Brief Account of the Destruction of the Indies, Apologetic History of the Indies,* and *A History of the Indies.* His enthusiastic accounts of the Indians inspired the worship of the "noble savage" in polite circles in eighteenth-century Europe. His strictures on the Spanish conquerors were used by the British and Dutch as propaganda against the fitness of the Spanish to own and govern colonial realms.

Francisco López de Gómara (1511-60) described the conquest of Peru and Mexico in his *General History of the Indies*. Employed by the family of Cortez, he was forced to overemphasize the conquest of Mexico. Fueter regards him as perhaps the ablest historian of the discoveries, but Professor Wilgus disposes of him as a writer who relied upon hearsay rather than documents and even resorted to outright fabrication. More reliable, perhaps, was José de Acosta (1539-1600), a Jesuit official in Peru, who wrote his *Natural and Moral History of the Indies* in part from first-hand information. It was colored by a Jesuit bias and by a moralizing tendency. Another general descriptive work was the *Geography and General Description of the Indies* (1574) by Juan López de Velasco, which was compiled from documents placed at the author's disposal by the Council of the Indies. The voyage of Magellan was described by one of his sailors, Antonio Pigafetta (1480-1534), in his *Magellan's Voyage Around the World*.

One of the main seventeenth-century works on Hispanic America was the *General History* by Antonio de Herrera y Tordesillas (1549-1625). His book, written under the commission of Philip II, appeared between 1601-15 and dealt with events to 1555. He never used documents widely but pilfered much directly from the works of Las Casas. He lapsed into the Humanist style and his work was full of rhetorical embellishments. In spite of his reliance on Las Casas, he did not share the latter's respect for the natives. His vastly popular work was much exploited as Spanish propaganda and distorted Spanish opinion of the conquests. Far more valuable was the *History of the New World* by the Peruvian Jesuit, Bernabé Cobo de Peralta (1582-1657), who based his book on first-hand observation.

The eighteenth century produced a number of important general works on the New World. Antonio de Ulloa's *Notes on the Americas* was published in 1772 and is rich in information on Hispanic America, especially on Peru and Ecuador. Antonio de Alcedo y Bexarano (1736-1812) issued his *Geographical and Historical Dictionary of the American West Indies* in 1789, a well-documented work in five volumes. Equally reliable was the *History of the New World* by Juan Bautista Muñoz (1745-99), 1793.

There were many works on special phases of the discoveries and the colonization of Hispanic America. The first important book on the early Spanish missions was that of Augustín Dávila Padilla (1562-1604) on *The History of the Province of Santiago in Mexico*. The work of the Catholic Church in converting the natives was recounted by Alonzo Fernández in his *Ecclesiastical History of Modern Times*, 1611. Not only the missions but also the native Indian creeds were dealt with by Gil González Dávila

(1577-1658) in his *Ecclesiastical Treatise* (1655). The Catholic documents, especially the papal bulls, bearing on the conversion of Hispanic America were collected by Joaquín de Ribadeneira y Barrientos in his *Manual,* published in 1755. The legal history of early Hispanic America was compiled by Juan de Solorzano Pereira (1575-1655) in his *Disputation on the Law of the Indies.* On the commercial law of the age the most valuable work was *The Spanish Rule of Trade in the West Indies* (1672) by José de Veitia Linaje (d. 1688). The military aspects of Hispanic America were best described by Bernardo de Vargas Machuca (1557-1662).

The special areas occupied by the Spanish and Portuguese in the New World were covered by many extended works. The first important book on Brazil was the *Da Asia* of João de Barros (1496-1570). Based mainly on authentic documents, it thoroughly covered the discovery and conquest of Brazil. Published between 1552 and 1615, it was written in clear and vigorous style. The book also dealt with Portuguese conquests in the East Indies and did much to wipe out the more preposterous myths of the day regarding that area. Another important work, covering likewise both Brazil and the East Indies, was the *General History of East India* (1603) by Antonio de San Roman. Equally valuable was the *Epitome of Portuguese History* by Manuel de Faria y Sousa (1590-1648), also treating both Brazil and the Portuguese East Indies. An important Jesuit history of Brazil was *The Chronicle of the Society of Jesus in Brazil* (1663) by Siman de Vasconcellos (1597-1671). A useful eighteenth-century book on Brazil was the *History of Portuguese America* (1730) by Sebastião Rocha Pitta (1660-1738).

Francisco de Xeres (b. 1504), a secretary of Pizarro, wrote his *Authentic Account of the Conquest of Peru* (1534) at the request of Pizarro, and it is usually regarded as the official record of the conquest. A comprehensive history of Peru was *The History of the Conquest of Peru* (1555) by Augustín de Zárate (c. 1492-1560). The author was a royal official in Peru and wrote from notes made while in the service. The best account of early Inca culture was the *Chronicle of Peru* (1553) by Pedro de Cieza de Léon (1518-60). The best known of the early chroniclers of Peru was Garciaso de la Vega (1539-1616), author of the *Commentaries on the Incas,* and *The General History of Peru.* Critics are not agreed on the merits of his works. Fueter dismisses them as the product of an uncritical eulogist of the Incas, while Wilgus proclaims them to be "an excellent authority for the early history of the country." The best account of the civil wars in Peru was the *History of Peru* (1571) by Diego Fernández (b. 1510). The conversion of the Peruvian Indians to Catholicism was most fully described by Pablo José de Arriaga (1562-1622) in his *Extirpation of Idolatry in Peru* (1621). The best early history of Chile was written by Alonso de Ovalle (d. 1650), and the conversion of Paraguay was treated by Antonio Ruíz de Montoya (1593-1652), who shared the sentiments of Las Casas on the natives.

The conquest of Mexico (New Spain) received the attention of a number of competent historians. The most valuable of the early works was *The True History of the Conquest of New Spain* by Bernal Díaz del Castillo (1492-1581). He was an able and spirited soldier and wrote his book in order to give proper credit to the bravery, exertions and deeds of heroism of the army and its officers. It is an animated narrative and presents the best contemporary account of the military equipment and methods of the conquistadores. The book is not only a graphic account of the actual conquest, but rich in acute observations concerning the new world and its inhabitants. Another important and authentic work was *The General History of the Occupation of New Spain* by Bernardo Sahagún (b. 1590). The most readable account of the conquest of Mexico written in this age was *The History of the Conquest of Mexico* by Antonio de Solís y Rivadeneyra (1610-86), the literary merits of which were far in excess of its historical accuracy. The brutalities of the conquerors were most graphically arraigned by Fernando de Alva Ixtlilzochitl (1568-1648), in his *Horrible Cruelties of the Conquerors of Mexico*. The best history of the conquest of New Mexico was embodied in *The History of New Mexico* (1610) by Gaspar de Villagrá (d. 1620). On Spanish California the most valuable work was Miguel Venegas' *Account of California* (1757). For Florida we have *The Account and Commentaries* of Alvar Nuñez Cabeza de Vaca (1490-1564); and the *Florida of the Incas* by Garcilaso de la Vega, the latter of which not even Professor Wilgus can defend as authentic history.

Writers in northern Europe also took an interest in writing about the discoveries and colonization or in compiling accounts of the various voyages of discovery. The first important Dutch work was the *New World or West Indies* of Joannes de Laet (1593-1649), treating with care the natural history of the New World, native customs and the process of colonization. Arnoldus Montanus (1625-83) dealt with the discoveries in North America, the West Indies and Brazil in his *New and Unknown World*. In 1678, John Esquemelin (Hendrick Smeeks) published his *American Sea-Rovers*, one of the first good accounts of the buccaneers and pirates. The most elaborate of all early Dutch collections of voyages was that published by Pieter van der Aa in 1707, in 127 volumes. Two representative German works on discovery and colonization were Gaspar Ens' *History of West India* (1612), and Johan Ludwig Gottfried's *New World and American History* (1655).

The earliest French collection of voyages of any note was the *Accounts of Various Curious Voyages* (1693-96) by Melchisedech Thévenot (1620-96). In 1707 the Abbé Bellegarde published his *Universal History of Voyages*, giving special attention to the Spanish voyages to America. Charlevoix's extensive writings on the discoveries will be described later. One of the most ambitious French works dealing with discovery and colonization was the *General History of Explorations* by Antoine Prévost d'Exiles (1697-1763). This was primarily a compilation and a publisher's enterprise, but it contained a mass of information. It appeared in several volumes between 1746 and 1754. It was appreciative of the natives but critical of the naïve enthusiasm of Las Casas. It reflected Montesquieu's point of view in looking at culture and institutions from the comparative point of view and emphasizing the influence of climate on social institutions. The work gave much space to a philosophical analysis of the formation and growth of native societies. A compresensive work in fourteen volumes was Antoine Touron's *General History of America since the Discovery* (1770). It gave special attention to the religious history of the New World.

The first English work on the expansion of Europe was Richard Eden's *Decades of the New World* (1555), based in part on the work of Peter Martyr. Next came *The Principal Navigations, Voyages and Discoveries of the English Nation* by Richard Hakluyt, which appeared in 1588 and again in enlarged form in 1600. Supplementing this, a quarter of a century later, was Samuel Purchas' *His Pilgrims* (1625-26), which embodied much of the Hakluyt material along with other descriptive matter collected by Purchas. An English work on Hispanic America, which was based on prolonged residence in the West Indies, was Thomas Gage's *New Survey of the West Indies* (1648). A comprehensive survey of the New World, drawn in part from the Dutch book by Montanus, was *America: being the latest and most accurate description of the New World* (1671), by John Ogilby (1600-76). At the opening of the eighteenth century Awnsham Churchill published in 1704 a famous body of materials, *A Collection of Voyages and Travels*. A year later, John Harris brought out his popular work on the history of voyages and travels, *A Library of Navigations and Itineraries*. A leading buccaneer turned editor when William Dampier (1652-1715) published his *Collection of Voyages* in 1715. John Campbell's *Concise History of the Spanish America* (1742) laid special emphasis on trade and commercial relations. English writers also devoted attention to special areas, a notable example being the *History of Brazil* by Robert Southey (1774-1843), a part of his projected but unfinished *History of Portugal*. Southey was fair and realistic in treating both the native Indian population and their European conquerors. He was especially impressed with the great future possibilities of Brazil.

The first well-known history of English colonization was the boastful and fanciful *General History of Virginia and New England* (1624) by Captain John Smith. Smith was the author of only a small section of the total work, most of which was compiled from anecdotes and reminiscences of the settlers. One of the notorious inventions of Smith was the Pocahontas legend, which ranks with the Washington cherry-tree story among the myths of popular American history. Dr. J. F. Jameson sarcastically but accurately remarks of Smith's work that "what is historical is not his, and what is his is not historical."[4]

Of quite a different class was Robert Beverley's *History . . . . of Virginia* (1705), written at the request of a London bookseller. It was a fairly scholarly summary of earlier documents and records, and it was written in a vivid style. More scholarly and conscientious, but less entertaining, was William Stith's *History of the First Discovery of Virginia* (1747).

The history of early New England was first recounted in respectable fashion in the *History of Plymouth Plantation* by Governor William Bradford (1590-1657) and in the *History of New England* by Governor John Winthrop (1588-1649). Bradford's account was a straightforward narrative colored by piety and the providential theory of history. He had gathered documents for his work over many years and the record was highly reliable. It covered the history of the settlement of the Plymouth colony down to 1646. Winthrop's dignified narrative was written in the annalistic form and described the history of the Massachusetts Bay Colony to the year 1648. It was not a history of New England as a whole, the title of the book being altered by a London publisher to enhance interest and sales. It was the best of the Puritan historical compositions in the New World.

Far more fearful and wonderful was *The Ecclesiastical History of New England* by Cotton Mather (1663-1728). It was a comprehensive affair, running from the alleged biblical prophecies of the settlement of New England to the history of higher education in Massachusetts. It included the lives of administrators, educators, ministers and other prominent personages, the history of Harvard College, the Indian wars, and the evidences of God's Providence in the course of the history of New England. In the latter respect, Mather applied the same theories that Bossuet adopted, only to a smaller area.

The most scholarly of all summaries of early New England history was the *Chronological History of New England* by Thomas Prince (1736), an unparalleled, meticulous and reliable anthology of New England antiquities to 1633. Far superior in breadth of historical conception and in literary skill was *The History of the Province of Massachusetts Bay,* by Thomas Hutchinson (1711-80), in three volumes. An American scholar and the last royal governor of Massachusetts, he wrote under the influence of the Rationalist attitude towards history. His history was reliable and judicious, and especially competent in treating legislative and institutional developments.

A number of British writers considered the Indians of North and South America and tried to convey to Europeans the facts about them. Adam Ferguson, in his *History of Civil Society,* had dealt rather favorably

[4] J. F. Jameson, *The History of Historical Writings in America* (Houghton, Mifflin, 1891), p. 11.

with them—a mild version of the "noble savage" attitude. This interpretation of American Indian culture was vigorously attacked by J. H. Wynne, in his *General History of the British Empire in America* (1770). He claimed that it was a waste of time to try to civilize and educate the Indians. A similar attitude was taken in the famous *History of America* by William Robertson, and in C. H. Arnold's *New and Impartial Universal History of North and South America* (1781). All of these were an attack on the tendency to eulogize the native population of the Americas. A more sane and moderate position—intermediate between the upholders of the "noble savage" attitude and the severe critics—was taken by James Adair, in his *History of the American Indians* (1775), in which he turned the method of Montesquieu's *Persian Letters* against European critics of the Indians; and in William Russell's *History of America* (1778), which tried to present the good and bad sides of the Indian and his culture. Russell suggested that Europeans who were horrified by the cruelties attributed to the Indians might well compare the Indian raids on the whites with the wars of medieval and early modern Europe, or of antiquity—even the biblical forays.

On the French explorations in the Mississippi the first important work was Marquette's *Voyages and Discoveries* (1681). Another very interesting and popular writer was the Belgian missionary, Louis Hennepin (b. 1640). He accompanied LaSalle on his expeditions. He wrote books on *The New Discoveries* and *A Description of Louisiana*. They are important for American discoveries and ethnography, though some of Hennepin's claims, such as the navigation of the Mississippi to its mouth, have been since found to be spurious. The most popular history of the French explorations and colonial enterprises in America was *The General History and Description of New France* by the French Jesuit traveler, Pierre François Xavier de Charlevoix (1682-1761). He compiled this from both records and much first-hand information. Though somewhat wordy, pretentious and uncritical, the work was extremely entertaining and it enjoyed a long popularity. Charlevoix also wrote accounts of Jesuit missionary enterprises in Japan and the Far East on the basis of the works of Kaempfer and others, as well as elaborate accounts of Haiti and Paraguay.

Far and away the most competent description and analysis of American Indian culture in this age was the *Customs of the American Savages Compared with the Customs of Early Times* by Joseph François Lafiteau (1681-1746), a French Jesuit missionary, whose sane and restrained presentation of the culture of the Hurons and Iroquois helped to lay the basis for the rise of social and cultural anthropology. Much the most intelligent of all the general histories of the new world prior to the nineteenth century was the *History of America* by the English Rationalist historian, William Robertson, which will be described later in this book.[5]

[5] See below, pp. 156 ff.

On the Near East the most popular works were Richard Knolles' *General History of the Turks* (1603), a well-informed book and so pleasingly written that it received warm praise from Samuel Johnson and Henry Hallam; Jean Chardin's *Travels into Persia and the East Indies*, published sporadically between 1686 and 1711 and much exploited by Montesquieu; Sir John Malcolm's admirable *History of Persia* (1815), written from the sources and first-hand information; and David Price's excellent chronological *Retrospect of Mohammedan History* (1821). These and other works helped to arouse an avid interest in Muslim culture and literature, which was further promoted by the translation of the *Arabian Nights*.

The first systematic account of early European contacts with Japan and the Far East since the time of Marco Polo was the *History of Japan* by a German physician, Engelbrecht Kaempfer (1651-1716). His work remained the chief popular source of European knowledge of Japan for a century or more, as did that of de Barros on the East Indies. Further light was thrown on the East Indies by William Marsden's *History of Sumatra* (1783), dominated by Rationalist historical notions. A universal work of travel and description was the voluminous *Travels to the East and West Indies,* published at Frankfort between 1590 and 1634 by Dirk de Bry. An accurate account of later stages of British conquests in India was contained in Robert Orme's *History of the Military Transactions of the British Nation in Indostan from 1745* (1778), a vivid history of military details. The history of the British East India Company was written sympathetically from the documents by John Bruce in his *Annals of the Honourable East India Company* (1810). But the first fairly complete history of explorations and colonization in India was James Mill's voluminous *History of British India* (1818), the work of a Utilitarian philosopher. It was highly informing, and written in a very critical tone— critical alike of Hindu civilization and of British rule in India. Mill's appraisal of Hindu civilization was about as unfavorable as that in Katherine Mayo's much discussed *Mother India* in our day. At the same time, judging the administration of the East India Company by the standards of Bentham, he found it sadly lacking in efficiency, justice and economy. Further information was thrown on the East Indies by the British imperialist, Sir Thomas Stamford Raffles, in his *History of Java* (1817), and by John Crawfurd in his *History of the Indian Archipelago* (1820), both rich in descriptions of native manners and customs.

Important information on South Africa was contributed by Sir John Barrow (1764-1848) in his *Travels Into . . . . Southern Africa.* Barrow also gathered together the first thorough collection relative to the ill-starred efforts to find a northwest passage to India, his *Voyages of Discovery and Research within the Arctic Regions.*

Travel literature and scientific geography were linked together early in the nineteenth century in the writings of men like Alexander von Humboldt and Karl Ritter. The general impression of the influences growing out of the period of discoveries upon historians was best popularized in *The Philosophical and Political History of the Settlements and Trade of Europeans in the East and West Indies,* by the promoter and journalist, Guillaume Thomas Raynal (1713-96). Published in 1771, it was not only something of a compilation of earlier works, but also indicated the reaction of the expansion of Europe upon European thought. A philosophical rendition of the views of Raynal was set forth in the work of François Jean Chastellaux (1734-88), *A Discourse on the Advantages and Disadvantages of the Discovery of America* (1787). The influence of the new geographical knowledge upon historical concepts at this time was illustrated by the works of Nicholas Lenglet-Dufresnoy (1674-1755), especially his *Methode pour étudier l'histoire,* and his *Methode pour étudier la géographie.*

But important as some of these writers may have been in altering the conventions of historical style and the interests of the historian, the general reaction of the expansion of Europe upon historical writing was less significant in its stimulation of the historians of the discoveries than in the resulting alteration of most phases of life and thought in the succeeding centuries. These new developments grew more or less directly out of the movement of expansion and indirectly wrought great changes in historical concepts and methods.

RATIONALISM AND HISTORICAL WRITING

No one of the indirect influences of the expansion of Europe upon historical writing was more important and more obvious than its aid in producing the new critical and naturalistic philosophy of which Bacon, Descartes and Locke were among the most conspicuous exponents. The exploration of the major portions of the earth's surface had not only demonstrated the great extent of the habitable portions of the globe, but had also shown that the supposed marvels and terrors in the unexplored regions were but an unfounded myth which failed to materialize.

During the same period that Da Gama, Columbus and Magellan were revealing the extent and nature of the surface of the globe, less picturesque figures were devoting themselves to an exploration of the universe, with results equally disastrous to the older theological traditions. The vast and immeasurable extent of the universe was apprehended to an elementary degree by Copernicus, Bruno, Galileo and Tycho Brahe. The notion of an orderly arrangement and functioning of the universe was established by the new laws of celestial mechanics, discovered and formulated by

Galileo, Kepler and Newton. To these major advances in science should be added the explanation of now commonplace natural phenomena through the notable progress in every field of natural science in the seventeenth century. The net result of all these advances was a serious challenge to the old theological interpretation of the world and man. The latter had been based primarily upon the concept of a God of arbitrariness, who was continually varying or suspending the laws of the universe to punish a recalcitrant prince or to answer the prayers of a faithful bishop.

The general implications of the above scientific discoveries were reduced to a fairly systematic body of philosophical thought by Francis Bacon, René Descartes and John Locke. Bacon especially emphasized the necessity of following the inductive method, Descartes suggested a mechanical interpretation of the universe, and Locke attempted to base knowledge and truth on human experience. The new discoveries and the new philosophy tended to produce a rationalistic interpretation of natural and social phenomena which abruptly challenged the older and then generally accepted view of miracles and wonders that had been so popular with Christian historians during the medieval period. The English Deists, such as Cherbury, Blount, Middleton, Tindal, Chubb, and especially Woolston and Hume, discredited with educated people the doctrine of the miraculous.[6] Finally, with the attacks upon the traditional views of the composition of the Old and New Testaments by Hobbes, Spinoza, Astruc, Reimarus and Ilgen,[7] the philosophy of wonder-working was undermined, not only through the evidence brought forward by natural science, but also by questioning the authenticity of the scriptural record in which the miracles were recorded. The gradual growth of toleration, especially in Holland and England, during the latter part of the seventeenth century and throughout the eighteenth century enabled these revolutionary ideas to obtain adequate expression and some general currency.

It was also inevitable that the new scientific discoveries and the new philosophy of nature should react profoundly upon the contemporary social philosophy. The idea of orderly development and continuity in social as well as natural processes was comprehended by such writers as Vico, Hume and Turgot. The older notion of social evolution as a gradual decline or retrogression from a primordial golden age was replaced in the writings of Fontenelle, Perrault, Vico, Voltaire, Hume, Turgot, Kant, Godwin and Condorcet by the concept of continual progress from lower stages of civilization. The need for miracles to justify history and the other sciences dealing with human activities was lessened by the growing

---

[6] Middleton's view of miracles deeply influenced Gibbon's ideas of Christianity.
[7] See above, pp. 19 ff.

prevalence of the Deistic doctrine of the inherent and reasonable "decency" of man—a notion widely at variance with the older views of the Christian Fathers and of Calvin, which stressed the depravity of mankind. Finally, the new discoveries and the secularization of natural and social philosophy produced a notable extension of the interests of the historian beyond the field of politics and religion.

In the writings of Voltaire, Raynal, Montesquieu and Heeren it became apparent that the trend towards a broader and sounder scope of history had begun to affect others than those who described the course of the explorations and colonization. This healthy tendency towards a wider scope of historical investigation and narrative was to some extent checked by the renewed impulse to political history that was stimulated by the rise of nationalism. But it gained a foothold from which it was not entirely dislodged until it was overwhelmingly reinforced by the renewed interest in social, economic, and intellectual topics which followed the scientific and industrial revolutions of the nineteenth century.

The reaction of this naturalistic philosophy and the new social philosophy upon historical writing appeared in the writings of what is conventionally known as the "Rationalist School" of historians, or the historians of the *Aufklärung*. While the writings of this school varied so greatly that it is customary to divide the writers into several groups, there was a fundamental unity of method and interest which makes it possible to summarize the general nature of the Rationalist historiography of the eighteenth century.

Much the most important innovation of this school was the general tendency to broaden the field of history, so that it would extend beyond the political intrigues of church and state and embrace the history of society, commerce, industry, and civilization in its widest aspects. The historians of the discoveries had shown a similar trend, but their work had been mainly confined to a discussion of the new world and they had not constituted a general European school of historians. With the Rationalists, no matter what the period or country dealt with, there was an effort to adopt a broad cultural approach to history and to introduce some embryonic sociological principles into historical analysis.

Scarcely less important was the attempt to discredit superstition and the theological theories of historical causation, and to substitute natural causes. The Rationalist historians accepted the general mechanistic theory of the universe and society which had been deduced by the Deists from Newtonian astrophysics. God directed the process, but he worked through His own natural laws. Everything in human history was a product of definite cause-and-effect relationships, but this did not prevent the Rationalist historians from believing in personal causes of a secondary nature. Indeed, at times they approached the "catastrophic" theory of causation in interpreting major movements or policies as the outgrowth of some single personal act. In general, they adhered to the notion that intellectual factors—in other words, ideas—are the dominating element in history. They thus laid special stress on intellectual history.

As a group, they held that the human mind is essentially the same the world over and that differences are due to contrasts in the social environment, that is, special types of manners and customs. The latter were traced by some of these historians to differences of geographical environment, especially differences in climate. Montesquieu and his school laid particular emphasis on these geographical influences. Voltaire contended that the three major forces which mould the minds of men are climate, government and religion. The Rationalist historians believed in inevitable progress and they thought that the greatest forward step ever taken by man was the freeing of the human mind from superstition and fear of the supernatural. Hence, they had a general feeling of assurance and satisfaction relative to the alleged superiority of their own age over any previous period in human history. Reason would destroy the evils inherited from the past and lead to a better future. Progress had been incredibly slow down to the sixteenth century, but the rate of human enlightenment had accelerated greatly thereafter.

Even the political history of the Rationalists was given a new and more promising cast. It was no longer limited to the field of political apologetics, but became a truly critical political history, as far as its attitude towards policies was concerned. It was not usually written by members of the governing classes nor under their patronage, but by representatives of the new *bourgeoisie* or third estate, who had little influence in the European governments at that period outside of England. It became an instrument of political criticism and of agitation for reform, but rarely for revolution. There was a general conviction, however, that only men who had taken some part in public affairs were able to deal competently with political history. They should at least be what we call "publicists," even if not statesmen or diplomats.

It must be remembered, however, that the critical advances brought about by the Rationalists were in evidence mainly in their attitude towards the general subject matter of their history. They were not exhibited to any comparable degree in their handling of the sources of information. As research scholars in the use and criticism of printed and manuscript sources they did not advance beyond the school of Mabillon. They used, generally with discrimination, the existing printed sources.

In the construction of their works the Rationalist historians were deeply interested in giving literary artistry to their compositions. They were as much interested in this as were the Humanists. But their notions of literary art differed greatly from those of the Humanists. They did not try to write affected Latin rhetoric, in imitation of Cicero, Livy, or Tacitus. They wrote a straightforward and distinguished style in the vernacular of their country. As Professor Black puts it:

> It was not a matter, be it observed, merely of finding the exact word, and of stitching the sentences together in such a way as to make the transition easy: the architecture of paragraphs, and indeed of whole chapters, was seriously considered, in order that emphasis might be properly controlled and justly distributed, the shades of meaning duly brought out, and the details grouped artistically.[8]

But the outstanding aspect of Rationalist historical writing was the aim of relating historical facts to a broad social, philosophical and humanitarian frame of reference, as we would call it today:

> The eighteenth century historians, whatever their other shortcomings may be, undoubtedly accomplished their assessment of the past with commendable vigour. There is never any doubt left in the mind of the reader what Voltaire and Hume, for example, think of the matters they describe. The important events of history are set in a wide framework, their bearings are indicated to the great moral background against which the drama of the race is enacted, and they are judged with respect to standards which the writers, rightly or wrongly, regard as ultimate. Hence it comes about that to all who look to history for more than factual instruction, who believe that a historical fact is not fully appreciated until it is placed in its philosophical as well as its purely causal relationships, the historians of the Age of Reason will never quite lose their charm; on the contrary, they will remain as perhaps the most brilliant examples of how human culture may be brought into fruitful contact with what would otherwise be a dead and, for the vast majority, a valueless past.[9]

The special historical philosophy of the Rationalist school, which was rather generally held by all of these writers, is worthy of emphasis here because it was fundamental to their historical writing. It determined their aims and much of their method in writing history and explains why, as a school, they laid so much stress upon history as "philosophy teaching by example"—a phrase which is attributed to the Rationalist statesman, Bolingbroke. Their enthusiasm for history arose in large part from their interest in the new naturalistic philosophy. They sought to resolve the apparent contradiction between the usual assumption of evil in the universe and their own thesis of the goodness of man. Finding it difficult adequately to prove the validity of their belief in the laws of nature and of nature's God solely by an appeal to reason, they sought aid in their perplexity by a careful examination of man's past experience on the planet.

[8] J. B. Black, *The Art of History* (F. S. Crofts and Company, 1926), pp. 17-18.
[9] *Ibid.*, p. 7.

They endeavored to prove that, even though there may be evil in the universe, evil in man existed only when he was coerced by an irrational and bigoted religion. Man gave evidence of evil in the past only in those "unhappy ages" when religion, especially Christianity, coerced him, and warped his otherwise essentially good nature. Conversely, the experience of man in the "happy ages" when religion and the Church were unable to dominate and control man shows what high levels and good conduct man can attain to under natural conditions. History is, thus, philosophy teaching by example in the broadest sense and it helped to point the moral in the Rationalist dogma. It was, roughly, the method of Orosius and Augustine reversed. Hence, the deep concern of the Rationalist historians with the "happy Chinese," the American Indians and others free from church domination, and their appreciation of Islam and Muslim culture. The scholarship of the Rationalist school was often "objective," but the basic moral of their story, whether it be the history of England or of the decline of Rome or of the Middle Ages, was always the same and predetermined. Their general conclusions were completed in advance before they began their research, for they knew what man was like before they began to ask history formally to give them the answer.

VOLTAIRE AND HIS SUCCESSORS

The founder of the Rationalist school of historians and the master mind of the movement was François Arouet, more commonly known as Voltaire (1697-1778), whose works were a partial answer to the earlier demands of Francis Bacon, Fénelon, and others for books on intellectual, cultural and social history. The dominating factors in Voltaire's political and historical philosophy were his faith in science and reason, his great admiration for the English civilization of his time, and his peerless powers as a critic. An apologist of an enlightened despotism that would allow the free development of *bourgeois* culture and prosperity, he saw in the England of Walpole his political ideal, and his agitation for reform in France was limited mainly to a desire to create in France what he beheld in England. Reason equipped the historian to deal intelligently with the past and enabled the statesman of the present to devise a better world for man to live in. As a critic, Voltaire has never been equaled in any age, primarily because of the fact that he was utterly devoid of reverence or false respect for any institution. He was, thus, wholly free to give full expression to his reactions against every phase of obscurantism.

The first important historical work by Voltaire was his life of Charles XII of Sweden, written in 1731. While it lacked an understanding of the institutional background and of the larger "logic of events" which, rather than Peter the Great, defeated Charles, the work was a masterpiece as literature and as a delineation of the character of Charles. Professor Black says of it:

> There is nothing superfluous, no straining after effects, no ornamentation, no undue intrusion of the author's opinions, no congestion, no digression: brevity, precision, lucidity, characterize every line. And the result is that the person of Charles XII stands out from the text as if he had been etched on steel.[10]

Voltaire's most polished historical work was *The Age of Louis XIV* (1751), which Fueter describes as "the first modern historical work." In it Voltaire broke wholly with the annalistic method, or even with any strict chronological system, and organized his work in accordance with the topical system of arrangement. Again, it was the first time that the civilization of a great European state had been described in its totality. And it was competent from the strictest critical standpoint. Voltaire read widely and intelligently in preparing to write the book and he mastered most of the sources for the period.

Voltaire's survey of the age of Louis was no mere skillful compilation; it was an attempt to exhibit the main currents of development in the whole life of a powerful state and a cultured society, set out in its contemporary political relationships. As was the case with the internationally minded Rationalists, there was little of that chauvinism in his book which disfigured the work of the political historians of the following century. The excellencies and defects of Louis and his period were pointed out with equal candor and clarity. His wars and religious bigotry were scathingly condemned and the cultural achievements of the age proportionately praised. From a literary standpoint, the work was a masterpiece. The major defect lay in Voltaire's failure to link up the age of Louis with the general evolution of European civilization. He did not place it intelligently against the picture of the development of modern culture as a whole.

Much less thorough, but even more significant was his *Essay on the Manners and Spirit of the Nations* (1756), generally regarded as the first universal history in the true sense of the term. It was planned as a vast *Kulturgeschichte* of all ages and peoples. Though Voltaire did not possess the knowledge or the leisure requisite for its successful execution and while the work was ill-proportioned and marred by serious omissions, it was, nevertheless, one of the great landmarks in the development of historical writing. It was the real foundation of the history of civilization in the modern sense. It was the first work in which due credit was given to the non-Christian contributions, especially of the Orientals and Muslims, to European civilization. It first put political history in its proper relation

---

[10] Black, *op. cit.*, pp. 63-64.

to economic and social history in the general development of humanity. It thoroughly undermined the theological and providential interpretations which had prevailed from Orosius to Bossuet.

Especially important was the abandonment of provincialism or even a European viewpoint. Voltaire not only dealt with the ancient civilizations, but also with the newly discovered primitive peoples. He helped to destroy the Humanist tendency to sanctify classical antiquity. He was especially critical of the Middle Ages, medieval Christianity and the medieval historians. He had little more use for the Protestant Reformers, whose supernaturalism and bigotry repelled him. It was only the Age of Reason which impressed him and he did not reach this in the *Essay,* which ended with the reign of Louis XIII. Voltaire looked upon human history as having been carried along chiefly by the clash of ideas and civilizations. Christianity challenged paganism. Mohammedanism came into conflict with Christianity. Protestantism rose to defy medieval Catholicism. In his own period, reason smote superstition of all types. The major defect of the *Essay* lay in its lack of unity and completeness. The commendable discussions of primitive culture and the Orient were not linked up with the rest of the picture. They were preliminary digressions. Classical antiquity was passed over rapidly. The story really got under way only with Charlemagne, and the treatment of the Middle Ages was fragmentary and uneven in emphasis.

Voltaire's chief French disciple was the philosopher Étienne de Condillac (1715-80), who published an *Ancient History* and a *Modern History* which brought in much more intellectual, cultural and social material than had Voltaire. It also came down far enough to include a treatment of the Age of Reason. Condillac stated clearly and precisely the Rationalist views of historical causation and laid much stress on the arts and sciences. In a special work he considered in detail the influence of commerce on politics and government.

Voltaire's mode of approach to history found several distinguished representatives in England and Scotland. There was, however, one important difference. Among the British writers there was little underlying impulse towards reform. In the case of the English historians of the period there was much of that same complacent self-satisfaction over the finality and perfection of English institutions that was evident in the legal works of Blackstone, which later aroused the fury of Bentham. This is to be explained in part by the fact that in England the *bourgeois* revolution in politics lay behind—it had been achieved in the seventeenth century. In France, still under despotism and the social exploitation of a decadent feudalism, the revolution lay ahead. Hence, the French intellectuals and historians were far more interested in reform. Moreover, their exclusion from politics explains their concentration on ideas to attain self-expression.

The best example of this lofty and complacent tendency in English historical writing at the time was David Hume (1711-76), author of the *History of England from the Invasion of Julius Caesar to the Revolution of 1698*. Hume was no conscious imitator of Voltaire. His historical writing grew out of his general philosophy, and this had taken shape before Voltaire wrote either his *Age of Louis XIV* or his *Essay*. The fact is that both were dominated by the general body of ideas common to the Enlightenment.

As one critic has observed, Hume's history was written as witches say their prayers—backwards. The volumes on the Stuarts (1603-88) appeared in 1750. They aroused such a storm that he wrote on the Tudors (1759) to defend his earlier volumes. Then, to round out the whole and to keep busy at pleasurable mental effort, he composed the early portion on English history from Caesar to Henry VII (1762). The whole history was the first relatively complete or "national" history of England, and this fact, together with Hume's entertaining style and his popular Rationalism, gave his book a wide reading public and large cultural influence.

Hume did not gather his materials as widely and thoroughly as Voltaire did for his *Essay,* to say nothing of his work on Louis XIV. Hume read mainly the easily accessible chroniclers and histories, being especially and unfortunately influenced by Clarendon's history of the great Civil War. His history was not only defective in scholarship, but at times even failed to provide an orderly narrative, dropping into unorganized memoranda of events. This was especially true where Hume should have been strongest, namely, in his sections on ideas, manners and customs. On the whole, one may say that Hume's mentality far outran his talents or industry as a professional historian. It was the philosophy, scepticism, and insight which permeated his volumes, far more than the historical facts contained therein, which gave his history permanent value. As a record of English history it was a rather sorry exhibit, but as an illustration of a powerful mind playing over historical materials it has rarely, if ever, been surpassed, and it has gained immortality on this account alone.

Hume believed that history is preëminently the record of the intellectual and moral ideas of mankind. But he chose to write a political history. Therefore, his historical work was, in its underlying pattern, an account of how ideas, morality and religion mold politics. It was also a judgment of politics from the standpoint of Hume's own notions in the realm of science, philosophy, religion and morals. He had no wish to promote a revolution. His aim was to be "entertaining and instructive"—in short, to promote urbane sophistication. Hume's antagonism to superstition and to orthodox Christianity made him contemptuous of the Middle Ages, which he regarded as a thousand years of cultural blank—a great trough in the graph of human development. This attitude also affected his view of the

Reformation and the English constitutional struggles of the seventeenth century. The fanaticism of the Protestant reformers and the bigotry and narrow-minded moral ideas of the English Puritans made him take a hostile attitude towards both the Reformation and the Puritan struggle against the English monarchy. Hume has been accused of being a Tory in politics and history. But he was not. He was anti-Whig because of his moral and religious emancipation and his aversion to revolution. Bitterly as his history of the seventeenth century was attacked, it went much further than any other work down to his time in the way of viewing the movement free from historical partisanship. As Professor Peardon writes:

> He attempted in his volumes on the Stuarts to handle the seventeenth-century struggles in an impartial spirit and with due regard to the historical setting in which the respective claims of King and Parliament were put forward. He saw that much might seem legal and constitutional to a Stuart monarch that would be correctly regarded as an attack on public liberty in the next century, and he emphasized the fact that the Constitution was not clearly outlined until after 1688. By so doing he brought a breath of realism into the atmosphere of rabid partisanship surrounding previous discussions of the seventeenth century.[11]

Hume's attitude towards religion also helped to clarify the historical atmosphere. It was a valuable corrective to the fanatical or biased histories of the English church and of English religious development written by devout Catholics and Protestants. The general import and permanent value of Hume's volumes on English history have been admirably summarized by Professor Black:

> They read as freshly today as when they were first penned, and there are many students, both inside and outside the professional ranks, who still find them satisfying and illuminating. The wonderful ease, directness, and perspicuity of the style in which they are expressed, together with the depth, wisdom, and concentrated experience distilled into them, make them, as Hume hoped they would be, "instructive and amusing" in the highest degree.[12]

A much abler technical historian than Hume was the Scotchman, William Robertson (1721-93). Robertson was, perhaps, the most competent technical historian of the English Rationalist school. Certainly, only Gibbon approached him in this respect. He had the instincts of a scholar, worked hard to master his materials, used his sources with discrimination, and had a real reverence for truth. As Professor Black says, "accuracy and general truthfulness" are the chief characteristics of Robertson's historical

---

[11] T. P. Peardon, *The Transition in English Historical Writing, 1760-1830* (Columbia University Press, 1933), p. 20.

[12] Black, *op. cit.*, p. 116.

writings. He wrote in a clear and effective manner, free from literary affectation. Swift and Defoe were his models of literary style. Gibbon was inspired to write his great history in part by his admiration of Robertson's language. Robertson also believed that history should be a dignified matter, in other words, that it should be a narrative of the doings of dignified personages—public figures of importance. This made it difficult for him to have due and proper interest in cultural, economic and social history, since much in such fields relates to the commonplace, both as to persons and events. "Dignified" history must all too often be only superficial political and military history.[13] Still Robertson was not unaware of cultural, economic, and social elements in history. He frequently alluded to them, but they could never become the basic substance of his work. Robertson was the least rationalistic of the major English historians of his group. He spent part of his life as a Protestant minister, and he believed the Reformation to have been caused primarily by Divine Providence. While not a fanatical Protestant, his Rationalism appeared chiefly in his treatment of the history of the Catholic church.

Robertson's four major works were *The History of Scotland* (1759); *The History of the Reign of the Emperor Charles V* (1769); *The History of America* (1777-94); and *An Historical Disquisition Concerning Ancient India* (1791). Most critics regard the *Charles V* as the ablest of the lot, but Professor Black, the foremost English authority on Robertson as a historian, inclines to the opinion that the *America* is the most impressive. As a matter of fact, as a finished and competent historical composition, the *History of Scotland* stands easily at the head of the list, in the same way that Voltaire's *Age of Louis XIV* is superior as a unified historical product to the *Essay*. On the history of Scotland, Robertson was a master for his day. He read most available sources, sifted them carefully, dealt with his material with relative impartiality, and wove everything into a smoothly flowing, interesting and dignified narrative. The gulf between his work and that of Buchanan was boundless.

Robertson's *Charles V* has been highly esteemed in large part because of the philosophical survey of the Middle Ages which was published as a separate volume, introductory to the main study which began with the sixteenth century. This was entitled *A View of the State of Society in the Middle Ages*. It was superior in scholarship and proportion to the medieval sections of Voltaire's *Essay,* and was surpassed as an interpretation of the Middle Ages only by Gibbon's work, among all the historical writings of the eighteenth century. Robertson's general attitude towards the cultural aridity of the Middle Ages was a little too harsh, though not so

---

[13] For a contemporary defense of this attitude towards history, see W. C. Abbott, *Adventures in Reputation* (Harvard University Press, 1936).

extreme as Hume's assessment. The author was antagonistic to Catholicism, though not nearly so fiercely as Voltaire. Yet he was one of the first to grasp the nature of political and institutional development in the medieval period and to emphasize leading economic and cultural influences in medieval progress, such as the Crusades, legal evolution, the growth of towns, commercial expansion, and the like. Robertson did, however, somewhat exaggerate the influence of the Crusades and he gave revived currency to the Legend of the Year 1000, which had come down from Ralph the Bald via the *Annals* of Baronius. With respect to the long and somewhat tedious body of the *Charles V*, the most notable fact was the attention paid to the "secondary" causes of the Reformation: namely, abuses in the church, excessive papal taxation, the revival of learning, the invention of printing, and so on. While it did not sufficiently emphasize the elements of nationalism and the rise of commerce and the middle class, it was the best work on the age of the Reformation written by any historian down to Robertson's period. It goes without saying that Robertson was a definite, though dignified, partisan of Luther and the Reformers.

The *History of America* was the most ambitious and the most original of Robertson's works. It also dealt with a more colorful and dramatic theme than any of his other books. The very nature of his subject compelled Robertson to depart more widely from conventional historical standards and interests and to introduce much material on manners and customs, and on the geographical background of both American aboriginal culture and the exploits of the explorers and conquerors. The *America* was weak in the discussions of the aborigines, but it was good on the life and exploits of the explorers, and really masterful for that day in the treatment of the nature and development of the Spanish imperial system. Even with the aborigines, Robertson was one of the first to suggest what has become the accepted doctrine, namely, that the American Indians came into the new world by way of the Bering Straits and Alaska. The *Disquisition on India* was a hurriedly compiled work, but it was very important in emphasizing the extent and importance of the commercial relations between East and West in antiquity and the Middle Ages.

Far the best known and most distinguished of the Rationalist writers as a historian was Edward Gibbon (1737-94). He was less original as a historian and less influential on the course of subsequent historical writing than Voltaire, and not superior to Robertson as a conscientious scholar. Yet his reputation as a historian, with the learned public outside of professional historians, far outruns that of either Voltaire or Robertson. This unique repute of Gibbon as a historian was due to a number of circumstances. His theme of the decline of Roman civilization and imperial institutions was one designed to capture the popular imagination. His enterprise was on the grand or epic scale. He organized his work with great skill, and his style was polished, pleasing and impressive. Moreover, his work was so surprisingly accurate, considering its period, that it proved reliable and usable for a century and a half. The *Decline and Fall of the Roman Empire* was not only popular; it has become immortal.

Gibbon, unlike any other of the major Rationalist historians, devoted his life mainly to historical reading and the writing of history. Voltaire was a man of letters, a publicist and reformer, Hume a philosopher, Robertson a clergyman and university principal, but Gibbon more or less consciously prepared himself for the career of a historian from his youth onward. Gibbon read widely on classical and medieval history for many years, but he used mainly the best printed sources. He had little interest in research in manuscripts. He had a lofty idea of the historian as the architect of a great literary and scholarly enterprise, and only supreme contempt for the mere copyist or research clerk, who has become the historian *par excellence* in our day. While his judgment as to the superiority of the real historian over the plodding compiler of monographs may have been correct, he did not appreciate fully enough that "histories" are possible only when the previous spade work has been done by the monograph compilers.

Gibbon had steeped himself in Roman antiquities and his original plan was to write a history of Rome down to Augustus. But in 1764 he decided to turn his attention to the history of Rome from Augustus to the fall of the Eastern Roman Empire in 1453. The great classic which resulted was called *The History of the Decline and Fall of the Roman Empire* (1776-88). It was fairly detailed for the period from A.D. 180 to A.D. 641, and then it provided a summary sketch of developments from 641 to 1453. But it swept into view later developments. For example, a classic summary of the cultural and institutional results of the Reformation is contained in Gibbon's *Decline and Fall*.

Gibbon's work was less definitely philosophical in tone than most other major works of the Rationalist historians. It was more of a literary epic. Gibbon gave more attention to the form and style of his work than to its pragmatic philosophical implications. So deep has been the impression of the general character of Gibbon's enterprise on the minds of men that the *Decline and Fall* has been described through the use of many and varied figures of speech. It has been compared to a brilliant rear-guard action, a Roman triumph, a grand *levée* of Louis XIV, a great Gothic cathedral, a rocky promontory over which break the waves of time, a lofty mountain range shifting in appearance with changes of light and shade—and so on. The style has been equally admired. Frederic Harrison wrote of Gibbon: "He was the consummate literary artist, who transmutes mountains of exact research into a complex mass glowing with life in all its parts, and glorious to contemplate as a whole." Perhaps the best brief summary of Gibbon's literary qualities, one of the outstanding aspects of his work as a whole, has been prepared by Professor Black:

> The gravity and dignity, the pomp and circumstance of the utterance are in keeping with the grandeur of the theme. . . . . Gibbon will not say the plain truth in a plain way, exactly as he perceives it. He must perforce pass it through a series of mysterious and complex processes, which polish, refine, and enrich, until eventually it emerges bedecked and bejewelled and splendid beyond recognition. But those who are in a mind to read the *Decline and Fall* as it was intended to be read—with intentness and deliberation, and with a due regard for the play of the author's wit— there is no more fascinating document in the world. In spite of its great length, and the imposing erudition which sometimes breaks through the crust and disconcerts the general reader, its buoyancy and animation are remarkable. The specific gravity of the style is so high that it seems capable of floating anything, from the interminable Persian and Byzantine wars to the abstruse theological disputes of the early Church and the technicalities of Justinian's legal reforms.[14]

It seems that Gibbon was influenced deeply by the major historians of Rome. From Livy he derived a notion of the eloquent flow of an epic narrative, from Tacitus a philosophical and pragmatic attitude towards historical materials, and from Polybius a high regard for accuracy and the broad understanding of public affairs. The notions of these historians towards the subject matter of history also affected Gibbon. He contended that "wars and the administration of public affairs" should be the major theme of history. Some material on social, economic and cultural history was introduced in Gibbon's narrative, but it was wholly incidental. Moreover, his "baroque style" was ill adapted to the handling of this type of historical subject matter.

Gibbon was passionately devoted to Rome and its history. He regarded its fall as a world calamity. In spite of his voluminous treatment, however, there was no systematic analysis of the fall of Rome. Gibbon recognized and described most of the causes now listed by specialists, but he did not weld them into a consistent theory of the decline of Rome. His most comprehensive explanation, derived perhaps from Montesquieu, was that the Roman Empire became too large, but he did not make it clear that largeness was fatal mainly because of the lack of contemporary methods of industry, transportation and communication. Gibbon wrote too early to sense this.

One of the most original and commendable of the innovations in Gibbon's work was his treatment of the origins of Christianity, for which he was admirably prepared by both study and personal experience. He had

14 Black, *op. cit.*, pp. 144, 175.

been successively a Protestant, a Catholic and a Deist. It was as the latter that he wrote the *Decline and Fall*. He was not as fiercely opposed to Christianity as Bury and some of his other interpreters have alleged. He adopted Hume's notion that one should look at religion as he would at any other social institution—in a naturalistic fashion. He treated the rise of Christianity, for the first time, in a fully objective manner. He accounted for its growth and development as he would have treated the evolution of any other religion or any secular institution; in short he dealt with the problem historically and not theologically. There was no assumption of its uniqueness or of any supernatural aid. As to the historical effects of Christianity, Gibbon was naturally critical and hostile. He regarded the Roman Empire as the greatest creation of mankind and felt that Christianity had played an important part in weakening and undermining it. Hence, he could not avoid being antagonistic to it. Yet he paid a tribute to its cohesive and sustaining powers, once the secular empire had disintegrated. And he understood clearly the cultural services of the Church during the Middle Ages, though, as a Rationalist, he could not hold in high regard the Age of Faith. Gibbon was also one of the first writers in Christendom to deal with the rise of Islam and with Muslim services to civilization in a reasonably fair and discerning fashion. And even if he made some mistakes in his interpretation of Byzantine history, it was a novelty and a contribution not to ignore it altogether, as most historians of the Middle Ages had done and as many of them have continued to do since his day.

It is a tribute to Gibbon's industry and scholarship that, over a century and a half after his work appeared, it is still highly regarded by scholars and, in conjunction with the critical and supplementary notes of Professor Bury, is today perhaps the best, and certainly the most readable general survey of the broad field which he covered.

Several lesser works showed the influence of Rationalism on historical writing in England. One of them was the *History of England* by Richard Henry (1718-90), originally planned in ten volumes. It was intended to be a great *Kulturgeschichte,* in which much attention would be paid to cultural, social and economic history. It was executed fairly faithfully and was a great departure from the usual political history. But the plan was laid out in a mechanical fashion, more like an encyclopedia than a historical work, and it was extremely dry reading, as such compilations are almost bound to be. While Henry was a Rationalist and sceptical of Christianity, he showed a great deal of credulity in dealing with pagan and biblical traditions and fables. He brought his book down only to 1547, from whence it was continued to 1603 by James Petit Andrews. The Rationalist history of Europe was adapted for youth in a pleasing manual by William Russell, in his *History of Modern Europe from the Fall of the Ro-*

man Empire to 1763 (1779-84). It was written in the form of letters from a nobleman to his son, and introduced much cultural and social history, though by no means as much as had been promised. It was a popular treatise for over half a century. Another popular manual of a comparable spirit, but covering world history, was Alexander Fraser Tytler's *Elements of General History* (1801), which attempted, without great success, to explain political history in terms of non-political influences. The author did, however, cleverly combine the topical and chronological arrangements. An interesting effort to harmonize the Rationalist and the providential philosophy of history appeared in the *Lecture on History* by the ardent Unitarian scientist and philosopher, Joseph Priestly (1733-1804). We shall have occasion to deal with Adam Ferguson's works a little further on.

A more considerable work was the four-volume treatment of the great Civil War and the Commonwealth by William Godwin (1756-1836), the eminent Rationalist, *The History of the Commonwealth of England*. If Godwin was frank in expressing judgments, he exercised independence and let his criticism fall on both sides. He felt that Charles I was one of the world's greatest criminals, but believed that his execution was a strategic blunder, helping to make the Restoration inevitable. He thought that Cromwell betrayed the friends of liberty and republicanism, but he paid a tribute to his ability and believed that if he had lived for another ten years he might have founded a new English dynasty.

A worthy disciple of Voltaire in England was William Roscoe (1753-1831), who wished to fill in the gap between the great histories of Gibbon and Robertson. Consequently, he devoted himself to a study of the Medici and the Renaissance popes, whom he admired as patrons of the arts and sciences. His major works were biographies of Lorenzo de' Medici and Pope Leo X, but they were in reality surveys of the history and culture of the age. Roscoe contrasted the glories of this period with what he regarded as the gloom and fanaticism of both medieval Catholicism and Reformation Protestantism.

While he formally believed in the workings of Providence in history and was of Protestant affiliations, Henry Hallam (1777-1859) really belonged in the tradition of Gibbon and the Rationalists. He had the same philosophic attitude towards the past, believing that history should teach a lesson to the present, shared the Rationalist depreciation of the culture of the Middle Ages, and showed a real interest in the history of society, thought and culture. He also resembled Robertson and Gibbon in his scholarly attributes. He was a learned gentleman, who studied informally, rather than a follower of the new critical research methods of men on the Continent like Niebuhr and von Ranke. But he was even more widely read in historical materials than Gibbon or Robertson and rather more faithful to his sources.

Hallam's first notable work was a general survey of medieval history from Clovis to Charles VIII in three volumes, *A View of the State of Europe During the Middle Ages* (1818). It was the first historical treatise in western Europe to rival Gibbon in impressiveness and scope. While inferior to Gibbon in style and color, it was much superior as an institutional history of the medieval period. Hallam rigorously excluded anecdotes, episodes and the personal interpretation of history, and devoted himself to institutional progress. The major defect of the work lay in the fact that the chapters of his book dealing with the various countries were separate monographs rather than a comparative study of European institutions during the medieval period. His judgment of the Middle Ages, while not actively hostile, was cold and unsympathetic, except for medieval England, which he admired and to which he gave disproportionate space. This was the main nationalistic strain in his work. Hallam's affinity with the Rationalist notion of the scope of history was to be discerned in his excursion into *Kulturgeschichte* in his concluding section on the general character of European civilization.

Most critics rate his *Constitutional History of England* from Henry VII to George III (2 vols., 1827) as Hallam's ablest work. It represented the Whig viewpoint, but was written from a detached, austere and sceptical point of view. He presented both sides of controversial periods and issues and advanced far beyond Hume in both knowledge and insight. With this book English constitutional and party history attained a new high level of dignity and reliability. Hallam's Whig preconceptions could be discerned in the fact that his main thesis was that England had always been fundamentally a constitutional monarchy, suffering periodic lapses into absolutism or anarchy. Hallam's longest work, and his major contribution to the history of thought and culture, was his four-volume *Introduction to the Literature of Europe in the Fifteenth, Sixteenth and Seventeenth Centuries,* for its time an unrivaled panorama of European intellectual and cultural history. Henry Thomas Buckle, who was a late echo of extreme English Rationalism, will be dealt with later in connection with the rise of the philosophy of history.[15]

In Germany, Voltaire found three followers in von Schlözer, Schmidt, and Spittler. August Ludwig von Schlözer (1735-1809) produced an ambitious excursion into *Universal History* of a rather schematic and wooden type, accepting the conventional date of creation. His main work was done in the history of Slavonic Europe, where he found his ideal in the enlightened despotism of Catherine II. His *History of Russia* appeared in 1769, and his *General History of the North* was published in 1772. They

[15] See below, p. 202.

were probably the best existing works on Slavonic Europe. Von Schlözer had limited powers of criticism, especially in regard to biblical matters, and had slight historical imagination and an unattractive style, but he was far the ablest philologist of the Rationalist school. He was also the outstanding apologist for enlightened despotism among Rationalist historians.

What Voltaire did for France, Hume for England, and Robertson for Scotland, was done for Germany by Michael Ignatz Schmidt (1736-94). His *German History,* to 1660, was one of the most finished products of Rationalism in historical literature. His style was excellent; he was cautious and accurate in the use of his sources; he was free from chauvinism; he was one of the first to handle the German Reformation in an impartial manner; and the scope of his work resembled Voltaire's in being a real history of civilization.

The smaller German states and the Christian church found their Rationalist historian in Ludwig Timotheus Spittler (1752-1810), author of histories of the lesser German states, a *Survey of the History of the European States* (1793), and a *History of the Christian Church* (1782). His work was at its best in dealing with the period nearest to his own day. He idealized the Middle Ages, and to him was due in part the origin of that rosy and romantic conception of the medieval period as one in which the main events were tournaments and the chief figures were the knights, *troubadours* and *minnesingers.* This became a popular idea with the Romanticist school later. Spittler was the first writer to handle the whole history of the Church from the Rationalist standpoint. His criticism was relatively mild, and he adopted the peculiar attitude of judging the Church from the standpoint of an instrument for advancing the cause of Rationalism. This attitude, as Fueter points out, was more of a contribution to historical humor than to historical scholarship or illumination.

An abler historian of the Church was Gottlieb Jakob Planck (1751-1833). Spittler had treated the history of the Church from the personal and episodical point of view. Planck dealt with it from the standpoint of the history of ideas and institutions. His *History of the Christian Constitution of Society* was an able study of the political organization of the medieval Church, the relations between church and state, and the efforts of the Church to assert its ascendency over the state. Planck also wrote extensively on the history of Protestant doctrine and theology, especially stressing the uniqueness of the Protestant notions of Christianity. He was, in a way, the founder of the comparative study of the Protestant denominations, superseding the partisan and hostile work of Bossuet. Planck was one of the more extreme believers, among Rationalist historians, in the accidental theory of history. In regard to the Reformation, he held that its accidental character proved that Providence must have been in favor of the outcome.

THE SCHOOL OF MONTESQUIEU

The rather advanced Rationalism of Voltaire and his school could scarcely gain general acceptance and sustained success in the eighteenth century, when it was far more advanced than the general level of contemporary thought. It had also some limitations inseparable from the first courageous attempt to reconstruct history and to bring it in harmony with the contemporary progress in scientific thought and social philosophy. It was natural, then, that there should be a reaction against many of its premises and methods. This was in part a recrudescence of obscurantism and in part an effort to correct some of the defects of the school of Voltaire. The stages in this reaction were gradual and clearly marked. It passed from the more moderate and conservative Rationalism of Montesquieu to the almost irrational sentimentalism of Rousseau, and ended in the mystic and idealistic vagaries of Romanticism. The school of Voltaire did not come to its own until it was revived with greater profundity by Buckle, Lecky, Morley, Leslie Stephen, Draper, White and Robinson, as a result of the reaction of nineteenth-century science and critical thought upon historical writing.

While Montesquieu's own works, as examples of historical criticism and investigation, were of no great value, his broader attitude toward general methodology was of the utmost significance. He was not at all violent or revolutionary in his political theory, and his literary affinities were with Humanism rather than Rationalism. He did, however, present certain phases of thought which were a marked improvement over Voltaire's notions. Accepting Voltaire's unanalyzed doctrine of the genius of a people, he tried to show how this was produced by the operation of natural forces, particularly climate influences. He first brought out clearly the fundamental proposition that the excellence of social institutions must be judged, not by an arbitrary and absolute standard, but by their relative adaptability to the spirit of the people whom they serve. Again, where Voltaire and his followers had dropped little more than casual observations, Montesquieu offered a synthesis of the various factors of historical development, which, though crude and incomplete, marked a considerable methodological advance. Finally, while the school of Voltaire had merely suggested the treatment of economic factors in connection with political development, Montesquieu and his followers laid much stress upon the profound influence of commercial and fiscal activities in the life of the state. The school of Montesquieu most faithfully represented the reaction of the Commercial Revolution on European historiography.

Montesquieu's own major excursion into history was a long essay on *The Causes of the Greatness and the Decadence of the Romans* (1734). It illustrated no advances in criticism of the sources or in scholarship. But it did give evidence of amazing power in interpreting the major trends and factors in Roman development and decline. He anticipated most of the chief explanations given today by specialists relative to the growth and disintegration of Roman politics and imperial power—laying special stress on the fact that the Empire grew too large and unwieldy for its economy. He was conspicuously a writer who did not let the trees obscure his vision of the forests. His notions of Roman decline had much influence on the writings of Gibbon.[16]

Since Montesquieu was primarily a political philosopher rather than a historian, his disciples were as numerous among the political theorists as among the avowed historians. J. L. De Lolme's *Constitution of England* and Adam Ferguson's *History of Civil Society* were works that most clearly exhibited the principles of Montesquieu in the field of political philosophy.

De Lolme's *Constitution of England* was first published in 1770. It followed Montesquieu's imaginative analysis in finding in the government of England a definite separation of governmental powers—executive, legislative and judicial—and in seeing therein the chief guaranty of individual liberty. De Lolme believed that the safety of the citizen is best assured by equality of laws and certainty of enforcement. He heartily opposed Rousseau's idea of government through the popular will. He held that the people are invariably victims of "the silent, powerful and ever-active conspiracy of those who govern."

Adam Ferguson, a Scotch social philosopher, wrote a *History of the Progress and Termination of the Roman Republic* (1782). He rivaled Montesquieu's power of reaching essentials in interpretation. He pointed out clearly the highly conjectural character of Roman history in the early period. He especially emphasized the institutional reactions of the Roman conquests and showed how the Republican system was no longer adequate for the crisis of the times. But his adamant libertarianism made Ferguson incapable of judging fairly those who wished to overthrow the republic and create the needed imperialistic system. Especially ridiculous was his eulogy of the venal and shortsighted Roman Senate of the last century of the republic. Ferguson's earlier *History of Civil Society* (1765) was the best account of social evolution ever written down to that time. It marked the real beginnings of historical sociology. He particularly stressed the importance of wars in early political progress.

If Montesquieu had few disciples among professional historians, he had at least one of the highest order in Arnold Hermann Ludwig Heeren

---

[16] For an admirable summary of Montesquieu's generalizations on Roman history, see Smith, *History of Modern Culture*, II, 265. See also Moritz Ritter, *Die Entwicklung der Geschichtswissenschaft* (Munich, 1919), pp. 210-32.

(1760-1842), one of that brilliant group of Göttingen professors of his period. His great work was entitled *Reflections Concerning the Politics, Intercourse and Commerce of the Leading Nations of Antiquity*. Its principles were those of Montesquieu, improved by the more scientific analysis of economic life which was embodied in the works of Adam Smith. With great skill Heeren attempted to reconstruct the commercial life of antiquity and to indicate its hitherto unsuspected influence upon the course of the history of the several ancient nations. Heeren was one of the best writers among the historians of his time. Abandoning all attempts at rhetorical flourish, he produced a most thoughtful work, written with clarity and coherence. Eduard Meyer, one of the ablest authorities on the history of the ancient nations, has called Heeren the pioneer among those who have attempted to deal with this field. Heeren's approach to history, linked up with contemporary scholarly methods, reappeared in Wilhelm von Heyd's *History of Commerce with the Levant in the Middle Ages* (1879). The comparative and geographical approach of Montesquieu to political problems was reflected in Heeren's *Handbook of the History of the European State Systems and their Colonies*. Heeren inspired Pertz's study of medieval sources, Waitz's work on constitutional history, and Ritter's interest in political geography.

Two British writers also illustrated Montesquieu's emphasis on the influence of commerce. Adam Anderson wrote a useful *Historical and Chronological Deduction of the Origin of Commerce* (1764), the medieval sections of which were rewritten and amplified by David Macpherson early in the nineteenth century. Macpherson also wrote a comprehensive and broadly conceived *History of European Trade with India* (1812). In the latter part of his work he resembled Raynal in considering the relation of the expansion of Europe to European civilization and the well-being of the human race.

Another historical disciple of Montesquieu was the Scotch historian, Gilbert Stuart (1742-86), a brilliant but erratic writer. He protested against the unsympathetic attitude towards the Middle Ages which had been taken by Hume and Robertson. In his *Historical Dissertation* on the English constitution, and his *View of European Society* he eulogized the alleged democratic political institutions of the primitive Germans and claimed that Anglo-Saxon England was purely Teutonic. He believed that the English constitution really originated in the backwoods of Germany. He was, thus, a forerunner of the Germanicists of the next century in England. He admired the early Middle Ages more than the later medieval period. He composed a whole series of works on the history of Scotland, designed to combat the views and interpretations given by Robertson in his *History of Scotland*.

ROUSSEAU'S DISCIPLES

Much less sound was another variation of the Rationalist school, that which followed the lead of Rousseau and formed the logical transition from Rationalism to Romanticism. There were a number of important differences between Rousseau and Voltaire in their attitude toward historical and social problems. In the first place, Voltaire was purely intellectual and critical and little moved by sentiment; Rousseau was almost pathologically emotional, sympathetic and sentimental. In the second place, Voltaire was realistic and practical; Rousseau was idealistic and utopian. Finally, Voltaire wrote from the standpoint of the *bourgeoisie,* praised enlightened despotism, and had little faith in the political ability of the illiterate masses; Rousseau wrote as an ardent exponent of the release of the masses from despotic political power.

Until the period of the French Revolution, Rousseau's views gained little currency in France, but in Germany he found several enthusiastic disciples. The first of Rousseau's German disciples was Isaak Iselin (1728-82), author of two volumes of *Philosophical Conjectures on the History of Humanity.* Iselin was also intrigued by the political doctrines of Montesquieu. The influence of Rousseau was manifest in the extended attention which Iselin gave to primitive society. Except for the writings of Lafiteau, his book was perhaps the best analysis of primitive culture and institutions that had yet appeared, though he fallaciously tried to distinguish between the state of nature and the savage state of man. Iselin's devotion to Montesquieu appeared in the extensive attention he gave to a comparative analysis of the civilization, manners and customs of the major peoples of history.

The most attractive of Rousseau's German disciples in the field of history was the poet-dramatist-historian, Freidrich Schiller (1759-1805), whose chief works were the *History of Rebellion of the Netherlands against the Spanish Rule,* and *The History of the Thirty Years' War.* His works presented a combination of the sentiment and pathos of Rousseau with the native powers of a great dramatist and poet. In his somewhat rhetorical history of the Dutch revolt he found an epic theme of deliverance from oppression, while in the description of the Thirty Years' War he saw in Gustavus Adolphus and Wallenstein the central figures of a great historical drama. It scarcely needs to be pointed out that in his masterly dramatic exercises there was little place for prosaic description of economic and cultural factors. He had great power in clear preliminary analysis of political movements, such as his remarkable account of the background of the Thirty Years' War. Once his narrative got under way, however, the poet and dramatist gained almost complete control over the historian, and his work, like that of Carlyle, was a contribution to great literature rather than to scientific history. As a stylist, Schiller imitated the Humanists more than the Rationalists.

A much more influential historian among his contemporaries, but incomparably inferior in every sense to Schiller, was Johannes Müller (1752-1809), once regarded as the ablest Germanic historian of his era. Indeed, he regarded himself as a second Tacitus. As Tacitus had eulogized the Roman republic, so Müller extolled a fictitious, glorified Middle Ages and advocated a return to its ideals and institutions. His most famous work was the *History of the Swiss Confederation*. Though possessing a memory rivaling Macaulay's and a zeal for the study of sources comparable to that of Fustel de Coulanges, he wholly lacked Macaulay's power of analysis, organization and narrative, and had none of the critical power of Fustel. Though he read all the available sources, he not only failed to possess the power to discriminate in their use or to digest them, but was also so devoid of critical power as to be unable to detect and exclude glaring contradictions in his own narrative.

These contradictions were in part due to the rapidly shifting nature of his own interests and convictions. To Rousseau's sentimental devotion to liberty he added a pedantic imitation of classical rhetoric. His Swiss history became an epic of freedom, combining the methods of Rousseau and Tacitus. Then he later became an admirer of Napoleon the conqueror. Müller's treatment of medieval Germany and Switzerland also helped along the trend towards hero worship and local color in the interpretation of the Middle Ages which became so popular with Chateaubriand, Walter Scott, and the Romanticists.[17] Combined with this was his admiration for the paternalistic medieval church. His work marked a transition from Rationalism to Romanticism in historical writing. Müller's *Twenty-four Books of General History,* planned but never completed, were significant only in their ambitious scope and in their emphasis on the hand of God in history.

Rather a representative of several of the phases of the Rationalist historiography than a complete disciple of Rousseau was Johann Gottfried Herder (1744-1803), important chiefly as one of the founders of the philosophy of history. His notable work—*Ideas for the Philosophy of the History of Humanity*—was a composite of many current doctrines. It combined Rousseau's exaggerated enthusiasm for the state of nature and freedom from authority, Voltaire's conception of the reality and permanence of national character, Montesquieu's doctrine of the relation between national character and physical environment, and the mystical conception, later elaborated by Hegel, of the gradual development of humanity toward a state of freedom. He had an evolutionary outlook, and he is

[17] See below, pp. 181 ff.

credited with being the "father of the historical sense" in Germany. His particular emphasis upon the uniqueness of national character and the organic unity of cultural evolution put him in direct line with the Romanticists and stimulated the trend towards nationalistic sentiment in historical writing. We shall consider his philosophy of history later.[18]

Friedrich Christoph Schlosser (1776-1861) took over Rousseau's conceptions through the mediation of Kant's "categorical imperative." In his *History of the Iconoclastic Emperors*, his unfinished *History of the World*, and his major work, *A History of the Eighteenth and Nineteenth Centuries*, he anticipated the position of Lord Acton that history should judge men sharply according to high moral standards. He passed judgment on historical events and public figures according to the principles of the Kantian precepts of individual morality. His work had a somber cast, due to his inordinate passion for Dante's *Divine Comedy*, and his books were full of harsh and hasty criticisms of a purely subjective nature. He was not a critical scholar, his treatment of political history was superficial, and he ignored social and economic history. His chief significance as a historian lies in the fact that he was one of the first notable writers to lay great emphasis upon the political importance and influence of a national literature. Schlosser's outlook had its greatest value years afterwards when scholars used it to correct the notions of Burckhardt and Symonds as to the uniqueness of the Renaissance and its separation from medieval culture.

Rousseau's devotion to liberty was reflected in the long *Universal History* of Karl von Rotteck (1775-1840). Rotteck fiercely attacked all suppressions of liberty in the human past, with the aim of combating the raids upon liberty by Napoleon, and by the reactionaries at the Congress of Vienna and thereafter. A brilliant and fervent writer, Rotteck's book became "the bible of Liberal Europe." It went through twenty-five editions by 1866 and was widely translated into other languages. Rotteck devoted himself mainly to political science in the later years of his life.

One of the ablest of Rationalist historians, Jean Charles Leonard Simonde de Sismondi (1773-1842) of Switzerland, is difficult to classify with any school. He had Voltaire's admiration for the *bourgeoisie*, he was impressed by Montesquieu's emphasis on the importance of commerce and economic factors in the development of civilization, he was fired with Rousseau's love of liberty, and he admired Gibbon greatly as a stylist. But he did not share the contempt of Voltaire or Gibbon for the Middle Ages, he rejected Montesquieu's emphasis on geographical factors, he departed from the democratic notions of Rousseau, and he had a far broader view of the content of history than Gibbon. His *History of the Italian Republics of the Middle Ages* praised the spirit of independence of the Italian city-

[18] See below, pp. 193-94.

states and showed its importance for their commercial supremacy. To Sismondi, the growth of the Italian communes marked "the rise of human liberty out of the muck of feudal degradation and tyranny." He gave more attention to commercial and other economic factors than any other Rationalist historian except Heeren. But he was not so clear on the re-action of economic factors on medieval political life. He could not discern their full effect on the politics of the medieval Italian cities. All in all, he reflected the attitude of the French Revolution towards medieval and Ren-aissance Italy, in the same way that Machiavelli and Guicciardini applied the spirit of the Renaissance to their age.

Sismondi's *History of the French* was especially good on the Middle Ages and showed the same broad attitude towards the subject matter of history. It was the first fairly complete history of France. Sismondi was also much interested in literature and wrote an important book on the history of southern European literature which reflected the influence of Madame de Staël. In this he revealed sympathies with Romanticism by portraying literature as the product of national character. Sismondi was a careful scholar for his time and, if he did not rival Gibbon as a literary artist, he wrote in a clear and dignified manner.

UNIVERSAL HISTORY

One of the most interesting developments promoted by the historical writing of the age of discoveries and Rationalism was the increasing popularity of world histories. Aside from the dry and stereotyped world chronicles which began with Africanus, Eusebius and Jerome, the only true world histories produced in Western Europe had been those of Orosius and those written during the period of Humanism by Sabellicus and Doglioni in Italy, François de Belleforest in France, Johannes Clüver in Holland, and Sir Walter Raleigh in England. And these were poor apologies for a universal history.

Then, at about the middle of the eighteenth century, world histories began to appear in ever increasing number, most of them very volumi-nous. This trend grew out of a number of influences. Humanism had aroused interest in classical antiquity. The Reformation and counter-Reformation had promoted concern with the history of the Christian church. The histories of the discoveries had given a world-wide scope to the vision of historians. The Rationalists had set the pace for ambitious historical projects. It was only natural that writers with imagination would aspire to bring together the whole story of man on this planet in a single historical enterprise. The first of these efforts to produce a universal history was the coöperative *Universal History from the Earliest Account of Time to the Present* (1736-65), compiled by a number of scholars, chiefly English. Among them were John Campbell, George Sale, John

Swinton, Archibald Bower and George Psalmanazar. While not a brilliant or independent work, it presented an unparalleled body of materials on all peoples in all ages, including those overseas. It was written from an orthodox Christian point of view, for the most part, and showed little critical power in handling biblical and antique myths. But it was the first reasonably complete world history ever written, it was fairly popular, and it helped greatly to introduce a more expansive conception of the history of the human race.

We have mentioned many of the other world histories of the next half-century or more in connection with the names of the various Rationalist historians who were their authors. It will suffice to enumerate them and others, in order to give some idea of their number and ambitious character. Two British writers contributed world histories after the original composite product, John Adams' *View of Universal History* (1795), and Alexander Tytler's *Elements of General History* (1801). August Schlözer's *Lectures on Universal History* appeared in 1772; Jacob Daniel Wegelin's *Universal History,* in 1775; Johannes Müller's incomplete *Twenty-four Books of General History,* in 1779; Johann Christoph Gatterer's immensely popular and relatively able *World History* in 1785-87; Karl Rotteck's *Universal History,* between 1812 and 1827; Cesare Cantu's *Universal History,* in 1837; Friedrich Schlosser's *World History for the German People,* between 1844 and 1856; François Laurent's *Studies on the History of Humanity,* in 1870; and Leopold von Ranke's *World History* was completed by one of his students after his death. Some of these were of great length, Rotteck's running to eleven volumes, Laurent's to eighteen, and Schlosser's to nineteen. There were other books of this type, but these are representative and will indicate the new interest in such works and the profusion in their production.

SCHOLARSHIP AND CHRONOLOGY

The critical attitude of scholarship was also carried to the treatment of the pagan texts and culture of antiquity. Scholars continued the work which had been launched by Scaliger, Casaubon and others in the period of Humanism. Richard Bentley (1662-1742) advanced the science of textual criticism as applied to ancient authors and prepared excellent editions of Homer and other eminent pagans. J. A. Fabricus put the study of Greek literature on a scientific basis, and Bernard de Montfaucon (1657-1741) brought together a general anthology of classical literature in his *Antiquité Expliquée.* The rise of the doctrine of progress served to dispel the reverential attitude towards the pagan past which had been encouraged by the more sentimental brand of Humanism. The new attitude was not the hostility of Orosius, but a sane view of pagan antiquity, disciplined by the historical outlook and the notion of the progress of culture. The critical study of the sources of ancient history in this period by Sigonius, Pouilly, Perizonius, Beaufort and others will be discussed later in connection with the rise of critical historical scholarship.[19]

Chronological studies were pursued along the lines laid down by Scaliger and Usher. Sir Isaac Newton gave attention to the problem in his *Chronologies of the Ancient Kingdoms,* but he revised the date of Creation in the wrong direction by placing it about 500 years nearer our time than had Scaliger and Usher. But others were making faint advances towards the expansive computations of our own day. The Deists, beginning with Charles Blount, being less held down by orthodox Christian conceptions and more influenced by the new science, were cordial towards longer estimates of time than Usher and his followers. Above all, the natural historians and geologists were coming to see that the orthodox date of Creation could not be harmonized at all with scientific notions of the history and age of our planet and of the life thereupon. The great French naturalist, Buffon, estimated that the earth must have an age of seventy-five thousand years.

This period also produced the conventional notions of historical periodization which are still accepted.[20] The general comprehension of two main periods in the human past, pagan antiquity and the Christian era, had been implicit in the Christian views of history. These two divisions were gradually transformed into Ancient History and the Middle Ages. The writers most influential in putting over this notion were Otto of Freising and Flavius Blondus. We have already noted Bodin's division of history into Oriental, Mediterranean and north European stages. The rise of Humanism and the Protestant Reformation suggested to other writers who lived after these events that perhaps a new era had dawned in the fifteenth or sixteenth centuries. There might be a modern age. This threefold division of history, which is still conventionally used, was first set forth by Gisebert Voëtius (1588-1676) in connection with church history. He suggested that there was an ancient period which came down to Augustine, an intermediate age from Augustine to Luther, and a new era since Luther's time. This notion was carried over to universal secular history by a Dutch Humanist, Christoph Keller (better known as Christian Cellarius, 1634-1717). He placed ancient history from Creation to Constantine, the Middle Ages between Constantine and the capture of Constantinople by the Turks in 1453, and modern history since 1453. These divisions are still more widely accepted than any other dating. By the time of Raynal many writers were coming to look upon the discoveries following 1492 as

[19] See below, pp. 240 ff.
[20] See also below, pp. 330-31.

more important than the Renaissance or Reformation in launching the modern era, but a wide acceptance of this notion did not come until the twentieth century.

THE ORIGINS OF THE THEORY OF PROGRESS

One of the most striking contributions of this age to a more truly historical attitude towards the human past was the gradual rise of an idea of progress. It is a significant fact that more than ninety-nine per cent of the period of man's existence upon the planet was passed through without any consciousness of the actual progress of human culture. Human development as far as the seventeenth century was natural and spontaneous, and in no sense the result of the collective effort to realize any conscious ideal of racial and cultural advancement.

The ancient Jews, holding to the doctrine of the Fall of Man, therefore believed perfection to be found in the past rather than to be sought in the future. The ancient pagans shared to some degree a comparable notion, namely, the dogma of a decline from a golden age. Even more popular with the Greeks and Romans was the conception of the cyclical nature of human development. Culture would rise to a certain point and then decline to a level comparable to that which had existed at the beginning. Then the process would start all over again and the cycle would be repeated. The Christians took over the Jewish notion of the Fall of Man and combined it with the pagan view of the decline from a golden age. Man could never expect any Utopia here on earth. The state of blessedness was to be attained only in the world to come. The final judgment and the end of things earthly was, according to the Christian view as stated in the Book of Revelation, to be preceded by unusually horrible and devastating earthly portents.

Gradually, however, there arose the conviction that better things might be in store for humanity here on this earth. Back in the thirteenth century Roger Bacon had a vision of what applied science might do for man. Montaigne had a glimmering of a new idea when he suggested that philosophy should be concerned with human happiness here on earth rather than with salvation in the life to come. Francis Bacon, Pascal, and Descartes united in decrying the authority of the past. Bacon and Pascal contended that the moderns were superior to the ancients and suggested that Utopia might be secured through applying science to human problems.

The doctrine of progress as it is conventionally understood began, however, with men like Bernard de Fontenelle (1657-1757). In his *Dialogues of the Dead* (1683) Fontenelle hardly went beyond the contention that the ancients were no better than the moderns, but five years later in his *Digression on the Ancients and the Moderns* he took a more advanced position. He held that the ancients and the moderns are essentially alike in a biological sense, there being no progress in this respect. In the fine arts, which are chiefly a spontaneous expression of the human spirit, there seems to be no law of progress. The ancient peoples achieved great things here, but the best modern works in art, poetry, and oratory equal the most perfect ancient examples. On the other hand, in science and industry we find an altogether different story. In these fields development is cumulative. There has been vast progress since antiquity and even greater things may be looked for in the future. Moreover, Fontenelle proceeded to state that unreasoning admiration for the ancients is a major obstacle to progress. It is doubtful if anybody, even in our own day, has more successfully stated the general principles involved in the problem of what we call progress than did Fontenelle.

Charles Perrault (1628-1703) was a contemporary of Fontenelle and expressed very much the same view in his *Parallel of the Ancients and Moderns* (1688-96). But he was so much impressed by what he regarded as the perfection of the culture of his own generation that he was not much concerned with future progress—if, indeed, he would have conceded that anything could be better than his own age. A more positive attitude towards future progress was taken by the Abbé de Saint-Pierre in his *Discours sur la polysynodie* (1718). He contended that progress was real and that the achievements of his own age were more notable than those of the era of Plato and Aristotle. He was particularly interested in social progress, and believed in the desirability of an academy of political science to guide social advance. He placed great faith in the power of a wise government and was a forerunner of Helvétius and the Utilitarians. Helvétius, who flourished in the middle of the eighteenth century, was the foremost of the French social optimists of this period. He believed thoroughly in the possibility of human perfection and thought it could be achieved effectively through universal enlightenment and rational education. He believed in the equality of man, and held that existing inequalities could be eliminated through education.

In the first half of the eighteenth century the Italian Giovanni Battista Vico (1668-1744), a philosopher of history,[21] worked out his conception of progress. He held that human progress does not take place directly or in a straight line. Rather, it takes the form of a spiral. There may seem to be cycles of development, but they never go back to the original starting-point. Each turn is higher than the preceding. A little later in France a more realistic historical theory of progress was worked out by Anne Robert Jacques Turgot (1729-81), himself an eminent contributor to the philosophy of history. He laid great stress upon the continuity of history and

[21] See below, pp. 192-93.

the cumulative nature of progress. He contended that the more complex the civilization, the more rapid human progress. Hence advance was extremely slow in primitive times, but has been greatly accelerated in the modern epoch. Even more optimistic was the distinguished writer of the French revolutionary period, Condorcet. He not only stated his belief in the reality of progress but presumed to divide the history of civilization into ten periods, each representing a definite stage in the development of mankind and human civilization. Nine of these periods had already been passed through, and the French Revolution and modern science were leading us to the brink of the tenth, which would produce an era of happiness and well-being the like of which had never been known.

There were other men who contributed variously to the notion of progress. The German philosopher Herder attempted to work out laws of progress based on the joint operation of nature and Providence. Immanuel Kant sought to prove the reality of moral progress. The English publicist William Godwin (1756-1836) believed that perfection might be obtained through the abolition of the state and property and the inculcation of reason through private instruction. Henri de Saint-Simon (1760-1825) followed the line of the Abbé de Saint-Pierre in holding that a definite social science must be provided to guide human progress. These notions culminated in the historical philosophy and sociology of Auguste Comte (1798-1857). He worked out a comprehensive system of "laws" concerning intellectual progress and formulated an expansive philosophy of history, embodying the division of the past into a large number of periods and subperiods, each characterized by some phase of cultural advance.

While the theory of progress has retained enthusiastic support from many since the time of Comte, pessimistic or chastened attitudes have also appeared. Some, like the German philosophers Friedrich Nietzsche and Oswald Spengler, have reverted to something similar to the doctrine of cycles characteristic of classical times. More common, however, has been the tendency to substitute the notion of change for that of progress. The latter implies that things are certainly getting better. Of this we are not now so certain, but we are aware of change in many phases of life and thought. Most important has been the recognition that change takes place rapidly in the realm of science and material culture and very slowly in institutions and morals. This discrepancy in the rate of progress as between material culture and social institutions—now called "cultural lag" —seems to have placed modern civilization in special jeopardy.[22]

[22] H. E. Barnes, *A History of Western Civilization* (Harcourt, Brace, 1935), II, 1101 ff.; and *Historical Sociology*, Part III, Philosophical Library, 1948.

SELECTED REFERENCES

J. E. Gillespie, *A History of Geographical Discovery, 1400-1800.* Holt, 1933.

M. W. Spilhaus, *The Background of Geography.* Lippincott, 1935.

A. P. Newton, ed., *Travel and Travellers of the Middle Ages.* Knopf, 1926.

Guilday, *Church Historians,* pp. 128-52.

Smith, *A History of Modern Culture,* Vol. II, chaps. vii-viii.

Flint, *Historical Philosophy in France,* pp. 234-339.

Ritter, *Die Entwicklung der Geschichtswissenschaft,* Book IV.

Wegele, *Geschichte der deutschen Historiographie,* Book III.

Fueter, *Histoire de l'historiographie moderne,* pp. 361-80, 415-516.

T. P. Peardon, *The Transition in English Historical Writing, 1760-1830.* Columbia University Press, 1933.

Adolf Rein, *Das Problem der europäischen Expansion in der Geschichtsschreibung.* Hamburg, 1929.

Geoffrey Atkinson, *Les Relations de voyages du XVIIe siècle et l'évolution des idées.* Paris, 1925.

Gilbert Chinard, *L'Amérique et la rêve exotique dans la littérature française au xvii et au xviii siècle.* Paris, 1934.

A. C. Wilgus, *Histories and Historians of Hispanic-America.* Pan American Union, 1942.

J. B. Black, *The Art of History.* Crofts, 1926.

Thompson, *History of Historical Writing,* Vol. II, chaps. xxxviii-xxxix.

H. L. Bond, *The Literary Art of Edward Gibbon.* Oxford Univ. Press, 1960.

Ferdinand Schevill, *Six Historians,* pp. 93-122. University of Chicago Press, 1956.

E. T. Oliver, *Gibbon and Rome.* Sheed and Ward, 1958.

F. E. Manuel, *The Age of Reason.* Cornell University Press, 1951.

————, *The Eighteenth Century Confronts the Gods.* Harvard University Press, 1959.

J. S. Spink, *French Free Thought from Gassendi to Voltaire.* Oxford University Press, 1960.

Romain Rolland et al., *French Thought in the Eighteenth Century.* David McKay, 1953.

J. H. Brumfitt, *Voltaire: Historian.* Oxford University Press, 1957.

R. R. Palmer, *Catholics and Unbelievers in Eighteenth Century France.* Princeton University Press, 1939.

F. C. Green, *Jean-Jacques Rousseau.* Cambridge University Press, 1955.

Friedrich Meinecke, *Die Entstehung des Historismus.* Munich, 1936. 2 vols.

G. M. Young, *Gibbon.* Appleton, 1933.

B. Pier, *Robertson als Historiker und Geschichtsphilosoph.* Leipzig, 1929.

W. C. Lehmann, *Adam Ferguson and the Beginnings of Modern Sociology.* Columbia University Press, 1930.

J. B. Bury, *The Idea of Progress.* Dover, 1955.

C. L. Becker, *The Heavenly City of the Eighteenth-Century Philosophers.* Yale University Press, 1932.

VIII

ROMANTICISM AND THE PHILOSOPHY OF HISTORY

THE REACTION OF ROMANTICISM AGAINST RATIONALISM

EVEN before Louis XVI had issued the royal edict directing an election of delegates to an Estates-General, the reaction against the frank and direct Rationalism of Voltaire had definitely commenced in the works of the disciples of Rousseau mentioned in the previous chapter. The French Revolution greatly stimulated this reaction. To the conservative element it seemed that the events of the French Revolution had finally demonstrated the futility of the Rationalist doctrines of catastrophic causation and the possibility of altering social institutions through the application of a few "self-evident dictates of pure Reason."

Unfortunately, this laudable attempt to correct the artificiality of the dogmas of Rousseau led to a reaction in the opposite direction which was even less valid and defensible than the theories of the Rationalists. Romanticism in historical writing meant a decided retrogression in the direction of obscuranticism, and was closely related to that reaction in political and social philosophy which is chiefly identified with the names of Burke, De Bonald, De Maistre and von Haller.[1]

The underlying historical premise of the historiography of Romanticism was the doctrine of the gradual and unconscious nature of cultural evolution in any nation. The Romanticists proclaimed the organic unity and unique development of all forms of national culture. There was a decidedly mystical strain in their thinking which maintained that these unconscious creative forces move and operate in a mysterious manner which defies direct intellectual analysis. It was held that cultural and constitutional development is subject to the influence of these mysterious forces of psychic power, which were later grouped by Leopold von Ranke and christened as the *Zeitgeist*. Great emphasis was laid upon national traditions and the alleged "ideas" which go to make up this spirit of the age and of the nation. These conceptions naturally led to a dogma of political fatalism, which represented the nation as powerless before the momentum of creative spiritual forces. Revolution was represented as par-

[1] Cf. W. A. Dunning, *A History of Political Theories from Rousseau to Spencer* (Macmillan, 1920), chap. v.

ticularly wicked and futile, and deserving of special condemnation. There grew up that philosophy of political "quietism," which fitted in excellently with the current laissez faire doctrines of the economists and political theorists.

Out of this tendency there developed, especially in England and the United States, that notorious and specious myth representing the Anglo-Saxon peoples as the perfect examples of political quietism and, hence, of inherent political capacity. An equally erroneous doctrine pictured the French as the typical instance of a revolutionary and unstable nation, utterly devoid of all political capacity.[2] This fundamental error did more than anything else to mar the accuracy of nineteenth century history and political philosophy, and has not even yet been fully eradicated. Again, the idea of the pure, indigenous and spontaneous nature of national culture led to a narrowing of the laudable cosmopolitan outlook of the Rationalists and to the centering of attention on national history.[3] Further, for each nation the period of particular fertility and promise for historical research was held to be the Middle Ages. This tendency was due in part to the strong conviction that this was the period of the "fixing" of the several national cultures and in part to the emotional sympathy of the Romanticists with many of the medieval mental reactions to the problems of existence and cultural development. The latter trend was also stimulated by the fact that so many Romanticists were either Catholics or were converted to Catholicism. Language was believed to be the most vital criterion of national uniqueness. This doctrine took its deepest root in Germany where language was perhaps the chief bond of nationality, and it led to the remarkable researches in philology associated with the names of Humboldt, Wolf, the brothers Grimm, and Lachmann.

In spite of their glorification of the nation, however, the historical writings of the Romanticists frequently became little more than a collection of biographies. This was due to the fact that the individual was more glamorous to them and that biography was very readily adapted to their literary flights. This trend, even in early Romanticism, shows that the Great Man theory was common long before Carlyle.

On account of the fact that the Romanticists maintained the hopelessness of any detailed intellectual analysis of historical causation, their philosophy of history ran in a vicious circle. Without giving any scientific explanation of the development of the spirit of a nation, they attributed the

[2] Cf. H. J. Ford, "The Anglo-Saxon Myth," *American Mercury*, September, 1924; and J. T. Shotwell, "The Political Capacity of the French," in *Political Science Quarterly*, March, 1909.

[3] While the emphasis of the Romanticists was distinctly nationalistic, there was also a strain of universalism in their philosophy, due in part to the fact that their interest in culture and historical philosophy had a world-wide sweep. Thus Herder collected material on the spirit of the songs of all nations and Schlegel wrote on world literature.

peculiarities of national institutions, laws, literature and government to the "genius" of the nation, and then represented national character as the product of the art, literature, laws and institutions of a people. But in spite of the semi-obscurantic tendencies and the philosophical vagaries of the Romanticists, we must give them credit for having emphasized the element of unconscious growth in historical development and for having stressed the vital truth of the organic unity of a cultural complex. There is, moreover, no escaping the fact that the Romanticists did have a broader, sounder and more truly historical conception of cultural and institutional development than the Rationalist historians as a group. And, while they romanticized and exaggerated the nature and importance of the Middle Ages, they rendered a service in correcting the Rationalist disdain for this period. It was left for Lamprecht, nearly a century later, to take over what was really valuable in the Romanticist doctrines and to work them over into his famous theory of historical development as a process of transformations and mutations within the collective psychology of both the nation and humanity.[4]

ROMANTICISM AND HISTORICAL WRITING

The expressions of Romanticism in historiography were many and varied. Its doctrines were introduced into the field of the investigation of legal origins by Edmund Burke, and were systematically employed here by Christian Haubold (1766-1824) and Karl Friedrich Eichhorn (1781-1854). The latter's *History of German Law and Institutions* was devoted primarily to the study of the growth of German law. Eichhorn, son of one of the first scientific students of oriental civilization, obtained from his teacher, Gustav Hugo (1764-1844), the idea that law is a product of national genius. Eichhorn was himself an intense patriot by reason of his experiences in the Napoleonic period and his chagrin over Jena-Auerstaedt in 1806. He proceeded to apply this nationalistic idea in a long work on the origins of Germanic law. He dealt with German law as a whole, showed its antecedents, and indicated the influence of all aspects of national culture upon its development. He particularly stressed the evolutionary character of law. His work was almost as stimulating to German nationalism as to German legal studies. Eichhorn's approach was carried further by Friedrich Karl von Savigny (1779-1861) in his *History of Roman Law in the Middle Ages*. This was a long and very scholarly work devoted to tracing the persistence of Roman law throughout the Middle Ages and to assessing its influence upon culture and institutions. He stimulated the founding of the *Zeitschrift der Savigny Stiftung*, which

[4] See below, pp. 316-17.

has published the most elaborate studies on the history of law. More an expression of Romanticism was Savigny's famous debate with Thibaut over the desirability of codifying German law. Such a notion was repugnant to a Romanticist, and Savigny vigorously attacked the proposal. His part in this memorable debate was the most able and dogmatic defense of the conception of law as the product of the national genius of a people.[5] The same point of view was embodied in *Legal Antiquities of the German Peoples* by the great philologist, Jacob Grimm (1785-1863), who used his vast knowledge of language and customs to demonstrate that law is the product of the "folk spirit."

Hitherto the Romanticist interest in law had been chiefly of a purely historical character, but Eduard Gans (1798-1839) broke with the tradition of Savigny, and, under the influence of Hegel, introduced a philosophical flavor into historical discussions of law. Working with this conception in mind, he traced the "unfolding" of the law of inheritance from ancient Chinese days to the German law of the Middle Ages. He also wrote on Roman law, indulging in several controversies with Savigny over its interpretation. It was in this period that the nationalistic interpretation of medieval origins began, involving the origins of Merovingian culture, of the manor, the towns, the guilds and the like. The German writers tended to uphold the Teutonic thesis, while the French defended the theory of the Gallo-Roman basis of medieval culture and institutions.

In the realm of literature and aesthetics the Romanticist point of view achieved notable expression in the works of the Grimm brothers, Chateaubriand, Madame de Staël, Villemain and Gervinus. The Grimm brothers gathered the incomparable collections of folk tales, fairy tales, and the like —the whole body of *Märchen* literature. François René Auguste de Chateaubriand (1768-1848), though always conservatively inclined, went through a notable intellectual transformation. He wrote his first important work, a *Historical, Political and Moral Essay on Revolutions* (1797), from the standpoint of an opponent of the French Revolution. He surveyed twelve major revolutions of the past to prove their waste, brutality and futility. But he conceded that the French Revolution was inevitable. In this work he shared the antipathy of the French *philosophes* to Christianity. Then, in 1799, he was, like Augustine, converted to Christianity at the death of his mother, and went through an equally overwhelming mental change. His emotions broke through their earlier bonds, and in 1802 his *Genius of Christianity* appeared. In this Chateaubriand stressed the powerful inspiration of Christianity to art and poetry and its stimulus to human progress and perfectibility. The book was characterized by beautiful verbal imagery, especially in its descriptions of nature. Chateau-

---

[5] See A. W. Small, *Origins of Sociology* (University of Chicago Press, 1925), chap. ii.

briand had visited the new world and made the most of his knowledge and observations and even more of his imagination. The thesis of *The Genius of Christianity* was further illustrated from history in a work on early Christianity, *The Martyrs* (1809). It was characterized by pious sentimentality, eulogy of the early Christians, and magnificent descriptions, especially of the forests of ancient Gaul, the life of the Christians in the catacombs, and Roman civilization under the empire. Chateaubriand exerted a powerful influence in creating an interest in pictorial description and in a sentimental version of Christian origins and development. His last mentioned works did more than any other books to destroy for a time the Rationalist notion of the Middle Ages. There was also a strong nationalistic note in Chateaubriand's *Martyrs* which helped to make the book very popular. He eulogized French Christianity, and one of the great passages is that on Pharamond, legendary king of France. Chateaubriand's virtues were, however, more literary than scholarly. As Professor Wright says of him: "Chateaubriand was one of the great *poseurs* and one of the worst liars and plagiarists in literature but he had qualities which partly justified him, and he influenced his times as perhaps no other man since Rousseau. He is the father of [French] Romanticism."[6]

Madame Anne Louise de Staël (1766-1816) was also an example of an interesting intellectual evolution. She was the daughter of Necker, the pre-Revolutionary minister of finance. Under the influence of Rousseau's notions, she espoused the more moderate doctrines of the French Revolution and the popular concepts of human progress and perfectibility. But she hated Napoleon as an alleged enemy of the Revolution and republicanism. So she left France and traveled widely, coming under the influence of Schlegel and Constant. Her work on the French Revolution anticipated that of De Tocqueville in holding that it was the natural outgrowth of eighteenth century conditions in France. Her most important book was her *Literature in Its Relation to the Moral and Political Condition of Nations* (1800). She used the history of literature to confirm her thesis that literary styles and models are a direct product of the social environment which, in turn, is deeply influenced by the geographical setting, especially by climate. This latter notion she obtained in part from Montesquieu. She maintained that democracy as a new social system required a new type of literary tradition. Her later and longer work on Germany (1810) showed that she had by this time come to be deeply affected by Christian Romanticism. In this last book she endeavored to instil the French ideals of nationality in Germany and to arouse an interest in German literature on the part of French readers.

[6] C. H. C. Wright, *A History of French Literature* (Oxford University Press, 1925), p. 619.

Abel François Villemain (1790-1867) was a professor of literature at the Sorbonne and one of the founders of comparative literature and literary criticism in France. His lectures were one of the first scholarly attempts at comparative European literature. He published portions of them as a *Sketch of French Literature in the Middle Ages* and a *Sketch of French Literature in the Eighteenth Century*. He followed the tradition of Madame de Staël and especially emphasized the dependence of literature at any time upon the prevailing body of ideas in the surrounding civilization. This line of criticism was carried further by Saint-Beuve and Taine.

We shall deal with Gervinus later on as an example of Romanticist historical writing. In the present connection, his most important work was his *History of German Poetry*. He endeavored to show the relationship between each stage of German literature and poetry and the culture out of which it grew. Gervinus had a definite political reason for writing this book and a curious attitude towards German literature developed out of it. He wished to divorce the best German minds of his day from their interest in poetry and to get them absorbed in German political reform and liberalism. Hence, while he eulogized the great German poets of the past, he contended that German genius had worn itself out in this field and that the final German poet of genius was Goethe.

The main English contributor to this school of historical and literary thought was Sir Walter Scott (1771-1832). He produced a great literature of his own, rather than writing about the history of literature. No other literary figure, not even Chateaubriand, did so much to arouse interest in medieval life and chivalry. He was the supreme literary artist in the use of local color in recreating the past. His *Ivanhoe, The Talisman,* and his novels on medieval Scotland exerted a great influence, not only on literary tastes but also upon the attitude towards the Middle Ages held by historians from Augustin Thierry to Andrew D. White. Scott wrote some strictly historical works, such as his voluminous *Life of Napoleon,* but they were unimportant compared to the influence of his historical novels upon the thought of serious historians.

While it is customary to date Romanticist historical writing from the disciples of Walter Scott and Chateaubriand, Professor Peardon and others have made it clear that this sort of historical writing got under way in England before the days of Chateaubriand and Scott. It was stimulated by primitivism, pietism and a romantic interest in the British Middle Ages. Racial doctrines also played a leading part. The medieval theories of the Trojan origin of the British, and other fantastic notions, were replaced by a rudimentary "Germanism"—the derivation of all important European races from the "Goths," and the weaving in of Anglo-Saxon history as a subordinate incident of Gothic triumph.

The new interest in Anglo-Saxon England was manifested in a number of works, but especially in those of John Whittaker and Sharon Turner. A bitter critic of Hume, Robertson, and Gibbon, Whittaker planned to reconstruct the real history of medieval England around a detailed *History of Manchester* (1771-75). He was only able to complete the sections dealing with the pre-Norman period. Whittaker sought to derive characteristic English institutions, such as parliament, feudalism and civil liberty, from the pre-Norman age. He did his best to bring out the "romantic glamor" of this early period in English history, and almost rivaled Bossuet in his ability to discern "the hand of God in history."

A later and far abler historian with similar views was Sharon Turner, whose chief work was a *History of the Anglo-Saxons* (1799-1805). He argued for the importance of more extended and accurate attention to the early history of Britain. He even recommended a careful study of the Anglo-Saxons before they came to England. He eulogized the rude Anglo-Saxons and contrasted them with the decadent Romans whom they superseded. We may here note the anticipation of that romantic "Germanism" which found full expression in *The Roman and the Teuton* of Charles Kingsley. His book was, however, the first reasonably accurate and adequate work on Anglo-Saxon England. His enthusiasm led him into a number of errors, such as the effort to derive the English Parliament from the Witanagemot and to find the jury in existence in Anglo-Saxon England. This was another anticipation of the genetic trends of the "Germanists" among English institutional historians. Turner's work on English history from the Norman Conquest to the sixteenth century was less valuable, but it gave unusual attention to medieval culture and literature and to the Continental contacts of Britain. Turner shared Whittaker's conviction that the main causative factor in history is Providence. He thought that God stands directly behind the convincing evidences of human progress.

The attempt to glorify and romanticize British medieval culture was to be seen in the works of John Pinkerton and Joseph Strutt, among others. Pinkerton's *History of Scotland* (1788-97) was an enthusiastic excursion into the recovery and praise of medieval British literature, especially British poetry of the period. Pinkerton was also a leader of the early racialists. He believed that the major European races were derived from the Goths, whom he identified with the Scythians as mentioned in ancient historical literature. He claimed that the Picts of Scotland were Gothic in origin. This Gothic obsession was a sort of eighteenth-century pre-Aryanism. In his *Complete View of the Dress and Habits of the People of England* (1796-99), and his *Sports and Pastimes of the People of England* (1801), Jacob Strutt adapted to Romanticist attitudes the interest in medieval social and cultural history which had earlier been manifested by the Rationalist school. His contention that sports are a better reflection of the spirit of a people than their wars or constitutional and diplomatic policies was both original and defensible.

The Romanticist approach was carried into the history of medieval British Catholicism by a Catholic, Joseph Berington (1746-1827), and an evangelical pair, the Milner brothers. Berington was a priest who shared the Romanticist zeal for liberty. As Spittler, from the Rationalist camp, had sought to find in the medieval Catholic church a servant of the cause of Rationalism, so Berington endeavored to show that the medieval English Catholic church had been a zealous partisan of civil liberty. He seized upon such instances as the case of Thomas à Becket. In his work on Abelard and Heloïse and other monographs, Berington eulogized medieval British and Continental Catholicism. But his *Literary History of the Middle Ages* (1814) was, curiously enough, critical of medieval literature and learning. In their *History of the Church of Christ* (1794-1809) Joseph and Isaac Milner showed unusual enthusiasm for Roman Catholicism, though they wrote from the evangelical side. They sought to show that true Christianity—the teaching of Jesus—persisted, whatever the external form of Christian organization. Hence, there were plenty of good Christians among the medieval Catholics. In taking this position, the Milners assailed the view of Protestant partisans and Rationalists alike, but they were most interested in discrediting the views of the Rationalists with respect to the nature of medieval Christianity. Their main position was that Christianity got its start in "Roman dress" and that the loyal historian of Christianity should not allow this fact to prejudice him in tracing the history of the Church.

The classic narrative school of Romanticist historians was not only dominated by the general theories enumerated in preceding pages, but also affected by the literary canons of the historical novels of Walter Scott with their great emphasis upon the element of local color. This tendency was really anti-historical, in that it aimed primarily to portray episodes in periods from the past in such a manner as to make them have the vividness and intimacy of contemporary events. It was a contribution to literature rather than to scientific history. Its main impulse to better historical writing lay in the fact that its literary attractiveness awakened a public interest in history on a wider scale than ever before. In due time, it brought into historical writing many eminent scholars, like Leopold von Ranke, whose individual contributions to historical knowledge were greater than those of all the narrative school of Romanticists combined. Of this narrative variety of Romanticist historical writing the most important products were the *History of the Conquest of England by the Normans,* and the *Narratives of the Merovingian Period* by Augustin Thierry (1795-1856); the *History of the Dukes of Burgundy, 1364-1483* by Amable de

Barante (1782-1866); the *History of the Italian States,* the *History of the Netherlands* and *Universal History* by Heinrich Leo (1799-1878); and *The History of the Nineteenth Century* by George Gottfried Gervinus (1805-71).

Thierry was inspired as a youth by reading Chateaubriand's *Martyrs,* and some years later by the novels of Walter Scott. These gave him interest in local color. Thierry wrote with a definite political philosophy—a devotion to the *bourgeoisie* and republicanism and a hatred for aristocracy which he derived in part from Saint-Simon. He believed that aristocracies were built upon conquest and manned by the foreign conquerors. He projected his hatred for the French aristocracy of his day into his treatment of the Middle Ages and endeavored to use history against them by representing the medieval nobility as a brutal, vulgar, and exploiting group. In his history of the Norman Conquest he used William the Conqueror and the Norman invasion of England to illustrate his thesis. In treating of the Merovingians he traced the French aristocracy back to a series of foreign intruders—first the Franks and then the Normans. There his hatred of aristocrats was intensified by his racial prejudices. Thierry was not over-critical in his use of historical materials. He rejected unreliable secondary authorities, but he had little power or interest in estimating the widely different authenticity of contemporary chronicles. He had, however, great powers of constructive historical imagination, an artistic sense and a lucid and attractive style. His political philosophy made his historical writings highly acceptable to *bourgeois* intellectuals in France. All these factors gave his works great popularity, though they are now rejected as anything like a true or balanced history of medieval France or England. More enduring was his editorial work on the medieval French communes which enlisted his *bourgeois* sympathies.

Barante was less capable as a historian than Thierry, but he was an even greater artist in the use of local color. Like Thierry, he was influenced by Scott. His interest was primarily absorbed in producing a thrilling narrative—something essentially true but yet as vivid as a historical novel. He chose for his theme the history of Burgundy in the age covered by the brilliant chroniclers, Froissart and Commines. What he tried to do was to weave together a narrative out of the contemporary sources—an eloquent paraphrase. He was lacking, however, in critical power to assess the relative accuracy of sources. Barante did not allow his own ideas, if he had any, to enter at all into his narrative. There was no reflection, interpretation, or philosophy in his work. But its stylistic charm gained for it an army of enthusiastic readers.

Leo best represented the narrative school of Romanticist historical writing in Germany. His most important work, that on the Italian city-states of the Middle Ages, recreated the medieval towns in terms of the local color of the medieval chroniclers. Though Leo as a youth had been imbued with the liberalism of Father Jahn, he turned more conservative and, while remaining formally Protestant, soon became a passionate apologist for medieval Catholicism, almost in the spirit of Chateaubriand. This trend appeared not only in his interpretation of the Middle Ages but also in his harsh judgment of the Jews, of Luther and the Reformation, and of the Dutch revolt against Catholic Spain. As a result of a quarrel with von Ranke and other bitter antagonisms he lost in popularity. His style was vivid and he was superior to Thierry or Barante in using sources with discrimination.

Gervinus was a student and disciple of Schlosser, but his interests were more political and less moral than those of his master. His dominating political prepossession was the liberalization of Germany. His notable history of German poetry was written for a political purpose—to prove that all great German poetry had already been written and that the poets of his day should turn their attention to politics. His most important book was a large *History of the Nineteenth Century,* which was especially taken up with the tracing of constitutional, democratic and republican tendencies and movements. He looked upon the battle for liberty as a struggle of the democratic ideas which had come in with the Reformation against the aristocratic heritage from the medieval Church, monarchy and nobility. This shows how little he really understood the Reformation, which in some respects strengthened the divine right of kings and royal absolutism. Gervinus inclined more towards the Rationalists than towards the Romanticists in one respect. He was not nationalistic in any reactionary sense. German unity, won at the sacrifice of liberalism, did not appeal to him.

A still further intensification of the subjective element in the narrative school was reached in the works of the "lyrical" and subjective group, Michelet, Carlyle and Froude, where an attempt was made not only to bring the reader in immediate touch with the local color of the events narrated, but also with the personal impressions and subjective attitudes of the author. The reader was expected to visualize the events related as taking place before his very eyes, and to share in the sensations of the narrator.

The *History of France* by Jules Michelet (1798-1874) was the most eloquent and dramatic product of French historical literature in any age. The author was dominated by a passionate attachment to his country, possessed a marvelous creative imagination, and wrote in a style notable for its word-painting and its power of symbolical representation. Michelet's romantic and dramatic attitude towards history remained unchanged throughout his life, but his political and religious attitudes and his temper altered markedly, and this change affected the tone of his historical writings. He started out as a devout Catholic, but became interested in liberalism and science. The study and translation of Vico's *Scienza Nuova* convinced him that science and faith could be harmonized, and in this spirit he wrote his earlier and minor works and attacked his major historical enterprise, *The History of France.* Then he became converted to the spirit of the French Revolution and took a prominent part in French liberal politics. The Catholic church was active in supporting French political reaction, and Michelet was thus gradually transformed into not only a radical democrat but also an anti-clerical. In this spirit he wrote the sections of the *History of France* which follow the Middle Ages. This accounts for the marked difference in spirit between the earlier and the later portions of his history.

To Michelet, history was "the drama of human liberty." He was not particularly interested in the philosophy of history, but rather in the full and rich exposition of the human drama in the past. He once wrote, "Augustin Thierry saw in history a narrative, Guizot an analysis. I call mine a resurrection." He was nationalistic in the sense of possessing a fervent love for "the spirit of the French people." Actually, he did more than any other French Romanticist historian to stimulate French nationalism. This he did not only in his history of France and the French Revolution, but also in his work, *The People,* a marvelous example of romantic nationalism. While Michelet searched out the sources of French history more thoroughly and industriously than any French narrative historian down to his day, he did not approach the sources, like von Ranke, to sift and weigh them. Rather, like Barante, he went to them to get local color for his narrative. He felt that the raw materials of historical drama can best be assembled from the sources. His *History of France* was a succession of great dramatic scenes rather than a tight and consecutive narrative. Particularly brilliant were the passages on the Templars and on Joan of Arc. In spite of his romantic and literary interests, however, his portrayal of the geographical basis of French history was the best summary ever written by a historian until very recent times. Michelet's account of the Middle Ages was not only a passionate review of the genesis of the French nation but also a tribute to French Catholicism which almost reminds the reader of Chateaubriand and actually won the latter's warm praise.

Then came the change in Michelet's temper and he jumped from the close of the Middle Ages to the French Revolution. His *History of the French Revolution* was both a marvelous literary performance and a liberal and anti-clerical polemic. He interpreted the French Revolution as the noble work of the emancipated French people, especially lauding Danton, and represented it as a great triumph over the oppression of the Church and the monarchy alike. He later filled in the gap in his history between the Renaissance and the French Revolution. This portion of his work was also colored by vigorous criticism of the French monarchy and aristocracy and of the French Catholic church. His condemnation of the St. Bartholomew massacre and of the revocation of the Edict of Nantes and the like were daring innovations. Both of these episodes were part of the national tradition of which Frenchmen were, on the whole, proud. This illustrates the power of Catholicism in the French historical perspective of that time. Michelet's bitterness towards the oppressors was accompanied by a compensating sympathy for the oppressed.

The least attractive personality of the group and the least worthy as a historian was the English author, Thomas Carlyle (1795-1881). In radical contrast to Michelet, he was possessed of a sour contempt for the masses and an equally exaggerated interest in the picturesque figures of history. He thought that "the common herd must be drilled, led and punished by their superiors." To Carlyle, history was but the "collective biography" of the conspicuous public figures through the ages.[7] Carlyle was as responsible as any other historian for the conventional disdain of the modern historian for those commonplace things of daily life which have often had incomparably greater influence upon social development than the dramatic personalities. His biographical interpretations, brilliant as they were in a literary sense, were more concerned with a subjective interpretation of the character of the personalities considered than with an intelligent appraisal of their public acts. Carlyle brilliantly indulged his prejudices in his *Letters and Speeches of Cromwell,* the *History of Frederick the Great,* and the *French Revolution.* While possessing only moderate value as sources of information, on account of the writer's uncontrolled prejudices, the utter absence of critical method, and the lack of well-organized published source material, they earned him the undisputed position as "the greatest of English portrait painters."

The work on Cromwell was a vigorous effort to vindicate the character of Cromwell, and in this it succeeded. But it was a feeble contribution to constitutional history and a complete failure in analyzing the economic and social factors involved in the civil war and commonwealth. The biography of Frederick the Great has been accurately called "the largest and most varied show-box in historical literature," and it provided vivid character sketches of the leading public figures of Frederick's time. But it failed utterly as an institutional history of the age of the enlightened despots. The *French Revolution* was a "series of tableaux," showing no deep understanding of the origins, nature, course or results of the great

---

[7] In theory, Carlyle held that history is the compilation of innumerable biographies, of the mighty and the humble: "Who was the greatest benefactor, he who gained the battles of Cannae and Trasimene or the nameless poor who first hammered out for himself an iron spade?" But, in practice, Carlyle gave attention and prestige to the mighty and ignored the humble when he did not express contempt for them.

movement. It accepted the absurd thesis that the French Revolution was from the beginning the product of a savage national mob. It was also inaccurate in many details as well as in the general picture. But the work was brilliant literature, rivaling the vastly different interpretation by Michelet, and it has been enormously popular from his day to ours with readers who seek entertainment rather than instruction. The best brief judgment ever passed on Carlyle as a historian was that of Leslie Stephen, who said of his writings that "phrase-making is not thought-finding."

While his name has been almost synonymous with chronic inaccuracy in historical narrative, Carlyle's disciple, James Anthony Froude (1818-94), was a much abler historian than his master. His faults were those of one who was constitutionally careless and faulty in memory rather than intentionally or dishonestly inaccurate. Froude had a keen appreciation of the value of critical methods and his work was the first extended English history written mainly on the basis of unpublished documents. The charge made by many of his contemporaries, and repeated by Fueter, that Froude consciously altered or forged his sources to square with his doctrines is not accepted today by the best and most impartial critics of his works. His *History of England from the Fall of Wolsey to the Defeat of the Spanish Armada* was an epic of English deliverance from the "slavery of Rome." His Carlylian attraction to great personalities found ample scope for expression in his portraits of Henry VIII, Burleigh and Knox. As a narrative writer he was approached among English historians only by Macaulay. "No other English historian," says Gooch, "has possessed a style so easy, so flowing, so transparent."

Froude, like Michelet, went through a profound psychological change, but it had been felt before he began his major historical work. Originally, he had been sympathetic with the High Church Oxford Movement, but his experience with it drove him in the opposite direction from that followed by Manning and Newman. He became an enemy of Rome and sympathetic with the English Reformation. He was encouraged by Carlyle to write from the original sources the first extended treatment of the English Revolt. He was governed by three notions or ideals—the evils of Rome, Carlyle's hero worship, and admiration for Macaulay as a story-teller. He excelled both Carlyle and Macaulay in his use of pathos. His handling of his theme combined to some degree Macaulay's narrative ability, Carlyle's capacity for portrait painting, and the method of a lawyer in organizing a long and telling brief. He defended Henry VIII warmly, but did not make him plausible as a political realist or present his work in the proper economic and political setting. Froude was less appreciative of Elizabeth and attributed her "greatness" to Burleigh. He was friendly to John Knox as the man who helped to save the British Reformation, and was hostile to the Catholic, Mary Queen of Scots. In spite of all its faults, Froude's work remains the most complete and original history of the English Reformation by a single author. Its excesses were prompted, and in part justified, by the scurrilous attacks on the English Reformation in Froude's day by the High Churchmen and neo-Catholics.

Russia contributed one notable historical work conceived under the influence of Romanticism. This was the *History of the Russian State* by Nicholas Karamazin (1766-1826), which carried the story of the Russians down to 1611. It pictured Russian development as due to the very special genius of the Russian people, which was derived mainly from their oriental heritage and their Eastern church. Karamazin criticized the liberalism and occidental culture of the West. His work was very popular with the anti-Western school of Russian thought. In Poland, the popular national historian, Joachim Lelewel (1786-1861), composed his *History of Poland in the Middle Ages* in harmony with the Romanticist conception of cultural evolution. There were Romanticist strains in the histories of such Italian writers as Carlo Troya, Luigi Tosti, Cesare Balbo and Cesare Cantu, but we shall treat them later in other connections.

The United States found its most distinguished representative of the school of Carlyle and Froude in John Lothrop Motley (1814-77), the friend and fellow-student of Bismarck, who devoted his life to a narration of the struggle of the Netherlands against Spain and the creation of a republic in the Netherlands. Surpassing even Michelet and Freeman in his passion for liberty, he found a most congenial subject in tracing the successful revolt of the Dutch and the establishment of their republic. For word-painting and vivid description of dramatic scenes only Carlyle has equaled him among historians writing in the English tongue.

Motley studied under Bancroft as a boy, learned German, and was encouraged to go to Germany to study. It was at Göttingen that he met Bismarck. Influenced by Bancroft's views of the American Revolution and by his own convictions relative to the virtues of liberty, he was led into an investigation of the rise of liberty and revolution among the Dutch. While, as a Unitarian, he was not a Protestant fanatic, Motley was convinced of the oppression of Rome. Hence, his *Rise of the Dutch Republic* was an eloquent polemic for liberty and republicanism and a vigorous diatribe against Catholicism and Spanish absolutism. William the Silent, whom Motley compared with Washington, was the hero of the book, and Philip and Alva the villains. The first work was followed by an equally vivid *History of the United Netherlands,* and then by the *Life and Death of John Barneveldt,* which was criticized by Dutch Calvinists because of its attack upon the Calvinist bigotry of the Statholder, Maurice. Motley worked long and patiently with the sources, and his work was relatively accurate in a factual sense. His prejudices and biases have been variously appraised, but no one can well question the literary brilliance and appeal of his writings or the nobility of the author's character.

While the conceptions of Romanticism gained some dominion over the minds of greater scholars, such as von Ranke, they served rather to stimulate the author's interest in history than to vitiate his scholarship. With its emphasis on the doctrine of the "genius of a nation" and its deep emotional basis, Romanticism was a powerful influence in stimulating the nationalistic historiography which dominated the historical writing of the nineteenth century.[8]

THE RISE OF THE PHILOSOPHY OF HISTORY

The philosophy of history did not first come into being in the age of Romanticism. It was implicit in the theory of progress of the seventeenth and eighteenth centuries, with which we have dealt in the preceding chapter. Indeed, the Christian historians from Eusebius to Bossuet had a very specific philosophy of history, based upon the Christian Epic. This received its classic expression in the works of Otto of Freising and Bossuet. But it was Romanticism which first promoted an unusual profusion of contributions to the philosophy of history. This influence spread beyond the literal Romanticists and affected the writings of some late Rationalists. There were good reasons for this stimulus of Romanticism to philosophizing about the course of mankind. The growth of interest in history promoted by Rationalism and Romanticism naturally produced a far greater body of reliable historical information upon which to generalize. Then the Romanticist position laid special stress upon the organic unity of national culture and the principle of development in culture and institutions. Finally, the somewhat mystical and sentimental attitude of the Romanticists towards the human past created an ideal mental atmosphere for speculating about that past.

There has been a long debate as to who was the "father" of the philosophy of history, candidates being presented for this honor all the way from Herodotus to Hegel, but it would seem a sensible compromise to select Vico as the first writer to produce an impressive system of historical philosophy. We have already referred to his "spiral" conception of progress.[9] According to Vico, the essence of historical development consisted of creations and alterations in the collective mind—changes in the character of the "human spirit"—from age to age. Like so many later philosophers of history, he postulated three major stages of historical development. To Vico these were the divine, the heroic and the human. The divine period was characterized by the dominion of the feelings and raw emotions in the world of spirit, and by theocracy in the realm of politics.

[8] See below, chap. ix.   [9] See above, pp. 175-76.

The heroic period displayed the powers of poetic imagination in the collective mentality, and gave rise to aristocracy in politics. The third period manifested positive knowledge in the collective mentality, and produced political freedom, embodied in constitutional monarchies and republics. As we made plain above, Vico believed that these triadic cycles repeat themselves, but never on the same level. There is a gradual spiral advance in the culture of mankind. Vico's ideas were in many ways in harmony with Romanticism, especially his notion of changes in the character of the collective spirit of mankind and his idea of the potency of God in history. As we have already pointed out, he directly inspired one of the leading Romanticist historians, Jules Michelet.

GERMAN CONTRIBUTIONS

While important philosophical reflections on historical development are to be noted in the writings of Rousseau, Turgot, Condorcet and others, in connection with their views of progress, the next important effort to work out a philosophy of history was that of Johann Gottfried von Herder in his four-volume *Ideas for the Philosophy of the History of Mankind*. Herder was a sort of border-line figure between Rousseauistic Rationalism and Romanticism, being listed as a Rationalist by some and a Romanticist by others. Herder believed the historical process to be the product of the interworkings of external environment and *Geist*, the latter being the dynamic totality of subjective impulses, for which there is no exact English equivalent. "Every civilization buds, flowers and fades according to natural laws of growth." Robert Flint has well summarized Herder's main propositions in his philosophy of history:

I. The end of human nature is humanity; and that they may realize that end, God had put into the hands of men their own fates.

II. All the destructive powers in nature must not only yield in time to the preservative powers, but must ultimately be subservient to the perfection of the whole.

III. The human race is destined to proceed through various degrees of civilization, in various revolutions, but its abiding welfare rests solely and essentially on reason and justice.

IV. From the very nature of the human mind, reason and justice must gain more footing among men in the course of time, and promote the extension of humanity.

V. A wise goodness disposes the fate of mankind, and therefore there is no nobler merit, no purer or more abiding happiness, than to coöperate in its designs.[10]

[10] Robert Flint, *The Philosophy of History in France and Germany* (Scribner, 1874), p. 386. Herder's genetic outlook was clearly stated in his earlier *Auch eine Philosophie der Geschichte* (1774).

From Herder to Hegel, historical philosophy was influenced by the theology and epistemology of the German Transcendental Idealists. So far as their historical perspective is concerned, these ponderous dialecticians were, in reality, little more than Lutheran theologians or Bossuets, who had merely changed their terminology. The Absolute is none other than God, and its unfolding in the world is the working of Providence.

A few years after Herder had published the first outline of his philosophy of history, another contribution to the subject came from the pen of the greatest of all German metaphysicians, Immanuel Kant (1724-1804), in his *Idea of a Universal History,* later elaborated at some points in his tract *Of Perpetual Peace.* It was Kant's thesis that the dynamic factor in history resides in the struggle in both the human personality and in society between selfishness and altruism—between individualism and collectivism. The first factor produces progress and the latter order. Civilization is the union of the two. The perfect state is one in which the maximum amount of creative individualism is combined with the minimum of state control essential to preserve order. It is the task of statesmanship to discover and introduce this ideal combination. Success in this requires peace, in order that all available civic intelligence may be devoted to the solution of this difficult problem. Therefore, Kant argued that the abolition of war is essential to the realization of an ideal state of civilization.

An extremely abstract conception of the philosophy of history appeared in the *Characteristics of the Present Age* by another German philosopher, Johann Gottlieb Fichte (1762-1814). He well nigh succeeded in divorcing the philosophy of history from history itself. He believed that the historical scheme of things, as designed by God, embraced five epochs: (1) the age of innocence, in which reason manifested itself only crudely in the form of blind instinct; (2) the age of authority, demanding the subordination of reason to passive obedience; (3) the age of indifference to truth, thus involving the complete rejection of reason; (4) the age of science, in which truth is revered above all other things and we become conscious of reason; and (5) the age of art, when humanity becomes free and beautifies itself as befitting the image of Absolute Reason. In his *Addresses to the German Nation* in 1807 Fichte held that the hope of the future lay with the German peoples. They were an *Urfolk* or unmixed race, possessing "hidden and inexhaustible springs of spiritual life and power." The Romance peoples were a *Mischvolk,* or a product of race mixture. Consequently, they had bloomed prematurely in civilization and even in Fichte's day were on the high road to decadence. It is no wonder that Fichte's doctrine was a strong stimulant to the growth of nationalism in Germany.[11]

A combination of intellectual mysticism with the belief in divinely-

11 Cf. H. C. Englebrecht, *Johann Gottlieb Fichte* (Columbia University Press, 1933).

guided progress appeared in the historical philosophy of Friedrich Wilhelm Joseph von Schelling (1775-1854), who was deeply influenced by Fichte. In his *System of Transcendental Idealism* he carried further Fichte's effort to unite nature and intelligence and show that they coöperated in the unfolding of the Absolute. "Nature is visible soul, and soul is invisible nature, and both advance incessantly by an uninterrupted succession of stages and gradation of forms." History is essentially a process of the self-revelation of the Absolute, in which Schelling discerned three stages: (1) that in which the forces of destiny or fate ruled, embracing the period of the ancient empires; (2) that in which fate gave way to nature and produced an ordered regularity in human affairs, beginning with the expansion of Rome and its conquests; and (3) the future, which will fully manifest in human affairs the dominion of Providence.

One of Schelling's disciples, Johann Goërres (1776-1848), anticipated roughly the recapitulation theory of Ernst Haeckel and G. Stanley Hall, holding that the human race passes through the same stages of development as the individual. Hence, he found in history four stages representing progress towards maturity: (1) the natural groupings of man determined by geography; (2) the enthnographic stage in which men separated into races, tribes and nations; (3) the ethico-political period which appeared with the rise of civilized states ruled by law; and (4) the religious stage, when man becomes capable of understanding the revelations of the Divine Word.

A widely influential philosophical interpretation of history was contained in *The Philosophy of History*, by Karl Wilhelm Friedrich von Schlegel (1772-1829). Schlegel contended that the central problem of philosophy is to determine how unity and harmony may be restored to the inner life of man—how the image of God, which has been lost, may be restored in the human personality. The major task of history is to trace this restoration of the image of God to mankind through the successive stages of human history. He wrote that the chief purpose of his philosophy of history was "to point out the progressive restoration in humanity of the effaced image of God, according to the gradation of grace in the various periods of the world, from the revelation given at the beginning, down to the middle revelation of redemption and love [the coming of Christ], and from that to the final consummation." Schlegel, accordingly, surveyed history from the early Chinese era to his own day in order to trace the gradually returning likeness of the Almighty in mankind. He became a Catholic in his quest for sufficient emotional assurance, and his treatment of the Middle Ages was colorfully eulogistic. As might be expected, he was highly critical of Protestantism, which he regarded as the product of man, while he interpreted Catholicism as the work of God.

Most famous of all the Germanic philosophies of history in this period was that of the impressive and pontifical dialectician, Georg Wilhelm Friedrich Hegel (1770-1831). Hegel's *Philosophy of History* was a highly subjective work—a record of the unfolding of the self-consciousness of freedom in the human spirit. Perhaps the best brief summary of it ever written is that penned by Robert Flint more than a half-century ago:

> The course of the sun is a symbol of the course of the spirit; and as the light of the physical sun travels from east to west, so does the light of the sun of self-consciousness. Asia is the determinate east or absolute beginning, and Europe the determinate west or end of history. Its great moments, stages or epochs are three in number—the Oriental, the Graeco-Roman, and the Modern or Germanic. In the first, the spirit slumbers ignorant and unconscious of that freedom which is its very essence, and patiently submits to civil and spiritual despotism, so that *one* only is free, and the rights of individuals are unknown; in the second, the spirit is awake to these rights in some, but not all its forms—it has a partial consciousness of its true nature, and *some*, but not all, are free; in the third, the spirit knows itself as what it is, as essentially free, and knows that *all* have inherent rights to rational freedom.[12]

Like that of Fichte, Hegel's philosophy of history had a strong nationalistic impulse. It implied that the Germans of the post-Reformation period were invested by Divinity with the mission of bringing the blessings of freedom to mankind. Though the analysis just given reveals the general pattern of Hegel's theory of history, progress itself comes as the result of conflict and synthesis. A movement or idea—thesis—gets under way. Then its opposite—antithesis—makes its appearance. Out of the clash comes an ultimate synthesis which marks a further step towards truth. The synthesis then becomes another thesis, and the process goes on. This Hegelian dialectic of progress had much influence on later historical thought, particularly through its adoption by Karl Marx and its exploitation in the service of a materialistic philosophy of history.[13] Hegel stimulated other important work in historical research, especially the magisterial studies of Greek philosophy by Eduard Zeller, and the investigation of Christian origins by Ferdinand Christian Baur. While Hegel's historical influence was felt in a double direction—Marxism and nationalism—it is the latter influence which is more prominent today. The celebration of his death centenary in 1931 was almost wholly nationalist.

The rise of biology and the notion of the social organism—the identity between the individual organism and society—influenced the philosophy of history as expounded in the *General Philosophy of History,* by Charles Christian Friedrich Krause (1781-1832), a student of both Fichte and

---

12 Flint, *op. cit.,* p. 515.
13 Cf. Sidney Hook, *From Hegel to Marx* (Reynal and Hitchcock, 1936).

Schelling. He held that humanity passes through stages of development which may be fruitfully compared with the life of man. First, we have primitive society, or the age of innocence and infancy with the race. Then we have the period of youth and growth, divided again into three states— that of polytheism from the ancient Orient through the era of Greece and Rome; next, the age of fanatical monotheism and clerical dominion, namely, the Middle Ages; and, finally, the period of freedom, in which all external authority over the mind is cast off. The ultimate epoch of humanity is one in which man masters both physical nature and society, bringing about the unity of all nations in a great and prosperous world-state. There is at least a faint anticipation of H. G. Wells in this view of human development and destiny.

The answer to and the negation of the Idealistic and Romanticist philosophy of history in Germany, appeared in the pessimistic and anti-Christian philosophy of Friedrich Nietzsche (1844-1900). But Nietzsche shared one point in common with the Romanticists, namely, his worship of the Great Man—the superman.

FRENCH, BELGIAN, AND ITALIAN WRITERS

A number of French writers also exemplified the Romanticist view of the course of history. Victor Cousin (1792-1867) became a disciple of Hegel and helped to introduce Hegelianism into France. In his lectures on the philosophy of history in 1828, Cousin depicted three main stages in human development: (1) the Infinite, when men depended wholly upon belief in gods; (2) the Finite, when reflection gave rise to a sense of personal freedom and power, but brought chaos into society; and (3) that of Union, which produces the ideal combination of the first two stages through uniting divine guidance with liberty. Cousin adopted a providential attitude and held that the course of human history is basically a revelation of "the government of God, gradually made visible." Cousin also took up the "great man" theory of his English contemporary, Thomas Carlyle. While great men reflect the spirit of their times, they sum up the essence of the individual and the universal and are all-important for the advancement of man. "Universal history is but the united biography of great men."

Théodore Jouffroy (1796-1842) produced an intellectualistic philosophy of history in his *Philosophy of History* (1825-27). He held, in a pre-Darwinian vein, that the main difference between man and the animals is that the animals remain unchanged while man advances. The changes in human ideas underlie and determine all other phases of human development. Therefore, the essence of the philosophy of history is to observe and analyze the modification of ideas and the reaction of these alterations on "the external facts of history"—that is, on manners, customs, institutions and states. There have been three major systems of civilization in human history—the Brahminic, the Mohammedan and the Christian. The Christian system is bound to conquer all others. In the Christian world there are three major nations, each with a definite mission to perform in the interest of improving civilization. The Germans are the nation of learning and erudition, and they contribute facts. The French are talented in philosophy—the interpretation of the facts discovered by the Germans. The English are the practical people who put the facts and philosophical theories to work in industry, public spirit, and constitutional government. These nations should recognize their special qualities and coöperate for the good of all humanity.

The ideas of Herder and Hegel reappeared, with some original modification and elaborations, in the Introduction to his translation of Herder, the *Introduction to the Philosophy of History,* by Edgar Quinet (1803-75). He shared Jouffroy's notion that ideas are the basic causative factor in human history and social development. He combined strong attachment for liberty with a devotion to republicanism, and held that republicanism must always protect liberty. Hence, his *Christianity and the French Revolution* was vigorously critical of the period of the Terror. Quinet viewed the historical process as the progressive realization of liberty and free-will —"history is from beginning to end the development and display of liberty, the continuous protestation of the mind of the human race against the world which oppresses and enchains it, the process through which the soul gradually secures and enlarges its freedom." Quinet was as enthusiastic for Protestantism as Schlegel was for Catholicism, and he looked upon Protestantism as the chief liberating factor in modern times. He believed that the French Revolution had failed primarily because it had failed to embrace Protestantism instead of the religion of Reason.

The other important remaining French contributions to the philosophy of history were a heritage from the age of Rationalism. The tradition began with Turgot, who set forth in his Sorbonne *Discourse on the Historical Progress of the Human Mind,* a clear anticipation of what became famous as Auguste Comte's three stages of the intellectual progress of mankind—the theological, metaphysical and scientific. Turgot wrote that:

> Before knowing the connection of physical facts with one another, nothing was more natural than to suppose that they were produced by beings, intelligent, invisible, and like to ourselves. Everything which happened without man's own intervention had its god, to which fear or hope caused a worship to be paid conforming to the respect accorded to powerful men—the gods being only men more or less powerful and perfect in proportion as the age which originated them was more or less enlightened as to what constitutes the true perfections of humanity.

But when the philosophers perceived the absurdity of these fables, without having attained to a real acquaintance with the history of nature, they fancifully accounted for phenomena by abstract expressions, by essences and faculties, which indeed explained nothing, but were reasoned from as if they were real existences.

It was only very late that from observing the mechanical action of bodies on one another, other hypotheses were inferred, which mathematics could develop and experience verify.[14]

The idea was taken up by the eminent French publicist and social philosopher, Count Claude Henri de Saint-Simon (1760-1825), a man of great originality and fertility of ideas, probably second only to Bentham in this respect in his age, but of little power in the way of consistent elaboration of doctrines. Saint-Simon contended that there were two major periods in the intellectual development of mankind, that of theological conjecture, and that of positive knowledge, which began with Bacon and Descartes. He shared the organic theory of history and stressed the similarities between individual and social development. History is the record of a succession of organic and critical periods. In organic periods of history, society is peacefully united by a common body of ideas and institutions. Then follows a critical period, preparatory to change and advance, which is characterized by social criticism, contending schools of thought, and a general unsettlement of older institutions.

A theological cast was emphasized in the philosophy of history by one of Saint-Simon's disciples, Philippe Buchez (1796-1866), in his *Introduction to the Science of History*. He stressed the influence of race on the development of nations and individuals and anticipated Herbert Spencer in holding that progress is cosmic and universal as well as human. But he did not share Spencer's naturalism. Rather, he believed as firmly as did Bossuet that the intervention of the Divinity has been the dominating force in the development of humanity and civilization. There have been four main stages of history, each characterized by a major revelation: (1) that made through Adam, which led to the rise of human institutions; (2) that given to Noah, which encouraged the origin of tribes and races; (3) that made to some unknown prophet among the sons of Shem and Japeth, involving the establishment of the sentiments of unity and equality and the notion of the division of labor; and (4) the revelation of truth and life through Jesus Christ. The doctrine of human solidarity and the universal and continuous nature of progress was expounded in the work on *Humanity* by Pierre Leroux (1798-1871), another disciple of Saint-Simon.

The classic elaboration of Saint-Simon's ideas, together with some orig-

14 Flint, *op. cit.*, p. 113.

inality on his own part, appeared in the extensive writings of Auguste Comte (1798-1857). Comte's most important works were voluminous treatises on *The Principles of a Positive Philosophy,* and *The Principles of a Positive Polity.* The first work presented Comte's ideas of intellectual development, and the latter and larger treatise gave his notions of both intellectual and social development. Comte held that the intellectual development of mankind had passed through three stages: the theological, the metaphysical, and the scientific or positive. The first was characterized by the dominion of the supernatural, the second by reliance upon metaphysical categories and assumptions, and the last by the growing influence of critical philosophy and scientific knowledge.

Comte divided his treatment of sociology into two sections—social statics and social dynamics. In the latter division he considered the problem of social evolution. He found three stages in social development as well as in intellectual growth. The first stage, essentially that of oriental society, was theological in mental outlook and militaristic in political and social expression. Then came the metaphysical and legalistic period, that of Greece, Rome and the Middle Ages, in which militarism still continued, but industry and civil liberty made headway, philosophical thought developed, and law established its reign. Finally, with the Industrial Revolution and the growth of modern science, there comes the scientific and industrial epoch in social development, dissipating superstition and devoting attention to industrial development. Comte's philosophy of history was taken over with only slight change by the eminent American sociologist, Franklin Henry Giddings,[15] and it also influenced the distinguished German historian, Karl Lamprecht.

Belgium produced an eminent philosopher of history in the incredibly prolific François Laurent (1810-87), long professor in the University of Ghent. His philosophy of history was contained in the last volume of an eighteen-volume compilation, *Studies on the History of Humanity.* This work was an elaborate universal history. Hence, Laurent knew more actual history [historical facts] than any other man who had written on the philosophy of history down to his time. But he failed to make very intelligent use of his extensive knowledge in his philosophy of history, which was a culmination and a sort of *reductio ad absurdum* of the theistic attitude—the attempt to put God into history on a grand scale. He criticized earlier philosophies of history for their alleged "fatalism"—"in Vico he sees only an advocate of ancient fatalism; in Voltaire and Frederick the Great, the fatalism of chance; in Montesquieu, of climate—in Herder, of nature—in Renan, of race; in Thiers, revolutionary fatalism; in Hegel, pantheistic fatalism; in Comte, positivistic fatalism; and in Buckle, the fa-

15 *Principles of Sociology* (Macmillan, 1896), Book II.

talism of general laws."[16] Laurent's own philosophy of history was an extreme theistic version, based on the idea that "history declares the glory of God." God was held to propel man irresistibly ahead towards modern civilization, Laurent thus giving us an admirable example of theological fatalism. The most interesting and important aspect of his history of philosophy related to his emphasis on the development of the principle of nationality and its contributions to the intellectual and moral evolution of the human race. He concluded with a rather noble plea for the unity and coöperation of the nations of the contemporary world.

Italians also turned their attention to the philosophy of history. Cesare Balbo (1789-1853) was a protagonist of papal leadership in the reunion of Italy. His philosophy of history was contained in his *Historical Meditations*. This was a late echo of Bossuet and an earnest statement of the providential theory of history. Guiseppe Ferrari (1812-76) was deeply influenced by Vico. He offered a philosophy of revolution devoted to the amplification of the idea that revolutions are constructive rather than destructive influences in human development. More important was the notion developed in his *Theory of Political Periods* (1874). He contended that human progress has been the result of the workings of certain fundamental principles, each of which dominates for a period of about 125 years. The dominion of each principle passes through four subperiods —preparation, efflorescence, reaction and dissolution. We shall refer below to the views of Benedetto Croce.

THE PHILOSOPHY OF HISTORY IN ENGLAND AND THE UNITED STATES

England has produced no avowed and systematic philosophers of history. There were English followers of the transcendental Idealists and of Hegel, as well as of Comte, but they did no more than introduce such philosophical ideas into England. Sometimes they prepared elaborate commentaries and carried on a powerful propaganda, as in the case of the introduction and dissemination of Comte's doctrines by Frederic Harrison and the Positivist Society.[17] But certain Englishmen, in the course of the nineteenth century, offered observations bearing upon the philosophy of history which were of more value and validity than all of the pontifical pretense and ponderous rationalizations which we have just reviewed, with the sole exception of the rather solid contributions of Auguste Comte. Most of them were written under the influence of the new materialism, naturalism, and evolutionary philosophy.

[16] Flint, *op. cit.*, p. 324.
[17] J. E. McGee, *Crusade for Humanity: The History of Organized Positivism in England* (Watts, 1931).

The history of humanity and the evolution of human culture were linked up with the doctrine of universal evolution in the writings of Herbert Spencer (1820-1903), especially in the second part of his *First Principles* and in his *Principles of Sociology*. Spencer held that social and cultural evolution conforms to the laws of cosmic evolution—a progressive integration of matter followed by increasingly perfect differentiation and coördination in the parts. Especially did Spencer divorce human history from the providential hypothesis. Social evolution, far from being directed by God, is not even consciously planned or controlled by man. The development of society is a naturalistic process, just like that of the cosmos as a whole. Spencer discerned three major stages of social development: (1) that of tribal or gentile society, emerging out of small and sporadic groupings; (2) the military age, during which the small tribal groups were welded together into states by war; and (3) the industrial period, when social effort is devoted primarily to industrial and productive ends.

Henry Thomas Buckle (1821-62) was an English follower of Rationalism, influenced also by the Positivism of Comte and by the new biological naturalism. In his famous *History of Civilization in England* he formulated certain naturalistic laws of historical development, which he planned to apply in detail to the history of England, but he died before he could complete the task. Buckle held, like Holbach, that man is simply a part of nature in general and, hence, that the laws of historical development can be reduced to natural laws. Such were: (1) the physical laws relating to the effects of soil, climate, wealth, and the aspects of nature upon man, with the conclusion that these geographical influences act in inverse ratio to the growth of intelligence—were strongest in primitive society and weakest in advanced civilization;[18] (2) moral laws, which are static, changeless and enduring—Buckle failed to appreciate the evolutionary attitude in this field; and (3) intellectual laws, to the effect that the unrestricted application of the scientific method has always been most beneficial to man and has most effectively hastened the development of civilization. Buckle illustrated these laws in a preliminary way through reference to the history of France, Spain, and Scotland, but he did not live to carry out his major plan—their application in detail to the history of English civilization.

Perhaps the most brilliant attempt to apply Darwinian principles to human development by an Englishman was contained in the *Physics and Politics* of the publicist and economist, Walter Bagehot (1826-77). He attempted to utilize Darwinism in a psychological interpretation of human development. He found that there had been three outstanding pe-

---

[18] Cf. Franklin Thomas, *The Environmental Basis of Society* (Century, 1925), pp. 87ff., 130ff., 199ff.

riods in human advance: (1) the custom-making period, or that of primitive society; (2) the age of the conflict of customs, or the period of
nation-making, which was brought about by the wars that amalgamated
tribal groups and made states of them; and (3) the age of discussion, by
means of which rigid customary beliefs and practices were gradually dis-
solved and subordinated to the reign of intelligence and free discussion.
The nation-making age produced the great empires of oriental antiquity.
The age of discussion began in Greece and Rome, but in the Middle Ages
there was a regression to something like the nation-making period of antiquity. Representative government, originating in the tribal assemblies
of the Germans, revived the age of discussion in modern times.

Sir Leslie Stephen (1832-1904), an eminent essayist, editor and publicist, was famed for his effort to divorce history from providential interpretations and to introduce an agnostic point of view. His most notable
work in this respect was his *Science of Ethics,* in which he endeavored to
create a naturalistic theory and interpretation of ethics, based on the Darwinian doctrine and defending the notion that the main purpose of sound
codes of behavior is to conserve group life and promote social development.

Robert Flint (1838-1910) was important chiefly for his historical studies
of the development of the philosophy of history in modern times. He was
a professor of divinity in the University of Edinburgh. His important
works here were *The Philosophy of History in Europe: France and Germany* (1874) and his study of the philosophy of Vico (1884). Those sections of the first-named work which dealt with France and Belgium were
expanded into a whole volume, *The Philosophy of History in France*
(1893), with the expectation that he would follow it by later volumes on
the philosophy of history in Germany and elsewhere and on his own views
of the philosophy of history. But he never published any further systematic material along this line. Flint ingeniously combined his own steadfast
theism with the traditions of British empiricism in his critical comments,
and was urbanely hostile to Transcendentalism and Hegelianism. His
chief service was to interest English and American readers in the writings
of others on the philosophy of history.

A curious hodgepodge of scientific naturalism and obscurantism appeared in the widely-read works of Benjamin Kidd (1858-1916), especially
his *Social Evolution.* Kidd looked upon history somewhat as Kant did,
in the sense of being a struggle between individual initiative and social
control. But, whereas Kant believed that the individualistic impulses were
the main incentives to progress, Kidd held that the group constraint of individualism constitutes the mainspring of human development. It was
Kidd's contention that reason would promote individualism and anarchy.
Therefore, the all-important social control must rest upon some powerful
super-rational force or sanction. This Kidd found to reside in religion.

Kidd accepted Spencer's idea of the military and industrial stages in social development. Christianity rescued humanity from the military stage, through its strong ultra-rational sanctions for right conduct and its altruistic ethical system. When Catholicism had performed its function and run its useful course, Protestantism appeared to let loose a flood of hitherto repressed or misdirected altruism. This altruism so gripped the ruling classes that they found themselves unable to resist the movement for democracy and social justice. Kidd thus sought to deny or obscure the Marxian theory that all gains have been made by the struggle of the lower classes against their masters.

The United States has shown much interest in the philosophy of history, especially on the part of the philosophical disciples of Hegel, Comte and others. The professional historians, at least after the days of Andrew D. White, had little use for it.[19] Morris, Harris, Royce and others introduced Hegel. John Fiske popularized Herbert Spencer's notions of cosmic evolution. John Dewey applied the Darwinian concepts to philosophy. Franklin H. Giddings adapted Comte's scheme in his interpretation of social evolution. Henry Adams suggested the subjection of historical data to scientific laws, especially the second law of thermodynamics, which elucidates the doctrine of the degradation of energy. More influential was his brother Brooks Adams' *Law of Civilization and Decay* and *The Theory of Social Revolution*. J. D. Forrest combined a modified Hegelianism with a thorough knowledge of historical facts in his *Development of Western Civilization*. But the historical movement of any scientific sort got under way so late in the United States that thoughtfully-inclined historians were more interested in the interpretation of history than in the older comprehensive schemes of the philosophy of history.[20]

RECENT TRENDS

There have been other contributions to the philosophy of history beyond those we have briefly reviewed. Karl Marx adapted the Hegelian dialectic to create a materialistic interpretation of history, representing technological and economic factors as the determining items in human and social development. Of these economic elements, the class struggle has been by far the most potent in its influence. Ultimately, according to Marx, the proletariat will overthrow their capitalistic exploiters and create a classless society.[21]

The eminent Italian aesthetician, Benedetto Croce, has presented a neo-

19 See, for example, G. B. Adams, "History and the Philosophy of History," in *American Historical Review,* January, 1909.

20 Cf. Shotwell, *Introduction to the History of History,* chap. xxvii. See below, pp. 355 ff.

21 M. M. Bober, *Karl Marx's Interpretation of History* (Harvard University Press, 1927).

Hegelian view of history, but has shifted the emphasis from logic to art.[22] History, to Croce, is a manifestation of reality in the present, which contains within itself the impressions from the past and the germs of insight into the future. It is the duty of philosophy to interpret these collective manifestations of reality at each stage of historical development. Croce thus calls for a close inter-relation between philosophy and history. Following the Idealist notion that there is no reality apart from Mind or Spirit, Croce declares that "in external essence, history is the story of the human mind and its ideals, in so far as they express themselves in theories and in works of art, in practical and moral actions." Croce is famous for his "common-sense" argument for the philosophy of history, to the effect that those who reject dignified and grandiose philosophical assumptions, and throw them out of the front door, usually sneak in some petty and mean philosophy through the back door. Hence, he implies, we might better frankly work with a worthy and honorable philosophy of history.

A lengthy and much discussed philosophy of history, appearing after the first World War, was embodied in the ponderous tomes of Oswald Spengler, *The Decline of the West*. The pompous pedantry and the showy but variable erudition bear along an underlying philosophy of historical pessimism which suggests in some respects the influence of Nietzsche. The cyclical theory of history is once again revived. Spengler discerns four great types of civilization though he mentions many others: the Indian, which started about 1800 B.C.; the Antique, beginning about 900 B.C.; the Arabian, starting with the Christian era and including the rise of Christianity and Islam; and the Western, which sprang up about A.D. 900. Each passes through a complete four-period cycle of spring, summer, autumn, and winter. Western civilization is now in its winter period and it may toss on the torch of culture to the yellow races of the East. While the general philosophy of the work is dubious and its conclusions highly debatable, one must admit that the book is immensely stimulating and that it throws off thousands of interesting suggestions. The ostensible learning has also impressed many readers. The Spengler "bubble" was burst in part as a result of the later publication of a little book on *Man and Technics* which proved Spengler almost illiterate on elementary principles of biology and anthropology.[23] Spengler was answered by Ludwig Stein, another Germanic philosopher, in his *Evolution and Optimism*.

An interesting development in our own day appeared in the work of the German historian and sociologist, Paul Barth (1858-1922), a close student of the historical philosophy of Hegel and his followers. Barth sought

[22] *American Historical Review*, January, 1934, p. 230. See also his *History: Its Theory and Practice* (Harcourt, Brace, 1921). Croce has wavered between various attitudes, one of which was a violent anti-historical position.

[23] Henry Hazlett, in the *Nation*, February 24, 1932.

to separate the philosophy of history from history and to take it over into sociology. He regarded the philosophy of history as the essence of sociology. His large and important work, *The Philosophy of History as Sociology* (1897, 1922), is both an important survey of the philosophy of history and an argument in support of his contention that the philosophy of history is sociology, a claim which most conventional historians have been only too glad to concede. Kurt Breysig, a follower of Lamprecht and an able sociological historian, has of late lapsed into the philosophy of history in his *Vom geschichtlichen Weden* [*On Historical Becoming*]. He has merged Marx and Hegel, stressing the potency of both material factors and ideals. His eulogy of leadership is especially notable. The most voluminous contributions to the philosophy of history in recent times are *The Study of History* by Arnold J. Toynbee, a gigantic work which appeared in twelve volumes between 1934 and 1961; and Pitirim Sorokin's *Social and Cultural Dynamics*, in four volumes (1937-1941). Toynbee studied the rise and fall of some twenty-two civilizations, the net result being, as Joseph Hergesheimer observed, to "bury the universe in an Anglican churchyard." Sorokin portrayed social evolution as fluctuating between recurring doomsdays and intervals of transitory well-being.

SELECTED REFERENCES

G. B. Adams, "History and the Philosophy of History," in *American Historical Review,* January, 1909.

D. S. Muzzey, ed., *Essays in Intellectual History Dedicated to James Harvey Robinson,* chaps. iv, x, xiii. Harper, 1929.

Fueter, *Histoire de l'historiographie moderne,* pp. 517-73, 647-57.

R. Flint, *The Philosophy of History in France and Germany.* Scribner, 1874.

———, *The Philosophy of History in France.*

G. P. Gooch, *History and Historians in·the Nineteenth Century,* chaps. ii-iv, ix-x, xvii, xxvi. Longmans, Green, 1952.

Thompson, *History of Historical Writing,* Vol. II, chaps, xl, xliv, xlvii.

Reinhold Aris, *History of Political Thought in Germany from 1789 to 1815.* London, 1936.

R. T. Clark, *Herder: His Life and Thought.* Univ. of California Press, 1955.

H. C. Englebrecht, *Johann Gottlieb Fichte.* Columbia University Press, 1933.

J. C. Herold, *Mistress to an Age: A Life of Madame de Staël.* Bobbs-Merrill, 1958.

L. M. Young, *Thomas Carlyle and the Art of History.* Univ. Pa. Press, 1939.

T. P. Donovan, *Henry Adams and Brooks Adams.* Univ. of Okla. Press, 1961.

Wegele, *Geschichte der deutschen Historiographie,* Books IV and V.

Rudolph Haym, *Die romantische Schule.* Berlin, 1914.

K. A. Poetzsch, *Studien zur fruehromantischen Politik und Geschichtsauffassung.* Leipzig, 1907.

Gottfried Salomon, *Das Mittelalter als Ideal in der Romantik.* Munich, 1922.

Peardon, *The Transition in English Historical Writing.*

Kenneth Bell and G. M. Morgan, *The Great Historians.* Macmillan, 1925.

IX

HISTORICAL WRITING UNDER THE INFLUENCE OF LIBERALISM AND NATIONALISM

NATIONALISM AND HISTORICAL WRITING

THE expansion of Europe was not only a powerful factor in arousing historical interest in non-European peoples and a strong impulse to the development of the new natural science and its accompanying sceptical philosophy; it was also the chief force in creating the modern national states out of the feudal monarchies of the later Middle Ages. By its contributions to the increase of the capital and other resources at the disposal of the monarchs, and to the creation of a loyal middle class, it enabled the kings to provide the hired officialdom and military forces, by means of which they crushed the opposition of the feudal nobility and brought into being the national state system.

The welling up of patriotic pride in these newly fashioned states led to the production of narratives glorifying the national past and to vigorous activity in collecting the priceless records of the achievements of the several nations from the most remote past. While this editing and collecting movement, in its earliest phases, goes back to the sixteenth century, it took on its modern form after the French Revolution, the Napoleonic Wars and the regeneration of Prussia had contributed so greatly to the creation of an ardent national self-consciousness in most of the European states. At this time, it was reinforced by the popular tenets of Romanticism, emphasizing the importance of national character and the imperishable "genius of a people."

Liberalism also strongly influenced nationalistic historical writing, especially in those countries where the monarchical and absolutist traditions were not overwhelmingly dominant. The liberal tradition was stimulated by the English revolutions of the seventeenth century, the American Revolution, the French Revolution, the Prussian War of Liberation, and the revolutions of 1830 and 1848. Writers like Rotteck, Gervinus, Dahlmann, Thierry, Michelet, Quinet, Macaulay, Freeman, Bancroft, Motley, and the like, well illustrate how the liberal impulse operated in creating nationalistic historical narratives.

The nationalistic impulse was augmented from another source in the middle of the nineteenth century by the malign influence of the notorious *Essay on the Inequality of the Human Races* (1854) by Count Joseph

Arthur of Gobineau (1816-82). Gobineau proclaimed the determining influence of racial qualities on the course of historical development, asserted the inherent superiority of the "Aryan" race, and held that racial degeneration is the inevitable result of its mixture with inferior races. His now utterly discredited doctrines gained great vogue, especially among nationalistic German historians and publicists.[1] This culminated in the Teutonic rhapsodies of Charles Kingsley and Houston Stuart Chamberlain, the Gallic ecstasy of Maurice Barrès, and the Saxon paeans of Kipling and Homer Lea. Not only was this doctrine effective in developing a still greater degree of chauvinism upon the part of the governing "races" but it also led to the persecution of minority "races," and to the consequent stimulation of their nationalistic sentiments.[2]

NATIONALISTIC HISTORICAL WRITING IN GERMANY

Perhaps the earliest state to begin a national historical literature was Germany in the days of Humanism and the old empire. The cultured Emperor Maximilian I (1493-1519) followed the example of Charlemagne in gathering at his court in Vienna some of the leading historical scholars of German Humanism. Conrad Celtis revived interest in the *Germania* of Tacitus and thus launched a controversy which lasted for nearly four centuries. Johannes Spiessheimer (1473-1529), better known as Cuspinian, made a critical study of the historical works of Jordanes and Otto of Freising. Irenicus, Peutinger and Beatus Rhenanus exhibited the spirit of Blondus in their researches into German antiquities. Their activity was soon smothered, however, in the controversies of the Reformation, and the interest in secular and national history waned. The collection of German historical sources began with the work of Simon Schardius (1535-73), Johann Pistorius (1546-1608), and Marquard Freher (1565-1614). Melchoir Goldast (1578-1635) produced his famous collection of documents dealing with medieval German history and public law, known as the *Monarchia romani imperii,* which was the standard German collection until the *Monumenta* had covered the same period and material in a more thorough fashion. The distinguished philosopher, Gottfried Wilhelm Leibnitz (1646-1716), was ambitious to provide a collection of the sources of German history which would rival those on French history that had been gathered by Duchesne.[3] He was not, however, able to obtain the ne-

---

[1] Contrary to the general impression, Gobineau did not have any large popular following in France. There he was looked upon as the French Nietzsche, that is, as anti-religious, anti-Christian, anti-nationalistic, and anti-democratic. The first French biography of Gobineau was published only recently.

[2] Cf. F. H. Hankins, *The Racial Basis of Civilization* (Knopf, 1926), chaps. i-v; and Théophile Simar, *The Race Myth* (Boni, 1925).

[3] See below, p. 212.

cessary imperial support and the larger project had to be abandoned. He merely produced a collection on the history of the Guelphs—the *Scriptores rerum brunsvicensium* [*Brunswick Annals of the Western Empire*] (1707-11)—a by-product of his history of the dynasty of Brunswick. Leibnitz stressed the necessity of copying the sources just as they were instead of correcting them.

The vast modern collection of the sources of German history, the justly famous *Monumenta Germaniae Historica,* was a product of the spirit of the War of Liberation and was begun by the leading German statesman of his time, Heinrich Friedrich Karl, Baron vom Stein. Discouraged by the reactionary tendencies of the period following the Congress of Vienna, Stein devoted his energies to the stimulation of popular interest in German history. Love of his fatherland was Stein's dominating motive. Failing to obtain government support for a collection of the sources of German history, he raised the necessary funds from the resources of himself and his friends, founded the *Gesellschaft für Deutschlands ältere Geschichtskunde* and, with rare good fortune, secured an editor of remarkable scholarship and energy in the Hanoverian archivist, Georg Heinrich Pertz (1795-1876). Pertz carried the burden of the editorship for half a century, aided by many of the ablest German scholars, most prominent of his colleagues being the famed constitutional historian, Georg Waitz. This magnificent and colossal compilation—the *Monumenta*—included the important sources of information regarding German history from the time of the Roman writers on the invasions through the Middle Ages. In 120 volumes, it was not finished until 1925. It was one of the major landmarks in the development of scientific historical writing since it made possible the productivity and accuracy of succeeding generations of historians. This great national collection has been supplemented by large collections dealing with the history of the many German states, the religious history of Germany, German foreign relations, and the deeds of leading rulers, such as Erdmannsdörffer's exhaustive collection on the reign of Frederick William the Great Elector.

National history in Germany was not limited to the collection of sources, but received expression in glowing narratives which usually found their theme in the glories of the German imperial past or in laudatory accounts of the later Hohenzollern achievements. The latter served as the basis of enthusiastic proposals for a Prussian revival of the glamour of the medieval empire. One of the most important personal influences in the rise of German nationalistic history was that of Johannes Müller, who had written of the German Middle Ages in colorful and romantic fashion. Schmidt, as we have seen, had written a history of Germany from the Rationalist standpoint, but his cosmopolitan outlook made his work unsatisfactory to the patriots. Friedrich Wilken initiated the nationalist narrative by an account of German prowess in the period of the Crusades, his extended *History of the Crusades* (1807-32). Heinrich Luden (1780-1847), under the spell of Johannes Müller's views of the medieval period, produced a long *History of the German People* [to 1235], in which he aimed to arouse national enthusiasm for the magnificence of medieval Germany. Johannes Voigt (1786-1863), in his *History of Prussia,* and his *History of Marienburg* contributed an epic dealing with the conversion and conquest of Prussia by the Teutonic Knights. Friedrich von Raumer (1781-1873) surveyed the achievements of the Hohenstaufens, thus popularizing the heroes of medieval Germany, and Gustav Stenzel (1792-1854) portrayed the deeds of the Franconian emperors with critical skill as well as patriotic edification. Wilhelm von Giesebrecht (1814-89) analyzed the formation of the medieval German Empire, in his *History of the German Imperial Era,* with a display of scholarship not less remarkable than his Teutonic fervor and rare literary powers.

Though Leopold von Ranke's history of the Reformation was a powerful influence in making Luther a great German national hero, it must be admitted that von Ranke and his immediate disciples shared something of the universal outlook of the Rationalists. But with the rise of the "Prussian school," nationalistic history in Germany became even more chauvinistic and dynastic. Even von Ranke, while he generally controlled his emotions, could not restrain his admiration for Prussia and the Hohenzollerns. His many works on Prussian history come closer than any other of his writings to nationalistic history. Ludwig Hausser (1818-67), wrote a vivid account of the Thirty Years' War and the Palatinate, and contributed a voluminous epic on the War of the Liberation in his *History of Germany, 1786-1815*. In the latter he emphasized the rôle of Prussia in liberating and unifying Germany. Maximilian Duncker (1811-86), the historian of antiquity, as a result of his work in editing the state papers of the great Hohenzollerns, developed a warm admiration for the dynasty which convinced him of its fitness to revive the imperial glories of the old Germany. Praise of Prussia also came from Adolph Schmidt (1812-87), in his *Prussia's German Policy* and his *History of Attempts at Unity Since Frederick the Great*. Schmidt stressed the unwavering devotion of Prussia to the cause of German unity.

The first massive panegyric of Prussianism was the work of Johann Gustav Droysen (1804-84), who deserted his early liberalism to become an almost sycophantic eulogist of the Hohenzollerns. His monumental *History of Prussian Policy* was marred not only by its grave prejudices in favor of the "mission" of the dynasty he admired, but also by the fact that it was almost wholly limited to the superficial field of Prussian foreign politics. It gave little attention even to domestic policy, to say nothing of its omission of the underlying social conditions and economic forces.

The story was picked up where Droysen had left it by Heinrich von Treitschke (1834-96). His *History of Germany in the Nineteenth Century* ranks with the histories of Michelet, Macaulay and Froude as one of the literary masterpieces of modern historiography. While it was charged with all of the vivid enthusiasm for the leadership of Protestant Prussia which fired the work of Droysen, Treitschke's history at least had the real merit of devoting adequate attention to the fundamental cultural forces in German national development.

Heinrich von Sybel (1817-95), the last of the three leaders of the Prussian school, began his work as a disciple of von Ranke by a brilliant work on the First Crusade and by a profound study of the origins of the German kingship. But the stirring political situation in the middle of the century led him away from the poise of his master and he became a thorough advocate of German unity through Prussian military leadership. His *History of the French Revolution* was a massive polemic against the whole movement, and its central theme was the old Romanticist dogma of the political incapacity of the French. From this spectacle of alleged political ineptitude Sybel turned to an account of the event which seemed to him to demonstrate the supreme capacity of his own nation in political affairs —the foundation of the German Empire by Bismarck. Von Sybel's voluminous work on *The Foundation of the German Empire by William I* showed wonderful power in the clear presentation of a mass of political and diplomatic details, but it was a highly partisan defense of Bismarck's politics and diplomacy.

By the time von Sybel had finished his work, history in Germany had become too weak a vehicle to serve as the leading instrument for advancing national aspirations. Its place was taken by the literary products of Peters, Tannenberg and the pan-German expansionists; of Bernhardi and the ultra-militarists; and of Chamberlain and the blatant Teutonists. The part played by the Prussian school of historians in the production of this state of national exaltation has been clearly revealed by Guilland.[4] How scientific history itself had triumphed over ardent nationalism among professional historians by the time of the World War was well illustrated by Otto Hintze's celebration volume, *The Hohenzollerns and Their Work* (1915), where even the temptations of a centenary volume could not drive a competent historian from his poise. Yet there was an occasional hangover of nationalistic history down to the World War period. Perhaps the last of the eminent line of German nationalistic historians was Dietrich Schäfer (1845-1929), a strong monarchist and nationalist, whose *Modern World History* and *German History* were extremely popular with German patriots.

---

[4] Antoine Guilland, *Modern Germany and Her Historians* (London, 1915).

The sources of Austrian history were first collected by Jerome Pez (1685-1762), a monkish savant, in his *Scriptores rerum Austriacarum veteres*. In the nineteenth century, they were not only collected in the German *Monumenta,* where the great scholar, Theodor Sickel (1826-1908), rendered valuable editorial assistance, but also in separate national collections, the *Fontes rerum Austriacarum,* published in over seventy volumes since 1849 by the Vienna Academy, and the new edition of Böhmer's *Regesta imperii,* edited by Caspar Julius von Ficker (1826-1902) after 1877 at Innsbruck.

Sickel, while a great scholar, was the first to create popular interest in the medieval past of Austria through his editorial work and his volumes on the Saxon emperors. Ficker was equally one of the erudite school, but his studies of comparative law led him to defend the kinship of the various German peoples. The great national narrative history of Austria was the monumental work of Alfred von Arneth (1819-97) on the times of Maria Theresa. Onno Klopp (1822-1903) recalled the imperial heroes of the Thirty Years' War and conducted an attack on Frederick the Great. He was the major apologist for the Hapsburgs. Helfert defended the antirevolutionary policies of Metternich, while Friedjung (1851-1920) presented in measured fashion Austria's case against Prussia in the final years of friction before 1866. His outlook was pan-German and anti-Hungarian.

NATIONALISTIC HISTORY IN FRANCE

Nearly a century after the beginnings of German national historical writing at the court of Maximilian, the French began to turn their attention to the analysis and collection of the sources of their national history. This movement may conveniently be dated from the publication of the *Franco-Gallia* of François Hotman in 1574. Other early examples of this tendency were the *Antiquités gauloises et françoises* of Claude Fauchet (1579); the *Annales Francorum* of Pierre Pithou (1588); the *Récherches de la France* of Étienne Pasquier (1611); and the material on the Crusades in the *Gesta Dei per Francos* (1611-17) of Jacques Bongars. The true beginning of the critical collection of sources appeared in the products of André Duchesne (1584-1640) who compiled the *Historiae Normannorum scriptores antiqui* (1619), and the *Historiae Francorum scriptores coaetanei* (1636 f.); in the "genealogies" and the *Gallia christiana* of the brothers Sainte-Marthe (1572-1650, 1655); in the critical editions of Villehardouin and Joinville by Charles du Frense du Cange (1610-88); and in the *Capitularia regum Francorum* of Étienne Baluze (1636-1718).

During the last half of the seventeenth century and the first half of the eighteenth this work of collecting sources was carried on mainly by the scholarly Benedictine monks of the Congregation of Saint Maur at Saint-Germain-des-Près in Paris, which was founded between 1618 and 1630 by Doms Martin Tesnière and Grégoire Tarisse. Their leader in historical scholarship was the indefatigable Jean Mabillon (1632-1707). Only a few of their more notable collections can be mentioned here. Dom Thierry Ruinart (1657-1709) prepared critical editions of Gregory of Tours and Fredegarius; Dom Edmond Martène (1654-1739), the *Thesarus novus anecdotorum seu collectio,* and the *Veterum scriptorum et monumentorum amplissima collectio;* Dom Bernard Montfaucon (1655-1741), *Les Monuments de la monarchie française;* Dom Martin Bouquet (1685-1749), the famous *Rerum Gallicarum et Francicarum scriptores,* which is still being continued under the title of the *Recueil des historiens des Gaules et de la France;* and Dom Antoine Rivet de la Grange (1683-1749) aided by Duclou, Poncet and Colomb, began that unique *Historie littéraire de la France* which was continued by the French Institute and the Academy of Inscriptions. They have at present come down to the fourteenth century. The Maurists also turned their attention to the history of the French provinces and gathered many valuable collections, the most famous of which was the *Historie générale de Languedoc* of Doms Vaisette and Vic (1730-49), later revised by Molinier.

In the latter part of the eighteenth century the laymen again came to the front, the most notable center of their activity being the *Academie des inscriptions et belles-lettres,* which had been founded by Colbert in 1663. The most valuable product of their labors was the large collection of *Ordonnances des roys de France* by E. J. de Laurière, Denis Secousse and L. G. de Bréquigny (1714-94). They also continued the *Histoire littéraire* and the *Gallia Christiana.* A further stimulus came when P. C. F. Daunou was appointed national archivist by Napoleon. He brought many foreign archives to Paris and also continued the work on the *Histoire littéraire* and the other great Benedictine collections. Jourdan, de Crusy and Isambert brought together a notable collection on French legal history, *Recueil général des anciennes lois françaises,* in twenty-eight volumes (1822-23). The first monumental collection of sources produced in the nineteenth century was the voluminous *Collection compléte des mémoires relatifs à l'histoire de France* by the Petitots and Monmerqué in 130 volumes (1819-29), on the period from Philip Augustus to 1763.

What Germany owed to Baron vom Stein for the gathering of the sources of German national history France owed to the statesman-scholar, François Guizot, who not only organized the movement for systematic scientific work in collecting and editing the sources of French history, but also was a historical scholar of ability who contributed some valuable books from his own pen. Before he left historical writing for the field of political activity he had published a collection of some thirty volumes coming down to the thirteenth century. In 1833 he organized the *Société de l'histoire de France*, which was first presided over by Barante and which has since included in its membership many of the most famous historians of France. The *Ouvrages publiés* of this society have amounted to over 350 well-edited volumes of source materials. Even more important was Guizot's initiative in inducing Louis Philippe to appoint a subcommittee of the Ministry of Public Education which was to devote itself to publishing the hitherto unpublished source material of French history. In 1836 the work began to appear in the monumental series, *Collection de documents inédits sur l'histoire de France*, of which about 290 volumes have thus far been published.

The early editorial associates of Guizot in this enterprise were Mignet, Thierry, Guérard and Raynouard. With the foundation of the *Société de l'École des Chartes* in 1829, the provision of competent editors was henceforth assured through the establishment of one of the world's leading historical institutes for training students in the use of documents—*L'École des Chartes*.[5] The *Documents inédits* are the official French counterpart of the German *Monumenta* and are even more valuable, in that they are confined entirely to the presentation of material never before published. Since 1881 the volumes have been published under the supervision of the *Comité des travaux historiques et scientifiques*. The elaborate source collection brought out by the *Bibliothèque de l'École des hautes études* also deserves mention.

The French have also advanced a step beyond any other nation in providing great collections of sources for a study of their history in modern times. This has been due primarily to the fact that no other European state has possessed a national event or movement in modern times quite comparable in picturesque or romantic interest to the French Revolution. In 1903, the Socialist historian and statesman, Jean Jaurès, succeeded in inducing the government to establish a committee of the Ministry of Public Instruction to supervise the publication of the unpublished documents dealing with the economic history of the French Revolution. This work has been carried on by leading French historians, and the *Collection de documents inédits sur l'histoire économique de la Révolution Française* has been appearing in successive volumes since 1906. About a hundred volumes have been printed thus far. The municipal government of Paris has been publishing the *Collection de documents relatifs à l'histoire de Paris pendant la revolution française* since 1888. In addition to these public collections, many collections of sources dealing with special phases of the Revolution have been made by enterprising scholars, among whom Al-

---

[5] J. T. Shotwell, "The École des Chartes," in *American Historical Review*, July, 1906.

phonse Aulard and his pupils have been most active. Aulard has also taken a leading part in editing the Paris collection mentioned above.

The French also vied with the Germans in the writing of nationalistic historical narrative. The publication of Chateaubriand's *Genius of Christianity* in 1802 gave a luster and romantic touch to the French past in the Middle Ages comparable to the effect produced in Germany by the writings of Spittler and Johannes Müller. His later work, *The Martyrs,* continued this influence. Claude Fauriel (1772-1844), in his *History of Southern Gaul under the German Conquerors,* anticipated Fustel de Coulanges and Jullian by contending for the primacy of the Roman and Gallic over Frankish culture in the formation of medieval civilization. Joseph Michaud (1767-1839), in a very popular book, *History of the Crusades* (1812-17), vividly portrayed the glories of the French in the period of the Crusades. François Raynouard (1761-1836), in his *Researches into the Antiquity of the Roman Language,* and his *Comparative Grammar,* drew a colorful picture of the medieval troubadours and proclaimed the supremacy of French among the Romance languages. Numa Denis Fustel de Coulanges (1830-89), while the father of scholarly medieval studies in France, helped to intensify the patriotic element in French historical writing by defending the thesis of the Roman origin of French institutions and culture and by attacking the popular Teutonic and Germanist dogmas. Hanotaux, Fagniez and Chéruel, much later, analyzed with both critical erudition and patriotic pride the centralization of the French monarchy by the great statesmen of the seventeenth century.

Alphonse de Lamartine (1795-1869), in a work which rivaled Carlyle in the realm of historical literature and was equally unscientific as history, set forth with fervid admiration the glories of the French Revolution, and especially the exploits of the Girondists. Michelet interpreted the Revolution as an epic of liberty and a crusade for the emancipation of the people. The notion that the basic purpose of the Revolution was to establish Fraternity was defended by Louis Blanc, in his *History of the French Revolution of 1789,* and in his *History of Ten Years* (1841), the latter of which dealt with the period from 1830 to 1840. François Mignet (1796-1884), the most scholarly French historian of the first half of the nineteenth century, made an implied attack on the Bourbon restoration in his *History of the French Revolution,* by representing the French Revolution as the necessary and inevitable outgrowth of the tendencies of the age and as the dawn of a new and better era in the history of the world. Louis Adolphe Thiers (1797-1877) wrote a long and popular history of the French Revolution from the standpoint of nineteenth-century liberalism. While critical of the Empire in his *History of the Consulate and the Empire,* Thiers praised the First Consul as the savior of France and of European civilization. Napoleon was defended in his imperial splendor by Frédéric

Masson, Albert Vandal, Henri Houssaye and Arthur Lévy. Masson wrote touchingly of Napoleon's private life, attacking the infidelity and triviality of Josephine, and the mediocre and parasitical character of the Bonaparte family, to which Napoleon showed such pathetic and fatal loyalty. Vandal represented Napoleon as peace loving and goaded to war by English jealousy. Houssaye defended Napoleon's military genius right down through Waterloo, and vigorously condemned the Bourbon restoration. Lévy presented Napoleon as a superhuman and faultless personality. The Napoleonic legend has played a large part in French nationalistic historical literature to this day, various points of view being defended by Taine, Aulard, Mathiez, Madelin and Sée. Paul Thureau-Dangin (1837-1913), in his *History of the July Monarchy,* while deploring its popular origin, appeared as the historical apologist of the July Monarchy. Pierre de la Gorce (1846-1934), in his *History of the Second Empire,* dealt with the Second Empire as an apologist of monarchy and clericalism, if not of the personality of Napoleon III. Émile Ollivier (1825-1913), in *The Liberal Empire,* dwelt with pride upon the liberal tendencies of the last decade of the Empire. Finally Gabriel Hanotaux, in one of the finest products of nationalistic historiography in France, *The History of Contemporary France,* described and defended the establishment and policies of the Third Republic.

Nor has France been lacking in general histories written from the national point of view. Charles Henault (1685-1770) wrote the first general history of France, his *Abridged Chronology of the History of France* (1744). This held the field until Sismondi's longer and more competent work appeared. Early in the nineteenth century Sismondi produced the first comprehensive history of France. It was written from the standpoint of an ardent liberal who castigated kings and bishops and lauded the liberal tendencies in the medieval communes. But Sismondi was a Genevan and, to some extent, a representative of the mild rationalism of Rousseau, and his work was not calculated to arouse intense patriotic enthusiasm. Much different, except in its liberalism, was the brilliant work of Michelet. This was not only a real contribution to French literature but also to the stimulation of patriotic pride, especially on the part of liberal Frenchmen. Henri Martin's *History of France,* which began to appear in 1883, was less brilliantly written than Michelet's but rested on sounder scholarship. For half a century it remained the popular national history of France on account of its logical arrangement, lucid presentation, urbane *bourgeois* liberalism, and its central theme of the steady growth of French national unity. It went through many revisions and elaborations. Less nationalistic, but immensely popular was Victor Duruy's *History of France.* The great coöperative *History of France* edited by Ernest Lavisse belongs to the field of erudite and critical rather than nationalistic historiography, but there is plenty of patriotic sentiment in it.

French nationalism was greatly stimulated by the sting of the defeat and injustices of 1870. While the scholarly French historians, such as La Gorce and Sorel, maintained an impartiality in treating of the war of 1870 which put to shame the biased apology of von Sybel, there was a great outburst of nationalistic ardor on the part of the "superpatriots" among their countrymen. These tendencies found expression, above all, in the fiery speeches, poetry and pamphlets of Paul Déroulède, the chief of the *Revanchards,* and in the brilliant polemics and eulogies of his admirer, that ardent Gallican and head of the League of Patriots, Maurice Barrès, whose study of French history had convinced him that "the French make war as a religious duty. They were the first to formulate the idea of a Holy War. It is not in France that wars are entered upon for the sake of spoil, but as a champion in the cause of God, as a knight upholding justice."

While the French showed more restraint after 1870 than the Germans, the situation was reversed after 1918. In Germany, the empire and Prussia were temporarily discredited. But in France victory and nationalism were rampant. In his own volumes in his series on *The National History of France,* Franz Funck-Brentano is amazingly patriotic and full of hatred and contempt for Germany. The patriotic flavor is not even absent from Gabriel Hanotaux's large coöperative post-war work, *The History of the French Nation.*

NATIONALISTIC HISTORY IN ENGLAND

England did not start any systematic collection of the sources of its national history until the beginning of the nineteenth century. Just before his death Gibbon had warmly urged the creation of a committee to edit and publish a collection of the works of all the medieval chroniclers of England. He appropriately recommended John Pinkerton as the editor-in-chief. But nothing came of this after Gibbon's death. In the year 1800 the Record Commission was created, but no real historian was connected with its labors until Sir James Mackintosh was appointed in 1825. In 1830, Nicholas Harris Nicolas called attention to the deplorable condition of the historical sources in England and his sharp criticism led to the creation of a more active and critical committee on the Record Commission in 1836. One outcome of this improvement was the edition of Parliamentary writs by Palgrave.

The Record Commission was discontinued in 1837, and the historical records were placed in charge of the master of the rolls. No systematic activity in the collection of sources, however, began until after the middle of the century. At this time, William Stubbs, the greatest of English medievalists before Maitland and the anglicized Russian, Vinogradoff, vigorously criticized the state of affairs in respect to the collection of sources for the history of England. Shortly afterwards, in 1857, Lord Romilly, the master of the rolls, was able to secure an appropriation from the government to publish the sources of English medieval history, and the general oversight of the project was conferred upon Thomas Duffus Hardy (1804-78), a careful, if not brilliant, scholar. The work of editing these sources was carried on by a number of English medievalists, among them Brewer, Gairdner, Canon Robertson, Giles and Dimock, but far the greatest figure was "the English Waitz," Bishop William Stubbs (1825-1901). For more than a quarter of a century after 1863 he gave much of his time to this work. This collection, which was finished in 1911 in 243 volumes, is known as the *Chronicles and Memorials of Great Britain and Ireland During the Middle Ages (Rerum Britannicarum medii aevi scriptores)* or, more briefly, as the *Rolls Series,* from the fact of its publication under supervision of the master of the rolls. It is the official British analogue to the *Monumenta* and the *Documents inédits.* Other important collections are the calendars of state papers, the parliamentary records and debates, the records of the privy council, and the like. Less pretentious collections have been provided by the Camden society and the Early English Text society. There should also be mentioned the great collection of the sources of English legal history executed by the Selden society, and the publication of the manuscript records of important voyages and explorations by the Hakluyt society.

The historiography of nationalism was hardly less forceful in England than in Germany or France. Its most conspicuous feature was a variant of the Aryan and Nordic myths. This dogma stressed the political superiority of the Anglo-Saxon peoples, and became very popular in the nineteenth century. It rested primarily upon the assumption that the Teutonic invaders of England had made a clean sweep of the early Briton and Celtic inhabitants and had created an England purely Germanic in culture and almost purely Germanic in race. A most vigorous statement of this view appeared in *The Saxons in England,* by John Mitchell Kemble (1807-57), which was published in 1849. The book not only taught this Anglo-Saxon doctrine to the English, but was widely read in Germany and served to furnish the German nationalists with further confirmation of their convictions regarding the Germanic "mission." Kemble believed that the English institutions of the nineteenth century were directly derived from Germanic sources.

Edward Augustus Freeman (1823-92) carried the argument still further in his *History of the Norman Conquest of England.* In this he not only accepted the Anglo-Saxon theory, but, being an ardent lover of liberty, he also espied the real origins of political liberty in the German *folk-moot,* particularly in its English manifestation. This myth, dating back to Rapin Thoyras and Montesquieu, and so thoroughly punctured by Fustel de Coulanges and Brunner, has been one of the most persistent and pernicious sources of error which have come from a pre-anthropological stage in historical studies. Even the calm and cautious Bishop Stubbs and the charming John Richard Green were also seduced by this fiction of a Teutonic England, which was to be challenged by Seebohm and modified by Maitland and Vinogradoff.

The leading popular emotional impulse to the Germanist interpretation came from the notorious work of the poet-historian, Charles Kingsley, *The Roman and the Teuton,* which was first published in 1864. Highly entertaining but almost wholly unscientific and non-historical, it did more to pervert the interpretation of early medieval history than any other book of its time. He idealized the "young and virile Teutonic forest children" with the ardor of a Las Casas, set them in marked and flattering contrast to the morally and physically decadent Romans of the "dying empire," and rejoiced in the destruction of the latter by the "human deluge" from the North. It is a sufficient commentary upon the accuracy of his work to note that the labors of scholarly medievalists for the last generation have discredited every one of his main theses. The book, however, gained a great popular vogue and no Englishman could well read it without desiring to trace his ancestry back to Arminius and Alaric.

Passing from the Middle Ages, where the national grandeur of Britain had been laid by the Teuton, one of the most intensely nationalistic of English historians, James Anthony Froude, described the glories of the English revolt from Rome.[6] Carlyle lauded the virtues of Cromwell and his associates of the Commonwealth. The Whig apologists, James Mackintosh, Hallam, and above all, Thomas Babington Macaulay, described the salvation of the world's liberties through the "glorious revolution" of 1688-89. Macaulay's *History of England* (1848-61) is the English counterpart of the histories of Treitschke and Michelet. It is the most brilliant of English contributions to historical literature, as well as a valuable, though partisan body of historical knowledge. The Earl of Stanhope's extended *History of England from the Peace of Utrecht to the Peace of Versailles* presented the history of eighteenth century England from the standpoint of a Tory approval of the British policies of that era. General William Napier praised English prowess in the Peninsular War in his *History of the War in the Peninsula* (1824-40) which was as frank an adulation of war as a factor in human society as was Bernhardi's work over half a century later. Sir Herbert Maxwell eulogized the "Iron Duke" in his

[6] See above, p. 190.

Life of Wellington (1899). Harriet Martineau, in her *History of England* (1877-78), dealt with the first half of the nineteenth century in a manner to emphasize the benefits of the Whig triumphs in that period. Finally, Sir John R. Seeley (1834-95), an example of both nationalism and erudition in historical writing, wrote with pride of the development of the British Empire in his *Expansion of England,* and his *Growth of British Policy.* Not only was Seeley a nationalist and an imperialist, but along with Freeman, he was chiefly responsible for holding English historiography in the narrow and limited channels of political history.

The great national history of England was John Richard Green's *Short History of the English People* (1874), which combined a discreet appropriation of the Germanist doctrines with primary interest in the development of English civilization as a mass culture. It gave much more space than customary to the development of British popular life. It became a classic and especially thrilled the British liberals. Green did the work over on a larger scale in his *History of the English People* (1880), which was far less widely read.

The growth of national enthusiasm which accompanied the work of Cecil Rhodes and the Boer War, did not fail to produce its nationalistic literature, which was as far removed from the scholarly grasp of Seeley as was the attitude of Bernhardi from that of von Sybel. Bernhardi found his English counterpart in Professor J. A. Cramb, who detected as a governing principle in England's past wars "that higher power of heroism which transcends reason." Curiously enough, as it had fallen to a renegade Englishman, H. S. Chamberlain, to produce the apotheosis of Germania, so it required an American, Homer Lea, to link up the future salvation of the world with the necessity of the universal triumph of Britannia, through the strengthening and preservation of "the scarlet circle of power that the Saxon has marked around the earth as has no other race before him."

NATIONALISTIC HISTORICAL WRITING IN OTHER EUROPEAN COUNTRIES

Italy shares the double honor of having been the first nation to provide a fairly complete collection of its sources of national history and of having produced the most indefatigable of all editors in Lodovico Antonio Muratori (1672-1750). From 1723 until his death in 1750 he brought together in the twenty-five folio volumes of the *Rerum italicarum scriptores* many of the extant sources of Italian history from 500 to 1500 A.D. So thorough was his work that it has only been deemed necessary in recent years to undertake a new edition of his collection. This has been in progress since 1900, at first under the supervision of Giosuè Carducci and Vitorio Fiorini and now under the control of the Italian Historical Institute. In 1833, Charles

Albert aided the movement to gather sources of Italian national history, and some twenty-two volumes were published under the title of *Monumenta historiae patriae*. Much material on the history of medieval Italy has been edited and published by the Italian Historical Institute in the collection, *Fonti per la storia d'Italia*.[7]

While the national narrative history, like the collection of sources, dates back to a more remote period in Italy than in the other states of Europe, namely, to the era of Humanism, it began in its modern phase with *The History of the Neapolitan Revolution of 1799,* by Vincenzo Cuoco (1770-1823). Here he recited the reason for its failure and maintained that Italian unity could only be achieved by Italians themselves. It would be necessary to create a national consciousness in Italy and a mental atmosphere favorable to revolution. Similar in spirit was *The History of Italy During the Revolutionary and Napoleonic Wars,* by Carlo Botta (1766-1837), which breathed the ardent liberalism that found expression in the politics of the period in the activities of the *Carbonari*. Carlo Troya (1785-1853), in his *Italy in the Middle Ages,* and Luigi Tosti (1811-97), in his *Lombard League* and *Boniface VIII,* surveyed the history of medieval Italy for evidence to support their plea for papal leadership in creating Italian unity. They eulogized Dante, the Church and the popes. D'Azeglio turned to both medieval and contemporary Italy to prove papal incapacity and to call attention to the promise of leadership in the house of Savoy. Cesare Balbo's *History of Italy* (1846) implied that both the pope and the house of Savoy might well collaborate in achieving Italian confederation. Guiseppe Ferrari (1812-76), in his *History of Revolutions in Italy* (1858), glorified the alleged constructive services of the struggles, violence and bloodshed which accompanied the battle for political liberty in medieval Italy. It was implied that a similar service might be rendered by revolution in Ferrari's age. In his later *Theory of Political Periods* [cycles], Ferrari, in a vein reminiscent of Vico, sought to put the philosophy of history at the service of the *Risorgimento*. Gino Capponi sought patriotic inspiration in the Renaissance and produced an able and extended *History of the Republic of Florence* (1875). Pasquale Villari (1827-1917) devoted his historical writings primarily to medieval and Renaissance Florence and her heroes, such as Savonarola and Machiavelli, using their memory to inspire the movement for Italian unity. Villari did much to popularize medieval Italian history. His work on the history of Florence was a masterpiece. But the historian who did for Italy what Martin did for France in popularizing the reading of national history was Cesare Cantu (1804-95), who produced the first complete national history of Italy on an ample scale. Pietro Colletta (1775-1831) set forth a stinging criticism

---

[7] 58 vols., 1887 ff.

of the cruelty and corruption of Bourbon rule in Sicily in his *History of Naples,* which was an encouragement to any uprising against the yoke of the foreigner. The extreme expression of Italian national sentiment after union was accomplished appeared in the poetry of Giosue Carducci and Gabriele d'Annunzio. With the coming of Fascism to Italy, nationalism was raised from a historical philosophy to the level of a religion.

The first collection of Spanish sources was not the work of Spaniards, but of the itinerant English scholar, Robert Beal (d. 1601), who published his *Rerum hispanicarum scriptores* in 1579-81. Nearly two centuries later, J. A. C. Bertodano produced his extensive collection of sources on diplomatic history (1740-52). The great national collection of sources, however, was not begun until the middle of the nineteenth century when Pidal, Salva and others started the *Colección de documentos inéditos para la historia de España,* which was completed in 112 volumes (1842-95). It deals mainly with the sixteenth century. In addition, the Royal Academy of History at Madrid has been publishing source material since 1851 in the collection entitled *Memorial histórica español.* The sources of medieval Spanish history have never been systematically collected, edited and published. Spain found her great national historian in Modesto Lafuente (1806-66). His monumental *General History of Spain,* which was intended to be a continuation of Mariana, appeared in thirty volumes from 1850 to 1867. It covered the period to 1833 and was continued after his death by Juan Valera. The grandeur and decadence of Spain was likened to that of Rome in the classic *History of the Decadence of Spain* (1854) by Antonio Cánovas. What Walter Scott did for Scotland, England, and France, was performed in the vastly popular historical novels of Perez Galdos.

In Bohemia, Czech nationalism did not initiate interest in history, as in other European states. Rather, it was history that tended to arouse nationalism in the first instance. To the vigorous patriotism of Frantisek Palacky's monumental *History of Bohemia* (1836-67), more than to any other source, the modern Czech national spirit owes its origin. In spite of the absence of government aid before 1919, there have been reasonably adequate collections of the sources of Czech history. Palacky and others since his day have edited the *Old Czech and Moravian Written Records,* in thirty-two volumes (1840-1918). The ablest of native Bohemian historical scholars, Anton Gindley, edited another collection, the *Monumenta historiae Bohemica* (1864-69). Special interest has been shown in the collection of material on Bohemian religious history. Count Franz von Lützow, in the period just before the World War, provided the best appreciation of John Huss as the Bohemian national hero. On the seventeenth and eighteenth centuries, the ablest national history was the work of Antal Rezek and Josef Svatek, *History of Bohemia and Moravia in Modern Times* (1892-97) A French scholar, Ernest Denis, and an American,

Robert J. Kerner, have made important contributions to Czech history, highly sympathetic with Bohemian aspirations.

The Hungarian government has been publishing the *Monumenta Hungariae historica* at Budapest since 1857. More than a hundred volumes have appeared. But for the earliest Hungarian sources one must consult the smaller collection, edited by Matthias Florianus, *Historiae Hungaricae fontes domestici* (1881-85). Historical circumstances have so inflamed Hungarian national sentiment that even the most scholarly Magyar historians remain highly patriotic. The first great national history of Hungary was the *History of Hungary* by Ignácz Fessler (1756-1839), which brought the story down to 1811. János G. von Mailath's history, written later, came down to 1848. No European historian has been more thoroughly united scholarship and patriotism than Henrik Marczali in his *Hungary in the Eighteenth Century* (1910), and his *History of Hungary* (1911). The official national history of Hungary is Ignácz Acsády's *History of the Hungarian Empire* (1904). The most extensive work is the coöperative *History of the Hungarian Nation* (1895-98) in ten volumes, edited by Alexander Szilágyi.

Though contemporary Poland had no independent government until 1919 to subsidize collections of Polish national history, the Academy of Sciences at Cracow began systematic collections in the seventies of the last century. Some of the more important collections were the *Scriptores rerum Polonicarum* (twenty-two volumes); the *Monumenta medii aevi historica res gestas Poloniae illustrantia* (eighteen volumes); and the briefer *Acta historica res gesta Poloniae* (twelve volumes). The partitions of Poland and the resulting zeal for emancipation were a powerful stimulus to nationalistic Polish history. The first important national historian of Poland was Joachim Lelewel (1786-1861), author of the *History of Poland in the Middle Ages*, and of *Poland: Her History*. While a Rationalist and a democrat in outlook, Lelewel wrote his history of Poland according to the Romanticist notion of the national soul and the collective genius of a people. Karol Szajnocha (1818-68) gained popularity by his reconstruction of the age of the Jagiellos. The foremost poet of Poland, the eminent patriot, Adam Mickiewicz (1798-1855), also contributed to the history of his country. His *Popular History of Poland* amply vindicated its title and did much to arouse general enthusiasm for the Polish past. The ablest of all the nationalistic histories of Poland was Jósef Szujski's *History of Poland* (1862-66), a work of great literary merit which especially extolled the ancient Polish republic. The foremost nationalistic historian of the Ukraine was Vyacheslav Lipinsky (1882-1931). He gave special attention to the historical rôle of the Ukrainian nobility. He interpreted Ukrainian history as a perpetual struggle to reëstablish Ukrainian independence, stressing the leadership of the Ukrainian nobility in this process.

In spite of the reactionary policies of the Russian government and the literary censorship, nationalistic historical writing got under way in the latter portion of the eighteenth century. Indeed, the nationalistic narrative was the only type which was safe under tsardom. The collection of the sources of Russian history has been mainly the work of the Russian Archeological Commission which was set up in 1835. It has collected the old Russian chronicles in the *Polnoe sobranie russkikh lietopisei,* in twenty-three volumes (1841-1916), and the *Russkaia istoricheskaia biblioteka,* in thirty-seven volumes (1872-94) on the Muscovite period, and many lesser collections on legal, economic and ecclesiastical history. The great collection of materials on foreign policy is that prepared by Féodor de Martens under the direction of the Ministry of Foreign Affairs, the *Recueil des traités et conventions,* in fifteen volumes (1874-1909). Since the Revolution of 1917 much material has been published on the history of Russian revolutionary movements.

The first comprehensive history of Russia of any scholarly pretentions was the *Russian History Since the Most Ancient Times* by Michael Shcherbotov (1733-90), which painted Russian national development in glowing terms and stressed the primary significance of the outstanding leaders in this achievement. More thorough and readable was *The History of the Russian State* by Nicholas Karamazin (1766-1826), which brought the story down to 1611, when the Romanovs appeared on the scene. It was conceived in Romanticist terms, stressing the national genius of the Russian people. Russian national culture was regarded as superior to that of the West because of its oriental heritage, its devoted church, and its aristocratic political institutions. Karamazin, like Shcherbotov, glorified the rulers as national heroes. Nationalism was extolled from the standpoint of the "western school" of Russian historians by Sergius Soloviev (1820-79), in his *History of Russia from the Most Ancient Times* (twenty-one volumes, 1851-79), which dealt in great detail with Russian history down to 1774. It was far more scholarly than any preceding work of its kind and was cordial to the westernization of Russia. Hence, it eulogized the achievements of Peter the Great. The most voluminous history of Russia ever written, Soloviev's work was too long to become a popular masterpiece. This latter distinction was achieved by his one-volume work, *Outline of Russian History* (1859). The enthusiasm of Russian liberals for their national history was aroused by Nicholas Kostomarov (1817-85), in his *Historical Monographs and Researches* (1872-79). While earlier writers had concentrated on leaders, Kostomarov emphasized the life, manners and customs of the Russian people in the course of their national development. His work was one of the best contributions to Russian ethnography. He also brought the Russian borderlands, especially the Ukraine, within his purview. What John Richard Green did for English national history was performed for Russia on a larger scale by Vasiliev Kluchevsky (1841-1911) in his *Course of Russian History*, which traced the evolution of Russian folk-life, institutions and nationality. It was a scholarly work and one of the masterpieces of modern historiography. Kluchevsky especially stressed the importance of Russian colonization and expansion, though he was not a professional pan-Slavist. Since the Revolution of 1917 there has been a natural tendency to depreciate the achievements and institutions of the tsarist era, but Pokrovsky has written a suggestive general Marxist survey of Russian history.

Belgian enthusiasm for the collection of sources of national history began with the attainment of independence in 1830. The great national collection is the *Collection de chroniques Belges inédits*, published in 179 volumes at Brussels by the Royal Historical Commission since 1836. The *Société d'émulation de Bruges*, published between 1839 and 1864 the fifty-six volumes of the *Recueil de chroniques, chartes, et autres documents concernant l'histoire et les antiquités de la Flandre occidentale*. In addition, Alphonse Wauters (1817-98) edited the great collection of communal charters, Louis Gachard (1800-85) edited the foreign archives of the period since the fifteenth century, and Paul Fredericq edited the documents on the Inquisition in Belgium and Holland. Wauters also wrote with feeling on the Belgian communes of the Middle Ages, and Gachard on the era of Charles V and Philip II. The great Catholic and Belgian counterblast to Motley's work, as well as to that of Prinsterer in Holland, was contained in the writings of Joseph Kervyn de Lettenhove (1817-91) on the sixteenth century, and in his general *History of Flanders*. He condemned William the Silent and his Protestant supporters and defended the position of Spain and the Catholic party. His somewhat chauvinistic and obscurantic work has been superseded by the admirable critical works of Paul Fredericq (1850-1920) and Henri Pirenne (1862-1935). In the writings of Fredericq, however, there was still a strong flavor of Flemish nationalism.

While Holland has not provided so complete a collection of national sources as Belgium, the Historical Society of Utrecht has been publishing important sources since 1863—the *Werken uitgegeven door het Historisch Genootschap te Utrecht*—and Prinsterer had edited the voluminous archives of the House of Orange. In 1902 a royal commission of the most eminent Dutch historians was appointed to arrange for the systematic publication of the manuscript sources of the history of Holland. Under the editorship of H. T. Colenbrander, it has published twenty-two volumes of *Gedenkstukken der algemeene geschiedenis van Nederland van 1795 bis 1840*. The most enthusiastic Dutch nationalistic narrative history was the *Handbook of the History of the Netherlands*, by Guillaume Groen van Prinsterer (1801-76). In this and in his *Maurice and Barnevelt*, Protestantism and the House of Orange received their vindication and eulogy. Prinsterer's volumes have now been rendered obsolete by the scholarly monographs of Robert Fruin (1823-99), one of the ablest of Dutch historians, and by the accurate and well-balanced general history of the Netherlands by Petrus Blok (1855-1929).

The Scandinavian nations have not been unproductive in the field of national historical writing. The sources have been collected in the following series, among others: the *Scriptores rerum Danicarum medii aevi,* edited by Jacob Langebek and his successors; the *Diplomatarium Norvegicum,* edited by C. C. A. Lange; and the *Scriptores rerum Sueciarum,* edited by Erik Gustav Geijer (1783-1847) and his associates. The nationalistic historical narrative was introduced in Denmark by Worsaae; in Norway by Keyser and Munch; and in Sweden by Geijer, Carlson and Fryxell. Johan Jacob Worsaae (1821-85) gave special attention to the early history of Denmark in his *Primeval Antiquities of Denmark* and his *Prehistory of the North.* He also dealt with the Danes in England. Jacob Rudolf Keyser (1803-64) cultivated particularly the colorful and romantic origins of Norway in his *History of the Norsemen.* He also gave much attention to the religious history of Norway. Far broader and more popular was the long *History of the Norwegian People* by Peter Andreas Munch (1810-63). Geijer's *History of the Swedes* [to Charles X] did much to promote popular interest in the early history of Sweden and its folk-life. Friedrich Carlson (1811-77) continued Geijer's monumental work. Andreas Fryxell (1795-1881) wrote a ten-volume *Essay on the History of Sweden* which gained wide popularity. These works have been succeeded by the more recent and scholarly national histories of Johannes Steenstrup and his associates on Denmark; Johan Sars, Knut Gjerset and Alexander Bugge on Norway; and Harold Hjarne and Emil Hildebrand on Sweden.

If there were available space it would be easy to demonstrate the very great, if not determining, influence of the study of the "glories" of their national past upon the rise of the nationalistic aspirations of the Balkan peoples since 1820. The well-known influence of Alexandru Xénopol's *History of the Roumanians of Trajan's Dacia* (1888-93) upon Roumanian nationalism is but a typical illustration of the influence of historical writing upon Balkan nationalism.[8]

JEWISH NATIONALISM

Surely, no account of the inter-relation of nationality and historiography in European modern times would be complete without some reference to the national historical literature of Judaism and Zionism. The

8 See also below, p. 321.

rise of Jewish nationalism in the last century was intimately related to the general development of the spirit of nationality in Europe during that period. This stimulated Jewish national spirit, both by the direct process of imitation and also through the persecution of the Jews, as a result of the growing chauvinism throughout continental Europe after 1870. The remarkable reaction which this growth of Jewish national sentiment had on the development of the interest of the Jews in their national history is readily apparent. Historical societies were formed in most leading modern states—the *Société des études juives,* founded in 1880; the Historical Commission of the Union of German-Jewish Congregations, appointed in 1885; the American-Jewish Historical Society, founded in 1892; and the English-Jewish Historical Society, created in 1895. These societies have done valuable work in compiling the sources of Jewish history and in arousing interest in its study. Especially to be noted is the *Regesten zur Geschichte der Juden im fränkischen und deutschen Reiche bis zum Jahre 1273,* published by the German-Jewish Historical Commission since 1887. Including an account of the Jewish persecutions in the medieval period, it has tended to arouse national resentment over past, as well as present, oppression of the Jews.

The Jews have also been stirred by the work of an able national historian, Heinrich Graetz (1817-91). Isaac M. Jost (1793-1860), in his *History of Judaism,* and his *History of the Israelites,* surveyed the history of the Jews, but he was too liberal, rationalistic, and impartial to serve as a truly national historian. Widely different was the work of Graetz, sometimes called the "Jewish Treitschke," *The History of the Jews from the Most Ancient Times to the Present.*[9] Conservative, basically orthodox, and fired with a warm enthusiasm for the past and future of his people, Graetz traced in an eloquent manner the history of the Jews from their origins to 1848, laying special stress upon their literary and spiritual development—in other words, upon those elements which contributed the most to the development and persistence of their national culture. He viewed the Jews as a "special spiritual type." Graetz's work was especially in line with the development of "Zionism," for he insisted that the true Messiah is the national spirit of the Jewish people and he discouraged further delay in awaiting the coming of a personal Messiah. Scholarship triumphed over nationalism, though the latter is not wholly absent, in S. M. Dubnow's *World History of the Jewish People from their Origins to the Present.*[10] In addition to the general histories of Graetz and Dubnow there should be mentioned the many histories dealing in a comprehensive fashion with the history of the Jews in the several European states. The *Jewish Encyclopedia* is both scholarly in nature and nationalistic in tone.

[9] 11 vols., 1853-75.   [10] 10 vols., 1925-29.

The persecution of the German Jews launched by Hitler and the Nazis has done more to revive Jewish nationalism than any other event of a century. Numerous works have been written since 1933, by Maurice Samuels and others, dealing with various aspects of Judaism and nationalism.

ARCHIVAL MATERIAL

In connection with this brief summary of the reaction of nationalism upon historiography in Europe some passing reference should be made to the growth and accumulation of archival material and its increasing accessibility to students. The development of the national states and their bureaucracies led to the develoment of a large volume of administrative "red tape" and to the growth of fixed diplomatic correspondence. From these sources a rich storehouse of historical material had accumulated in the national, ecclesiastical and private archives by 1800. Before they could be generally useful to historians, however, the sources in the archives had to be classified and centralized and made public to accredited historians. Before the nineteenth century there was a marked disinclination to open the archives to historians.[11] In the matter of centralization and classification of archival material France has taken the lead, due chiefly to the large number of highly-trained archivists provided by l'École des Chartes. At the present time only England is exceedingly backward among the major European states in providing for a systematic arrangement and classification of its archival material. One of the major defects of even well-classified archives is the frequent absence of the most important materials in the form of private letters and memoranda which the statesmen and diplomats have removed from the files. For this reason, Bismarck once declared that public archival material is of little value for writing realistic diplomatic history. Sir Edward Grey set a precedent by leaving most of his private papers in the Foreign Office when he laid down his duties as Secretary of State.

In the same way that national pride and competition led to the compilation of the great source collections of national history, so it forced the several European states at various dates during the nineteenth century to open the national archives to historical scholars. In addition, the liberal-minded Pope Leo XIII opened the Vatican archives in 1881 and secular scholars for the first time had the privilege of examining the treasures that Cardinal Baronius had first made use of. Down to the period of the World War, however, complete freedom was not accorded anywhere in the use of archival material, scholars being excluded from the more recent documents. For instance, the Vatican archives were accessible only to 1815,

---

[11] Cf. Gooch, *History and Historians in the Nineteenth Century*, pp. 12-13.

those of France to 1830, those of Russia to 1854, and those of England to 1860. In America, scholars like Gaillard Hunt labored to put the collection of archival material of the United States upon the same high plane that it has reached in most European countries.

After the first World War a new era dawned in the opening of archives to scholars. This was due to the desire to abolish secret diplomacy and to establish the real responsibility for the World War. The process was begun by the Bolsheviks and followed quickly by the Germans and Austrians. This action forced the English and then the French to follow suit. Not only were the archives opened, but the more important diplomatic documents on the generation prior to the War were published on an unparalleled scale.[12] After the second World War the Allies captured and carried away great masses of German documents but have been reluctant to publish their own. The Russians were especially secretive instead of forcing the Western Allies to publish their materials, as was the case after 1918.

NATIONALISTIC HISTORICAL WRITING IN THE UNITED STATES

The United States has never provided a great official collection of the sources of its national history comparable to those prepared by the European countries. This has been due in part to the particularism inherent in the American federal system and in part to the fact that the Federal government has been too much absorbed in the details of routine legislation and the demands of party politics to be able to concentrate its attention on furthering intellectual interests. The true American counterpart of the European movement in collecting the sources of national history, which was associated in Europe with the names of Muratori, Pertz, Guizot, Nicolas, Hardy and Stubbs, was found in the rather pathetic attempt of Peter Force (1790-1868) in the thirties of the last century to obtain adequate government support for his *American Archives,* which were designed to constitute a complete collection of the sources of the history of the United States from the period of discovery to the formation of the Constitution.[13] Its psychological and historical affinity with the European movement is clearly indicated by Force's statement of his aims. "The undertaking in which we have embarked is, emphatically, a national one; national in its scope and object, its end and aim." After a painful process of protracted importuning, Force received a Federal appropriation which allowed him to begin publishing his *Archives* in 1837, but the government aid was soon withdrawn and the material published was but an insigni-

---

[12] See below, pp. 281 ff.

[13] Cf. J. S. Bassett, *The Middle Group of American Historians* (Macmillan, 1917), pp. 261 ff.

ficant fraction of what he had planned to include. Owing to the fact that American historical scholarship was then a generation behind that of Europe, Force was primarily a hard-working antiquarian compiler rather than a scholarly editor like Waitz, Mignet, Guérard, or Stubbs, and the national loss from the cessation of his work was much less notable than would have been occasioned by a discontinuance of the *Rolls Series,* the *Monumenta* or the *Documents inédits.*

The collections which have been published have been primarily the result of the enterprise of individuals, publishing companies, and the historical societies of the several states of the Union. The process began with the publication of Jared Sparks' *Diplomatic Correspondence of the American Revolution,* in twelve volumes (1829-30), his *Life and Writings of Washington* in twelve volumes between 1834 and 1837, and several other compilations.[14] The most ambitious attempt to make a thorough collection was the work of Mr. Hubert Howe Bancroft (1832-1918) in the last half of the nineteenth century, in his collection of the sources of the history of the Pacific states, to be used in his coöperative thirty-nine-volume *History of the Pacific States.* Unfortunately, he did not follow the example of Stein and secure the aid of a Pertz, but trusted to his own untrained guidance the execution of the project, with the result that the work often was lacking in critical scholarship and careful editing. An incomparably more scholarly work was the coöperative history of the colonization of America, edited by Justin Winsor—the *Narrative and Critical History of America.* Though this contained much source material, it was primarily a narrative work giving a critical review of the sources rather than publishing them.

Parallel with this movement went the publication of source material by the various states in the large collections of colonial records and archives. In the great majority of cases, however, these collections were prepared by erudite antiquarians rather than by men trained as critical historical editors, and there was little uniformity in the methods employed. Some of these state collections have, however, been of a very high order, the most notable being, perhaps, the extensive series dealing with the exploration and settlement of the Middle West by Reuben G. Thwaites of Wisconsin, and the documents on the history of New York State, edited by Alexander C. Flick. Local historical societies have been numerous and often very active in collecting the sources of local history. They have often coöperated with state historical societies in such work. Another mode of collecting sources was exhibited in the editions of the messages and papers of the presidents and of the writings of the chief statesmen by numerous scholars. These have varied widely in quality, reaching the highest level,

[14] Bassett, *op. cit.,* pp. 80 ff.

perhaps, in W. C. Ford's *Writings of Washington*, Gaillard Hunt's *Writings of James Madison*, P. L. Ford's *Writings of Jefferson*, and J. B. Moore's *The Works of James Buchanan*.

The United States has not been lacking in editorial ability of the highest order, for in men like Worthington C. Ford, John Franklin Jameson, Paul Leicester Ford and Gaillard Hunt were to be found the equals of Pertz, Waitz, Guizot, or Stubbs. The great defect has been the lack of concerted planning and of continued and adequate government aid. Promising beginnings in the right direction are to be seen in W. C. Ford's edition of the *Journals of the Continental Congress, 1774-89*, Max Farrand's edition of the *Records of the Federal Convention of 1787*, and the scholarly products of the Carnegie Institution under John Franklin Jameson's direction. John Bassett Moore has labored with almost Benedictine patience and productivity in the preparation of his monumental series dealing with the documentary history of diplomacy. There should be mentioned the valuable collection of sources dealing with the history of labor in America which has been prepared by Professor John R. Commons and his associates. Miss Adelaide Hasse has begun an invaluable series of volumes describing and classifying the sources for American economic and social history which are available in the public documents of the various commonwealths. On the whole, however, the United States has been incomparably delinquent in the thorough and scholarly collection of the sources of its national history, and it cannot seek refuge behind any assertion that this has been due to a lack of rabid nationalistic emotions, or ample financial resources.

If this country has not kept abreast of European developments in the editorial aspect of national historiography, it can lay claim to having produced historians as ardently patriotic as a Treitschke, a Michelet, or a Froude. Nationalism in American historiography has, naturally, centered mainly about the romantic period of colonization and the struggle for American independence. American historians have surrounded this period with a halo comparable to that given to the early national history of Germany and France by Johannes Müller and Chateaubriand.

The chief figure in the creation of this national epic of migration and deliverance was George Bancroft (1800-91), whose early years fell in that period of national bumptiousness and florid democracy, the thirties and forties of the last century. His voluminous work was entitled *The History of the United States from the Discovery of America*.[15] To Bancroft, one of the first Americans to be trained in a German seminar, the history of the formation of the American republic was no modest secular achievement of ordinary mortals, but a veritable *Aeneid*. In it Augustus was re-

[15] 10 vols., 1834-87.

placed by Washington. It exhibited in its succession of scenes "the movement of the divine power which gives unity to the universe, and order and connection to events." In florid rhetorical style, Bancroft represented the process of colonization as the flight of brave spirits from oppression, characterized the American Revolution as a crusade of wholly virtuous and disinterested patriots in behalf of the liberties of civilized humanity, described the American Constitution as the creation of a group of unique mental giants, never before equaled and not to be matched at any later epoch, and regarded their work as even more notable than its makers. The pathetic inaccuracy of all of his major dogmas can only be appreciated after a careful perusal of the scholarly treatment of the same topics by George Louis Beer, C. H. Van Tyne, Carl Becker, S. M. Eliot, M. C. Tyler, H. L. Osgood, C. W. Alvord, C. M. Andrews, S. G. Fisher, Max Farrand, C. A. Beard and A. M. Schlesinger, among others. The damage done to sane perspective in American history by his works was almost incalculable, if not irreparable. The myth was perpetuated in the long Puritan apology of John G. Palfrey (1796-1881), *The History of New England,* and was repeated in a less vigorous form in Henry Cabot Lodge's *History of the English Colonies in America,* which at least had the merit of arousing·interest in colonial life.

Through his pride in American exploits in behalf of liberty and democracy, John Lothrop Motley was encouraged to study the comparable movement among the Dutch when they rebelled against Spanish tyranny and established a republic.[16] Francis Parkman (1823-93), turning from the Anglo-Saxon phobia of Bancroft, first gave full credit to the work of France in colonizing the new world. In a number of thorough and interesting volumes, he found that the record of heroism had not been wholly monopolized by the English and German colonists. While Parkman gave his attention to the French in the North and West, William H. Prescott (1796-1859), famous also as a historian of early modern Spain, found his American theme in the conquest and colonization of Central and South America by the Spanish. He also produced a brilliant description of the splendor of the native American civilizations of Mexico and Peru. His *History of the Conquest of Mexico,* and *The History of the Conquest of Peru* were literary masterpieces, but need modification in the light of subsequent archeological work. Alfred T. Mahan (1840-1914), impressed by the exploits of the small American navy in the Revolution and the War of 1812, was encouraged to make a study of the influence of naval supremacy upon the history of the past. His two main works were *The Influence of Sea Power on History, 1660-1783,* and *The Influence of Sea Power on the French Revolution and Empire, 1793-1812.* Few books

[16] See above, pp. 191-92; and D. A. Pease, *Parkman's History,* Yale Press, 1953.

have been more influential in stimulating the disastrous growth of modern naval armaments. The cementing of the national union through the efforts of the Federalists was glorified in the works of Richard Hildreth (1807-65) and John Church Hamilton (1792-1882). Hildreth, as an anti-Puritan, answered Palfrey on this point, praised Federalism, and criticized Jefferson. Hamilton, the son of the great statesman of Federalism, defended his father's policies in his *History of the Republic*. The blessings of the "pure" democracy of the Jacksonian epoch were set forth in the essays and addresses of Bancroft, who believed that he detected the very "voice of God" in the acclaim of Jackson's followers. Theodore Roosevelt (1858-1918), in *The Winning of the West*, described the process of American expansion westward with the buoyant and ill-concealed pride of an admirer of the West and an ardent patriot and national imperialist. He also popularized Mahan's work. The German-American, Hermann von Holst (1841-1904), in his *Constitutional and Political History of the United States*, beheld in the struggle over slavery one more great episode in the eternal conflict between righteousness and iniquity. He was also inspired by the triumph of nationalism in this country and saw in it a lesson to his German countrymen in their struggle for unity. Professor John William Burgess (1844-1931), author of *The Middle Period, The Civil War and the Constitution*, and *Reconstruction and the Constitution*, beheld in the success of the North in the Civil War not only a justification of his own nationalistic political philosophy, but also a sure manifestation of Teutonic genius in the field of political unification and organization.

On the whole, however, by the time the Civil War and Reconstruction periods had come to be subjects for serious historical analysis, the objective scholarship of the critical and erudite school, led by Professor William A. Dunning, had begun to prevail and the "American epic" passed out of scholarly works, to be preserved mainly in the school texts of succeeding generations.

The task of rationalizing the Bancroftian epic and of adapting it to the prevailing tendencies of the latter part of the nineteenth century fell to the philosopher-historian, John Fiske (1842-1901). Through his amiable Spencerian rationalism and his eulogy of the rise of the middle class he best summed up the prevailing spirit of the educated Americans of his time. By his vivid and attractive style and his primary concern with the period of discovery, colonization and revolution he attracted a following which probably entitled him to the position of the most popular national historian of the last generation. He was the prophet of the new era in the interpretation of Anglo-American relations. This replaced the Puritan and American epic of Bancroft by an account of the rise and triumph of the middle class in both England and America—"an epic of the English speaking peoples."

Fiske was as fully convinced as Burgess of the supreme political capacity of the Teutonic branch of the "Aryans." He held that the first instance of self-government in recorded history was to be seen in the Teutonic village-community, which was an "inheritance from prehistoric Aryan antiquity," and he believed that "American history descends in unbroken continuity from the days when stout Arminius in the forests of northern Germany successfully defied the might of imperial Rome."

Fiske, however, stressed the element of liberty as the surest criterion of political capacity, rather than the elements of order and authority which had found favor with Burgess. England under Gladstone seemed far better adapted than Germany under Bismarck to furnish an edifying example of the attainment of complete political liberty, and the then popular theory of a wholly Teutonic England was an ethnic argument in favor of such an undertaking. Therefore, instead of conducting the Muse of Liberty directly from the "German forest primeval" to the Federal Constitutional Convention of 1787, Fiske arranged a detour in her migration to the new world which would guide her to America by the way of the "glorious revolution of 1688." In this revolution, conceived in the work of the English *bourgeoisie,* "freedom both political and religious was established on so firm a foundation as never again to be shaken, never again with impunity to be threatened, so long as the language of Locke and Milton and Sydney shall remain a living speech on the lips of men."

Working hand in hand with George Otto Trevelyan, Fiske tried to show how the American Revolution was but the perfect fulfilment of the spirit of 1688. He pictured it as the work of Whigs on both sides of the Atlantic in the heroic effort to check and crush the autocratic tendencies of a Tory squirarchy and the unconstitutional tyranny of a "German king," and to preserve for the world the liberties embodied in the English Bill of Rights. He dwelt with pride upon the establishment of the American Federal Republic and regarded it as the great contribution of the western hemisphere to the solution of political problems. It reconciled the liberty of the New England town meeting with the existence of large political aggregates. Fiske contemplated with unmixed pleasure the progress of the middle class in its political and economic conquest of the American continent in the nineteenth century. Just before his death at the opening of the twentieth century, he was deeply gratified to see his own country at last assume its part of the "white man's burden" by retaining the Philippines. Not at all a militarist, he looked upon this as a most significant step in that process of bringing the world under the peaceful domination of "the two great branches of the English race which have the mission of establishing throughout the larger part of the earth a higher civilization and a more permanent political order than any that has gone before."

While Fiske introduced the Germanic and Anglo-Saxon myth into popular history in this country, its establishment in respectable academic history was the work of Herbert Baxter Adams (1850-1901) and John William Burgess (1844-1931). Both were trained in Germany. Adams established the famous historical seminar at the Johns Hopkins University, where he trained many eminent historians and political scientists, among them Woodrow Wilson. The best example of the application of the Germanic theory to American institutions was contained in the work of one of Adams' students, George Elliott Howard's *Introduction to the Local Constitutional History of the United States,* published in 1889. Burgess started his work at Amherst College and then founded the famous school of political science at Columbia University. But many of his students were too keen to be taken in by the Teutonic myth. The Germanic doctrine was spread mainly in his writings and in the public addresses of Nicholas Murray Butler. Perhaps the best expression of smug American nationalism today is that exemplified in Wilbur Cortez Abbott's *The New Barbarians.*

Nationalistic history has appeared elsewhere in the New World. Source material on the Dominion of Canada has been collected in ample fashion in the Dominion Archives at Ottawa and in the archives of the several provinces. The history of Canada was reviewed at length from the French-Canadian viewpoint by François Garneau, and from the Canadian Loyalist standpoint by William Kingsford. Both works have now been superseded by the scholarly coöperative histories of Canada edited by George M. Wrong and Hugh H. Langton, and Adam Shortt and Arthur G. Doughty. The best one-volume history of Canada is George M. Wrong's *The Canadians.*

The sources of Latin American history have been elaborately collected from the Spanish archives and in the Latin American states. Characteristic are the collection of Argentine documents edited by the faculty of philosophy and letters of the University of Buenos Aires, the collection of Chilean documents edited by José Medina, and the Mexican collection edited by M. O. y Berra. General histories of Latin America have been written by Juan Ortega y Rubio, Diego Barros Arana, Francisco García Calderón, Carlos Navarro y Lamarca, and others. The stirring period of independence has been especially cultivated by Bartolomé Mitre (1821-1906). There have been a number of important works produced on particular countries. Among these are the histories of Brazil by Francisco Adolpho Varnhagen, João Manuel Pereira da Silva, José Francisco da Rocha Pombo, Manoel de Oliveira Lima and Felisbello Firmo de Oliveiro Freire; of Argentine by Mitre, Mariano Pelliza, Martín García Mérou, Vicente Gambón, Vicente Fidel López, and Ricardo Levene; of Chile by Benjamín Vicuna Mackenna, José Torbido Medina, Miguel Luís Amunátegui, Diego Barros Arana, Domingo Amunátegui y Solar and Gonzalo Bulnes; of Peru by Mariano Felipe Paz Soldán, Sebastián Lorente and Nemesio

Vargas; of Central America by Lorenzo Montúfar y Rivera Maestre, Antonio Batres Jáuregui, Pedro Zamora Castellanos and José N. Rodríguez; and of Mexico by Luís Pérez Verdía, Luíz Gonzáles Obregón, Niceto de Zamacois, Enrique Santibañez, Emilio Rabasa and Gregorio Quintero.

HISTORY AND NATIONALISM

The net result of growth of nationality and of nationalism upon historiography has been very diverse and a mixed blessing. Its fortunate results have been, above all, the provision of great collections of source material which would otherwise never have been made available, and the training of many excellent historians in the process of compiling and editing of the sources. The deplorable effects have centered about the creation of a dangerous bias of patriotism. This has not only hampered the calm, objective and accurate handling of historical facts, even by highly trained historians, but it also contributed in no small degree to the great increase in chauvinism which led to the calamity of 1914. The responsibility of the nationalistic historians in this regard was well stated by Professor H. Morse Stephens: "Woe unto us! professional historians, professional historical students, professional teachers of history, if we cannot see written in blood, in the dying civilization of Europe, the dreadful result of exaggerated nationalism as set forth in the patriotic histories of some of the most eloquent historians of the nineteenth century."[17] It would be fortunate, indeed, if this were all, but for every patriot made by a Treitschke, a Michelet, a Froude or a Bancroft, hundreds have been charmed by the naïve but vicious bumptiousness of third-rate textbook compilers who have imitated the bias of the masters without their literary virtues.[18] The nature and the effect of these textbooks upon the past generation have been indicated for this country by Mr. Charles Altschul and Miss Bessie L. Pierce, and for France and Germany by Professor J. F. Scott. England has not fallen behind any of these nations in this respect. With the rise of totalitarianism in both Fascist and Communist countries and the coming of the second World War nationalistic fervor and bias returned on a scale unprecedented in contemporary times.

ECCLESIASTICAL HISTORY

It should be pointed out in passing that the zeal for collecting historical source material was not limited to the sources of secular history. In the

[17] H. M. Stephens, "Nationality and History," in *American Historical Review*, January, 1916, p. 236.

[18] Bessie L. Pierce, *Public Opinion and the Teaching of History in the United States* (Knopf, 1926); J. F. Scott, *Patriots in the Making* (Appleton, 1916), *The Menace of Nationalism in Education* (Macmillan, 1926); Mark Starr, *Lies and Hate in Education* (London, 1929); and C. E. Merriam, *The Making of Citizens* (University of Chicago Press, 1931).

same way that gathering the sources of national history was begun by Duchesne in the seventeenth century, so activity in collecting the sources of ecclesiastical history was initiated at this same period and has been continued to the present time. The first complete collection of the writings of the Church Fathers was gathered and published by Jacques Migne in his *Patrologiae cursus completus, graeca et latina,* in 382 volumes between 1844 and 1864. While, like Bancroft's *History of the Pacific States,* it was a publisher's rather than a scholar's enterprise, it has been of immense value to students. The failure of Migne to use the best texts in all cases led to the attempt to produce better collections of patristic literature. Since 1866 the Vienna Academy has been publishing a carefully-edited collection of the writings of the Latin Fathers, and in 1897 the Berlin Academy began to issue an edition of the Greek Fathers. The collection of material dealing with the lives and deeds of the saints, which was begun by Bolland in the middle of the seventeenth century, is still in progress.[19] A collection of the acts of the Church Councils, by Labbe and Cossart, appeared in the latter half of the seventeenth century and was taken up again by Étienne Baluze in 1783. In 1685, Jean Hardouin started another collection and in the middle of the eighteenth century Gian Mansi compiled the most complete of all collections of the Councils, *Sacrorum conciliorum nova et amplissima collectio,* in thirty-one volumes, a new edition of which, in fifty-six volumes, was completed in Paris in 1924. At the same time that Mansi was preparing his collection of conciliar material, Mainardi published his edition of papal bulls. In the latter half of the nineteenth century Philipp Jaffé and August Potthast produced scholarly collections of papal *regesta* to the year 1304, and Paul Kehr recently completed the publication of the latest and most complete compilation of this type of material. On the whole, the collections of source material for the history of the Church are today fully equal to those for the secular history of Europe. Nor has the psychological exaltation been less in the case of the ecclesiastical historians. Cardinal Hergenröther wrote with as much feeling on the Catholic church as his fellow-countryman, von Treitschke, did on Prussia and the German nation. The *Catholic Encyclopaedia* systematically collected the official Catholic position on historical matters.

The Protestants, of course, wrote with equal feeling. We have already called attention to this literature. Merle d'Aubigné matched the vehemence of any of the Catholic writers mentioned above, and even the scholarly David Schaff showed a very definite Protestant bias. The Schaff-Herzog *Encyclopaedia* embalmed the Protestant viewpoint.

[19] See above, pp. 132-33.

SELECTED REFERENCES

C. J. H. Hayes, *The Historical Evolution of Modern Nationalism.* Long and Smith, 1931.

Fueter, *Histoire de l'historiographie moderne,* pp. 608-18, 629-87.

Gooch, *History and Historians in the Nineteenth Century,* chaps. v, viii, xi-xv, xvii-xviii, xxi-xxii.

Michael Kraus, *A History of American History.* Farrar and Rinehart, 1938.

———, *The Writing of American History,* chaps. iv-vi, x. University of Oklahoma Press, 1953.

H. H. Bellot, *American History and Historians.* University of Oklahoma Press, 1952.

Harvey Wish, *The American Historian.* Oxford University Press, 1960.

David Levin, *History as Romantic Art.* Stanford University Press, 1959.

R. R. Ergang, *Herder and the Foundations of German Nationalism.* Columbia University Press, 1931.

G. S. Morris, *Hegel's Philosophy of the State and of History.* Scott, Foresman, 1892.

P. M. Hammer, ed., *A Guide to Archives and Manuscripts in the United States.* Yale University Press, 1961.

D. H. Thomas and L. M. Case, *Guide to the Archives of Western Europe.* University of Pennsylvania Press, 1959.

Thomas Pressly, *Americans Interpret Their Civil War.* Princeton University Press, 1954.

D. R. Van Tassel, *Recording America's Past, 1607-1884.* University of Chicago Press, 1960.

Peardon, *The Transition in English Historical Writing.*

Wegele, *Geschichte der deutschen Historiographie,* Books IV-V.

Antoine Guilland, *Modern Germany and Her Historians.* London, 1915.

Gustav Wolf, Dietrich Schäfer and Hans Delbruck, *Nationale Ziele der deutschen Geschichtsschreibung seit der französischen Revolution.* Gotha, 1918.

Louis Halphen, *L'Histoire en France depuis cent ans.* Paris, 1914.

Benedetto Croce, *Storia della storiographia italiana nel seclo decimo nono.* Bari, 1921. 2 vols.

P. J. Blok, *Geschichtschreibung in Holland.* Leiden, 1924.

J. F. Jameson, *Historical Writing in America.* Houghton, Mifflin, 1891.

J. S. Bassett, *The Middle Group of American Historians.* Macmillan, 1917.

Thompson, *History of Historical Writing,* Vol. II, chaps. xliii-xlv, xlviii.

W. T. Hutchinson, ed., *The Marcus W. Jernegan Essays in American Historiography.* University of Chicago Press, 1937.

John Fiske, *American Political Ideals.* Harper, 1885.

Wilgus, *Histories and Historians of Hispanic-America.* Pan American

B. L. Pierce, *Civic Attitudes in American School Textbooks.* University of Chicago Press, 1930.

J. F. Scott, *Patriots in the Making.* Appleton, 1916.

———. *The Menace of Nationalism in Education.* Macmillan, 1926.

Bell and Morgan, *The Great Historians.*

X

THE RISE OF CRITICAL HISTORICAL SCHOLARSHIP

THE ORIGINS OF CRITICAL HISTORICAL SCHOLARSHIP

PROFESSOR George Peabody Gooch, in his scholarly and informing account of the development of historiography in the nineteenth
century, points out that prior to the nineteenth century historical
science labored under four serious handicaps: (1) the catastrophic
theory of historical causation and the contempt for the medieval period
which had characterized the Rationalist school; (2) the absence of adequate collection of original sources and of any organization of archival
materials; (3) the widespread lack of critical methods in handling historical materials; and (4) the failure to provide for any systematic and competent teaching of either the subject matter or methods of history.

It has already been pointed out how the Romanticists had corrected
some faults of the Rationalists by insisting upon the law of continuity in
historical development and by looking upon the medieval period as the
most fruitful age for historical research. We have also briefly indicated
how the pride of exuberant nationalism led to the provision of magnificent collections of source material for the history of every leading modern
nation. It now remains to trace the rise of critical scholarship in the field
of history, and to show how the scholarly methods were widely disseminated and permanently retained through the appearance of the professional teacher of history.

It was made clear in an earlier chapter how the promising rise of critical methods in the use of historical materials, as an incidental phase of
Humanism, and as exemplified in the works of Blondus, Beatus Rhenanus, Vadianus and Zurita,[1] had been checked and smothered in the
fierce religious controversies of the period of the Reformation and counter-Reformation. By the beginning of the eighteenth century, however,
the volume of religious polemic was tending to decline. It was again possible to resume to some degree an objective attitude and to begin anew
the dispassionate search for historical truth.

The development of scientific historical method passed through two
natural and normal stages: first, the rise of those auxiliary sciences—such

---

[1] See above, pp. 105, 111-13, 119.

as diplomatic, chronology, paleography, epigraphy and lexicography—which would enable the historian to ascertain the genuineness of a document; and, second, the growth of internal or interpretive criticism, which passes beyond the mere establishment of the authenticity of a document and examines the credibility of its author as a witness of historical facts.

Even the early days of this new critical scholarship brought a rigorous appraisal of preceding historical writing. From De Pouilly to Duncker, the chronicles of the ancient Orient were critically appraised. Grote and others examined the major Greek historians. De Pouilly, Perizonius, Beaufort and Niebuhr assessed the historians of Rome. The Maurists, the Bollandists, Mosheim and Tillemont dealt with the church historians. From Goldast to Waitz, from Fauriel to Fustel, and from Sharon Turner to Stubbs, the medieval chroniclers were subjected to critical dissection. Von Ranke won his spurs in historical scholarship by a classic analysis of the Humanist historians, expecially Villani, Machiavelli and Guicciardini. Fauriel, Muratori, Leibnitz and the editors of the great collections dealt with the sources of national history. The new scholarship thus moved into every field.

The first of the important steps in the growth of modern historical science was primarily the work of those same Benedictine monks of the Congregation of Saint-Maur who had been so active in the preliminary period of the collection of the sources of French history.[2] Their priority in this scholarly movement seems to have been due in part to the fact that, not being a militant order, they did not have to appear as vigorous apologists for Catholicism. They also had the advantage over lay writers of not being compelled to glorify a particular city, province, family or dynasty. In the quiet library of their monastery they devised and elaborated indispensable items in the mechanics and technique of the modern historian.

The leader of the historical scholars of the order was Jean Mabillon (1632-1707), who, in collaboration with Luc d'Achery, created the science of diplomatic—or the critical method of determining the authenticity of documents. In 1675 a Jesuit historian, Daniel von Papebroch, made a sweeping claim that many of the documents upon which the Maurists had relied were worthless. Mabillon devoted the next six years to the preparation of his reply, and in 1681 his opponent was crushed under the erudition of the *De re diplomatica,* which remained the standard treatise on the subject until it was displaced in the last generation by the volumes of Sickel, Ficker and Giry. The basis of modern paleography and archeology was laid by Dom Bernard Montfaucon (1655-1741) in his *Paleographia graeca* and his *L'Antiquité expliquée et réprésentée en figures.*

While a layman, Charles du Fresne du Cange had founded historical lexicography in his *Glossarium mediae et infimae latinitatis* (1678), the Benedictines left their impress upon this field in the famous revision and expansion of Du Cange's work by Dom Carpentier (1768). Finally, in a great coöperative work begun by Dantine and Durand, and finished in 1790 by Dom Clément, *L'Art de vérifier les dates,* chronology was at last taken from the hands of Eusebius and Jerome and put on a scientific foundation. Clément went far beyond Scaliger in his systematic analysis of chronology.[3] Of course, the Benedictines did not limit their efforts wholly to the perfecting of methods of research, but applied these methods in the production of those voluminous works and source collections on church and national history of which mention is made in other sections of this work.

The advances in scientific method which the Maurists brought into existence can scarcely be overestimated. Before this time there had either been no attempt to cite sources or else the citations had been hopelessly confused; there had been no general practice of establishing the genuineness of a text; there had been little hesitancy in altering the text of a document to improve the style. The work of Leibnitz was the only notable exception. Now documents were searchingly examined as to their authenticity, the text was quoted with exactness, and the citations of sources were invariably included and given with scrupulous accuracy.

It is, however, easily possible to overestimate the modernity of the Maurists; they were as near to Timaeus as to von Ranke or Gardiner. Their critical methods were almost wholly limited to external or textual criticism—to an examination of the genuineness of the document. They were greatly inferior to the school of Voltaire in examining the credibility of contemporary authorities and generally regarded the contents of an authentic primary source as almost identical with absolute historical truth. Neither did they possess anything of the Romanticist conception of cultural evolution. They were nearer to erudite antiquarians than to modern scientific historians. Nor were they sceptical of ecclesiastical tradition. They labored under the pious conviction that the truth would substantiate the contentions of the Church. Ironically enough, they provided their Rationalist contemporaries and successors with a large supply of scholarly information with which to rout the ecclesiastics.

Almost identical with the Benedictines' method was the work of the Jansenist, Louis Sebastian de Tillemont (1637-98), author of two notable works on the history of the Church and the Roman Empire to about A.D. 515. His product was highly objective, being primarily a mosaic pieced together from sources which were selected so that they would harmonize

[3] See above, p. 117.

but not altered as to text or facts. It was one of the earliest of modern historical works to include a critical discussion of the principal sources for each period. This solid work, designed as a pillar of Christian doctrine, was one of the chief sources used by the sceptical Gibbon.

One of the earliest German exemplifications of the new critical methods came in the history of German law. The prolific German physician and savant, Hermann Conring (1606-81), wrote a learned *Historical Commentary on the Origins of German Law,* which is regarded by many as the true beginning of the scientific study of German legal origins. Another example of the new erudite methods was the researches into the history of the Guelphs carried on by the German philosopher, Gottfried Wilhelm Leibnitz (1646-1716), in his *Brunswick Annals of the Western Empire.* Indeed, in an article written in 1679, two years before Mabillon had published his critical notions, Leibnitz had clearly stated the same basic ideas as those advanced by the Maurists. Leibnitz's ideals first received application on a large scale in *The History of the Germans under the Merovingians* by Johann Jakob Mascov (1689-1761), who used his sources critically and rejected the conventional legends. He continued his historical writings by an equally critical survey of the medieval empire. His book was the best history of the early Germans prior to the work of Schmidt.[4]

A further step was taken towards the development of internal criticism by the industrious Italian, Lodovico Muratori, who made a number of advances over his master, Mabillon. He was as critical of miracles as Blondus and departed widely from the Benedictine practice of regarding contemporary sources as infallible. Rapin Thoyras (1661-1735) combined the methods of Mabillon and Muratori with some faint anticipation of the Romanticist conception of historical development in his *History of England,* which long remained the chief source on the Continent for the history of seventeenth-century England. He anticipated Montesquieu in attributing English liberties to precedents in the German backwoods. Finally, in the coöperative *Universal History* produced by the English scholars, Campbell, Sale, Swinton, Bower and Psalmanazar, to which we have already called attention, the erudite school published the first scholarly and fairly complete universal history in all historical literature. Although thoroughly pious in its approach, it has been called by no less authoritative a critic than Fueter "the first universal history worthy of the name."

While Vadianus,[5] Muratori and Thoyras had shown at least some elementary insight into the credibility of contemporary, or "primary," sources, the beginning of systematic internal criticism of historical documents must be attributed to the Jesuits. Having been put upon the defen-

---

[4] See above, p. 164.   [5] See above, pp. 111-12.

sive by the Protestant onslaughts, they were compelled to examine the sources of ecclesiastical history to discover what portion of the old traditions and legends would bear the test of scientific scrutiny. By this means they hoped to eliminate the damaging criticism of the Church by Protestant historians who ridiculed the many crude and obviously false legends connected with the Catholic past. The chief example of this Jesuit criticism was the monumental *Acta Sanctorum,* begun by the Belgian Jesuits under Bolland's direction in 1643.[6] Here the sources bearing on the lives of the various saints were arranged according to age and authenticity.

A much healthier and more expansive spirit of criticism was exhibited by Pierre Bayle (1647-1706) in his *Historical and Critical Dictionary,* and in his criticism of Maimbourg's history of Calvinism. Bayle took special delight in pointing out the grave discrepancies between the views and opinions of authorities contemporary with the events described and he did not hestitate to extend his methods to the examination of "sacred" history. Indeed, Bayle demolished the idea of sacred history. One of the most damaging criticisms of such historical ideals as those of the Maurists came from an English Deist, Conyers Middleton (1683-1750). In his *Introductory Discourse* and his *Free Inquiry,* he emphasized the unreliability of the Church Fathers as historians of the rise of Christianity. He stressed the fact that this was an age which forged and falsified as a matter of course.[7]

Since the period of Humanism the historical writers of classical antiquity had been generally regarded with a reverent confidence second only to that accorded the Church Fathers. Valla, as we have seen, had questioned some assertions of Livy. But the first really critical student of Roman antiquities was Carlo Sigonio, better known as Sigonius (1524-84), who ranked with Scaliger and Casaubon as one of the greatest scholars of the age. He dealt sceptically with the whole field of Roman history, law and antiquities, going far more extensively into matters than Blondus had done. A Dutch scholar, Jakob Voorbroek, known as Perizonius (1651-1715), author of a critical *Latin Grammar* and of the *Animadversiones historicae* (1685), critically appraised the sources of early Roman history and challenged their adequacy and authenticity. Even more severe was Louis Lévesque de Pouilly (1691-1750), a French moralist and historian, who slashingly attacked the historians of early Rome. He was even more destructive than Beaufort and Niebuhr later, in that he believed that it would never be possible to reconstruct reliably the early history of Rome. De Pouilly also attacked the credibility of the conventional sources for Assyrian history. The study of early Roman history was considered even

---

[6] See above, pp. 132-33.

[7] His book was an early anticipation of such works in our own generation as Joseph Wheless' *The Church Founded on Lies and Forgeries* (Knopf, 1930).

more thoroughly by Louis de Beaufort (d. 1795) in his *Dissertation On the Uncertainty of the Early Centuries of Roman History*. Beaufort proved in detail the divergences in the accounts of the early Roman period by the great classical authorities. He held that this situation indicated that the history of Rome before the third century B.C. rested almost wholly on legendary material. The work of Beaufort marked a break with Humanism in attitude and method as well as in style. Niebuhr took up the history of Rome where Beaufort's critical work had left it.

French historians of the new critical tradition also turned their scholarship to the history of their own country. In his *History of France* (1713), Gabriel Daniel anticipated Mascov by his vigorous criticism of the historical fables and legends enveloping the Merovingian age. The most obscure member of the early critical school, but perhaps the ablest historical scholar before Niebuhr, was Jean Baptiste Dubos (1672-1740). His *Critical History of the Establishment of the French Monarchy in Gaul* was the first attempt to turn the new critical methods upon the study of institutions. In as objective a spirit as that exhibited by von Ranke, he examined the documentary sources for the early history of France and anticipated Fauriel and Fustel de Coulanges in contending that the Merovingians had mainly adopted rather than displaced Roman culture in Gaul. He also foreshadowed the Romanticists in possessing a grasp upon the conception of the gradual, organic development of civilization which was vastly superior to the catastrophic theory of the contemporary Rationalists. Less critical than Dubos' work, but more truly historical was the *History of Osnabruck* by Justus Möser (1720-94), regarded by many as the first real constitutional history, in that it revealed the manner in which political institutions develop out of the deeper social and economic forces in the life of a state. A much subtler and more finished historian of German public law and imperial institutions was Johann Stephen Pütter (1725-1807), who analyzed with astuteness and accuracy the evolution of German public law and imperial political institutions.

A disciple of Möser, Barthold Georg Niebuhr (1776-1831), is conventionally regarded as the creator of modern historiography. If, however the foregoing discussions have shown anything, it is that no single personality or school can be regarded as having brought into existence the totality of modern historical science. Niebuhr, a Dane, called to the new University of Berlin by Humboldt in 1810, best exemplified the tendency to synthesize the progressive and critical methods of his predecessors. He was familiar with the work of Perizonius, De Pouilly and Beaufort in criticizing the unreliability of early Roman history. He was influenced by Savingy's Romanticism in the study of the evolution of legal and political institutions. He followed Möser in his penetrating analysis of the development of these institutions. Finally, he applied to the sources of early Roman history the critical methods which had been adopted by Wolf in his epoch-making studies of the authorship of the Homeric poems. Niebuhr's *Roman History* was the first book to combine the best of the newer critical methods with the constructive principles of institutional history. It was the chief source of inspiration for the historical work of his greater successors, Leopold von Ranke and Theodor Mommsen.

Before considering the revolution in historical writing produced by Leopold von Ranke, we should pause to notice two contributions made by the critical school to historical science and historical method—following the line of Bodin's famous *Method for Easily Understanding History*. A German savant, Johann Martin Chladni, wrote a *General Science of History* in 1752. In this he considered intelligently and critically such matters as the general nature of historical evidence, the character of historical materials, the rôle of personalities, historical probability and causation, and the problems of historical interpretation. Equally interesting was the *Rational Plan for a Universal History* by Jacob Daniel Wegelin (1721-91). He examined the special problems of the historian, criticism of sources, sifting and organization of historical data, synthesis in universal history, and the nature of social and cultural development. Wegelin later applied these theories in a large *Universal History* of Europe.

LEOPOLD VON RANKE AND THE GERMAN SCHOOL

Leopold von Ranke (1795-1886) first became interested in history through his studies in classical literature, an examination of the ideas of Romanticism, and reading Niebuhr. His practical activity as a historian was initiated by his discovery of the wide divergencies between the various accounts of the events in fifteenth-century Italian history, as presented by the leading contemporary authorities of that century. This led to the publication in 1824 of his *History of the Romance and Germanic Peoples, 1494-1535*. Its most significant portion was the appendix, which was entitled *A Critique of Modern Historical Writers* and was devoted to an analysis of the sources of information for the period that he had covered. This did for internal and interpretative criticism what Mabillon's treatise on diplomatic had done for external criticism, or the critical study of the authenticity of texts.

It was von Ranke's great contribution to historical method to have insisted that the historian must not only use strictly contemporary sources of information, but also must make a thorough study of the personality, "tendencies," activities and opportunities of the author of each document in order to determine, as far as possible, the "personal equation" in his record of events.

There were two other fundamental characteristics in the historical

technique of von Ranke: (1) the conception derived from the Romanticists that every nation and age is dominated by the prevalent set of
ideas, called *Zeitgeist* by von Ranke; and (2) the doctrine that the
historian must view the past wholly freed from the prejudices of the present and must narrate the events of the past as they actually happened—
wie es eigentlich gewesen.

His defects have been pointed out by later writers to be: (1) his failure
to exhaust the sources available for any subject upon which he wrote;
(2) a primary concern with political events and dominating personalities,
to the neglect of the more fundamental facts of economic and social history, and even of institutional political life; (3) a pietistic bias in favor of
a providential theory of history; and (4) undue enthusiasm for Luther,
the Hohenzollerns and Prussia.

While he ranged over the entire history of Europe and the world and
left an enduring mark upon every field, it was von Ranke's contributions
to historical method and to the teaching of history which were most influential upon the later development of historiography. To historical method he contributed primarily through his formulation of the principles of
the internal criticism of documents and his insistence upon entire objectivity in the treatment of the past. The influence he exerted upon historical scholarship through his teaching was probably even greater than the
effect of the exemplification of his methods in his own written works.
That fundamental instrument for the advancement of historical scholarship in the academic world—the historical seminar—was founded by von
Ranke in 1833 and it served to train not only many leading German historians, but historical students from all over the world who came to study
in the historical laboratory which he maintained during half a century.
When von Ranke became too aged to conduct his seminar with effectiveness, his foremost pupil, Georg Waitz, adopted the methods of his master
at the University of Göttingen.

With the work of von Ranke the foundations of modern historical
scholarship were finally laid. The progress since his time has consisted
primarily in the further refinement of critical methods and their general
dissemination among a continually growing body of historical scholars.
This steady extension of scientific historical scholarship has been, in part,
the result of the direct imitation of von Ranke's methods by his students
and, in part, the outcome in other countries of those same scholarly conditions and developments which had made the work of von Ranke possible.

In Germany, the growth of the critical school of historiography was
primarily the result of the work of von Ranke. Among his pupils were
Köpke, Jaffé, Waitz, von Giesebrecht, and von Sybel, who perpetuated their
master's methods in their own writings and teaching. Waitz, the ablest of
German constitutional historians, probably surpassed von Ranke in the

thoroughness and exactness of his scholarship. The existence of impulses to critical scholarship independent of von Ranke was demonstrated by the case of Theodor Mommsen (1817-1903), who revolutionized the study and writing of Roman history.

Von Ranke's leading disciples were Waitz, von Sybel and von Giesebrecht. In the generation since their day German historians applied and improved the methods of von Ranke.[8] Heinrich Gerdes and Karl Hampe surveyed medieval Germany. Bernhard Kugler treated the Crusades with thoroughness. August Müller wrote the most satisfactory political history of the Muslim world. The era of the Renaissance and Reformation has best been covered by Robert Davidsohn, Friedrich von Bezold, Georg von Below, Gustav Wolf, Karl Brandi, Otto Scheel, Willy Andreas, Georg Mentz, and Adolph Hausrath, the latter the foremost biographer of Luther. The standard account of the counter-Reformation and the Thirty Years' War is that by Moritz Ritter. An equally excellent work is that by Bernhard Erdmannsdörffer on the period from 1648 to 1740. The works of Hans Prutz, Reinhold Koser, and Otto Hintze, on the history of Prussia, show the marked progress in scholarship and poise since the days of Droysen. Koser has produced the best biography of Frederick the Great which, though sympathetic, removes the halo about his head created by Carlyle and Droysen. Eugen Guglia has written extensively on Maria Theresa. Karl von Heigel treated the period from Frederick to Napoleon.

The most impressive general history of Germany in the nineteenth century was that by Adelbert Wahl. The period of the War of Liberation and the reforms of Stein and Hardenberg has been thoroughly treated by Wilhelm Oncken, Max Lehmann, Friedrich Meinecke, Hans Delbrück, and Gerhard Ritter, the latter one of the most productive of contemporary German historians. The following period, down to 1870, has been most competently dealt with by Erich Marcks, Arnold Meyer and Hermann Oncken. Veit Valentin produced the best work on the Revolution of 1848. A vast literature has grown up around Bismarck, the struggle for German unity, and the formation of the Empire. Among the more important books are those by William Maurenbrecher, Wilhelm Oncken, Erich Brandenburg, Johannes Ziekursch, Max Lenz, Otto Becker, Erich Marks and Erich Eyck. The best biographies of Bismarck are those by Marks, Eyck and Arnold Meyer, that by Eyck being a vigorous criticism from the liberal point of view. The period from 1870 to 1914 is best treated by Gerhard Ritter, Hermann Oncken, Brandenburg, Ziekursch, and Gottlob Egelhaaf. Erich Eyck has produced the best history of the Weimar Repub-

---

[8] In the remainder of this chapter dates of authors and titles of books will be eliminated to save space and increase readability. Readers may supply such data, if they wish, by consulting *A Guide to Historical Literature,* edited by G. M. Dutcher, W. H. Allison and others (Macmillan, 1931). A new edition edited by G. F. Howe *et al.* was issued in 1961.

lic. Hans Grimm and Ernst von Salomon have provided the only respectable preliminary judgments on the period of Hitler and National Socialism. Friedrich Meinecke, regarded by many as the ablest German historian since Von Ranke, is especially known for his able studies of political ideas. Fritz Hartung produced the best constitutional history of Germany. Werner Sombart's history of capitalism was the most impressive German work in the field of economic history, and Hans Delbrück easily surpassed all others as an authority on German military history. The history of German foreign policy from the Bismarckian era to 1914 was most competently handled by Otto Becker, Veit Valentin and Erich Brandenburg. Alfred von Wegerer produced the most competent account of the causes of the first World War. The most indefatigable editor in recent German historical work was Friedrich Thimme.

Scientific historical scholarship was introduced into Austria by Sickel, Ficker and Arneth. The ablest of contemporary Austrian historians was Heinrich Ritter von Srbik, author of a monumental biography of Metternich and of a leading treatment of the years leading to the Austro-Prussian War of 1866. Alfons Dopsch is one of the ablest institutional historians of our day and contributed exceedingly original and important works on the social history of Western Europe from the Roman Empire to the age of Charlemagne. Oswald Redlich was the ablest Austrian medievalist. Karl von Inama-Sternegg contributed notably on the economic history of Germany in the Middle Ages. August Fournier produced perhaps the best biography of Napoleon. Alexander Helfert defended the reactionary tendencies of the mid-nineteenth century. Heinrich Friedjung treated with detailed scholarship the period from 1848 to 1866, and also contributed an important work on the relations of Austria-Hungary with the Balkans. Joseph Redlich produced a brilliant and learned work on Austria-Hungary from 1848 to 1867. Alfred Pribram, Ludwig Bittner, and Hans Ueberberger covered the diplomatic developments preceding 1914. Alfons Huber and Hugo Hantsch produced the best general histories of Austria, and Hans von Zwiedeneck-Südenhorst wrote one of the finest histories of Germany in the nineteenth century.

The general nature of Germanic historical scholarship, as exemplified in the adoption of critical methods, is best observable in the coöperative work edited by Wilhelm Oncken, *Allgemeine Geschichte in Einzeldarstellungen*; and in the *Bibliotek deutscher Geschichte,* edited by Hans von Zwiedineck-Südenhorst. The most erudite synthesis of historical methodology was Ernst Bernheim's classic *Lehrbuch*, supplemented by the works of Gustav Wolf and Wilhelm Bauer.

In addition to the new critical scholarship in German political history, great progress has also been made in the field of church history since the days of the Magdeburg Centurians. Interest in this subject was revived by Johann Mosheim (1694-1755) and August Neander (1789-1850). Notable in the field of church history have been the works of Emil Schurer, Paul Wernle, K. H. von Weizsäcker, Eduard Meyer, Ernst von Dobschütz and Hans von Schubert on Christian origins; of Karl Hase and Wilhelm Möller on the general history of the Christian church; of Ludwig von Pastor, Erich Casper, Johannes Haller, Friedrich Nippold, and D. F. Strauss on the Papacy; of Carl von Hefele, Joseph Hergenröther and Hubert Jedin on the church councils; of Paul Hinschius, Aemilius Richter and Rudolph Sohm on canon law; of Julius Köstlin and Karl Holl on Luther and his times; of Albert Hauck on the German church; of Ernst Tröltsch on the social teachings of the Christian church; of Adolph Harnack on the history of Christian dogma; and of Franz Kraus on Christian archeology and art.

German scholarship has taken a leading position in the recovery of our knowledge of the ancient world. In fact, the scientific study of oriental antiquity was launched by Maximilian Duncker. Karl Lepsius founded modern Egyptology. Adolph Erman wrote what is still the best account of the social history of Egypt. Hugo Winckler devoted himself to Mesopotamia. But far the greatest Orientalist who has ever lived was Eduard Meyer, who dealt in magisterial fashion with the history of antiquity from the Stone Age to the rise of Christianity. August Boeckh founded the scientific study of Greek inscriptions. Otfried Müller was the first to make a scientific use of mythology in reconstructing early Greek and Roman history. On Greece we have the important works of Ernst Curtius, Adolph Holm, George Busolt, Karl Julius Beloch, Benedictus Niese and Ulrich Wiliamowitz-Moellendorf, Eduard Zeller's exhaustive studies of Greek philosophy, Theodore Gomperz's unrivaled history of Greek thought, and Wilhelm Christ's exhaustive review of Greek literature. The scientific study of Roman history was first soundly established by Theodor Mommsen, the most original mind ever devoted to this field. Since his day such scholars as Wilhelm Ihne, Hermann Desau, Hermann Schiller, Vicktor Gardthausen, Karl Nitzsch, and Otto Seek have enriched our knowledge of Roman history. Paul Krueger was the foremost student of Roman law, Ludwig Friedländer produced the most notable study of Roman life and manners, Georg Wissowa established himself as the foremost student of Roman religion, and Wilhelm Teuffel compiled the standard history of Roman literature. But the overtowering figure—even far surpassing Mommsen—among not only German but among all students of ancient history, was Eduard Meyer (1855-1930), whose *Geschichte des Altertums* was the first history of the ancient world written from the sources and with a mentality commensurate with the task. He will probably rank as the foremost scholar that historical writing has produced down to our day.

CRITICAL HISTORICAL WRITING IN FRANCE

The growth of critical historical scholarship in France owed something to German influences and some of the leading French historians, such as Gabriel Monod, were trained by German masters like Waitz. But, on the whole, the progress of historical scholarship in France was primarily an indigenous development. To Niebuhr might be compared Claude Fauriel, who was the inspiration of Guizot and his associates. While Guizot did not equal von Ranke in exact scholarship or in productivity, he was superior to Ranke in ability for historical synthesis and analysis, and was just as capable and active as an editor. His influence in stimulating historical scholarship in France was almost comparable to that exerted by von Ranke in Germany, though Guizot lacked the power wielded through a long-continued seminar.

The precise scholarship of Waitz found its first French counterpart in the works of François Mignet on sixteenth-century Europe and on the French Revolution. They foreshadowed present French historiography, not only by their high critical standards, but also by their almost uncanny powers of causal analysis and their remarkable lucidity in exposition. Mignet was also a talented editor of documents. Following Mignet came Fustel de Coulanges, who exerted an influence comparable to that of Waitz in Germany in stimulating scientific medieval studies in France. In spite of the nationalistic controversy which Fustel stirred up by his denial of Teutonic predominance in shaping the institutions of the Merovingians, he was primarily an exacting scholar with unwavering avidity for the sources. But the perfection of exact historical methods in France was not principally due to the work of a few individuals, as in the case of von Ranke and Waitz in Germany. It was rather a result of the labors of many scholars and teachers in the greatest of the world's institutes for training historians in the refined methods of criticism—L'École des Chartes, which began its work in 1829.[9] The names of Leopold Delisle, Benjamin Guérard, Gabriel Monod, Achille Luchaire, Auguste Molinier, Arthur Giry and Paul Viollet are indicative of the quality of work produced by the institution. In Alphonse Aulard, France possessed a scholar whose detailed and masterly knowledge of a brief period of national history could be equaled among the world's historians only by S. R. Gardiner in England, and many of the myths surrounding the French Revolution have at last been put to rest. The finest representative collection of modern French historical scholarship is to be found in the coöperative *Histoire générale,* and *Histoire de France* edited by Ernest Lavisse.

We shall enumerate only briefly the leading members of the recent generation of French scholars. Henri Hubert has surveyed the history

[9] Cf. Shotwell, "The École des Chartes," *American Historical Review*, July 1906.

of the ancient Celts. Camille Jullian has carried on the methods of his master, Fustel de Coulanges, in a thorough history of ancient Gaul. Fustel de Coulanges, André Berthelot and Ferdinant Lot have distinguished themselves by studies of the later Roman Empire and the beginnings of medieval Europe. Gustave Bloch and Lot have contributed some striking monographs on the transition from Roman to medieval civilization. Charles Diehl has devoted his attention to the revival of the eastern empire under Justinian and the course of Byzantine history. Henri Lammens, Émile Gautier, Henri Saladin, Edouard Driault, Clément Huart, and others have contributed notably to the study of Muslim history. Feudalism has been analyzed by Charles Seignobos, Achille Luchaire, Jacques Flach, Paul Guilhiermoz and Charles Petit-Dutaillis. Luchaire was the foremost authority on France during the eleventh, twelfth and thirteenth centuries. René Grousset produced what is probably the best work ever prepared on the Crusades. Charles Langlois has traced the decline of the Capetians and written the classic account of the reigns of Philip III and Philip the Fair. Town life in the Middle Ages has received the attention of Arthur Giry, who also has contributed the standard treatise on diplomatic. Eugène Viollet-le-Duc is a foremost authority on medieval French art and architecture. Charles Bémont is easily the leading French student of medieval England, though Ferdinand Lot has done notable work in early French and English medieval history. Charles Bayet holds a place of eminence for his investigation of the medieval German Empire, and he has also done signal work on the Byzantine Empire. Alfred Coville is a master of the period of the Hundred Years' War. Christian Pfister has contributed important monographs to medieval history, the history of Nancy and the administrative policy of Henry IV.

The fifteenth century has received the able attention of Petit-Dutaillis and Pierre Champion. Henri Lemonnier, Pierre Imbart de la Tour, Lucien Romier, Jean Mariéjol and Henri Hauser are leading authorities on the history of France in the sixteenth century. Imbart de la Tour is the main French authority on the Protestant Reformation. Gabriel Hanotaux and Georges d'Avenel have analyzed the France of the early seventeenth century. Pierre Clément is the chief authority on Colbert, and Joseph Dedieu on the Huguenots. Ernest Lavisse and Arthur de Boislisle have mastered the age of Louis XIV, and Lavisse, also the foremost French historian of Prussia, holds as well the first place among French editors of coöperative historical works. Henri Vast has brilliantly surveyed the political history of France in the later seventeenth and eighteenth centuries and the Napoleonic era. Our understanding of the eighteenth century has also profited by the labors of Aimé Chérest, Camille Bloch, Henri Carré and Philippe Sagnac on the political history of

France and Europe, while Albert Sorel mastered the international relations of the eighteenth century to an unparalleled degree. The institutional and intellectual history of the eighteenth century has been enriched by the recent labors of Henri Sée.

There have been important developments in the study of the French Revolution since the time of Aulard. Albert Mathiez discarded Aulard's bourgeois interpretation and championed Robespierre and the fourth estate. He added much on the economic and social history of the period, as also did Georges Lefebvre, who occupied a position intermediate between Aulard and Mathiez in interpreting the Revolution. He is now the most highly respected among French authorities on the Revolution. The best critical summary of the Revolution from a conservative point of view was produced by Louis Madelin, who became the leading authority anywhere on Napoleon and first placed Napoleonic studies on a thoroughly scholarly basis, where a start had been made by Edouard Driault. Emile Bourgeois, Georges Weill and Georges Laronze covered the period from Napoleon to the Third Republic. The latter has been best surveyed by Gabriel Hanotaux, Pierre Renouvin, Daniel Halévy and Georges Bonnefous. Henri Aron produced a remarkably well-balanced history of the Vichy regime.

Jean Mariéjol is the leading French authority on modern Spain, as is Georges Blondel on modern Germany and Austria to 1914. Ernest Denis and Louis Léger have dealt ably with Austria-Hungary, Bohemia and Poland. Elie Halévy became the leading authority in any country on nineteenth-century England. Alfred Rambaud did distinguished work on the Byzantine Empire, Slavonic Europe, French civilization, and colonial expansion. Charles Seignobos produced a classic history of civilization. Henri Sée was the foremost authority on French economic life.

The French historians have made important contributions to the scholarly history of the Christian church. Alfred Loisy is a leading critic of New Testament literature and an authority on the pagan mystery religions which influenced Christianity. Charles Guignebert has written in almost as brilliant a style as Renan, and with far greater scholarship, on Jesus and the development of Christianity. Louis Duchesne has produced the classic account of the early centuries of Christianity. André Lagarde [Joseph Turmel] has prepared an admirable survey of medieval Christianity, while Felix Rocquain has written learnedly on the history of the medieval papacy and on the French wars of religion. Pierre de la Gorce is the author of a massive religious history of the French Revolution. Debidour and Emile Chénon dealt with the church and state in the nineteenth century. The great coöperative works have been the general history of the Church edited by Augustin Fliche and Gaston Martin, and the vast dictionary of Catholic theology.

French historians have taken a special interest in the problems of

French colonial expansion. Others than Rambaud have devoted themselves to this subject. Among the more notable have been Émile Levasseur, Eugène Fallex, Édouard Petit and Arthur Girault. Charles de la Roncière has written the foremost history of the French navy.

The French also have contributed in an important way to the reconstruction of the history of antiquity. Early in the nineteenth century, Jean Champollion deciphered the Egyptian languages. A half-century later, Auguste Mariette took up Egyptology where Lepsius had left it and was the outstanding Egyptologist before Maspero. Sir Gaston Maspero was the foremost historian of antiquity before Eduard Meyer published his classic work. Eugène Cavignac is the author of the only general history of antiquity which has even approached Meyer's in comprehensiveness and vision. Louis Delaporte has written a good survey of Mesopotamian civilization. Jacques De Morgan discovered the famous Code of Hammurabi. Georges Perrot and Charles Chipiez have compiled the outstanding history of ancient art. Paul Giraud, the favorite pupil of Fustel de Coulanges, devoted himself to both Greek and Roman history. There are also the admirable works of Gustave Glotz on Cretan civilization, the Greek city state and Greek economic life. Auguste Bouché-Leclercq is a master of the Hellenistic period. Cavignac has written extensively on Greek economic history, and Alfred and Maurice Croiset are established as leaders in the history of Greek thought and literature. Victor Duruy wrote the first general histories of Greece and Rome from the sources. Gustave Bloch, Léon Homo and Joseph Declareuil have treated the political and legal evolution of Rome, and Victor Chapot has surveyed the provinces of the empire. Paul Louis and Jules Toutain are authors of standard works on the economic history of Rome. René Cagnat and Victor Chapot are leaders in the history of Roman art.

What von Ranke and Waitz achieved for the improvement of the teaching of history in Germany was accomplished in France by Jean Victor Duruy, Ernest Lavisse, Charles Bémont and Gabriel Monod. The latter, one of the most scholarly and stimulating teachers of history who has yet lived, greatly improved the seminar method which had been introduced by Duruy. In conclusion, no sketch of French historical scholarship would be complete without proper recognition of the unparalleled ability of French historians to unite careful scholarship with a broad interpretation of historical material, an admirable lucidity of expression, and rare powers of synthetic organization.

HISTORICAL SCHOLARSHIP IN ENGLAND

Even more than in France, critical historical scholarship in England was a native product. Beginning in the work of such men as Lingard, Freeman, Stubbs, Green, Lecky, Creighton and Seeley, it reached its highest point in Samuel Rawson Gardiner's work on the stirring events of the first half of the seventeenth century. For thorough mastery of all the available sources for a limited period and the ability to organize these in an intelligible narrative, Gardiner had but one rival among European historians, Alphonse Aulard, and the objectivity of his work surpassed that of the Frenchman. The English have never, however, provided anything comparable to the École des Chartes or the Historical Institute at Vienna for the training of young historians in the methods of exact critical scholarship. The great repertoires of the best products of recent English historical scholarship are the coöperative works—the *Cambridge Ancient History*, the *Cambridge Medieval History*, the *Cambridge Modern History*, and the series on English history edited by Hunt, Poole and Oman. J. H. Clapham produced the outstanding work on the economic history of England.

The history of Roman Britain has been most carefully investigated by T. Rice Holmes, R. G. Collingwood, J. L. Myres, and Francis Haverfield. The Anglo-Saxon period was studied in scholarly fashion by Charles Oman, Thomas Hodgkin, and Charles Plummer. J. H. Round, H. W. C. Davis, F. M. Powicke, and F. M. Stenton are the leading historians of Norman England. Round severely criticized Freeman, and Stenton has revised some of Round's conclusions. On the Plantagenets there are the important works of L. F. Salzman, C. W. C. Oman, G. M. Trevelyan, T. F. Tout, F. M. Powicke and Alice S. Green. William S. McKechnie, in an exhaustive work, dissipated the myths which surrounded the Magna Carta. James Wylie produced a monumental work on the period of the houses of Lancaster and York. The greatest of all English medievalists was Frederic William Maitland, whose primacy here is comparable to that of Waitz in Germany and Fustel in France. His best work was done on English medieval law. His only rival as a medievalist was the anglicized Russian, Paul Vinogradov. Edward Jenks contributed highly original works on medieval law and political institutions. The chief English authority on the Byzantine Empire was John Bagnell Bury, one of the most versatile and competent historians the world has known. Charles Oman and Norman Baynes have also dealt with Byzantine affairs. Stanley Lane-Poole, Thomas W. Arnold, D. S. Margoliouth, De Lacey O'Leary, and Reynold Nicholson are leading writers on Muslim civilization. Ernest Barker has written brilliantly on the Crusades. Foremost student of medieval geography and contacts with the Far East is Sir Raymond Beazley. James Bryce and H. A. L. Fisher wrote of the medieval German Empire. The great authority on the Lancaster-York era is James Gairdner.

On the Tudors the main authorities are Gairdner, A. F. Pollard, H. A. L. Fisher, A. D. Innes, G. W. Prothero and Mandell Creighton. Pollard and Fisher are among the most stimulating of recent English historians. The classic works on the Stuart period are those by Gardiner and Charles Firth. More recently the period has been studied by G. M. Trevelyan, F. C. Montague, Richard Lodge, G. N. Clark and Keith Feiling. Trevelyan's *Eng-*

land Under the Stuarts is the most brilliant piece of writing on this century since Macaulay's *History of England.* C. G. Robertson, I. S. Leadam, William Hunt and Louis Namier wrote on the Hanoverians. Here also fall the biographical works of George Otto Trevelyan on Fox, of Morley on Burke, of Rosebury and Williams on the elder Pitt, and of Stanhope and J. Holland Rose on the younger Pitt. Nineteenth-century Britain has been covered by S. J. Low and L. C. Sanders, G. M. Trevelyan, J. A. R. Marriott, Spencer Walpole, Justin McCarthy and Gilbert Slater. On this age we also have such notable biographies as Morley's life of Gladstone, and Monypenny and Buckle's life of Disraeli. Charles Masterman and C. L. Mowat wrote on the aftermath of the first World War in Britain. A. J. P. Taylor analyzed the origins of the second World War.

The history of British colonies, the development of the British Empire, and the growth of British colonial policy have been discussed by John A. Doyle, H. E. Egerton, Arthur B. Keith, Richard Jebb, A. D. Innes, J. A. Williamson, and Harry H. Johnston, the latter the foremost authority on the colonization of Africa. But the most detailed treatment of British colonization and imperialism is contained in several elaborate cooperative works — *The Historical Geography of the British Colonies*, edited by Charles P. Lucas; *The Cambridge History of the British Empire*, edited by J. Holland Rose and others; and *The Oxford Survey of the British Empire*, edited by Herbertson and Howarth. John W. Fortescue is the foremost historian of the British army, and William L. Clowes of the navy.

Stanley Leathes, A. J. Grant and J. S. C. Bridge are leading authorities on the political history of France. F. C. Montague and J. R. M. Macdonald have investigated the history of eighteenth-century France. H. Morse Stephens projected a systematic work on the French Revolution, but the best treatment of this subject by an Englishman is that of J. M. Thompson. J. H. Rose is the undisputed English authority on the Napoleonic period.

European politics and international relations in the last century have been dealt with by G. P. Gooch, W. A. Phillips, R. B. Mowat, Edward Hertslet, J. A. R. Marriott and others. In addition, there should be mentioned the exhaustive scholarship of Adolphus W. Ward with respect to all things connected with the political history of modern Germany, the detailed studies of William H. Dawson on the modern German Empire, and the writings of G. P. Gooch on contemporary Germany; the scholarly work of R. N. Bain, R. W. Seton Watson, D. M. Wallace, F. H. Skrine and W. Miller on Scandinavian, Slavonic and eastern Europe; the books of Bernard Pares and E. H. Carr on Russia; the survey of Italian unification by B. King and G. M. Trevelyan; and the work of M. Hume on Spain.

Church history has not been neglected in England. The most impressive achievement was an early effort, Henry Milman's *History of Latin Christianity*. The most notable products in this field since Milman were the works of H. M. Gwatkin and F. J. Foakes-Jackson on the early

church; of H. K. Mann on the popes; of G. C. Coulton and H. B. Work-
man on the medieval church and Reformation; of Charles Beard and T.
M. Lindsay on the Reformation in general, and of James Gairdner and
R. W. Dixon on the Reformation in England; of R. W. Church and F.
W. Cornish on the religious movements of the last century; of H. W.
Clark on the non-Conformists; and the monumental cooperative history
of Stephens and Hunt.

English scholars have made important contributions to the history of
antiquity. George Rawlinson was the first great English orientalist and
his works were important in their day. William Flinders Petrie ranks as
one of the able Egyptologists of our day. T. Eric Peet has also done notable work on Egyptian history. Leonard Woolley, Leonard Hall and Sidney Smith are the foremost English students of ancient Mesopotamian history. John Garstang and David Hogarth have investigated the history of
the Hittites. Harry R. H. Hall has made an able synthesis of the political
aspects of the ancient history of the Near East. George Grote wrote the
first scholarly history of Greece. Sir Arthur Evans has taken the lead in
the scientific reconstruction of our knowledge of Cretan civilization. J. L.
Myres has done brilliant work on the races of ancient Greece. The works
of Alfred Zimmern, J. P. Mahaffy and Gilbert Murray have done much
to add to our knowledge of the institutional and cultural history of
Greece. J. B. Bury has written an excellent survey of Greek history. T.
Eric Peet has investigated the "pre-history" of Italy. A. H. J. Greenidge
has contributed to all phases of Roman history. William Heitland has
produced the standard political history of the Roman Republic. William
Arnold has investigated the government of the Roman Empire. T. Rice
Holmes is the leading authority on Caesar's conquest of Gaul. W. Warde
Fowler has made important contributions to Roman social and religious
history. The *Cambridge Ancient History*, edited by J. B. Bury and others,
is far and away the best synthesis of the facts and scholarship of ancient
history. J. L. Myres has ranged over the whole field of ancient history and
is the only Englishman who might have duplicated the feat of Eduard
Meyer if he had seen fit to do so. The best history of classical scholarship
from ancient times to the modern age is the work of John E. Sandys.

Of the teachers of history in England who have done the most to inspire their pupils with the ideals of modern criticism and with an interest
in historical investigation, Freeman, Seeley, Acton, Maitland, Tout, and
Pollard, perhaps, had the widest and most salutary influence.

In the same way that Robertson's *History of Scotland* marked a great
advance over the earlier work of George Buchanan, so the solid histories
of Scotland by Peter Hume Brown, Andrew Lang and John Hill Burton
have moved on far ahead of Robertson. The standard histories of Ireland
have been written by Edward D'Alton, Florence Wright, Edmund Curtis,
Robert Dunlop, Stephen Gwynn, Mary T. Hayden, and Eleanor Hull.

CRITICAL HISTORICAL SCHOLARSHIP IN OTHER EUROPEAN COUNTRIES

The "heavy hand of censorship" has held back the development of historical scholarship in Russia, a case in point being the frustration of Vasiliev Bilbasov's ambitious project for a definitive biography of Catherine II. In spite of this, there have been a number of Russian historical scholars of the highest order. Among those who have devoted themselves to the general history of Russia were Sergius Soloviev, Sergius Platanov and Vasiliev Kluchevsky. Soloviev produced the first exhaustive history of Russia according to the new scholarly technique, and Kliuchevsky's work is probably the ablest institutional history of Russia. Alexander Kornilov wrote a highly competent history of the internal politics of modern Russia, and M. N. Pokrovsky surveyed all Russian history from the Marxian point of view in a scholarly and highly suggestive work. Paul Miliukov excelled in the interpretation of the general course of Russian political development, viewed from the liberal angle. Maksim Kovalesky, in a brilliant work, analyzed the social basis of the evolution of Russian political institutions, and Vasiliev Sergieevich traced the course of Russian legal and political development. Ludwik Kulczycki wrote the definitive history of the Revolution of 1905, and Leon Trotsky has produced a monumental history of the Revolution of 1917.

Russian historians have also made extremely important contributions to the history of other countries. For example, Ivan Luchitsky revolutionized our knowledge of the state of the French peasantry on the eve of the French Revolution, Alexander Savin illuminated English agrarian history in early modern times, while Paul Mitrofanov has produced one of the best accounts of the era of Joseph II of Austria. Some of the most distinguished work done by Russian historians has been the product of exiles. Paul Vinogradov fled from the intolerance of the tsars and became the ablest medievalist in England after the death of Maitland. He also did distinguished work on the general history of law and legal institutions. Mikhail Rostovtsev and Alexander Vasiliev fled from the Bolshevists. The former has established himself as one of the major authorities on classical history, especially the economic history of the Hellenistic period and of Rome. The latter has written the best general history of the Byzantine Empire. The Bolsheviks are developing the most extensive corps of Marxian historians that the world has known. Their work has been directed by Pokrovsky and his successors, such as M. N. Tikhomirov, M. A. Alpatov and A. L. Sidorov.

Spain has produced some scholarly historians, such as Pedro José Pidal, an authority on the age of Philip II; Rafael Altamira y Crevea, historian of Spanish civilization; Eduardo Pujol Pérez, who has traced the development of Spanish social institutions; and Eduardo Hinojosa, historian of the development of Spanish law and legal institutions. Scholarly history in Italy owed something to Muratori, but more to Ranke and the Ger-

man school, whose influence was marked upon such writers as Pasquale
Villari, Bartolomeo Malfatti, de Leva and Domenico Comparetti. Guiseppe de Leva wrote a classic history of Italy during the reign of Charles V.
Alfredo Comandini has produced the first scholarly and satisfactory history of Italy in the nineteenth century. Francesco Ruffini has mastered the
period of Cavour. But perhaps the greatest activity of recent Italian scholars has been evidenced in the field of Roman history. Corrado Barbagallo
has reopened the whole question of the credibility of the traditional early
history of Rome. Guglielmo Ferrero startled the scholarly world by his
daring re-interpretation of Roman history. Emilo Costa has produced a
highly valuable history of Roman law.

Modern historical scholarship has found competent representatives in
Switzerland. Johannes Dierauer, Karl Dändliker and Barthold van Muyden have produced able general histories of Switzerland. Eduard His has
written the best history of Swiss public law. Alfred Stern is the author of
what is generally considered the outstanding political history of Europe
from 1815 to 1870. Eduard Fueter has made important and original contributions to the history of Switzerland, to the history of Europe since the
French Revolution, and to the history of modern historical writing. In
Belgium, Herman van der Linden and Henri Pirenne have produced able
general histories of Belgium, and Pirenne was also the author of notable
studies of medieval cities, of Belgian democracy, and of medieval economic history. Isaak Gosses, Nicolaas Japikse, P. J. Blok and Pieter Geyl produced scholarly histories of the Netherlands; Herman Colenbrander,
perhaps the foremost Dutch historical scholar, is the master of the era of
the French Revolution and Napoleon in Dutch history; and Robert Fruin
is the outstanding authority on the constitutional history of the Netherlands. Historical scholarship in Denmark is best exemplified by the histories of Denmark by Johannes Steenstrup, Aage Friis and their associates.
In Norway the ablest historians are Knut Gjerset, and Alexander Bugge
and his collaborators; and in Sweden we have an anthology of the best
historical work in the coöperative history of Sweden by Emil Hildebrand
and his associates.

In Poland, the old nationalistic history of writers like Lelewel has been
replaced by the scholarly history of Poland produced by August Sokolowski and Adolf Inlender. Kamil Kantak is the author of a definitive work
on the history of the Catholic church in Poland, written from the pro-Catholic standpoint. In Czechoslovakia the school of Palacky has been
replaced by the scholarly histories of the country, such as those by Josef
Pekar and Václav Novotný. The chief historical ornament of contemporary Hungary was Henrick Marczali, author of the best general history
of Hungary and a special authority on Hungarian constitutional history.
Eugen Horvath did excellent work on Hungary and the origins of the

first World War. In Rumania the era of Xénopol was replaced by the leadership of such able scholars as Nicolae Iorga. The first scholarly history of Serbia was that by Stanoje Stanojevic, the man who, perhaps unwittingly, revealed the complicity of the Serbian government in the murder of Franz Ferdinand in 1914.

CRITICAL HISTORICAL WRITING IN THE UNITED STATES

The origins of modern critical scholarship in the field of American history date back only to about the period of the close of the American Civil War. American scholarship owed its start very largely to the influence of Germany. In the first quarter of the nineteenth century George Bancroft had attended the lectures of Heeren at Göttingen, then studied at Berlin, and later was a friend of von Ranke. Since Bancroft was not a university teacher, he had little influence on scientific historical methods in the United States, but the origins of the German prestige in this country must be attributed to him. The real beginnings of the systematic introduction of the improved methods of German historical scholarship into the United States took place in the year 1857, when Henry Torrey succeeded Sparks at Harvard, Francis Lieber assumed his professorship at Columbia, and Andrew D. White accepted a chair of history at the University of Michigan. All of these men had been trained in Germany and established a direct contact between German and American scholarship. Professor White had also been profoundly influenced by Guizot, and his teaching was never limited to the narrowly episodical and political history which attracted the extreme disciples of von Ranke and the Prussian school.

A still greater impulse to the sound establishment of historical scholarship in America came when Herbert Baxter Adams instituted the teaching of history in Johns Hopkins University in 1876, immediately after the conclusion of his studies in Göttingen, Berlin and Heidelberg. To Adams was due not only the establishment of the seminar method of instruction in America, but also the organization and creation of the first great training school for historians in the United States. There was scarcely a great American university at the opening of the twentieth century which did not have in its department of history one or more men trained in the Johns Hopkins seminar. The literary products of this seminar were the first conspicuous exemplification in America of the newer critical historical scholarship and of the historical theories of the Teutonic school.

Another leading personal influence in the introduction of the German methods and ideals was that of Professor John William Burgess, who began his work at Amherst in 1873, after having studied in Göttingen, Leipzig and Berlin. In 1880, he founded the famous Faculty of Political

Science at Columbia, which came to rival and later to overshadow the Johns Hopkins seminar. Professor Adams, while appreciating the value of the exact German methods, had a healthy confidence in the ability of American professors to interpret and apply the new methods. But Professor Burgess was convinced that, at best, Americans could be but lame and halting imitators of Germanic genius, and he induced most of his graduate students to finish their studies in Germany. As Professor Adams has expressed it: "The students of Professor Burgess went to Berlin in shoals. They went in such numbers that they began to be called the 'Burgess School.' They all went to hear Droysen lecture, and came home with trunks full of Droysen's *Preussische Politik* and of the writings of Leopold von Ranke."[10]

In addition to the work at Johns Hopkins and Columbia, Michigan fostered the new methods under Charles K. Adams, and Cornell under President White, Moses Coit Tyler and George Lincoln Burr. About this same time Ephraim Emerton and Edward Channing, at Harvard, carried further those beginnings in the newer historical scholarship which had been made by Henry Adams in the seventies. At the present time, the new scholarship has permeated the whole American university world and American students of history need no longer, as Professor Gooch would seem to imply, seek their training abroad. In the seminars of such scholars as Herbert L. Osgood, William A. Dunning, George Burton Adams, J. F. Jameson, Frederick Jackson Turner, George Lincoln Burr, Edward Channing, Edward G. Bourne, Dana C. Munro, Charles H. Haskins, Ferdinand Schevill, Carl Becker, C. H. McIlwain, Guy S. Ford, D. S. Muzzey, Evarts Greene, and others, the serious American student has received training in refined critical methods quite equal in most respects to anything to be obtained abroad. The French influence has to some degree displaced the German in recent years and most American medievalists finish their training in the École des Chartes, a substitute for which scarcely exists in America. A number of American scholars, such as H. B. Adams, E. G. Bourne, Henry Johnson, B. A. Hinsdale, N. M. Trenholme, F. M. Fling, H. E. Bourne, W. H. Mace, J. M. Vincent, Earl Dow, F. H. Foster, Allen Johnson, H. C. Hockett, and R. M. Tryon, have made worthy contributions to the elaboration of historical methodology, but nothing has appeared in this field in America that in any way rivals the works of Bernheim, Wolf or Langlois and Seignobos.

Any account of the introduction of the modern methods of historical writing in America would be incomplete without some mention of the work of Professor Albert Bushnell Hart of Harvard. While he did not

[10] H. B. Adams, *The Study of History in American Colleges and Universities* (Richmond, 1898).

contribute notably to the further refinement of critical methodology in historiography by his own works, there can be no doubt that he has been a leader in promoting scholarly contributions to the field of American history and government, in his capacity as an editor, and in popularizing scholarly methods. He fruitfully linked up the American idea of mass production with historical scholarship.

The application of the more critical methods to the field of American history has resulted in works worthy to rank with the best European products and has thoroughly reconstructed the earlier notions of American national development. The period of colonization has been examined by Professor Herbert Levi Osgood, a student of Professor Burgess and von Ranke. His monumental seven-volume work on the *History of the English Colonies in America* constituted the highest level to which exact American scholarship has attained on a large scale, and was worthy to rank with the writings of Gardiner and Aulard. The relation of the colonies to British foreign policy has been recast in a number of volumes by George Louis Beer, L. H. Gipson, and others. Charles M. Andrews united critical scholarship with a far broader conception of history than Osgood possessed, and has established for himself the position of the foremost historian of our colonial life. James Truslow Adams completed the work of Charles Francis Adams in "debunking" the Puritan myth and has written the best books on the colonial history of Massachusetts. E. G. Bourne and Herbert Eugene Bolton brought a new perspective into our study of colonial history by joining Prescott's interests with exact scholarship and emphasizing the importance of Spanish colonization for the early history of North America. As a careful conventional historian of the American colonial period, Evarts B. Greene has succeeded to the position once held by Professor Osgood. Professor Clarence W. Alvord, in a scholarly and original work, *The Mississippi Valley in British Politics,* for the first time showed the full significance of the problems of British imperial administration west of the Alleghenies in the preliminaries of the American Revolution, and finally rescued the study of the beginnings of that conflict from the obsession with Boston Harbor. Arthur M. Schlesinger has made clear the economic and commercial background of the American Revolution. S. G. Fisher, A. C. Flick, W. H. Siebert, M. C. Tyler and C. H. Van Tyne have at last dealt fairly with the Loyalists. Van Tyne has produced the best history of the American Revolution. The most original work on the intellectual background of the Revolution and on the interpretation of the Revolution has come from the pen of Carl L. Becker. The study of the period of the formation and adoption of the American Constitution has finally been secularized through the detailed and critical research of Professor Max Farrand, and the brilliant essay of Professor Beard on the economic basis of the Constitution.

Professor John Bach McMaster has surveyed the first seventy years of our national development not only with scholarship, but with a broader approach than has been attained in any other comprehensive American historical work. He did much to make social history popular in this country. Much more limited in its scope, but even more scholarly was Henry Adams' detailed historical account of American politics and foreign policy in the administrations of Jefferson and Madison. Professor Frederick Jackson Turner and his students, such as Frederick L. Paxson and others, have combined something of the scholarship of Osgood with the originality and the breadth of interest of McMaster in the study of colonizing the West and expanding the frontier. Their work has in all scholarly ways superseded the vigorous and interesting survey by Theodore Roosevelt. Professor Turner's "school" was one of the best illustrations in America of the combination of exact scholarship with the synthetic tendency in modern historiography.[11] The anti-slavery epic of von Holst has been modified as a result of better presentation of the southern viewpoint in the writings of William E. Dodd, Ulrich B. Phillips and others.

The period of the Civil War and Reconstruction was dealt with in a calm and temperate fashion by James Ford Rhodes in a detailed work. The period of the Civil War and its antecedents has been thoroughly handled by Allan Nevins and J. G. Randall. The subsequent generation has been covered in an exhaustive manner by Professor William A. Dunning and his students. Ellis P. Oberholtzer, a disciple of Professor McMaster, produced a detailed narrative of the history of the people of the United States after the Civil War, interpreted in the original and comprehensive spirit of his master. The whole period of national history has been sketched in a careful and dispassionate manner by James Schouler, and Professor Channing partly completed an ambitious attempt to trace the history of the United States from the period of colonization to the present in a work which may fairly be called our great national history in the better sense of that term. The best summary survey of American history in keeping with the erudite tradition and scholarship is probably D. S. Muzzey's *The United States of America*. The constitutional history of the United States has been handled competently by A. C. McLaughlin, E. S. Corwin and J. S. Landon.

The character of the best American historical scholarship in the first generation of those who had imbibed the newer critical methods is to be discovered in the coöperative *Narrative and Critical History of America*, edited by Justin Winsor. A comprehensive and representative repertory of American scholarship of more recent type is to be found in the *American Nation*, edited by Professor Albert Bushnell Hart. More comprehen-

---

[11] Turner's ideas have of late been attacked by Louis M. Hacker and others. See the *New Republic,* June 5, 1935.

sive was the *Chronicles of America*, edited by Allen Johnson. H. S. Commager and R. B. Morris have just completed the editing of a new *American Nation* project.

In addition to investigation of the history of their own country, American historians have made important contributions to many other periods and phases of history. Professor James Henry Breasted deservedly earned a place among the leaders of modern Egyptology. He first applied machine-age techniques to excavating the remains of the ancient Near East. Jack Finegan reconstructed the chronology of this age and area. R. W. Rogers, Morris Jastrow, A. T. Olmstead and G. S. Goodspeed have done creditable work on the history of Babylonia and Assyria. Professor W. S. Ferguson was the world's foremost authority on Greek imperialism and Hellenistic Athens. W. L. Westerman has dealt in an original fashion with the provinces of the Roman imperial system and the social history of antiquity, with particular attention to ancient slavery. Tenney Frank, Frank F. Abbott and Grant Showerman wrote ably on the economic, social and cultural history of Rome. G. W. Botsford and W. E. Caldwell ranged over classical antiquity with insight and scholarship. J. W. Swain, A. A. Trever and Ralph Turner synthesized the whole of ancient history.

In the field of medieval history George Lincoln Burr mastered the Carolingian period and medieval culture, and was easily the leading authority in Europe or America on the history of toleration. L. M. Larson has investigated the early medieval history of England, and James Westfall Thompson has dealt with the growth of the French monarchy under Louis VI and with German medieval history. Dana C. Munro, one of our ablest medievalists, devoted himself particularly to a study of the Crusades. The part played by the Normans in the history of medieval Europe has been investigated by Charles H. Haskins with a thoroughness and precision not equalled by any other American or European scholar. Few English scholars could rival George Burton Adams' knowledge of the constitutional history of medieval England. Ernest F. Henderson summarized the results of modern scholarship dealing with medieval and modern Germany. Ephraim Emerton contributed scholarly and detailed manuals covering the entire medieval period. Lynn Thorndike has presented an original synthesis of the best modern scholarship dealing with the Middle Ages, and has compiled a colossal work on medieval thought and science. Henry Osborn Taylor has furnished the best general survey of the intellectual history of this period. In summarizing and synthesizing the history of medieval Europe, in its political, social, and economic aspects, James Westfall Thompson occupies a preëminent place, not only among American, but among all medievalists.

Ferdinand Schevill has excelled in the cultural history of the Renaissance and has written a masterly history of Florence. Preserved Smith stood out preëminently among American students of the Reformation. E. M. Hulme has summarized our knowledge of the Renaissance and Reformation. The original and now generally accepted thesis that the expansion of Europe rather than the Renaissance or the Reformation marked the dawn of the modern world has furnished the center of orientation for the stimulating works of W. R. Shepherd, W. C. Abbott, J. B. Botsford, J. E. Gillespie and E. P. Cheyney. Professor Shepherd's work in the field of the expansion of Europe ranks with the work of F. J. Turner as one of the more profoundly original historical interpretations brought forth by American historians. Our knowledge of the French Revolution and the Napoleonic period has been enriched by the works of H. M. Stephens, F. M. Fling, W. M. Sloane, Henry E. Bourne, and Carl Becker and his students such as Leo Gershoy and Louis Gottschalk. William Roscoe Thayer dealt with the history of Italy from the end of the Napoleonic régime to the completion of unification. Henderson, Schevill and G. S. Ford have treated the history of modern Germany. R. B. Merriman has compiled a pretentious work on the Spanish Empire. Excellent work has been done on English history by E. P. Cheyney, L. M. Larson, A. L. Cross, W. E. Lunt and others. Cheyney has written the standard work on the last years of the reign of Elizabeth. C. H. MacIlwain has produced scholarly works on the history of political theory and on the origins of representative government. A. H. Lybyer has been the main American historian to devote special attention to the history of Byzantine civilization and the Turks. C. M. Andrews and C. D. Hazen have contributed standard political narratives on the history of modern Europe. In Professor John Bassett Moore the United States has the most productive and authoritative student of the history of international law and diplomacy. D. J. Hill, J. W. Foster, A. C. Coolidge, C. R. Fish, C. C. Tansill, W. L. Langer, J. W. Swain, R. J. Sontag, Parker T. Moon, R. L. Buell, G. H. Blakeslee, and S. F. Bemis have contributed to the study of contemporary international relations. W. L. Langer, S. B. Fay and R. J. Sontag produced standard histories of the diplomacy leading to World War I. The best work on American entry was C. C. Tansill's *America Goes to War*. D. L. Hoggan has written the only comprehensive work on the causes of World War II.

Among the American historians who have shown special competence in the field of Hispanic-American history have been W. R. Shepherd, H. E. Bolton, W. S. Robertson, J. F. Rippy, H. I. Priestly, Bernard Moses, C. W. Hackett, C. H. Haring, E. C. Barker, C. E. Chapman, Frank Tannenbaum, D. M. Dozer, D. G. Munro, Hubert Herring, and C. L. Jones. Scientific history has come to Hispanic America itself in the works of Barros Arana, Ortegay Rubio, Alejandro Álvarez, Oliveira Lima and others. Carl Wittke and J. B. Brebner have given special attention to Canadian history, and J. T. Shotwell edited an extensive series on Canadian-American relations. Significant books on the Far East have been produced by S. K. Hornbeck,

Tyler Dennett, K. S. Latourette, E. T. Williams, H. M. Vinacke, P. J. Treat, A. W. Griswold, Nathaniel Peffer, Paul H. Clyde, and others.

Church and religious history have attracted a large number of American students. Henry Charles Lea's many vast monographs on the medieval Church entitled him to rank with European scholars like Harnack, Denifle and Duchesne. G. P. Fisher, Philip Schaff and Williston Walker sketched the whole history of the Christian Church. A. C. McGiffert won an international reputation by his edition of Eusebius and later made important contributions to the history of the early Church and the history of Christian thought. The rise of the medieval Church has received the attention of J. C. Ayer and A. C. Flick. Flick has also written the best introduction to the decline of the medieval Church. The period of the Reformation has been covered by the monographs of Preserved Smith, Emerton, S. M. Jackson and H. E. Jacobs. David Schaff, Jackson and W. W. Rockwell have contributed to this field by valuable editorial labors, and Professor Rockwell has been especially active in keeping Americans in touch with the latest developments in European scholarship in this field. Schaff, Potter and Jackson have edited a comprehensive history of American churches. Peter Guilday has done much to promote Catholic historical scholarship in the field of American church history, and has written able biographies of leading American Catholics.

The interest of European historians in ancient and medieval history— a lingering effect of Humanism and Romanticism—left its impress upon American scholarship, and for a time led to the relative neglect of modern history. The younger generation of historians, however, by devoting their energies primarily to modern history, have tended to make a salutary break with tradition and are promising to equal in volume and quality the contributions that their former teachers made to the study of the Middle Ages. The series edited by W. L. Langer on *The Rise of Modern Europe* is the best and latest example of this laudable trend. The *Journal of Modern History*, launched by C. P. Higby and others in 1929, has been influential in encouraging this movement.

Historical biography in the United States has tended to take the form of a great number of brief biographies, such as the *American Statesmen Series,* the *Riverside Biographical Series,* and the *Dictionary of American Biography* rather than being limited to a few notable figures. Among the better biographies are the following: S. E. Morison of Columbus, Carl Van Doren of Franklin, D. S. Freeman of Washington, A. J. Beveridge of Marshall, Nathan Schachner and Broadus Mitchell of Hamilton, Gilbert Chinard of John Adams, Dumas Malone of Jefferson, Irving Brant of Madison, W. P. Cresson of Monroe, S. F. Bemis of John Quincy Adams, J. S. Bassett of Jackson, C. M. Wiltse of Calhoun, Beveridge and J. G. Randall of Lincoln, Freeman of Lee, L. P. Stryker of Johnson, Allan Nevins of Cleveland, Nevins and J. T. Flynn of Rockefeller, Herbert Croly of Mark Hanna,

Margaret Leach of McKinley, H. F. Pringle and H. K. Beale of Theodore Roosevelt, Pringle of Taft, A. S. Link of Woodrow Wilson, and Frank Freidel and A. M. Schlesinger, Jr., of F. D. Roosevelt.

Like natural science and other fields of learning, historical science had become a coöperative affair by the latter part of the nineteenth century. National historical societies were formed to act as clearing-houses for historical investigation and controversy. Historical journals were created to give publicity to existing research and to provide reviews of current historical literature. This made possible scholarly coöperation on an international scale. The *Historische Zeitschrift* was founded in 1859, the *Revue historique* in 1866, the *Revista storica italiana* in 1884, the *English Historical Review* in 1886, and the *American Historical Review* in 1895. Exchange professorships were common during the generation before the World War, especially exchanges between the United States and European countries.

While the erudite school prided itself upon complete freedom from philosophy and upon absolute objectivity, this "objectivity" itself became a philosophical bias—what the Germans call *Historismus*— with definite results which Charles Austin Beard pointed out with cogency in his sprightly article, "That Noble Dream," in the *American Historical Review* for October, 1935. To this topic we may devote a few critical comments.

THE ASSUMPTIONS UNDERLYING OBJECTIVE HISTORICAL WRITING

We may briefly subject the dominating tenets of erudite scientific historiography to critical examination. It has long been assumed that the perfection of historical science is only a matter of securing an increasingly perfected adoption of the ideals of von Ranke and his school. Once external and internal criticism had been mastered, it would be possible to reconstruct the past just exactly as it was. We are now in possession of critical knowledge which sharply challenges this body of assumptions.

In the first place, modern psychology has completely undermined the assumptions of those who uphold the ideals of complete historical objectivity. It has shown that no truly excellent piece of intellectual work can be executed without real interest and firm convictions. The notion that the human intellect can function in any vital form in an emotionless and aimless void is obviously contrary to the most elementary teachings of psychology. The assertion of the erudite school that we must approach historical problems with no preconceived notions, actually means that we should have no unorthodox notions. Members of the erudite school are replete with preconceived notions, but they are the opinions and dogmas that are currently received and approved by the historical guild.

Again the fetish of historical "facts," basic in the underlying assumptions of the erudite school, will not stand the test of critical analysis. Every historical situation is essentially unique, never again to be repeated in its entirety. A fact takes on uniqueness and completeness however, in relation to all the other aspects of the total historical situation. A historical fact refers to a specific concatenation of circumstances which was both born and terminated at the moment of its occurrence. When we say that we have discovered a historical fact we actually mean only that we have acquired information which allows us to make a highly subjective and incomplete reconstruction of one or more of the elements which once existed in a now extinct historical situation. No one can ever entirely re-create this historical entity and, in general, we make of a historical fact essentially what we put into it as a result of our subjective imagination.

The naïve assumption of many historians that there are concrete and integral entities known as historical facts lying about in profusion in our collections of historical sources is actually an animistic vestige. It has not yet been adequately exploded by the intrusion of critical and scientific thinking into the historical field. Such a conception is akin to the earlier scientific notion of the simple integral atom which has since been revealed to be as complex as our universal system.

In a brilliant paper on "What Are Historical Facts?" read before the American Historical Association at Rochester, New York, in December, 1926, Professor Carl L. Becker exploded once and for all this basic illusion regarding historical facts.[12] He exposed relentlessly the fallacy involved when we talk about the "hard facts" or the "cold facts" of history. "By virtue of talking in this way, the facts of history come in the end to seem something solid, something substantial like physical matter, something possessing definite shape and clear, persistent outline—like bricks and scantlings; so that we can easily picture the historian as he stumbles about in the past, stubbing his toe on the hard facts if he doesn't watch out." Taking as his theme one of the simplest and least challenged "facts" he could recall in the course of history, namely, the statement that Caesar crossed the Rubicon, Professor Becker showed the difficulty of arriving at certainty as to how, when or why Caesar crossed the Rubicon. He indicated the wide diversity of opinion as to the importance of this fact, according to the subjectivity of the chronicler. He showed the essential irrelevance of this fact, except in so far as it formed one element in a larger historical totality which it would be difficult if not impossible completely to restore and restate. "A thousand and one lesser 'facts' went to make up the one simple fact that Caesar crossed the Rubicon; and if we had some one, say James Joyce, to know and relate all these facts, it would no doubt

[12] P. L. Snyder, ed., *Detachment and the Writing of History: Essays and Letters of Carl Becker*, pp. 141 ff.; see also pp. 3-28. Cornell University Press, 1958.

require a book of 794 pages (i.e. *Ulysses*) to present this one fact that Caesar crossed the Rubicon."

In other words, the simple historical fact, which has long been the cornerstone of erudite and respectable historiography, proves to be the illusion of the simple-minded and the inadequately informed:

> The simple historical fact turns out not to be a hard, cold something with clear outline and measurable pressure like a brick. It is, so far as we can know it, only a symbol, a simple statement which is a generalization of a thousand and one simpler facts which we do not for the moment care to use and this generalization itself we cannot use apart from the wider facts and generalizations which it symbolizes. And, generally speaking, the more simple a historical fact is, the more clear and definite and probable it is, the less use it is to us in and for itself. . . . . This symbol is what the historian deals with—this symbol; and perhaps the safest thing to say about a symbol is not that it is in fact either true or false, but only more or less appropriate.

If the very foundation of the work of the erudite group is an illusion, then it is obvious that we cannot place complete confidence in the adequacy or reliability of the completed edifice. The whole structure must be regarded as little more than a tedious and laborious fantasy, though it may be the best that we can get.

These observations by Professor Becker, which are developed with thoroughness in his paper, obliterate the underlying conceptions of von Ranke and his followers as thoroughly as Einstein, Planck, Schroedinger, and Heisenberg have obliterated the old physics from Newton to Helmholtz. It is manifestly impossible to create the past *wie es eigentlich gewesen*. Now that this paper by Professor Becker has been published it should have the same place in historical science that the theory of indeterminacy occupies in contemporary physical science.

It is obvious, then, that the fundamental conception of the erudite school, namely, that they can discover the data of history in absolute, precise, unchangeable entities known as historical facts, which in any given situation are invariably the same and may be viewed uniformly by all honest investigators, is an illusion born of a pre-psychological age. The essence of the matter has been well stated by Professor A. A. Goldenweiser:

> The historian is of necessity a selector of events. His interpretation, moreover, is not separable from the selection, rather does the former determine the latter, at least in part. When the historians tell us that they merely record, that "the facts speak for themselves," they simply delude themselves. The facts, of course, do not speak: the historian speaks for

them or makes them speak, and what they say depends upon the m[...]
his wand.[13]

Another basic criticism may be leveled against this worship of historical facts; namely, that the erudite historians have approached them and
gathered them as though they existed in a void and were not related to
an active agent, *homo sapiens*. A major number of the scholarly historians
of the past and present have approached their documents without the
slightest technical preparation in the way of understanding human behavior. Indeed, they have been for the most part unconscious of the need
for any such preparation.[14] As far as their practical activities in gathering
and narrating facts are concerned, the deeds they recounted might equally well have been performed by any other one of the numerous orders of
mammals, or indeed by mere wooden puppets moved about by the hand
of Fate. In other words, the erudite historians, while assuming to recount
the deeds of mankind in the past, have ignored the central element in the
drama—the nature and behavior of man. While pretending to write the
story of mankind they have virtually left man out of the picture. They
have not only been concerned with elusive and essentially illusory data,
namely, historical facts. They also have neglected the only disciplines
which could in any way give these facts greater reliability and reality;
namely, those biological and social sciences which can give us an understanding of the nature of man, whose past behavior has created the constituent elements in what passes for a historical fact. As James Harvey
Robinson made clear, without this essential knowledge of the ways of
man, we can only reconstruct the "face and appearance" of things in the
past, remaining essentially ignorant of the underlying and all-important
realities of history.[15]

The persistent contention of the erudite school that the essential subject matter of history is past politics has been so frequently attacked and
so thoroughly discredited that it is both a waste of time and needless
cruelty once again to marshal the arguments against this position. We
can do no better than repeat Frederick Harrison's classic statement that
Freeman's ideals of history ignored nine-tenths of the human past. It is
plain enough that political activities constitute but a small fraction of the
interests and expressions of mankind. Therefore, if history is to be a record of all that man has done, thought and hoped, it cannot well limit itself to a record of his past political achievements and aspirations. Further,

[13] A. A. Goldenweiser, "The Nature and Tasks of the Social Sciences," *Journal of Social
Philosophy,* October, 1936, p. 12.

[14] For a spirited defense of the value to the historian of ignorance of human and social
facts see Abbott, *Adventures in Reputation,* pp. 211 ff.

[15] J. H. Robinson, "Newer Ways of Historians," in *American Historical Review,* January, 1930.

inasmuch as political data are of a secondary and resultant order, instead of being primary and determining, political history cannot well serve as the framework about which to organize the non-political materials.

The most telling indictment of the erudite school is probably that which may be drawn against their thesis that research and the accumulation of facts constitute the total obligation and the supreme achievement of the historian. As an actual matter of fact, historical research is but the first or preliminary stage of historical work. Research is indispensable to history, but it does not constitute history in any true or complete sense of the term. It is only when the results of historical research have been sifted, analyzed, organized and interpreted by a mind thoroughly equipped with an understanding of human nature and social institutions that historical research may be said to have contributed in any fundamental way to permanently valuable historical writing.

The real historian is not the plodder or compiling clerk who gathers the facts from a diversity of sources. He is, rather, the one who takes this raw material, evaluates it, and organizes it in such a fashion as to illuminate our minds with respect to the nature of the past and the manner in which the past has produced the present. It requires a far higher order of mind to produce historical synthesis than to carry on historical research, and it is for this reason that there are many research students and few real historians.

The erudite school has tended to confuse the excavators, the steel workers, the brick-makers and the hod-carriers of their profession with the architects. It has tended to create a profession which rests satisfied merely to attain competence in the inferior function of assembling historical materials. It has thereby discouraged interest in truly historical endeavor.

So long as the mere technique of research is viewed as the final measure of historical prowess, there is little hope that the great majority of individuals in the historical field will wish to go beyond this stage of endeavor. Indeed, it is unlikely that they will realize that any area of potential historical activity actually lies beyond the responsibilities and achievements of an accurate recording clerk.

No less indefensible is the characteristic thesis of the conventional school that there is no essential difference in the inherent value of historical achievements—that the significance of a piece of historical work is to be measured solely by the relative accuracy of the facts which have been gathered, irrespective of whether or not they throw light upon any important problem connected with the evolution of society and civilization. If history is to have any significance beyond pedantic exhibitionism, we must admit that historical materials are valuable in the degree to which they explain the present. We need not necessarily discourage research in highly esoteric fields which happen to interest a particular investigator, but that does not carry with it the implication that a study of Prussian diplomacy in the seventeenth century is as valuable as an equal amount of time expended upon a study of factors contributing to the growth of capitalism, the middle class and nationality in western Europe in this same century.

It is obvious to thoughtful persons that historical facts present no significance whatever until they have been selected, sifted, analyzed and interpreted to show their bearing upon the flow of civilization. To stop with the mere gathering and narration of the facts would be equivalent to the procedure of a scientist who never went beyond laboratory experiments and writing his observations in a notebook. It is universally agreed that the relevant results of science only emerge when the outcome of a large body of long-continued researches justify the formulation of a tentative scientific law. In like manner, we shall ultimately come to recognize that true history makes its appearance only when a large body of accumulated facts lend themselves to: (1) the possibility of a valid historical synthesis; and (2) the interpretation of these materials in such a way as to indicate the bearing of past developments upon contemporary conditions.

An equally effective attack can be made upon the contentions of the erudite school relative to excessive caution in historical conclusions. One of the most revered hypotheses of the respectable school is that historical scholarship is better exemplified by conclusions that fall seventy-five per cent short of the truth than by those that stray one per cent beyond it.[16]

We must recognize that absolute historical truth is a complete fiction, and that at best we can only hope for approximations that are partly the result of accurate research, partly the result of lucky accidents of interpretation, and partly the product of special ingenuity and subtlety on the part of a particular historian. At the same time, conclusions which fall seventy-five per cent short of an apparent approximation are likely to be as divergent from the truth as conclusions which go seventy-five per cent beyond it. The conventional historical contention as to understatement is as preposterous as it would be to allege that ten gallons are closer to a barrel than thirty-four gallons. If this historical dogma were applied to geographical science it would mean that it would be sounder and wiser to say that the earth is two thousand miles in circumference than twenty-six thousand miles. Approximation to accuracy, not mere caution, should be the goal of the historian.

Closely related to this obsession with understatement is the widely held conviction that historical scholarship stands in inverse relation to the amount of material published by an individual—that consistent refusal to publish is somehow a proof of the individual's exacting standards. There

[16] Well exemplified by the concluding chapter of S. B. Fay's notable *Origins of the World War*.

is, of course, everything to be said in favor of hesitating to publish immature work or unfinished research. But it is another matter to assume that failure to publish historical works is of itself alone necessarily an indication of exacting scholarship. It may just as well be a dignified cover for indolence. In those cases where it is obvious that men who are reluctant to publish do possess the highest standards of scholarship and a vast fund of historical information, then the situation is one which indicates a problem of psycho-pathology rather than of scholarship. It is probably a case of "anxiety neurosis" in most instances. Most of those who refuse to publish do present their materials to students in the form of classroom lectures, frequently of a graduate school character. It is obvious that material which is accurate enough to set forth before advanced technical students of history must be fit to see the light of day in printed form. If a man feels that his facts are not substantial enough to print, he should recognize that they are not suitable for any form of public presentation. To be sure, these observations must not be regarded as any justification of the hasty printing of premature or "half-baked" historical works.

It is not difficult to riddle the idealized conception of the model historian according to the hypothesis of the erudite school. An individual attaining this ideal of an entirely emotionless being, devoid of all human passions and prejudices, probably would present a well-nigh classical case of pseudo-feeble-mindedness.[17] Human life is, in reality, a vital and dynamic affair and can only be discovered, recreated and interpreted by a person as vital as the data which he uses.

The threadbare slogan of the conventional historian that we should "seek light without heat" also is little capable of defense. As far as we know, there is nothing which generates light without heat except the firefly or "lightning bug," and it is not unfair to compare many a conventional historian, with his aimless accumulation of scattered and disorganized historical materials, with the futile and aimless wanderings of this fugitive insect that flits about with no discernable object and no definite results.

Professor Ferdinand Schevill, who has met all the qualifications imposed upon the successful historian by the erudite school but has escaped to a singular degree the paralyzing limitations implicit in these ideals, has admirably summarized the weakness of the conventional position:

> Is it not possible to make entirely too much of non-partisanship and objectivity as the great desiderata for the writer of history? To be completely objective is to be as dry and colorless as an adding-machine, and that surely is a literary ideal which the historian should and the reader will resist as inhuman. What we have a right to demand of a historian is that he be honest, capable of subjecting his feelings to his understanding,

---

[17] Cf. W. H. Burnham, *The Normal Mind* (Appleton, 1924), chap. xviii.

trained to read documents critically, and ready to grub patiently for the facts and to form his judgment under their direction.[18]

It is probable that of all the psychic factors paralyzing the vitality and effectiveness of historical writing, the good-taste obsession is one of the most far reaching and the most damaging in its influence. While even the very erudite historians are frequently subject in practice to the warping influence of partisan fury or religious conviction, they are all prepared to admit in theory that such things are damaging to that clarity of vision and impartiality of analysis which are believed to be indispensable prerequisites of the historian.

Good taste in historical writing and analysis, however, is something in which most conventional historians veritably glory. There is not even any real comprehension of the fact that good taste, as conventionally understood, is probably a greater handicap to contemporary historiography than any of the recognized prejudices and passions which historians have been formally combating for a generation. They do not comprehend that it is as difficult for a "gentleman"—according to the qualifications for that status which are accepted by the respectable American historians—to be an effective historian as it is for the scriptural rich man to enter the kingdom of heaven.

It is now well understood by students of dynamic psychology that those intimate matters of personal life, which are taboo in respectable historical biographical studies, are of major significance in explaining the personality and the behavior-patterns of an individual, past or present. (It goes without saying that we do not restrict the term "intimate matters" solely to sex interests and activities.) The conventional historian, in assuming a mythological ideal as his model historian, has created mythological figures as the subjects of his multifarious biographical efforts. Moreover, the identification of historical good taste with conservative *bourgeois* economic and social ideals leads historians to be very timid in recognizing the importance of material factors in historical development. The economic interpretation of history is associated with Socialism, any sympathy with which is an extreme manifestation of bad taste.

Likewise, the initial assumption of invariable nobility of character and purpose and of non-earthly interests and motives upon the part of historical characters practically nullifies from the outset the value of any biographical effort, or of any historical synthesis based upon a compilation of biographical material. The only assumptions which can by made by a creditable and up-to-date biographer are that his subject of study was obviously a human being functioning as human beings are revealed to be-

[18] Introduction to Hermann Oncken, *Napoleon III and the Rhine* (Knopf, 1928), pp. xvii-xviii.

have by physiologists, psychologists, psychiatrists, and social scientists. The shock which such a naturalistic hypothesis brings to the recondite historian is well illustrated by James Truslow Adams' contribution to the composite work, *Living Philosophies*,[19] in which he clings to a truly medieval conception of human qualities.

A writer should start with the assumption of essential humanity on the part of the personality to be studied and with technical preparation in the way of knowledge of human behavior. He should then proceed to gather, organize and interpret his facts so as to reveal the manner in which this particular example of human machinery has operated from birth to death, whether his life proves to be a singular evidence of altruism and devotion to human justice, or a unique exemplification of human arrogance, selfishness, corruption, and oppression.

Especially absurd is the idea we may not speak frankly of the work of a historian until he is dead—that we may denounce Ralph the Bald with impunity, but must not question the motives of a living historian. This means that the misrepresentations of historians must be allowed to stand and do damage for perhaps forty years before they may be demolished in workmanlike fashion. This notion is certainly preposterous and is not accepted as thoroughly in Europe as in the United States. Beyond its disservice to historical science, this attitude is not sporting. It is far fairer to attack a historian while he is alive and can defend himself.

One of the most serious results of the good-taste mania is the tendency of scholarly historians to have two different opinions on matters which are strongly controversial. Such, for example, are the questions of responsibility for the World War and the nature and progress of the Communist experiment in Soviet Russia. An intelligent but discreet professor will have a candid and logical view, based upon the facts, which he freely expresses to intimate friends and to advanced students in the privacy of his graduate seminar. But when it comes to public papers, articles, and books, he all too frequently abandons his private and scholarly convictions and tempers his declarations to conform with prevailing opinion in the historical guild. The deviation between these two views may be wide and striking.[20] What would be said of a scientist who, in private, expressed a belief in evolution but in public still clung to the dogma of special creation? The fierce nationalists like Droysen, von Sybel and von Treitschke were at least candid. They may have distorted history by patriotic ardor, but they were patriots in private as well as in public. They may have been wrong, but there was no doubt about where they stood.

We may fairly say that the good-taste complex is by all odds the most

---

[19] Simon and Schuster, 1933.
[20] M. H. Cochran, *Germany Not Guilty in 1914*, Introduction.

important source of obscuring truth among respectable historians today. In these circles good taste is as powerful an obstacle to truth, honesty, candor, and accuracy today as was fierce partisanship or obsessed patriotism some generations ago. It is obvious that no sane critic would urge vulgarity or anything else which is legitimately regarded as offensive in historical writing. There can be no objection to the utmost refinement in expression. It is the suppression of candor, forthrightness, and fundamental integrity of thought which makes historical good-taste so fatal to sound historical writing. The matter of refinement is not at all involved. Historians like James Harvey Robinson, Carl Becker, Preserved Smith and Ferdinand Schevill, for example, have shown that the highest degree of intellectual candor can coexist with the most extreme refinement of expression.

Of course, as an actual matter of fact, the erudite school has never realized in any true sense its ideal of good taste in attaining the mountain top of dominion over all human passions and prejudices. What it has done in reality has been to bring professional approval to the fashionable biases of any particular period, the most impressive illustration of this being the warm professional acclaim of the abusive and myth-mongering historians during two World Wars.

In the last two decades of the nineteenth century it was fashionable to present a Teutonic or Anglo-Saxon interpretation of European and American history. The individual who dared to set forth the Gallic point of view of writers like Fustel de Coulanges was regarded as a victim of a grossly warped outlook. Since 1914 it has become equally fashionable to repudiate the Teutonic and Anglo-Saxon hypothesis and to find France the real custodian and preserver of civilization through the ages.

SELECTED REFERENCES

H. B. Adams, *Methods of Historical Study*. Johns Hopkins Press, 1884.

A. W. Small, *Origins of Sociology*, chaps. iii-v. University of Chicago Press, 1924.

Guilday, *Church Historians*, pp. 212-415.

Wegele, *Geschichte der deutschen Historiographie,* Book V.

Ritter, *Die Entwicklung der Geschichtswissenschaft,* Book V.

Fueter, *Histoire de l'historiographie moderne,* pp. 387-99, 574-614.

Gooch, *History and Historians in the Nineteenth Century,* chaps. vi-vii, xii, xviii-xxvii.

Thompson, *History of Historical Writing*, Vol. II, chaps. xxxvii, xli-xlii, xlv, xlvii.

Schevill, *Six Historians*, pp. 125-190.

B. E. Schmitt, ed., *Some Historians of Modern Europe.* University of Chicago Press, 1942.

S. W. Halperin, ed., *Some Twentieth Century Historians.* University of Chicago Press, 1961.

Herman Ausubel *et al., Some Modern Historians of Britain.* Dryden Press, 1951.

———, *Historians and Their Craft.* Columbia University Press, 1950.

R. L. Schuyler, ed., *Frederic William Maitland.* University of California Press, 1960.

Gertrude Himmelfarb, *Lord Acton.* University of Chicago Press, 1952.

H. F. Helmolt, *Leopold von Rankes Leben und Werken.* Leipzig, 1921.

S. Steinberg, ed., *Die Geschichtswissenschaft der Gegenwart in Selbstdarstellungen.* Leipzig, 1925-26. 2 vols.

Guilland, *Modern Germany and Her Historians.*

G. A. H. von Below, *Die deutsche Geschichtsschreibung von den Befreiungskriegen bis zu unseren Tagen.* Munich, 1924.

Gustav Wolf, *Einführung in das Studium der neueren Geschichte.* Berlin, 1910.

Halphen, *L'Histoire en France depuis cent ans.*

Louis Halphen, *et al., Histoire et historiens depuis cinquante ans.* Paris, 1927-28. 2 vols.

Croce, *Storia della storiografia italiana.*

P. N. Miliukov, *Main Currents of Russian Historiography.* Moscow, 1898.

Kraus, *A History of American History.*

———, *The Writing of American History,* chaps. viii, ix, xi-xii.

M. E. Curti, ed., *Theory and Practice in Historical Study.* Social Science Research Council, 1946.

Elizabeth Stevenson, *Henry Adams: A Biography* Macmillan, 1955.

J. R. Cameron, *Frederick William Maitland and the History of English Law.* University of Oklahoma Press, 1961.

Henri Marrou, *De la connaissance historique.* Paris, 1956.

William Dray, *Laws and Explanation in History.* Oxford University Press, 1957.

Fritz Wagner, *Geschichtswissenschaft.* Berlin, 1951.

———, *Moderne Geschichtsschreibung.* Berlin, 1960.

H. W. Odum, ed., *American Masters of Social Science.* Holt, 1928.

A. M. Schlesinger *et al., Historical Scholarship in America.* American Historical Association, 1932.

J. M. Vincent, *Historical Research*: an Outline of Theory and Practice. Smith, New York, 1929.

C. G. Crump, *History and Historical Research.* London, 1928.

Allen Johnson, *The Historian and Historical Evidence.* Scribner, 1926.

C. V. Langlois and Charles Seignobos, *Introduction to the Study of History.* Holt, 1912.

Ernst Bernheim, *Lehrbuch der historischen Methode und Geschichtsphilosophie.* Leipzig, 1908.

XI

THE WORLD WARS: THE FALL AND RISE OF
HISTORICAL SCHOLARSHIP

THE WORLD WARS AND THE CLASH OF NATIONALISM
WITH SCHOLARSHIP IN HISTORICAL WRITING

HISTORICAL scholarship, by 1914, seemed to have attained a very high degree of impartiality. Patriotic sentiments were subordinated to the desire to tell the truth. Of course, important historical works were still being produced which were dominated by patriotic ardor, but these were the exception rather than the rule. The historian who allowed patriotism to distort his judgment or ruffle his mental calm was very sharply criticized. Special pride was taken in the ability to deal impartially with sharply controverted subjects and with topics that involved patriotic pride.

Then came the first World War, and there was a revival of patriotic enthusiasm on the part of historians, which temporarily carried historical writing back, in psychological temper at least, to the generation before von Ranke. Compared to the writings of historians on the World War between 1914 and 1920, the strictures of Fustel de Coulanges against the Germanists, and the interpretation of the Franco-Prussian War by von Sybel were almost calm and measured historical analysis. Indeed, it is probably no exaggeration to say that not since the days of the Magdeburg Centurians and Baronius, of Knox and Maimbourg, had there been so much bias and such ferocity in the general run of historical writing. And it was not merely the lesser lights of the historical profession who were upset and driven from objectivity. The man who was the most eminent of living historians, Eduard Meyer, was thrown off his balance as well as the mediocre plodders of the profession. And the nationalistic hysteria affected historians in all countries. The various governments published "official documents" on the crisis of 1914 to justify their policy. They were shamefully altered and falsified and historians aided in this falsification. Not since the days of the early Christian Fathers had historical documents been juggled so casually and extensively.

Early in the war a large number of eminent German professors drew up a "manifesto" setting forth the German view of the issues and merits of the conflict. Many historians were among its signers. It was purely accidental that history has since rather thoroughly vindicated their general position. It was not lack of emotion which made it possible for them to approximate the truth more closely than Entente scholars. Nor had they any knowledge of the documentary secrets which have since tended to confirm their allegations. Eduard Meyer turned aside from work on his *Geschichte des Altertums* to compose a diatribe against the British Empire. Georg von Below eulogized the Hohenzollerns and lauded the German position in the war. Dietrich Schäfer defended with enthusiasm the program of the pan-Germans. These are only the most notable of a host of similar efforts to buttress the German case by an appeal to history.

The French historians were even more active, lyrical and vehement than the German savants.[1] Ernest Lavisse was almost by common consent the dean of French historians in 1914, and he was noted for his former enthusiasm for German culture, but he took the lead in assailing the Germans after 1914. In April, 1915, he roundly denounced a neutral proposal to promote a discussion of war issues and peace conditions by belligerent intellectuals. In many speeches and articles he besmirched the Germans. In a Sorbonne address he said of Germany: "She poisons opinion in the same way as she poisons the air and poisons wells. She is the great poisoner of the earth." Lavisse addressed the German delegation to the Paris Peace Conference as follows: "You are here before your judges, to answer for the greatest crime in history. You are going to lie, for you are congenital liars. But beware, lying is awkward when you know that those who are listening to you and are looking at you know that you are lying." Alphonse Aulard, the world-famed historian of the French Revolution, wrote in similar terms of the Germans: "Lying is the national industry of the Germans, their very system of government. It is on lies that the Hohenzollerns established the Prussian power, and later, for the benefit of Prussia, the German power." Aulard also lamented the fact that an armistice was signed with the Germans. He wished them pursued and massacred. Henri Hauser, famous expert on the sixteenth century, bitterly attacked the German pacifists. Georges Blondel, a leading French historian of modern Germany, compiled extended diatribes against the Germans, accusing them of desiring to establish a military dictatorship over the planet. As an editor, Lavisse eagerly published the superficial contributions of German renegades like Richard Grelling and excluded from his pages the substantial articles of honest German experts like Count Maximilian Montgelas. Émile Bourgeois, eminent historian and publicist, upheld the lamblike innocence of Russia. Georges Renard, Socialist and leading economic historian, supplied propaganda for the Anti-German League, which aimed to boycott all things German.

---

[1] The most damaging exposure of the French historians is contained in Georges Demartial, *La Guerre de 1914: comment on mobilisa les consciences* (new ed., Paris, 1926).

In England, Wickham Steed composed fanciful tales of war origins, denounced the Austrians and extolled Serbia. R. W. Seton-Watson defended the southern Slavs and assaulted the Austro-Hungarian policies. J. W. Headlam, biographer of Bismarck, actually shared with H. G. Wells the organization and production of anti-German propaganda in England. For this service he was knighted as Sir J. W. Headlam-Morley. With few exceptions, such as Raymond Beazley, F. W. Hirst and F. C. Conybeare, the English historians fell into line. And Hirst was primarily an economist and Conybeare a biblical scholar. Even the solid and venerable economic historian, Archdeacon William Cunningham, actually attacked the English pacifists for digging up the Sermon on the Mount, and contended that it was the highest moral duty of the English soldiers to kill as many Germans as possible.[2] His bloodthirsty sermons were collected, printed and distributed by the Society for the Propagation of the Gospel.

It was in the United States, however, that the largest number of eminent historians broke loose from their intellectual moorings and outdid Bancroft in their patriotic enthusiasm.[3] This was mainly due to the fact that the United States was in no real danger of attack. In the absence of the actual sound of real cannon fire, the American mob had to be stirred up by a cannonade of fierce but fictitious rhetoric. Propaganda was indispensable for building up American morale and bloodlust. The few American historians who held tenaciously to their pre-War objectivity—Sill, Schevill, Thompson, Henderson, Shepherd, Preserved Smith, and others —were shamefully treated and at times denounced as intellectual traitors. Even more bitter was the attack on alleged pro-Germans like Professors Burgess and Sloane. The most obsessed of the historical war propagandists, William Roscoe Thayer, was twice elected president of the American Historical Association. The warnings of H. Morse Stephens, presented in his presidential address before the American historians a year before we entered the War, proved of no avail.

The leadership in preparing fierce invective against the Germans was taken by William Roscoe Thayer, Charles Downer Hazen, William Stearns Davis, Munro Smith, Albert Bushnell Hart, Earle E. Sperry, R. McNutt McElroy, E. Raymond Turner, Bernadotte Schmitt, and Claude Halstead Van Tyne. Most amazing of all, perhaps, was the case of George Lincoln Burr. He was one of the half-dozen ablest American historians and the leading authority on tolerance. But even he insisted, in spite of his advanced years, in donning khaki and drilling with the boys on the Cornell campus.

[2] C. E. Playne, *Society at War* (Houghton Mifflin, 1931), p. 218.

[3] See the sprightly and invaluable memoir by C. Hartley Grattan, "The Hist   : Cut Loose," in the *American Mercury*, August, 1927, reprinted in H. E. Barnes, *I*   *t of Truth and Justice* (National Historical Society, 1928), pp. 142 ff.

Certain universities coöperated in producing comprehensive statements of the philosophy of hate and anti-Germanic history. Perhaps the most notable example was the *War Book* of the University of Wisconsin, but many other institutions published similar documents. The most impressive defection from objectivity was the organization of the National Board for Historical Service by Professors J. T. Shotwell and Guy S. Ford, and its overt alliance with the Creel Bureau—the official government department of propaganda. Professor Shotwell had rivaled James Harvey Robinson as a leader of the new history in the United States. His associates on the National Board read like an honor roll of the most eminent and venerable American historians—most of the men who had really established historical scholarship in the United States. American historical writing became organized for mass production in propaganda. Other distinguished historians wrote openly for such patriotic societies as the National Security League and the American Defense Society. Not only were the Germans berated as an inferior and contemptible nation, but stress was laid upon our invaluable heritage from Britain. The American Revolution almost seemed to have been a rash and lamentable mistake. For nearly a decade after the war most of the men elevated to the presidency of the American Historical Association were those who had been conspicuous for their professional services to the Allies.[4]

THEN CAME THE DAWN

While bias and emotion prevailed in the minds of most historians for a decade or more after 1918, a definite reaction soon set in among a minority. New sources of information replaced the carefully-edited official documents which the various governments had published during the war. Scholars who had controlled their emotions during the war, or others who recovered from their patriotic orgy, devoted themselves to a study of these documents. The result was that within a decade we had a more complete and accurate knowledge of the causes of the first World War than we had of the causes of the Franco-Prussian War in 1914.

If historical writing during the war left a deep stain upon the record of historical scholarship, the work of able historians after the war was over, dealing with the preliminaries of 1914, constitutes one of the most remarkable and commendable examples of productive historical scholarship in a century. We may now consider briefly the reasons for and the nature of this renaissance of scholarship after the war closed.

Down to the time of the first World War it was the universal practice for governments to keep their documents relating to foreign politics secret for

---

[4] Barnes, *In Quest of Truth and Justice*, Part II.

from forty to sixty years after the event. In 1914, for example, the documents bearing on the Franco-Prussian War of 1870 had not been published with any completeness by either France or Germany. How was it possible, then, for historians, only a quarter of a century since 1914, to talk with an air of finality concerning those who brought on the World War?

The situation is wholly novel in human experience.[5] As a result of the revolutions in Russia, Austria, and Germany in 1917-18, new governments appeared on the scene which had no reason for desiring to conceal the facts that might possibly discredit the preceding royal régimes. Indeed, they hoped that the documents in the foreign offices would actually show that the imperial governments had been responsible for bringing on the Great War. They believed that such proof would help to maintain the revolutionary governments in power. They felt that popular hatred of the older régimes would be likely to spring up from the knowledge that the monarchical governments had been responsible for the horrible sufferings which the World War had produced.

Therefore, the Austrian and German governments voluntarily published a full and complete edition of the documents in their respective foreign offices bearing on the crisis of 1914: the so-called *Red Book* in Austria and the *Kautsky Documents* in Germany. The Germans subsequently published all of the important documents on the whole period from 1870 to 1914, the famous *Grosse Politik*, edited by Friedrich Thimme and others, thus allowing the facts to speak for themselves as to German foreign policy in the half-century before the war and challenging the other states to do likewise. Austria later published a briefer collection of eight volumes on the period from 1908 to 1914—*Oesterreich-Ungarns Aussenpolitik von der Bosnischen Krise 1908 bis zum Kriegsausbruch 1914,* edited by Ludwig Bittner and Hans Uebersberger. They covered chiefly the relations of Austria with Serbia, and constitute the basis for the Austrian case against the Serbs and Russians.

Much progress has been made, as well, in the publication of the documents in the foreign offices of Allied countries. In fact, Russia was the first country to make public such materials, starting with the publication of the notorious Secret Treaties of the Entente in November, 1917. The Russian Bolshevik government did not systematically publish its docu-

---

[5] For a comprehensive summary and analysis of the scholarly literature on the causes of the first World War, see H. E. Barnes, *Genesis of the World War* (Knopf, 1928), Appendix; and *World Politics* (Knopf, 1930), chap. xxi. For an instructive hangover of wartime trickery see *A Guide to Historical Literature,* p. 396. It is the custom of the editors to refer to reviews of books from different standpoints and representative of all shades of opinion. In handling my *Genesis of the World War,* Frank Maloy Anderson, himself a "bitter-ender," ignored the many and authoritative reviews of a favorable type and listed only severely hostile reviews, some of them anonymous.

ments, but allowed French and German scholars, such as René Marchand and Friedrich Stieve, to have access to the archives and to make adequate selections. The Stieve collection, known as *Der diplomatische Schrift-wechsel Iswolskis,* is the standard edition and its honesty and adequacy cannot be successfully challenged. The secretary of the Russian embassy in London, B. de Siebert, copied and made available for publication the exchanges between St. Petersburg and London in the years immediately before the war. E. A. Adamov has edited the documents on Russia's crucial diplomatic struggle to get control of the Straits.

The British government was the first non-revolutionary government voluntarily to publish its documents bearing on the outbreak of the World War. This it began in the autumn of 1926. Eleven volumes of these *British Official Documents on the Origins of the War,* 1898-1914, have been published covering the period from 1898 to 1914. They are well edited by G. P. Gooch and H. W. V. Temperley.

Though the French did not publish their documents for over a decade after 1914, we could discover most of the essential facts concerning the French diplomacy of the period in the Russian and British documents, for the French were allied to Great Britain and Russia. Such check-ups as were made by Demartial, von Wegerer, and others, showed that the French *Yellow Book* of the war period—full of forgeries and omissions —was perhaps the most seriously distorted of any of the apologetic publications issued during the War. It was rivaled in this respect only by the Russian *Orange Book.* Due to the continued taunts of impartial scholars throughout the world and to the demands of the friends of truth in France, the French government at last reluctantly announced in 1928 that it would publish the documents in its foreign office bearing on the crisis of 1914, and on the diplomacy of the years since 1871. As Robert Dell pointed out, however, in a trenchant article in the London *Nation* of January 14, 1928, the nature of the committee entrusted with the task of selecting and editing the documents gave little assurance of candor, integrity, or absolute completeness in the publication. No anti-official or revisionist historians were included on the editorial committee:

> The French Government having at last recognized that it cannot with decency refrain any longer from any publication of the diplomatic documents concerning the origin of the war, has appointed a commission of forty-eight persons to superintend their publication. Three of the four secretaries of the Commission are government officials, and the Commission includes thirteen other permanent officials of the *Quai d'Orsay* and diplomatists, most of whom were intimately concerned with the events leading to the war. Such a commission is a guarantee of bad faith. The French Government will never publish all the documents, for their publication would show that many of the documents in the French *Yellow*

Book of 1914 were faked or even forged. That has already been proved by M. Georges Demartial in his little book, *L'Evangile du Quai d'Orsay,* to which no reply has been or can be made.

The first volumes of these *Documents diplomatiques français, 1871-1914,* appeared in 1929 and bore some marks of selection and adroit editing. But the volumes thus far published are far superior in accuracy to any other French collections in this field. During the war the Germans raided the Belgian archives and they published a great collection of Belgian diplomatic documents under the title of *Zur europäischen Politik, 1897-1914,* edited by Bernhard Schwertfeger. Milosh Boghitschewitsch edited a collection of documents on Serbian diplomatic history before 1914, *Die Auswärtige Politik Serbiens, 1903-1914,* but he was not allowed to use the Serbian archives. The United States is also publishing its diplomatic documents of the war period. This information explains how we can talk authoritatively about war guilt so soon after the conflict. For the first time in human history, a generation which had lived through a great war could know the facts as to its origins.

In addition to the authoritative documents, most of the important participants in the diplomatic crisis of 1914, the Kaiser, von Bethmann-Hollweg, von Jagow, von Tirpitz, von Moltke, Falkenhayn, Pourtalès, von Schoen, Lichnowsky, Hoyos, Conrad, Musulin, Sazonov, Schilling, Rosen, Dobrorolski, Poincaré, Viviani, Paléologue, Asquith, Grey, Churchill, Bertie, Buchanan, Haldane, and Nitti—have published memoirs or diaries giving their versions of the crisis. Izvolski was prevented by death from finishing his memoirs, but his letters, preserved in reasonable completeness, have been edited and published. They tell more than his memoirs could ever have been expected to reveal. Count Leopold Berchtold was prevented from finishing his memoirs on account of Entente interference with the free use of the documents in Vienna.

While these books must be used with caution, they often enable us to understand the documents more fully and to comprehend better the motives of the diplomats who either launched or failed to prevent the war. In addition, it has been the privilege of the present writer to interview in person many of those prominent in the diplomacy of 1914 and to induce them to clear up as far as possible obscure or controverted points.[6] The nature and significance of all of this vast body of material has been admirably described in a remarkable book published in 1927 by George Peabody Gooch, a leading British authority. It is entitled, *Recent Revelations of European Diplomacy.* Subsequently revised and extended, it is fair, accurate, judicious, and reasonably complete, though at times somewhat overpolite to myth-mongers in high places.

[6] *New York Times Current History Magazine,* July, 1928.

It was only natural that the more critical and scholarly approach to the origins of the first World War first made headway in Germany. Historians in Allied countries had been forced to garble the facts far more extensively in order to make out a good case for the Entente cause. We have already referred to the editorial work in publishing the German documents from 1870 to 1914. A number of German scholars have reviewed the history of German diplomacy in the pre-war period. The ablest of these books is Erich Brandenburg's *Von Bismarck zum Weltkriege,* one of the best studies of diplomacy in the era before the World War. The same period is covered in the work of Veit Valentin on German foreign policy. The crucial epoch of Bülow's chancellorship has been dealt with by Johannes Haller. Most complete of all these studies of pre-war German diplomacy are the several volumes by Otto Hammann, long connected with the German foreign office. Hermann Lutz has given us the most competent survey of the diplomacy of England under Sir Edward Grey and has also produced one of the most thorough and restrained summaries of the onset of the World War, written from the latest documents. Friedrich Stieve drew from his study of the Russian documents the information which enabled him to write the most complete and reliable study of the diplomacy of Izvolski and Poincaré. This is supplemented by the monographs of Major Gunther Frantz on the military phases of Russia's entry into the World War, including the fateful mobilization order of July 30, 1914. The most exacting student of the crisis of 1914 in Germany is Count Maximilian Montgelas, a master of detail and a clear expositor. He has also provided from the new British documents a trenchant summary of the diplomacy of Sir Edward Grey. Alfred von Wegerer, editor of the *Kriegschuldfrage,* has done the most to promote a reconsideration of the problems of war responsibility and has himself delivered a smashing blow at the indictment of Germany formulated by Entente diplomats at the Versailles Conference. The most readable of all German accounts of war origins is Theodor Wolff's *The Eve of 1914,* which is generally accurate although too harsh on Berchtold. Even more absorbing is Ludwig Reiners' recent work, *The Lamps Went Out in Europe* (1955). Certain German writers, like Hermann Kantorowicz, have allowed their hatred of the Hohenzollerns to color their judgments and to continue the wartime mythology. Kantorowicz's writings also are warped by his evident Anglomania. The role of Austria in the crisis of 1914 has been treated by Alfred Pribram, Ludwig Bittner, Hans Uebersberger and O. H. Wedel. But the case for Austria and Berchtold still awaits an adequate presentation. In Holland the leader of the investigation of pre-war diplomacy was Nicholaas Japikse.

The official and academic historians in France long remained formally correct in their account of the coming of the World War—that is, they defended the essential innocence of France. A representative example of this kind of writing is the account by two eminent diplomatic historians, Bourgeois and Pagès. Even the much-praised work by Pierre Renouvin is only a more than usually adroit apology for the official French position. Of a similar tone is the work of Jules Isaac. If, however, the French historians have not recovered from their "shell shock," many courageous French journalists and publicists have done so. Notable among them have been Pevet, Dupin, Morhardt, Margueritte, Judet and Lazare. But the most competent and indefatigable of them all has been M. Georges Demartial, formerly an honored official of the French colonial office. He has been a veritable thorn in the side of the official falsifiers and apologists, and his work is characterized by extended knowledge of the documents and by meticulous accuracy in statement. Georges Michon has written a very able and reliable account of the development of the Franco-Russian alliance which played a great part in leading Europe into war. A brilliant French publicist, Alfred Fabre-Luce, provided the best balanced French account of the crisis of 1914. Alcide Ebray has critically examined the Treaty of Versailles and shown its relation to the errors in war propaganda. He has also studied in detail treaty violations since 1815 in Europe, blasting the popular charge that Germany has been the only state to reduce an important treaty to a "scrap of paper."

In England, the struggle for truth was kept alive during the war and immediately thereafter by E. D. Morel, already famed for his exposure of the nefarious doings of Leopold of Belgium in the Congo. The first devastating critique of the official English version of war origins was embodied in Lord Loreburn's *How the War Came,* which has since been amply vindicated by the British documents. G. P. Gooch has been especially active and industrious in bringing about a better understanding of the diplomatic background of the World War. He wrote the first masterly survey of European diplomacy from 1878 to 1920, and has given us our best review of the new literature of scholarly disillusionment. G. Lowes Dickinson wrote the most satisfactory English summary of the diplomacy of 1914 and the previous decade. Sir Raymond Beazley produced the sanest brief summary of the facts concerning the crisis of 1914 that has appeared in any country. Irene Cooper Willis and Caroline E. Playne have brought out the most adequate surveys of the war hysteria and propaganda in England during the World War. As in France, most of the academic historians, well represented by R. B. Mowat, are traditional and official in their version of how the war came. One of the later important English books on war origins, H. W. Wilson's *The War Guilt,* faithfully continues the wartime illusions and propaganda. John Morley's *Memorandum on Resignation* proved that Britain had decided to go to war before Belgium was even mentioned in the Cabinet meetings. The best

Canadian account of the crisis of 1914 and its diplomatic antecedents is the work of an eminent Canadian barrister, J. S. Ewart.

In Russia, the Bolshevik government had little interest in whitewashing the old tsarist régime. Therefore, it has facilitated the investigation of war origins, and Professors Adamov and Pokrovsky have taken the lead. Milosh Boghitschewitsch, formerly a Serbian diplomat, has written several monographs on the responsibility of Serbia for the World War, but he has been denied access to the Serbian archives. Official Serbia has carefully safeguarded her secrets regarding pre-war diplomacy though it was a Serbian historian who revealed that Pashitsch and the Serbian cabinet knew of the plot to assassinate the Austrian archduke weeks in advance of the murder.

In spite of Fascism and censorship, Italian historians have made valuable contributions to our knowledge of war origins. Leaders in this work have been Corrado Barbagallo, Augustino Torre and Count Alberto Lumbroso. The latter is noted for his emphasis on the economic and commercial factors back of 1914 and for his criticism of British diplomacy.

In the United States, journalists were the first to criticize the official version of the causes of the first World War and our entry into it. Such were the works of Francis Nielson, Albert Jay Nock and John Kenneth Turner. The first important historian to puncture the Entente myth was Sidney Bradshaw Fay, whose articles in the *American Historical Review* in 1920-21 aroused interest and consternation throughout the civilized world. Eight years later, Professor Fay published the most complete and competent of all accounts of the diplomatic causes of the World War. It was seriously marred only by an inadequate comprehension of the Austrian case, which defect has been somewhat mitigated in later editions. The first comprehensive American attack on the Entente propaganda was the work of an American jurist, Frederick Bausman's *Let France Explain* (1922). American scholars have made important contributions to the study of European diplomacy before 1914. Especially substantial have been Mildred Wertheimer's analysis of the pan-German league, William L. Langer's account of the origins of the Franco-Russian alliance, F. L. Schuman's thorough presentation of French diplomacy, E. F. Henderson's critique of Sir Edward Grey, and the able summary of the whole pre-war period by R. J. Sontag. But the most thorough and competent history of European diplomacy before 1914 is the still incomplete work of William L. Langer. It promised to be the best diplomatic history in any language of the half-century before 1914. A highly competent summary of the new attitude is contained also in J. W. Swain's *Beginning the Twentieth Century*. Bernadotte Schmitt once gave much promise as a student of pre-war diplomacy but his complete work turned out to be a vast apology for the official wartime view of German guilt and mendacity. It was pulverized in detail by M. H. Cochran.

American writers have attacked the traditional view of the entry of the United States into the first World War. The ablest of such books are those by C. H. Grattan, Walter Millis and especially C. C. Tansill. J. K. Turner's assertions regarding the importance of economic, especially banking, interests in putting the United States into the World War have been amply vindicated on the basis of documentary material, especially that revealed by the Nye Committee. Nearly twenty years after 1918, Newton D. Baker denied any banker influence on our entry. Much valuable information on this subject is contained in the voluminous life of Woodrow Wilson by Ray Stannard Baker. In a careful study of Claude Kitchin's activities in 1914-18, Professor Alex M. Arnett has demonstrated the reality of the famous Sunrise Conference, and has shown that Wilson had decided to put this country into the war on the side of the Allies many months before the resumption of submarine warfare by Germany. The academic historians are, for the most part, still quiescent or traditional. Charles Seymour, in particular, has persistently defended the wartime illusions. The hangover of the wartime fixations is well illustrated by the statement of James Thomson Shotwell, made before the New York Credit Men's Association in 1936: "This nation took on the task which history assigned to us. It was not to protect our pocketbooks, but it was the old-time spirit of America that, when our flag is attacked on the high seas, this country does not fail to respond." This hardly explains why we had failed to respond to the more numerous British attacks on our flag on the high seas—even the flying of our flag on British ships. It was not until 1938 that a professor published a definitive work on our entry into the war, Charles C. Tansill's *America Goes to War,* a book worthy to rank with that by Fay.

One important reason why academic historians in Entente countries have been so reluctant to change their views as to war responsibility is the fact that many were called in as technical advisers to those who fashioned the post-war treaties. These historians felt a sort of parental responsibility for the Treaty of Versailles and other treaties of the time. They regarded it as in part their treaty. Since these treaties were based on the wartime views of war responsibility, the historians involved had a vested interest in maintaining conventional notions on the subject.

DIVISIONS OF SCHOLARLY OPINION ON WAR GUILT

The writers who have dealt with the general problem of war responsibility may be divided into three classes: (1) the bitter-enders; (2) the salvagers; and (3) the revisionists. These terms have been those employed by the present writer in discussing the historiography of the war-guilt controversy and, for better or worse, have come into common usage as a means of classifying and discriminating between the several groups of writers dealing with the subject.

The bitter-enders are those who, with access to the new documents, still adhere essentially to the wartime view of the predominant responsibility of the Central powers for the World War. The leading members of this group have been Heinrich Kanner, Hermann Kantorowicz, Emil Ludwig, Richard Grelling, Émile Bourgeois, Georges Pagès, Antonin Debidour, Wickham Steed, R. W. Seton-Watson, J. W. Headlam-Morley, H. W. Wilson, Charles Downer Hazen, E. Raymond Turner, William Stearns Davis, Earl E. Sperry, and Frank Maloy Anderson.

The salvagers represent writers who cite the latest documentary references bearing upon the problem of war responsibility, but still cling to the view that the Central Powers were primarily responsible for the coming of the World War. The leading salvagers are Pierre Renouvin, R. B. Mowat, Bernadotte Schmitt, Charles Seymour, Preston W. Slosson, M. T. Florinsky, and Eugen Fischer.

The revisionists are made up of those writers who have examined the contemporary documentary evidence on war guilt and have been led thereby to modify the wartime conceptions of the causes of the war. They have been wrongfully identified with writers like John Maynard Keynes and others who have recommended the revision of the Treaty of Versailles on the ground of its economically unwise features. The revisionist writers agreed also to the proposal to revise the Treaty of Versailles, but the revision with which they were primarily concerned was the revision of our older views as to war responsibility. It is only because they have been compelled to revise their views on this subject that they have also recommended a revision of the post-war treaties which rest upon the war-guilt clause of the Treaty of Versailles.

The revisionists are divided into two camps. The moderate group believe that the major guilt in 1914 attaches to the Entente, but that the Central Powers must be assigned considerable responsibility. Among the moderate revisionists are Sidney B. Fay, J. F. Scott, J. S. Ewart, Hermann Lutz, G. Lowes Dickinson, G. P. Gooch, Corrado Barbagallo, Augusto Torre, and Victor Margueritte. The more uncompromising revisionists hold that, though Germany and Austria lacked adroitness in 1914, neither desired a European war. They also contend that the moral justification involved in the Austrian attack upon Serbia and the German support of Austria was far greater than that of Russia in attacking Austria and of France in supporting Russia. They maintain that the primary military responsibility for the war is to be found in the premature general mobilization of the Russian army. This group is made up of such writers as Max Montgelas, Friedrich Stieve, Gunther Frantz, Erich Brandenburg, Paul Herre, Alfred von Wegerer, Hermann Aall, Nicolaas Japikse, Georges Demartial, Mathias Morhardt, Gustave Dupin, Alfred Fabre-Luce, F.

Gouttenoire de Toury, Alberto Lumbroso, M. N. Pokrovski, E. A. Ada-
mov, E. D. Morel, Raymond Beazley, M. Edith Durham, Irene Cooper
Willis, Ferdinand Schevill, W. E. Lingelbach, M. H. Cochran, P. T.
Moon, W. L. Langer, A. H. Lybyer, Joseph Ward Swain, Frederick
Bausman, and the present author.

The renaissance of scholarship also produced decently accurate and
objective histories of the first World War. Representative of these are
war histories by individual authors, such as John Buchan, Hermann
Stegemann and Maximilian Montgelas; coöperative histories like that
edited by Max Schwarte; and critical memoirs, like those by General Max
Hoffmann. The most ambitious work by a single author is that by Gabriel
Hanatoux, but it is pretty well shot through with French patriotic pride
and the defense of the stupidities of the French high command at the beginning of the war. The incredible incompetence and irresponsibility of
most of the high command during the World War has been exposed by
such writers as B. H. Liddell Hart, J. W. Wheeler-Bennett and others, in
literature almost as startling as the revisionist studies of pre-War diplomacy. By all odds the most impressive product of the World War in the
field of historical writing was the monumental *Economic and Social History of the World War,* edited by James T. Shotwell, in more than two
hundred volumes. Its collaborators were gathered from the scholars of all
important countries, and the series is the most gigantic example of successful coöperative work in the history of historical writing. Sponsored
and subsidized by the Carnegie Endowment for International Peace, and
intended as a definite aid to peace, its main practical use probably was
actually to serve as a handbook for those who directed the second World
War. The ablest summary of the generation that made and finished the first
World War is J. W. Swain's *Beginning the Twentieth Century.*

In states where Fascism prevailed, extreme nationalism perpetuated
the biases of wartime historical writing. In remote areas of historical
studies, which do not relate to current national issues, scholarship might
still maintain a foothold. But scholarship in dealing with the contemporary period all but disappeared from such countries.

Hegel is said to have remarked that the only lesson we learn from history is that we learn nothing from history. This was never more thoroughly
demonstrated than by the behavior of historians in all countries during
the second World War, even by those who had been in mature years during the first World War and some of them leading revisionists later. On a
vastly greater scale than in the first World War, historians entered into
various government departments, new and old, to participate in propaganda with little concern for historical facts, and they wrote books, articles
and reports as biased as any which appeared between 1914 and 1918. The
war was portrayed on all sides as a veritable "holy war." There was no

observable dissent from this point of view on the part of historians in any country involved in the war.

Revisionism and a return to factual objectivity after the war was far more vigorously opposed by most historians than following 1918. There developed what came to be known as a "historic blackout." Nearly all of the few revisionist books that were published appeared in the United States, where Professor Tansill's *Back Door to War* matched his *America Goes to War* for objectivity and scholarship. Virtually no revisionist books by eminent historians appeared anywhere in Europe until the publication of A. J. P. Taylor's *Origins of the Second World War* in 1961.

There might have been some return to historical realism and truth if enough time had been allowed to lapse. But the war was hardly over when the Cold War began during the Truman administration on March 12, 1947. From then onward, hatred of Russia and Communism (or defense of them in Russia) was added to the still continuing hatred of Germany and Italy, or of Russia and her western Allies. As the well-known British historian, A. J.P. Taylor, observed in the *Manchester Guardian*: "In the Cold War, apparently, even the world of scholarship knows no detachment. The academic historians of the West may assert their scholarly independence even when they are employed by a Government department; but they are as much 'engaged' as though they wore the handsome uniform designed for German professors by Dr. Goebbels."[7]

SELECTED REFERENCES

M. H. Cochran, *Germany Not Guilty,* 1914, chap. i. Stratford Press, 1931.

H. E. Barnes, *The Genesis of the World War,* chap. ii, App. Knopf, 1929.

———, *World Politics in European Civilization,* chaps. xxi-xxiii. Knopf, 1930.

———, *In Quest of Truth and Justice,* Part II. Nat. Hist. Soc. , 1928.

———, ed., *Perpetual War for Perpetual Peace.* Caxton Printers, 1953.

G. P. Gooch, *Recent Revelations of European Diplomacy.* Longmans, 1928, and later supplements.

Arthur Ponsonby, *Falsehood in Wartime.* Allen and Unwin, 1928.

I. C. Willis, *England's Holy War.* Knopf, 1928.

Georges Demartial, *Comment on mobilisa les consciences.* Paris, 1926.

H. C. Peterson, *Propaganda for War.* University of Oklahoma Press, 1939.

J. M. Read, *Atrocity Propaganda, 1914-1919.* Yale University Press, 1941.

Russell Grenfell, *Unconditional Hatred.* Devin-Adair, 1953.

René Wormser, *The Myth of the Good and Bad Nations.* Regnery, 1954.

Hermann Lutz, *German-French Unity.* Regnery, 1957.

D. F. Fleming, *The Cold War and Its Origins.* 2 vols., Doubleday, 1961.

Louis Morton, "Pearl Harbor in Perspective: A Bibliographical Survey," *U.S. Naval Institute Proceedings,* April, 1955.

[7] *Loc. cit.,* January 19, 1961; see also H. E. Barnes, "Revisionism and the Promotion of Peace," *Liberation,* Summer, 1958; and H. E. Barnes, ed., *Perpetual War for Perpetual Peace,* Caxton Printers, 1953, especially chap. i.

James Harvey Robinson

XII

BROADENING THE PERSPECTIVE AND INTERESTS OF THE HISTORIAN

THE EXPANSION OF HISTORICAL INTERESTS IN CONTEMPORARY TIMES

THE critical and erudite historians perfected the technique for the accurate determination of historical facts, as far as they can be recovered or reconstructed by the historical scholar. But they did little to broaden the conceptions of the historians as to what facts are worth recovering. They rested content, for the most part, with the older notions of the subject matter of history. As a rule, religious and political interests have been dominant throughout the greater part of the course of the development of historical writing. Among the Jews, most of the historical writing was occupied with proof of God's tender and unique solicitude for "the Seed of Abraham." Patristic, medieval and Reformation historical writing was shot full of supernaturalism, always endeavoring to make clear God's somewhat vacillating and changeable will towards man. This motif dominated the succession of works from Chronicles-Ezra-Nehemiah, through Augustine, Orosius, Otto of Freising, Baronius, Bossuet, Paley, Merle d'Aubigné, Montague Summers, and Henry Osborn Taylor. Even in our own day distinguished historians dogmatically assure us of God's existence and detail his attributes. For example, Henry Osborn Taylor, a leader in European intellectual history, and former president of the American Historical Association, concluded one of his latest books with the assurance that:

> God exists: we may be as sure of Him as ever; it is only the rational proofs of God that change and lose their validity. The sense of the divine, the strength and comfort of belief in God, may still be the grandest verity of human life; may still assure us that here and forever all things shall never cease to work together for good to them that love God, who rest in the sure harmony of relationship with the divine and omniscient and omnipotent love. . . . . Human progress still points onward through the action of the free intelligence, the righteously resolving will, and the ever more enlightened love of God and Man. . . . . Through many conflicts and in many ways, but always in the way of freedom, the human soul has been emerging, and has been gathering, as it were, affinity to God, in whom lies its immortality.[1]

[1] H. O. Taylor, *The Freedom of the Mind in History*, pp. 293-97.

On the whole, however, the last half-century has been characterized by a notable and healthy secularization of historical writing. Not only has the interest in supernaturalism enormously declined, but there has also been a distinct abatement of the feeling of dogmatic assurance about the nature of God and his specific will with respect to the human race. The findings of modern science and biblical criticism have not only undermined the older dogmatics and apologetics. They have also made it woefully apparent how inadequate are the orthodox conceptions of the extent, nature and control of the cosmos. In the face of this situation, the informed and thoughtful historian hesitates to deliver himself of theological opinions or to assume to possess the confidence of God, even though admitting that cosmic problems today are infinitely more impressive and interesting than they could possibly have been to Augustine or Luther.[2]

The other obsession of the conventional historian—an absorption in political events and episodes—has died harder and is still a potent force opposing the development of a more rational and inclusive type of historical writing. The political tradition has a heritage as venerable as the theological. Among the Jews the political and the religious preoccupations were blended. With Herodotus historical interest was partially secularized and relatively concentrated on political entities, though "the father of history" was less an offender in this respect than any of the other major historians of classical antiquity, and gave liberal consideration to cultural elements and contrasts. From Thucydides to Freeman, Droysen and Rhodes, however, the great majority of the distinguished historians who did not devote themselves to advancing the cause of Christianity or one of its multitudinous sects were engrossed in a study of divers events, episodes, and anecdotes relating to political, diplomatic, or military history. Droysen, Freeman, Seeley and Schäfer frankly and aggressively proclaimed manly history to be "past politics," though some erratic minds might busy themselves with the more effeminate history of economic life, social institutions, literature, or the fine arts.

To a very considerable degree this political obsession in modern times was due to two influences, not entirely distinct—the Hegelian theory of the state and the spirit of nationalism. The philosophy of Hegel had emphasized the state as the noblest of God's mundane achievements, and Hegel's philosophy had enormous vogue among the German savants who founded the science of history in its modern form in the first half of the last century. Added to this was the sentiment of nationalism, which flourished with particular virulence during the French Revolution and the Napoleonic period, and was given a more substantial technological basis

[2] Cf. J. H. Leuba, *God or Man?* (Holt, 1933); and J. H. Robinson, *The Human Comedy* (Harper, 1936).

by the Industrial Revolution. The French memories of the Revolutionary and Bonapartist glories, the German inspiration from the War of Liberation and the unification of the empire, the Italian ecstacy over the ultimately consummated ambition for a united Italy, which had inspired Dante and Machiavelli as well as Mazzini, the English enthusiasm over the peninsular campaign and Waterloo, as well as the new imperial expansion after 1870, and the pride of the Americans over the foundation of the Federal Republic and its preservation intact after a great civil war, all served to warm the hearts of the great historians of the nineteenth century. And along with these purely political foundations of nationalism went others of a psychological and cultural sort, such as the doctrine of racial and cultural superiority. Hegelianism and nationalism, in combination, proved amply adequate to hold most historians firmly in the service of political history.

One would find less to complain of concerning the devotion of these historians to political history if they had actually promoted a study of political institutions and contributed to an increase of our knowledge concerning the development of the state and its various organs. But the major part of this political history was perverted through the operation of two influences flowing mainly from the effects of Romanticism upon historical writing. One was the Romanticist theory that history should be vivid and interesting, and hence, that the finest sort of historical material was to be discovered in dramatic episodes. The other was the view, drawn largely from Carlyle and his disciples, that history is collective biography. Hence, the personal element loomed large in this variety of historiography. On account of the triumph of this combination of ideals and aspirations, most of the political history of the last century was primarily biographical and episodical, and threw little light upon the general problems of the origins and evolution of the major political institutions. It is scarcely an exaggeration to say that generalized works on constitutional history like those by Waitz, Fustel, Maitland, Luchaire, Esmein, Viollet, Flach, Brunner, and G. B. Adams were more enlightening with respect to the history of the state than the achievements of scores of comparably scholarly conventional political historians of the day. Amazing detail concerning essentially irrelevant topics was, then, the characteristic thing about the respectable historical writing of the last century.

Moreover, an exclusive devotion to even the dynamic and vital political and legal history of the type represented by Brunner, Esmein, Flach, Maitland and Adams can hardly be defended. The state is not the whole of human society or culture. It is but the umpire of the social process, the arbiter of conflicting social and cultural interests, many of which are more fundamental than the state. All of them taken together supply the dynamic and creative elements in the development of man and society, significant as the state may be in rendering their impulses, interplay and conflicts more constructive and less disintegrating and disastrous. Moreover, the detailed study of the state's evolution is the province of political science rather than of history.

In spite of the fact that most respectable historians in every modern state, and particularly in Europe, remain faithful worshippers at the political shrine, there has been revolutionary progress in the last half-century in the way of expanding the scope of the historian's interests. This has probably been due to the remarkable cultural changes of the period, to the advances made in the natural and social sciences, and to the greater independence and liberty of scholars, which have allowed able and original historians to execute their ambitions and to express their conceptions with relative freedom. The remarkable progress in science, technology and economic institutions, with the resulting social and cultural changes, has led to a great increase of interest in the history of science and technology, and in economic and social history. The rise of psychology, anthropology, and sociology has introduced new lines of approach to the study of man and his activities in society, and has furnished added guidance in the execution of such projects. The exaggerated interest of Burckhardt and Symonds in the Renaissance was an important factor in arousing a greater concern with the history of literature and the fine arts. Along with some disastrous influences mentioned above,[3] Romanticism served to broaden the ken of the historian by interesting him in religion as a universal institution, as well as in philosophy, art, and letters. Attention should also be called to the influence of the growing popularity of Ph.D. degrees in promoting the new history. At first the dissertations were unusually dry, minute, and conventional. But in time it became necessary to find so many new subjects that the distressed professors were forced to approve topics which lay far outside the field of the usual political and diplomatic history. Once the breach was made, further departures became easier and more marked. Not a little credit for the rise of a broader interest in history must be assigned to the personal insight, originality, and courage of the historians who have so largely fashioned the new history. Looking at the change broadly, it may be safely maintained, without any suspicion of national vanity or arrogance, that the movement for a more dynamic and comprehensive type of history has gained a much firmer hold in the United States than elsewhere, and has been received with the least cordiality and greatest resistance in Great Britain.

The fundamental tenet of the exponents of the broader type of history is that it is the function and duty of the historian to describe every phase of the development of the culture and institutions of a people, though any

[3] See above, pp. 179 ff.

particular historian may select that aspect of the history of civilization which interests him most. It must be conceded that one interested in the history of Anglo-Saxon literature or the Irish learning of the sixth century is as truly a historian as he who traces the evolution of the Witanagemot or the vicissitudes of the Saxon dynasty. This does not mean that it is unnecessary for the historian to discriminate at all in weighing and estimating the importance of events, but the idea of dynamic historical writing does oppose strenuously the notion that any one phase of human achievement so transcends all others in importance that we are justified in concentrating on one aspect of culture and ignoring the others. What the new historian pleads for is not the substitution of a new fetish for the political obsession, but rather for the recognition of the necessity of describing the development of every phase of the life and culture of a society. It is obvious that, with the widening of the historical field in this manner, the execution of a well-rounded history of even a single national state will require the coöperation of a large number of enthusiastic and tolerant experts. No one person could well hope to master every phase of the history of a single society during even a brief period. The great historical works of the future seem destined to become coöperative products.

Many historians, then, no longer remain content to chronicle the doings of public figures in the field of politics. They have tended to become interested in the whole realm of human achievement on our planet—intellectual, economic, social, political, scientific and esthetic. They have been aided in this by the progress of modern astronomy with its new chastening cosmic perspective, by the development of the evolutionary point of view with respect to life and culture, by the rise of psychology and social science, by the progress of modern industrialism and urban life, and by the growing secularism of the contemporary era. There were notable anticipations of this attitude towards history in the period of Rationalism and Romanticism, but contemporary developments have been far more varied and voluminous. And they have been founded upon wider and more substantial knowledge and have been disciplined by a more accurate technique of historical research.

INTELLECTUAL HISTORY

One of the first of the various salutary efforts to break with the narrow tradition of political history and to substitute interest in the evolution of human culture that we shall consider is what has been called "intellectual history," or a review of the transformations of ideas, beliefs and opinions held by the intellectual classes from primitive times to our own. Protagonists of this approach to history contend that, in the same way that the human mind is the integrating factor in the human personality and its behavior, so the prevailing intellectual attitudes in any age are the most important unifying and organizing influence in the development of human culture.

The possible significance of this type of history was forecast by Francis Bacon in his *De Augmentis,* when he wrote: "No man hath propounded to himself the general state of learning to be described and represented from age to age, as many have done the works of nature and the State civil and ecclesiastical; without which the history of the world seemeth to me to be as the statue of Polyphemus with his eye out; that part being wanting which doth most show the spirit and life of the person." The same position was held by Dr. Samuel Johnson, who stated in *Rasselas*: "There is no part of history so generally useful as that which relates to the progress of the human mind, the gradual improvement of reason, the successive advances of science, the vicissitudes of learning and ignorance, which are the light and darkness of thinking beings, the extinction and resuscitation of arts, and the revolution of the intellectual world." A notable impulse to this line of approach was also given by the French sociologist, Auguste Comte, who worked out a philosophy of history based in part on his general conception of the major stages in the evolution of mental attitudes, which he postulated as the theological, metaphysical, and scientific. An even more important contribution was made by G. Stanley Hall in his development of genetic psychology, which was built upon the notion that the evolution of the human mind might be studied historically from its origins in the mental life of the earliest organisms to its present manifestations in modern man. Genetic psychology was supplemented by social psychology, as advanced by Bagehot, Tarde, Durkheim and others. W. E. H. Lecky, Andrew D. White, John W. Draper and Joseph McCabe aroused much interest in this field by their assaults upon obscurantism and their presentation of the intellectual progress of Europe.[4]

The first contemporary historian to devote systematic attention to this field was Karl Lamprecht of Leipzig (1856-1915). Lamprecht admitted the general anticipation of his position by Comte, but he worked out a far more elaborate scheme. To him, the basis of any adequate periodization of history is to be found in the prevailing collective-psychological dominants that have succeeded one another in history. These are what give character to the culture of each period as well as prepare the way for that of the next.[5] Though he originally postulated and elaborated this scheme to apply to German history alone, he was later pleased to find that it seemed well adapted as a framework about which to organize the general

[4] Cf. H. E. Barnes, *Psychology and History* (Century Company, 1925).
[5] See below, pp. 316-17.

history of human culture. His disciple, Kurt Breysig, has devoted his latest efforts to a study of the influence of ideas on the course of history.

While admitting the validity of Lamprecht's general thesis that the dominant socio-psychological traits of any era constitute the most fundamental basis about which to organize the trends in cultural development as a whole, many historians, in sympathy with Lamprecht's general point of view, have held that his particular interpretation was too rigid, subjective and schematic to be suitable for precise application to the interpretation of the intellectual history of Europe. They look upon it as one more example of that somewhat subjective and artificial effort to divide the history of mankind into "stages" of development, which has characterized much of the anthropological, sociological, and "culture-historical" writing on social and cultural evolution, particularly among German writers. It has all too frequently sacrificed accuracy in the interest of order, unity, and simplicity of organization and exposition. This criticism has led to the development of a more pragmatic and flexible method of organizing and presenting the intellectual development of Europe, namely, a study of the actual nature of and changes in the prevailing opinions and intellectual attitudes in western society from oriental times to the present day, without any commitment to a specific type of interpretation or any rigid prearranged scheme of organization.

In executing this newer and more scientific approach to intellectual history, the most active figure was Professor James Harvey Robinson (1863-1936), formerly of Columbia University. Professor Robinson developed his interest and competence in this field in connection with a highly original course in the history of the intellectual class in Europe, which he launched as an experiment a generation ago. It grew into much the most popular and influential course ever offered in the department of history in that institution. His delimitation of the field and his general conceptions as to its nature and scope can best be discovered by consulting the syllabus which he prepared for use in connection with this course, entitled *An Outline of History of the Western European Mind*. This he amplified somewhat in his *Mind in the Making, The Humanizing of Knowledge,* and *The Human Comedy,* which have done more than any other works to arouse an intelligent popular interest in this field. His long promised *magnum opus* on the intellectual history of Europe was never published.[6] Rather, the substantial scholarly products of his stimulus are to be found in the achievements of his students and disciples, the most notable of which are the remarkable works of Preserved Smith on the period of Humanism and the Reformation, and on *A History of Modern Culture,* of Lynn Thorndike on the *History of Magic and Ex-*

---

[6] The field is, however, covered in a far more voluminous fashion than Robinson ever contemplated in H. E. Barnes *et al., An Intellectual and Cultural History of the Western World.* 2 vols., Dover Publications, 1962.

perimental Science in the Middle Ages, of Miss Martha Ornstein on the rise of the scientific societies in the seventeenth and eighteenth centuries, Howard Robinson's work on Bayle, Carl Becker's study of French and American political thought, and J. H. Randall's comprehensive treatment of modern intellectual history. More recently, attention has been paid to intellectual history by F. B. Artz, Crane Brinton, Eugen Weber, E. N. Johnson, M. E. Curti, H. S. Commager, and others.

While it is to Professor Robinson and his followers that we owe the demarcation and cultivation of intellectual history as one of the most promising fields of historical study, there have been many notable contributions to the subject by those who have, in many cases, not been aware of the formal existence of such a line of historical activity. They have been led on by an interest in some phase or period of the history of thought. As representative of such labors which have enriched the content of intellectual history might be mentioned the works of Lévy-Bruhl, Wundt, Goldenweiser, Bartlett, Paul Radin, Marett and Wissler on primitive thought; the contributions of Breasted, Erman, Rogers, Jastrow, Robertson Smith, and Winckler to the thought of the ancient Orient; the studies of classical thinking by Gomperz, Christ, Croiset, Aust, Zeller, Wissowa, Fowler, and others; Harnack's great history of Christian dogma, Lea's study of the medieval Inquisition, and the works of Taylor, Poole, Rashdall, Haskins, and De Wulf on medieval thought; the monumental surveys of Humanistic scholarship by Voigt and Sandys; the studies of the rise and influence of modern Rationalism by Lecky, Morley, Benn, Stephen, and Robertson; Merz's unmatched account of European thought in the last century; the studies of mental sciences by Dilthey, Rickert, and Windelband, and Meinecke's original notions of the intellectual history of modern politics; the histories of social thought by Stein, Barnes and Becker, and Sorokin; and the histories of national thought by such writers as Schmidt, Fischer, Lévy-Bruhl, Faguet, Croce, Stephen, Patten, Riley, Parrington, Curti, and others. In no other field are there richer sources than for intellectual history, nor have the books cited above been surpassed for scholarship.

THE HISTORY OF SCIENCE

Closely related to intellectual history is the history of science. Indeed, there is almost a causal relation between them, because the prevailing intellectual attitudes will generally determine the state of the development of science and the position accorded to it in the cultural complex. Naturally, the history of science has as yet attracted little favorable or fruitful attention from professional historians. The historians have been more closely in touch with the literary and academic traditions, which, until very recently, have looked scornfully upon natural science. The Industrial Revolution and the varied applications of our growing scientific knowledge, which have revolutionized modern material culture, have made it increasingly difficult, however, for the historian to ignore the ever-growing importance of science in the development of man and society. Slowly, a few of the more progressive historians have joined with scientists in cultivating this extremely significant phase of cultural history. Down to the present time, however, most of the work in this field has been done by the scientists, not always with the best results, because of lack of proper training in historical method and expression. When historians have dared to enter the field of the history of science they have been handicapped by their elementary knowledge of natural science. Better training on both sides is desirable.[7]

Some important representative contributions to the history of science by scientists and philosophers are the general histories of science by Dannemann, Ginsburg, Sedgwick and Tyler, Libby, Dampier-Whetham, George Sarton, and others; the valuable essays on various phases of the history of science and thought edited by Dr. Singer; the surveys of ancient science by Cantor, Milhaud, Bouché-Leclerq, Berthelot and Duhem; the research into medieval science by Duhem, Singer, Sarton, and others; the monographs on the rise of modern science by Shipley and Wolf; and Merz's remarkable survey of the growth of contemporary science in the second volume of his *History of European Thought in the Nineteenth Century*. In addition to these works on certain periods of the development of science there have been particular works covering the history of some special science, as, for example, the works of Osborn, Singer, Locy, Cajori, Mach, Thorpe, Bauer, Garrison, Sudhoff and Sigerist on the history of biology, mathematics, physics, chemistry and medicine. In particular, there should be mentioned the notable work of George Sarton and Frederick Brasch in stimulating active interest in the history of science on the part of both scientists and historians, Sarton's important activities as an editor and investigator in the history of science, and the notable bibliographic work done by Dr. Aksel G. S. Josephson on the history of science. Sarton's general history of science is the most ambitious and competent undertaking ever launched in this field.

A considerable number of progressive historians have evinced an enthusiastic interest in the history of science, such as Lamprecht and his followers in Germany, Henri Berr and his group in France, F. S. Marvin in England, and James Harvey Robinson in the United States, to whom in this country should also be joined the names of Breasted, Haskins,

---

[7] Cf. George Sarton, *The Study of the History of Science* (Dover, 1957).

Thorndike, Smith and Randall. There have been, however, but two comprehensive works of enduring significance produced by professional historians dealing with the field of the history of science, namely, Lynn Thorndike's *History of Magic and Experimental Science during the first Thirteen Centuries of the Christian Era*,[8] and C. H. Haskins' *Studies in the History of Medieval Science*. It may be safely predicted, however, that historians can no longer complacently ignore the history of science. A generation hence, it may well occupy as much of their attention as the history of constitution-making, something which seems forecast by the giving over of section meetings of the American Historical Association to the history of science.

THE HISTORY OF TECHNOLOGY

It is obvious that the history of technology, especially in relation to its bearing upon changes in culture and social institutions, is intimately associated with the history of science. If one regards technology in the broad sense as essentially identical with applied science, it is evident that natural science makes its contact with practical life and culture chiefly through the medium of technology. The importance of technology for history can be readily shown by calling attention to the fact that the history of progress in material culture is predominantly a record of the development of technology. It is the existing mechanical technique which determines the degree to which man can conquer and exploit nature and adapt it to his use. This achievement is virtually material culture in its dynamic setting. Whether or not one cares to accept the hypothesis of the determining nature of material culture in its relation to other cultural factors and human institutions, it can scarcely be denied that material culture is an extremely important conditioning influence, affecting all other aspects of human life and expression. The two major stages in the progress of technology have been: (1) the development of the tool, and (2) its displacement by the machine. The outstanding illustration of the revolutionary influence of changes in technology is, of course, the Industrial Revolution, which, resting upon a series of scientific and technological changes in spinning and weaving, iron and steel manufacture, transportation methods and communication, has profoundly altered the whole complexion and direction of modern civilization.

Important as the history of technology might be, then, for an understanding of cultural and institutional development, it must be admitted that historians have not as a class seriously interested themselves in this field. This is a situation which is not surprising when one reflects that

[8] Followed by his two volumes on late medieval science.

while for generations the books on modern history devoted many chapters to a relatively unimportant political episode, the French Revolution, the first general textbook on modern European history to include even a chapter on the Industrial Revolution was Robinson and Beard's *Development of Modern Europe,* published in 1907. Nevertheless, the problem has been attacked from various angles and notable contributions have already been made.

The archeologists and cultural anthropologists have done much to supply us with a knowledge of the origins of material technique—the appearance and development of various tools—and certain apparent laws or processes governing the origin, development, and transmission of material culture. Some of these data in their earlier form were brought together in a theoretical and descriptive synthesis by Otis T. Mason in his *Origins of Invention,* and have recently been popularized in more modern fashion in the works of the Quennells and Wissler. From the so-called "prehistoric" period to the Industrial Revolution little has been done except in specialized histories of various lines of technological advance. The history of the mechanical progress involved in the Industrial Revolution has been worked out in such books as those by Usher, Kaempffert, Mumford and others. Then there have been various indispensable studies made of the history of specific types of technical progress, such as that in the textile industry, the iron and steel industry, transportation methods on land and sea, the modern chemical industry, the coal industry, the rubber industry, the application of modern methods of exploiting electricity and so on.[9]

General histories of technology have been executed by Vierendeel, Usher, Derry and Williams, Fiske, Klemm, and by Charles Singer and his associates in their massive coöperative work. A suggestive effort was made by Thorstein Veblen, carrying further the impulse of Karl Marx, to visualize the process of technological evolution as a whole and set it in its proper place in cultural history and socio-economic evolution. He also tried to find in it certain important suggestions as to the solution of some major economic and social problems of the present day. His attitude is less thoroughly and effectively developed by such writers as Hobson, Sombart and Ogburn. In recent decades it has been revived and expanded by the group of writers interested in the challenging "technocracy" movement.

It probably would not be reckless to predict that within a generation professional historians will be undertaking seriously and systematically the task of investigating the relation of technical development to human and cultural evolution. This is foreshadowed in the interest already shown in the subject by such historians as Lamprecht, Berr, Robinson,

[9] For a summary and appraisal of the books on contemporary technology, mainly in English, see the bibliographies at the close of chaps. vii-viii and xx of Vol. II of my *History of Western Civilization* (Harcourt, Brace, 1935).

Marvin, Shotwell and others, though, unfortunately, their interest has as yet borne little specific literary fruit. The first really satisfactory attempt to trace the evolution of technology and to relate it to the history of civilization was embodied in Lewis Mumford's *Technics and Civilization*.[10] The theme has been developed by Singer and his colleagues, and by Siegfried Giedion in his *Mechanization Takes Command*, and has been ably popularized by Roger Burlingame, especially in his *Machines that Built America*.

ECONOMIC HISTORY

The history of economic processes and institutions is directly related to the history of technology, inasmuch as our economic life is the product of applying the existing mechanical technology to the exploitation of nature, as conditioned by social attitudes and legal institutions, especially the ownership of property and the differentiation and status of economic classes. The economic historian, then, must start with the aid of the technician and end with that of the sociologist. The history of the economic life of the peoples of our planet is almost entirely a nineteenth-century development.

Economic life, like the data of science, has savored of the commonplace and has been disdained by historians whose romantic imagination and literary traits have inclined them towards the majestic achievements of kings, generals, statesmen, diplomats and gentlemen. The earliest systematic interest in economic history came incidentally as an aspect of the rise of economic science in the period of mercantilism and physiocracy, during which the writers illustrated their points by more or less dubious economic history. The best of this sort of work appeared incidentally in Adam Smith's *Wealth of Nations*. Montesquieu was impressed by the importance of commercial relations in the development of man and culture, and Raynal shortly afterward attempted to estimate the significance of the expansion of Europe and the Commercial Revolution for European history. It was in the spirit of Montesquieu that Heeren, the brilliant Göttingen professor, wrote the first great book on economic history —his history of antiquity in the light of the economic life and commercial relations of the age. Some further interest in economic history was stimulated by the controversy over trade policies in the first half of the nineteenth century, and by the development of the German school of historical economists. Real interest in economic history came chiefly, however, after the Industrial Revolution had exerted sufficient influence to call attention to the great significance of economic factors in history.

In the development of economic history there have been two major stages or types. The first was represented by the carrying over of the con-

---

[10] Harcourt, Brace, 1934.

cepts and methods of descriptive political history into the realm of economic history. The succession of economic events was described and chronicled in a purely narrative fashion, in case the treatise was a general one. In other cases, the minute monographic investigation of some special problem in political or diplomatic history was paralleled in economic history by an intensive study of the development of some particular economic institution or practice, or its special manifestation at a specific time. In either case, the scholarship might be of a most severely accurate and disciplined sort and the special contribution of real, if limited, importance. But there was relatively little effort to relate the economic activities described to the general institutional life of the society as a whole, or to portray the historical development of man and society as an interplay of economic and other factors in cultural growth. Examples of this preliminary type of economic history may be found in such well known works as those by Rogers, Gibbins, Ashley, Cunningham, Unwin, Lipson, Clapham, Warner, Inama-Sternegg, Mavor, Usher, Heaton, Bogart, Lippincott, Coman and Carman; and in monographic works too numerous to be cited here. The most ambitious work along this line is the *Universal History of Labour* by Georges Renard and his associates. Henry David and his associates have produced another impressive coöperative work, an *Economic History of the United States.*

A more significant, dynamic, and synthetic type of economic history has gradually been built up which does make the effort not only to narrate the progression of economic events, but also to describe the evolution of economic institutions. The first important step along this line came in the work of the early German historical school of economists, led by Roscher. A more advanced step was taken when an attempt was made to indicate, as far as possible, the inter-relation between the development of economic institutions and other social institutions. While there had been earlier anticipations of this approach from Aristotle onward, the systematic formulation of this attitude was the contribution of Karl Marx, though work from this angle may be carried on without any adherence to the socialistic theory of economic reconstruction which Marx postulated. This statement is confirmed by the fact that the most important work done in this field has been the product of writers like Kovalevsky, Schmoller, Sombart, Bücher, Weber, Levasseur, Hobson, Webb, Hammond, Tawney, Veblen, Commons, Gras, Faulkner, Kirkland, Dorfman, Cochran, Miller, and Clough, some of whom are leading critics of orthodox Marxian doctrine.

It is evident that this highly developed type of economic history must be based upon an adequate knowledge of sociology, which alone can furnish the writer with a sufficiently broad grasp upon the laws and patterns of interinstitutional development to allow him to handle such problems successfully. In general, it may be said that writers in this field have been successful in proportion to their sociological point of view.[11] In the United States this dynamic approach to economic history has been largely the result of the work of Thorstein Veblen and his disciples, who have made it a basic phase of the new or institutional economics. Perhaps the most interesting fact about the development of economic history of both types is that, with few exceptions, most of the work done in this field has been executed by economists rather than historians. It is of more than casual interest that with chairs in political, diplomatic and constitutional history of every country and age abounding, there are at the present time not a half-dozen chairs of economic history in all of the history departments of the United States combined. Indeed, the only one known to the author is that at the University of Minnesota.

SOCIAL HISTORY

Social history has been another of the relatively recent additions to the achievement of making history more inclusive in scope and more vital in content. This movement started nearly a century ago with such works as those by Riehl and Freytag, who attempted to arouse an interest in the German past, not so much by recalling the glorious fictions of the Holy Roman Empire or the Hohenzollern mission as by reconstructing the social life and customs of medieval and modern Germany.[12] This sort of work, particularly in the case of Freytag, was less a systematic treatment of the development of social institutions than a collection of word-pictures, scenes, anecdotes and episodes descriptive of the intimate daily life of the people. This approach has been developed through a large number of studies of the manners and customs of different ages and periods, conceived and executed on the basis of antiquarian interest rather than an aspiration towards broad historical synthesis. The works of Ludwig Friedländer on Roman imperial life and of Paul Lacroix on medieval manners and customs afford good examples of this type of social history. A step in advance was taken by those who attempted to give greater space and attention to social factors in the history of peoples in works of descriptive narration, conceived and executed more strictly according to historical than antiquarian notions. This type of achievement was embodied in such well-known works as Traill and Mann's *Social England*, Rambaud's survey of French civilization, Blok's *History of the Dutch People,* Alta-

---

[11] A major difficulty in bringing about the writing of good economic history lies in the fact that few historians have much knowledge of economics, while it is a rare economist who has any grasp of history. A first-rate economic historian should be conversant with historical method, economics, sociology, science, technology, psychology and philosophy, and have a flair for literary expression. The fact that the conventional approach was still most popular was proved by the limited response to my *Economic History of the Western World*, Harcourt, Brace, 1937.

[12] See below, p. 312.

mira's sketch of Spanish civilization, McMaster's monumental work on the national period in American development, and its continuation since the Civil War by his disciple, Oberholtzer.

More significant still is that type of social history which attempts to indicate the general patterns of social development, as created and modified by the interaction of the various types of institutions and forces and the struggles of different social classes and groups. This approach assumes social development to be a genetic and cumulative process. Writers who have, in varying degrees, promoted this variety of dynamic social history have been Lamprecht, Steinhausen, Gothein, Goetz, and Nitzsch in Germany; Fustel de Coulanges, Berr and his associates in France; John Richard Green, Maitland, Vinogradoff, Pollard, Slater, J. L. and Barbara Hammond, Sidney and Beatrice Webb, and Clapham in England; Barbagallo and Ferrero in Italy; Kluchevsky in Russia; and Shotwell, Turner, Simons, Fox, Kendrick, Hacker, Carman, Becker, Dodd, Hayes, Cheyney, Schlesinger, Faulkner and Bowden in the United States. The coöperative work on American social and cultural history edited by A. M. Schlesinger and D. R. Fox furnishes a good illustration of the status of social historiography in the United States today.

Some writers, more historical sociologists than social historians, have carried this development still further and have attempted to ascertain the laws of social growth, to detect repetitions in history, and to ascertain the facts as to cause and effect in history; in other words, to reduce history to a somewhat quantitative and schematic brand of genetic social science. Examples of work of this type have been the contributions of Comte, Buckle, Hobhouse, Giddings, Müller-Lyer, Breysig, Alfred Weber, Teggart, Wallace, Forrest and Sorokin.

INSTITUTIONAL POLITICAL HISTORY

These newer trends in economic and social history have reacted in an important manner upon political and legal history. The respectable type of political history in the nineteenth century was primarily anecdotal and episodical, and rarely presented a clear picture of political development, to say nothing of its general ignoring of the relation between political institutions and other forces in national history. Even where the author was fairly well trained in the science of politics he usually buried the threads of constitutional and institutional development under such a mass of biographical, anecdotal and episodical material that only the most patient and competent reader could make use of his product. An admirable illustration of this was S. R. Gardiner's long-popular *Students' History of England*. The broader and more synthetic view, which looked upon political development as essentially the outcome of conflicts, pressures, forces and adjustments in society at large, led to the appearance of what may be called institutional political history.

Here the genetic point of view is adopted, attention centered on institutional changes rather than on episodes and personalities, the leading stages of political evolution indicated, and the economic and social basis of politics expounded. This approach was faintly anticipated as early as the last half of the eighteenth century by Justus Möser in his *History of Osnabruck*. De Tocqueville, Fustel de Coulanges, Lacombe, Luchaire, Viollet, Flach and Petit-Dutaillis carried on the work in France. Schmoller, while an economist rather than a historian, stimulated historical writing of this sort in Germany. Nitzsch's volumes were a good example of it. Brunner, Waitz, Gneist and Duguit forwarded this type of work from legal and constitutional points of view. Maitland, Vinogradoff, Edward Jenks, Pollard, and the Webbs have led the way in England. Miliukov well represented this trend in Russian historiography. It was also basic in the political analysis in Ferrero's work on Roman history. In America the most extensive contribution to institutional political history is to be found in Osgood's history of the English colonies to the Revolution, though it is somewhat archaic in its failure to give adequate attention to the interplay of economic, social and political factors. It did, however, divorce colonial history from the prevailing tendency to bury the development of colonial institutions under an impenetrable shell of biographical, episodical and anecdotal detail. It also stimulated institutional surveys of local political units by competent students. McIlwain has done notable work on medieval government and on the English legal and political background of American institutional history. More adequate attention to social and economic factors in the colonial period has been given by C. M. Andrews and J. T. Adams. The closest approximation to such European achievements as those by Maitland and his school and the Webbs is to be found in Adams's constitutional history of England, Beard's monographs on the constitutional and early national period, and his largely unpublished lectures on American constitutional history, in Hacker and Kendrick's *History of the United States Since the Civil War*, and in the books and lectures of W. E. Dodd and Billington. Most suggestive contributions to a prospectus of what is yet to be achieved in American institutional political history have been supplied by Turner, Beard, Schlesinger and Becker. It must be admitted, however, that no political historian has yet given evidence of that grasp upon interinstitutional processes in the growth and operation of political institutions which has been characteristic of such sociological studies of social and political evolution as those by Bagehot, Gumplowicz, Ratzenhofer, Michels, Weber, Oppenheimer, Kovalevsky, Loria and Bentley.[13]

[13] The nearest approach has been E. McC. Sait's *Political Institutions*, Appleton-Century, 1938.

LEGAL HISTORY

This more profound approach to the evolution of political institutions on the basis of economic and social history has also affected the history of law and juristic institutions. Writers of this school have divorced the study of legal development from metaphysical and theological concepts, and have shown the mundane and social nature of legal origins and transformations, indicating how law adjusts itself to changing social conditions at large. Those to whom we owe the most for this epoch-making transformation of legal history are Gumplowicz in Austria; Gierke, Ihering, Brunner, Kohler, Kantorowicz, and Berolzheimer in Germany; Maitland, Pollock, Jenks, Vinogradoff and Laski in England; Esmein, Duguit and Charmont in France; Vaccaro in Italy; and Holmes, Wigmore, Cardozo, Roscoe Pound, and their disciples in the United States.[14]

WORLD HISTORY AND THE WORLD POINT OF VIEW

Closely connected with the scientific and economic development of the last century has been the recent trend towards eliminating the insularity and provincialism of much historical writing in the past, and the substitution of a world point of view. It is becoming increasingly clear that even the internal political history of one state can scarcely be understood without reference to influences coming from without its boundaries. It is even more evident in this age of easy and rapid contacts of peoples on a worldwide scale that all types of modern history must, in a real sense, be world history and must adopt an international point of view. This salutary departure has been forwarded by the many writers on world politics and international relations in recent years. H. G. Wells has attempted to write a universal history with this point of view dominant at all times. An effort has been made to bring this same thesis to bear upon the history of modern times by more scientific historians such as Fiske, Seeley, Hayes, Botsford, Abbott, Gillespie, Fueter, Keller, and Flick. But the most fundamental and comprehensive attempt to indicate the significance of world history for the development of modern civilization has been the contribution of Professor W. R. Shepherd of Columbia University in his lectures on the expansion of Europe. From this day on, all adequate types of historical work must have a world outlook. Impressive cooperative world histories have been edited by Wilhelm Oncken, Walter Goetz, Gustave Glotz, Louis Halphen, Henri Berr, Eugène Cavaignac and Maurice Croi-

[14] See H. E. Barnes, *Social Institutions*, Prentice-Hall, 1942, chap. xi.

zet, culminating in the UNESCO project after the second World War, edited by Julian Huxley and Ralph E. Turner.

GENERAL CULTURAL HISTORY

An important contribution to broadening the scope of history is to be found in the increasing evidences of *Kulturgeschichte* in its most general sense, such as the history of art, literature, manners and customs, printing, music, and all other expressions of national culture. With such a multiplicity of interests forced upon the historian by the acceptance of the concepts of the new history, it is evident that historical writing in the future must be more and more a coöperative effort, to which writers will contribute according to their special interests and training, and the products of no group can be despised if their work is accurate and reliable.[15]

HISTORY AND SOCIAL INTELLIGENCE

The last aspect of the new history which we may note here is the recent effort to make history at once scientific and pragmatic, namely, useful to us who are alive today. Pragmatic history of a sort has been, of course, common in the past, notorious examples being such works as the Book of Chronicles-Ezra-Nehemiah, and Orosius' *Seven Books of History Against the Pagans*. More recently the effort has been made to survey history from different points of view, so as to generalize from the assured results of historical scholarship in such a manner as to put the facts of history at the disposal of the statesman, reformer and thoughtful citizen. Well-known examples of such attempts are Marvin's *Living Past*, and *The Century of Hope*, Robinson's *Mind in the Making*, and *The Human Comedy*, Wallace's *Trend of History*, Wells' *Outline of History*, and Van Loon's *Story of Mankind*. Probably the most stimulating of all have been the works of Robinson and the volumes of the Unity Series edited by F. S. Marvin.

Whatever one may think of the degree of success exhibited in such preliminary achievements, it would seem that unless history can lend itself to such pragmatic use, when objectively and cautiously exploited, it must be, as far as practical human significance is concerned, essentially irrelevant—a chaste but arid type of intellectual entertainment.[16] And it would appear that, so far as we are concerned today, the basic practical use of history is to show the development of our culture from primitive origins, to suggest progress in spite of important oscillations and retrogressions, and to demonstrate that the present is so different from the past as to preclude the possibility of drawing many specific and direct analogies for our generation from the past experience of the race. In other words, it is prob-

15 For a monumental example of such a contribution to historical writing see Maurice Parmelee, *A History of Modern Culture*, Philosophical Library, 1961, and of a coöperative work, Ralph Gabriel, ed., *The Pageant of America*, 15 vols., Yale University Press, 1926 ff

16 Cf. Robinson, *The Human Comedy*, especially chaps. i, iv; and R. L. Heilbroner, *The Future as History*, Harpers, 1960.

able that the chief practical utility of pragmatic history is the aid it may render in that laudable effort to lessen the influence of the "dead hand" over those who today must plan a more efficient and happy future for the race.

SELECTED REFERENCES

C. L. Becker, "Some Aspects of the Influence of Social Problems and Ideas upon the Study and Writing of History," in *Publications of the American Sociological Society*, 1912.

J. H. Robinson, *The New History*. Macmillan, 1911.

———, *Mind in the Making*. Harper, 1921.

———, *The Human Comedy*. Harper, 1937.

———, "New Ways of Historians," *American Historical Review*, January, 1930.

W. G. Beasley and E. G. Pulleyblank, *Historians of China and Japan*, Oxford, 1961.

H. K. Beale, ed., *Charles A. Beard*. University of Kentucky Press, 1954.

C. W. Smith, *Carl Becker: On History and the Climate of Opinion*. Cornell University Press, 1956.

Thompson, *History of Historical Writing*, Vol. II, chaps. li-lv.

Kraus, *The Writing of American History*, chap. xiv.

Howard Odum, ed., *American Masters of Social Science*. Holt, 1927.

H. E. Barnes, *History and Social Intelligence*. Knopf, 1926.

———, *The New History and the Social Studies*. Century, 1925.

———, *Social Institutions*. Prentice-Hall, 1942.

F. J. Teggart, *Prolegomena to History*. University of California Press, 1916.

———, *Processes of History*. Yale University Press, 1918.

———, *The Theory of History*. Yale University Press, 1925.

A. A. Goldenweiser, *History, Psychology and Culture*. Knopf, 1933.

White, *The Evolution of Culture*.

G. E. Dole and R. L. Carneiro, eds., *Essays in the Science of Culture*. Crowell, 1960.

Joseph Dorfman, *The Economic Mind in American Civilization*. 5 Vols., Viking, 1946-1959.

E. R. A. Seligman, *The Economic Interpretation of History*. Columbia University Press, 1907.

T. K. Derry and T. I. Williams, *Short History of Technology*. Oxford Univ. Press, 1961.

Crane Brinton, *Ideas and Men*. Prentice-Hall, 1950.

H. G. Wells, *Experiment in Autobiography*. Macmillan, 1934.

W. W. Wagar, *H. G. Wells and the World State*. Yale University Press, 1961.

Lewis Mumford, *Technics and Civilization*. Harcourt, Brace, 1934.

C. A. Beard, *The Economic Basis of Politics*. Knopf, 1922.

H. J. Laski, *A Grammar of Politics*. Yale University Press, 1925.

Fritz Berolzheimer, *The World's Legal Philosophies*. Macmillan, 1912.

Roscoe Pound, *Interpretations of Legal History*. Macmillan, 1923.

XIII

THE RISE OF KULTURGESCHICHTE: THE HISTORY OF CIVILIZATION AND CULTURE

THE RISE OF INTEREST IN KULTURGESCHICHTE

ONE of the most important and novel developments in the history of historical writing in contemporary times has been a growing interest in the history of human life and culture in the past. In the preceding chapter the varied character of this broadening of historical interests beyond affairs of church and state has been briefly described. In this chapter an effort will be made to survey some major contributions to the history of civilization which have been made by progressive-minded historians.

By common consent, the real beginning of modern *Kulturgeschichte* dates from the publication of Voltaire's *Age of Louis XIV,* and his *Essay on the Manners and Spirit of Nations,* the character of which we have already described.[1] The universal histories, promoted by the rise of Romanticism, also contained much material on the history of civilization.[2] The next major contribution to cultural history came in the famous *History of Art in Antiquity* by Johann Joachim Winckelmann (1717-68). Published in two volumes in 1764, it was the first able history of ancient art, laying special stress upon the art of the Greeks. In Greek art Winckelmann discerned as major features its loftiness, purity and admirable sense of proportion. The book had a wide influence upon scholars, poets, and artists, especially upon Romanticist students of cultural history. But it did not greatly affect the professional historians, who remained devoted to recounting the story of public affairs and the actors therein.

Early in the next century came the effort, in the works of Madame de Staël and Sismondi, to make the history of literature a branch of the history of civilization and of social history. Gervinus followed soon after with his history of German poetry. Then Heeren stressed the importance of commerce in the cultural and institutional history of antiquity. Eduard Zeller, under the inspiration of Hegel, devoted a long life to his magisterial history of Greek philosophy. One of the earliest avowed histories of

---

[1] See above, pp. 153-54.
[2] *Ibid.*, pp. 171-72.

civilization was the *General History of European Civilization* by the French historian and publicist, François Guizot (1787-1874), which appeared in 1828. It surveyed European development from the Roman Empire to the eighteenth century, laying special stress upon the rise of *bourgeois* ideas and the growth of representative government. It well reflected the conservative middle-class historical ideals of the first half of the nineteenth century in France.

Next came those developments which we associate with Henry Thomas Buckle, and John William Draper, his leading disciple. We have already discussed Buckle's contributions to history.[3] They combined a eulogy of intellectual freedom, with emphasis on the influence of geographical factors and food resources upon the growth of culture. From these assumptions an American physician and chemist, John William Draper (1811-82), wrote a comprehensive *History of the Intellectual Development of Europe* (1863), strongly skeptical in tone but disappointing as an intellectual history of Europe. Even more sharply anti-clerical was his courageous *History of the Conflict between Science and Religion.* Written in a similar intellectual temper were two books by an Irish historian, which were perhaps the most remarkable examples of historical precocity in the whole history of historical literature. These were the *History of the Rise and Influence of Rationalism in Europe* (1865), and the *History of European Morals from Augustus to Charlemagne* (1869) by William Edward Hartpole Lecky (1838-1903). Lecky's work on Rationalism was a landmark in the history of the intellectual emancipation of the West from such ideas as those of Augustine and Calvin. Another powerful British exponent of free thinking and agnosticism was Sir Leslie Stephen (1832-1904), famed for his *History of English Thought in the Eighteenth Century,* and for his *The English Utilitarians.* The next important example of this literature was the work of an American scholar, publicist and educator, Andrew Dickson White (1832-1918), president of Cornell University. His monumental *History of the Warfare of Science with Theology in Christendom* was, in reality, a historical justification of his own life work in the cause of intellectual freedom and toleration. It was probably the most impressive of all "free-thought" historical enterprises and one of the most thrilling and absorbing historical books ever penned.

Another development appeared in some important historical works, mainly by Germans, that devoted special attention to the history of life, manners and customs. This school really dates from Jacob Grimm and his historical work on the German language, legal customs, folk tales, fairy tales and the like. One of the earliest and most important of these

[3] See above, p. 202.

writers was Wilhelm Heinrich Riehl (1823-97), pioneer in both *Kultur-geschichte* and descriptive sociology in Germany. He gathered his material not only from documents, but even more from extensive travels in Germany. His major work was *The Natural History of the People as the Basis for German Social Politics,* which appeared in four volumes between 1851 and 1864. Riehl's historical doctrines were based upon the assumption that geographical factors, such as climate, topography and the like, account in the main for cultural diversity. He held that social conditions and occupations also play their part in the process. The peasants are naturally provincial and the townspeople cosmopolitan and progressive. He believed that the family is the social cell and the great social stabilizer. Riehl was at his best in dramatic characterizations of German local life and culture in the seventeenth and eighteenth centuries. He was very weak and inadequate in historical generalization and in appreciation of the genetic evolution of culture. He was preëminently a descriptive social historian. Riehl was much impressed with the cultural importance of art and music and devoted a great deal of attention to them in his main work and in special works on German art and music. In addition to his own works, he edited a large coöperative series on *The Land and People of Bavaria.*

In the work of Gustav Freytag (1816-95) we find a fusion of nationalistic and cultural history. Freytag came to the study of German social and cultural history after scholarly training in philology and the history of the drama. His major work in the field of cultural history was his *Scenes from German History* [*Bilder aus der deutschen Vergangenheit*] which appeared in five volumes between 1859 and 1862. It covered the history of the life of the German people from their origins to the nineteenth century. Freytag held that the life of the people was the outstanding feature which gave unity to the history of the German nation. He stressed the organic nature of national culture in a manner reminiscent of the Romanticists. He agreed with Guizot that the middle class provides the backbone of national life and culture. His work included much more political and military history than Riehl's writings, and he provided colorful pictures of the major German national heroes—Charlemagne, Barbarossa, Luther, Frederick the Great and the like. Yet Freytag was no sentimental worshipper of the past, as Riehl was to a considerable degree. He made it clear that life becomes more harsh and provincial as we recede from the present. Freytag's work possessed great literary charm and intriguing anecdotal intimacy.

More scholarly in a conventional sense and more strictly historical were three other works on German civilization. Karl Nitzsch (1818-80) wrote a *History of the German People to the Peace of Augsburg,* which was published posthumously in three volumes from 1883 to 1885. Nitzsch gave attention to economic, social and intellectual, as well as political, history, and he possessed unusual powers in the reconstruction of medieval German institutional life. He also wrote an important history of the Roman republic, which was not so obviously a contribution to cultural history. Perhaps the major Catholic contribution to *Kulturgeschichte* was the voluminous *History of the German People at the End of the Middle Ages* by Johannes Janssen (1829-91), which appeared in eight volumes from 1877 to 1894. It took as its theme the life of the masses, giving also much attention to the history of social life and culture. His picture of German society on the eve of the Reformation was a masterpiece, but scholars question his contention that German civilization attained its highest development at the close of the Middle Ages.

The final fruition of the school of Riehl and Freytag came in the work of their admirer, Georg Steinhausen (1866-1933), who brought out an able *History of German Culture* in 1904, and also wrote a number of more specialized works on different phases and periods of German cultural history. While he differed from Freytag in eliminating the state entirely from consideration in cultural history, he equaled Freytag in his talent for rendering significant and entrancing the most minute details of daily life. In the history of esthetics he did not match Burckhardt in originality, though he had a better knowledge of the formal facts. This type of historical interest, from Riehl to Steinhausen, was reflected in the *History of French Civilization* by Alfred Rambaud (1842-1905), in John Richard Green's popular books on English history, in the six-volume social history of England, edited by H. D. Traill and J. S. Mann (1901-4), and in the voluminous history of the American people by John Bach McMaster.

More interested in literature and esthetics than in life and institutions was the Swiss scholar, Jacob Christoph Burckhardt (1818-97), author of the most brilliant survey of the Renaissance and of a realistic study of Greek civilization. Burckhardt studied history under Boeckh and Ranke, and art under Kugler. He was also influenced by the Romanticist yearnings for art and literature. The work upon which his fame mainly rests, *The Civilization of the Renaissance,* appeared in 1860. Burckhardt seized upon what he conceived to be the basic psychological trait of the period—the emergence of individualism—with great brilliance and success. It remains, after three-quarters of a century, the most original and engaging work on the Renaissance by any single author. Its main weakness lay in the failure of the author to appreciate the gradual development of the Renaissance out of the Middle Ages. He portrayed it as a more sudden and dazzling episode than the facts warranted. Yet, Burckhardt was no indiscriminate worshipper of all aspects of the Renaissance. He fully recognized its brutal and seamy side, but believed that this was the price exacted for its glamorous achievements in the realm of esthetics. Burckhardt's *History of Greek Civilization* was a much longer work and was a distinguished historical achievement. It cast off all romantic reverence for the Greeks and dealt with Hellenic civilization in a fair but realistic fashion. But the book never made the stir created by his treatment of the Renaissance. Burckhardt's range of interests in cultural history was amazingly wide, a fact well revealed when the collection of his essays and lectures was published by his students in 1918 on the hundredth anniversary of his birth.

Burckhardt's views of the Renaissance were expressed in more complete and unrestrained form in the work of his English admirer, John Addington Symonds (1840-93), biographer of Dante and Michael Angelo and author of *The Renaissance in Italy,* which was published in seven volumes from 1875 to 1886. While a student of Dante and his times should have known better, Symonds stressed even more than Burckhardt the sharp break between the Middle Ages and the Renaissance. To Symonds, the Renaissance was not only the springtime of humanity in the West; it was also an age devoted to promoting freedom and humanitarianism. Symonds saw a direct intellectual and moral line of descent from the Renaissance through the Reformation to the French Revolution. They were all spiritually akin. Symonds' description of Renaissance culture and personalities was forceful and written with great charm. His general theories as to the place of the Renaissance in western history have, however, been greatly modified.

The cultural history of classical antiquity was illuminated by Ludwig Friedländer (1824-1909). His early interests were in Homeric scholarship, but he fell under the influence of Mommsen, Riehl, Freytag and Burckhardt, and produced his *Roman Life and Manners Under the Early Empire* in three volumes between 1862 and 1871. It presented almost unequaled pictures of many sides of a great civilization—the first two centuries of the Roman Empire. Manners, customs, life, travel, art, antiquities, and many other aspects were described with much charm, intimacy and vividness. Friedländer was more of a colorful and dramatic antiquarian than a dynamic historian of civilization in his approach. More comprehensive in time but less detailed were the three works of Sir Samuel Dill (1844-1924), *Roman Society from Nero to Marcus Aurelius, Roman Society in the Last Century of the Western Empire,* and *Roman Society in Gaul in the Merovingian Age.* Dill wrote in clear and attractive fashion and had superb powers in interpreting his materials. His last work was the least satisfactory of the three, and was much inferior to that of the French historian, Ferdinand Lot, or of the brilliant work of Alfons Dopsch on the economic and social life of the Carolingian era. The cultural, as well as the political, history of Rome from the fall of the empire to the Renaissance was provided in the colossal *History of the City of Rome in the Middle Ages* by Ferdinand Gregorovius (1821-91), published in eight volumes between 1859 and 1872. Gregorovius also wrote a less complete book on *The History of the City of Athens in the Middle Ages.* He was a prodigious worker and writer and ranged over many subjects from early Greek history to the question of socialism in the writings of Goethe.

Economic development was brought within the field of *Kulturgeschichte* in such important works as those by Karl von Inama-Sternegg (1843-1908) and Maksim Kovalevsky (1851-1916). The former wrote a monumental economic history of Germany, laying special stress on the importance of agrarian developments. The latter, under the influence of Spencerian evolutionary concepts, produced an even more ambitious treatise, a comprehensive economic history of Europe. He also wrote at length on the rise of modern democracy and on the derivation of modern Russian institutions from their ancient laws and customs.

The most pretentious effort by any historian, prior to the Lamprecht era, to write a general history of civilization was that embodied in the *General Cultural History from the Earliest Times to the Present,* by the scholarly Swiss writer, Otto Henne-am-Rhyn (1828-1914), which appeared in seven volumes between 1877 and 1897. Considering the scope of the task and the period of its execution, the work was remarkably well done and remains one of the major individual accomplishments in cultural history and historical synthesis. Henne-am-Rhyn was an amazingly prolific writer on cultural history. In addition to this large general work, he wrote a cultural history of the German people, a cultural history of the Jewish people, a cultural history of the Crusades, a work on the place of women in cultural history, and an account of the cultural import of German folk tales. Produced in the Lamprecht epoch, but in part independent of Lamprecht's personal influence, was the great work edited by Paul Hinneberg, *The Culture of the Present: Its Origins and Destiny,* which appeared in thirty-seven volumes between 1905 and 1921.

The influence of the new science of anthropology upon cultural history in Germany was best exemplified in the work of Julius Lippert (1839-1909), especially in his *Kulturgeschichte der Menschheit* [translated into English as *The Evolution of Culture*]. He applied in discriminating fashion the evolutionary notions of writers like Morgan and Spencer to cultural data, but he also emphasized the importance of the diffusion of culture. Further, he believed that the dynamic factors in human history were cultural rather than biological and geographical. He was, thus, one of the first "cultural determinists." Within each cultural complex he emphasized the potency of ideas. Lippert wrote other books on the evolution of religious ideas and rites, the history of the family, and the history of

German manners and customs. Not only cultural history but also historical sociology owed much to his writings and influence.

The most aggressive champion of *Kulturgeschichte* and the most discussed person in connection with its development in recent times was Karl Lamprecht of Leipzig (1856-1910). Lamprecht's first important work was a long and original treatise on the economic history of medieval Germany, with special attention to the Moselle area. Here he indicated his interest in the history of economic groups and economic mass movements as affecting the social history of a people. This attitude he obtained in part from Karl Marx, though Lamprecht was not an orthodox Marxian. He was also much influenced by Nitzsch and by Auguste Comte's suggestion that history should be viewed as successive stages in the collective psychology of humanity, and he was affected as well by the doctrine of evolution.

All of these notions went into his monumental *German History,* which appeared in twelve volumes from 1891 to 1909, and was supplemented by three volumes on the most recent period. In this work Lamprecht organized his materials around the fundamental notion that each major era possesses a dominant collective-psychological trait which governs the age. History is the record of the influence and succession of these "psychic dominants." The primitive stage was symbolic in its group psychology; the early Middle Ages, typical; the later Middle Ages, conventional; the age of the Renaissance and Enlightenment, individualistic; the period of Romanticism, subjective; and the post-Industrial Revolution epoch, one of nervous tension. Lamprecht did not ignore political history, but he subordinated it to economic and cultural history. His interest in economic history led him to lay special stress on economic factors in German development, and he also gave unusual attention to the history of art and music. Not only did Lamprecht write voluminously; he was also an eager and effective controversialist and did much to promote his views of history. He had considerable influence on Lacombe and Berr in France, Ferrero and Barbagallo in Italy, Pirenne in Belgium, and W. E. Dodd and Carl Becker in the United States.

While Lamprecht did not found a formal school in Germany, he left a strong influence. In 1909 his admirers enabled him to found the *Institut für Kultur-und-Universalgeschichte* at Leipzig to carry on the training of scholars in his tradition. A number of his disciples have done important work. Kurt Breysig, in his *Cultural History of Modern Times,* applied Lamprecht's general ideas to a systematic survey of the cultural evolution of the modern world. Breysig's work is even more rigorously schematized and generalized than Lamprecht's. In late years, Breysig has devoted himself to intellectual history and the philosophy of history in his *On Historical Becoming*. Eberhard Gothein has made valuable contributions to the study of the Renaissance and to the history of the Jesuits and the counter-

Reformation, and was a contributor to the Hinneburg series. Walter Wilhelm Goetz has edited the *Archiv für Kulturgeschichte*; has written important monographs on the age of the Renaissance and the Reformation, accounts of the cultural history of Assisi and Ravenna, and a cultural history of Germany; and has edited the *Propylaen Weltgeschichte,* a magnificent and profusely illustrated universal cultural history. Rudolph Kötzschke is an expert on medieval economic history, especially the agrarian history of the medieval period. Bernhard Groethuysen is one of the eminent contributors to the up-to-date interpretation of the Renaissance and Humanism, and has written an account of the rise of the *bourgeois* spirit in France. The progress of cultural history in Germany has been hastened by the work of Lamprecht and his followers. This, together with his influence abroad, has tended to transform a previously sporadic and casual interest in cultural history into a fairly well organized movement in this direction.

German cultural history was merged with historical sociology in the writings of Franz Carl Müller-Lyer (1857-1916), psychologist, physiologist, and historical sociologist. His historical system was a fusion of the terminology of Spencerian evolution, the "stage" theory of the evolutionary anthropologists, and the Marxian materialistic theory of history. He believed that one could reduce the historical development of institutions and culture to definite laws. He held that there is a general uniformity of cultural and institutional development the world over, in which the divergencies are local and of relatively trivial character. His handling of technological and economic development was especially suggestive. His general theoretical views were of the type which are now accepted only with severe reservations by critical anthropologists, sociologists, and historians, but his handling of concrete materials was often very clever and suggestive. Müller-Lyer wrote on the evolution of everything from tools to love. His most important theoretical work has been translated into English as *The History of Social Development.* Even more schematic and sweeping and more up to date in its mastery of historical materials is Alfred Weber's *Kulturgeschichte als Kultursoziologie* (1935), perhaps the ablest effort yet produced to merge cultural history with a highly generalized sociological interpretation of human institutional development. It treats of the evolution of typical civilizations as viewed through the sociological approach.

In France, the traditions of cultural development, embodied in the philosophy of history and historical sociology of Auguste Comte, were kept alive by René Worms and other French disciples of Comte. The next important French contribution to the development of cultural history came in the work of several able and original students of literature and literary critics, Hippolyte Taine, Charles Sainte-Beuve and Ernest Renan.

Taine, historian of English literature and of the French Revolution, believed that history must be a science and that human culture is a product of the race, social environment, and the historical occasion. Sainte-Beuve, a talented literary critic, wrote an admirable cultural history of the Jansenists, his *History of Port Royal*. Renan was an urbane Rationalist, a charming essayist and a great Semitic scholar. He did much to link up "free thought" with cultural history.

An important impulse to cultural history in France appeared in the work of Jacques Philippe Tamizey de Larroque (1828-98), who showed the relation of archeology and letters to cultural history. His own most important writings were on French archeology and the social and religious history of the Middle Ages. Another stimulating approach to the subject appeared in the books of Paul Lacombe (1834-1919), whose chief work was *History Regarded as a Science* (1894). Lacombe stressed the view of history as a genetic science of the development of institutions, and contrasted sharply the conventional history of events with what he regarded as the vastly more important history of the development of human institutions. He understood the mutual interdependence of history, thus conceived, and historical sociology. In his own narrative writings he devoted attention to literary history, and to the history of political, economic and educational institutions. Lacombe had no little influence on Henri Berr, the chief contributor to the idea of historical synthesis in France and editor of one of the most ambitious of all coöperative works on *Kulturgeschichte*. Two of the more eminent and broad-minded of the distinguished French historical scholars, Alfred Rambaud (1842-1905) and Charles Seignobos, wrote well-known histories of civilization. Rambaud produced the best history of French civilization, and Seignobos wrote an introductory history of all western civilization. Georges Renard, himself an authority on economic history from primitive to contemporary times, has edited much the best coöperative work on general economic history from primitive days to our own, *The Universal History of Labor*. This sort of work has tended to bring history down to earth and arouse interest in the development of material things and the destiny of the common man. It is at the furthest extreme from the historical ideals of Pufendorf, Robertson and Gibbon, who felt that history is a record of the doings of prominent public figures and high courtiers. Renard has also contributed an important monograph on the social and institutional basis of national literature. It is a scientific and modernized treatment of the attitudes first introduced by Madame de Staël and Sismondi.

The foremost French exponent of historical synthesis and of the history of civilization in France is Henri Berr. His general theoretical position was set forth in his work, *Historical Synthesis,* published in 1911. Ten years later he expanded his views and answered his critics in his *Tradi-*

tional History and Historical Synthesis. Berr makes a fundamental distinction between erudite summaries and scientific historical synthesis. He also carefully differentiates between the latter and the old a priori philosophy of history. Berr undertook the heavy responsibility of editing what was the most ambitious coöperative work on the history of civilization ever attempted down to that time—*The Evolution of Humanity,* in about one hundred volumes. In the introduction to this he presents his general theory of historical synthesis in its most compact form:

> Without claiming that the method of scientific synthesis can actually be fixed for history in any definite fashion it may be assumed—at least, as a tentative hypothesis—that the facts of which human evolution is woven, can be grouped in three quite distinct orders. The first are the contingent, the second the necessary, and the third those that relate to some inner logic. We shall try to make use of and to harmonize the very diverse explanations that have been attempted, by endeavoring to show that the whole content of human evolution falls into these general divisions of contingency, necessity and logic. It seems to us that by this tripartite division, history receives both its natural articulation and its whole explanation. Indeed, this classification opens up a deeper view of causality. It invites us to probe into the mass of historical facts and to attempt to disentangle three kinds of causal relations: mere succession, where the facts are simply determined by others: relations that are constant, where the facts are linked to others by necessity: and internal linkage, where the facts are rationally connected with others. On this view of the nature of the causes operating in history, a synthesis may not appear easy, but it is at least conceivable. . . . .
>
> Although profoundly scientific in intention this series will not, for that reason, be any the less alive. It has been supposed, quite erroneously, that the introduction of science into history is opposed to life, that the resurrection of the past is the privilege of art. It is analysis which reduces the past to a dust-heap of facts; what erudition collects is saved not from death but from oblivion. Synthesis resurrects the past, otherwise than does intuition, and better. Its task as defined by Michelet, "the resurrection of the whole of life not merely in its surface aspects but in its inner and deeper organisms," cannot be fulfilled by genius; but science can accomplish it by deepening its theory of causality and endeavoring, through its synthesis, to reconstitute the interplay of causes.

It may be said that the series lived up to the high expectations of the editor. Excepting only the English edition, which has been notably extended, it is the most comprehensive of all contributions to the history of human civilization. Most of the contributors are French specialists in one or another phase or period of the history of civilization. Another contemporary French historian who has taken an active interest in historical synthesis is Louis Halphen, an authority on Roman and early medieval civilization, and co-editor with Philippe Sagnac of a large history of civilization, *Peoples and Civilizations,* in twenty volumes. Gustave Glotz, one of the most important contributors to the Berr series, is also editing an elaborate *General History,* with emphasis on the history of civilization. The latest work on the history of civilization in France by a single author is the *Universal Cultural History* by the French physiologist and historian of science, Charles Richet. He regards the history of science as the most important element in the development of human culture. Hence, his two-volume work on the general history of civilization carries the story down to 1789 in the first volume. Most of the striking scientific and technical advances in human history have taken place since that date. Richet's attitude is a valuable corrective of the former disproportionate emphasis placed on ancient and medieval history. In any brief review of cultural history in France one would have to mention the erudite savant, Salomon Reinach (1858-1932), a voluminous and independent contributor to the history of art, literature, and religion in innumerable able volumes.

In England, the chief workers in the cause of historical synthesis since the days of Buckle have been Francis Sydney Marvin and Arnold Toynbee. Marvin's *Living Past* and *The Century of Hope* are able introductions to historical synthesis and interpretation. A sincere friend of peace, he has edited many coöperative volumes in the *Unity Series* devoted to tracing the history of civilization and emphasizing the international character of western civilization. Arnold Toynbee's *Study of History* is the most ambitious project in historical synthesis ever attempted by a single author. J. B. Bury, himself the author of a charming little volume on the history of the freedom of thought and of a larger treatise on the theory of progress, has rendered important services to the history of civilization in an editorial capacity. As planner of the *Cambridge Ancient History,* and the *Cambridge Medieval History,* he allowed for extended treatments of economic and social history, philosophy, science, art, and religion, though of course these great sets are primarily political history. An interesting brief coöperative cultural history is contained in the so-called *"Legacy"* series— *The Legacy of Israel,* edited by Edwyn Bevan and Charles Singer; *The Legacy of Greece,* edited by R. W. Livingstone; *The Legacy of Rome,* edited by Cyril Bailey; *The Legacy of Islam,* edited by T. W. Arnold and Alfred Guillaume; and *The Legacy of the Middle Ages,* edited by C. G. Crump and E. F. Jacob. Sir John Hammerton has done much to promote work in cultural history. He has edited magnificent collections of pictorial reconstructions of the past—*Wonders of the Past* and the like, and he has edited the most serviceable history of civilization ever published in the English language, *A Universal World History,* in eight volumes, lavishly illustrated. C. K. Ogden, in collaboration with the present writer, has undertaken the task of editing an even more complete *History of Civilization* than that projected by Berr. It embodies both the Berr and Renard series and many additional volumes supplied by English, American and German scholars. It is the most formidable and comprehensive of all coöperative histories of civilization.[4] The best history of English civilization is the coöperative set, *Social England,* edited by H. D. Traill and H. S. Mann. H. G. Wells in his *Outline of History* did more than anyone else since John Richard Green to arouse the interest of English readers in non-political history.

Historians in other parts of Europe have contributed to the growth of interest in the history of civilization. One of the ablest and most original of all national cultural histories is the *History of Spanish Civilization* by Rafael Altamira. More complete, but giving less attention to cultural history than the work of Altamira, is the *History of Spain and Its Influence in Universal History* by Antonio Ballesteros. In Italy, Pasquale Villari, who contributed important works to the cultural history of the late medieval period and the Renaissance, strongly emphasized the importance of historical synthesis. While sharply critical of the old grandiose philosophy of history, Villari held that the task of the historian is not completed until he has arranged his facts in a logical and orderly synthesis. Benedetto Croce, while on the one hand trying to dress up and render more palatable the old philosophy of history, has also made important contributions to the history of European and Italian art, literature, and esthetic theory. Guglielmo Ferrero's *Greatness and Decline of Rome* reflects the influence of Lamprecht's emphasis on the importance of collective psychological factors in historical development. Corrado Barbagallo is the editor of the chief Italian journal devoted to cultural history and has himself written one of the finest of all general histories of civilization.

Henri Pirenne, in Belgium, influenced by Lamprecht and Lacombe, executed a broadly conceived history of Belgium, as well as contributing notably to the history of medieval economic and urban life. In Rumania, Alexandru Xénopol (1847-1920) not only wrote a stirring national history, but also produced important books discussing the nature and problems of historical science, his *Fundamental Principles of History,* and his *Theory of History.* Carefully differentiating between the nature and problems of the natural and the social sciences, including history, he contended that history might be regarded as a genetic social science. Laws of historical causation can be worked out for general historical patterns and trends, if not for individual historical events. The only significant historical facts are those which have important social relationships and consequences. One of Xénopol's leading disciples, Nicolae Iorga, in his *Essay on the Synthesis of the History of Humanity,* attempts a general history of civilization and human progress which gives evidence of broad vision, keen

---

[4] See H. E. Barnes, *History and Social Intelligence* (Knopf, 1926), pp. 55 ff.

insight, and no little learning. Russian interest in cultural history has been manifested in many works already mentioned—Kovalevsky's economic and institutional histories, Vinogradov's work on the social history of the Middle Ages and the history of law, Paul Miliukov's writings on Russian institutional and legal history, and Rostovtsev's magisterial work on the early cultural history of southern Russia and the social and economic history of the ancient world. From Czechoslovakia have come the scholarly writings of Thomas Masaryk on Slavonic thought and literature.

We have already noted the earlier evidences of an interest in cultural history in this country in the works of Draper, M. C. Tyler, White, and Henry Adams. In the twentieth century, the main figure in the United States devoted to the promotion of cultural history has been James Harvey Robinson (1863-1936). He was little influenced by Lamprecht or European innovators, though he was familiar with their work. His progress from an ultra-scholarly conventional student of constitutional history to a detached observer of the "human comedy," as he called it, was a gradual, informal, and personal affair.[5] From biology he derived the genetic point of view, and he slowly but effectively applied this outlook to the interpretation of historical materials. Becoming interested in the French Revolution, he moved back gradually, as he once said, from the guillotine to the fist-hatchet. He summarized his views in his widely discussed *New History,* published in 1911, but his influence was exerted mainly through his revolutionary textbooks on European history and his uniquely stimulating teaching. He projected an ambitious intellectual history of Europe, but never completed it. His students did the productive writing. James T. Shotwell edited a large set of sourcebooks on the history of civilization —*Records of Civilization,* and he was a pioneer in promoting interest in social and economic history in the United States. Lynn Thorndike has written the most complete work on medieval science and thought. He has also brought out a brief general introduction to the history of civilization. Carl Becker, a student of both Robinson and Turner, has written with much discernment on the thought of the seventeenth and eighteenth centuries. Preserved Smith distinguished himself in the cultural history of the Reformation and launched into what might have been the most stimulating history of modern culture by one author. Howard Robinson has cultivated the period of Rationalism and has written the best work in English on Pierre Bayle. Charles Austin Beard, Benjamin B. Kendrick, A. M. Schlesinger, D. R. Fox, Harold Faulkner, Harry J. Carman, and others have carried the Robinsonian interests and outlook over into the field of American history. Fox and Schlesinger have edited the most complete and up-to-date history of American social life and culture,

---

[5] See H. E. Barnes, in H. W. Odum, ed., *American Masters of Social Science* (Holt, 1927), pp. 321 ff; J. H. Robinson, *The Human Comedy* (Harper, 1937); L. V. Hendricks, *James Harvey Robinson,* New York, 1946.

A History of American Life. Independent of the Robinsonian stimulus, Ferdinand Schevill, probably the most sensitive and discerning exponent of *Kulturgeschichte* in the United States, has written able works on Siena and Florence, the latter a masterly contribution to our understanding of the culture of the Renaissance. Frederick J. Teggart has written most extensively on the theoretical foundations and assumptions of the new history. Hispanic American achievements in cultural history are illustrated by the works on Mexican civilization by Vicente Riva Palacio and Jesús Romero Flores, and on Argentine civilization by Romulo D. Carbia.

CULTURAL HISTORY AND THE MAJOR EPOCHS IN HUMAN HISTORY

We have now traced the development of cultural history through major landmarks in its development. It remains to point out some outstanding contributions to the cultural history of the various periods of human advance since preliterary times. We can only call attention to outstanding works, chosen from the multiplicity of volumes which exist in the field. Whatever the paucity of books which have been devoted to a conscious defense of *Kulturgeschichte* and however recent the trend as an organized historical movement, there have been a multitude of special works which deal with some particular field of cultural development. The reader who wishes some approximation to completeness may consult with profit the titles listed under "cultural history" in successive sections of the *Guide to Historical Literature*.

The introduction to all cultural history must be found, of course, in cultural anthropology—the account of cultural development in the long period of human development which we now designate as the preliterary period. The works in the field of preliterary archeology, which have already been summarized, provide the fundamental basis of cultural history.[6] Theodor Mommsen never heard of the "Ice Age" until near the close of his life, but today all respectable books on ancient history begin with an account of the preliterary period. Eduard Meyer's *Geschichte des Altertums* has a whole preliminary volume on anthropology. *The Cambridge Ancient History* opens with two magnificent chapters on preliterary culture by J. L. Myres. The achievements of scholarship in this field to date are admirably summarized in George Grant MacCurdy's *Human Origins*. We must consult also the works on primitive institutions and culture and on the principles of cultural development which have been written by the cultural anthropologists. Here we may begin with the old classic of E. B. Tylor, *Anthropology,* and pass on to the more up-to-date formulations in such books as Franz Boas' *Mind of Primitive Man,* and *Anthropology and Modern Life*; A. L. Kroeber's *Anthropology*; R. H.

[6] See above, pp. 4-8.

Lowie's *Primitive Society* and *Introduction to Cultural Anthropology*; Alexander Goldenweiser's *Early Civilization* and *History, Psychology and Culture*; L. A. White's *Evolution of Culture*; Clark Wissler's *Man and Culture*; A. M. Tozzer's *Social Origins and Social Continuities*; Harold Peake's *Early Steps in Human Progress,* and Gustav Schwalbe's *Anthropologie.* These works constitute the threshold of history and remove much of the mystery from the "dawn of history." The achievements of man which brought him to literary civilization are described, the processes of human and group behavior are analyzed, and the principles and patterns of cultural development are clarified, as far as the known sources permit. The cultural and institutional transition from primitive society to historical civilization is best summarized in Jacques de Morgan's *Oriental Prehistory*; Max Blanckenhorn's *The Stone Age in Palestine, Syria and North Africa*; V. Gordon Childe's *The Dawn of European Civilization* and *The Most Ancient East*; and Moret and Davy's *From Tribe to Empire.*

On the everyday life of ancient Egypt Adolph Erman's *Life in Ancient Egypt* is still the the classic account. A new edition by a competent scholar was prepared some thirty years after the original work appeared. Erman has also summarized Egyptian literature and thought. A much briefer but more up-to-date account of Egyptian culture has been provided by Georg Steindorff in *The Pharaonic Empire in Its Prime.* Not only is there much cultural history in James H. Breasted's able histories of Egypt, but he has also written special works on religion and thought in Egypt and on the dawn of ethical and humanitarian movements in Egypt. Morris Jastrow's *Civilization of Babylonia and Assyria* is a readable and authoritative account of most phases of Mesopotamian culture, and Jastrow has also taken a place in the front rank as an authority on the religion of ancient Mesopotamia. The most complete and up-to-date survey of Mesopotamian civilization is Bruno Meissner's *Babylonians and Assyrians.* R. W. Rogers, Clément Huart, M. N. Dhalla, P. M. Sykes, A. V. W. Jackson and others have reviewed the important contributions of ancient Persia to western civilization. The sections on the art of the Orient in Georges Perrot's and Charles Chipiez' *History of Art* are still the best treatment of the art of the ancient Near East, though there are more recent manuals, such as Jean Capart's *Lectures on Egyptian Art.* The early volumes in the Hammerton *Universal History of the World* are especially good on the cultural history of preliterary times and the Near Orient. Fresh and original treatments are to be found in the volumes by Moret, Davy, Delaporte, Huart, and others on the Orient in the "History of Civilization Series." There is also much splendid cultural material in the *Cambridge Ancient History*; and in Ralph Turner's *The Great Cultural Tradition.* Max Weber and J. E. Hertzler have surveyed the social thought of oriental antiquity.

Passing on to Greece, we have an admirable survey of the Cretan and

Aegean civilization in the recent work of Gustave Glotz. One of the most prolific contributors to the elucidation of Greek culture was the Irish scholar, Sir John P. Mahaffy, who wrote on nearly every aspect of Greek culture and history. While somewhat discursive and over-eulogistic, the enthusiasm and industry of Mahaffy were commendable and he did much to arouse popular interest in the culture of ancient Greece. More discriminating and concise have been the writings of the English humanists, Gilbert Murray and G. Lowes Dickinson. The best introduction to Greek culture in a single volume is the coöperative *Companion to Greek Studies* edited by Leonard Whibley. More complete is the German work, *Introduction to Antique Learning,* edited by Alfred Gercke and Eduard Norden. On the civilization of Greece and Rome there is the excellent series, *Our Debt to Greece and Rome,* edited by George D. Hadzsits and David M. Robinson, and the comparable German series edited by Otto Immisch. Greek philosophy has been authoritatively summarized by Eduard Zeller, Theodor Gomperz and Wilhelm Windelband. Ernest Barker has written a monumental work on Greek political philosophy. Hugo Berger, Auguste Bouché-Leclercq and Pierre Duhem have dealt with Greek science. Otto Kern, Jane Harrison, Lewis R. Farnell and Erwin Rohde have made valuable and extended contributions to the history of Greek religion. The history of Greek literature has been handled in detail by Alfred and Maurice Croiset and by Wilhelm von Christ. Greek art is surveyed and interpreted by Percy Gardner, Maxime Collignon and Johannes Overbeck. The relevant volumes in the Hammerton Series, the "History of Civilization," and the *Cambridge Ancient History* are of high value for the cultural history of both Greece and Rome.

On Rome we have the invaluable general introduction to all aspects of Roman culture in the *Companion to Latin Studies,* edited by Sir John E. Sandys. Roman social history has been handled by Marion Park, Frank F. Abbott, William Warde Fowler, Samuel Dill and Ludwig Friedländer The literature on Roman religion is especially rich. Here we have, among others, the standard works of Jesse B. Carter, Warde Fowler, Georg Wissowa, Gaston Bossier, Alfred Loisy, Franz Cumont and Terrot R. Glover. The writings of the last three authors are especially valuable for a study of the conflict of religions in the Roman Empire. The growth of Roman literature is surveyed by John W. Duff, Eduard Norden and Wilhelm S. Teuffel. Roman art has been studied intelligently by Henry B. Walters, René Cagnat, Victor Chapot, Franz Wickhoff, and G. T. Rivoira. The history of classical scholarship since Greek and Roman days has been covered thoroughly in the monumental work of Sir John R. Sandys. The transition from Roman to medieval civilization has especially claimed the attention of Henri Pirenne, Ferdinand Lot, Alfons Dopsch, Christopher Dawson, M. L. W. Laistner, E. K. Rand, Eleanor Duckett and H. O. Taylor, and others.

All material on the origins and growth of Christianity is necessarily a phase of cultural history. We can only note some of the more important contributions. There are a number of worthy general histories of the Christian church, of which that by William Möller is characteristic. On the history of Christianity as a whole there are the excellent works by Charles Guignebert on Jesus and the evolution of Christianity. Emil Schurer has written an authoritative history of the Jews in the early Christian era, and Louis Duchesne, Arthur C. McGiffert and Henry M. Gwatkin have treated the early history of the Church. The writings of Shirley Jackson Case on early Christianity are especially rich in social and cultural history. The works of Henry Charles Lea on the medieval Church are still the masterpieces on the subject. Walter Adeney has provided the most useful account of the Greek or Eastern church. The co-operative work of Georges Goyau and his associates on *The Vatican, the Popes and Civilization* is the best work on the cultural history of the Catholic church. Alexander C. Flick has analyzed the decline of the medieval Church. The age of the Reformation has received especially fruitful attention from Thomas M. Lindsay, Preserved Smith, Ludwig von Pastor, Ernst Troeltsch, Max Weber and others. George P. Fisher, Adolph Harnack and Arthur C. McGiffert have produced the most satisfactory histories of Christian thought and dogma. Gustav Krüger is the master of the history of early Christian literature. A stimulating account of Christian art has been worked out by Josef Strzyowski. The cultural history of the great rival of Christianity, the religion of Islam, has been cultivated by such writers as Stanley Lane Poole, Sir Thomas W. Arnold, De Lacey O'Leary, Duncan B. Macdonald, Reynold Nicholson, Edward G. Browne, Sir Richard F. Burton, Henri Lammens, Henri Saladin, Clément Huart, Ignaz Goldziher, Bernard Carra de Vaux, and others.

A scholarly and stimulating discussion of the nature and spirit of medieval civilization is contained in Henry Adams' *Mont-Saint-Michel and Chartres.* Tamizey de Larroque has done important work on French archeology, the history of the medieval communes, and medieval cultural and religious history. Medieval manners and customs have been presented in detail in Paul Lacroix's many able works. Henry Osborn Taylor's *Medieval Mind* and Reginald Lane Poole's *Illustrations of the History of Medieval Thought* are important representative works on medieval intellectual history. Maurice De Wulf has done the best work on medieval philosophy. Charles Homer Haskins and Lynn Thorndike have contributed notably to the history of medieval thought and science. Stephen d'Irsay, Hastings Rashdall, Heinrich Denifle and Haskins are leading authorities on medieval education, schools and universities. Maximilianus Manitius has provided the best comprehensive survey of medieval Latin literature, and Karl Krumbacher is the author of the standard work on the medieval

Greek, or Byzantine, literature. William Lethaby has produced the best general survey of medieval art, Charles Diehl and O. M. Dalton have written the standard manuals on Byzantine art, while Ralph Adams Cram, Sir Thomas G. Jackson and Eugène Viollet-le-Duc have produced the best works on medieval architecture. The ablest criticism of the whole medieval complex is embodied in the works of George Gordon Coulton.

An introduction to the cultural history of modern times is provided by John Herman Randall's *Making of the Modern Mind*. What promised to be the most satisfactory cultural history of modern times in any language, the *History of Modern Culture*, by a superbly competent historian, Preserved Smith, was abandoned after two volumes had been published. Egon Friedell's *Cultural History of the Modern Age* contains many brilliant generalizations and original interpretations, but it is frequently erratic and is based in part on the dubious theoretical position of Oswald Spengler. There is a great deal of cultural history in the series on *The Rise of Modern Europe*, edited by William L. Langer. It is the closest approach in the English language to a coöperative cultural history of modern times. The Renaissance has been dealt with in up-to-date fashion by Gothein, Goetz, Groethuysen, Brandi and others in works already mentioned. Emile Gebhart threw much light on the relations between the later Middle Ages and the Renaissance and showed why the Renaissance started in Italy. He did especially important work on the relation between late medieval mysticism and pietism and the early Christian Renaissance. Robert Davidsohn and Ferdinand Schevill have produced the classic histories of Renaissance Florence. Henry Osborn Taylor, Ferdinand Schevill, Albert Hyma and Edward P. Cheyney have been American leaders in recent studies of this age. Preserved Smith and Ernst Troeltsch have done excellent work on the cultural history of the Reformation, and Walter Goetz on the counter-Reformation. The ablest general works on the economic history of modern times have been those by Kovalevsky and Werner Sombart. On leading countries we have able economic and social histories, such as those of Lamprecht's disciples in Germany, of the Webbs and Hammonds in England, of Levasseur in France, and of Dorfman, and David and associates in the United States.

The most important books on modern philosophy, thought and science are those of Harald Höffding and Abraham Wolf, John Morley's books on the French Rationalists, and John T. Merz's voluminous study of thought and science in the nineteenth century. F. J. C. Hearnshaw has edited a series of remarkably useful works on social and political thought from the Middle Ages to the twentieth century. Harold J. Laski excels as a historian of modern political ideas, especially the rise of liberalism. The art of the Renaissance has been described by Bernard Berenson and others, modern painting by Frank J. Mather, Jr., and modernistic art by Thomas

Craven, Clive Bell, C. J. Bulliet, and others. Literary history has been covered in numerous important surveys of national literature, such as the *Cambridge History of English Literature,* Émile Faguet's history of French literature, Francisco Garcia Blancho's account of Spanish literature, Francesco de Sanctis' survey of Italian literature, and Wilhelm Scherer's history of German literature through the age of Goethe. Wilhelm Dilthey and Heinrich Rickert made brilliant and original attempts to place intellectual history on a scientific basis, though they distinguished sharply between natural and social science, and Friedrich Meinecke has done notable work in studying liberalism and nationalism as dominant intellectual concepts of the nineteenth century. In the United States Carlton J. H. Hayes has done much to promote interest in the history of nationalism.

No country has provided better systematic work on its cultural history than the United States. Arthur M. Schlesinger and Dixon R. Fox have edited a *History of American Life* in twelve volumes, a real *Kulturgeschichte* of the highest order. The fifteen-volume *Pageant of America,* edited by Ralph H. Gabriel, is admirable for its illustrations as well as its text. Woodbridge Riley has done some of the best work on the history of American thought and philosophy. Vernon L. Parrington wrote an unusually original history of American literature against its social background. The writings of Van Wyck Brooks on American literature were especially thoughtful and stimulating. Even more thorough is the *Cambridge History of American Literature.* Samuel Isham, Frank J. Mather, Jr., Lorado Taft, Fiske Kimball, T. E. Tallmadge and Oliver Larkin have treated the history of American art in its various phases.

This rapid and necessarily sketchy survey of some of the notable contributions to cultural history probably will impress the reader with the magnitude, volume, and variety of the writings in this field, especially if he remembers that the works here mentioned are but the more important or representative ones chosen from the totality of such products in recent times. His conclusion, on contemplating this vast literature, is likely to be that cultural history has definitely triumphed over the older political and military history. But it is necessary to bear in mind that the majority of this material has not been written by professional academic historians. Most of the authors have been students of literature, art, religion, sociology, economics, science, philosophy, and the like. But we may be thankful for this broadening and illuminating material, whether written by professional historians or others. The most promising development is the increase in the number of professional historians who are taking an interest in various aspects of cultural history. It is this fact which supplies the chief foundation for the hope and prediction that history ultimately will come more and more to be identified with the history of civilization and culture.

As of the present writing, the most ambitious and commendable effort to describe the whole course of human civilization has been Will Durant's voluminous *Story of Civilization,* now projected in ten volumes of which seven are published. It is doubtful if any professional historian could have performed the feat with such comprehensive competence.

SELECTED REFERENCES

Gooch, *History and Historians in the Nineteenth Century,* chap. xxviii.

Fueter, *Histoire de l'historiographie moderne,* pp. 652-57, 708-52.

Ritter, *Die Entwicklung der Geschichtswissenschaft,* pp. 421-61.

Becker, "Some Aspects of the Influence of Social Problems and Ideas upon the Study and Writing of History," *loc. cit.*

Guilday, *Church Historians,* pp. 321 ff.

Robinson, *The New History.*

Barnes, *The New History and the Social Studies.*

Muzzey, *Essays in Intellectual History Dedicated to James Harvey Robinson.*

Thompson, *History of Historical Writing,* Vol. II, chap. lv.

Odum, *American Masters of Social Science,* chapters on James Harvey Robinson and Frederick Jackson Turner.

L. V. Hendricks, *James Harvey Robinson.*

M. E. Curti, *Frederick Jackson Turner.* Mexico City, 1949.

Beale, *Charles A. Beard.*

Smith, *Carl Becker: On History and the Climate of Opinion.*

Schmitt, *Some Historians of Modern Europe,* chaps. i, x, xix-xxi.

Halperin, *Some Twentieth Century Historians,* pp. 1-39, 277-298.

Ausabel *et al., Some Historians of Modern Britain,* chaps. 8-10, 15, 20, 22.

Kraus, *The Writing of American History,* chap. xiv.

J. C. Levenson, *The Mind and Art of Henry Adams.* Houghton Mifflin, 1957.

Philip Bagby, *Culture and History.* University of California Press, 1960.

Ernst Schaumkell, *Geschichte der deutschen Kulturgeschichtschreibung.* Leipzig, 1905.

R. Kötzschke and A. Tille, *Karl Lamprecht.* Gotha, 1915.

E. J. Spiess, *Die Geschichtsphilosophie von Karl Lamprecht.* Erlangen, 1921.

Steinberg, *Die Geschichtswissenschaft der Gegenwart in Selbstdarstellungen.*

Halphen *et al., Histoire et historiens depuis cinquante ans.*

Halphen, *L'Histoire en France depuis cent ans.*

Henri Berr, *L'Histoire traditionelle et la synthèse historique.* Paris, 1921.

Croce, *Storia della storiografia italiana.*

Blok, *Geschichtschreibung in Holland.*

Miliukov, *Main Currents of Russian Historiography.*

Kurt Breysig, *Die Meister der entwickelnden Geschichtsforschung.* Breslau, 1936.

J. B. Bury *et al., Evolution in Modern Thought,* chap. ix. Boni and Liveright, 1915.

H. G. Wells, *The Science of Life.* Doubleday, Doran, 1931. 2 vols.

Clark Wissler, *Man and Culture.* Crowell, 1923.

W. F. Ogburn, *Social Change.* Viking Press, 1922.

XIV

HISTORY AND THE SCIENCES OF MAN

THE NEW COSMIC ORIENTATION

IN this chapter we shall deal with the intellectual and cultural developments and the progress in human knowledge which have served to broaden the perspective and enrich the subject matter of history and to aid the historian in reconstructing the civilization of the past. First, we must consider the reaction of the new astronomical outlook upon the perspective of the historian.

The new astronomy and celestial mechanics, starting from Newton's preliminary synthesis, have much more than vindicated the brilliant intuition of Giordano Bruno with respect to the plurality of worlds and the similarity between the heavenly bodies and the earth in material composition. Distant planets, such as Uranus and Neptune, have been discovered, the existence of which proves the unsuspected extent of our own solar system. But much more significant has been the development of instruments which have enabled us to detect innumerable and, in many cases, almost incalculably distant and complex solar systems. Our cosmic outlook has required adjustment not merely to the disconcerting notion of a plurality of worlds, but also to the vastly more impressive concept of an almost infinite plurality of universes. This has led to the necessity of a much chastened revision of the cosmology of Greek science, Hebrew tradition and the Christian Epic. The relative insignificance and modernity of the earth have become impressively apparent.

With the growing recognition of this fact has come the scientific vindication of Montaigne's suspicion that it is highly improbable that God has a meticulous and inquisitorial interest in each passing thought and every casual act of the individual man. This new astronomy, far more than evolutionary biology, has dealt a death blow to the supernatural and providential theory of historical causation.

Further, the enormous demands upon the element of time required by the newly realized cosmic chronology make the assumed date of the creation of the universe in 4004 B.C. seem almost as naïve and inadequate a concept as the crudest creation tale of any known primitive people. The new cosmic time perspective introduced by astrophysics is much more impressive than the older geological perspective. It stands towards the latter much as the geological outlook did towards the Mosaic chronology. The discoveries of Fraunhofer, Michelson, Einstein, Shapley and

Jeans are supplanting not only Adam, Noah and Moses but also the work of Lyell, Geikie, Chamberlin and others, as the foundation upon which the historian is basing his notions of time perspective and historical relativity.

What astronomy has done for the cosmos at large, geology and paleontology have done for our conception of the genesis and antiquity of our own planet, which is, from the cosmic viewpoint, an exceedingly minute celestial juvenile. Historical and structural geology have proved the naturalistic evolution of the earth, the relatively immense expanse of time required for its development, and the fact that the geologic period prior to the origin of life on the planet probably vastly exceeds that which has elapsed since. Paleontology, as the true historical background of evolutionary biology, has revealed the gradual development of organic life on the earth, the progression of the types of plant and animal life, and the genetic connection between extinct and existing genera and species. Above all, it has revealed a somewhat paradoxical situation with regard to man. From the standpoint of the evolution of organic life as a whole, he is a strikingly modern arrival. Yet, as contrasted with the older orthodox view of the duration of his mundane existence, he possesses an amazing antiquity.

The reception of the new cosmic and time perspective by historians has been paralleled by a comparable decline in the prestige of the supernaturalism which buttressed the older Creation hypothesis. The outlook of supernaturalism, which lay back of conventional history almost down to the present generation, has been challenged, not only indirectly through the development of the natural and social sciences, which have thoroughly discredited the traditional *Weltanschauung,* but also directly through the critical and historical study of the "sacred" documents in which the supernatural hypothesis has been embodied.[1] In this manner, the alleged documentary basis of supernaturalism has been completely undermined, and the "warfare between science and theology" is finally resolved into naught for the educated classes.

THE SIGNIFICANCE OF THE EVOLUTIONARY HYPOTHESIS FOR HISTORY

Among the various intellectual and scientific influences which have revolutionized the perspective, orientation, and ideals of dynamic historical writing there is little doubt that the evolutionary hypothesis must be assigned the foremost place. And our notion of evolution must transcend the biological limitations of Darwinism and embrace universal evolution in the Spencerian sense. As a general concept, the evolutionary hypothesis merely insists that all portions of the known cosmos, great or

[1] See above, pp. 19-22.

small, have been produced by naturalistic causes which bring about both progress and regression. It also implies, in agreement with the ancient hypothesis of Heraclitus, that change is the great basic principle of the cosmos. As such, the evolutionary hypothesis is in no way involved in theological controversy. It rests upon no dogmatic position as to the part taken by God in this process of cosmic development and in no way pretends to have received from Him any revelation as to His purposes in bringing into being the multitudinous celestial bodies which make up the cosmic equipment. It may well be that this view of cosmogenesis possesses infinite significance for those who concern themselves with the supernatural, but a consideration of the teleological import of the evolutionary hypothesis is a problem for the philosopher and theologian and not for the biologist or historian.

The theory of evolution is, of course, by no means a wholly new phase in the thought-stream of western civilization. Its history is as old as that of reflective thinking itself, beginning with the pre-Socratic philosophers of ancient Greece. Not even Herbert Spencer himself stated more adequately the general concepts and implications of cosmic evolution than did Lucretius in the age of Cicero, and Lucretius asserted that his exposition was but an inferior version of the doctrines of his master, Epicurus, who lived three centuries earlier. A general revival of this evolutionary interpretation of nature followed the growth of science and Romanticism during the eighteenth and nineteenth centuries. But this line of thought gave rise to relatively little controversy until it included man himself within the scope of its generalizations. Spencer elaborated the thesis of universal evolution and showed its varied pertinent applications to the whole range of human intellectual activity. Darwin devoted himself primarily to the biological phases of the problem and indicated that the evidence for man's development from lower forms of organic life was far more convincing than any which could be adduced for the orthodox view of a special and recent creative act. His thesis was warmly espoused and effectively defended and disseminated by such scholars as Haeckel, Huxley, Romanes and Wallace. The cultural and historical implications of the evolutionary notions were expounded by writers as varied as J. M. Robertson, W. E. H. Lecky, Leslie Stephen, Karl Lamprecht, J. W. Draper, Andrew D. White and Henry Adams. So effective have been their efforts that the concept of evolution is probably the most useful and potent working hypothesis in our present cultural equipment and intellectual life, doubted and opposed only by well-meaning but uninformed Fundamentalists such as William Jennings Bryan, John Roach Straton and Jasper Cortenus Massee and by Catholic apologists of similar intellectual temper.[2]

---

[2] Cf. Robinson, *The Human Comedy.* chap. ii.

Even the major aspects of the significance of the evolutionary hypothesis for history are numerous and impressive. Perhaps the most striking is its denial of the transcendentalist philosophy. Plato felt that his esthetic nature, as well as his epistemology, was outraged by the conception of a shifting reality, but such seems to be the nature of things. If there is anything in the realm of nature which is perfect, final and changeless, its existence has not yet been revealed to any type of scientist. Paradoxically enough, it seems that the principle of change is almost the only "changeless" and invariable cosmic principle.

This view of the matter is even more disconcerting to the piously inclined when its implications are transferred from the realm of the natural to that of the social. The thought that rocks and plants may change their character is less impressive to many than the fact that human institutions, opinions, and beliefs are evolutionary in character and relative in nature, permanence, and value. The notion that our particular convictions with respect to such things as God, biblical inspiration, the validity and permanence of monogamy, democracy, the protective tariff, and unlimited fecundity may be of purely human derivation, are the exact opposite of the opinions held on these subjects by others, and may very well be wholly mistaken, is to many appalling, but such are the unavoidable conclusions which the evolutionary doctrine forces upon us.[3] The evolutionary hypothesis is especially cogent when applied to the development of our social institutions. Our culture and institutions represent society's crude and awkward efforts to adjust itself to the conditions of life in any given region. No human institutions have existed in their present form from the beginning; all are the changing products of perpetual readjustment to altering environmental and technological factors. Conduct and institutions are, thus, mundane in their origin and their later traits, and are not divinely created or inspired. The only valid test of the excellence and adequacy of an institution is its efficient adaptation to the needs of the group in a particular region at any given time. Institutions and morals are, then, transient and relative, the product of man and society, and subject to the possibility of artificial human alterations for better or worse.

Somewhat disconcerting, likewise, is the genetic point of view, as opposed to the earlier notion of providential causation. It now appears that all phenomena of which we at present have any knowledge are the product of natural causes, working in an evolutionary manner. One stage is the outgrowth of another. Given a definite set of forces operating upon concrete materials under certain conditions, there will be an invariable outcome. Man may, to some degree, alter the materials and the circumstances upon which and under which natural forces operate, but he is

[3] W. G. Sumner, *Folkways* (Dover, 1959); and Barnes, *Social Institutions*.

subject to the results of the collaboration of natural factors and his own intellect, and he cannot safely sink back upon the regressive delusion that, somehow, God will surely care for him. If, to some, this is disconcerting, to others it is a dynamic and appealing challenge to human ingenuity and initiative.

The immediate application of evolutionary biology to historical problems is most direct and pertinent in the fields of genetic psychology, genetics, and eugenics. G. Stanley Hall and later writers have shown in impressive works that the human mind must be viewed as an evolutionary product, quite as much as the body, and have thus made genetic psychology the natural introduction to intellectual history.

The old Christian and democratic notions were erected upon the belief in the essential equality of all men. Biology and psychology have proved that there is no more obvious or disastrous error than this. As change is the fundamental principle of the cosmos, so variegation and differentiation are the primary principles of organic life, including man. Differences in capacity for potential achievement, then, rather than identity of ability, are the most conspicuous fact about humanity, and also one of the most frequently ignored elements in current social and historical philosophy. While one must be on his guard against the excessive emphasis of the Galton-Pearson school upon purely biological factors at the expense of the potency of environmental and educational influences, yet one of the two major factors in social progress is physical excellence in the population. There is no evidence of a strong people or an enduring civilization in the past which has been based upon the ascendency of inferior and deteriorating physical types in the population. In fact, it is apparent that one potent cause for the cycles of civilization and the rise and fall of cultures is the differential birth rate, whereby the abler ruling classes decrease in fertility and leave the matter of population increase to the inferior biological classes, thus creating a process of biological counter-selection. No historian can today be regarded as intellectually and professionally well equipped who is ignorant of the biological philosophy of Francis Galton, Karl Pearson, Vacher de Lapouge, and Otto Ammon.

Important as biological factors may be in human society, there is a danger in attempting to transfer biological concepts directly to social situations and to assume that processes of observed importance in the organic life of the individual apply without qualification or reservation to society. That there are interesting analogies between the organism and society cannot be denied, though these may have little more practical significance than the analogy between the atom and a universal system. Further, there may be some biological processes which have an important application to the functioning of human society, but the distinct differences in the two situations must be calculated and allowed for before the propriety of the analogy can be admitted. Probably the most serious error which has resulted from this effort to apply biological concepts directly to social processes has been the assumption that war plays the same constructive part in social and cultural evolution that the struggle for existence does in the realm of organic life. That this was ever fully the case is doubtful, and it is an absurdly grotesque doctrine when applied to war under modern conditions and in the present cultural setting.

The evolutionary hypothesis has been influential in shaping the orientation of certain types of scholars in the historical field. Notable in this respect have been the works of Spencer, Drummond, Lecky, Leslie Stephen, Allen, Lang, Schurman, Kidd, Hobhouse, Fiske, and Sutherland in the history of religion and ethics, and the contributions of Post, Maine, McLennan, Bagehot, Letourneau, Kovalevsky, Ritchie, and Morgan, among others, to the history of law and politics. In general, however, the main impression which the evolutionary hypothesis has left on history has been to create in the alert historian's mind a perception of the genetic nature of the social process, and to give a firm basis for a sound theory of historical development. As James Harvey Robinson was wont to say, it was the biologists who gave the historians the idea of development, i.e., true historical-mindedness.

THE ANTHROPOLOGICAL CONTRIBUTION TO HISTORY

The discussion of the importance of the evolutionary hypothesis for history leads directly to a consideration of the relation of anthropology to the new or dynamic history. In fact, it is through the various fields of anthropology that evolutionary concepts have made some of their most significant contacts with contemporary thought. As Professor Marett has very appropriately said:

> Anthropology is the whole history of man as fired and pervaded by the idea of evolution. Man in evolution—that is the subject in its full reach. Anthropology studies man as he occurs at all known times. It studies him as he occurs in all parts of the world. It studies him body and soul together—as a bodily organism, subject to conditions operating in time and space, which bodily organism is in intimate relation with a psychic life, also subject to those same conditions. Having an eye to such conditions from first to last, it seeks to plot out the general series of the changes, bodily and mental together, undergone by man in the course of his history. Anthropology is the child of Darwin. Darwinism makes it possible. Reject the Darwinian point of view and you must reject anthropology also . . . . with Darwin, then, we anthropologists say: Let any and every portion of human history be studied in the light of the whole history of mankind, and against the background of the history of living

things in general. It is the Darwinian outlook that matters. None of Darwin's particular doctrines will necessarily endure the test of time and trial. Into the melting-pot must they go as often as any man of science deems it fitting. But Darwinism as the touch of nature that makes the whole world kin can hardly pass away. At any rate, anthropology stands or fails with the working hypothesis, derived from Darwinism, of a fundamental kinship and continuity amid change between all the forms of human life.[4]

The significance of anthropology for history is obviously extensive and varied. First and foremost is the fact that it alone can furnish that type of knowledge about the early development of man which is indispensable to any intelligent study of so-called ancient history. A generation ago it was customary to open books on ancient history with a discussion of the separation of the sons of Noah and the re-peopling of the earth, due to the heroic procreative efforts of these worthies and their descendants. This sometimes occurred despite the fact that the same book might refer to the fact that ancient Egyptian civilization had reached remarkably high levels of civilization years before the date traditionally assigned to the "creation" of Adam. Such hopeless inconsistencies and confusion could only be removed by entirely wiping away the Hebraized chronology of Julius Africanus, Eusebius, and Usher, and taking as the background of ancient history the facts well established by anthropology relative to the infinitely long period of human development prior to the dawn of literary history.

Not only does this new approach to history remove the strange and mysterious elements from the "dawn of history"; it also makes this very term intelligible. There was no break between the so-called "prehistoric" and historic periods. There has been a slow and steady, though not necessarily uniform, process of unbroken development since the appearance of mankind upon the planet a million or more years ago. The art of writing is the main achievement which definitely separates the historic from the prehistoric, and this was but one phase of human cultural achievement. It was not until centuries after its origin that writing was sufficiently perfected to exert any revolutionary influence upon human culture and conduct.

When one attempts to make an inventory of cultural progress before the invention of the art of writing—including such things as the varied technique of hunting and fishing, the domestication of animals, the origins of agriculture, the foundations of the textile industry in spinning and weaving, important progress in art, the origins of settled life, artificial habitats, highly developed forms of social coöperation, the definite appearance of private property in chattels and perhaps in land, and some considerable advances in government and law—he begins to comprehend

---

[4] R. R. Marett, *Anthropology* (Holt, 1910), chap. i.

the vital importance of the cultural heritage we have received from the preliterary period, and the vast significance of material that was omitted from history textbooks only a generation ago.

Another reason for the value of a knowledge of anthropology to the historian resides in the fact of the survival of primitive institutional life and psychic traits in our present-day society. There is hardly a contemporary institution that does not have its roots in primitive origins or that can be accurately understood and interpreted without an adequate knowledge of its genesis. Our institutions associated with religion, property, sex, government, law, and ethics have not only been erected on primitive foundations, but even contain within their present-day forms and expressions a large admixture of primitive heritages. If we properly understood these facts, there would be little ground for chauvinism, cultural arrogance, and conservatism. The facts would tend to convince us of the lack of that uniqueness, divine revelation, perfection, and permanence with which we are wont to clothe and adorn our institutions. A perusal of Hutton Webster's *Rest Days,* for example, should be more disconcerting to an intelligent exponent of Sunday observance legislation than any amount of theological argumentation. Especially is most of the ceremonialism of contemporary life based on primitive origins. One could scarcely suggest more entertaining and edifying, and at the same time more disconcerting, reading than an exposition of cultural vestiges such as is contained, for example, in the third volume of Herbert Spencer's *Principles of Sociology.*

Nor are we free from psychic traits which, with some variations and transformations, we share with savages and barbarians. Among these are the tendency to jump at conclusions, to see more in situations than actually exists, to think symbolically, to look at certain phases of experience in a highly mystical manner, to trust to the efficacy of words and phrases, and the varied modern perpetuations, variations and re-adaptations of primitive belief in mana, animism, totemism, fetishism, taboos and naïve superstitions. No general categorical statement can be made about the degree to which primitive thought survives in the modern period, because its perpetuation varies greatly among the different phases of contemporary culture. In science, we have departed rather completely from the primitive outlook and modes of thinking, while in religion and ethics the orthodox thoroughly retain a pseudo-rationalized and enormously elaborated primitive mysticism and supernaturalism. The primitive element in other phases of our thinking varies between the two extremes. For example, in politics we still rely upon rhetoric, which was but a Hellenic elaboration of shamanistic incantations and formalistic deliverances of chieftains. An understanding of this fact of primitive survivals in our contemporary mental traits and psychic interpretations is of particular value for workers in the field of intellectual history. Anthropology thus links up genetic psychology with the intellectual development of mankind. Books like those of Wundt, Lévy-Bruhl, Paul Radin, Goldenweiser, and others constitute as much the logical threshold of intellectual history as do those of Osborn, Burkitt, Peake, Tyler, Déchelette, Wilder, Cleland, and MacCurdy the proper introduction to the history of human material culture.

An extremely important contribution to the technique of historical analysis has been put at the service of history by the anthropologists; namely, that of interpreting the evolution of human culture and of explaining its similarities and parallels, its variations and divergencies. Of course, this technique has no pertinence for the conventional student of history, who is interested only in "unique" episodes and anecdotes, but it is indispensable to any historian who seeks to be scientific in treating the history of civilization and culture.

Both similarities and differences in the cultures of various areas have attracted observers from the time of Herodotus and earlier. The similarities have created the greatest problems in explanation and interpretation, even if they have excited less interest than the differences. Variations seem to be readily understandable on the basis of the diversity of race, geographic environment, ethnic contacts and the stages of cultural development. With cultural similarities the case is different. How can we explain, for example, the presence of pyramids in both Egypt and Central America, or the similarity of weapons and pottery designs in widely separated areas?

The first effort of cultural anthropologists to explain these phenomena of cultural parallelisms and identities was identified with the work of such men as Spencer, Tylor, and particularly Morgan and Letourneau. They worked on the basis of the theory of Bastian with respect to the unity of the human mind, the doctrine of a direct and determining influence of geographic environment upon culture, and the evolutionary hypothesis of uniform and orderly development of institutions from the simple to the complex. They then constructed a hypothetical evolutionary scheme of institutional development. Finally they devoted themselves to seeking, rather indiscriminately, concrete information to substantiate this predetermined outline of social evolution. As a general proposition, this school maintained that cultural identities are due to internal causes rather than to external contacts between groups. They thus laid stress upon independent development and upon the fertility of human inventiveness, even though these might be rather sharply conditioned by physical surroundings and certain definite traits of the human mind.

A theory taking the directly opposite view was suggested by Julius Lippert and E. B. Tylor, apprehended by Ratzel, and definitely developed by Fritz Graebner, Sir G. Elliot Smith, Foy, Ankermann, W. Schmidt, W. J. Perry, and Rivers. This group holds that cultural similarities and identities are due wholly to the contact of groups and the resulting diffusion of culture. They question the frequent occurrence of independent invention of implements and customs. In order to maintain their thesis, some of the more extreme members of this school, such as Graebner and Smith, have contended that diffusion existed between areas separated by seemingly impassable distances and insuperable obstacles. In spite of some exaggerations, however, this school has made very valuable suggestions as to the migration of cultures and institutions. Their labors are especially significant in aiding the investigation of the dissemination of material culture.[5]

More satisfactory than a one-sided exaggeration of either the doctrine of independent development or of diffusion is the historico-psychological line of analysis which has been developed by Professor Boas and his students in this country, and accepted to some considerable degree by such anthropologists as Marett and Ehrenreich in Europe. This school has no presuppositions or assumed hypotheses, but aims to investigate the actual facts with respect to the nature and genesis of any particular cultural complex. As a result, they have found that both independent development and diffusion have been involved in creating most cultural situations. The alacrity, however, with which one cultural group will adopt contributions from another varies widely according to the specific phase of culture to be borrowed. Peoples borrow most readily material culture, and most reluctantly religious beliefs and practices.

The cultivation of this critical method has led to a considerable revision of the earlier theories concerning social evolution. It has been shown that many of the alleged identities are merely superficially such, and has further proved that real identities do not always imply similar antecedents or exactly the same subsequent developments. In other words, this method has modified somewhat the older views concerning the orderly and uniform nature of institutional evolution, as summarized in such work as *Ancient Society* by Lewis H. Morgan.[6] Notable diversity seems to be the rule of nature as expressed in social development over the planet. In his *Evolution of Culture*, White has adapted the theories of Morgan to the factual content of anthropology.

It should be evident, then, that no one can be regarded as adequately equipped to deal with the fields of institutional and cultural history who has not mastered the type of material available in such books as Boas' *Mind of Primitive Man*; Wissler's *Man and Culture*; Kroeber's *Anthro-*

---

[5] The diffusionist controversy is still active. The American critical anthropologists are its most severe critics. It has greater support in Europe, where new converts are being made, such as A. C. Haddon, V. Gordon Childe, W. J. Perry, Bronislaw Malinowski, A. C. Hocart, and others. The best brief discussions of the matter are G. Elliot Smith *et al., Culture: The Diffusionist Controversy* (Norton, 1927); and Effie Bendann, *Death Customs* (Knopf, 1930), pp. 1-20.

[6] Cf. B. J. Stern, *Lewis Henry Morgan*, University of Chicago Press, 1931; and Carl Resek, *Lewis Henry Morgan*, University of Chicago Press, 1960.

pology; Lowie's *Culture and Ethnology* and *Primitive Society*; Golden-weiser's *Early Civilization*; Dixon's *Building of Cultures*; Müller-Lyer's *History of Social Development*; Linton's *Study of Man* and White's *Evolution of Culture*. A great service has been rendered to the laudable aim of linking up anthropology with dynamic history by Professor A. L. Kroeber, who, in the last two chapters of his excellent general work on anthropology, has set forth a most suggestive survey of human history from the paleolithic age to contemporary civilization, interpreted in the light of the anthropological approach.

While there have been a large number of philosophical historians, such as Buckle, Draper, Spengler, and Cheyney, who have offered various hypothetical laws regarding human development or decline, the only school that has made any serious contribution to this problem is that of Lamprecht and Breysig, and many feel that their formulations embody in their methodological assumptions much the same errors that characterized the Morganian anthropology. Among the few historians who have mastered the newer technique of cultural anthropology have been Eduard Meyer, J. L. Myres, James Thomson Shotwell, James Harvey Robinson, and F. J. Teggart.

In regard to such matters as race and religion, anthropology has done much to aid the historian in freeing himself from chauvinism and bigotry. A generation ago, even the most objective and distinguished of historians were laboring under the spell of Gobineau, with his grotesque theories of the superiority of the white race and of the alleged Aryan group within the white race. With the possible exception of the obsession of national superiority, which grew out of it in large part, there has probably never been an influence more disastrous to historical objectivity than the mythology connected with the notion of the uniformity and rigidity of race, and the "proof" of the superiorities and deficiencies flowing therefrom.

Modern critical physical anthropology has shown the elusive nature of the very concept of race and the difficulties in discovering any invariable physical criteria of sufficient significance to identify it. It has proved the hopeless intermixture of the subdivisions of the white race, as well as the wide degree of diversity of types within each of these. Moreover, it has shown that, far from there being a lordly and superior Aryan race, there never has been any such thing as an Aryan race of any sort. Further, Professors Boas and A. F. Chamberlain have shown that differences in cultural attainment on the part of various races can be adequately explained without involving the hypothesis of differences in innate racial capacity. They have indicated the difficulty of proving the comprehensive superiority of races when the element of adaptation to the native environment is taken into consideration. In short, the problem of race is at present so vague, confused, and indeterminate that it not only should, but must, be treated cautiously by the historian, whatever psychology and biology may later bring out of the chaos in the way of ascertainable and verifiable facts. The following summary of Charles Darwin's racial ancestry, by Karl Pearson, is an impressive proof of the futility of the racial hypothesis in history:

> Too often is this idea of close association of mentality and physique carried into the analysis of individuals within a human group, i.e., of men belonging to one or another of the many races which have gone to build up our population. We talk as if it was our population which was mixed, and not our germplasm. We are accustomed to speak of a typical Englishman. For example, Charles Darwin; we think of his mind as a typical English mind, working in a typical English manner, yet when we come to study his pedigree we seek in vain for "purity of race." He is descended in four different lines from Irish kinglets; he is descended in as many lines from Scottish and Pictish kings. He has Manx blood. He claims descent in at least three lines from Alfred the Great, and so links up with Anglo-Saxon blood, but he links up also in several lines with Charlemagne and the Carlovingians. He sprang also from the Saxon Emperors of Germany as well as from Barbarossa and the Hohenstaufens. He had Norwegian blood and much Norman blood. He had descent from the Duke of Bavaria, of Saxony, of Flanders, the Princes of Savoy, and the Kings of Italy. He had the blood in his veins of Franks, Alamans, Merovingians, Burgundians, and Langobards. He sprang in direct descent from the Hun rulers of Hungary and the Greek emperors of Constantinople. If I recollect rightly, Ivan the Terrible provides a Russian link. There is probably not one of the races of Europe concerned in folk-wanderings which has not a share in the ancestry of Charles Darwin. If it has been possible in the case of one Englishman of this kind to show in a considerable number of lines how impure is his race, can we venture to assert that if the like knowledge were possible of attainment, we could expect greater purity of blood in any of his countrymen?[7]

Especially is it necessary to be wary of such preposterous products of the neo-Gobinesque literature as Madison Grant's *Passing of the Great Race,* and its crop of debased imitations. This is as bad an expression of the racial fallacy as the Aryan lore of Max Müller and his generation, which was revived by Hitler and the Nazis in Germany.

Physical anthropologists and students of population from the biological standpoint have, however, called attention to the importance of differences of traits and ability on the part of members of the same race and group. This goes to the roots of the problem of democracy. Anthropologists have indicated, moreover, that significant materials for history and culture may exist in such social processes as a differential birth rate, racial mixture, and emigration.

[7] *Scientific Monthly*, November, 1920, pp. 435-36. The ablest history and critique of the race fallacy is F. H. Hankins, *The Racial Basis of Civilization*, Knopf, 1926.

Likewise, anthropology has done much to lessen bigotry in dealing with the problem of the history of religion. The anthropological approach to the analysis of religious origins has shown the remarkable similarity of the raw material of religion, of the forms of reaction to the supernatural the world over among all peoples, and of the psychic behavior patterns associated with religious phenomena. They have made clear the large amount of uniformity in the basic core of religious institutions and ceremonies, however they may differ in the external form of their expression. This technique of analysis has been applied to both Judaism and Christianity by such students as Marett, Robertson Smith, Wellhausen, Hubert and Mauss, Gardner, Conybeare, and others. It has been amply shown that no claim for historical or cultural uniqueness can be supported by the facts in either case. In other words, anthropology applied to the study of religious phenomena gives that long-time perspective and comparative point of view which, in combination, furnish the best possible basis for tolerance and understanding. And if anthropology proves that bigotry and arrogance as between Jew and Gentile, Buddhist, Mohammedan and Christian to be without foundation, how much more absurd appear the quarrels between Catholics and Protestants, Methodists and Presbyterians or Northern and Southern Baptists? Works like Lowie's *Primitive Religion,* Marett's *Threshold of Religion,* and *Sacraments of Simple Folk,* Reinach's *Orpheus,* Carpenter's *Comparative Religion,* Moore's *History of Religion,* and Larson's *Religion of the Occident* furnish the best possible background for one who is to pursue the history of the religious institutions of any particular people.

ARCHEOLOGY AND HISTORY

The remaining phase of anthropology which has been of great service to dynamic history is the so-called "prehistoric" archeology, which has opened up to us that vast period of preliterary history, far longer in duration than the age of written history and nearly as important in basic achievements.[8] Cultivated from the days of Thomsen and Boucher de Perthes to Déchelette and MacCurdy, this is perhaps the most exact and impressive branch of "prehistory." In a very real sense, it serves as the bridge between evolutionary biology and human culture by tracing the material evidence for man's gradual passage from the simian to the distinctly human stage of physique and culture. In the first place, preliterary archeology offers definite proof of the long existence of human life and culture before the origins of written records. Whatever the actual nature of man's derivation or creation, archeology shows that not even the most heroic allegory or exegesis can harmonize the Christian chronology with

[8] See above, pp. 4-8.

the demonstrable existence of human artifacts with an antiquity of several hundred thousand years. In the second place, as has been made clear above through the brief catalogue of the cultural contributions in the preliterary period, archeology produces an impressive exhibit of the cultural equipment of man at about the time usually assigned to the creation of Adam, an equipment which was not greatly extended in the material realm until the Industrial Revolution. It is prehistoric archeology, then, which has supplied, for the most part, that type of information which actually makes anthropology the "threshold of history." Books like those by the Quennells and Harold Peake on everyday life in the preliterary ages constitute the ideal popular introduction to the history of society and material culture, and remove, as we have seen, all of the element of mystery and confusion from the "dawn of history."

The contribution of the archeologists to a better understanding of historic eras is far better known. A century ago our knowledge of Oriental history was limited to certain vague and dubious references in the Old Testament, Berossos, Herodotus, Josephus and a few antique chroniclers. Now we have a definite and reasonably complete record of the civilizations of Egypt, Mesopotamia, Persia, Anatolia, Syria, the Aegean, and Crete. The great majority of this invaluable information has been due to archeological excavations. In the case of Crete and the Etruscans, archeology is our main guide since scholars have not fully mastered these languages. While we can rely rather more upon literary sources for classical than for Oriental history, much of our accurate knowledge of Greek history before Herodotus and of Roman history before 390 B.C. depends upon archeological work. One of the best, but perhaps the least known of the services rendered to history by archeology has been the work done on Gallic archeology by Déchelette. This has shown the high civilization of Gaul before Caesar's time, and has rescued Gaul from the obscurity into which it had fallen as a result of the self-interested slanders of Julius Caesar and the contempt of the Teutonic historians. The intelligent approach to the history of western Europe is now found in the investigation of the old Gallic civilization north of the Alps, which endured from the age of the lake dwellers through the days of Clovis, and made innumerable contributions to the cultural and institutional history of Europe.[9] Ellis H. Minns has revolutionized our knowledge of southern Russia in ancient times in his *Scythians and Greeks*. American archeology has given us our extended knowledge of the native Indian culture, though this is of less historic value, because of the intrusion of European cultures and the failure of the indigenous Indian culture to develop extensively thereafter.

[9] See H. E. Barnes, *History of Western Civilization* (Harcourt, Brace, 1935, 2 vols.), Vol. I, chap. xii.

THE NEWER PERSPECTIVE OF HISTORICAL DEVELOPMENT

Perhaps the most impressive and significant result of the exploitation of biology and anthropology in the service of history is the new perspective of historical development, namely, the changes produced by the newer approach to history in our interpretations of the past and the future of man.

The authoritative view of human origins, accepted even by most scholars down to the last generation, was that systematized by Archbishop James Usher in his *Annals of the Old and New Testaments,* published in 1650. It was still further refined shortly after by Vice Chancellor Lightfoot of Cambridge, who held that man made his appearance in response to a definite creative act on Friday, October 28, 4004 B.C. at 9 A.M. Man had, thus, a definite providential origin, and his surroundings and equipment were likewise a product of God's labors and foresight.

The perspective and outlook provided for history by biology and anthropology is exactly the reverse. The new viewpoint rests upon the concept of the vast period of demonstrable existence of man on the earth and the far greater antiquity of his prehuman ancestry. The biological improvement and cultural progress of man have both been a gradual development. As we retrace the steps of human and social evolution we do not come upon Paradise but upon a bestial state. Without denying cases of definite retrogression in the past and without entering into the debatable problem as to the physical betterment of the race, there is no doubt of the possibility of infinite cultural and institutional improvement, if we are ever able fully to exploit the potential resources of the human intellect. Instead of the depressing orientation of orthodoxy, we may substitute a dynamic and optimistic view of history, though it is impossible to defend successfully any teleological interpretation or to hold that the planet may not at some time be snuffed out of existence by a slight cosmic disturbance, readjustment or new equilibration.

Down to some forty or fifty thousand years ago cultural progress was paralleled, and probably accelerated, by biological development, but there is little evidence of any biological and neurological improvement since the time of the appearance of the Cro-Magnon type (homo sapiens). Consequently, human progress has become more and more dependent upon advances in culture and ideas. We have come to rely more definitely on nurture and less and less on nature, though this in no way implies a disbelief in the potency of superior human types or in the efficacy of the eugenic program, if actually introduced. As to the possibility of artificially accelerating human progress and cultural achievements, there is no doubt about our power to improve our material culture. Our achievements since the Industrial Revolution in this regard have been stupendous beyond comparison. The great problem, as Veblen and Ogburn have well stated, is whether we can secure anything like a parallel improvement of the institutional aspects of our social heritage or whether civilization will perish because of a fatal disparity between our technology and our social institutions.

The historical orientation gives us, however, some considerable ground for patience in attempting to work out institutional improvements. The recognition of the long and tedious process of reaching our present state may well act as a safeguard against too great pessimism about the apparent slowness of contemporary amelioration and reform. We are moving more rapidly in most ways than ever before, even though there is no certainty that we are going in the right direction or rapidly enough. No civilization has long been able to stagnate safely. Progress or decline seems to be the law of nature. The one menacing element in our present situation—which did not exist earlier—is the potency of our new technology for human and cultural destruction. If war can be averted until our intelligence has had more opportunity to play upon the complex problems of today, we may be able in time to bring our institutional life up to something like the plane of efficiency that now characterizes technology.

The new historical perspective also furnishes a vastly more satisfactory basis for considering the problem of progress than that possessed by writers like Vico, Turgot, Kant, and Condorcet, who first developed the foundations of our modern doctrines of progress in the eighteenth century. Not only were they ignorant of modern biology, psychology, and social science, but they also were denied a knowledge of the slow development of human culture in the million years before Adam. Nor could they fully forsee the marvelous advances in science and technology that have come about since their day. Modern anthropology, history, and the advances in natural and social science have for the first time furnished the basis for at least a tentative theory of progress, though it must be frankly admitted that the advances in certain lines of culture have been far more notable and demonstrable than in others. And of course, all criteria of progress are to a certain degree subjective.

HISTORICAL CHRONOLOGY AND PERIODIZING HISTORY

The history of historical chronology is itself an interesting phase of the history of history. This has already been described and can be touched upon but lightly in this place.[10] Down to the time of the Christian Fathers, there was little general interest in chronology because even the his-

10 See above, pp. 12-16, 117, 133.

torians had generally failed "to discover the past." As a matter of fact, as Professors Webster and Shotwell have made clear, it was the priest rather than the historian who discovered time and the calculation of dates. The great majority of historical writing down to the Christian period had been contemporary history, or else the references to the past were vague and inexact from the chronological standpoint. While the historian is today able to construct a passable chronology of oriental history from the regnal lists and other court records, these peoples themselves possessed no systematic historical chronology. The Greek historians never worked out more than the most elementary chronology, and this not until Timaeus, about 300 B.C., introduced the method of determining it by reference to the Olympiadic years. The Romans were ultimately more successful in devising a fairly practical chronology, dating their events on the basis of the alleged founding of Rome in 753 B.C. But this system quite obviously made no effort to carry the historian's vision over the broad sweep of time back to the dawn of history, though Nepos did initiate the process of preparing comparative chronological tables.

Grotesque as was the patristic chronology, it did have the merit of attempting to work out a scheme which would encompass the totality of historic time. To be sure, the Christian hypothesis of the creation of man at a period not more remote than six thousand years before Christ was pathetically inadequate for the attainment of this objective. The selection of Hebrew history as the basis of comparative chronological tables, moreover, gave an absurdly exaggerated place to the history of Jews and distorted the perspective of Oriental history, but at least the Christian chronographers sized up the problem involved in the chronology of the past. From that time to our own day students of historical chronology have been occupied chiefly in rendering more exact this chronology laid out by Julius Africanus, Eusebius and Jerome, these labors sometimes taking the form of the effort to be more specific, as in the case of Usher and Lightfoot, or more scientific and reliable, as in the case of scholars like Scaliger and Clément.

In general, all types of historical chronology down to our own generation have been miserably inadequate and misleading. The criteria have been highly subjective, usually based upon some special religious or national episode, whether it be the birth of Christ, the Hegira or dynastic mutations in the Far East. None of these have any such objectivity or universal cultural validity as to make them suitable for the chronology of world history. Even more serious is their invariable inadequacy from the standpoint of the time element. All are notoriously modern or recent in their point of departure, 6000 B.C. being the most ancient date allowed for the creation in even the most expansive of the orthodox chronologies.

A reconstruction of the chronology of human advance on the basis of biological and anthropological knowledge would fall into something like the following form. The most general background of history is the astronomical, which reveals the enormous extent of the cosmos, and the insignificance of the size and past existence of our own planet. This is doubtless at once the most impressive and the most indeterminate phase of the background of human evolution. Then come the geological ages in the development of the earth, the period before the origin of life doubtless being far longer in extent than that since the beginnings of primordial living matter. Since the origins of life we have a guide in the record afforded by paleontology, which covers a period so long that no cautious geologist will venture to express it in terms of years, but must run to more than a billion. Very late in terms of geological time, in the Tertiary period, man emerged about five million years ago.

From this time onward we have at our disposal the chronology worked out in preliterary archeology from Thomsen to Mortillet, Déchelette and MacCurdy. This is divided into the Stone Age, with its subdivisions of eolithic, paleolithic and neolithic, each with elaborate and awesomely christened subperiods; and the Metal Age, running through copper, bronze, iron and steel periods. The chronology of the Stone Age is being drastically revised. The beginnings of the eolithic go back more than two million years, of the paleolithic more than a million, and of the neolithic to at least fifteen to twenty thousand. The copper age may have begun in Egypt as early as 4000 B.C. The bronze age proper appears in the Aegean around 2600 B.C. The iron age was initiated by the Hittites in Anatolia about 1350 B.C., and by the peoples of Hallstatt in Austria about a century later. The iron age may be said to embrace western civilization from the fourteenth century B.C. to the Industrial Revolution, which produced the true age of steel, with all of its implications and ramifications. Perhaps the most fundamental periodization of the history of mankind since the beginning of the metal era would be that of: (1) the pastoral and agrarian age, characterized primarily by psychological and cultural provincialism, stagnation, and repetition, which dominated society down to the coming of the Industrial Revolution; and (2) the dynamic contemporary era of capitalism, industrialism, and urban civilization.

Yet it will be easily perceptible that this reasonable summary of the newer and more comprehensive chronology is but a partial and incomplete one, as it lays stress primarily on material culture. Here is where the greatest progress has been made and where changes and developments are most readily detected and demonstrable. It is quite evident that for certain other phases of cultural evolution quite another scheme of periodization would be essential, even though the one offered above might include more characteristic aspects of the mutations of civilization than any other. Further, most specific historical dating is still based upon the event arbitrarily selected by Dionysius Exiguus and Bede, namely, the birth of Christ. While this will probably serve for practical purposes as the well as any other, the special reasons for utilizing it, as they appeared to medieval writers, have ceased to be regarded as valid by most progressive historians. A more logical date would probably be 4236 B.C., the supposed date of the adoption of the Egyptian solar calendar and the earliest verifiable date in the history of mankind. Back of this we can never expect any dating more exact than culture periods, ages, eras, and eons.

It should be clear enough to any thoughtful person that these new conceptions in regard to chronology have a revolutionary bearing upon the older conventional efforts in the way of the periodization of history. Our present mode of historical periodization is one which took its origin in a wholly arbitrary and accidental way, and possesses no valid grounds for its triumph or continuance. To the Christian Fathers there had been but two important periods in human development: (1) that of the unspeakable paganism between the creation of Adam and the birth of Christ, alleviated only by the shining exception of the divinely guided Jewish culture; and (2) the glorious age which dawned with the coming of the Savior. This conception of periodization was continued during the medieval period, largely because the work of Orosius, who had done the most to fix this division in the European cultural heritage, remained the approved manual of universal history until the world history of Sabellicus was produced during the age of Humanism. In the writings of Otto of Freising one discovers a combination of the outlook of Orosius with some faint perception of the significance of the period which separated Otto from the Augustinian age. But Flavius Blondus was perhaps the first to think of the Middle Ages as a somewhat distinct period, characterized by the rise of new states in northwestern Europe following the decline of Roman power. Jean Bodin divided human history into the Oriental, Mediterranean, and North European stages. It seems that our conventional present-day trilogy of ancient, medieval and modern history is due primarily to the influence of a Dutch Humanist, Christoph Keller [Cellarius].[11]

The childish inadequacy of this periodization is evident to any thoughtful historian. In the first place, it ignores more than nine-tenths of the period of human existence upon the planet. In the second place, there are no such general cultural synchronisms among the peoples of the earth as will allow of a definite periodization of universal history. A comparison of the state of culture in Egypt, Mesopotamia, India, China, Britain, and California in 4000 B.C. will show the great diversity of cultures included

---

[11] See above, pp. 16, 172.

under a single arbitrary temporal synchronism. A further *reductio ad absurdum* would be afforded by comparing the civilizations of Aix-la-Chapelle and Constantinople in A.D. 800, or of England, Russia, and China in A.D. 1825. In the third place, such a scheme is inadequate even for the periodization of a single state, as one can readily observe by comparing the culture of Germany in A.D. 500 with that of the court of Emperor Frederick II—both falling in the so-called "medieval period."

If we are to retain these old terms and categories, we must extend their scope to cover a far broader sweep of years. In a general way, we might say that ancient history would seem most logically to include the period from the origins of man to the close of the paleolithic age; medieval history the neolithic age; modern history the era from the age of metals to the Industrial Revolution; and contemporary history the period since the Industrial Revolution. But it is a question as to whether we need to hold at all to the older nomenclature. Further, it is certain that all scientific periodization in the future will need to be highly pluralistic, discriminating, and specialized. In certain phases of culture, like technology and economic institutions, there seems to be a definite pattern of accumulation and progress. But art and religion appear to obey no such formula, and there will continue to be wide divergences between the cultures of the various states of the world. Hence, it would seem that the periodizing of the future will need to be confined to some one definite type of cultural development in a single state or culture area.[12] This may produce pedagogical confusion, but it will be productive of greater historical accuracy and discrimination. The suggestion of Lamprecht that we should give up the old methods of periodizing and adopt one which is founded upon the succession of dominant types of collective psychology has in it much to commend it to the historian, whether or not he accepts as valid Lamprecht's own proposal for socio-psychological periodization. Finally, of course, the conception of the continuity of history challenges any plan for the arbitrary periodization of history.

GEOGRAPHICAL FACTORS IN HISTORICAL DEVELOPMENT

The German philosopher Herder suggested that human history is essentially the changing expressions of *Geist,* as diversified and modified by external surroundings. Of the latter the physical environment is the most important. But historians fell under the influence of Hegel with his zest for Absolutes and the state and of Carlyle with his notion of great men acting as the instruments of Providence. So history in the nineteenth cen-

[12] Cf. Lewis Mumford, *Technics and Civilization* (Harcourt, Brace, 1934).

tury languished under the spell of constitutionalism, nationalism, and the enchantment of biological episodes and anecdotes. Karl Ritter was scarcely noticed, Buckle was laughed to scorn, and Ratzel largely unheeded. Even in our own day, a scholarly American historian has revealed the majestic migration of *Geist* across the American continent, heedless alike of economic interests and geographic sections.[13] Gradually, however, historians have become conscious that the actions of man cannot be fully understood or adequately described when divorced from their physical setting. We have some notable instances of an increasing appreciation by historians of the significance of the impressive body of material being placed at their disposal by the students of physiography and anthropo-geography.

The interest in the relation between geographic factors and social institutions and human culture is almost as old as history itself. The "father of medicine," Hippocrates, a contemporary of Herodotus and Thucydides, apparently contributed the first systematic essay on the subject, incidental to an effort to ascertain the effects of climate and other physical factors on the types and pathogenesis of disease. He ended by discovering reasons why the Greeks, as inhabitants of the "middle climate," were superior to the weaklings of the south and the barbarians of the north. Aristotle confessed his satisfaction with his interpretation, and Cicero indicated how this view really substantiated Roman superiority. Aquinas revived the Aristotelian concepts in the medieval period, and they appeared again slightly later in the writings of Ibn Khaldun (1332-1406), this time enriched by the Muslim knowledge of geography. Bodin showed how geography had conspired with God to make the French a great nation, and offered suggestions as to how its study might aid statesmen in avoiding revolutions. Richard Mead and John Arbuthnot, two English physicians of the first half of the eighteenth century, exploited the new discoveries in physics and meteorology in order to build up interesting, if not convincing, interpretations of weather and climatic influences on man. Montesquieu's classic effort to erect a philosophy of history and a science of jurisprudence upon geographic foundations was based chiefly upon the theories of Arbuthnot and the descriptive material brought together in Chardin's *Travels*. In the first half of the nineteenth century, Karl Ritter, building upon the sound knowledge accumulated as a result of the labors of such explorers as Alexander von Humboldt, founded the science of anthropo-geography in its modern sense. His impulse inspired the work of later systematizers such as Peschel, Guyot, and particularly, Friedrich Ratzel and Elisée Reclus. In addition to the systematic work by Ratzel, Reclus, and later writers, such as Richthofen, Brunhes, Vallaux, Vidal de

---

[13] E. D. Adams, *The Power of Ideals in American History* (Yale University Press, 1913). The latest exponent of a neo-Hegelian view of history is the Italian philosopher, B. Croce. See above, p. 205.

la Blache, Semple and Huntington, many significant contributions have been made to special phases of the subject by Demolins, Cowan, Metchnikoff, Mackinder, LePlay, Geddes, Hahn, Huntington, Ward, Dexter, Hellpach and others.[14]

The bearing of such works upon historical exposition and interpretation is obvious. The anthropo-geographers mentioned above have touched upon well-nigh every environmental factor operating upon human society, and have provided a well articulated picture of the relation between man and nature. Demolins and Cowan have laid stress upon the importance of topography and routes of travel, as well as of natural barriers to invasion and contacts. LePlay and Geddes have analyzed the river-basin as the basis of the natural geographic region in modern industrial society. Mackinder has indicated the importance of strategic geographic position in the history of national expansion and international relations. Hahn and Ward have provided systematic manuals touching upon all phases of climatic influences upon man. Ellsworth Huntington has supplemented their contributions by a daring and original hypothesis of climatic oscillations, with which may have been associated many important historic migrations of peoples and the decline of historic cultures. Hellpach, Dexter, Huntington and Leffingwell have made a beginning in the investigation of the effect of weather and seasonal changes on human energy and activity. Huntington has, in his *Earth and Sun,* set forth the hypothesis of the fundamental unity of solar, climatic and weather influences upon the course of civilization.

In addition to these works on broad geographic influences upon the course of civilization, a number of geographers have devoted themselves to the specific relation between environmental factors and history. Reclus and Fairgrieve have indicated the relation between geography and universal history, a task which has been more recently and far more thoroughly executed by Brunhes and Vallaux, and Lucien Febvre. The significance of the river valley setting in early oriental civilizations has been analyzed by Léon Metchnikoff. Philippson has provided a monumental study of the bearing of the geographical factors in the Mediterranean basin on oriental and classical history. He has been followed in more popular works by Semple and Newbigin. Newbigin has analyzed in detail Balkan geography in relation to Balkan history. Nissen has supplied the classic study of Italian geography. Vidal de la Blache and Brunhes have dealt in great detail with the geographical factors in French history. Mackinder has worked out the best geographical study of Great Britain, while Richthofen, Kretschmer, Partsch, Penck, and Goetz have made notable contributions to the historical geography of central Europe, and Kropotkin

[14] Cf. Franklin Thomas, *The Environmental Basis of Society*, Century, 1925, the best general summary of geographical theories of history.

and others have dealt with the geographic factors involved in the history of Slavonic Europe. In America, the geographic elements in our history have been successfully investigated by Semple, Brigham and J. Russell Smith. Mention should also be made of the helpful contributions of the economic geographers such as Chisholm, McFarlane, Goetz and J. Russell Smith to economic history.

Historians have followed the lead of the geographers in devoting attention to the geographic influences which have shaped the development of specific historic areas or national states. H. B. George and J. K. Wright have made an effort to show the general bearing of geography on history, particularly political and military history. J. L. Myres has presented an interesting and stimulating survey of the geographic basis of the rise of the earliest historic cultures. The historians of oriental antiquity have studied so thoroughly the river-valley environment of these cultures that the Nile and the Tigris and Euphrates have become classic examples of alleged geographic determinism. Curtius and Zimmern have set forth in detail the relation between the geography of the Greek peninsula and the rise and nature of Greek civilization. Duruy provided, a half-century ago, a sketch of Italian geography in its relation to Roman history which has never yet been supplanted. Harnack recognized the geographic factors affecting the spread of Christianity. Beazley has done valuable work on the background of medieval historical geography. Michelet and Jullian described with thoroughness the geographical background of French history. Green supplied the classic survey of the bearing of the physical features of Britain upon English history, while Lucas has shown how geographic factors have influenced the nature and course of British imperial expansion. Riehl indicated in a penetrating manner the relation between Germanic geography and the evolution of German society and culture. Spilhaus has treated the geographical origins of the expansion of Europe and the progress of colonization. With respect to the United States, Payne has described the relation of the physical features to the period of exploration and settlement, Winsor has shown the historic significance of the Mississippi basin, and Hulbert has provided much descriptive detail on the routes of travel utilized in the conquest of the continent. But it has remained for Frederick Jackson Turner and his disciples to work out in convincing detail the relation between the geographic regions of the United States and its sectional and national history. Finally, the German scholar, Helmolt, edited a pretentious universal history, based upon a moderate acceptance of Ratzel's views concerning the relation between geography and history.

In spite of the promising beginnings mentioned above with respect to the recognition of the significance of the physical environment for the historic development of a people, most conventional historians have devoted little attention to geographic factors; indeed, one may doubt if many historians even yet are vividly conscious of their existence or potency. And those who have asumed to give some thought to this subject have scarcely realized that the topographic and economic, not the political, map is the vital one by means of which to discover the operation of geographic factors in historical development. If one were to turn to most modern historical works he would discover twenty political maps to one topographic map. Historical geography to the average history teacher is still little more than "chromatic politics," chronologically considered, with chief interest in the shifts of political boundaries.

Along with the dominating interest in episodes, it is probable that the chief reason for this apathy, if not antipathy, on the part of historians towards geography is the erroneous impression that an interest in geography implies an acceptance of the materialistic doctrine of geographic determinism. The problem is not to be viewed in this light, but rather as a matter of man and nature evolving together. To employ the phrase of Ratzel, every geographical problem must be studied historically, and every historical problem must be studied geographically." The varied geographical influences operate quite differently in the successive periods of technological evolution. Further, as the critical anthropologists of the Boas school have amply demonstrated, there is no possible ground for a belief in complete geographic determinism, beyond such broad considerations as that the costume designs of the natives of the Belgian Congo would scarcely be practicable north of the Arctic circle. There are vastly different cultures existing in approximately the same geographic environment, while highly similar civilizations are to be found in fairly divergent types of physical surroundings. Culture seems to be the dynamic element in history, interacting with many other factors, among the most potent of which are the natural surroundings and physical resources.

While geographical considerations are important for all phases of history, they are of special significance for dynamic social history. Material culture and the attendant social institutions appear to be primarily the outgrowth of the application of a specific technology to the natural resources. Both are indispensable to any flourishing economy. Modern Italy is a good example of a country relatively backward economically, in spite of remarkably proficient technicians. It has lagged because of a lack of mineral resources for a development of the iron and steel industries. Russia prior to 1917 (or 1928) presented the opposite example of industrial retardation due to lack of modern technology to exploit unusually rich mineral resources. In this interplay, technology is the dynamic and geography the latent factor. A threadbare example of the alteration of geographic influences with a transformation of science and technology is the influence of the Mediterranean Sea and the Atlantic Ocean. Once barriers to travel and causes of cultural isolation, they have, since the invention of the art of navigation, first by galley and sail-boat and later by steam-vessels, become major agencies in the development and expansion of civilization from the beginning of the third millenium B.C. to our own day. Likewise waterpower sites, once largely useless because of inaccessibility or remoteness from sea and settled territory, may now be utilized through the generation and transmission of electrical power.

One of the most interesting recent examples of the growing rapprochement between history and geography is the interest in regional geography and sectional history. French geographers, following Vidal de la Blache, have done much to promote the intensive study of natural geographic regions, which mark out the ideal and logical basis for the development of a social and cultural unity. This concept has been appropriated by LePlay's disciples in France and by Patrick Geddes in Scotland as the basis of a suggestive theory of social reform. While many European historians, such as Lamprecht and Schmoller, have analyzed the relation between certain geographic sections and the economic life contained therein, the man who has done most to cultivate this field has been Professor Frederick Jackson Turner. Taking as his key to the interpretation of American history the logical, if novel, thesis that it has been primarily a process of pushing westward a frontier and pioneer society from the Atlantic seaboard to the Pacific, he has shown how this general movement has been diversified by the varied geographic areas traversed. While, in a sense, the development of the United States has been a matter of expanding area and power, it has in another sense been characterized by social, economic, cultural, and political diversity, due mainly to differences in geographical setting and resources. This sectional divergence has been a source of strength and power, through a sort of regional division of labor and coöperation. But it has, at the same time, been a cause of much difficulty in the matter of maintaining political unity and loyalty. It may be predicted that, in the future, historians will turn their attention from exclusive concern with so artificial a unit as the state, and concentrate upon attempts to trace the history of, and interaction between, natural geographic regions and their social and cultural products. And it may be that, in the future, political entities will conform to appropriate and convenient geographic settings instead of being determined according to the arbitrary considerations of dynastic ambition and national pride.

And, finally, to pass from the basic geographic unity in the natural region to the opposite extreme, it may be pointed out that since the expansion of Europe overseas from 1500 onward, and particularly since 1870, world geography has become a subject of ever greater importance to the historian. No one can hope to write intelligently of European expansion unless he is familiar with the natural features and resources of the discovered, colonized or exploited areas. To a certain extent this interest in world geography may be said to have expanded history in space, much as geology, biology and anthropology have extended the scope of its time perspective and chronological orientation.

THE INTERPRETATION OF HISTORY

By the close of the nineteenth century, as we have seen, vast collections of source material had been brought together and the machinery of historical scholarship perfected, as far as it related to the handling of historical information. We have already made it clear how these developments came about. But in most cases the labors of historians had resulted only in the collection of the data of history. The student of history was in a condition not unlike that in which the physicist, chemist, or biologist would find himself if supplied with a vast number of notebooks containing carefully set down records of countless experiments and observations, but without any real attempt to interpret the significance of this mass of material or to derive from it scientific laws of general applicability. The determination on the part of the majority of historians to resist being diverted from the discovery of facts and the narration of successive events was not without some justification a half-century ago. The memory of the grotesque attempts of the philosophers to exploit the facts of history to substantiate their fantastic views of historical development[15] was fresh in their minds and, moreover, the facts upon which any sound interpretation could be based had not yet been fully gathered.

It would, however, betray clouded thinking to hold that this gathering of facts marks the final completion of the task of the historian, no less than it would be for the scientist to contend that his work is at an end when he has tabulated his observations.[16] The careful and painstaking interpretation of historical materials, far from being unscientific and wholly aside from the task of the historian, in reality constitutes the final rounding out of the scientific method in history and gives some meaning and significance to the vast array of assembled facts. This vital fact has been effectively stated by Professor James Harvey Robinson and A. F. Pollard:

> History, in order to become scientific, had first to become historical. Singularly enough, what we now regard as the strictly historical interest was almost missed by historians before the nineteenth century. They narrated such past events as they believed would interest the reader; they commented on these with a view of instructing him. They took some pains to find out how things really were—*wie es eigentlich gewesen*. To this ex-

---

[15] See above, pp. 192 ff.   [16] *Ibid.*, pp. 266 ff.

tent they were scientific although their motives were mainly literary, moral, or religious. They did not, however, in general, try to determine how things had come about—*wie es eigentlich geworden*. History has remained for two or three thousand years mainly a record of past events, and this definition satisfies the thoughtless still. But it is one thing to describe what once was; it is still another to attempt to determine how it came about.[17]

Facts—I make the avowal at the risk of the laughter of pedants—are only a secondary consideration from my point of view, and they will only be used as illustrations. That phrase is perhaps unlucky; at least it has lately caused some innocent merriment. And, indeed, one's facts should be correct; but their meaning is greater than the facts themselves, and it is with the meaning of historical facts that I am now concerned. It is only when we penetrate the outer husks of facts that we can reach the kernel of historic truth. A fact of itself is of little value unless it conveys a meaning. There is a meaning behind all facts, if one can only discover it; but to discover the meaning of facts is commonly the last object at which the writers of textbooks aim. Facts are stated as though their statement were more important than to understand them, as though the end of education were to make the youthful mind a lumber-room of facts, instead of an efficient instrument, trained to perform the duties of life and to discover the features of truth.[18]

As Comte suggested and Professor Shotwell has made clear, the prevailing types of historical interpretation through the ages have faithfully reflected the dominating intellectual interests of the successive eras. The supernatural epics of the ancient Orient were superseded by the mythological and philosophical interpretations of the thinkers of classical antiquity. With the general acceptance of Christianity, the classical mythology was replaced by the dualistic, eschatological and providential conception, derived in part from the Persians, which dominated historical interpretation from Augustine to Bossuet. With the expansion of Europe and its violent shock to the old intellectual order, there arose the critical and rationalistic school of Bacon, Descartes, Voltaire, Hume and Gibbon. On account of its being too far in advance of the intellectual orientation of the times, this tended to lapse into the dualism of Kant and the romanticism and idealism of Herder, Fichte, Schlegel, Schelling and Hegel. We have already noted its reaction on historical writing. The growth of nationalism following the French Revolution tended to give temporary precedence to the political mode of interpretation. But the great transformations which constituted the scientific and industrial revolutions of necessity doomed so superficial a view to an ephemeral existence. The un-

[17] Robinson, *The New History*, p. 62.
[18] A. F. Pollard, *Factors in Modern History* (Knopf, 1928), pp. 2-3.

precedented breadth and depth of modern knowledge and intellectual interests have produced a number of interpretations of historical development, most of which represent the outgrowth of some outstanding development of the last hundred years.

With the growth of modern natural science and the critical attitude in the appropriation of knowledge, the effort to formulate a magnificent and systematic philosophical scheme for the organization and presentation of historical development, such as was devised by Augustine, Otto of Freising, Bossuet, and Hegel, has notably declined. Scepticism of any formal philosophy of history seems to be a necessary accompaniment of our increasing knowledge of the infinite complexity of social and historical phenomena. These grandiose attempts to reduce the course of history to a framework of such simplicity savor too much of the a priori method, now thoroughly discredited.

To take the place of the older dogmatic philosophy of history there have developed what may be called "interpretations" of historical data.[19] These at present differ from the older philosophy of history in the absence of any teleological element and in the rejection of the deductive method. They aim solely to emphasize and bring into higher relief those factors, which, according to the various schools of interpretation, seem to have been most influential in producing the civilizations of the past and of today. It is, in short, the attempt to supplement Ranke's rather aimless search for what occurred in the past by at least an humble effort to explain how the present order came about. Instead of being less scientific than the older program of Ranke, it really constitutes the completion of scientific method in historiography, in the same way that the formulation of the major generalizations and laws of natural science constitutes the logical completion of the task of gathering data by observation in the field and by experimentation in the laboratory.

At present some seven definite schools of historical interpretation are set forth by representatives of the modernized students of historical phenomena, each of which has made an important contribution to our knowledge of historical development. They are in no sense mutually exclusive, but are rather, to a large degree, supplementary. They may be designated as: (1) the personal, biographical or "great man" theory; (2) the spiritual or idealistic; (3) the scientific and technological; (4) the economic; (5) the geographical; (6) the sociological; and (7) the synthetic or "collective psychological." It may be pointed out in passing that, in the main, the conventional type of historian either clings to the outworn theory of political causation, or holds that historical development is entirely arbitrary and obeys no ascertainable laws.

[19] See above, pp. 192 ff. The most complete survey of the main interpretations of history is contained in H. E. Barnes, *The New History and the Social Studies*, Century, 1925.

The best known of these schools of historical interpretation, and the only one to which the conventional historians accord much consideration, is that which found its most noted representatives in the Romanticists, Carlyle and Froude, who claimed that the great personalities of history are the main causative factors in historical development—that history is collective biography. This view is, of course, closely allied to the catastrophic interpretation of the eighteenth-century Rationalists. Perhaps the most distinguished contemporary adherents to this view have been Émile Faguet, W. H. Mallock, Karl Pearson, William Roscoe Thayer, William A. Dunning, Emil Ludwig, Claude Bowers, and Allan Nevins.

A belated offshoot of the idealism of von Schelling and von Schlegel is to be found in the so-called spiritual interpretation of history, which has had its most ardent advocates in Rudolph Eucken, Shailer Matthews, H. O. Taylor and R. W. McLaughlin. Professor Matthews thus moderately and modestly defines this view of history: "The spiritual interpretation of history must be found in the discovery of spiritual forces coöperating with geographic and economic to produce a general tendency toward conditions which are truly personal. And these conditions will not be found in generalizations concerning metaphysical entities, but in the activities of worthful men finding self-expression in social relations for the ever more complete subjection of physical nature to human welfare."[20] Viewed in this sense, far removed from the earlier transcendentalism, this type of interpretation can be said to have a considerable affinity with the "great man" theory and apparently aims to reconcile this doctrine with the critical and synthetic interpretation, under cover of a common theological orientation. Closely conformable to this mode of interpretation are E. D. Adams' attempt to connect the historical development of the United States with a succession of dominant national ideals, the origins and basis of which are not adequately explained, and Croce's effort at a general synthesis and defense of the idealistic interpretation.

The attempt to view human progress as directly correlated with the advances in natural science and technology received its first great exposition in the writings of Condorcet, and was revived by Comte and Buckle. Aside from the attention given to it by students of the history of science, such as Dannemann, Sarton, Duhem, Tannery, and others, this phase of historical interpretation has been sadly neglected by recent historians, though F. S. Marvin, Lewis Mumford, Lynn Thorndike, C. H. Haskins, A. Wolf, A. P. Usher and Charles Singer have shown its real potentialities. It has been emphasized incidentally by Lamprecht, Seignobos, Shotwell, Robinson, and Preserved Smith in their synthetic inter-

[20] Shailer Matthews, *The Spiritual Interpretation of History* (Harvard University Press, 1916).

pretation of history, but it remains the least exploited, and yet perhaps the most promising of all the special phases of historical interpretation. Its adherents claim a more fundamental causal importance than can be assigned to the economic interpretation, in that they contend that the prevailing state of scientific knowledge and its technical interpretation will determine the existing modes of economic life and activities. Even Karl Marx admitted the validity of this contention.[21]

The contributions of the economic school of historical interpretation, which was founded by Feurbach and Marx, and has been carried on by a host of later and less dogmatic writers, such as Rogers, Ashley, Tawney, the Webbs, Hammond, Schmoller, Sombart, Gide, Loria, Veblen, Simons, Beard, Hacker, and Simkhovitch, are too familiar to call for any additional elaboration. In its best and most generally accepted form, this doctrine contends that the prevailing type of economic institutions and processes in society will, to a very large degree, decide the nature of the resulting social institutions and culture. In spite of occasional exaggerations, no phase of historical interpretation has been more fruitful or epoch-making.

Immediately related is the geographical interpretation of history, which began with Hippocrates and continued through the writings of Strabo, Vitruvius, Bodin, Montesquieu and Buckle. It was revived and given a more scientific interpretation in the hands of such writers as Ritter, Ratzel, Reclus, Semple, Brunhes, Vallaux, Demolins and Huntington. Since the days of Ritter few progressive historians have ventured to chronicle the history of a nation without having acquired some knowledge of its geography. The significance of this trend has already been indicated above.

The sociological interpretation of history goes as far back as the Arab, Ibn Khaldun; was developed by Vico, Turgot, Ferguson, Condorcet, Comte and Spencer; and has had its ablest modern representatives in Giddings, Ogburn, Thomas, Hobhouse, Müller-Lyer and Alfred Weber. Giddings admirably described this theory as "an attempt to account for the origin, structure and activities of society by the operation of physical, vital and psychical causes, working together in a process of evolution." As a genetic social science, sociology works hand in hand with cultural anthropology in the effort to explain the repetitions and uniformities in historical causation.

The latest, most inclusive and most important of all types of historical interpretation, and the one which perhaps most perfectly represents the newer history, is the synthetic or "collective psychological." According to this type of historical interpretation, no single category of "causes" is suf-

---

[21] A. H. Hansen, "The Technological Interpretation of History," *Quarterly Journal of Economics*, November, 1921.

ficient to explain all phases and periods of historical development. Nothing less than the collective psychology of any period is sufficiently powerful to dominate the historical development of that age. It is the task of the historian to discover, evaluate, and set forth the chief factors which create and shape the collective view of life and determine the nature of the group struggle for existence and improvement. Perhaps the best summary formulation of this viewpoint is that general intellectual conditions at large will normally determine the prevailing attitude towards science and technology. Science and technology create and control the type of economic institutions. These, in turn, gradually build up a set of "connective" or defensive institutions, taking specific character from underlying economic life. These are social institutions and mores, forms and policies of government, types of legislation and jurisprudence, educational theories, public opinion and expressions of the press, approved modes of conduct, and general *Weltanshauung*. Every age thus has in it both the heritage from the past and the germs of future change, but the most dynamic factor is invariably the intrusion of new ideas through contact with outside cultures. The most eminent leaders of this school of historical interpretation, though with widely divergent antecedents and points of view, have been Lamprecht, Ferrero, Tarde, Lévy-Bruhl, Fouillée, Seignobos, Durkheim, Marvin, Robinson, Shotwell, Becker, Preserved Smith, Randall, and J. K. Hart.

HISTORY AND THE SOCIAL SCIENCES

One of the most promising of the newer developments in the study of history along more progressive lines has been the growing interest on the part of historians in the social sciences, or, as they have come to be more generally known in teaching circles, "the social studies." This has been a natural result of the development of a more dynamic point of view in both history and the social sciences. History cannot safely be ignored by social scientists because of the significance of the problems of genesis for all the social sciences. The history of social institutions, economic processes, the state, law, and prevailing and approved forms of conduct, are among the most vital phases of sociology, economics, political science, jurisprudence and ethics. It should be the function of all valid and worth-while history to furnish ample data on these matters. To be sure, much of the past historical literature has not had this objective in mind, and it has been difficult to utilize or exploit for such a purpose. But we may expect that, more and more, historians will be guided by the knowledge that their labors will be in part futile if they do not illumine the genesis of the various institutions with which we are today familiar.

Likewise, if the historian is to describe the evolution of the leading types of institutions he must have some decent elementary knowledge of the various social sciences which deal with these major institutions. One of the reasons for the futility and irrelevance of most of the dramatic and episodical political history in the past is the fact that historians have been woefully ignorant of even the crude and formal political science which was at their disposal. Otherwise, they would scarcely have wasted their time in spinning out in great detail personal anecdotes and episodes. They would have given attention to those matters which illustrate the development of the various constitutions, organs of government, party machinery and other aspects of political life. This does not mean, of course, that the personal element in descriptive history can ever be wholly ignored, but it does mean that a discriminating selection of personal activities should be made, so that what is described will have some bearing on various forms of institutional life or will illustrate some definite type of personality reaction.[22]

In short, it is as necessary for the historian who is to write intelligently about the history of society, the state, law, or economic life to possess a knowledge of sociology, political science, jurisprudence and economics, as it is to know something of chemistry in order to write on the history of chemistry. The only reason why such knowledge of the social sciences has not been generally recognized as a prerequisite for historical writing is the persistence and prevalence of the notion of the adequacy of rule-of-thumb and common-sense methods in history and the social sciences. Nothing of this sort would be tolerated in the natural sciences. It is at once amusing and unfortunate to note: (1) the insistence by the historian upon intensive training in paleography, diplomatic, lexicography and the principles of internal and external criticism, in the effort to secure accurate texts and narratives, and (2) the co-existent ignoring of adequate training in the only group of studies which can make it possible for the historian intelligently to organize and interpret his materials.

The most striking evidence of a change of attitude on the part of historians with respect to the social sciences came in the appointment of a commission on the social studies in the schools under the auspices of the American Historical Association in 1929. Obtaining a large sum of money from the Carnegie Corporation, the commission carried on an ambitious program of investigation and published a number of daring and suggestive volumes.[23] This stood in marked contrast to the attitude of the historians back in 1903, when they gave evidence of marked hostility to the

---

22 Cf. H. D. Lasswell, *Politics: Who Gets What, When, How* (McGraw-Hill, 1936).
23 See A. C. Krey, ed., *Conclusions and Recommendations of the Commission of the Social Studies* (Scribner, 1934), and the fifteen volumes of special studies by the commission.

social science movement as exemplified by Professor Franklin Henry Giddings' famous address before them, "A Theory of Social Causation."

Psychology was at one time scarcely looked upon as a social science. It was viewed as a study of the mental processes of an individual. It was not long, however, before it came to be conceded that no study of individual mental processes can be complete or satisfactory without a consideration of inter-mental activity, of the interaction of mind on mind in society. This has promoted the growth of a special branch of psychology which concentrates on the relation between minds, namely social psychology.

History may derive from psychology most important information relative to the nature of the motivation, patterns, and controls in human actions and beliefs.[24] The mind is the unifying and integrating factor in the organism and society alike, and it should be obvious that it is impossible for a historian to understand the behavior patterns of men in the past without a knowledge of the general psychology of human behavior. Since there appears to have been no fundamental change in the psychophysical basis of the mind or the basic behavior patterns since the dawn of written history, the psychology of man today will apply to the analysis of past historical personalities and group situations, provided adequate data are available. Nothing is more apparent in conventional historical writing, particularly in biographical writing, than the pathetic lack of a knowledge of technical psychology on the part of even many of the most talented literary biographers, with the result that all too often grotesquely superficial explanations are offered for personal motives and actions. It is probably not an exaggeration to state that the average historical biography is fully as weird as Freud's *Leonardo da Vinci*, though in quite a different way. The influence of psychology on biography is illustrated by the writings of Lytton Strachey, Andre Maurois, Gamaliel Bradford and others. Beyond this matter of a better understanding of personal behavior, psychology in conjunction with sociology indicates how individual action is modified by social settings and contacts, as well as by custom and tradition.

The interchange between history and psychology should be reciprocal and mutually beneficial. History supplies the psychologist with much concrete material illustrative of human action in the past, from the period of savagery to our own day, while the data are almost invariably incomplete, history affords examples of almost every character type which is of interest to the psychologist, and gives at least some slight clue to their behavior patterns under varying conditions. As the sources become more adequate, we may hope that, ultimately, history will serve as a major laboratory for the psychologist.

Inasmuch as men have always lived in groups of greater or less extent

[24] Cf. H. E. Barnes, *Psychology and History* (Century, 1925), for a detailed treatment of this important subject. See also W. L. Langer, "The Next Assignment," *American Historical Review*, January, 1958.

and density, it is obvious that sociology, or the science of the life and activities of men in groups, will have much of value to offer to history.
Sociology attempts to catalogue and analyze the various geographical,
biological, psychological and economic forces which affect the place and
mode of group life. It likewise aims to describe and interpret the results
of this group life in social behavior patterns, folkways and mores, and
the more permanent institutional controls and guides. Embracing, as it
does, both the causes and results of group life, it is the basic social science
and the only one which can hope to give a generalized view of the social
process and of social causation as a whole. Since history, in no small part,
is devoted to describing the behavior of groups in economic, political, military, esthetic and religious situations, it should be apparent that the accuracy and insight of the historian would be materially enhanced by a
knowledge of the elementary principles of sociology.

On the other hand, history can be of the utmost value to sociology in
furnishing it with concrete data concerning both a cross-section of any
given society at a particular time, and the dynamic aspects of social and
institutional change. While many conventional and literary historians
vigorously resent this view of the function of history in regard to sociology,
there can be no doubt that one of its most fruitful services will come to be
the assembling, consciously or unconsciously, of the raw materials of dynamic sociology. And the more accurate and discriminating history becomes in its factual content, the more pertinent its findings will be for sociology and, incidentally, for the illumination and edification of mankind.

Economics, as the science of man's acquisition and utilization of material goods, takes its departure from psychology and sociology. Human
motives, as they function in relation to the wealth-getting activities of
man, can be comprehended properly only upon the basis of an adequate
appreciation of human impulses in general. Likewise, group action for material gain and increased productivity requires for competent analysis an
understanding of the general principles and laws of group action. While
one cannot accept an unqualified statement of the doctrine of the economic interpretation of history, in the sense of complete economic determinism, no sane person can well doubt the great importance of economic
factors in society. In some eras they have apparently possessed a truly determining potency. This seems especially to be the case with the period
since A.D. 1750. An economic interpretation of the rise of modern and contemporary society, while doubtless leaving out many interesting factors,
would unquestionably be closer to the truth than any other. And during
no period in the history of mankind can the influence of the economic
factors in society be ignored or denied.

Such being the case, the historian must treat of economic activities, and
he can hardly hope to do so competently without some acquaintance with

the science of the creation and utilization of material wealth. Particularly is this true of modern and contemporary history. In this field nothing more than a superficial description of our highly complex economic system could be produced by any historian unless he had previously mastered economic theory and institutional economics.

And history is not without its potential services to the economist in putting at his disposal the dynamics of economic development. This is not only true of modern times, but even of the ancient period. For example, the Oriental Institute at Chicago has recently recovered a large body of material on prices and taxes over a long period of Assyrian history which is of real importance for the economist and economic historian. The great contribution of the German school of historical economists, in their reaction against the static dogmatism of the classical school, lay in their insistence upon the relativity and the changing nature of economic institutions. The body of economic theory, which emerges as an explanation and rationalized justification of every economic system, is likewise relative. The older history was guilty of amazing superficiality and oversight in ignoring the economic life of the past, because it was absorbed in the dramatic and cared little for the commonplace things of daily life. Still, much of importance for the economists interested in the genesis of economic motives and institutions is incidentally preserved in the historical documents and narratives that have thus far been produced by Clio's devotees. Unsatisfactory as the available information may be, it is impossible to obtain an adequate perspective for the study of the economic life of the present without the genetic sweep which history alone can furnish. History, moreover, provides the economist in many cases with illuminating examples of the relation between economic and other institutions. The validity of the preceding generalizations was confirmed in the impressive work of Joseph Dorfman, *The Economic Mind in American Civilization.*

Political science, or the science of the state, its organs and functions, must likewise be based upon psychology and sociology. The foundations of political obedience must be discovered through a study of the psychology of subordination and of the habits of leadership and emulation.[25] Institutionalized obedience, as exemplified by the reactions of citizens to the state, also requires the intervention of the sociologist to explain the origin of the folkways and mores that cement this particular cake of custom. And life in political groups cannot be interpreted without an understand-

[25] Cf. C. E. Merriam, *Political Power* (McGraw-Hill, 1934); H. D. Lasswell, *Psychopathology and Politics* (University of Chicago Press, 1930); and *Politics: Who Gets What, When, How?*; Bertrand Russell, *Power: A New Social Analysis*, Norton, 1938; and Thurman Arnold, *The Symbols of Government*, Yale University Press, 1935.

ing of how group life in general has developed and of how the state has gradually evolved out of earlier social institutions.

Historians, even of the conventional political school, have been more willing to admit that political science is of value for their subject than they have been to concede the worth of any other social science. The great majority of the distinguished historians of the last century concentrated their attention upon activities in the political realm. Few, however, were adequately grounded in systematic political science. Only the institutional, legal and constitutional historians, like Waitz, Brunner, Flach, Viollet, Maitland, Vinogradoff, and Adams, were really concerned with tracing the history of political processes. The majority simply contented themselves with a narration of episodes in the careers of politicians or diplomats. The scientific political historian of today recognizes, however, that it is a naïve procedure to attempt to deal with the history of political institutions without first learning the nature of fundamental political principles and the basic forms of political institutions. Likewise, the historian, because of the long duration of the political obsession, can furnish the political scientist with rather more genetic data than he can put at the disposal of any other social science. But, unfortunately, much political history written in the past was so highly dramatized, episodical, and anecdotal that most of the vast detail available is of slight practical service.

What has just been said of political science applies equally to jurisprudence, for law is but the expression of the social will as conveyed through the state. Since much of the writing of the conventional political historian concerns legislation, he can scarcely afford to remain ignorant of the science of law, while the student of jurisprudence can escape the sterility of the natural law and analytical schools only by grasping the significance and mastering the content of the genetic approach.

Finally, with respect to ethics, while it is no longer regarded as the function of the historian to follow the precedent of Tacitus, Schlosser, and Lord Acton in passing sharp judgments upon historic characters, on the basis of highly personal and subjective ethical dogmas, it is desirable that historians should know something about the processes whereby standards of human conduct are evolved and enforced. Unfortunately, ethics has no such status of assured achievement as a science as that to which psychology, sociology, economics, and political science can lay claim. Almost without exception, all that has passed for ethics in the past is nearly worthless, simply because the prerequisites of any reliable ethical science in biology, ethnography, psychology, and sociology did not exist. What pretended to be a science of conduct was merely a priori philosophizing and guess-work, in most cases the rationalized defense of the bigotry, biases, and complexes of the particular writer. A new era is beginning, however, and in such works as those of Letourneau, Ratzel, Sumner, Westermarck, Hobhouse, Kropotkin, and others, which supply illuminating ethnographic material on the variety and genesis of moral codes; in the attempt to base ethical theory on the facts of biology, psychology, and sociology by Stephen, Duprat, Ellis, Dewey, Hayes, Groves, Givler, Tufts, Drake and others; and in the attack upon the transcendental and puritanical codes by Shaw, Mencken, Joad, Aldous Huxley and their disciples, there is foreshadowed the dawn of a science of conduct, with which the historian will do well to keep himself in touch.

The historians have supplemented the ethnographers in supplying concrete information concerning the various forms of conduct which have prevailed among mankind, though the services of the historians in this connection have been less notable than might easily have been the case. They have rarely been interested in manners and customs, and when they have treated of moral conduct they have not usually been objective, but have judged it by some artificial standard, instead of giving an unemotional exposition. Further, the historians have too often followed the Protestant and Puritan *Ethik* in viewing morality as solely a matter connected with sex. Yet, in works like those by Lecky, Myers, McCabe, and others, valuable material has been assembled, not seriously warped by Christian ardor. There are innumerable contributions by historians to the history of conduct in special periods and areas, even if there has been little conscious effort among historians to develop a special department of history devoted to the evolution of various forms of conduct in relation to sex, property, recreation, and general orientation towards life.

NEWER METHODS IN THE TECHNIQUE OF TEACHING AND STUDYING HISTORY

While the major aspect of the progress in historiography since Ranke has consisted in the rise of a far broader perspective, there have been important improvements in the earlier and traditional lines of development. In the first place, while little has been achieved in scholarship that was not implicit in the methodological system of von Ranke, there have been important improvements in both the critique and the technique of historical methodology since von Ranke's time. The fundamental principles of historical criticism have been refined and systematized in the admirable works of Bernheim, Wolf, Langois and Seignobos, and others, so that the beginner may now have at his disposal an extended discussion of historical scholarship and methodology. Elaborate bibliographies of the historiography of the various countries have been prepared by Paetow, Langlois, Molinier, Monod, Dahlman-Waitz, Gross, Williams, and Channing, Hart and Turner. These are supplemented by current lists of the new works which appear, published in the various technical historical journals, and the student is thus enabled to keep thoroughly abreast of the literature in his field.[26] Remarkably thorough and accurate guides to the vast collections of sources of national and ecclesiastical history, which were gathered during the nineteenth century, have been prepared by Potthast, Chevalier, Gross, and others, and the modern student may thus locate in a few minutes in any great library sources which might have necessitated months of fruitless searching in any earlier generation. Again, archives, public and private, have been opened more freely to historical scholars since the first World War—a real revolution in regulations having taken place since 1918. Guides to these archives have in some cases been carefully prepared. Nor should one neglect to point out the great contribution to efficiency, expedition and accuracy in historical investigation which has come about from the general introduction of card catalogues, filing systems, loose-leaf notebooks and elaborate schemes for indexing and cross-reference.[27] Even more sensational has been the provision of new methods of reproducing documents, such as making photostats and microfilming. This has made possible the wide circulation, distribution, and storing of documents which are not security risks.

Just as important as the advances in bibliographic and other mechanical aids has been the great extension and improvement of the teaching profession in the field of history. Under the guidance of trained scholars, the members of graduate historical seminars, though of mediocre literary talent, may contribute more exact knowledge to the field of history in their abstruse and esoteric dissertations than was contained in many volumes of the older and popular literary history.

In general, there has been little change in the external forms of historical instruction in the last generation. The lecture and seminar methods are still the most widely used for all types of advanced instruction. Perhaps the most significant innovation has been the introduction of the so-called "project method," which is based upon the salutary notion that the teaching of the history of the past shall be directed primarily toward indicating its bearing upon the leading problems of today. While capable of exaggerations and distortions, this method, when cautiously used, gives more promise of making the study and teaching of history vital than any other which has thus far been proposed. It has, however, made little progress in the universities and colleges, where the professors have usually been able to resist any threat to make history less dignified by rendering it more practical and serviceable in the education and guidance of mankind.

While there can be no doubt that the science of history has profited enormously through the organized activity and coöperation which has

[26] See Coulter and Gerstenfield, *Historical Bibliographies*.
[27] Jacques Barzun and H. G. Graff, *The Modern Researcher*, Harcourt, Brace, 1957.

been promoted by university historical instruction, it has, like all forms of organized and professionalized effort, a negative and deplorable side. Particularly important in this respect is the operation of this system in retarding the progress of newer concepts as to the nature and purpose of history, and the modes of teaching it most successfully. This situation is mainly due to the fact that the great revolution in the attitude towards history has come since the older historians now teaching received their training, and has for the most part been the work of younger men.[28] But these younger men must perforce teach in departments presided over in many cases by historians with views much more venerable and antique than those harbored by their younger and more progressive subordinates. In many cases the latter will successfully repress their unorthodox convictions about historical method and interpretation.

A frequent expedient utilized further to hamstring progressive instructors is close supervision of the type of courses which they are allowed to offer, in this way making well-nigh impossible introduction of much novel material. While time will ultimately remedy this situation, it is not without significance that perhaps a majority of men who have shaped and are shaping the new history are not now teaching in university departments of history. Another phase of the technique of impressing upon progressive young historians the virtues of "solidity" and "stability of viewpoint" is the arrangement that, in the award of official honors in historical associations, preferment and precedence shall obviously and ostentatiously go to those whose notions on the subject of history have been egregiously respectable, and distinguished by a fine sense of propriety and eminent good taste.

The situation in regard to history, is, of course, not in any sense unique but is characteristic of university instruction in general. Here, since the days of Abelard, formal success has normally gone to the conformist with no troublesome new ideas, or to the potentially progressive person whose good sense and discretion have led him into efficient practice of the remarkably pertinent and helpful precept lifted by Descartes from Ovid, *bene qui latuit bene vixit* (loosely but fairly translated as "He lives best who hides his ideas most effectively").

MODERN TECHNOLOGY AND HISTORICAL NOVELTIES

Among the most striking and colorful of the recent developments in the field of history are those which have grown out of various aspects of the new technology. Most of them relate to the provision of a more com-

---

[28] This statement is made, of course, with qualifications and exceptions. Some of the older men in the profession, such as Robinson, Shotwell, Carl Becker, Breasted, and the like, have shown more interest in the new history than some of the newcomers in the field.

prehensive and rapid portrayal of current historical events. They are associated especially with the modern daily newspaper, the moving pictures, especially the newsreels, and the radio.

The modern newspaper presents an unusually comprehensive survey of current history, local, national, and foreign. The facts are set forth for readers in an amazingly short time after their occurrence. Within twenty-four hours the contemporary newspaper reader may learn more about important world affairs than would have been known a year later at the time of the American Civil War. The recent invention of radio-pictures supplements the verbal news by immediate visual presentation of events and personal figures.

This journalistic information is relatively reliable, in spite of the speed demanded on the part of correspondents and the selective process through which the news passes before it is put down in print in newspaper columns. These remarkable achievements are made possible chiefly through the marvellous technological efficiency of modern printing, the facilities for the rapid transmission of information, and the work of well-organized news-gathering agencies like the United Press, the Associated Press and the like, which have experts in all parts of the world ready to pounce like a hawk on every possible item of news. Through the medium of the modern newspaper, then, the historian of current affairs is supplied with an instrument which is complete and efficient to a degree which his prototype of a century ago could not even have imagined in his most expansive moments. If he is too busy or indolent to sort out this information for himself, there are weekly journals which will do it for him, incidentally interpreting the current news.

Newspaper files are coming to be regarded as among the richest collections of raw materials for the historian of periods since the newspaper became an important news-gathering agency. This brings up the interesting question of the relative reliability of journalism and formal history. "Mere journalism" and "mere journalist" are favorite epithets of the historian with respect to newspaper products and personalities. Yet it is probable that the better journalistic writings are as reliable as the historical narratives which are constructed out of them. The trained journalist in the field is unusually well fitted to gather, organize and transmit his materials. He has had long experience in rapid observation and accurate recording. He has background, insight, and specialized technique for his task. His product, under normal conditions, is likely to be a faithful reproduction of the events. Even in the midst of popular hysteria like World War conditions, the journalist is not likely to be more at the mercy of his emotions than the professional historian.

These journalistic products are ultimately bound up and placed in library files. After a generation or so, the professional historian comes along and settles down to work. He turns the pages, now yellow with age, copies and paraphrases. In due time, he has a mosaic compounded of the work of hundreds of reporters. The historian possesses the advantage of better perspective on the events recorded in the newspapers, and he can check and compare the reports submitted in the various newspapers. Yet, his results cannot, in the end, be more accurate than the sources which he has used.

Over against the better perspective of the historian there are a number of advantages possessed by the original reporters. They witnessed the events at first hand. They were specialists in the art of witnessing events. They lived at the time and were thoroughly acquainted with the whole setting of the events described in their dispatches. The historian comes on the scene far later and is relatively out of psychic touch with the peoples and events involved. He can never have more than a secondhand and remote contact with the issues, events and peoples he is seeking to describe. In these ways, he is at a great disadvantage when compared to the trained journalist on the spot. His superior long-time perspective can hardly offset these disadvantages. Therefore, it is a moderate statement to hold that history based on journalism can hardly be as reliable as the better contemporary journalism itself.

The excellence of the journalistic technique can be further illustrated by reference to journalists turned historians. Such a case is that of Professor Allan Nevins of Columbia University. For years he was a distinguished journalist, but was not taken especially seriously by professional historians. He produced several impressive historical books and was then drafted into the professorial ranks, whereupon he came to be regarded, and rightly, as a leading light of the historical profession. It is obvious that he remains as much of a journalist, so far as training is concerned, in a professorial post at Columbia University as in a journalistic position on the *New York World*. The example of Professor Hans Kohn is another case in point.

Supplementing the newspaper is the great agency for speedy presentation of current historical events in visual form, the newsreels of the moving picture world. They bring current events before millions each week in colorful fashion, with a minimum of intellectual effort on the part of the observers. Professional historians are now turning to the moving-picture to present historical pageants, not merely reviews of current events but carefully staged reproductions of notable occurrences long past.

Of late years, the radio has entered prominently into the field as an instrument for the dissemination of news in speedy fashion. It has served to render world news almost instantaneous. This is well illustrated by Admiral Byrd's flight across the South Pole in 1930. The *New York Times,* through its own radio station in New York, knew of Byrd's exploit as soon as it was known to his own associates. It picked up Byrd's message from his plane when it was being sent to his base station. The news bulletins given many times daily by radio stations bring local and world events to many millions without the necessity of their leaving their homes. In the "March of Time" and similar radio programs not only current history is presented, but also reproductions of historical events in the past. Hundreds of millions listened in on the coronation of George VI and sixteen years later more millions saw his daughter crowned by means of television. The American Historical Association has recently sponsored a radio program. It is interesting to observe in this connection that history, which began as oral narratives in the folklore of early peoples, is now returning in part to transmission by word-of-mouth methods. When moving pictures and sound recordings of future crossings of the "Rubicon" are made, we may be able to go further than we can now in preserving "historical facts" and in making it possible for historians to reproduce them.[29]

In 1930, Karl Bickel, then head of the United Press, made the following prediction: "The twist of the dial and the throw of a switch will enable you, in your sitting room, to see and hear the Kentucky Derby, to have a better vision of a great prize fight or athletic contest than even the boxholders, to range the world, attending the theatre or opera, visiting important banquets, sitting in the Congress in Washington, or viewing an airplane meet in Africa."[30] When this forecast was made it seemed as fantastic as a trip to the moon. Today, this and much more have become a commonplace in every household owning a television set.

Technology has also revolutionized the mode of recovering a knowledge of ancient civilizations. The Potassium-Argon technique makes it possible to date remains as far back as two million years.[31] Airplane surveys are made prior to starting important excavations. Indeed, promising excavation sites are even discovered through airplane investigations. When excavations begin, the steam-shovel has superseded the spade for all but the closer and finer work. Much more rapid excavation is thus brought about. Then airplane pictures may be made of excavated ruins, thus making possible the portrayal of archeological achievements in a much more complete and efficient manner than ever before. The last historical project of the late James Henry Breasted was the gathering and presentation of an aërial panorama of the archeology of the ancient Near East.

Therefore, if technology has created a whole new social world for the historian to deal with, it has also rendered great aid to historians in the task of handling many historical problems, from the ancient civilizations of Mesopotamia and Yucatan to the latest happenings in current history.

[29] See above, pp. 267-69.

[30] Bickel, *New Empires* (Lippincott, 1930), p. 43.

[31] For these sensational new methods of dating early remains, see L. J. Briggs and K. F. Weaver, "How Old Is It?" in *National Geographic Magazine*, October, 1958; and G. H. Curtis, "A Clock for the Ages: Potassium-Argon," *Ibid.*, October, 1961.

SELECTED REFERENCES

Robinson, *The New History.*

Shotwell, *An Introduction to the History of History,* chap. xxvii.

H. E. Barnes, *Historical Sociology,* Philosophical Library, 1948.

————, *The New History and the Social Studies.*

H. E Barnes and Howard Becker, *Contemporary Social Theory.* Appleton-Century, 1940.

————, *Social Thought from Lore to Science,* Vol. II.

E. C. Hayes, ed., *Recent Developments in the Social Sciences.* Lippincott, 1927.

W. F. Ogburn and Alexander Goldenweiser, *The Social Sciences.* Houghton Mifflin, 1927.

Pendelton Herring, *The Social Sciences in Historical Study.* Social Science Research Council, 1954.

H. M. Parshley, *Science and Good Behavior.* Bobbs-Merrill, 1928.

E. P. Cheyney, *Law in History and Other Essays.* Knopf, 1927.

Dray, *Laws and Explanations in History.*

Patrick Gardiner, *The Nature of Historical Explanation.* Oxford University Press, 1957.

Harlow Shapley, *Of Stars and Men.* Beacon, 1958.

White, *The Evolution of Culture.*

Jacques Barzun, *Race, A Study in Superstition.*

R. G. Hoxie *et al., A History of the Faculty of Political Science, Columbia University.* Columbia University Press, 1955.

B. F. Hoselitz, ed., *A Reader's Guide to the Social Sciences.* Glencoe Free Press, 1959.

Paul Tillich, *The Interpretation of History.* Scribner, 1936.

Muzzey, *Essays in Intellectual History Presented to James Harvey Robinson.*

V. F. Calverton, ed., *The Making of Man.* Modern Library, 1931.

Goldenweiser, *History, Psychology and Culture.*

F. H. Hankins, *The Racial Basis of Civilization.* Knopf, 1926.

MacCurdy, *Human Origins.*

Grahame Clark, *World Prehistory.* Cambridge Univ. Press, 1961.

R. V. D. Magoffin and E. C. Davis, *The Romance of Archeology.* Holt, 1929.

Stanley Casson, *The Progress of Archeology.* McGraw-Hill, 1935.

C. R. Knight, *Before the Dawn of History.* McGraw-Hill, 1935.

J. C. McDonald, *Chronologies and Calendars.* London, 1927.

Franklin Thomas, *The Environmental Basis of Society.* Century, 1925.

Seligman, *The Economic Interpretation of History.*

R. W. McLaughlin, *The Spiritual Element in History.* Abingdon Press, 1926.

C. A. Beard, *A Charter for the Social Sciences in the Schools.* Scribner, 1932.

————, *The Nature of the Social Sciences.* Scribner, 1934.

P. V. N. Myers, *History as Past Ethics.* Ginn, 1913.

R. M. Tryon, *The Social Sciences as School Subjects.* Scribner, 1935.

Paul Klapper, *The Teaching of History.* Appleton, 1926.

XV

THE NEW HISTORY AND THE FUTURE OF HISTORICAL WRITING

INTRODUCTORY CONSIDERATIONS

WE shall endeavor in this chapter to present a conciliatory appraisal of the new history, to outline the program implied in its assumptions and aspirations, and to indicate the preparation essential to its cultivation. Whatever the defects in this presentation, such an exercise is valuable, as the new history cannot be successfully cultivated in an aimless or indifferent manner. We must know what we want to achieve and how to secure such results.

The first question, one raised with subtlety and cogency by Professor Carl Becker in his review of the writer's *New History and the Social Studies* in the *Saturday Review of Literature* for August 15, 1925, relates to the actual nature and scope of the new history and to the validity of its claim to novelty. It generally has been held that the new history means a type of historical writing which has abandoned the Freemanesque conception of the adequacy of history as "past politics," anecdotally selected and episodically expounded. It is conventionally presented as a mode of historical exposition which attempts, in the broadest way, to reconstruct the history of civilization in its totality—being, as Professor Robinson expresses it, "all that we know about everything that man has ever done or thought or hoped or felt." As a notion of the scope of the new history, this view is, in a rough, general way adequate and accurate, but even more fundamental has been the triumph of the genetic orientation.

But this revised and more expansive conception of the scope and task of history carries with it by firm implication another equally fundamental requirement: namely, a type of training adequate to allow the aspiring historian to execute the exacting and extensive tasks of his profession with confidence and success. This broader training must consist primarily in such a grasp upon the nature of man and of his relationships with his natural and social environment as will enable one to cope with the difficult problem of reconstructing the divers phases of the history of civilization. He must also be equipped to analyze that institutional evolution which preserves the record of man's gradual conquest of his material surroundings and his ever greater success in organizing the coöperative efforts of the race. In other words, those looking forward to work in the new history must be grounded in biology, anthropogeography, psychology and sociology. They must also be specially trained in the social sciences and in such branches of science or esthetics that are most relevant to the particular aspect of historical writing in which they intend to engage.[1]

We shall discuss in a later section of this chapter the preparation essential to a competent exploitation of the new history, but we will do well to insist at the outset upon the fact that our revised notions of the desirable nature of history not only imply an ambitious extension of the range of the historian's interests. They require also an equally comprehensive expansion of the preparation that is indispensable to any work in this field which is likely to inspire confidence or to possess permanent value. It has been suggested by some that all that is needed to write the new history is a change of heart[2]—that one only has to change his mind to be able to turn from dealing with the genesis of the Holy Alliance or the break-up of the Whig party to an analysis of class-conflicts in antiquity, the history of medieval natural science, a psychoanalysis of Voltaire, the economics of the Continental system, the evolution of modern jurisprudence, or the progress in medicine since the downfall of the Hippocratic lore. It is stated in the Scriptures that no man, merely by taking thought, can add one cubit to his stature. It may be safely contended that it is much more difficult, merely by taking thought, suddenly to transform one's self from a conventional narrator into a cultural or institutional historian. The new history implies both a new program as to the content of history and a new set of qualifications for the practice of history.

So much for the scope of the new history; what about the legitimacy of its claim to alleged novelty? In its implications as a range of historical interests wider than politics and diplomacy, there can be no valid claim for absolute or unique novelty. The first comprehensive historical work, Herodotus' *History of the Persian War*, was, as we have seen, in many ways a contribution to cultural history. In every subsequent age there have been writers whose interest in the past transcended military campaigns and party conflicts, if only to expend itself on the miracles achieved by a saint's femur or the ravages wrought by witches. The chief claim to novelty which the "new history" can make with respect to the scope of its subject matter is the degree to which this broader point of view has gained acceptance in the present age. In previous generations the writers on the history of culture were lonely and often despised individuals. Today, perhaps a majority of the younger historians have seriously embraced the prospectus of the new history, and some of the older exponents of conventional historical writing have capitulated or are showing signs of

[1] The writer has argued this position at length in his *New History and the Social Studies.*

[2] Cf. Becker, *loc. cit.*

weakening morale, something far more significant and more provocative of rejoicing than the conversion of the ninety and nine exuberant youths. The triumph of the evolutionary viewpoint and the genetic attitude, leading the historian to be chiefly interested in showing how the present order has come into being, is, moreover, truly novel and unique. There was little of this in Herodotus. This is the real new history at its best.[3]

In its conception of the preliminary preparation necessary to study and write history, the contentions of the new history are also unquestionably novel. Down to the time of von Ranke, while there were a few writers like Polybius and Mabillon who insisted on special training and qualifications for the historian, it was generally held that literary ambitions and a flowing style qualified any person to attack history in a serious fashion. Von Ranke and his successors declared that one must prepare for historical work by intensive training in the principles of documentary criticism and historical bibliography. The contention that the historian must be thoroughly equipped with knowledge in the social sciences is a much more recent position. The social sciences have only recently arrived at that state where their subject matter is sufficiently reliable to serve as a dependable foundation for historical insight and analysis. The notion that history must rely upon the social sciences as much as upon diplomatic or paleography is a very late discovery indeed. It will probably be ultimately conceded that the most original and novel section of Professor Robinson's revolutionary work, *The New History*—that manifesto of the new historical order—was the chapter, "New Allies of History." The new history, then, is new in the sense of the more general acceptance of a broader set of interests by most historians, and is also novel in its genetic orientation and its recognition that a more extensive preparation is necessary for a competent execution of its tasks.[4]

SOME PHASES OF THE TRIUMPH OF THE NEW HISTORY

The development of the new history seems to have been the product of many different factors and influences. In the first place, there have been a number of writers whose individual interests combined a deep concern with the past and a wider outlook upon it than that afforded by politics, diplomacy and military strategy. With Wilhelm Riehl it was a romantic story-teller's interest in the national past; with Freytag, a dramatist's projection of creative insight into the past of his own country; with Burckhardt, an esthete's appreciation of artistic achievements in the great

---

[3] The theoretical basis of this position is well stated by Professor Teggart in his *Prolegomena to History; The Process of History;* and *The Theory of History;* and by James Harvey Robinson in his *Human Comedy* (Harpers, 1936).

[4] See Barnes, *The New History and the Social Studies, passim.*

epoch of Italian art; with Voltaire, Renan, Draper, and Andrew D. White, the Rationalist's omnivorous appetite for facts relating to the intellectual emancipation of the race; with Green, the craving of a sensitive and cultured soul for a more adequate portrayal of the social basis of his country's greatness; with McMaster, the appreciation by a practical-minded engineer of the engrossing nature of the story of national development as illustrated by the life and interests of all classes.

Another powerful influence was that exerted by the evolutionary hypothesis, particularly the genetic interests of the biologists. As Professor Robinson often stated, it was the biologists who first taught the historians the principle of development and the genetic attitude which must be regarded as the cornerstone of the more vital phases of the new history.[5] The dominating concern of the historian of the new dispensation with how things have come about has been due chiefly to the reaction of the evolutionary philosophy upon the more alert and receptive historical minds. The historical point of view, then, was missed by the historians for three thousand years and had to be supplied by the natural scientists, though Abbé de Saint-Pierre, Turgot and Condorcet in the eighteenth century caught glimpses of a posible science of social change.[6]

This genetic interest in tracing the origins of things came at a time when civilization had been profoundly revolutionized by great scientific, technological and economic transformations, so that indicating the development of culture and institutions could no longer mean merely constitutional history, party development, the genesis of diplomatic entanglements or the genealogy of dynasties. It had to involve such matters as the development of the dynamo, surgical anesthesia, international exchange, radio-activity, syphilo-therapy, mental hygiene, mechanical devices, the factory system, the internal combustion engine, the Bessemer process, the printing press, and a host of other achievements which had never disturbed the thought of the complacent Freeman. In other words, the impulse to find out how the present order had arisen arrived at a time when the prevailing civilization no longer presented itself in the guise of a few gentlemen struggling for economic privilege, political prestige, or the power to amuse themselves at the expense of the poor puppets who constituted the standing armies of despots more or less benevolent. The genetic trend virtually forced an interest in the history of civilization.

[5] It should, perhaps, be emphasized that this "teaching" of the genetic viewpoint by the biologists and other natural scientists was for the most part indirect and unintentional. Few natural scientists have applied the principles of their own discipline to social phenomena. When it comes to social matters, the scientists have rarely been "genetic" in their attitudes; they have all too often been static and reactionary. The late Henry Fairfield Osborn was a conspicuous example of this trend.

[6] See above, pp. 174 ff.

The genetic method of tracing development led thoughtful students to the next and final stage in the evolution of the new history, namely, the effort to interpret historical evolution in such a fashion as to discover what significance, if any, attaches to the mutations of civilizations and the genesis of social institutions. The more up-to-date type of historian no longer hopes to discover the will of God or the ultimate destiny of mankind in the record of the past, as did those who were wont to view history as philosophy teaching by example. Yet it must be conceded that the more significant events in the past are those which have relevance for the guidance of present or future generations. Further, the only real value which history possesses lies in its potential aid in enabling us better to understand, control and redirect our own civilization.

In the work of putting together these various impulses to the formulation and launching of the new history the chief figures have been Karl Lamprecht, Henri Berr, James Harvey Robinson, F. J. Teggart, F. S. Marvin, Arnold Toynbee and Sir J. A. Hammerton.

Lamprecht's system grew out of his interest in cultural anthropology, the psychological approach of Wundt, Comte's attempt at a psychological interpretation of human progress, and his own wide cultural interests, extending from economic evolution to musical history. Whatever one may think of Lamprecht's system and historical formulations, his work was the first to launch on a wide scale the controversy that has finally ended in the definite triumph of the new history.

Henri Berr has not only written learnedly on the theoretical aspects of historical synthesis, but has, as we have seen, also edited a stupendous series—*L'Evolution de l'humanité*—designed actually to achieve this synthesis. His theoretical background is to be found in a sociological view of institutional evolution, a desire to introduce a scientific attitude toward historical causation, the elaboration of a so-called logic of historical synthesis, and a world point of view, making his conception of historical synthesis truly coextensive with a study of the history of humanity as a whole.

Unlike Lamprecht, Berr and Teggart, James Harvey Robinson did not evolve any system of theoretical principles in regard to history. His conversion to dynamic history came gradually and empirically. It would appear to the writer that the explanation is to be found in the fact that he was an unusually thoughtful and intellectually inquisitive individual, and the new history, after all, is little more than thoughtful history. The beginnings of Robinson's secession from conventional history are to be found in his genetic attitude toward the French revolution. This took him ever backward toward the origins of humanity. As he himself expressed it, he moved in the twenty years which followed his initial work as lecturer at the University of Pennsylvania from the slime of modern politics back to the primordial slime out of which life itself was born. Likewise, he was greatly influenced by the biologists' evolutionary and genetic bent. As he came to understand better how thought and culture have gradually developed, he became more interested in the significance of the historical process. This converted him to the view of the primary importance of the interpretation of historical materials. Robinson's undisputed primacy in the movement towards the new history in the United States was due to the popularity of his textbooks, his success as a teacher in one of the great graduate schools of the country, his mild and amiable persuasiveness as a propagandist of the newer attitudes, and the number, loyalty, and persistence of his followers.

Of all the important writers on the newer methods and attitudes in history, no other suffered more from the discrepancy between his merits and his influence than Professor Teggart. Unquestionably the foremost writer in this country, if not in the world, on the theoretical basis of the new history as a science of social change, he has remained practically unknown and without influence outside the circle of his few students. This has been due to his preference to play a lone hand—denying the significance of what most others have done and refusing to associate himself actively with those who have succeeded in establishing the new history.

F. S. Marvin was not a professional historian; he was an enlightened social philosopher and publicist. Yet he has done as much as anybody in England to arouse an interest in the new history and to promote its development. A believer in the reality of progress, the potency of science and technology in human welfare, and the need of peaceful world relations, he founded the Unity Series, which along with his own books, notably *The Living Past*, have greatly stimulated the new history. Toynbee's suggestive program of comparing the rise and fall of civilizations was ruined by his extreme theological premises which made his vast work a theodicy rather than a history. Sir J. A. Hammerton has promoted the new history chiefly as an editor. Most notable is his *Universal History of the World* (1933) in eight volumes, the most impressive publication in the field of the new history in England.

The new history has recently met with a surprising support in Italy. It was foreshadowed by the much-discussed book of Ferrero, *The Greatness and Decline of Rome,* and has received powerful support from the eminent philosopher, Benedetto Croce. The progressive Italian historians were led by Corrado Barbagallo, author of a brilliant history of civilization, and they have as their organ the notable journal, the *Nuova Revista Storica,* launched in 1917.

A PROSPECTUS OF THE NEW HISTORY

It was once held that any one who could supply himself with a quill pen and an ink pot could be a historian if he saw fit to copy some inscriptions from gravestones in a local churchyard or to prepare an essay on Cleopatra to be read before a local sewing circle. There have been thoughtful and progressive historians in our own day who decry the effort to define and demarcate the field of history and who would rest content with urging any one who so desires to jump in and do his level best by tackling whatever historical problem may intrigue him.

It seems to the writer that the correctness of this position can scarcely be conceded unless one is willing to admit that every person who mixes Seidlitz powders is a physician and that all who provide themselves with sharp butcher knives are to be encouraged to go out at once and practice surgery. Even the older and much simpler episodical and anecdotal history suffered from lack of a well-thought-out methodology. The new history will certainly be impaired unless there is a general consensus as to its program and as to the training essential to the execution of its aspirations. It will require as much agreement, unity and coöperation as now exists in the medical, legal, or engineering professions.

The program of the new history with regard to the scope of its interests is by definition all inclusive. It is the recording of everything which has happened in the past. Nothing which has taken place in the past can be ruled out as non-historical in any strict or literal sense. But this does not mean either a sloppy indifference or an inchoate anarchy. The fact that the historian of the newer type admits the historical nature of everything which has taken place in the past, from the incantations of primitive shamans to the cosmetic habits of Solomon's wives, the invention of the steam engine, and the texture of the mattresses which supported Washington's manly form during his slumbers on the way from Virginia to Massachusetts, does not mean that he is equally interested in all of these matters or believes them uniformly important. It is doubtless true that a man is likely to do good work only in a field in which he is interested. If one must be a historian and has an overpowering passion to investigate the evolution of naval strategy in Switzerland he should be encouraged to do so. But he should not be led to regard such an exercise as of equal importance with studies of the Industrial Revolution or with research into the history of contemporary science.

A common-sense attitude must prevail. The relative significance of historical materials is to be determined, in part, by the nature of the period in which they fell, and in part by their bearing upon contemporary life, but in either case practically and immediately by the purpose the writer has in mind.

The two chief tasks of the new history are: (1) to reconstruct as a totality the civilizations of the leading eras in the past; and (2) to trace the genesis of contemporary culture and institutions. In the first of these problems the relative importance of the divers aspects of human culture should be determined by the significance they possessed in the age we wish to reconstruct. In attempting to reconstruct civilization of the age of Pericles the criterion of the importance of events and interests should be the estimates placed upon them by the Periclean age, not by those of the period of the historian. It is this fact which would make it very difficult, if not quite impossible, for a pure, pious, dry, unesthetic, and celibate professor of history in a Kansas denominational college to depict with skill the civilization of the age of Alexander or Augustus. He would be as much shocked by Greek and Roman sex mores as by the total absence of the Sunday school, the anti-cigarette laws and the prohibition of alcohol. This is one reason why the Christian historians have so distorted their accounts and estimates of pagan culture. A civilization whose philosophy was concerned with teaching people how to live happily could scarcely be appreciated and interpreted by an age whose all-absorbing passion was to prepare people to die safely.

On the other hand, when one is occupied with the second of the main tasks of the new history—namely, tracing the development of the characteristic traits and institutions of contemporary life—the criterion of the relative significance of the different aspects of culture must be their cogency and relevance with regard to the present age. Religion was infinitely more characteristic of the Middle Ages than science, yet with reference to contemporary civilization the history of science in the Middle Ages is more significant than the study of medieval religious life. If one should attempt faithfully to portray the Hellenic civilization as a whole he would have to assign far more space to the astrologers than to the Hellenistic astronomers, but if he is interested primarily in indicating the genesis of contemporary civilization, then the work of Aristarchus and Hipparchus would have to be regarded as more significant than the work of all the astrologers in the whole of classical antiquity. If one were to give a true picture of the intellectual interests in the Protestant Reformation one would need to deal far more with such issues as justification by faith than with the incidental economic views of Luther, Calvin, and other leaders. Yet, with respect to the evolution of the culture of today the Protestant defection from the Catholic economic opinions and practices was of infinitely greater moment than all of the theological issues of that age combined. To the medievalist, Roger Bacon must appear as primarily a medieval character in his interests and activities, while to the genetic historian the interesting things about Bacon are his few flashes of modernity and his incidental references to the virtues of the inductive and observational method and the implications of future mechanical invention.

These few examples will suffice to indicate that the practical importance of historical events and cultural manifestations is not monistic or absolute, but dual and perhaps pluralistic. Every fact of history has its relative significance with respect to: (1) its importance in the age of which it was a part; and (2) its bearing upon the genesis of contemporary culture. No student of history can approach his problems with intelligence or competence without fully recognizing the reality of this differential appraisal of historical material and being guided by the aim he has in mind.

It has been usually assumed that any historian in a single work can adequately execute both of these tasks, namely, to recreate a civilization and to indicate its relation to the present age. But it is doubtful if this is wholly true. The wide difference in the relative importance of the same materials, when viewed from one or the other of these two angles of interest is likely to lead to serious distortion in one or the other of the phases of the twofold achievement, if not in both of them.

It will also be apparent that if one is interested in tracing the genesis of a civilization other than his own, the criterion of the importance of materials must be their relevance with respect to the civilization whose origins one is investigating. Thus, to one investigating the genesis of Greek civilization, the importance of Egyptian data would have to be decided by their particular contribution to Hellenic culture rather than by their relative significance in Egyptian civilization or their importance for one's own day.

Some may complain that these tests of the significance of historical materials are relative and pragmatic. Is there no absolute and transcendental test? Apparently not, beyond the fact that, in the last analysis, the value of historical materials in explaining our contemporary civilization far transcends any other significance they may have.

This brief discussion of the all inclusive scope of the vision and interests of the historical practitioner of the new school and of the twofold criterion of the relevance of historical subject matter leads naturally to the problem of the organization of historical materials in the light of the newer concepts and attitudes.

In the old days the situation was relatively simple. The skeleton of political and military history was always present and was looked upon as wholly adequate to serve as the framework for the construction of the complete epic of humanity. The conceptions of the new history are as destructive of this primitive simplicity and guilelessness of the older history as modern astrophysics, evolutionary biology, and biblical criticism have been of the simple faith and comforting dogmas of our fathers. We must now recognize not only that the political staging is utterly inadequate for the construction of the complete edifice of history, but also that no one category of historical events or facts can serve as the basis for the organization of historical materials. There is no single key to the riddle of historical causation. At times one or another factor may rise to a position of transcendent importance, but no single "cause" or "influence" has been dominant throughout all of human history.

In a rough and tentative way it may be held that the chain of historical causation is something like the following: We have as the two relatively constant factors in history the original nature of man and the geographical environment in a given area, but these cannot be said to be absolutely static, and they are so involved with other conditioning influences that their interaction is continually varying in nature and extent. The original nature of man, reacting to a particular form of geographic stimulation, will produce a characteristic outlook on life. The latter will in turn control to a considerable degree the extent to which science and technology can emerge and develop. The state of technology will rather sharply condition the nature of the economic life which can exist in any age and area. The economic institutions tend to have a powerful conditioning, and sometimes a determining influence over the other institutions and cultural elements: social, political, juristic, religious, ethical, educational and literary.

Yet this is, in reality, an over-simplified statement of the historical process. Cause and effect are continually acting and interacting upon each other. A few basic mechanical inventions, such as printing or new methods of transmitting information, may so alter the life of man as completely to transform the dominating psychology of any age. Again, certain psychological and cultural factors may at times have sufficient power to obstruct the obvious dictates of economic advantage and material prosperity. The skein of historical development is a tangled and complicated one. It is a profound historian who can solve the problems of historical causation in any single epoch, to say nothing of making an effort to formulate a universally valid interpretation of human history as a whole.

Some who are alert enough to observe the collapse of the political scaffolding which once supported the laboriously active historians, will attempt to seek solace in the thought that if we cannot use political events as the framework of historical efforts, we can at least fall back upon national entities and write the story of the evolution of French culture, Italian culture, Spanish culture, and so on. But here we shall once more have to take the joy out of life. The whole conception of national history was inseparably linked up with the Romanticist myth of "national genius," the political fetish, and the assumption of political causation. When one looks at history from the standpoint of the evolution of culture and institutions, it at once becomes evident that there can be no such thing as national history. Dynastic changes, partisan politics, and diplomatic intrigues may by definition be strictly national affairs, even though they rarely are completely so in practice, but cultural and institutional development is not, never has been, and never can be a strictly national matter.

A national history of the automobile, the printing press, or the microscope is no less unthinkable than a cultural history of France or Germany taken by themselves alone. It may be diverting to the scholar and gratifying to historical curiosity to study the ways in which internationally derived and conditioned phases of culture are especially developed or markedly restrained within the confines of any state. But any national history of culture and institutions is bound to be both artificial and trivial when compared to a study of cultural genesis as a process which knows no such things as the artificial boundary lines drawn by dynastic ambition or economic avarice.

We may, then, continue to study the nationalistic conditioning of culture, but certainly not the nationalistic evolution of culture. National history will go down to oblivion before the new history no less certainly than political history, when viewed as the foundation for the organization and presentation of historical facts. A nation was once viewed as a political entity. Then Renan, Zangwill, Zimmern and others denied its political basis and described it as a cultural unity. We shall probably have to go one step further and designate a nation as a misleading cultural illusion —a cultural psychosis or a sort of cultural dementia. For students of the problem of nationalism and of the questions of war and peace the above considerations have deep significance, but we cannot enter into these matters in this chapter.

Driven from his previous havens of refuge in the political framework of history and the nationalistic mode of compartmentalization, the disconcerted historian of the old school may at least contend that he can dig in and take his bearings within the shelter and moorings provided by the conventional historical chronology of ancient, medieval and modern history. But, as we have made clear above, the relentless expositor of the new history can give him even less quarter here than with respect to the theory of political causation and nationalistic orientation.[7]

It can easily be shown that a chronology based simply upon a sequence of basic years is of no vital significance whatever. The continuity of history proves the futility of any sharp division between successive eras. It is, moreover, a truism of theoretical anthropology and cultural history that the various elements in the cultural complex have sharply contrasting rates of development, as well as that the religious and esthetic aspects of culture seem to obey no demonstrable laws of evolution or progress. If we

[7] See above, pp. 345-49.

mean by modernity social adequacy and scientific validity, then the ethics of the Greeks were far more modern than those of John S. Sumner or Bishop Manning. The artistic life of the Renaissance was, likewise, far richer and more expansive than that of today. It is obvious, then, that there can be no scientific type of chronology which is based upon the hypothesis of a uniform rate of development of all types of culture and institutions. Further, the tempo of cultural evolution varies greatly from one part of the earth to another. Imagine trying to describe under the caption of "ancient civilization" the cultures of China, Scandinavia, South America, Gaul, Mesopotamia, and India in 1000 B.C., or under the heading, "contemporary civilization" the cultures of China, England, Germany, Russia and Brazil in A.D. 1890. It would seem, as we pointed out in the previous chapter, that the only chronology which can possess any validity whatever, must be a highly specialized one, based upon and descriptive of nothing more than the development of certain limited phases of culture or certain specific institutions within a relatively homogeneous cultural area. The conventional historian may retort that he might as well have no chronology at all. He would have some ground for this opinion.

The old-line historian may protest in despair that this means insufferable confusion, anarchy, and complexity. We must frankly admit that for the time being it does, but this is not a situation for which the advocates of the new history are in any sense responsible. It simply indicates that historians are beginning to awaken to the situation which faces us in every aspect of life today. It means that history is coming to be contemporary in its outlook and is beginning to recognize what the theologian, philosopher, sociologist and student of ethics have come to recognize long ago. It signifies nothing more than that the symbolic historical ostrich has at last raised his head from the sands of medievalism and Humanism and has given the twentieth-century world a thorough appraisal.[8]

In the place of the rustic simplicity of life conditions, changing little from century to century, and instead of an illusory sense of security obtained from credulous and uncritical reliance upon a primitive cosmology and a few naïve religious dogmas, our ostrich now beholds the rapidly changing mechanical and urban civilization of an industrial age. He can witness a disconcertingly expansive cosmology and the grave questioning of all the assumptions upon which man has been wont to justify his alleged place in the cosmos and his notions of safety before both the mundane and supernatural worlds. These startling changes in historical events and situations are forcing a similar revolution in historical concepts, aims, and methods. It is little wonder that the first impulse of the historical ostrich is to make another dive into the sand.

[8] See above, pp. 292 ff.

In other words, the historian is only facing the implications of executing his craft in the light of twentieth-century knowledge and methods, in the same way that we are all faced with the readjustments forced upon us by the fact of really living in the contemporary era. Fifty years ago a cultured citizen of the United States could have felt wholly adequate and secure buttressed by faith in the classical languages, the doctrines of the Atonement, the protective tariff, and the Republican party. Today the same individual would be faced by the perplexities and gnawing uncertainties imposed by the impressive contemporary astrophysics which proves the insignificance of our planet and by implication of man himself, by scepticism concerning the whole socio-economic complex upon which the tariff system rested, and by a growing recognition of the utter incompetence of the Republican and Democratic parties alike, if not of the actual political incapacity of mankind when confronted by the complexities of the contemporary age. The changes of outlook forced upon an alert professor of history in a university by the transformations of the last fifty years are no less profound and numerous.

If it be alleged that only a few superior minds could cope with the implications of this view of the tasks and obligations of the historian, it may be answered that the housewife can no longer practice medicine nor the barber surgery, yet medicine and surgery have both flourished to an unprecedented degree since scientific limitations upon the personnel of the profession have been both recognized and imposed. In the future we probably shall have to differentiate more sharply between the true historian and the record clerk.

In emphasizing the primary importance of the genetic approach to the origins of contemporary society, we touch upon one of the few real lessons which history has for mankind. It must be obvious to all thoughtful persons that social and cultural situations in the past were so different from those of the twentieth century that we can draw little of value for ourselves from the experiences of remote historic ages. Yet, by tracing back to their beginnings our own culture and institutions, we can not only better understand our own age but can also destroy that reverential and credulous attitude toward the past which is the chief obstacle to social and intellectual progress and the most dangerous menace to society.[9]

It might be pointed out, in passing, that if history should come to be chiefly occupied with tracing the genesis of contemporary culture and ininstitutions, many of the problems mentioned above in connection with the general organization of historical material and the conflicting theories of historical chronology would automatically disappear, for the problem in each case would be the origins and development of a single institution

---

[9] Cf. Robinson, *The Human Comedy*, *passim*.

or cultural manifestation, though its history would usually be involved
with that of related aspects of culture.

THE DESIRABLE TRAINING FOR THE NEW HISTORY

If the new history is to be a success, it will be conceded without argument that it must train an ever larger group of enthusiastic workers in
this field in such fashion as to render them capable of carrying on competent research and synthesis. If the older history suffered because of the
inadequate training of its devotees, such would be much more the case
with the new history, which requires a far wider range of preparatory
studies. It may, of course, be conceded that a unique genius might be
able to execute commendable work of this type with no extensive training,
but we are not here concerned with genius. Though it may be more difficult for them to succeed here, the new history, like the old, will have to
depend to a large extent for its recruits upon earnest and devoted plodders who will need to be strengthened, sustained and guided by thorough
and accurate training in craftsmanship.

It must be insisted that the new history is essentially a science of cultural reconstruction and institutional genesis. It may be freely conceded
that the distinguished historians of the new school will be those who, like
Robinson, Becker and Beard, add to scientific precision and erudition
a high degree of creative ability in that type of artistry essential to
the skillful reconstruction of civilizations and the astute tracing of the
genesis of ideas and institutions. This is as evident as that the great diagnostician in medicine is something above and beyond a trained technical
physician, but he could not be a great diagnostician without having first
been a competent medical scientist. Least of all should literary artistry be
confused with historical prowess.[10] The clever essayist, as such, is no more
a historian than a painter who produces a chromatic masterpiece designed
to reproduce the likeness of St. Peter or Charles I. Van Dyke was as
much entitled to rank as a historian as Carlyle. Hogarth was as truly a
historian as Macaulay.

It has been contended that the chief reason for the lack of influence
exerted by history upon public life and opinion is the absence of stylistic
distinction on the part of recent writers. It would appear to the present
writer that the real reason has been the handicaps imposed upon the historical profession by archaic conceptions of the nature, scope and purpose
of historical writing, by pedantic exhibitionism, by the choice of obscure
topics, by rotarian notions of good taste, and by the exploitation of historical writing for the purpose of promoting academic advancement and

---

[10] For the opposite view see Trevelyan, *Clio: a Muse.*

professional friendships instead of trying to illuminate humanity and advance human welfare. Even a Sombart or a Veblen will have his host of eager readers when there is something substantial to constitute an ultimate reward for the painful perusal of his pages. There is no denying the need of good writing, but it should be good writing by good historians; in other words, good historical writing in the best sense of that term.

In particular, we must look into the theory of the uniqueness and mysterious nature of significant historical situations, conceding the unique and elusive character of conventional "historical facts."[11] The so-called drama of history is the record of the responses of biochemical entities to terrestrial stimulation. Human responses are no more mysterious or unique than the behavior of other animals or the reaction of organic tissues and inorganic substances as studied in the laboratory.[12] The deliberations of the National Constituent Assembly in the French Revolution were as much a purely naturalistic product as the antics of the simians in the Bronx Park zoo. A historical situation may be unique in a strictly temporal sense, but it cannot be unique from a scientific point of view. It is the product of human behavior which can be analyzed scientifically. Further, it cannot be too much emphasized that such aspects of a historical situation as are unique are those which are the least relevant. Historical phenomena can be understood only to the degree that they are brought within the scope of the cogent type of scientific analysis, as provided by the relevant natural and social sciences.

Nor can one hope to prepare for the task of the historian merely through antiquarian research or by the acquisition of a vast body of conventional historical facts. The person who gathers and edits a large number of inscriptions is no more a historian, however valuable his services may be to learning and to history, than is the person who collects and classifies antique furniture for a museum of fine arts. And the person who has committed to memory W. L. Langer's *Encyclopedia of World History* is not by this fact alone qualified as a historian.

The basis of all technical training in the new history will, of course, remain the conventional instruction in the technique of documentary research. It will be as necessary as ever for the beginning historian to be thoroughly grounded in the principles of research in documents, inscriptions, and monuments. Indeed, the training here will need to be more extensive than ever. In ancient history today the student not only has to be familiar with the collections of inscriptions, but must also be a master of prehistoric archeology and papyrology, neither of which disturbed the serenity of Curtius or Mommsen. He may also have to be familiar with the

---

[11] See above, pp. 267-68.
[12] For a contrary mystical view see Alexis Carrel, *Man, the Unknown* (Harper, 1935).

technique of mechanical excavation and aërial photography. In modern history there is real need for a wider technical knowledge than was ever required for research in medieval documents. The embryonic medievalist, once he had mastered his Latin, Greek, and Arabic and the auxiliary sciences essential to documentary criticism, was ready to go ahead when provided with a glossary of theological terms and his DuCange to guide him in regard to medieval usages. The student who would execute research in contemporary times must face an infinitely greater range of requirements. He must be familiar with bookkeeping and accounting, the rudiments of technology, the elements of corporation finance, the terminology of contemporary political science, the fundamentals of transportation, the rudiments of evolutionary biology, the essentials of applied electro-physics, and a host of other manifestations of contemporary civilization, if he is to be able to read with any intelligence the documentary sources which contain the raw materials of his profession.

Next to this basic technique of documentary research would come the acquisition of the truly historical outlook, which is to be found in a thoroughgoing acquisition of the evolutionary point of view. The historian should be as completely conditioned to thinking in terms of genesis as the physician is to dealing in terms of diagnosis and prognosis. He should be a master of the basic processes of cosmic, biological, cultural, and institutional evolution, and should accustom himself to think always of man in terms of the nomenclature and processes of evolution. Evolution should be to the historian what dynamics is to the physicist. In other words, we should insist that the person who intends to be a historian should at the outset be historically minded.

Then the historian must master the fundamental facts and principles of anthropogeography, as interpreted by the most up-to-date exponents of regional geography, whose viewpoint is that of cultural anthropologists. A book such as Lucien Fevbre's *Geographical Introduction to History* will illustrate what is meant. The historian should, in particular, study carefully the physical and social geography of the area in which he expects to be a specialist. The practitioner of the new history must recognize at the outset that what has hitherto passed for historical geography, namely, a familiarity with changing political boundaries and battle sites, useful as such knowledge may be, is not in any sense the geography of history. He should, as well, be accustomed to thinking in terms of the three main stages of the geographic conditioning of history, such as outlined by Leon Metchnikoff and Professor J. K. Wright: namely, the fluvial, thalassic and the oceanic. He must also give due consideration to S. C. GilFillan's thesis relative to the "coldward course of progress." He should likewise be familiar with the basic historical significance of that worldwide contact

of cultures, so effectively described by Professor W. R. Shepherd in studying the historical significance of the expansion of Europe.

The student of the new history must be thoroughly acquainted with
man and his behavior, normal and abnormal. He must have mastered the
rudiments of physiological chemistry and endocrinology. No person unfamiliar with the glandular basis of human behavior can hope to interpret
intelligently the conduct of men, past or present. One must be as familiar
with the action of the adrenal glands as with Potthast or Bernheim. It is
probable that adrenalin played as large a part as pan-Slavism in Sazonov's
decision upon war in July, 1914. Likewise, the intelligent and properly
equipped historian must be familiar with the more common types of abnormal behavior associated with the major varieties of human pathology.[13]
Statesmen, diplomats and supreme court judges have usually been men of
advanced age, and certainly no one could hope to understand the conduct
of the aged unless acquainted with the behavior patterns associated with
arteriosclerosis and senile-dementia. Obviously, no one unfamiliar with
the effects of syphilis could offer an adequate interpretation of the acts of
some of the leading European monarchs, statesmen, and diplomats.
Chronic nephritis and dyspepsia are often more illuminating in explaining a person's behavior than his politics, education, religion, or economic
investments. An understanding of the behavior patterns associated with
the major psychoses and epilepsy is likewise indispensable.

Human behavior cannot be understood when sharply separated from
that of other animals, particularly that of our fellow simians. Hence the
necessity for full acquaintance with comparative psychology. A book like
Yerkes' *Almost Human,* the best and most reliable popular exposition of
simian psychology, is indispensable to anyone who would attempt a realistic interpretation of human behavior. The beginner blessed with an
adequate sense of humor should supplement this with Clarence Day's
This Simian World. The real fact that man is only a little higher than
the apes is of much greater significance to the understanding historian
than the dubious assurance that he is only a little lower than the angels.
Behavioristic psychology, with its stress upon social conditioning, is all
important to the historian who desires to interpret a personality in relation to his early life and social surroundings. And this must be supplemented by psychoanalytical psychology, which throws a flood of light
upon the unconscious motivation of conduct and insists upon an investigation of the intimate facts of personal history and daily life if one is to
learn the secret springs of human behavior in the case of any individual.
Finally, there must be adequate acquaintance with the facts of social psychology to make clear the effect of crowd-psychological situations upon

---

[13] Cf. Charles MacLaurin, *Post Mortems of Mere Mortals* (Doubleday, Doran, 1930);
James Kemble, *Idols and Invalids* (Doubleday, Doran, 1936); and Langer, 'The
Next Assignment," *loc. cit.*

man and to indicate the multifarious interactions between group and individual.

Anthropology must be cultivated, not only for its emphasis upon the evolutionary basis of man and his institutions, and for its clarification of the new time-perspective of human development, but even more for the elucidation of the laws and processes of cultural advance. There is more to be learned about the fundamental principles of historical development from such books as White's *Evolution of Culture*, Wissler's *Man and Culture*, Goldenweiser's *History, Psychology and Culture*, Kroeber's *Anthropology*, and the like than from the dozen best books yet written on formal historical method. More than any of the other new auxiliary sciences, anthropology is veritably the threshold to history, from the standpoint of both chronology and methodology.

No one can engage competently in the new history who is not familiar with sociology—the basic and elemental social science, introductory to all others—as well as with the special social sciences of economics, political science, jurisprudence, ethics, and the like.[14] History is a record of man's development as conditioned by his social environment. Hence, it is quite impossible to interpret this record intelligently without a scientific knowledge of the facts and processes of group life as explained by sociology and the special social sciences. Further, if one expects to execute a type of work which calls for more than average knowledge of some special social science, this latter must be thoroughly mastered. For example, no one should think of attempting detailed work in economic history who is not thoroughly trained in every leading branch of modern economics and in economic statistics. If one hopes to write in the field of the history of science or esthetics, he must add to his general preparation a specialized familiarity with the natural sciences or the fine arts.

Many who might admit the validity of the above ambitious and exacting program of preparation for the new history will contend that it is simply impossible for any single individual to meet such requirements. Such objection appears to the writer specious and inaccurate. It will be easy enough to achieve such a preparation, once its necessity is understood to the same degree that the requisite special preparation for medicine and engineering is now fully recognized and admitted. We have already our premedical courses in the colleges, and our professional medical courses which follow. In due time we shall have our "prehistory" courses and our professional schools of history and the social sciences where the foregoing educational program can be fully realized. It will require no more time than is now so largely wasted through unplanned and uncoordinated efforts in our colleges and universities. All of the requirements

---

[14] See above, pp. 360 ff.

for the successful student of the new history could easily be met in the seven years now occupied by our conventional history students in securing the A.B. and Ph.D. degrees. We should then have something substantial when we get through with the preparatory process. Our post-graduates would no longer need to be what former President Clarence Little of the University of Michigan has described as the pedantic and narrow-minded specialist who knows more than any other living person about the suspenders of Henry VIII and does not care to know about anything else.

Some might cantankerously contend that few of the present expositors of the new history can meet the test just laid down in regard to the desirable preparation of the historian. The indictment would be correct. No doubt Professor Robinson would have been the first to admit that he was but an amiable and humble novice with respect to almost every phase of the preparation of the student of the new history which we have sketched, but he might also retort that if he had his life to live over again he would be adequately prepared. And he could further contend with justice that the character of what he has been able to accomplish with inadequate preparation is the best proof of the excellent results we may expect from the thoroughly trained students of the future.

CONCLUSIONS WITH RESPECT TO THE NEW HISTORY

The following are the main points which we have attempted to establish thus far in this chapter:

1. The new history is more than a new conception of the scope and purpose of history. It carries with it the obligation of a far more profound and varied type of preparation for the career of the historian.

2. It is new in the wider degree to which the broader view of history has been accepted, in the recognition of the importance of the social sciences in the training of the historian, and in the conquest of history by the genetic point of view derived from the biologists and the evolutionary philosophers.

3. Down to the present time the exponents of the new history have found it necessary to engage in a campaign of persistent propaganda and education, associated most notably with the names of Lamprecht, Berr, Robinson, Teggart and Marvin. They have now definitely won the victory and can henceforth concentrate their energy upon perfecting the basis of the new history and upon providing for the training of those who will be competent to practice the new history.

4. The two chief tasks of the new history are to reconstruct as completely as possible the civilizations of the past and to trace the development of the leading social institutions of today. Of these two, the latter is by far the more important. The contributions which it may make to

the better understanding of our own age is the chief, if not the only real service of history. Some would add a third task, namely, the formulation of a theory of social causation or a generalized study of social change, but this sort of investigation would appear to fall more appropriately within the field of historical sociology.

5. No single category of historical events can be regarded as adequate to furnish the skeleton for the organization of the whole story of the historical evolution of human culture; least of all can political events. With the advent of cultural and institutional history there must pass into oblivion not only the previous political scaffolding of history, but also the conventional history of nations and the accepted historical chronology.

6. There is no single cause which determines the course of historical events. The historian must adopt a tentative and empirical attitude toward historical causation and accept a pluralistic outlook.

7. The naïve simplicity and dogmatic certainty of the older history must be abandoned as illusory and misleading. The complexities, uncertainties, confusion, and dynamic nature of the problems which face the historian of today are only the symptoms of the age as a whole—-the inevitable result of the historian's discovery that he is living in the twentieth century.

8. In training the prospective practitioner of the new history it is necessary to abandon at the outset the notion of history as a literary art or a mode of antiquarian recreation. The casual literary artist who exploits historical material is no more of a historian than a painter who depicts an alleged historical scene. History is the science of the reconstruction of past civilizations and of the genesis of our present-day culture. Hence, those who would follow the career of the historian must master all the types of information involved in recreating the human past and in tracing the development of the human present. This will require a careful planning of studies from undergraduate days onward, comparable to the foresight and specialization now found in preparation for medicine and engineering. In short, we can no longer continue to write and teach history without considering the nature and behavior of man.[15]

RECENT TRENDS AND THREATS IN HISTORICAL WRITING

The first edition of this book was composed in 1936-1937 shortly after the publication of my *History of Western Civilization*, which was probably the most widely reviewed and discussed substantial historical book published in the United States in the 1930's, as Wells' *Outline*

---

[15] For a discussion of the merits of the new history, see the observations of **Crane** Brinton and myself in the *Journal of Social Philosophy*, January, 1936.

of History had been in the 1920's. After reading hundreds of reviews of my book I was convinced that the great threat to the validity of historical writing was to be found in the clash of opposing ideologies. This probably remains true, if one considers the civilized world as a whole. The ideological struggle is, perhaps, even more bitter now if one extends his perspective to the conflict between the so-called Free World and all the Communist nations. But the ideological pressures which impressed me in 1936 were those in the Western World itself between Fascism and Communism.

The validity of historical books was appraised chiefly with respect to whether their content squared with Fascist or Communist gospel. Since in this country there were virtually no scholars who supported Fascism, the ideological estimate of my book was based chiefly on the extent to which it squared with Marxist doctrine. This was especially true of appraisals by younger historians. It is no exaggeration to state that of all the critical attacks on the *History of Western Civilization* for other than controversial details at least half of these blasts were due to my failure to follow Marx faithfully, despite the fact that I gave more attention to economic factors and forces than pleased most conventional historians.

This particular variety of ideological threat to objective historical writing, which was so rampant in the 1930's, has now all but disappeared, especially in the United States. Any historians who still esteem Fascist ideology keep their thoughts very much to themselves. The Cold War has also put an end to the tendency to make conformity to Marxism a test of sound historical writing outside of the Iron Curtain countries.

Since the earlier portion of this chapter dealt with the rise and growth of the new history, it may be well at this point to indicate that the enthusiasm for this broader pattern and content of history has distinctly declined in the last twenty-five years.

In the United States the growing popularity of the new history in the late 1920's and the 1930's was due in part to the "social science movement" which was powerfully promoted by the Social Science Research Council, which had access to Rockefeller funds, and by the liberal grant of the Carnegie Corporation to the American Historical Association to make a study of the relation of the social sciences to historical writing and education in general. The liberalism and the social interests of the New Deal generation encouraged an interest in civilization as a whole.

With the coming of the second World War, the absorption with martial affairs and politics and a general trend towards conservatism were reflected in the attitude of historians. By the close of the war, the most popular text for history of civilization courses was one in which the "civilization" was mainly on the title page, one which was actually less of an example of the new history than James Harvey Robinson's famous *History of Western Europe*, which appeared in 1903. Newspapers, led by *The New York Times*, attacked the social studies approach and called for a return in history teaching and writing to a "sound" political core and frame of reference.

It would be untrue to declare that the stream of the new history has dried up but it is certain that the speed and depth of its current have notably declined. The inflated martial ardor and concern with things military are bound to be increased with the veritable obsession of historians with the Civil War during its centennial decade. Along with the increased chauvinism of the postwar period has come a new and heavy emphasis on recent history—what is called "Presentism"—which carries to the opposite extreme the tendency of the older type of history to stop with the French Revolution or, at the most, boldly to dare to come down to 1871.

What has been regarded since the second World War as the chief threat to historical integrity and stability is something which must, if one is honest and realistic, be branded a fiction and a fantasy. It is a product mainly of escapism and an overcompensated sense of guilt, arising from the unwillingness of historians to recognize and condemn the actual menaces to historical integrity and candor. I have reference here to what is known in the historical craft as "historical relativism." In this sinful behavior the two chief culprits are alleged to have been the especially eminent and distinguished historians and former presidents of the American Historical Association, Carl L. Becker and Charles A. Beard.

The essentials of this wicked "relativism," so far as Becker, Beard, and those sympathetic with their point of view are concerned, are the following veritable historical truisms: (1) that historical events are so complex and elusive that no later historian, however well trained, honest, and industrious, can ever fulfill Leopold von Ranke's dream of reconstructing the past exactly as it was; (2) that what the public, including the historians, accepts as historical truth at any time will depend as much upon the mental climate of the period as on the validity of the facts themselves; (3) that what is accepted as truth by historians and the public will shift markedly from time to time due to emotional factors; and (4) that the main value of such facts as can be discovered and tentatively stated lies in the extent to which they can help us to understand the past and present and plan for the future. Becker never vigorously exposued this fourth item in the broad relativist creed but Beard did so with ardor, especially in the later years of his life.

We have seen that Becker first stated his convictions relative to the elusive nature, complexity, and incomplete character of historical facts in 1926.[16] Beard's statement of the same general position was made in his presidential address before the American Historical Association in 1933.[17] He elaborated it in later articles.[18]

The self-evident fact that what passes for historical truth is what the people accept as truth at any time had been a commonplace among social scientists, especially social psychologists, for at least a generation before Becker discussed historical "facts" in 1926. It was set forth as early as 1913 by William A. Dunning in his presidential address before the American Historical Association, when he said that "whatever a given age or people believes to be true *is* true for that age and people." Any historian who claims that historians are immune to any such conformity to public opinion can expect nothing more than a horselaugh from anybody familiar with the behavior of historians since 1914, all after the tenets of so-called scientific and objective history had been established and formally accepted for a quarter of a century. Why any informed person should have been disturbed by such a truism is difficult to understand.

Whether historical facts are to be prized for their pragmatic role in helping us to understand the past and present and plan for the future or are justified solely as a matter of limited professional pride and idle curiosity is surely a matter of opinion. But certainly the pragmatic approach is the more helpful and illuminating. Robinson went even further than Beard in arguing for the utilitarian and pragmatic view of historical facts. He proclaimed that the "objective historian" is an historian without any object and, hence, a rather useless person unless somebody comes along to utilize the facts he has collected.

In the opinion of the writer of this book, the whole row about relativism was a diversionary tempest-in-a-teapot designed in part to distract attention from the unwillingness of historians to face up to the

[16] See above, pp. 267 ff. In toned-down form it appeared in his presidential address before the American Historical Association in 1931, entitled "Everyman His Own Historian." It was elaborated in an unpublished paper on "Historical Evidence." See also Crane Brinton and H. E. Barnes, "The New History: Twenty-five Years After," *Journal of Social Philosophy*, January, 1936.

[17] "Written History as an Act of Faith," *American Historical Review*, January, 1934.

[18] "That Noble Dream," *American Historical Review*, October, 1935; and "Currents in Historiography," *Ibid.*, April, 1937. For the best analysis of the basis and development of Beard's historical ideas, see G. D. Nash, "Self-education in Historiography: The Case of Charles A. Beard," *Pacific Northwest Quarterly*, July, 1961.

real and vital threats to their profession. It was about like being distressed over a case of German measles or chicken-pox in the midst of an epidemic of typhus or bubonic plague. The irrational nature of the mental currents which often affect public and historical judgments was well described in his presidential address on "The Next Assignment" before the American Historical Association by William L. Langer in 1957.[19] The brief flirtation of some historians with *Historismus*, phenomenology, and the sociology of knowledge was even less of a justification for excitement than relativism.

Far more menacing to historical accuracy and insight and to the public weal are the trends towards a reversion to conditions during the disintegration of the Roman Empire when the Roman intelligentsia "lost their nerve," as Gilbert Murray described it. They turned to various mystery religions which offered them a promise of purification from earthly sins and a blessed immortality. Especially popular was the neo-Platonic philosophy which decried reason, held science in slight esteem, and extolled faith and credulity. Today, we can witness a comparable tendency for disturbed intellectuals to seek refuge in some such form of philosophy as existentialism or a dogmatic religion. The breakdown of supernaturalism and the threats to the contemporary nationalistic, democratic, and capitalistic regime have created a mental confusion not unlike that which accompanied the downfall of classical civilization.

The best exemplification of this trend in the historical field has been the immense popularity of Arnold J. Toynbee's *The Study of History*. Despite the fact that Toynbee is unquestionably the most learned living historian, his historical framework rested on theological aberrations, oddities, curios, and vestiges which should appall any reasonably well-informed college student. The fragility of the intellectual and theological scaffolding was revealed in devastating fashion by the Dutch historian, Pieter Geyl, in his *Use and Abuse of History* (1955) and *Debates with Historians* (1957).[20]

An even greater threat to the future of history lies in the manner in which the war fervor and its accompanying emotions have been revived

[19] For discussions of the "relativism" issue see the articles in the *American Historical Review* for October, 1956, by Perez Zagorin, Leo Gershoy and W. A. Williams; Cushing Strout, *The Pragmatic Revolt in American History: Carl Becker and Charles A. Beard*, Yale University Press, 1958; B. T. Wilkins, *Carl Becker*, Harvard University Press, 1961, chaps. vii-x; and C. W. Smith, *Carl Becker: On History and the Climate of Opinion*, Cornell University Press, 1956, especially chap. iii. This last otherwise excellent book is marred by an amazing and rather ridiculous attempt to find similarities between the relativism of Becker and the "Ingsoc" of Orwell's *Nineteen Eighty-four*, which advocated the suppression and destruction of historical facts and the deliberate falsification and distortion of historical information.

[20] On Toynbee, see H. E. Barnes, ed., *An Introduction to the History of Sociology*, chap. xxxvii, University of Chicago Press, 1948.

in the bosoms of historians since 1939. This time they have not been permitted to cool off and regain their composure, as was the case after 1918. We have dealt with this situation in earlier pages.[21] What this has done to sound historical ideals and practices was well stated by the eminent British naval historian, Russell Grenfell:

> To you and me who lived in the mentally free world of pre-1914, the determined rush of the historical Gadarenes into the sea of falsehood and distortion has been an astounding phenomenon. Which of us could have believed, in that first decade of the century, that the values which then seemed so firmly established in the historical profession could disappear so easily and rapidly, leaving only a tiny company of unheeded and derided protestors to lament their loss?[22]

The main reason that historians never had an opportunity to return to reasonable objectivity since 1939 is that no sooner was the hot war over in 1945 than the Cold War began early in 1947 during the administration of President Truman. The animus of the historians was quickly extended from Germany and Italy to Russia, China and other Communist nations. Most of this additional hatred was sincere, although some was surely synthetic and expressed for protective purposes, especially on the part of historians of violently pro-Communist fervor before 1945. How this has affected historical independence and open-mindedness has been well stated by Professor A. J. P. Taylor, an eminent British historian and author of *The Origins of the Second World War*. Writing of *Between War and Peace*, by Herbert Feis, the most productive and one of the most distinguished of the so-called court historians of our time, Taylor observes that Feis's book is:

> A State Department brief, translated into terms of historical scholarship. . . . Dr. Feis' conclusions were not derived from the evidence; they were assumed as self-evident, before the book was begun. . . . There was a time when historians shook off their national commitments and wrote as though observing from another planet. Indeed, when American historians wrote on the origins of the first World War they leaned over backwards so far that they became partial to the German side. In the Cold War, apparently, even the world of scholarship knows no detachment. The academic historians of the West may assert their scholarly independence even when they are employed by a government department; but they are as much "engaged" as though they wore the handsome uniforms designed for German professors by Dr. Goebbels.[23]

[21] See above, chap. xi, and especially pp. 290 ff.

[22] Letter to the writer, December 23, 1952. See my "Revisionism and the Promotion of Peace," *Liberation*, Summer, 1958.

[23] *Manchester Guardian*, weekly edition, January 19, 1961. See also the observations of another eminent British historian, Herbert Butterfield, on "Official History: Its Pitfalls and Criteria," in his *History and Human Relations*, Macmillan, 1952, pp. 182-224.

The most disquieting aspect of this bureaucratic control over historical writing and the identification of historical "truth" with governmental policy is that it is the first step, and a very important one, into the condition of history in the Orwellian nightmare of "Nineteen Eighty-four" society. Here we have complete and rigorous conformity of historical writing to the daily trends and dogmas of party whims, wishes, and tastes, and as much forging, suppression, and destruction of documentation as is required to bring about this result. The following passage from Orwell's book indicates the spirit that dominates historical writing under the tenets of Ingsoc, the ideological frame of reference of the "Nineteen Eighty-four" system:

> History is continuously rewritten. This day-to-day falsification of the past, carried out by the Ministry of Truth, is as necessary to the stability of the regime as the work of repression and espionage carried out by the Ministry of Love. . . . Past events have no objective existence, but survive only in written records and in human memories. The past is whatever the records and the memories agree upon. And since the Party is in control of all records, and is equally in control of the minds of its members, it follows that the past is whatever the Party chooses to make it. . . . To make sure that all records agree with the orthodoxy of the moment is merely a mechanical act. But it is also necessary to remember that events happened in the desired manner. And if it is necessary to rearrange one's memories or to tamper with written records, then it is necessary to forget that one has done so.[24]

This historical procedure under Ingsoc involves the deliberate suppression and destruction of all existing documentation which conflicts with what passes for historical truth at any moment.

Many readers will feel that we are still far removed from any such situation as that portrayed above. The truth is that we are already in just such a historical regimen. It is merely a matter of degree. Aside from a few despised "revisionist" historical volumes, there has been no historical writing since 1939, even in the Free World, which has substantially challenged or departed from the basic policy of the country of the writer.

It is well established that important documents dealing with the diplomacy of the second World War have been suppressed or destroyed. Approximately forty volumes of documents on recent American foreign policy have been awaiting publication for years but little has been done to carry out the publication program, even though the funds were long

[24] George Orwell, *Nineteen Eighty-four*, pp. 213–215, Harcourt, Brace, 1949.

since provided and an official promise of speedy publication was made back in May, 1953. The documents finally published on such important wartime summit conferences as those at Yalta and Teheran were often badly distorted and some were suppressed. The Pearl Harbor investigations revealed the suppression, distortion or destruction of crucial documents dealing with the responsibility for the catastrophe.

It may be that the situation is not such as should lead to any panic in the historical ranks—and it surely will not do so, because there is no general disposition on the part of historians to question current trends—but it is very disquieting to historians who cling to earlier ideals of integrity and veracity, to close on what is surely the most extreme understatement included in this book.

A NOTE ON THE HISTORY OF THE HISTORY OF HISTORY

A friend of the writer, when told of the present enterprise, observed that it would not be long before somebody would be writing "a history of the history of history." An article on this subject in some good historical magazine would, indeed, be illuminating and helpful, and it may be hoped that it will be forthcoming. There would certainly be no more appropriate way in which to close this brief survey of the history of historical writing than to summarize what has been done in this field down to date.

Perhaps the first step towards a consideration of earlier historical writing came in the work of Polybius when he reviewed and criticized the methods and results of previous antiquarian writings on Roman history. Most Greek and Roman historical writing was, as we have seen, contemporary history. Hence, there had been few preceding writers on any era, and the earlier historians of the period could not be systematically discussed and criticized. Then came the review of pagan and Jewish historical writers by the early Christian chronologists from Julius Africanus to Jerome. Throughout the Middle Ages the medieval annalists and chroniclers considered previous historical works, if only to copy them into their own manuscripts. More systematic investigation into the historians of the past arose during the controversies of the Reformation and the counter-Reformation. The Magdeburg Centurians, Cardinal Baronius and others critically reviewed the writers on ecclesiastical history from Apostolic days to the sixteenth century. Then the Humanists, from Flavius Blondus to Sigonius and Lévesque de Pouilly, analyzed the writers on ancient and medieval history. The early students of biblical criticism, from Aben Ezra to Astruc and Reimarus, looked into the historical sources of Holy Writ. These lines of study were carried on by the Rationalist and Romanticist historians, to be systematically and consciously cultivated when the movement towards the collection of the sources of national history got under way and modern critical historical scholarship made its appearance. The great editors, such as Muratori, Waitz, Guizot, Molinier, Guérard, Stubbs, and the like, critically appraised the writings of the early Christian writers and the medieval chroniclers. The scholars, like Niebuhr, Waitz and von Ranke, critically assessed the historians of antiquity, the Middle Ages and the Renaissance.

The work of the editors promoted the first notable crop of books which can in any literal way be regarded as histories of historical writing. These were the guides to the sources of national history—brief summaries of the leading historians of the national past, chiefly medieval and early modern writers. The first of these was the small guide to German historical writing issued by Friedrich Dahlmann in 1830, *The Sources of German History* [*Quellenkunde der deutschen Geschichte*]. It was revised by George Waitz, and passed through many editions. The eighth one, edited by Paul Herre in 1912, is an enormous volume. It classifies and describes briefly the works on German history in the German language prior to 1912. Even more complete for the Middle Ages was Wilhelm Wattenbach and Otto-kar Lorenz, *The Historical Sources for Germany in the Middle Ages* [*Deutschlands Geschichtsquellen im Mittelalter*]. In France, Gabriel Mo-nod's *Bibliography of the History of France* performed a service compar-able to that executed for German history by the Dahlmann-Waitz *Quellenkunde*. What Wattenbach and Lorenz did for German history Au-guste Molinier, Henri Hauser, Émile Bourgeois and André Louis did for French history in their elaborate works on *The Sources of the History of France,* bringing their catalogue and criticisms down to 1715. An Ameri-can scholar, Charles Gross, prepared the authoritative survey of the Eng-lish medieval historians in his *Sources and Literature of English History,* continued through the Stuart period by Godfrey Davies. Most other European countries have provided comparable guides to their past histori-cal writings. These can be found listed in the *Guide to Historical Litera-ture.* Channing, Hart and Turner prepared the authoritative guide to the writings on American history.

An excellent introduction to the history of medieval historical writing was provided in the "Early Chroniclers of Europe" series of James Gaird-ner, Gustav Masson, and Ugo Balzani, covering England, France and Italy, and also giving some material on German medieval historians be-cause of the close connection of Germany and Italy in the Middle Ages. For more detail on German medieval historical writing one will find it necessary to turn to the works of Wattenbach and Lorenz. A brief survey and appraisal of all historical writing since the close of the Middle Ages is to be found in the invaluable *Manual of Historical Bibliography* by the French savant, Charles V. Langlois. Also very useful was Charles Kendall Adams' *Manual of Historical Literature,* which listed and described most of the important historical works in English, French, and German which had appeared prior to 1889. It is now supplemented by the important *Guide to Historical Literature,* planned and edited by George M. Dutcher, William H. Allison, and others, and giving especial attention to works which have appeared between 1889 and 1930.

While such works as those mentioned above were monumental contributions to scholarship and provided introductions to historical writing, they were only incidentally histories of historiography. Perhaps the first important work which may fairly be called a conscious history of historical writing was Robert Flint's *The Philosophy of History in Europe: France and Germany,* which appeared in 1874. During the next twenty years Flint expanded the section on French historians into a whole volume, but never published the enlarged treatment of German historians. The book was more than a history of the philosophy of history, since it dealt with Rationalist, Romanticist, nationalistic and early scholarly historical writing as well as with formal philosophies of history. During the period since Flint's book was published, there have been many works on the history of historical writing. Since they have all appeared within recent years it will be best if we describe them in connection with successive periods of history rather than list them in confusing fashion according to the date of their publication.

For a survey of the whole period of antiquity no other work compares with James T. Shotwell's *Introduction to the History of History.* It covers historical work from primitive society to the early Christian chronologists. Professor Shotwell intended to publish a book dealing with the entire history of historical writing, forecast by his excellent article, "History," in the *Encyclopedia Britannica,* but he has brought out only this first section. There is no other comprehensive work on the historiography of antiquity in any language. On the Near Orient the most valuable work is that of a sociologist, Joyce O. Hertzler's *The Social Thought of the Ancient Civilizations.* James H. Breasted's *Ancient Records of Egypt* provides a survey of the more important historical writings of the ancient Egyptians. Important also is Adolf Erman's *The Literature of the Ancient Egyptians.* For the historical writings of ancient Mesopotamia we have the excellent introduction in A. T. Olmstead's *Assyrian Historiography.* There is no comparable work on Babylonian historiography. Translations of many of the historical texts are provided in Robert F. Harper's *Assyrian and Babylonian Literature,* in G. A. Barton's *The Royal Inscriptions of Sumer and Akkad,* and in D. D. Luckenbill's *Ancient Records of Babylonia and Assyria.* There are many introductions to the historical writing of the Hebrews, of which George Foote Moore's *Literature of the Old Testament* is the best starting point. On the historical writing of the ancient Greeks we have the charming work of John B. Bury, *The Ancient Greek Historians,* which includes a brief survey of Roman historiography. A comparable work on Roman historical writing is that of Wilhelm Soltau, and there are technical surveys of the sources of Roman history by Arthur Rosenburg, *Introduction to Roman History and Its Source Materials,* and by Hermann Peter, *The Historical Literature of the Roman Empire to the Time of Theodosius I.* Peter has also written an illuminating book on the capitulation of antique history to rhetoric, *Truth and Art* [*Wahrheit und Kunst*]. There are many works on individual Greek and Roman historians, of which the books of Glover on Herodotus, of Grundy, Abbott and Cornford on Thucydides, and of Bossier on Tacitus are representative.

On the historiography of Christianity the best introductions are Gustav Krüger's *Early Christian Literature,* and Pierre de Labriolle's *History and Literature of Christianity.* There is a good brief catalogue of the medieval ecclesiastical historians in André Lagarde's *The Latin Church in the Middle Ages.* More complete is Moritz Ritter's *Christian and Medieval Historical Writing,* first published in the *Historische Zeitschrift,* in 1911. All works on medieval historical writing naturally deal with Christian chroniclers. Peter Guilday has edited a valuable volume containing accounts of representative Catholic historians from Eusebius to the historians of the last half of the nineteenth century like Denifle and Pastor.

The best introduction to the historical writing in the early Middle Ages is C. J. H. Hayes, *Introduction to the Sources Relating to the Germanic Invasions.* There are good introductory works on the medieval chroniclers by Professors Tout and Jenkins, and Dr. Stanley Lane-Poole, and an excellent monograph on historical method in the Middle Ages by Miss Schulz. We have already called attention to the "Early Chroniclers of Europe" series, which, together with the work of Wattenbach, constitutes the best survey of medieval historical writing in western Christendom. The only introduction in English to the Byzantine historians is that interspersed throughout A. A. Vasiliev's *History of the Byzantine Empire,* which also contains (I. 13-54) a good review of all modern historical writing on the eastern empire in the Middle Ages. The only detailed material on Byzantine historical writing is contained in Karl Krumbacher's classic work on *The History of Byzantine Literature from Justinian to the End of the Eastern Roman Empire.* For the Muslim historians we have the brief work of D. S. Margoliouth, *Lectures on Arabic Historians,* and the admirable monograph of Nathaniel Schmidt on *Ibn Khaldun,* the ablest of the Muslim historical writers.

There is no single comprehensive work on the historical writing of the Renaissance, though there are special treatments like the works of Schevill, Morley, Gebhart, and Gervinus on the Florentine historians and of Joachimsen on the German Humanist historians. Nor is there any comprehensive summary of the historical writing of the Reformation, but we have the monumental technical review of the sources for the age in Gustav Wolf's *Sources of the History of the German Reformation*. For the whole modern period, including an excellent account of historical writing in the period of the Renaissance and Reformation, there is the admirable *History of Modern Historiography*, by the able Swiss scholar, the late Eduard Fueter. Adolf Rein has written the best survey of the influence of oversea expansion on European historical writing in *The Problem of European Expansion in Historical Writing*. The preëminent historians of the age of Rationalism—Voltaire, Hume, Robertson, and Gibbon—are discussed in John B. Black's *The Art of History*, a brief work but one of the most intelligent and readable of all books on the history of historical writing. For the historiography of Romanticism the best discussion that we have is in the books of Robert Flint, mentioned above, though Fueter has some excellent summaries of these writers. The historiography of nationalism and the rise of scholarly and critical historical writing are splendidly described and intelligently evaluated in George Peabody Gooch's *History and Historians in the Nineteenth Century*. The more recent period, which is only briefly sketched in Gooch, is covered in the composite French work by Louis Halphen and others on *History and Historians of the Last Fifty Years* (1927), and in the work edited by Steinberg on *The Historical Science of the Present in Individual Exposition*.

There are a number of histories of historical writing treating the several countries of the West. Germany is most satisfactorily dealt with. The whole history of German historical writing in modern times is surveyed in Franz von Wegele's *History of German Historiography since the Rise of Humanism*. The nationalistic school is examined in Antoine Guilland's *Modern Germany and her Historians*. The nineteenth century is handled with appreciation by Georg Below in his *German Historical Writing from the War of Liberation to Our Own Day*. The best account of the development of nationalistic and scholarly history in France is contained in the work of Louis Halphen, *History in France During the Last Hundred Years*. Benedetto Croce has written an extended account of Italian historical writing in the last century. There is no complete account of English historical writing, though there is much material on English historians of the nineteenth century in Gooch's book. The only important special work on English historical writing is Thomas P. Peardon's *The Transition in English Historical Writing, 1760-1830*, an able account of the period from Hume to Lingard. It deals with Rationalism, Romanticism, and the origins of nationalistic historical writing. Petrus Block has given us an important book on *Historical Writing in Holland*, while Paul Miliukov has written several monographs on Russian historical writing, including one on *Main Currents of Russian Historiography*. J. Franklin

Jameson, many years ago, wrote an excellent introduction to American historical writing, *The History of Historical Writing in America,* coming down through the great literary historians, Motley, Parkman, Prescott, Bancroft, and the like. This group, together with Force and the compilers, were treated more thoroughly by John S. Bassett in his *Middle Group of American Historians;* and by David Levin in his *History as Romantic Art.* The more recent period has been summarized by Theodore Clark Smith, William A. Dunning, Allan Nevins and A. M. Schlesinger and his associates. Michael Kraus's *A History of American History,* and the Marcus W. Jernegan *Essays in American Historiography,* covered, for the first time, the whole history of American historical writing. The only extended account of the rise and character of cultural and institutional history is the present writer's *The New History and the Social Studies.* There is an intelligent discussion of the rise of the notion of history as a social science in F. J. Teggart's *Prolegomena to History, The Processes of History,* and *The Theory of History.* It has only been since the revised edition of this book was published in 1938 that we have finally been provided with a reasonably complete survey of the history of historical writing by combining James Westfall Thompson's two-volume work on the *History of Historical Writing* (1942), with Michael Kraus' *The Writing of American History* (1953), and by the symposium, *The Development of Historiography* (1954), edited by M. A. Fitzsimons, A. G. Pundt, and C. E. Nowell.[25]

SELECTED REFERENCES

Robinson, *The New History.*

————, "New Ways of Historians," *loc. cit.*

H. E. Barnes, ed., *An Introduction to the History of Sociology,* chaps. xxxvii, xlvi. University of Chicago Press, 1948.

————, *The New History and the Social Studies.*

————, *History and Social Intelligence.*

Barnes and Becker, *Contemporary Social Theory.*

Jacques Barzun, *The House of the Intellect.* Harper, 1959.

Smith, *Carl Becker: On History and the Climate of Opinion.*

B. T. Wilkins, *Carl Becker.* Harvard University Press, 1961.

Cushing Strout, *The Pragmatic Revolt in American History.* Yale University Press, 1958.

Donald Sheehan and H. C. Syrett, eds., *Essays in American Historiography.* Columbia University Press, 1961.

[25] For an excellent summary survey of the literature on the history of history and historiography, see the bibliography in the *Encyclopedia of the Social Sciences,* 15 vols., Macmillan, 1932, Vol. VII, pp. 389-91.

Lee Benson, *Turner and Beard*. Glencoe Free Press, 1960.

Dexter Perkins and J. L. Snell, *The Education of Historians in the United States*. McGraw-Hill, 1962.

E. T. Gargan, ed., *The Intent of Toynbee's History*. Loyola Univ. Press, 1961.

R. G. Collingwood, *The Idea of History*. Oxford University Press, 1946.

Allan Nevins, *The Gateway to History*. Appleton-Century, 1938.

Louis Gottschalk, *Understanding History*. Knopf, 1950.

Geoffrey Barraclough, *History in a Changing World*. University of Oklahoma Press, 1956.

Pieter Geyl, *The Use and Abuse of History*. Yale University Press, 1955.

———, *Debates with Historians*. Philosophical Library, 1957.

George Orwell, *Nineteen Eighty-four*. Harcourt, Brace, 1949.

C. L. Becker, *Everyman His Own Historian*. Crofts, 1935.

Karl Lamprecht, *What Is History?* Macmillan, 1905.

Odum, *American Masters of Social Science*.

Schaumkell, *Geschichte der deutschen Kulturgeschichtschreibung*.

Karl Heussi, *Die Krisis des Historismus*. Tübingen, 1932.

E. H. Carr, *What Is History?* Knopf, 1962.

INDEX

CATALOG OF DOVER BOOKS

Language Books and Records

Say It language phrase books

These handy phrase books (128 to 196 pages each) make grammatical drills unnecessary for an elementary knowledge of a spoken foreign language. Covering most matters of travel and everyday life each volume contains:

Over 1000 phrases and sentences in immediately useful forms — foreign language plus English.

Modern usage designed for Americans. Specific phrases like, "Give me small change," and "Please call a taxi."

Simplified phonetic transcription you will be able to read at sight.

The only .completely indexed phrase books on the market.

Covers scores of important situations: — Greetings, restaurants, sightseeing, useful expressions, etc.

These books are prepared by native linguists who are professors at Columbia, N.Y.U., Fordham and other great universities. Use them independently or with any other book or record course. They provide a supplementary living element that most other courses lack. Individual volumes in:

Russian 75¢	Danish 75¢	Italian 75¢
Hebrew 75¢	German 75¢	Spanish 60¢
Japanese 75¢	Portuguese 75¢	Swedish 75¢
Dutch 75¢	French 60¢	Modern Greek 75¢
Esperanto 75¢	Norwegian 75¢	Yiddish 75¢
	Polish 75¢	Turkish 75¢

English for Spanish-speaking people 60¢
English for Italian-speaking people 60¢
English for German-speaking people 60¢

Large clear type. 128-196 pages each. 3½ x 5¼. Sturdy paper binding.

Say It Correctly language records

These are the best inexpensive pronunciation aids on the market. Spoken by native linguists associated with major American universities, each record contains:

15 minutes of speech — 12 minutes of normal but relatively slow speech, 2 minutes at normal conversational speed

120 basic phrases and sentences covering nearly every aspect of everyday life and travel — introducing yourself, travel in autos, buses, taxis, etc., walking, sightseeing, hotels, restaurants, money, shopping, etc.

32 page booklet containing everything on the record plus English translations and an easy-to-follow phonetic guide

Clear, high fidelity quality recordings

Unique bracketing system and selection of basic sentences enabling you to expand the use of your SAY IT CORRECTLY records with a dictionary so as to fit thousands of additional situations and needs

Use this record to supplement any course or text. All sounds in each language are illustrated perfectly for you. Imitate the speaker in the pause which follows each foreign phrase in the slow section and you will be amazed at the increased ease and accuracy of your pronunciation. Available, one language per record, for

French	Spanish	German
Italian	Dutch	Modern Greek
Japanese	Portuguese	Swedish
Russian	Polish	Hebrew
English (for German-speaking people)		Arabic
English (for Spanish-speaking people)		Serbo-Croatian
		Turkish

7″ (33⅓ rpm) record, album, booklet. $1.00 each.

Trubner Colloquial Manuals

These unusual books are members of the famous Trubner series of colloquial manuals. They have been written to provide adults with a sound colloquial knowledge of a foreign language, and are suited for either class use or self-study. Each book is a complete course in itself, with progressive, easy to follow lessons. Phonetics, grammar, and syntax are covered, while hundreds of phrases and idioms, reading texts, exercises, and vocabulary are included. These books are unusual in being neither skimpy nor overdetailed in grammatical matters, and in presenting up-to-date, colloquial, and practical phrase material. Bilingual presentation is stressed, to make thorough self-study easier for the reader.

COLLOQUIAL HINDUSTANI, A. H. Harley, formerly Nizam's Reader in Urdu, U. of London. 30 pages on phonetics and scripts (devanagari & Arabic-Persian) are followed by 29 lessons, including material on English and Arabic-Persian influences. Key to all exercises. Vocabulary. 5 x 7½. 147pp. Clothbound $1.75

COLLOQUIAL PERSIAN, L. P. Elwell-Sutton. Best introduction to modern Persian, with 90 page grammatical section followed by conversations, 35 page vocabulary. 139pp.
Clothbound $1.75

COLLOQUIAL ARABIC, DeLacy O'Leary. Foremost Islamic scholar covers language of Egypt, Syria, Palestine, & Northern Arabia. Extremely clear coverage of complex Arabic verbs & noun plurals; also cultural aspects of language. Vocabulary. xviii + 192pp. 5 x 7½.
Clothbound $1.75

COLLOQUIAL GERMAN, P. F. Doring. Intensive thorough coverage of grammar in easily-followed form. Excellent for brush-up, with hundreds of colloquial phrases. 34 pages of bilingual texts. 224pp. 5 x 7½. Clothbound $1.75

COLLOQUIAL SPANISH, W. R. Patterson. Castilian grammar and colloquial language, loaded with bilingual phrases and colloquialisms. Excellent for review or self-study. 164pp. 5 x 7½.
Clothbound $1.75

COLLOQUIAL FRENCH, W. R. Patterson. 16th revision on this extremely popular manual. Grammar explained with model clarity, and hundreds of useful expressions and phrases; exercises, reading texts, etc. Appendixes of new and useful words and phrases. 223pp. 5 x 7½.
Clothbound $1.75

COLLOQUIAL CZECH, J. Schwarz, former headmaster of Lingua Institute, Prague. Full easily followed coverage of grammar, hundreds of immediately useable phrases, texts. Perhaps the best Czech grammar in print. "An absolutely successful textbook," JOURNAL OF CZECHO-SLOVAK FORCES IN GREAT BRITAIN. 252pp. 5 x 7½. Clothbound $3.00

COLLOQUIAL RUMANIAN, G. Nandris, Professor of University of London. Extremely thorough coverage of phonetics, grammar, syntax; also included 70 page reader, and 70 page vocabulary. Probably the best grammar for this increasingly important language. 340pp. 5 x 7½.
Clothbound $2.50

COLLOQUIAL ITALIAN, A. L. Hayward. Excellent self-study course in grammar, vocabulary, idioms, and reading. Easy progressive lessons will give a good working knowledge of Italian in the shortest possible time. 5 x 7½. Clothbound $1.75

Other Language Aids

AN ENGLISH-FRENCH-GERMAN-SPANISH WORD FREQUENCY DICTIONARY, H. S. Eaton. An indispensable language study aid, this is a semantic frequency list of the 6000 most frequently used words in 4 languages—24,000 words in all. The lists, based on concepts rather than words alone, and containing all modern, exact, and idiomatic vocabulary, are arranged side by side to form a unique 4-language dictionary. A simple key indicates the importance of the individual words within each language. Over 200 pages of separate indexes for each language enable you to locate individual words at a glance. Will help language teachers and students, authors of textbooks, grammars, and language tests to compare concepts in the various languages and to concentrate on basic vocabulary, avoiding uncommon and obsolete words. 2 Appendixes. xxi + 441pp. 6½ x 9¼. T738 Paperbound $2.45

NEW RUSSIAN-ENGLISH AND ENGLISH-RUSSIAN DICTIONARY, M. A. O'Brien. Over 70,000 entries in the new orthography! Many idiomatic uses and colloquialisms which form the basis of actual speech. Irregular verbs, perfective and imperfective aspects, regular and irregular sound changes, and other features. One of the few dictionaries where accent changes within the conjugation of verbs and the declension of nouns are fully indicated. "One of the best," Prof. E. J. Simmons, Cornell. First names, geographical terms, bibliography, etc. 738pp. 4½ x 6¼. T208 Paperbound $2.00

CATALOG OF DOVER BOOKS

DICTIONARY OF SPOKEN RUSSIAN, English-Russian, Russian-English. Based on phrases and complete sentences, rather than isolated words; recognized as one of the best methods of learning the idiomatic speech of a country. Over 11,500 entries, indexed by single words, with more than 32,000 English and Russian sentences and phrases, in immediately useable form. Probably the largest list ever published. Shows accent changes in conjugation and declension; irregular forms listed in both alphabetical place and under main form of word. 15,000 word introduction covering Russian sounds, writing, grammar, syntax. 15 page appendix of geographical names, money, important signs, given names, foods, special Soviet terms, etc. Travellers, businessmen, students, government employees have found this their best source for Russian expressions. Originally published as U.S. War Department Technical Manual TM 30-944. iv + 573pp. 5⅝ x 8⅜. T496 Paperbound **$2.75**

DICTIONARY OF SPOKEN SPANISH, Spanish-English, English-Spanish. Compiled from spoken Spanish, emphasizing idiom and colloquial usage in both Castillian and Latin-American. More than 16,00 entries containing over 25,000 idioms—the largest list of idiomatic constructions ever published. Complete sentences given, indexed under single words—language in immediately useable form, for travellers, businessmen, students, etc. 25 page introduction provides rapid survey of sounds, grammar, syntax, with full consideration of irregular verbs. Especially apt in modern treatment of phrases and structure. 17 page glossary gives translations of geographical names, money values, numbers, national holidays, important street signs, useful expressions of high frequency, plus unique 7 page glossary of Spanish and Spanish-American foods and dishes. Originally published as U.S. War Department Technical Manual TM 30-900. iv + 513pp. 5⅜ x 8. T495 Paperbound **$1.75**

DUTCH-ENGLISH AND ENGLISH-DUTCH DICTIONARY, F. G. Renier. For travel, literary, scientific or business Dutch, you will find this the most convenient, practical and comprehensive dictionary on the market. More than 60,000 entries, shades of meaning, colloquialisms, idioms, compounds and technical terms. Dutch and English strong and irregular verbs. This is the only dictionary in its size and price range that indicates the gender of nouns. New orthography. xvii + 571pp. 5½ x 6¼. T224 Clothbound **$2.75**

LEARN DUTCH, F. G. Renier. This book is the most satisfactory and most easily used grammar of modern Dutch. The student is gradually led from simple lessons in pronunciation, through translation from and into Dutch, and finally to a mastery of spoken and written Dutch. Grammatical principles are clearly explained while a usefuly, practical vocabulary is introduced in easy exercises and readings. It is used and recommended by the Fulbright Committee in the Netherlands. Phonetic appendices. Over 1200 exercises; Dutch-English, English-Dutch vocabularies. 181pp. 4¼ x 7¼. T441 Clothbound **$2.25**

INVITATION TO GERMAN POETRY record. Spoken by Lotte Lenya. Edited by Gustave Mathieu, Guy Stern. 42 poems of Walther von der Vogelweide, Goethe, Hölderlin, Heine, Hofmannsthal, George, Werfel, Brecht, other great poets from 13th to middle of 20th century, spoken with superb artistry. Use this set to improve your diction, build vocabulary, improve aural comprehension, learn German literary history, as well as for sheer delight in listening. 165-page book contains full German text of each poem; English translations; biographical, critical information on each poet; textual information; portraits of each poet, many never before available in this country. 1 12″ 33⅓ record; 165-page book; album. The set **$4.95**

ESSENTIALS OF RUSSIAN record, A von Gronicka, H. Bates-Yakobson. 50 minutes spoken Russian based on leading grammar will improve comprehension, pronunciation, increase vocabulary painlessly. Complete aural review of phonetics, phonemics—words contrasted to highlight sound differences. Wide range of material: talk between family members, friends; sightseeing; adaptation of Tolstoy's "The Shark;" history of Academy of Sciences; proverbs, epigrams; Pushkin, Lermontov, Fet, Blok, Maikov poems. Conversation passages spoken twice, fast and slow, let you anticipate answers, hear all sounds but understand normal talk speed. 12″ 33 record, album sleeve. 44-page manual with entire record text. Translation on facing pages, phonetic instructions. The set **$4.95**

Note: For students wishing to use a grammar as well, set is available with grammar-text on which record is based, Gronicka and Bates-Yakobson's "Essentials of Russian" (400pp., 6 x 9, clothbound; Prentice Hall), an excellent, standard text used in scores of colleges, institutions. Augmented set: book, record, manual, sleeve **$10.70**

SPEAK MY LANGUAGE: SPANISH FOR YOUNG BEGINNERS, M. Ahlman, Z Gilbert. Records provide one of the best, and most entertaining, methods of introducing a foreign language to children. Within the framework of a train trip from Portugal to Spain, an English speaking child is introduced to Spanish by a native companion. (Adapted from a successful radio program of the N. Y. State Educational Department.) Though a continuous story, there are a dozen specific categories of expressions, including greetings, numbers, time, weather, food, clothes, family members, etc. Drill is combined with poetry and contextual use. Authentic background music is heard. An accompanying book enables a reader to follow the records, and includes a vocabulary of over 350 recorded expressions. Two 10″ 33⅓ records, total of 40 minutes. Book. 40 illustrations. 69pp. 5¼ x 10½. T890 The set **$4.95**

MONEY CONVERTER AND TIPPING GUIDE FOR EUROPEAN TRAVEL, C. Vomacka. A small, convenient handbook crammed with information on currency regulations and tipping for every European country including the Iron Curtain countries, plus Israel, Egypt, and Turkey. Currency conversion tables for every country from U.S. to foreign and vice versa. The only source of such information as phone rates, postal rates, clothing sizes, what and when to tip, duty-free imports, and dozens of other valuable topics. 128pp. 3½ x 5¼. T260 Paperbound **60¢**

Literature, History of Literature

ARISTOTLE'S THEORY OF POETRY AND THE FINE ARTS, edited by S. H. Butcher. The celebrated Butcher translation of this great classic faced, page by page, with the complete Greek text. A 300 page introduction discussing Aristotle's ideas and their influence in the history of thought and literature, and covering art and nature, imitation as an aesthetic form, poetic truth, art and morality, tragedy, comedy, and similar topics. Modern Aristotelian criticism discussed by John Gassner. lxxvi + 421pp. 5⅜ x 8. T42 Paperbound **$2.00**

FOUNDERS OF THE MIDDLE AGES, E. K. Rand. This is the best non-technical discussion of the transformation of Latin pagan culture into medieval civilization. Covering such figures as Tertullian, Gregory, Jerome, Boethius, Augustine, the Neoplatonists, and many other literary men, educators, classicists, and humanists, this book is a storehouse of information presented clearly and simply for the intelligent non-specialist. "Thoughtful, beautifully written," AMERICAN HISTORICAL REVIEW. "Extraordinarily accurate," Richard McKeon, THE NATION. ix + 365pp. 5⅜ x 8. T369 Paperbound **$1.85**

INTRODUCTIONS TO ENGLISH LITERATURE, edited by B. Dobrée. Goes far beyond ordinary histories, ranging from the 7th century up to 1914 (to the 1940's in some cases.) The first half of each volume is a specific detailed study of historical and economic background of the period and a general survey of poetry and prose, including trends of thought, influences, etc. The second and larger half is devoted to a detailed study of more than 5000 poets, novelists, dramatists; also economists, historians, biographers, religious writers, philosophers, travellers, and scientists of literary stature, with dates, lists of major works and their dates, keypoint critical bibliography, and evaluating comments. The most compendious bibliographic and literary aid within its price range.

Vol. I. THE BEGINNINGS OF ENGLISH LITERATURE TO SKELTON, (1509), W. L. Renwick, H. Orton. 450pp. 5⅛ x 7⅞. T75 Clothbound **$3.50**

Vol. II. THE ENGLISH RENAISSANCE, 1510-1688, V. de Sola Pinto. 381pp. 5⅛ x 7⅞. T76 Clothbound **$3.50**

Vol. III. AUGUSTANS AND ROMANTICS, 1689-1830, H. Dyson, J. Butt. 320pp. 5⅛ x 7⅞. T77 Clothbound **$3.50**

Vol. IV. THE VICTORIANS AND AFTER, 1830-1914, E. Batho, B. Dobree. 360pp. 5⅛ x 7⅞. T78 Clothbound **$3.50**

EPIC AND ROMANCE, W. P. Ker. Written by one of the foremost authorities on medieval literature, this is the standard survey of medieval epic and romance. It covers Teutonic epics, Icelandic sagas, Beowulf, French chansons de geste, the Roman de Troie, and many other important works of literature. It is an excellent account for a body of literature whose beauty and value has only recently come to be recognized. Index. xxiv + 398pp. 5⅜ x 8. T355 Paperbound **$1.95**

THE POPULAR BALLAD, F. B. Gummere. Most useful factual introduction; fund of descriptive material; quotes, cites over 260 ballads. Examines, from folkloristic view, structure; choral, ritual elements; meter, diction, fusion; effects of tradition. editors; almost every other aspect of border, riddle, kinship, sea, ribald, supernatural, etc., ballads. Bibliography. 2 indexes. 374pp. 5⅜ x 8. T548 Paperbound **$1.65**

CATALOG OF DOVER BOOKS

MASTERS OF THE DRAMA, John Gassner. The most comprehensive history of the drama in print, covering drama in every important tradition from the Greeks to the Near East, China, Japan, Medieval Europe, England, Russia, Italy, Spain, Germany, and dozens of other drama producing nations. This unsurpassed reading and reference work encompasses more than 800 dramatists and over 2000 plays, with biographical material, plot summaries, theatre history, etc. "Has no competitors in its field," THEATRE ARTS. "Best of its kind in English," NEW REPUBLIC. Exhaustive 35 page bibliography. 77 photographs and drawings. Deluxe edition with reinforced cloth binding, headbands, stained top. xxii + 890pp. 5⅜ x 8. T100 Clothbound **$6.95**

THE DEVELOPMENT OF DRAMATIC ART, D. C. Stuart. The basic work on the growth of Western drama from primitive beginnings to Eugene O'Neill, covering over 2500 years. Not a mere listing or survey, but a thorough analysis of changes, origins of style, and influences in each period; dramatic conventions, social pressures, choice of material, plot devices, stock situations, etc.; secular and religious works of all nations and epochs. "Generous and thoroughly documented researches," Outlook. "Solid studies of influences and playwrights and periods," London Times. Index. Bibliography. xi + 679pp. 5⅜ x 8.
T693 Paperbound **$2.75**

A SOURCE BOOK IN THEATRICAL HISTORY (SOURCES OF THEATRICAL HISTORY), A. M. Nagler. Over 2000 years of actors, directors, designers, critics, and spectators speak for themselves in this potpourri of writings selected from the great and formative periods of western drama. On-the-spot descriptions of masks, costumes, makeup, rehearsals, special effects, acting methods, backstage squabbles, theatres, etc. Contemporary glimpses of Molière rehearsing his company, an exhortation to a Roman audience to buy refreshments and keep quiet, Goethe's rules for actors, Belasco telling of $6500 he spent building a river, Restoration actors being told to avoid "lewd, obscene, or indecent postures," and much more. Each selection has an introduction by Prof. Nagler. This extraordinary, lively collection is ideal as a source of otherwise difficult to obtain material, as well as a fine book for browsing. Over 80 illustrations. 10 diagrams. xxiii + 611pp. 5⅜ x 8. T515 Paperbound **$2.75**

WORLD DRAMA, B. H. Clark. The dramatic creativity of a score of ages and eras — all in two handy compact volumes. Over ⅓ of this material is unavailable in any other current edition! 46 plays from Ancient Greece, Rome, Medieval Europe, France, Germany, Italy, England, Russia, Scandinavia, India, China, Japan, etc. — including classic authors like Aeschylus, Sophocles, Euripides, Aristophanes, Plautus, Marlowe, Jonson, Farquhar, Goldsmith, Cervantes, Molière, Dumas, Goethe, Schiller, Ibsen, and many others. This creative collection avoids hackneyed material and includes only completely first-rate works which are relatively little known or difficult to obtain. "The most comprehensive collection of important plays from all literature available in English," SAT. REV. OF LITERATURE. Introduction. Reading lists. 2 volumes. 1364pp. 5⅜ x 8. Vol. 1, T57 Paperbound **$2.25**
Vol. 2, T59 Paperbound **$2.25**

PLAY-MAKING: A MANUAL OF CRAFTSMANSHIP, William Archer. With an extensive, new introduction by John Gassner, Yale Univ. The permanently essential requirements of solid play construction are set down in clear, practical language: theme, exposition, foreshadowing, tension, obligatory scene, peripety, dialogue, character, psychology, other topics. This book has been one of the most influential elements in the modern theatre, and almost everything said on the subject since is contained explicitly or implicitly within its covers. Bibliography. Index. xlii + 277pp. 5⅜ x 8. T651 Paperbound **$1.75**

MASTERPIECES OF THE RUSSIAN DRAMA, edited with introduction by G. R. Noyes. This only comprehensive anthology of Russian drama ever published in English offers complete texts, in 1st-rate modern translations, of 12 plays covering 200 years. Vol. 1: "The Young Hopeful," Fonvisin; "Wit Works Woe," Griboyedov; "The Inspector General," Gogol; "A Month in the Country," Turgenev; "The Poor Bride," Ostrovsky; "A Bitter Fate," Pisemsky. Vol. 2: "The Death of Ivan the Terrible," Alexey Tolstoy "The Power of Darkness," Lev Tolstoy; "The Lower Depths," Gorky; "The Cherry Orchard," Chekhov; "Professor Storitsyn," Andreyev; "Mystery Bouffe," Mayakovsky. Bibliography. Total of 902pp. 5⅜ x 8.
Vol. 1 T647 Paperbound **$2.00**
Vol. 2 T648 Paperbound **$2.00**

EUGENE O'NEILL: THE MAN AND HIS PLAYS, B. H. Clark. In many respects America's most important dramatist, no source-book has previously been published on O'Neill's life and work. Clark analyzes each play from the early THE WEB to the recently produced MOON FOR THE MISBEGOTTEN and THE ICEMAN COMETH revealing the environmental and dramatic influences necessary for a complete understanding of these important works. Bibliography. Appendices. Index. ix + 182pp. 5⅜ x 8. T379 Paperbound **$1.25**

THE DRAMA OF LUIGI PIRANDELLO, D. Vittorini. All 38 of Pirandello's plays written between 1918 and 1935 are analyzed and contrasted in this authorized study. Their cultural background, place in European dramaturgy, symbolic techniques, and plot structure are carefully examined by a renowned student of Pirandello's work. Foreword by Pirandello. Biography. Synopses of all 38 (many untranslated) works. Bibliography. xiii + 350pp. 5⅜ x 8.
T435 Paperbound **$1.98**

THE HEART OF THOREAU'S JOURNALS, edited by O. Shepard. The best general selection from Thoreau's voluminous (and rare) journals. This intimate record of thoughts and observations reveals the full Thoreau and his intellectual development more accurately than any of his published works: self-conflict between the scientific observer and the poet, reflections on transcendental philosophy, involvement in the tragedies of neighbors and national causes, etc. New preface, notes, introductions. xii + 228pp. 5⅜ x 8. T741 Paperbound **$1.45**

H. D. THOREAU: A WRITER'S JOURNAL, edited by L. Stapleton. A unique new selection from the Journals concentrating on Thoreau's growth as a conscious literary artist, the ideals and purposes of his art. Most of the material has never before appeared outside of the complete 14-volume edition. Contains vital insights on Thoreau's projected book on Concord, thoughts on the nature of men and government, indignation with slavery, sources of inspiration, goals in life. Index. xxxiii + 234pp. 5⅜ x 8. T678 Paperbound **$1.55**

THE HEART OF EMERSON'S JOURNALS, edited by Bliss Perry. Best of these revealing Journals, originally 10 volumes, presented in a one volume edition. Talks with Channing, Hawthorne, Thoreau, and Bronson Alcott; impressions of Webster, Everett, John Brown, and Lincoln; records of moments of sudden understanding, vision, and solitary ecstasy. "The essays do not reveal the power of Emerson's mind . . . as do these hasty and informal writings," N.Y. Times. Preface by Bliss Perry. Index. xiii + 357pp. 5⅜ x 8. T477 Clothbound **$1.85**

THE GIFT OF LANGUAGE, M. Schlauch. Formerly titled THE GIFT OF TONGUES, this is a middle-level survey that avoids both superficiality and pedantry. It covers such topics as linguistic families, world histories, grammatical processes in such foreign languages as Aztec, Ewe, and Bantu, semantics, language taboos, and dozens of other fascinating and important topics. Especially interesting is an analysis of the word-coinings of Joyce, Cummings, Stein and others in terms of linguistics. 232 bibliographic notes. Index. viii + 342pp. 5⅜ x 8. T243 Paperbound **$1.85**

Orientalia and Religion

ORIENTAL RELIGIONS IN ROMAN PAGANISM, F. Cumont. A study of the cultural meeting of east and west in the Early Roman Empire. It covers the most important eastern religions of the time from their first appearance in Rome, 204, B.C., when the Great Mother of the Gods was first brought over from Syria. The ecstatic cults of Syria and Phrygia — Cybele, Attis, Adonis, their orgies and mutilatory rites; the mysteries of Egypt — Serapis, Isis, Osiris, the dualism of Persia, the elevation of cosmic evil to equal stature with the deity, Mithra; worship of Hermes Trismegistus; Ishtar, Astarte; the magic of the ancient Near East, etc. Introduction. 55pp. of notes; extensive bibliography. Index. xxiv + 298pp. 5⅜ x 8. T321 Paperbound **$1.75**

THE MYSTERIES OF MITHRA, F. Cumont. The definitive coverage of a great ideological struggle between the west and the orient in the first centuries of the Christian era. The origin of Mithraism, a Persian mystery religion, and its association with the Roman army is discussed in detail. Then utilizing fragmentary monuments and texts, in one of the greatest feats of scholarly detection, Dr. Cumont reconstructs the mystery teachings and secret doctrines, the hidden organization and cult of Mithra. Mithraic art is discussed, analyzed, and depicted in 70 illustrations. 239pp. 5⅜ x 8. T323 Paperbound **$1.85**

CHRISTIAN AND ORIENTAL PHILOSOPHY OF ART, A. K. Coomaraswamy. A unique fusion of philosopher, orientalist, art historian, and linguist, the author discusses such matters as: the true function of aesthetics in art, the importance of symbolism, intellectual and philosophic backgrounds, the role of traditional culture in enriching art, common factors in all great art, the nature of medieval art, the nature of folklore, the beauty of mathematics, and similar topics. 2 illustrations. Bibliography. 148pp. 5⅜ x 8. T378 Paperbound **$1.25**

TRANSFORMATION OF NATURE IN ART, A. K. Coomaraswamy. Unabridged reissue of a basic work upon Asiatic religious art and philosophy of religion. The theory of religious art in Asia and Medieval Europe (exemplified by Meister Eckhart) is analyzed and developed. Detailed consideration is given to Indian medieval aesthetic manuals, symbolic language in philosophy, the origin and use of images in India, and many other fascinating and little known topics. Glossaries of Sanskrit and Chinese terms. Bibliography. 41pp. of notes. 245pp. 5⅜ x 8. T368 Paperbound **$1.75**

Philosophy, Religion

GUIDE TO PHILOSOPHY, C. E. M. Joad. A modern classic which examines many crucial problems which man has pondered through the ages: Does free will exist? Is there plan in the universe? How do we know and validate our knowledge? Such opposed solutions as subjective idealism and realism, chance and teleology, vitalism and logical positivism, are evaluated and the contributions of the great philosophers from the Greeks to moderns like Russell, Whitehead, and others, are considered in the context of each problem. "The finest introduction," BOSTON TRANSCRIPT. Index. Classified bibliography. 592pp. 5⅜ x 8.
T297 Paperbound **$2.00**

HISTORY OF ANCIENT PHILOSOPHY, W. Windelband. One of the clearest, most accurate comprehensive surveys of Greek and Roman philosophy. Discusses ancient philosophy in general, intellectual life in Greece in the 7th and 6th centuries B.C., Thales, Anaximander, Anaximenes, Heraclitus, the Eleatics, Empedocles, Anaxagoras, Leucippus, the Pythagoreans, the Sophists, Socrates, Democritus (20 pages), Plato (50 pages), Aristotle (70 pages), the Peripatetics, Stoics, Epicureans, Sceptics, Neo-platonists, Christian Apologists, etc. 2nd German edition translated by H. E. Cushman. xv + 393pp. 5⅜ x 8.
T357 Paperbound **$1.75**

ILLUSTRATIONS OF THE HISTORY OF MEDIEVAL THOUGHT AND LEARNING, R. L. Poole. Basic analysis of the thought and lives of the leading philosophers and ecclesiastics from the 8th to the 14th century—Abailard, Ockham, Wycliffe, Marsiglio of Padua, and many other great thinkers who carried the torch of Western culture and learning through the "Dark Ages": political, religious, and metaphysical views. Long a standard work for scholars and one of the best introductions to medieval thought for beginners. Index. 10 Appendices. xiii + 327pp. 5⅜ x 8.
T674 Paperbound **$1.85**

PHILOSOPHY AND CIVILIZATION IN THE MIDDLE AGES, M. de Wulf. This semi-popular survey covers aspects of medieval intellectual life such as religion, philosophy, science, the arts, etc. It also covers feudalism vs. Catholicism, rise of the universities, mendicant orders, monastic centers, and similar topics. Unabridged. Bibliography. Index. viii + 320pp. 5⅜ x 8.
T284 Paperbound **$1.75**

AN INTRODUCTION TO SCHOLASTIC PHILOSOPHY, Prof. M. de Wulf. Formerly entitled SCHO-LASTICISM OLD AND NEW, this volume examines the central scholastic tradition from St. Anselm, Albertus Magnus, Thomas Aquinas, up to Suarez in the 17th century. The relation of scholasticism to ancient and medieval philosophy and science in general is clear and easily followed. The second part of the book considers the modern revival of scholasticism, the Louvain position, relations with Kantianism and Positivism. Unabridged. xvi + 271pp. 5⅜ x 8.
T296 Clothbound **$3.50**
T283 Paperbound **$1.75**

A HISTORY OF MODERN PHILOSOPHY, H. Höffding. An exceptionally clear and detailed coverage of western philosophy from the Renaissance to the end of the 19th century. Major and minor men such as Pomponazzi, Bodin, Boehme, Telesius, Bruno, Copernicus, da Vinci, Kepler, Galileo, Bacon, Descartes, Hobbes, Spinoza, Leibniz, Wolff, Locke, Newton, Berkeley, Hume, Erasmus, Montesquieu, Voltaire, Diderot, Rousseau, Lessing, Kant, Herder, Fichte, Schelling, Hegel, Schopenhauer, Comte, Mill, Darwin, Spencer, Hartmann, Lange, and many others, are discussed in terms of theory of knowledge, logic, cosmology, and psychology. Index. 2 volumes, total of 1159pp. 5⅜ x 8.
T117 Vol. 1, Paperbound **$2.00**
T118 Vol. 2, Paperbound **$2.00**

ARISTOTLE, A. E. Taylor. A brilliant, searching non-technical account of Aristotle and his thought written by a foremost Platonist. It covers the life and works of Aristotle; classification of the sciences; logic; first philosophy; matter and form; causes; motion and eternity; God; physics; metaphysics; and similar topics. Bibliography. New Index compiled for this edition. 128pp. 5⅜ x 8.
T280 Paperbound **$1.00**

THE SYSTEM OF THOMAS AQUINAS, M. de Wulf. Leading Neo-Thomist, one of founders of University of Louvain, gives concise exposition to central doctrines of Aquinas, as a means toward determining his value to modern philosophy, religion. Formerly "Medieval Philosophy Illustrated from the System of Thomas Aquinas." Trans. by E. Messenger. Introduction. 151pp. 5⅜ x 8.
T568 Paperbound **$1.25**

THE PHILOSOPHICAL WORKS OF DESCARTES. The definitive English edition of all the major philosophical works and letters of René Descartes. All of his revolutionary insights, from his famous "Cogito ergo sum" to his detailed account of contemporary science and his astonishingly fruitful concept that all phenomena of the universe (except mind) could be reduced to clear laws by the use of mathematics. An excellent source for the thought of men like Hobbes, Arnauld, Gassendi, etc., who were Descarte's contemporaries. Translated by E. S. Haldane and G. Ross. Introductory notes. Index. Total of 842pp. 5⅜ x 8.
T71 Vol. 1, Paperbound **$2.00**
T72 Vol. 2, Paperbound **$2.00**

THE CHIEF WORKS OF SPINOZA. An unabridged reprint of the famous Bohn edition containing all of Spinoza's most important works: Vol. I: The Theologico-Political Treatise and the Political Treatise. Vol. II: On The Improvement Of Understanding, The Ethics, Selected Letters. Profound and enduring ideas on God, the universe, pantheism, society, religion, the state, democracy, the mind, emotions, freedom and the nature of man, which influenced Goethe, Hegel, Schelling, Coleridge, Whitehead, and many others. Introduction. 2 volumes. 826pp. 5⅜ x 8.
T249 Vol. I, Paperbound **$1.50**
T250 Vol. II, Paperbound **$1.50**

LEIBNIZ, H. W. Carr. Most stimulating middle-level coverage of basic philosophical thought of Leibniz. Easily understood discussion, analysis of major works: "Theodicy," "Principles of Nature and Grace," Monadology"; Leibniz's influence; intellectual growth; correspondence; disputes with Bayle, Malebranche, Newton; importance of his thought today, with reinterpretation in modern terminology. "Power and mastery," London Times. Index. 226pp. 5⅜ x 8.
T624 Paperbound **$1.35**

AN ESSAY CONCERNING HUMAN UNDERSTANDING, John Locke. Edited by A. C. Fraser. Unabridged reprinting of definitive edition; only complete edition of "Essay" in print. Marginal analyses of almost every paragraph; hundreds of footnotes; authoritative 140-page biographical, critical, historical prolegomena. Indexes. 1170pp. 5⅜ x 8.
T530 Vol. 1 (Books 1, 2) Paperbound **$2.25**
T531 Vol. 2 (Books 3, 4) Paperbound **$2.25**
2 volume set **$4.50**

THE PHILOSOPHY OF HISTORY, G. W. F. Hegel. One of the great classics of western thought which reveals Hegel's basic principle: that history is not chance but a rational process, the realization of the Spirit of Freedom. Ranges from the oriental cultures of subjective thought to the classical subjective cultures, to the modern absolute synthesis where spiritual and secular may be reconciled. Translation and introduction by J. Sibree. Introduction by C. Hegel. Special introduction for this edition by Prof. Carl Friedrich. xxxix + 447pp. 5⅜ x 8.
T112 Paperbound **$1.85**

THE PHILOSOPHY OF HEGEL, W. T. Stace. The first detailed analysis of Hegel's thought in English, this is especially valuable since so many of Hegel's works are out of print. Dr. Stace examines Hegel's debt to Greek idealists and the 18th century and then proceeds to a careful description and analysis of Hegel's first principles, categories, reason, dialectic method, his logic, philosophy of nature and spirit, etc. Index. Special 14 x 20 chart of Hegelian system. x + 526pp. 5⅜ x 8.
T254 Paperbound **$2.00**

THE WILL TO BELIEVE and HUMAN IMMORTALITY, W. James. Two complete books bound as one. THE WILL TO BELIEVE discusses the interrelations of belief, will, and intellect in man; chance vs. determinism, free will vs. determinism, free will vs. fate, pluralism vs. monism; the philosophies of Hegel and Spencer, and more. HUMAN IMMORTALITY examines the question of survival after death and develops an unusual and powerful argument for immortality. Two prefaces. Index. Total of 429pp. 5⅜ x 8.
T291 Paperbound **$1.65**

THE WORLD AND THE INDIVIDUAL, Josiah Royce. Only major effort by an American philosopher to interpret nature of things in systematic, comprehensive manner. Royce's formulation of an absolute voluntarism remains one of the original and profound solutions to the problems involved. Part one, 4 Historical Conceptions of Being, inquires into first principles, true meaning and place of individuality. Part two, Nature, Man, and the Moral Order, is application of first principles to problems concerning religion, evil, moral order. Introduction by J. E. Smith, Yale Univ. Index. 1070pp. 5⅜ x 8.
T561 Vol. 1 Paperbound **$2.25**
T562 Vol. 2 Paperbound **$2.25**
the set **$4.50**

THE PHILOSOPHICAL WRITINGS OF PEIRCE, edited by J. Buchler. This book (formerly THE PHILOSOPHY OF PEIRCE) is a carefully integrated exposition of Peirce's complete system composed of selections from his own work. Symbolic logic, scientific method, theory of signs, pragmatism, epistemology, chance, cosmology, ethics, and many other topics are treated by one of the greatest philosophers of modern times. This is the only inexpensive compilation of his key ideas. xvi + 386pp. 5⅜ x 8.
T217 Paperbound **$1.95**

EXPERIENCE AND NATURE, John Dewey. An enlarged, revised edition of the Paul Carus lectures which Dewey delivered in 1925. It covers Dewey's basic formulation of the problem of knowledge, with a full discussion of other systems, and a detailing of his own concepts of the relationship of external world, mind, and knowledge. Starts with a thorough examination of the philosophical method; examines the interrelationship of experience and nature; analyzes experience on basis of empirical naturalism, the formulation of law, role of language and social factors in knowledge; etc. Dewey's treatment of central problems in philosophy is profound but extremely easy to follow. ix + 448pp. 5⅜ x 8.
T471 Paperbound **$1.85**

CATALOG OF DOVER BOOKS

MIND AND THE WORLD-ORDER, C. I. Lewis. Building upon the work of Peirce, James, and Dewey, Professor Lewis outlines a theory of knowledge in terms of "conceptual pragmatism." Dividing truth into abstract mathematical certainty and empirical truth, the author demonstrates that the traditional understanding of the a priori must be abandoned. Detailed analyses of philosophy, metaphysics, method, the "given" in experience, knowledge of objects, nature of the a priori, experience and order, and many others. Appendices. xiv 446pp. 5⅜ x 8.
T359 Paperbound **$1.95**

SCEPTICISM AND ANIMAL FAITH, G. Santayana. To eliminate difficulties in the traditional theory of knowledge, Santayana distinguishes between the independent existence of objects and the essence our mind attributes to them. Scepticism is thereby established as a form of belief, and animal faith is shown to be a necessary condition of knowledge. Belief, classical idealism, intuition, memory, symbols, literary psychology, and much more, discussed with unusual clarity and depth. Index. xii + 314pp. 5⅜ x 8.
T236 Paperbound **$1.50**

LANGUAGE AND MYTH, E. Cassirer. Analyzing the non-rational thought processes which go to make up culture, Cassirer demonstrates that beneath both language and myth there lies a dominant unconscious "grammar" of experience whose categories and canons are not those of logical thought. His analyses of seemingly diverse phenomena such as Indian metaphysics, the Melanesian "mana," the Naturphilosophie of Schelling, modern poetry, etc., are profound without being pedantic. Introduction and translation by Susanne Langer. Index. x + 103pp. 5⅜ x 8.
T51 Paperbound **$1.25**

SUBSTANCE AND FUNCTION, EINSTEIN'S THEORY OF RELATIVITY, E. Cassirer. In this double-volume, Cassirer develops a philosophy of the exact sciences that is historically sound, philosophically mature, and scientifically impeccable. Such topics as the concept of number, space and geometry, non-Euclidean geometry, traditional logic and scientific method, mechanism and motion, energy, relational concepts, degrees of objectivity, the ego, Einstein's relativity, and many others are treated in detail. Authorized translation by W. C. and M. C. Swabey. xii + 465pp. 5⅜ x 8.
T50 Paperbound **$2.00**

*THE ANALYSIS OF MATTER, Bertrand Russell. A classic which has retained its importance in understanding the relation between modern physical theory and human perception. Logical analysis of physics, prerelativity physics, causality, scientific inference, Weyl's theory, tensors, invariants and physical interpretations, periodicity, and much more is treated with Russell's usual brilliance. "Masterly piece of clear thinking and clear writing," NATION AND ATHENAEUM. "Most thorough treatment of the subject," THE NATION. Introduction. Index. 8 figures. viii + 408pp. 5⅜ x 8.
T231 Paperbound **$1.95**

CONCEPTUAL THINKING (A LOGICAL INQUIRY), S. Körner. Discusses origin, use of general concepts on which language is based, and the light they shed on basic philosophical questions. Rigorously examines how different concepts are related; how they are linked to experience; problems of the field of contact between exact logical, mathematical, and scientific concepts, and the inexactness of everyday experience (studied at length). This work elaborates many new approaches to the traditional problems of philosophy—epistemology, value theories, metaphysics, aesthetics, morality. "Rare originality . . . brings a new rigour into philosophical argument," Philosophical Quarterly. New corrected second edition. Index. vii + 301pp. 5⅜ x 8
T516 Paperbound **$1.75**

INTRODUCTION TO SYMBOLIC LOGIC, S. Langer. No special knowledge of math required — probably the clearest book ever written on symbolic logic, suitable for the layman, general scientist, and philosopher. You start with simple symbols and advance to a knowledge of the Boole-Schroeder and Russell-Whitehead systems. Forms, logical structure, classes, the calculus of propositions, logic of the syllogism, etc., are all covered. "One of the clearest and simplest introductions," MATHEMATICS GAZETTE. Second enlarged, revised edition. 368pp. 5⅜ x 8.
S164 Paperbound **$1.75**

LANGUAGE, TRUTH AND LOGIC, A. J. Ayer. A clear, careful analysis of the basic ideas of Logical Positivism. Building on the work of Schlick, Russell, Carnap, and the Viennese School, Mr. Ayer develops a detailed exposition of the nature of philosophy, science, and metaphysics; the Self and the World; logic and common sense, and other philosophic concepts. An aid to clarity of thought as well as the first full-length development of Logical Positivism in English. Introduction by Bertrand Russell. Index. 160pp. 5⅜ x 8.
T10 Paperbound **$1.25**

ESSAYS IN EXPERIMENTAL LOGIC, J. Dewey. Based upon the theory that knowledge implies a judgment which in turn implies an inquiry, these papers consider the inquiry stage in terms of: the relationship of thought and subject matter, antecedents of thought, data and meanings. 3 papers examine Bertrand Russell's thought, while 2 others discuss pragmatism and a final essay presents a new theory of the logic of values. Index. viii + 444pp. 5⅜ x 8.
T73 Paperbound **$1.95**

TRAGIC SENSE OF LIFE, M. de Unamuno. The acknowledged masterpiece of one of Spain's most influential thinkers. Between the despair at the inevitable death of man and all his works and the desire for something better, Unamuno finds that "saving incertitude" that alone can console us. This dynamic appraisal of man's faith in God and in himself has been called "a masterpiece" by the ENCYCLOPAEDIA BRITANNICA. xxx + 332pp. 5⅜ x 8.
T257 Paperbound **$1.95**

THE SENSE OF BEAUTY, G. Santayana. A revelation of the beauty of language as well as an important philosophic treatise, this work studies the "why, when, and how beauty appears, what conditions an object must fulfill to be beautiful, what elements of our nature make us sensible of beauty, and what the relation is between the constitution of the object and the excitement of our susceptibility." "It is doubtful if a better treatment of the subject has since been published," PEABODY JOURNAL. Index. ix + 275pp. 5⅜ x 8.
T238 Paperbound **$1.00**

THE IDEA OF PROGRESS, J. B. Bury. Practically unknown before the Reformation, the idea of progress has since become one of the central concepts of western civilization. Prof. Bury analyzes its evolution in the thought of Greece, Rome, the Middle Ages, the Renaissance, to its flowering in all branches of science, religion, philosophy, industry, art, and literature, during and following the 16th century. Introduction by Charles Beard. Index. xl + 357pp. 5⅜ x 8.
T40 Paperbound **$1.95**

HISTORY OF DOGMA, A. Harnack. Adolph Harnack, who died in 1930, was perhaps the greatest Church historian of all time. In this epoch-making history, which has never been surpassed in comprehensiveness and wealth of learning, he traces the development of the authoritative Christian doctrinal system from its first crystallization in the 4th century down through the Reformation, including also a brief survey of the later developments through the Infallibility decree of 1870. He reveals the enormous influence of Greek thought on the early Fathers, and discusses such topics as the Apologists, the great councils, Manichaeism, the historical position of Augustine, the medieval opposition to indulgences, the rise of Protestantism, the relations of Luther's doctrines with modern tendencies of thought, and much more. "Monumental work; still the most valuable history of dogma . . . luminous analysis of the problems . . . abounds in suggestion and stimulus and can be neglected by no one who desires to understand the history of thought in this most important field," Dutcher's Guide to Historical Literature. Translated by Neil Buchanan. Index. Unabridged reprint in 4 volumes. Vol I: Beginnings to the Gnostics and Marcion. Vol II & III: 2nd century to the 4th century Fathers. Vol IV & V: 4th century Councils to the Carlovingian Renaissance. Vol VI & VII: Period of Clugny (c. 1000) to the Reformation, and after. Total of cii + 2407pp. 5⅜ x 8.
T904 Vol I   Paperbound **$2.50**
T905 Vol II & III Paperbound **$2.50**
T906 Vol IV & V   Paperbound **$2.50**
T907 Vol VI & VII Paperbound **$2.50**
The set **$10.00**

THE GUIDE FOR THE PERPLEXED, Maimonides. One of the great philosophical works of all time and a necessity for everyone interested in the philosophy of the Middle Ages in the Jewish, Christian, and Moslem traditions. Maimonides develops a common meeting-point for the Old Testament and the Aristotelian thought which pervaded the medieval world. His ideas and methods predate such scholastics as Aquinas and Scotus and throw light on the entire problem of philosophy or science vs. religion. 2nd revised edition. Complete unabridged Friedländer translation. 55 page introduction to Maimonides's life, period, etc., with an important summary of the GUIDE. Index. lix + 414pp. 5⅜ x 8.
T351 Paperbound **$1.85**

ASTROLOGY AND RELIGION AMONG THE GREEKS AND ROMANS, Franz Cumont. How astrololgy developed, spread, and took hold of superior intellects, from ancient Babylonia through Rome of the fourth century A.D. You see astrology as the base of a learned theology, the influence of the Neo-Pythagoreans, forms of oriental mysteries, the devotion of the emperors to the sun cult (such as the Sol Invictus of Aurelian), and much more. The second part deals with conceptions of the world as formed by astrology, the theology bound up with them, and moral and eschatological ideas. Introduction. Index. 128pp. 5⅜ x 8.
T581 Paperbound **$1.35**

AFTER LIFE IN ROMAN PAGANISM, Franz Cumont. Deepest thoughts, beliefs of epoch between republican period and fall of Roman paganism. Contemporary settings, hidden lore, sources in Greek, Hebrew, Egyptian, prehistoric thought. Secret teachings of mystery religions, Hermetic writings, the gnosis, Pythagoreans, Orphism; sacrifices, nether world, immortality; Hades, problem of violent death, death of children; reincarnation, ecstasy, purification; etc. Introduction. Index. 239pp. 5⅜ x 8.
T573 Paperbound **$1.35**

History, Political Science, Americana

THE POLITICAL THOUGHT OF PLATO AND ARISTOTLE, E. Barker. One of the clearest and most accurate expositions of the corpus of Greek political thought. This standard source contains exhaustive analyses of the "Republic" and other Platonic dialogues and Aristotle's "Politics" and "Ethics," and discusses the origin of these ideas in Greece, contributions of other Greek theorists, and modifications of Greek ideas by thinkers from Aquinas to Hegel. "Must" reading for anyone interested in the history of Western thought. Index. Chronological Table of Events. 2 Appendixes. xxiv + 560pp. 5⅜ x 8.
T521 Paperbound **$1.85**

CATALOG OF DOVER BOOKS

THE ANCIENT GREEK HISTORIANS, J. B. Bury. This well known, easily read work covers the entire field of classical historians from the early writers to Herodotus, Thucydides, Xenophon, through Poseidonius and such Romans as Tacitus, Cato, Caesar, Livy. Scores of writers are studied biographically, in style, sources, accuracy, structure, historical concepts, and influences. Recent discoveries such as the Oxyrhinchus papyri are referred to, as well as such great scholars as Nissen, Gomperz, Cornford, etc. "Totally unblemished by pedantry." Outlook. "The best account in English," Dutcher, A Guide to Historical Lit. Bibliography, Index. x + 281pp. 5⅜ x 8.
T397 Paperbound **$1.50**

HISTORY OF THE LATER ROMAN EMPIRE, J. B. Bury. This standard work by the leading Byzantine scholar of our time discusses the later Roman and early Byzantine empires from 395 A.D. through the death of Justinian in 565, in their political, social, cultural, theological, and military aspects. Contemporary documents are quoted in full, making this the most complete reconstruction of the period and a fit successor to Gibbon's "Decline and Fall." "Most unlikely that it will ever be superseded," Glanville Downey, Dumbarton Oaks Research Lib. Geneological tables. 5 maps. Bibliography. Index. 2 volumes total of 965pp. 5⅜ x 8.
T398, 399 Two volume set, Paperbound **$4.00**

A HISTORY OF ANCIENT GEOGRAPHY, E. H. Bunbury. Standard study, in English, of ancient geography; never equalled for scope, detail. First full account of history of geography from Greeks' first world picture based on mariners, through Ptolemy. Discusses every important map, discovery, figure, travel, expedition, war, conjecture, narrative, bearing on subject. Chapters on Homeric geography, Herodotus, Alexander expedition, Strabo, Pliny, Ptolemy, would stand alone as exhaustive monographs. Includes minor geographers, men not usually regarded in this context: Hecataeus, Pytheas, Hipparchus, Artemidorus, Marinus of Tyre, etc. Uses information gleaned from military campaigns such as Punic Wars, Hannibal's passage of Alps, campaigns of Lucullus, Pompey, Caesar's wars, the Trojan War. New introduction by W. H. Stahl, Brooklyn College. Bibliography. Index. 20 maps. 1426pp. 5⅜ x 8.
T570-1, clothbound, 2-volume set **$12.50**

THE EYES OF DISCOVERY, J. Bakeless. A vivid reconstruction of how unspoiled America appeared to the first white men. Authentic and enlightening accounts of Hudson's landing in New York, Coronado's trek through the Southwest; scores of explorers, settlers, trappers, soldiers. America's pristine flora, fauna, and Indians in every region and state in fresh and unusual new aspects. "A fascinating view of what the land was like before the first highway went through," Time. 68 contemporary illustrations, 39 newly added in this edition. Index. Bibliography. x + 500pp. 5⅜ x 8.
T761 Paperbound **$2.00**

AUDUBON AND HIS JOURNALS, J. J. Audubon. A collection of fascinating accounts of Europe and America in the early 1800's through Audubon's own eyes. Includes the Missouri River Journals —an eventful trip through America's untouched heartland, the Labrador Journals, the European Journals, the famous "Episodes", and other rare Audubon material, including the descriptive chapters from the original letterpress edition of the "Ornithological Studies", omitted in all later editions. Indispensable for ornithologists, naturalists, and all lovers of Americana and adventure. 70-page biography by Audubon's granddaughter. 38 illustrations. Index. Total of 1106pp. 5⅜ x 8.
T675 Vol I Paperbound **$2.00**
T676 Vol II Paperbound **$2.00**
The set **$4.00**

TRAVELS OF WILLIAM BARTRAM, edited by Mark Van Doren. The first inexpensive illustrated edition of one of the 18th century's most delightful books is an excellent source of first-hand material on American geography, anthropology, and natural history. Many descriptions of early Indian tribes are our only source of information on them prior to the infiltration of the white man. "The mind of a scientist with the soul of a poet," John Livingston Lowes. 13 original illustrations and maps. Edited with an introduction by Mark Van Doren. 448pp. 5⅜ x 8.
T13 Paperbound **$2.00**

GARRETS AND PRETENDERS: A HISTORY OF BOHEMIANISM IN AMERICA, A. Parry. The colorful and fantastic history of American Bohemianism from Poe to Kerouac. This is the only complete record of hoboes, cranks, starving poets, and suicides. Here are Pfaff, Whitman, Crane, Bierce, Pound, and many others. New chapters by the author and by H. T. Moore bring this thorough and well-documented history down to the Beatniks. "An excellent account," N. Y. Times. Scores of cartoons, drawings, and caricatures. Bibliography. Index. xxviii + 421pp. 5⅜ x 8⅜.
T708 Paperbound **$1.95**

POLITICAL PARTIES, Robert Michels. Classic of social science, reference point for all later work, deals with nature of leadership in social organization on government and trade union levels. Probing tendency of oligarchy to replace democracy, it studies need for leadership, desire for organization, psychological motivations, vested interests, hero worship, reaction of leaders to power, press relations, many other aspects. Trans. by E. & C. Paul. Introduction. 447pp. 5⅜ x 8.
T569 Paperbound **$2.00**

THE EXPLORATION OF THE COLORADO RIVER AND ITS CANYONS, J. W. Powell. The thrilling first-hand account of the expedition that filled in the last white space on the map of the United States. Rapids, famine, hostile Indians, and mutiny are among the perils encountered as the unknown Colorado Valley reveals its secrets. This is the only uncut version of Major Powell's classic of exploration that has been printed in the last 60 years. Includes later reflections and subsequent expedition. 250 illustrations, new map. 400pp. 5⅜ x 8⅜.
T94 Paperbound **$2.00**

FARES, PLEASE! by J. A. Miller. Authoritative, comprehensive, and entertaining history of local public transit from its inception to its most recent developments: trolleys, horsecars, streetcars, buses, elevateds, subways, along with monorails, "road-railers," and a host of other extraordinary vehicles. Here are all the flamboyant personalities involved, the vehement arguments, the unusual information, and all the nostalgia. "Interesting facts brought into especially vivid life," N. Y. Times. New preface. 152 illustrations, 4 new. Bibliography. xix + 204pp. 5⅜ x 8.   T671 Paperbound **$1.50**

GARDNER'S PHOTOGRAPHIC SKETCH BOOK OF THE CIVIL WAR, Alexander Gardner. The first published collection of Civil War photographs, by one of the two or three most famous photographers of the era, outstandingly reproduced from the original positives. Scenes of crucial battles: Appomattox, Manassas, Mechanicsville, Bull Run, Yorktown, Fredericksburg, etc. Gettysburg immediately after retirement of forces. Battle ruins at Richmond, Petersburg, Gaines'Mill. Prisons, arsenals, a slave pen, fortifications, headquarters, pontoon bridges, soldiers, a field hospital. A unique glimpse into the realities of one of the bloodiest wars in history, with an introductory text to each picture by Gardner himself. Until this edition, there were only five known copies in libraries, and fewer in private hands, one of which sold at auction in 1952 for $425. Introduction by E. F. Bleiler. 100 full page 7 x 10 photographs (original size). 224pp. 8½ x 10¾.   T476 Clothbound **$6.00**

Art, History of Art,
Graphic Arts, Handcrafts

ART STUDENTS' ANATOMY, E. J. Farris. Outstanding art anatomy that uses chiefly living objects for its illustrations. 71 photos of undraped man, woman, and child are accompanied by carefully labeled matching sketches to illustrate the skeletal system, articulations and movements, bony landmarks, the muscular system, skin, fasciae, fat, etc. 9 x-ray photos show movement of joints. Undraped models are shown in such actions as serving in tennis, drawing a bow in archery, playing football, dancing, preparing to spring and to dive. Also discussed and illustrated are proportions, age and sex differences, the anatomy of the smile, etc. 8 plates by the great early 18th century anatomic illustrator Siegfried Albinus are also included. Glossary. 158 figures, 7 in color. x + 159pp. 5⅝ x 8⅜.   T744 Paperbound **$1.45**

AN ATLAS OF ANATOMY FOR ARTISTS, F Schider. A new 3rd edition of this standard text enlarged by 52 new illustrations of hands, anatomical studies by Cloquet, and expressive life studies of the body by Barcsay. 189 clear detailed plates offer you precise information of impeccable accuracy. 29 plates show all aspects of the skeleton, with closeups of special areas, while 54 full-page plates, mostly in two colors, give human musculature as seen from four different points of view, with cutaways for important portions of the body. 14 full-page plates provide photographs of hand forms, eyelids, female breasts, and indicate the location of muscles upon models. 59 additional plates show how great artists of the past utilized human anatomy. They reproduce sketches and finished work by such artists as Michelangelo, Leonardo da Vinci, Goya, and 15 others. This is a lifetime reference work which will be one of the most important books in any artist's library. "The standard reference tool," AMERICAN LIBRARY ASSOCIATION. "Excellent," AMERICAN ARTIST. Third enlarged edition. 189 plates, 647 illustrations. xxvi + 192pp. 7⅞ x 10⅝.   T241 Clothbound **$6.00**

AN ATLAS OF ANIMAL ANATOMY FOR ARTISTS, W. Ellenberger, H. Baum, H. Dittrich. The largest, richest animal anatomy for artists available in English. 99 detailed anatomical plates of such animals as the horse, dog, cat, lion, deer, seal, kangaroo, flying squirrel, cow, bull, goat, monkey, hare, and bat. Surface features are clearly indicated, while progressive beneath-the-skin pictures show musculature, tendons, and bone structure. Rest and action are exhibited in terms of musculature and skeletal structure and detailed cross-sections are given for heads and important features. The animals chosen are representative of specific families so that a study of these anatomies will provide knowledge of hundreds of related species. "Highly recommended as one of the very few books on the subject worthy of being used as an authoritative guide," DESIGN. "Gives a fundamental knowledge," AMERICAN ARTIST. Second revised, enlarged edition with new plates from Cuvier, Stubbs, etc. 288 illustrations. 153pp. 11⅜ x 9.   T82 Clothbound **$6.00**

THE HUMAN FIGURE IN MOTION, Eadweard Muybridge. The largest selection in print of Muybridge's famous high-speed action photos of the human figure in motion. 4789 photographs illustrate 162 different actions: men, women, children—mostly undraped—are shown walking, running, carrying various objects, sitting, lying down, climbing, throwing, arising, and performing over 150 other actions. Some actions are shown in as many as 150 photographs each. All in all there are more than 500 action strips in this enormous volume, series shots taken at shutter speeds of as high as 1/6000th of a second! These are not posed shots, but true stopped motion. They show bone and muscle in situations that the human eye is not fast enough to capture. Earlier, smaller editions of these prints have brought $40 and more on the out-of-print market. "A must for artists," ART IN FOCUS. "An unparalleled dictionary of action for all artists," AMERICAN ARTIST. 390 full-page plates, with 4789 photographs. Printed on heavy glossy stock. Reinforced binding with headbands. 7⅞ x 10⅝.
                                          T204 Clothbound **$10.00**

CATALOG OF DOVER BOOKS

ANIMALS IN MOTION, Eadweard Muybridge. This is the largest collection of animal action photos in print. 34 different animals (horses, mules, oxen, goats, camels, pigs, cats, guanacos, lions, gnus, deer, monkeys, eagles—and 21 others) in 132 characteristic actions. The horse alone is shown in more than 40 different actions. All 3919 photographs are taken in series at speeds up to 1/6000th of a second. The secrets of leg motion, spinal patterns, head movements, strains and contortions shown nowhere else are captured. You will see exactly how a lion sets his foot down; how an elephant's knees are like a human's—and how they differ; the position of a kangaroo's legs in mid-leap; how an ostrich's head bobs; details of the flight of birds—and thousands of facets of motion only the fastest cameras can catch. Photographed from domestic animals and animals in the Philadelphia zoo, it contains neither semiposed artificial shots nor distorted telephoto shots taken under adverse conditions. Artists, biologists, decorators, cartoonists, will find this book indispensable for understanding animals in motion. "A really marvelous series of plates," NATURE (London). "The dry plate's most spectacular early use was by Eadweard Muybridge," LIFE. 3919 photographs; 380 full pages of plates. 440pp. Printed on heavy glossy paper. Deluxe binding with headbands. 7⅞ x 10⅝.
T203 Clothbound **$10.00**

THE HUMAN FIGURE, J. H. Vanderpoel. Every important artistic element of the human figure is pointed out in minutely detailed word descriptions in this classic text and illustrated as well in 430 pencil and charcoal drawings. Thus the text of this book directs your attention to all the characteristic features and subtle differences of the male and female (adults, children, and aged persons), as though a master artist were telling you what to look for at each stage. 2nd edition, revised and enlarged by George Bridgman. Foreword. 430 illustrations. 143pp. 6⅛ x 9¼.
T432 Paperbound **$1.45**

ANIMAL DRAWING: ANATOMY AND ACTION FOR ARTISTS, C. R. Knight. The author and illustrator of this work was "the most distinguished painter of animal life." This extensive course in animal drawing discusses musculature, bone structure, animal psychology, movements, habits, habitats. Innumerable tips on proportions, light and shadow play, coloring, hair formation, feather arrangement, scales, how anmials lie down, animal expressions, etc., from great apes to birds. Pointers on avoiding gracelessness in horses, deer; on introducing proper power and bulk to heavier animals; on giving proper grace and subtle expression to members of the cat family. Originally titled "Animal Anatomy and Psychology for the Artist and Layman." Over 123 illustrations. 149pp. 8¼ x 10½.
T426 Paperbound **$2.00**

PRINCIPLES OF ART HISTORY, H. Wölfflin. Analyzing such terms as "baroque," "classic," "neoclassic," "primitive," "picturesque," and 164 different works by artists like Botticelli, van Cleve, Dürer, Hobbema, Holbein, Hals, Rembrandt, Titian, Brueghel, Vermeer, and many others, the author establishes the classifications of art history and style on a firm, concrete basis. This classic of art criticism shows what really occurred between the 14th century primitives and the sophistication of the 18th century in terms of basic attitudes and philosophies. "A remarkable lesson in the art of seeing," SAT. REV. OF LITERATURE. Translated from the 7th German edition. 150 illustrations. 254pp. 6⅛ x 9¼.
T276 Paperbound **$2.00**

THE MATERIALS AND TECHNIQUES OF MEDIEVAL PAINTING, D. V. Thompson. Based on years of study of medieval manuscripts and laboratory analysis of medieval paintings, this book discusses carriers and grounds, binding media, pigments, metals used in painting, etc. Considers relative merits of painting al fresco and al secco, the procession of coloring materials burnishing, and many other matters. Preface by Bernard Berenson. Index. 239pp. 5⅜ x 8.
T327 Paperbound **$1.85**

THE CRAFTSMAN'S HANDBOOK, Cennino Cennini. This is considered the finest English translation of IL LIBRO DELL' ARTE, a 15th century Florentine introduction to art technique. It is both fascinating reading and a wonderful mirror of another culture for artists, art students, historians, social scientists, or anyone interested in details of life some 500 years ago. While it is not an exact recipe book, it gives directions for such matters as tinting papers, gilding stone, preparation of various hues of black, and many other useful but nearly forgotten facets of the painter's art. As a human document reflecting the ideas of a practising medieval artist it is particularly important. 4 illustrations. xxvii + 142pp. D. V. Thompson translator. 6⅛ x 9¼.
T54 Paperbound **$1.25**

VASARI ON TECHNIQUE, G. Vasari. Pupil of Michelangelo and outstanding biographer of the Renaissance artists, Vasari also wrote this priceless treatise on the technical methods of the painters, architects, and sculptors of his day. This is the only English translation of this practical, informative, and highly readable work. Scholars, artists, and general readers will welcome these authentic discussions of marble statues, bronze, casting, fresco painting, oil painting, engraving, stained glass, rustic fountains and grottoes, etc. Introduction and notes by G. B. Brown. Index. 18 plates, 11 figures. xxiv + 328pp. 5⅜ x 8.
T717 Paperbound **$2.00**

HAWTHORNE ON PAINTING. A vivid recreation, from students' notes, of instruction by Charles W. Hawthorne, given for over 31 years at his famous Cape Cod School of Art. Divided into sections on the outdoor model, still life, landscape, the indoor model, and water color, each section begins with a concise essay, followed by epigrammatic comments on color, form, seeing, etc. Not a formal course, but comments of a great teacher-painter on specific student works, which will solve problems in your own painting and understanding of art. "An excellent introduction for laymen and students alike," Time. Introduction. 100pp. 5⅜ x 8.
T653 Paperbound **$1.00**

CATALOG OF DOVER BOOKS

METHODS AND MATERIALS OF PAINTING OF THE GREAT SCHOOLS AND MASTERS, C. L. Eastlake.
A vast, complete, and authentic reconstruction of the secret techniques of the masters of painting, collected from hundreds of forgotten manuscripts by the eminent President of the British Royal Academy: Greek, Roman, and medieval techniques; fresco and tempera; varnishes and encaustics; the secrets of Leonardo, Van Eyck, Raphael, and many others. Art historians, students, teachers, critics, and laymen will gain new insights into the creation of the great masterpieces; while artists and craftsmen will have a treasury of valuable techniques. Index. Two volume set. Total of 1025pp. 5⅜ x 8.
T718 Paperbound **$2.00**
T719 Paperbound **$2.00**
The set **$4.00**

AFRICAN SCULPTURE, Ladislas Segy. First publication of a new book by the author of critically acclaimed AFRICAN SCULPTURE SPEAKS. It contains 163 full page plates illustrating masks, fertility figures, ceremonial objects, etc., representing the culture of 50 tribes of West and Central Africa. Over 85% of these works of art have never been illustrated before, and each is an authentic and fascinating tribal artifact. A 34 page introduction explains the anthropological, psychological, and artistic values of African sculpture. "Mr. Segy is one of its top authorities," NEW YORKER. 164 full-page photographic plates. Bibliography. 244pp. 6 x 9.
T396 Paperbound **$2.00**

PRIMITIVE ART, Franz Boas. This authoritative and exhaustive work by a great American anthropologist covers the entire gamut of primitive art. Pottery, leatherwork, metal work, stone work, wood, basketry, are treated in detail. Theories of primitive art, historical depth in art history, technical virtuosity, unconscious levels of patterning, symbolism, styles, literature, music, dance, etc. A must book for the interested layman, the anthropologist, artist, handicrafter (hundreds of unusual motifs), and the historian. Over 900 illustrations (50 ceramic vessels, 12 totem poles, etc.). 376pp. 5⅜ x 8.
T25 Paperbound **$1.95**

DESIGN MOTIFS OF ANCIENT MEXICO, J. Enciso. This unique collection of pre-Columbian stamps for textiles and pottery contains 766 superb designs from Aztec, Olmec, Totonac, Maya, and Toltec origins. Plumed serpents, calendrical elements, wind gods, animals, flowers, demons, dancers, monsters, abstract ornament, and other designs. More than 90% of these illustrations are completely unobtainable elsewhere. Use this work to bring new barbaric beauty into your crafts or drawing. Originally $17.50. Printed in three colors. 766 illustrations, thousands of motifs. 192pp. 7⅞ x 10¾.
T84 Paperbound **$1.85**

DECORATIVE ART OF THE SOUTHWEST INDIANS, D. S. Sides. A magnificent album of authentic designs (both pre- and post-Conquest) from the pottery, textiles, and basketry of the Navaho, Hopi, Mohave, Santo Domingo, and over 20 other Southwestern groups. Designs include birds, clouds, butterflies, quadrupeds, geometric forms, etc. A valuable book for folklorists, and a treasury for artists, designers, advertisers, and craftsmen, who may use without payment or permission any of the vigorous, colorful, and strongly rhythmic designs. Aesthetic and archeological notes. 50 plates. Bibliography of over 50 items.
T139 Paperbound **$1.00**

PAINTING IN THE FAR EAST, Laurence Binyon. Excellent introduction by one of greatest authorities on subject studies 1500 years of oriental art (China, Japan; also Tibet, Persia), over 250 painters. Examines works, schools, influence of Wu Tao-tzu, Kanaoka, Toba Sojo, Masanobu, Okio, etc.; early traditions; Kamakura epoch; the Great Decorators; T'ang Dynasty; Matabei, beginnings of genre; Japanese woodcut, color print; much more, all chronological, in cultural context. 42 photos. Bibliography. 317pp. 6 x 9¼.
T520 Paperbound **$2.00**

ON THE LAWS OF JAPANESE PAINTING, H. Bowie. This unusual book, based on 9 years of profound study-experience in the Late Kano art of Japan, remains the most authentic guide in English to the spirit and technique of Japanese painting. A wealth of interesting and useful data on control of the brush; practise exercises; manufacture of ink, brushes, colors; the use of various lines and dots to express moods. It is the best possible substitute for a series of lessons from a great oriental master. 66 plates with 220 illustrations. Index. xv + 177pp. 6⅛ x 9¼.
T30 Paperbound **$1.95**

JAPANESE HOMES AND THEIR SURROUNDINGS, E. S. Morse. Every aspect of the purely traditional Japanese home, from general plan and major structural features to ceremonial and traditional appointments—tatami, hibachi, shoji, tokonoma, etc. The most exhaustive discussion in English, this book is equally honored for its strikingly modern conception of architecture. First published in 1886, before the contamination of the Japanese traditions, it preserves the authentic features of an ideal of construction that is steadily gaining devotees in the Western world. 307 illustrations by the author. Index. Glossary. xxxvi + 372pp. 5⅝ x 8⅜.
T746 Paperbound **$2.00**

FOUNDATIONS OF MODERN ART, A. Ozenfant. An illuminating discussion by a great artist of the interrelationship of all forms of human creativity, from painting to science, writing to religion. The creative process is explored in all facets of art, from paleolithic cave painting to modern French painting and architecture, and the great universals of art are isolated. Expressing its countless insights in aphorisms accompanied by carefully selected illustrations, this book is itself an embodiment in prose of the creative process. Enlarged by 4 new chapters. 226 illustrations. 368pp. 6⅛ x 9¼.
T215 Paperbound **$1.95**

CATALOG OF DOVER BOOKS

BYZANTINE ART AND ARCHAEOLOGY, O. M. Dalton. Still the most thorough work in English—both in breadth and in depth—on the astounding multiplicity of Byzantine art forms throughout Europe, North Africa, and Western Asia from the 4th to the 15th century. Analyzes hundreds of individual pieces from over 160 public and private museums, libraries, and collections all over the world. Full treatment of Byzantine sculpture, painting, mosaic, jewelry, textiles, etc., including historical development, symbolism, and aesthetics. Chapters on iconography and ornament. Indispensable for study of Christian symbolism and medieval art. 457 illustrations, many full-page. Bibliography of over 2500 references. 4 Indexes. xx + 727pp. 6⅛ x 9¼. **T776 Clothbound $7.50**

METALWORK AND ENAMELLING, H. Maryon. This is probably the best book ever written on the subject. Prepared by Herbert Maryon, F.S.A., of the British Museum, it tells everything necessary for home manufacture of jewelry, rings, ear pendants, bowls, and dozens of other objects. Clearly written chapters provide precise information on such topics as materials, tools, soldering, filigree, setting stones, raising patterns, spinning metal, repoussé work, hinges and joints, metal inlaying, damascening, overlaying, niello, Japanese alloys, enamelling, cloisonné, painted enamels, casting, polishing coloring, assaying, and dozens of other techniques. This is the next best thing to apprenticeship to a master metalworker. 363 photographs and figures. 374pp. 5½ x 8½. **T183 Clothbound $8.00**

SILK SCREEN TECHNIQUES, J. I. Biegeleisen, Max A. Cohn. A complete-to-the-last-detail copiously illustrated home course in this fast growing modern art form. Full directions for building silk screen out of inexpensive materials; explanations of five basic methods of stencil preparation—paper, blockout, tusche, film, photographic—and effects possible: light and shade, washes, dry brush, oil paint type impastos, gouaches, pastels. Detailed coverage of multicolor printing, illustrated by proofs showing the stages of a 4 color print. Special section on common difficulties. 149 illustrations, 8 in color. Sources of supply. xiv + 187pp. 6⅛ x 9¼. **T433 Paperbound $1.55**

A HANDBOOK OF WEAVES, G. H. Oelsner. Now back in print! Probably the most complete book of weaves ever printed, fully explained, differentiated, and illustrated. Includes plain weaves; irregular, double-stitched, and filling satins; derivative, basket, and rib weaves; steep, undulating, broken, offset, corkscrew, interlocking, herringbone, and fancy twills; honeycomb, lace, and crepe weaves; tricot, matelassé, and montagnac weaves; and much more. Translated and revised by S. S. Dale, with supplement on the analysis of weaves and fabrics. 1875 illustrations. vii + 402pp. 6 x 9¼. **T209 Clothbound $5.00**

THE STANDARD BOOK OF QUILT MAKING AND COLLECTING, Marguerite Ickis. A complete easy-to-follow guide with all the information you need to make beautiful, useful quilts. How to plan, design, cut, sew, appliqué, avoid sewing problems, use rag bag, make borders, tuft, every other aspect. Over 100 traditional quilts shown, including over 40 full-size patterns. No better book on the market. Index. 483 illus. 1 color plate. 287pp. 6¾ x 9½. **T582 Paperbound $2.00**

DESIGN FOR ARTISTS AND CRAFTSMEN, L. Wolchonok. The most thorough course ever prepared on the creation of art motifs and designs. It teaches you to create your own designs out of things around you — from geometric patterns, plants, birds, animals, humans, landscapes, and man-made objects. It leads you step by step through the creation of more than 1300 designs, and shows you how to create design that is fresh, well-founded, and original. Mr. Wolchonok, whose text is used by scores of art schools, shows you how the same idea can be developed into many different forms, ranging from near representationalism to the most advanced forms of abstraction. The material in this book is entirely new, and combines full awareness of traditional design with the work of such men as Miro, Léger, Picasso, Moore, and others. 113 detailed exercises, with instruction hints, diagrams, and details to enable you to apply Wolchonok's methods to your own work. "A great contribution to the field of design and crafts," N. Y. SOCIETY OF CRAFTSMEN. More than 1300 illustrations. xv + 207pp. 7⅞ x 10¾. **T274 Clothbound $4.95**

BASIC BOOKBINDING, A. W. Lewis. Enables the beginner and the expert to apply the latest and most simplified techniques to rebinding old favorites and binding new paperback books. Complete lists of all necessary materials and guides to the selection of proper tools, paper, glue, boards, cloth, leather, or sheepskin covering fabrics, lettering inks and pigments, etc. You are shown how to collate a book, sew it, back it, trim it, make boards and attach them in easy step-by-step stages. Author's preface. 261 illustrations with appendix. Index. xi + 144pp. 5⅜ x 8. **T169 Paperbound $1.35**

THE UNIVERSAL PENMAN, George Bickham. This beautiful book, which first appeared in 1743, is the largest collection of calligraphic specimens, flourishes, alphabets, and calligraphic illustrations ever published. 212 full-page plates are drawn from the work of such 18th century masters of English roundhand as Dove, Champion, Bland, and 20 others. They contain 22 complete alphabets, over 2,000 flourishes, and 122 illustrations, each drawn with a stylistic grace impossible to describe. This book is invaluable to anyone interested in the beauties of calligraphy, or to any artist, hobbyist, or craftsman who wishes to use the very best ornamental handwriting and flourishes for decorative purposes. Commercial artists, advertising artists, have found it unexcelled as a source of material suggesting quality. "An essential part of any art library, and a book of permanent value," AMERICAN ARTIST. 212 plates. 224pp. 9 x 13¾. **T20 Clothbound $10.00**

CATALOG OF DOVER BOOKS

LETTERING AND ALPHABETS, J. A. Cavanagh. This unabridged reissue of LETTERING offers a full discussion, analysis, illustration of 89 basic hand lettering styles — styles derived from Caslons, Bodonis, Garamonds, Gothic, Black Letter, Oriental, and many others. Upper and lower cases, numerals and common signs pictured. Hundreds of technical hints on make-up, construction, artistic validity, strokes, pens, brushes, white areas, etc. May be reproduced without permission! 89 complete alphabets; 72 lettered specimens. 121pp. 9¾ x 8.
T53 Paperbound **$1.25**

DECORATIVE ALPHABETS AND INITIALS, ed. by Alexander Nesbitt. No payment, no permission to reproduce any one of these 3924 different letters, covering 1000 years. Crisp, clear letters all in line, from Anglo-Saxon mss., Luebeck Cathedral, 15th century Augsburg; the work of Dürer, Holbein, Cresci; Beardsley, Rossing Wadsworth, John Moylin, etc. Every imaginable style. 91 complete alphabets. 123 full-page plates. 192pp. 7¾ x 10¾.
T544 Paperbound **$2.25**

THREE CLASSICS OF ITALIAN CALLIGRAPHY, edited by Oscar Ogg. Here, combined in a single volume, are complete reproductions of three famous calligraphic works written by the greatest writing masters of the Renaissance; Arrighi's OPERINA and IL MODO, Tagliente's LO PRESENTE LIBRO, and Palatino's LIBRO NUOVO. These books present more than 200 complete alphabets and thousands of lettered specimens. The basic hand is Papal Chancery, but scores of other alphabets are also given: European and Asiatic local alphabets, foliated and art alphabets, scrolls, cartouches, borders, etc. Text is in Italian. Introduction. 245 plates. x + 272pp. 6⅛ x 9¼.
T212 Paperbound **$2.25**

CALLIGRAPHY, J. G. Schwandner. One of the legendary books in the graphic arts, copies of which brought $500 each on the rare book market, now reprinted for the first time in over 200 years. A beautiful plate book of graceful calligraphy, and an inexhaustible source of first rate material, copyright free, for artists, art directors, craftsmen, commercial artists, etc. More than 300 ornamental initials forming 12 complete alphabets, over 150 ornate frames and panels, over 200 flourishes, over 75 calligraphic pictures including a temple, cherubs, cocks, dodos, stags, chamois, foliated lions, greyhounds, etc. Thousand of calligraphic elements to be used for suggestions of quality, sophistication, antiquity, and sheer beauty. Historical introduction. 158 full-page plates. 368pp. 9 x 13.
T475 Clothbound **$10.00**

THE HISTORY AND TECHNIQUES OF LETTERING, A. Nesbitt. The only thorough inexpensive history of letter forms from the point of view of the artist. Mr. Nesbitt covers every major development in lettering from the ancient Egyptians to the present and illustrates each development with a complete alphabet. Such masters as Baskerville, Bell, Bodoni, Caslon, Koch, Kilian, Morris, Garamont, Jenson, and dozens of others are analyzed in terms of artistry and historical development. The author also presents a 65 page practical course in lettering, besides the full historical text. 89 complete alphabets; 165 additional lettered specimens. xvii + 300pp. 5⅜ x 8.
T427 Paperbound **$2.00**

FOOT-HIGH LETTERS: A GUIDE TO LETTERING (A PRACTICAL SYLLABUS FOR TEACHERS), M. Price. A complete alphabet of Classic Roman letters, each a foot high, each on a separate 16 x 22 plate—perfect for use in lettering classes. In addition to an accompanying description, each plate also contains 9 two-inch-high forms of letter in various type faces, such as "Caslon," "Empire," "Onyx," and "Neuland," illustrating the many possible derivations from the standard classical forms. One plate contains 21 additional forms of the letter A. The fully illustrated 16-page syllabus by Mr. Price, formerly of the Pratt Institute and the Rhode Island School of Design, contains dozens of useful suggestions for student and teacher alike. An indispensable teaching aid. Extensively revised. 16-page syllabus and 30 plates in slip cover, 16 x 22.
T239 Clothbound **$6.00**

THE STYLES OF ORNAMENT, Alexander Speltz. Largest collection of ornaments in print— 3765 illustrations of prehistoric, Lombard, Gothic, Frank, Romanesque, Mohammedan, Renaissance, Polish, Swiss, Rococo, Sheraton, Empire, U. S. Colonial, etc., ornament, Gargoyles, dragons, columns, necklaces, urns, friezes, furniture, buildings, keyholes, tapestries, fantastic animals, armor, religious objects, much more, all in line. Reproduce any one free. Index. Bibliography. 400 plates. 656pp. 5⅝ x 8⅜.
T557 Paperbound **$2.25**

Dover publishes books on art, music, philosophy, literature, languages, history, social sciences, psychology, handcrafts, orientalia, puzzles and entertainments, chess, pets and gardens, books explaining science, intermediate and higher mathematics mathematical physics, engineering, biological sciences, earth sciences, classics of science, etc. Write to:

> Dept. catrr.
> *Dover Publications, Inc.*
> *180 Varick Street, N. Y. 14, N. Y.*